W9-BZI-179

Praise for

A Country of Vast Designs

"*A Country of Vast Designs: James K. Polk, the Mexican War, and the Conquest of the American Continent* is Robert Merry's brilliant biography and history of that time. Merry goes far toward righting the injustice done by historians who have denied this great man his place in the pantheon of presidents."

—Creators Syndicate/ Review in Pat Buchanan's column

"Tackles a compelling but largely uncharted era in American history: the flurry of western expansion that bridged the Age of Jackson to the politics of the Civil War. In three grand strokes, Polk transformed the geopolitical outlook of the continent for centuries to come, expanding the nation by a third and solidifying its claim to the Pacific . . . Merry's book offers a fresh perspective, and a glimpse of how things can work out differently."

—*Washington Monthly*

"[A] wide-ranging, provocative analysis of the controversial presidency of James K. Polk."

—*Publishers Weekly*

"A crucial architect of modern America, James K. Polk deserves to be elevated out of the mists of history. In this engaging book, Robert Merry does just that, recapturing the passions and personalities of a forgotten era in American life."

—Jon Meacham, author of *American Lion: Andrew Jackson in the White House*

"Merry is a wonderful writer, lively and very clear-eyed, and he tells a fascinating chapter in American history. Long neglected, James K. Polk turns out to be a rich, memorable figure, a war president whose will to conquest achieved the modern map of America."

—Evan Thomas, author of *Sea of Thunder*

"In Polk's single four-year term, the United States added Western lands from New Mexico through Washington State. Robert Merry skillfully draws a comprehensive portrait of Polk's extraordinary successes in a time of bitter politics and explains why this intense leader remains underappreciated."

—David O. Stewart, author of *Impeached: The Trial of President Andrew Johnson and the Fight for Lincoln's Legacy*

ALSO BY ROBERT W. MERRY

*Sands of Empire: Missionary Zeal, American
Foreign Policy, and the Hazards of Global Ambition*

*Taking On the World: Joseph and Stewart Alsop—
Guardians of the American Century*

A Country of

Vast Designs

James K. Polk, the Mexican War, and the
Conquest of the American Continent

ROBERT W. MERRY

Simon & Schuster Paperbacks

NEW YORK   LONDON   TORONTO   SYDNEY

Simon & Schuster Paperbacks
A Division of Simon & Schuster, Inc.
1230 Avenue of the Americas
New York, NY 10020

First Simon & Schuster trade paperback edition November 2010

SIMON & SCHUSTER PAPERBACKS and colophon are registered
trademarks of Simon & Schuster, Inc.

For information about special discounts for bulk purchases,
please contact Simon & Schuster Special Sales at
1-866-506-1949 or business@simonandschuster.com.

The Simon & Schuster Speakers Bureau can bring authors
to your live event. For more information or to book an event,
contact the Simon & Schuster Speakers Bureau at
1-866-248-3049 or visit our website at www.simonspeakers.com.

Designed by Paul Dippolito

Map by Marilyn Gates-Davis

Manufactured in the United States of America

5   7   9   10   8   6

The Library of Congress has cataloged the hardcover edition as follows:
Merry, Robert W., date.
A country of vast designs : James K. Polk, the Mexican War, and the
conquest of the American continent / Robert Merry.
p.   cm.
1. Polk, James K. (James Knox), 1795–1849.   2. Presidents—United States—
Biography.   3. United States—Politics and government—1845–1849.
4. United States—Territorial expansion—History—19th century.   I. Title.
E417.M1153 2009
973.6'1092—dc22
[B]   2009024131
ISBN 978-0-7432-9743-1
ISBN 978-0-7432-9744-8 (pbk)
ISBN 978-1-4391-6045-9 (ebook)

INSERT PHOTO CREDITS: © The Corcoran Gallery of Art / Corbis: 1; James K. Polk
Memorial Association, Columbia, Tennessee: 2, 10, 12; Jill Lang, 2009, used under license
from Shutterstock.com: 3; PictureHistory: 16, 29; Library of Congress: 4, 5, 7, 9, 11, 15,
18, 19, 21, 26, 28, 30, 31; Wikimedia Commons: 6; © Corbis: 8, 20; © Bettmann/Corbis:
13, 24; The Ohio Historical Society: 14; The Library Company of Philadelphia: 17;
© iStockphoto.com/Hulton Archive: 22; Courtesy, Special Collections, The University
of Texas at Arlington Library, Arlington, Texas: 23; Courtesy of the Bancroft Library,
University of California, Berkeley: 25; Wikipedia: 27.

To Susie,
Who brightens my life like the dawn's first
sunlight over the Cascades

CONTENTS

A Country of
Vast Designs

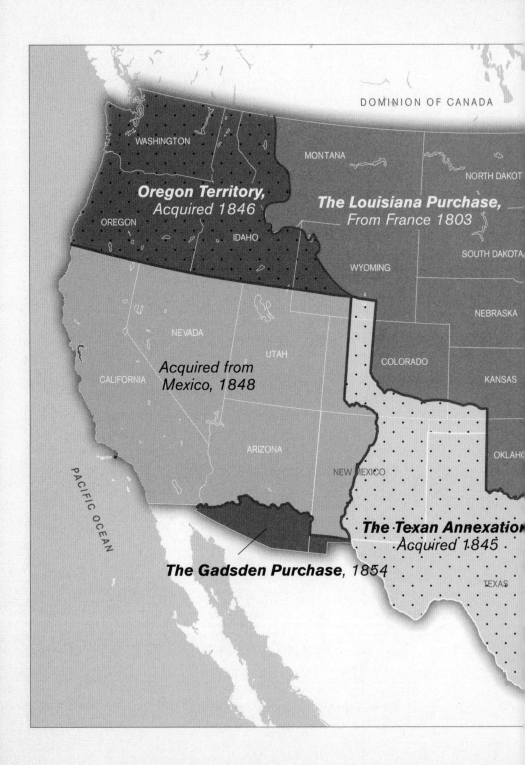

DOMINION OF CANADA

WASHINGTON

MONTANA

NORTH DAKOT

Oregon Territory,
Acquired 1846

The Louisiana Purchase,
From France 1803

OREGON

IDAHO

SOUTH DAKOTA

WYOMING

NEVADA

NEBRASKA

UTAH

*Acquired from
Mexico, 1848*

COLORADO

CALIFORNIA

KANSAS

ARIZONA

OKLAHO

NEW MEXICO

The Texan Annexatio
Acquired 1845

The Gadsden Purchase, *1854*

PACIFIC OCEAN

TEXAS

WISCONSIN

MINNESOTA

IOWA

MISSOURI

ARKANSAS

LOUISIANA

MICHIGAN

ILLINOIS

INDIANA

OHIO

KENTUCKY

TENNESSEE

MISSISSIPPI

ALABAMA

NEW YORK

PENNSYLVANIA

WEST
VIRGINIA

VIRGINIA

The United States,
1783

NORTH
CAROLINA

SOUTH
CAROLINA

GEORGIA

VERMONT

MAINE

NEW
HAMPSHIRE

MASSACHUSETTS

RHODE
ISLAND

CONNECTICUT

NEW JERSEY

DELAWARE

MARYLAND

WASHINGTON,
D.C.

ATLANTIC OCEAN

FLORIDA

*Ceded by Spain,
1819*

GULF OF MEXICO

INTRODUCTION:
RITUAL OF DEMOCRACY

The Emergence of an Expansionist President

PRECISELY AT SUNRISE on the morning of March 4, 1845, the roar of cannon shattered the dawn's early quiet of Washington, D.C.—twenty-eight big guns fired in rapid succession. Thus did the American military announce to the nation's capital that it was about to experience the country's highest ritual of democracy, the inauguration of the nation's executive leader and premier military commander. James Knox Polk was about to become that leader and commander. On this morning he was ensconced along with his wife, Sarah, at the National Hotel on Pennsylvania Avenue, known popularly as Coleman's, just ten blocks east of the White House. That night the two of them would be residing at the presidential mansion.

At forty-nine, Polk would be the youngest of the country's eleven presidents—and, in the view of his many detractors, the most unlikely. Until the previous May of 1844, when he had emerged unexpectedly as the Democratic Party's presidential nominee, few had imagined the man would ever rise to the presidency. Indeed, just a year earlier his political career had appeared in ruin following his third campaign for Tennessee governor. He had won the office in 1839 but had been expelled two years later by a backwoods upstart known as Lean Jimmy Jones, who had greeted his exacting rhetoric and serious demeanor with lighthearted buffoonery. Trying again in 1843 to outmaneuver this unlikely rival, he once again failed, causing friend and foe alike to dismiss his political prospects.

But those observers hadn't grasped Polk's most powerful trait—

his absolute conviction that he was a man of destiny. Throughout his political life he had been underestimated by his rivals in the Whig Party and also by some of his own Democratic colleagues. When he had captured his party's presidential nomination, the country's leading Whig newspaper sneered in derision. "This nomination," declared the *National Intelligencer*, "may be considered as the dying gasp, the last breath of life, of the 'democratic' party." The newspaper said it couldn't imagine a "less imposing" opponent.

It was true Polk lacked the soaring attributes of the era's two rival political giants, Andrew Jackson and Henry Clay. He didn't possess Jackson's forceful presence or his blunt-spoken way of attracting men instantly to his cause and his side. Nor could he match the lanky Clay's famous wit, his smooth fluency with the language, his ability to amuse and charm those around him even as he slyly dominated them. By contrast, Polk was small of stature and drab of temperament. Upon his Washington arrival for the inauguration, some of his former colleagues noted he appeared thinner than before, and one wit suggested if he hadn't had his coats cut a size or two large, "he would be but the merest tangible fraction of a President."

Polk lacked the skills and traits of the natural leader. His silvery gray hair, in retreat from his forehead but abundant elsewhere, was brushed back across his head and allowed to flow luxuriantly below his collar. His probing blue eyes, deep set under dark brows, reflected a tendency toward quick and rigid judgment. Seldom did his thin lips convey any real mirth or jocularity, and the powerful jaw that jutted from his countenance signaled a narrowness of outlook tied to a persistence of resolve. Polk lacked the easy manner and demeanor that bespoke friendship and camaraderie. He didn't much like people. What he liked was politics, the art and challenge of moving events in the favored direction, which for Polk meant the direction most favored by Democrats. People thus were a means to an end, figures on a vast civic chessboard of national destiny, to be directed and positioned in such a way as to move the country where he wanted to move it. Though a man of conviction and rectitude, he often allowed himself to become encased in his own sanctimony.

These traits shrouded the real James Polk, whose analytical skills and zest for bold action often placed him in position to outmaneuver his adversaries. He understood the forces welling up within the national polity and how they could be harnessed and dominated. He was a master in the art of crafting an effective political message. And he never allowed himself to be deflected from his chosen path by the enmity of his foes or their dismissive regard toward him or their unremitting opposition.

Besides, he enjoyed the friendship and mentorship of Andrew Jackson, Old Hickory, the country's most popular figure and its dominant political voice for the past twenty years. Jackson had been a longtime friend of the Polk family, had watched young James grow up, had counseled him on whom to marry and how to manage his career. So now on this momentous morning, as he began his day at Coleman's and prepared for the events ahead, his inauguration must have seemed the most natural thing in the world even as he knew it struck most others as utterly accidental.

From a window of his suite that morning, Polk could see the prospect of rain reflected in a charcoal sky. Yet the enthusiasm of democracy was running high. For days Washington had teemed with all manner of people thronging there for the festivities—"office seekers and office-expectants, political speculators and party leaders without number, and of every caliber," as the *Intelligencer* put it, adding that the crowd also included "strangers of every rank in life, and every variety of personal appearance." Hotels and boardinghouses were sold out, and some halls and bars spread pallets upon their floors to accommodate wayworn arrivals.

At ten o'clock the cannon roared again as part of a succession of inauguration day salutes, this one signaling the ceremonial procession was to begin forming at the western end of Pennsylvania Avenue for the mile-and-a-half ride up the boulevard to the Capitol. At precisely that time, as if summoned by the cannon, the rain began a steady downbeat. Up went a multitude of umbrellas. A British journalist, surveying the scene from the west end of the avenue, said it looked like "a long line of moving umbrellas, terminating at the Capitol, the dome of which towered up like a gigantic umbrella held aloft by some invisible hand."

Leading the procession was the inauguration's chief marshal and his aides, bedecked in silks and ribbons and carrying distinctive batons of officialdom: branches of "young hickory," alluding to Polk's nickname as protégé of Old Hickory. The marshals were followed by various local military units as well as leading officers of the day. Then came members of the area's clergy and behind them the open carriage transporting President-elect Polk and his predecessor, John Tyler of Virginia. Next in line came the justices of the Supreme Court; then the diplomatic corps; members and ex-members of Congress; participants at the Democratic convention in Baltimore that had nominated Polk the previous May over New York's Martin Van Buren, the former president who had hungered for a White House return; then governors and ex-governors.

A place in the procession had been reserved for ex-presidents, but only one such dignitary was in town that day, and he had declined the honor. That was John Quincy Adams, the New England moralist and political ascetic who had been expelled from the White House by Andrew Jackson sixteen years before. He had salved the wounds of defeat by taking up duties as an outspoken member of the House of Representatives, whence he waged unrelenting war upon Democratic aims. He had greeted Polk's election with near despair. "I mused over the prospects before me," he had written, "with the impression that they portend trials more severe than I yet have passed through."

The many military bands within the procession played lively marches to stir a buoyant mood among the throngs jammed compactly along the avenue. The rain may not have dampened the mood, but it drenched everything else. Military plumes began to droop, the white silk badges of the marshals stuck fast to their soaked black coats, and pretty dresses absorbed water. Meanwhile, in the shelter of the Capitol, the Senate was called to order precisely at eleven o'clock. Like the streets and plazas outside, the galleries and nearby stairwells were filled to overflowing. The chamber bustled with the arrival of special guests—Supreme Court justices, House leaders, the District of Columbia marshal. Polk and his designated vice president, George M. Dallas of Pennsylvania, appeared precisely at eleven-forty amid much interest and bustle on the floor and in the galleries.

The next order of business was the swearing in of George Dallas, then fifty-two. His most distinguishing physical characteristic was a head of thick flowing hair, white as milk, which accentuated his dark eyebrows and a broad face that displayed friendly resolve. Sarah Polk considered him an "elegant man, exceedingly handsome and gentle." He had served in the U.S. Senate at an early age, then held jobs as Pennsylvania attorney general and U.S. minister to Russia. He was part of a Democratic faction in his state that seemed in perpetual conflict with another faction led by Senator James Buchanan, designated as Polk's new secretary of state. The issue seemed to be who would control Pennsylvania's Democratic patronage, and Dallas had expected his vice presidential elevation to settle the question in his favor. "I am resolved that no one shall be taken from Pennsylvania [into the Polk administration] who is notoriously hostile to the Vice-President," he had written to a friend amid rumors that Buchanan might be tapped for Polk's cabinet. "If such a choice be made my relations with this administration are at an end." Such a choice was made, and Dallas promptly cast aside his private threat. But the animosities constituted a political reality that Polk needed to monitor.

At around eleven-forty-five, the Senate's president pro tempore, Willie P. Mangum of North Carolina, administered the oath of office to Dallas, who then delivered a brief speech marked by appropriate democratic platitudes mixed with appropriate expressions of humility. "The citizen whom it has pleased a people to elevate by their suffrages from the pursuits of private and domestic life," he intoned, "may best evince his grateful sense of the honor . . . by devoting his faculties, moral and intellectual, resolutely to their service. This I shall do; yet with a diffidence unavoidable to one conscious that almost every step in his appointed path is to him new and untried."

History doesn't record whether, as Dallas droned on, some in the audience perhaps found their minds wandering to thoughts of forthcoming political battles. Many of those assembled were destined to play major roles in those battles. James Polk had studied these men with his hallmark attention to detail and penetration of human traits and foibles. Polk knew his first priority would be keeping his party together, and down on the Senate floor he could see just how difficult that would be. He needed to look no further than to two of the Senate's most powerful and willful Democrats—Missouri's Thomas Hart Benton and South Carolina's George McDuffie—who pressed their convictions with a white-hot intensity that often melted any prospect for measured political behavior. Though both proudly carried the Democratic imprimatur, each reserved for the other a degree of political vitriol seldom directed at members of the opposition Whigs.

McDuffie, a senator since December 1842 and his state's governor before that, was a protégé and ally of South Carolina's fiery John C. Calhoun. An oval-faced man with dark, deep-set eyes and a recessive chin, McDuffie represented the extreme states' rights views that had emerged with South Carolina's efforts during Jackson's presidency to "nullify" federal laws distasteful to the state. Andrew Jackson had quashed this rebellion by threatening to hang Calhoun and any other traitors who sought to rend the hallowed union. But the sentiments behind it continued to percolate in some southern precincts, most notably in South Carolina.

Thomas Hart Benton despised those sentiments. He was a man given to flights of outrage that unleashed in turn torrents of outrageous rhetoric. John Tyler called him "the most raving political maniac I ever knew." Benton was an imposing man with a big face, full of crags, and a beak of a nose. He spoke with authority and an air suggesting he didn't have much patience for the mutterings of lesser men, a category that seemed to include most of those with whom he came into contact. He fancied himself a fighter, and he had a history of several duels to prove it. As a young man in Tennessee, he became embroiled in an altercation with Andrew Jackson that quickly escalated into an angry gun battle. Benton had been a protégé of Jackson and his aide-de-camp during the War of 1812, but the younger man had become enraged at Jackson's decision to serve a friend as second at the friend's duel with Benton's brother, Jesse. Jesse took a bullet to the buttocks, which proved humiliating, and Thomas Benton blamed Jackson for fostering the duel. The brothers trashed Jackson's name throughout Nashville with such abandon that the proud Jackson went after the two of them outside a downtown saloon with a riding whip. It ended with multiple wounds for Benton and a bullet-shattered shoulder for Jackson that nearly claimed his life. Concluding Tennessee was now enemy territory, Benton promptly set out for Missouri, where he emerged as its leading politician. When the territory became a state in 1821, it sent Benton to the U.S. Senate, where he nurtured his identity as a man of absolute independence. Though a proud Democrat, he could never be counted on to adhere with any consistency to the party line. He adhered only to the Thomas Hart Benton line.

Benton had awarded his political loyalty to former President Van Buren, and he felt rage toward the Democratic politicians who had maneuvered to deny Van Buren his party's nomination at the Baltimore convention. Polk studiously had avoided any overt action that could be construed as inimical to Van Buren's ambitions. Though Benton publicly had accepted Polk's denials, privately he wasn't so sure. But about George McDuffie and John C. Calhoun he harbored no doubts. They were the enemy.

The issue was Texas annexation and, just behind it, slavery. Texas had exploded onto the political scene quite unexpectedly when Tyler had negotiated an annexation treaty with this Southwest country that had secured its independence from Mexico through force of arms. It turned out that annexation was hugely popular in the United States, but an instinctive wariness emerged within the political establishment. Many politicians feared war with Mexico, which had never accepted or recognized Texas independence. They feared also an intensification of the slavery issue as the country grappled with the question of whether this vast new territory would be free or slave. Both Van Buren, the presumed Democratic presidential candidate, and Clay, the assured Whig candidate, had declared their opposition to immediate annexation, and both saw their presidential hopes destroyed in the bargain. Polk, attuned to political sentiment and attentive to

Jackson's expansionist instincts, had immediately embraced annexation, and this had helped boost him to the presidency.

Now, with the rain-soaked multitude about to witness Polk's swearing in, the Texas issue still loomed large over the political landscape, generating acidic animosities within the party and the country. Benton was convinced McDuffie and other anti–Van Buren southerners harbored desires to bring Texas into the Union as a slave state so the expanded slave empire could form its own country. He had railed against "this long-conceived Texas machination . . . an intrigue for the presidency, and a contrivance to get the Southern States out of the Union." McDuffie just as adamantly insisted the North harbored secret aims of surrounding, squeezing, and ultimately destroying the slave culture. Asked if South Carolinians would continue to submit to oppression, he had replied, "Before answering that question, I will ask—Are you *men*—are you *South* Carolinians . . . or are you *curs*—which, when kicked, will howl, and then come back and lick the foot that has inflicted the blow?"

Clearly, bringing these two men under the same political tent would not be easy.

It was nearly noon when the Senate assemblage made its way to the temporary platform constructed over the vast stairways of the Capitol's east portico. First to emerge, to "cheers of welcome," were Tyler and Polk, walking side by side but with the president-elect occupying the ceremonial position to the left of the outgoing president. A British journalist in attendance described Polk as "looking well, though thin and anxious in appearance." Behind them were their wives and behind them various dignitaries. Sarah Polk, though not a true beauty, possessed a magnetism that had served her well as a politician's wife. Her enveloping warmth was viewed by many family friends as an antidote to her husband's stiff demeanor. She had a Spanish appearance, with black hair, large dark eyes, olive skin, thin expressive lips, and an oval face. One high-toned Pennsylvanian noted that she "dresses with taste" and called her "a very superior person." He added, "Time has dealt kindly with her personal charms, and if she is not handsome she is at least very prepossessing and graceful."

On this day she wore a gown of satin with a neckline that dropped into a V and with stripes of deep red and silvery gray. The waistline was tight and the sleeves long. Over it she wore a sand-colored wool coat with a quilted rose taffeta lining. On her head, protecting her from the rain, was a velvet bonnet the same color as the red of her dress. Clearly she wished to make a statement with her manner of dress on this day. Dallas wrote to his wife that he found her "rather too showy for my taste . . . [but] I go for the new lady."

At the appointed time, before the swearing in, Polk stepped forward to deliver his inaugural address "to a large assemblage of umbrellas," as John Quincy Adams wryly noted in his diary. Standing at the front of the platform, protected from the rain by an umbrella held by a servant, Polk sought to quicken the hearts of Democrats while assuaging fears of Whigs and others. Passing quickly over his own humility in accepting the awesome responsibilities and his resolve to seek divine guidance in discharging those responsibilities, he moved directly to the central tenets of the Jacksonian creed. Warning against federal usurpation of governmental prerogative beyond the limits of the Constitution, he pledged "to assume no powers not expressly granted or clearly implied" in that document. He extolled the executive veto as protection against a capricious or despotic majority. He vowed to fight any threats to the union, thus serving notice that state actions aimed at nullifying federal laws or dissolving the Union would encounter the kind of military resistance Jackson had directed at South Carolina. Polk denounced any kind of federal bank, any national debt, and any tariffs crafted specifically for the protection of particular industries. "The raising of revenue should be the object, and protection the incident," he declared.

On foreign policy, Polk declared his expansionist vision. He celebrated the recent actions in behalf of Texas annexation and warned against any interference from Mexico or any other continental power. And he served notice that the United States considered its title to the full Oregon Territory to be "clear and unquestionable"—a bold statement given that his country and Britain had occupied those lands jointly for twenty-two years and had pledged mutually to negotiate a disposition of the matter at some point in the future. Just eighty years before, noted Polk, the country's small population had been confined to the east side of the Alleghenies. Since then, "our people, increasing to many millions, have filled the eastern valley of the Mississippi, adventurously ascended the Missouri to its headsprings, and are already engaged in establishing the blessings of self-government in valleys of which the rivers flow to the Pacific. . . . To us belongs the duty of protecting [these settlers] adequately wherever they may be upon our soil."

It was pure Jacksonian rhetoric in both substance and style. Indeed, the first draft had been crafted by Amos Kendall, Jackson's brilliant word maestro from his own presidential days. But Jackson himself wasn't there to hear it. In declining health for months, he now was dying. "I thank my god that the Republic is safe & that he had permitted me to live to see it, & rejoice," Jackson had written the previous fall, upon hearing of Polk's election. Jackson's absence was balanced by the absence of his great political rival, Henry Clay, whose defeat in November's presidential balloting had been his third such subjection. Clay remained at his vast Kentucky estate, Ashland, pondering how it happened that, after years of contending with Old Hickory, he now had to deal with his equally hostile young protégé.

Polk delivered his inaugural remarks, according to Washington's *Daily Globe,* "in a voice so firm and distinct, as to be heard by almost every individual present." But the response from the crowd was more polite than enthusiastic, suggesting perhaps his voice hadn't carried over the din of rain falling upon umbrellas. In any event, now it was time for the country's eleventh president to be sworn in, and Chief Justice Roger B. Taney stepped forward. Taney was a Jackson appointee whose robes of impartiality never fully shrouded his Democratic sympathies. "I feel so truly rejoiced at your election as President . . . ," he had written Polk in November, "that I must indulge myself in the pleasure of offering my cordial congratulations. . . . I need not say with what pleasure I shall again meet you in Washington, & see you entering upon the high station to which you have been so honorably called." Taney held what the *Illustrated London News* would describe as "a richly gilt Bible," presented to Sarah Polk by Alexander Hunter, chief marshal of the District of Columbia. At Taney's prompting, Polk uttered the famous thirty-five words affirming faithfully to execute the presidential office and to "preserve, protect and defend the Constitution of the United States." Then he was president, and another 28-gun salute roared its affirmation.

The new president and the man he had just replaced left the platform, again side by side. But this time Polk occupied the ceremonial position at Tyler's right. The official parade formed up once again into what Quincy Adams called a "draggle-tail procession thinned in numbers," and the president and first lady were escorted back to the White House, where they greeted visitors through much of the afternoon. The evening agenda included two inaugural balls—one at Carusi's Hall, at ten dollars a ticket; another at the National Theatre at five dollars. Intent on making yet another fashion statement, Sarah ventured forth in a marine blue velvet dress with a cape described by one biographer as "deeply fringed." Quincy Adams, whose self-exile from the day's activities didn't preclude his pouring wry pronouncements into his diary, reported that Polk attended both galas, "but supped with the true-blue five-dollar Democracy."

The next day Polk assumed the duties of a presidential term that he had promised would be his only claim upon the office. Ahead of him were four tumultuous years of American expansionism that would transform his country and set it upon a new course. But when he relinquished power in March 1849 he would be a spent force, politically and physically. His greatest accomplishments would live on in a vast expanse of territory in the West and Southwest, now part of the United States. But he himself would not last much beyond his hour of eminence. Within four months of leaving office, he would be dead.

1 · YOUNG HICKORY

The Making of a Jackson Protégé

BEGINNING IN SUMMER 1717 there arrived upon American shores a new breed of immigrant from the British Isles, far different from the Puritans, Quakers, and Cavaliers who had already settled in their chosen locales. The new arrivals came from the borderlands of northern England, northern Ireland, and the Scottish Highlands, and they emerged in undulating waves that deposited a quarter-million souls in the New World over nearly sixty years. The borderland migrants were a rustic folk, largely Presbyterian in religious provenance. The men were lanky and fit, with faces leathered through outdoor toil. They displayed distinctive habits of dress—hats made of felt, loose-fitting shirts made of sackcloth, wood shoes. The young women displayed a frolicsome sensuousness that seemed shocking to many of the earlier arrivals. They wore tight-fitting dresses with short skirts. Men and women alike showed a notable casualness and openness toward sex and nudity, and social sanctions against wayward personal behavior were mild compared to those of earlier migrants. The menfolk displayed a liberal attitude toward spirituous liquors and a fighting spirit more intense than their work ethic. There was a strain of cultural conservatism among these people; they were strongly attached to their ancestral ways.

The borderland migrants arrived not seeking religious freedom, as their predecessors had done, but rather to escape economic travail. Hence they came largely from a lower socioeconomic station than the folks who had settled earlier in Massachusetts, Delaware, and Virginia. The vast majority were small farmers, farm laborers, and mechanics. But they displayed a defiant pride that would have far-reaching political impact in the New World, particularly in the lush western regions beyond the Alleghenies that would become their favored frontier destination. As one historian would later put it, "Extreme inequalities of material condition were joined to an intense concern for equality of esteem." They demanded respect, often with a social insolence that surprised and irritated those who considered themselves of higher rank. Ultimately this trait would manifest itself in a powerful strain of political populism—a suspicion of entrenched elites, hostility toward wealth and power, a conviction that the new American democracy should be guided by the virtue and wisdom of ordinary folk. This was the heritage, outlook, and politics of Andrew Jackson—and also of his protégé, James K. Polk, twenty-eight years younger than his mentor.

The two men shared also a similar family consciousness. While the vast majority of borderland migrant families were poor and always had been poor, about one to 2 percent came from the landed gentry of Britain's borderlands. They migrated to America not to better their station but to retain it, and they remained intensely conscious of their family heritage. However impoverished they may have become in the course of their journey to America or during their struggles once they got there, they never lost their sense that they came from exalted levels of society. Jackson's mother taught him from earliest childhood to think of himself as a gentleman, and she taught him that his Scots-Irish grandfather had been a well-to-do linen weaver and merchant and his father a comfortable farmer with substantial acreage in the old country. And Polk proudly traced his lineage back eight centuries to a Saxon nobleman named Undwin and to Undwin's descendants who held sway over vast estates and political decision-making throughout their long Scottish ascendancy.

To Polk all this was vastly more significant than his inauspicious birth in a one-room log cabin at a time of economic transition for his family. The first of ten children, he was born November 2, 1795, in Mecklenburg County, North Carolina, to Samuel and Jane Knox Polk. His mother, a rigid Presbyterian of sharp intellect and strong character, came from an established North Carolina family. James's father, four generations removed from the family's New World founder, Robert Bruce Polk (or Pollock, as the family had been known up to that time), was a sturdy farmer of simple virtues whose robust drive for advancement overcame a rather limited imagination. When young James was eleven, the family set out on the arduous five-hundred-mile journey to the Duck River region of Tennessee territory, between the Smoky Mountains and the Mississippi River. Beleaguered and angry Indians posed mortal dangers that stirred the combative juices of these borderland settlers, whose fighting spirit was rendered all the more intense by the richness of the prize they sought. The region's fertile soil promised abundant wealth for those who survived, and the path of betterment was well established in the country's frontier out-lands: venture forth to a thinly populated area and accumulate large expanses of cheap or free land; develop as much acreage as possible for farming; when land prices rise with the arrival of subsequent pio-neers, sell undeveloped lands at elevated prices; use the profit to fur-ther develop the retained acreage and perhaps venture also into the law or commercial enterprises.

Sam Polk's father and uncle had pursued this formula successfully in North Carolina. Then, early in the new century, they had leveraged it further in the West by selling high-priced North Carolina land and purchasing much larger tracts of low-cost Tennessee acreage. They set-tled in what would become Maury County, south of Nashville, and founded James Polk's lifelong hometown, Columbia. Hence when Sam Polk followed them there in 1806, the way was paved for him to pros-per quickly if he was willing to invest long days of toil and plenty of sweat. Sam's father, Ezekiel, not only accumulated a thousand acres of rich-soil land but also fathered fourteen children, who in turn produced for him ninety-two grandchildren and 307 great-grandchildren.

One of Ezekiel's grandchildren, of course, was young James, but he would give the old man no great-grandchildren. Most likely this resulted from a medical development in his young life that must have had a searing impact on the lad's consciousness. He was a bright and studious boy with an early zest for learning. But he was weak and sickly, unable to do even modest physical chores without wilt-ing under the strain. The boy's father got him apprenticed to a local merchant so he could pursue a trade that wouldn't tax his physical strength. James hated the mercantile life and even more so the termination of his formal schooling. Then when he was seventeen the doctors finally diagnosed his ailment—urinary stones, which were slowly sapping his health. The only solution was surgery, a highly risky and painful procedure in those days before modern anesthetics.

Sam Polk bundled up the lad in the back of his wagon and took him to Danville, Kentucky, residence of an acclaimed medical pioneer named Ephraim McDowell. The doctor performed a surgery that can only be described as a necessary barbarity. With brandy his only sedative, young James was placed on his back with his legs secured by straps high in the air. With a knife the doctor cut into the perineum, through what would become known as the pelvic floor. He then used a pointed instrument called a gorget to cut through the prostate and into the bladder. A scoop or forceps was used to remove the stones. However hellish, it was a medical success. But, knowing what we know now about the nerves that line the prostate and control much of the sexual function, it would seem likely the operation left the young man impotent or sterile, perhaps both.

In any event, following his recovery he resumed his formal schooling with enthusiasm. At a small Presbyterian academy near Columbia, he proved "diligent in his studies, and his moral conduct was unexceptional & exemplary," according to a recommendation submitted later by the school. During subsequent studies at the Murfreesboro Academy, he displayed what a school document called "literary merit and moral worth." He was admitted to the University of North Carolina as a sophomore and was graduated three years later with first honors in both mathematics and classics. At the university he developed a personal outlook and pattern of behavior that would guide him through life: He never considered himself brilliant, and he knew he lacked the outsized personal characteristics that propelled some others through life with apparent ease. Yet he discovered that he had a highly functional mind, and if he applied himself with diligence and avoided diversions, he could excel beyond his peers. He acquired a seriousness of purpose and intensity of ambition that would become hallmark traits. They complemented the physical appearance that settled upon him in adult-hood. Just above medium height, he was not at first glance an imposing figure. But he conveyed a pleasant countenance marked by his strong oval face and prominent chin. He carried himself with a dignity and self-confidence that led many to see him eventually as a man of mark.

Upon graduating, he studied law under Felix Grundy, the state's most acclaimed lawyer and a former member of Congress. Taking a shine to the earnest young man, Grundy offered social connections and personal guidance as well as legal training. Within two years Polk was admitted to the bar, and with Grundy's help and his own fami-ly's prominence he didn't have any trouble acquiring clients. Soon his practice was sufficiently lucrative so he could branch out as clerk of the state Senate at Murfreesboro. It was at this time, in 1819, that he met Sarah Childress, then sixteen. At a high-toned reception to honor a prominent Tennessean named William Carroll (later governor), he saw young Sarah's reflection in a large mirror. "She's beautiful," he thought and began making his way through the crowded room to where she had been talking with General Jackson, a longtime family friend of the Childresses as well as the Polks. By the time he got there she was gone. But then he saw her talking with Anderson Childress, a classmate from his Murfreesboro Academy days. It turned out the young woman was Childress's sister—the same person Polk had met years earlier when she was a young girl. Anderson asked Sarah if she remembered James from their encounters years earlier.

"Why, of course I do," replied the self-possessed young lady.

Anderson later offered James a ride home in the family carriage, and the two got to know each other better.

But the young man was slow to pursue her as a marriage compan-ion—until Jackson slyly intervened. When Polk sought the General's counsel on how he might pursue his political ambitions, Jackson said he should take a wife and become an established member of society. Polk asked if Jackson had anyone in mind.

"The one who will never give you trouble," his mentor replied. "Her wealthy family, education, health, and appearance are all supe-rior. You know her well."

"You mean Sarah Childress?" asked Polk. Then, "I shall go at once and ask her."

They were married on the evening of January 1, 1824. By then the intensely ambitious Polk had been elected to the state legislature and was eyeing a run for Congress the following year. He also had joined the Tennessee militia, in which he eventually would rise to the rank of colonel.

With Jackson's endorsement he won the congressional seat in August 1825 and headed to Washington the following December. In reaching the capital, he entered into a political crucible defined largely by the political rivalry and personal animosity between two men—Andrew Jackson and Henry Clay. It isn't possible to understand Polk's emergence without understanding its political context. And nothing illuminates that context more clearly than the awesome tensions, political and personal, between the men known throughout the nation by their colloquial nicknames Old Hickory and Prince Hal—arguably the two greatest political figures to emerge in the second generation era of American politics.

There were similarities between the two. Born in the Southeast's Piedmont region, both sought opportunity across the Alleghenies in the boisterous western lands of Tennessee and Kentucky. Both gravitated to the law and gained early prominence in civic affairs—Jackson as judge and military officer, Clay as politician and diplomat. Both hungered for national fame and influence. Both married into prominent frontier families. And both harbored profound feelings of patriotism and viewed themselves as protectors of the Founders' civic legacy and dream of American greatness.

Beyond such similarities the two men could not have been more different. While Clay was playful in conversation, Jackson was stolid and upright. While Clay viewed politics as a game of intrigue in which the pursuit of victory was nearly as sweet as victory itself, Jackson considered politics a deadly serious business involving unbending principle. While Clay easily could forgive the most cutting rhetoric directed against him and expected the same from his adversaries, Jackson never forgot a slight he considered gratuitous. Clay moved with ease through any crowd or situation and brought forth an audacious eloquence based on his mastery of the language in all of its richness, range, and nuance. Jackson's eloquence was of a different cast—blunt, no-nonsense, unadorned language aimed directly at ordinary folk and betraying a depth of conviction and passion that moved people with its simplicity and common wisdom. Clay loved the legislative game that called forth his eloquence, wiles, and mastery of issues and people. Jackson hated the ceaseless debates and self-important maneuvering that characterized Congress.

But it was the variance in their political views that framed the pivotal debates of their era. Clay wanted the power of federal Washington brought to bear boldly in behalf of domestic prosperity. Almost single-handedly he crafted a philosophy of governmental activism and devised a collection of federal programs and policies he considered essential to American prosperity. He called it the American System, and it would become the bedrock of his Whig Party. Jackson abhorred the very thought of concentrated power in Washington, which he believed would lead inevitably to corruption and invidious governmental actions favoring the connected and powerful at the expense of ordinary citizens. He wanted political power to remain diffuse and as close to the people as possible. These two outlooks, personified by these two men, would drive political events surrounding nearly all the major issues of their day: protective tariffs, the Bank of the United States, public works, public lands—and, ultimately, American expansion into Texas, Oregon, New Mexico, and California.

JACKSON'S life and legend would serve as inspiration for James Polk throughout his life. Born 1767 in the Waxhaw region of the Carolinas, Jackson grew up in deprivation. His father had died before his birth, and his mother moved with her three boys into the plantation home of her sister and brother-in-law, the Crawfords, who had eight children of their own. With his mother busy earning her keep through household devotions and the Crawfords focused on their own offspring, the skinny lad quickly learned self-reliance. He developed an independent, pugnacious demeanor, always ready to fight for his interests and never willing to surrender even when bigger boys beat him up. He had almost no formal schooling, and his lack of mastery over spelling and grammar would become something of an identity scar in later life, ridiculed by political opponents frustrated by his tendency to rise in society despite these limitations. Young Jackson grew up quickly during the Revolution, when the Carolinas were ravaged by the British force known as Tarleton's Raiders. Judged too young to carry a rifle, the thirteen-year-old served as courier and scout. At one point, caught in a firefight, young Jackson witnessed a cousin killed at his side. Later he became a prisoner of war. When a British officer ordered the young rebel to polish the officer's boots, Jackson defiantly refused—and almost lost his life when the enraged officer brought down a sword upon his head. Jackson managed to deflect the blow but gashes on his hand and head left lifelong scars only slightly more apparent than his lifelong hatred of the English.

During these travails, the boy lost his two brothers to war and his mother to cholera. After Independence, orphaned and alone at seventeen, Jackson apprenticed in the law at Salisbury, North Carolina, and developed a reputation as a wild young man who drank, gambled, and roistered. But his commanding presence slowly gained dominance over his wilder tendencies. Tall, well proportioned, and always well dressed, he carried himself in polite society with dignity and courtliness. The intense gaze of his welkin blue eyes suggested an immense self-regard. One young woman of the area wrote that he possessed "a kind of majesty I never saw in any other young man."

At twenty-one, in search of financial betterment, he left North Carolina for the fledgling outpost of Nashville, in what would become Tennessee. He practiced law, acquired property, became a merchant of eastern goods, married a young divorcée named Rachel Robards, and took up with the territorial militia.* He became Tennessee's first congressman in 1796 and later served a one-session stint as U.S. sena-

---

* Rachel's actual marital status at the time of their wedding was in question, which resulted in later allegations of scandal that enraged the devoted husband.

tor. But he thrived particularly in the militia. Frontier citizens could accept a certain lassitude in their prosecutors, judges, and politicians, but not in their elected military leaders. Those were times when the area lost a man, woman, or child to Indian attack every ten days or so, and the tenuous existence of pioneer whites necessitated the highest degree of competence in their military commanders. Jackson possessed the desired attributes—quickness of mind, boldness of action, an ability to gain sway over other men, a deep sense of rectitude. And his occasional impetuousness and flashes of temper only added to his commanding mystique. In 1802, at thirty-five, he was elected major general of the Tennessee militia.

There followed a number of years when his military exploits and personal proclivity for roustabout conduct seemed in conflict. His reputation as a man out of control lingered as a result of a number of duels, that notorious gunfight with Thomas Hart Benton and his brother, and a tendency toward hotheaded reactions to presumed slights and insults. And yet, with the outbreak of the War of 1812, as major general of the United States Volunteers and later in the Regular Army, he ran up a string of military victories against the Creek Indians and the British that brought him national attention and widespread adulation. Displaying a toughness that stirred his troops to identify him with the hardness of hickory, he acquired his famous nickname. A noted example was the day he put down a mutiny of disgruntled troops by ordering artillery guns to be pointed at the troops as he confronted them. He then demanded that the mutineers return to their posts or he would order the guns to be fired, destroying them and himself in one barrage. The action stunned the wayward soldiers into subjection. Bringing his troops back into line, he destroyed elements of the Creek Indian tribe bent on terrorizing settlers in Mississippi. And he devastated a British army seeking to seize New Orleans and its strategic dominance over the Mississippi River Valley. The British reported 2,037 dead, wounded, and missing on that fateful January day in 1815, while Jackson's troops suffered only thirteen killed. Instantly he became a national hero and potential presidential contender. Subsequent military exploits against the Seminole Indians and a stint as governor of Florida Territory bolstered his countrywide standing. And yet he invited detractors with displays of defiance and a tendency to substitute his own judgment for those of his superiors. Most often he was right on the merits, but these traits provided an opening for critics to suggest he couldn't be trusted with power. By the 1820s, Jackson was probably the country's most revered figure, but also one of its most controversial.

A DECADE YOUNGER than Jackson, Clay soared to national prominence at a younger age. Born in 1777 into a comfortable Virginia family of yeoman farmers, he was one of eight siblings, four of whom died in infancy. His father, a planter and rousing Baptist minister, died when Henry was four. His mother remarried a plantation owner and militia captain named Henry Watkins. Aside from witnessing the ransacking of his home by Tarleton's Raiders shortly after his father's death, the boy grew up in comfort amid trappings of culture and learning. He didn't apply himself much to the meager formal education then available in rural Virginia. As he later explained with characteristic self-absorption, "I always relied too much upon the resources of my genius." Indeed, it was clear to all who knew the strapping youngster that he possessed special qualities of intellect and spirit. At sixteen, he became secretary to George Wythe, one of the state's top jurists, who gave the lad a sterling education in the law and civic affairs as well as entrée to the highest Richmond society. Four years with Wythe and another with Richmond lawyer Robert Brooke provided young Clay with enough background to pass his bar examination. He then set out for Kentucky, where his mother and stepfather had gone some years before.

He settled in Lexington, connected with other Wythe protégés, established a law practice, married, and prospered. He became known as brilliant, industrious, and dependable, and the town's residents soon were exchanging stories about this exciting young man who seemed always ready with an amusing quip or flight of eloquence on some intriguing topic. He was not without character flaws. His wit some-

times veered into the outrageous, and he displayed a weakness for
gambling, dueling, and indulgence with women. He also harbored a
certain intellectual arrogance, manifest in a biting invective directed
at those he considered less brainy than himself. Bored by a loquacious
man who suggested he spoke for posterity, Clay interjected, "Yes, and
you seem resolved to speak until the arrival of your audience."

Gravitating inevitably to politics, he served a number of terms in
the Kentucky legislature and twice was elected to fill vacancies in the
U.S. Senate before settling on a House career in 1810, at age thirty-
three. Such was the young westerner's reputation as a legislator that
his colleagues promptly elected him speaker upon his House arrival.
He thrived in the role and distinguished himself further when President James Madison sent him to Europe to help negotiate the Treaty
of Ghent ending the War of 1812. There he encountered John Quincy
Adams, who didn't much care for Clay's inveterate dissipations. An
early riser, Adams became increasingly disgusted to see, at the start
of his day, Clay heading off to bed after a night of drinking and card-
playing. When his diplomatic mission ended, he returned to the
House and his old job as speaker. In that role he brought off one of the
most difficult and commendable legislative feats of his generation—
the Missouri Compromise bills of 1820–1821, which sought to maintain a delicate balance of political power between slave and free states
and thus prevent the slavery issue from sundering the Union. Immediately Clay was hailed as the Great Compromiser, the "savior of his
country." His national standing was unrivaled by any other American
save Andrew Jackson.

Despite his brilliance, Clay displayed a tendency to misread political forces and trends and thus tread into unnecessary thickets. An
early example occurred after President James Monroe recalled Andrew
Jackson to military service in 1817 to subdue a wave of Seminole
Indian attacks against frontier Americans. Jackson's orders allowed
him to pursue the Seminoles to their protected enclaves in Spanish
Florida and to clean up operations there. Jackson invaded Florida,
crushed the desultory Spanish defenses, burned Seminole villages at
will, and created an international incident by hanging two British

subjects convicted in a military court of assisting the Seminoles in their murderous raids. Most Americans rejoiced, but some expressed shock. Juices of indignation flowed in Congress, and a censure measure emerged in the House.

On January 20, 1819, Speaker Clay rose to address the matter, and everyone knew he would not be kind. The galleries were so packed that one witness wondered if they could hold up under the weight. "Even the outer entries were thronged," he added, "and yet such silence prevailed that tho' at a considerable distance I did not lose a word." At times harsh, witty, admonitory, outraged, outrageous, amusing, and devastating, Clay spoke for two hours and never lost his audience. "Beware," he warned, "how you give a fatal sanction . . . to military insubordination. Remember that Greece had her Alexander, Rome her Caesar, England her Cromwell, France her Bonaparte, and, that if we would escape the rock on which they split, we must avoid their errors." Many in the galleries gasped, for he had just called Jackson a likely tyrant. He immediately disavowed any intent to assault Jackson's character, but such disclaimers couldn't wash away the force of his earlier words, and Jackson now was Clay's lifelong enemy. It was a major political blunder, as Quincy Adams quickly perceived. "His opposition to Jackson," wrote Adams, "is now involuntary, and mere counteractive." Jackson could hate with a vengeance, and now he would never pass by an opportunity to cut down his rival.

POLK'S WASHINGTON ARRIVAL in 1825 followed a powerful political development that would mark the beginning of Jackson's political ascendancy and ensure the frustration of Clay's lifelong presidential ambition. Some months before, on February 17, word spread through official Washington that President-elect John Quincy Adams had offered the job of secretary of state to Clay. And Clay had accepted. This was big news. As House speaker, Kentucky's consummate dealmaker had engineered Adams's rise to the presidency after the 1824 election had failed to produce a majority winner and the presidential contest had fallen to the House. Clay had even rebuffed the clear political sentiment of his own state to give Kentucky's House delegation to Adams rather than Jackson. Everyone knew that four of the country's six presidents had reached the White House from the job of secretary of state. Thus, to all appearances, the presidency—indeed, American democracy itself—had been bartered in a backroom deal closed off to the scrutiny and reach of the nation's voters.

Over at Gadsby's Tavern near the Capitol, where Jackson had taken up residence the previous December 7, the Old General received the news from an agitated supporter named Richard M. Johnson. The General exploded into one of his famous fits of rage. "So you see," he scribbled onto a letter to his loyal friend William B. Lewis, "the *Judas* of the West has closed the contract and will receive the thirty pieces of silver. . . . Was there ever witnessed such a bare faced corruption in any country before?" In Jackson's view, Clay's acceptance confirmed Washington rumors of a "corrupt bargain." He wrote: "When we behold two men political enemies, and as different in political sentiment as any men can be, so suddenly unite, there must be some unseen cause to produce this political phenomenon." His reaction, he told Lewis, was to "shudder for the liberty of my country."

Four men had vied for the presidency in 1824—Adams, Clay, Jackson, and former Georgia senator and cabinet secretary William H. Crawford. Jackson had received 154,000 votes to Adams's 109,000, while Clay and Crawford each had around 47,000. But in the Electoral College, Clay had come in fourth with 37 electoral votes, to 99 for Jackson, 84 for Adams, and 41 for Crawford. Under the Constitution, since no one had received an electoral majority, the House would choose the president from among the top three finishers. Clay was out, but he could still play kingmaker. "I cannot believe," he had written, referring to Jackson's most famous military victory, "that killing 2,500 Englishmen at New Orleans qualifies for the various, difficult and complicated duties of the Chief Magistracy." He considered Jackson a mere "military chieftain," unfit for the presidency. So his resolve to thwart Jackson and elevate Adams was natural enough.

But accepting the job at State was something else entirely. Clay knew it would look bad, but he wanted the position, and the one it

could lead to, with an almost desperate ambition. Besides, his arrogant confidence in his own political skills convinced him that he could
handle any political difficulties that might arise from his decision. So
he accepted the offer—and ensured the ascendancy of the one man
whose political career he most wished to thwart. Jackson now held
an almost unimaginable opportunity to drive out this rival administration at the next election. Employing rhetoric that included words
such as "cheating," "corruption," and "bribery," he set out on a four-
year campaign to destroy the Adams presidency and, with it, the Clay
ascendancy.

INTO THIS POLITICAL maelstrom stepped young James Polk, just
thirty when he began his congressional career bent on lending his
vote and voice to the furtherance of the Jackson career. In March
1826 he delivered his maiden floor speech favoring a constitutional
amendment to ensure that presidents were elected by direct popular vote—and never by the House. With a certain youthful sophistry,
he quoted selectively from the Constitution's preamble, the Federalist Papers, and various politicians to demonstrate that the Framers
clearly intended presidential elections to be decided by the people at
large. This was entirely false, but Jackson duly offered praise from his
estate outside Nashville, known as the Hermitage.

"Your speech . . . I have read with much pleasure," wrote the General, "and I can assure you is well received by all your constituents,
and gives you a strong claim to their future confidence." Later, when
Polk sent his mentor a long letter filled with inside Washington intelligence, the General responded warmly: "I feel greatly obliged to you
for the information . . . and I duly appreciate those feelings of friendship which dictated the communication."

In 1827, Polk won reelection in what was now a safe district. The
same year the Democrats took control of the House and promptly
replaced the pro-Adams speaker with a loyal Jacksonian, Andrew Stevenson of Virginia. "It was a great triumph," an elated Polk wrote a
friend. Returning to Washington for the next session of Congress, Polk

took with him the twenty-three-year-old Sarah, who had remained in Columbia, much to her dismay, during Polk's first-term trips to the federal capital. The young congressman's wife quickly emerged as his conspicuous helpmate, handling his correspondence and dealing with boarding matters at the couple's house on Pennsylvania Avenue. When Polk gave a speech on the House floor, Sarah often could be seen watching from the gallery. It was clear to friends and acquaintances that Polk was much enamored of his young wife. In one letter to a friend he extolled her stamina and good cheer during their stagecoach travels. She seldom needed to stop for rests, he said, and complained about the arduous trips far less than he did himself.

The Polks' return to Washington coincided with growing optimism among Democrats about Jackson's presidential prospects the next year. Already his forces were working furiously to position their man for victory, and the effort gave Polk further opportunity to attach his career to that of his mentor. He enlisted in the Nashville Central Committee, a pro-Jackson operation set up to parry any campaign allegations against the General. And there would be many, including murder, adultery, dueling, gambling, drinking, cockfighting, and swearing. Clay, mastermind of Adams's reelection campaign, knew Jackson's defeat required that his heroic image be shredded, and he set out to do that by dredging up for attack every indiscretion or misstep in his long career. Many of the allegations were spurious. One particularly vicious handbill alleged that Jackson's execution of six militiamen for desertion during the Creek War was actually murder as they merely had wanted to depart the military at the close of their enlistments. Polk helped gather evidence showing their crimes actually had included mutiny as well as desertion.

Meeting with Jackson and his allies in the summer of 1828, Polk discussed whether the General should defend himself publicly against the multiple allegations. Polk favored a dignified public address. But later he thought better of it and sent Jackson a letter saying so. "Treat every thing that has or may be said," he suggested, "with silent contempt." Jackson appreciated the counsel so much that he wrote upon the page, "My friend Col Polk's letter to be kept as a token of his real friendship." Replying to his protégé, he wrote, "I receive my Dr. Sir, your letter as the highest evidence of your sincere friendship, & as such have treasured it up."

The campaign unfolded amidst a subtle transformation in presidential politics that translated into opportunity. Through the nation's early decades, presidential elections had been in the hands of state legislators and other local men of prominence, who selected the electors who in turn selected the president. The idea was that the people themselves would not be directly involved in the process and would defer instead to the elites. Property restrictions also served to curtail voter involvement and hence voter interest in presidential elections. But, responding to a wave of populism emerging in the West, more and more states were choosing electors by popular vote and eliminating property requirements. The result was the emergence of a mass electorate, and any candidate who could reach these new voters could blow away the opposition. Jackson understood this; Adams and Clay missed it.

Jackson also understood that his central allegation of the campaign—the so-called corrupt bargain between Adams and Clay—was just the kind of message that would resonate with this new broad electorate. He would exploit this to the hilt, notwithstanding the lack of evidence that any quid pro quo deal had ever been struck. Besides, President Adams was embracing most of the major elements of Clay's American System—protective tariffs, federal internal improvements such as roads, bridges, and canals, even a bold concept to create a national university. Jackson opposed all this, and he was sure the expanded electorate would oppose it too. Thus, a new political alignment was emerging. On one side were Adams and Clay representing the Republicans' old Madisonian wing, which favored positive national legislation to promote economic development. Aligning with them were the remnants of the declining Federalists led by the impassioned and golden-voiced senator from Massachusetts, Daniel Webster. The other side included Jackson, Georgia's William Crawford, and Missouri's Thomas Benton, now a committed Jacksonian despite the earlier unpleasantness in Nashville. These men led a fac-

tion that opposed greater concentrations of federal power for any purpose. They also felt disturbed by Adams's earnest agitations against
slavery and, as national expansionists, faulted the administration for
not moving more aggressively to secure western territory for settlement by dealing with Indian land titles there.

It turned into an intense and nasty campaign before it ended with
a sweeping Jackson victory in November 1828. Jackson carried 56
percent of the popular vote to Adams's 43.6 percent; he also carried
178 electoral votes to Adams's 83. What's more, Jackson's Democrats
swept both houses of Congress by significant margins. Adams, fore-
seeing the calamity, had slipped into a depression at the thought of a
man such as himself, so admired and respected by czars, prime ministers, and brilliant intellectuals, being so unceremoniously discarded
by his own countrymen at the hands of a political ruffian. All he
could do, he concluded, was "await my allotted time. My own career
is closed." Clay missed the coming wave. "I yet think that Mr. Adams
will be reelected," he told Webster as the vote totals made their way
to Washington. His campaign rhetoric betrayed his misplaced optimism. "I would humbly prostrate myself before Him, and implore
his mercy, to visit our land with war, with pestilence, with famine,
with any scourge other than this military rule or a blind and heed-
less enthusiasm for mere military renown." Such words only enraged
Jackson all the more—and underscored a political casualness toward
the country's well-being that Jackson found scandalous.

Returning to his Ashland estate in Lexington for an extended
respite from affairs of state, Clay refused to see Jackson's victory as a
repudiation of his American System but rather as an accident of history that would be reversed as soon as the people perceived Jackson's
political incompetence. "We must but passively await the inevitable fragmentation of Jackson's alliance," he wrote a friend. But soon
it became apparent that Jackson was far more formidable than his
opponents had anticipated. And within three years Clay's congressional friends were begging him to return to the fray. "Everything valuable in the government is to be fought for," wrote Webster to Clay,
"and we need your arm in the fight." Indeed, the congressional oppo-

sition had sought to thwart Jackson at every turn but usually ended up outmaneuvered. When Jackson nominated a New Hampshire editor named Isaac Hill for a minor position in his administration, the Senate blithely rejected the man. The president quickly moved to get New Hampshire Democrats to redress this wrong by electing Hill to the very senatorial body that had repudiated him. When Jackson sought to get New York's Martin Van Buren, emerging as a presidential favorite, confirmed as minister to London, again the Senate turned thumbs-down. This time the Old General simply tagged Van Buren, now a subject of great sympathy among Democrats, to be vice president in his second administration. "You have broken a Minister and made a Vice-President," Thomas Benton sneered at one disgruntled Van Buren opponent.

Throughout the forthcoming political struggles unleashed by Jackson's bold brand of politics, Polk would be well positioned to help his mentor—and reap plenty of benefit in the process. Jackson long had demonstrated shrewdness in finding bright and effective men who would rally to his cause. Now as president he needed many such followers, and he could not find a better man than Polk to serve his interests in the House. Though hardly eloquent, Polk's rhetoric cut through to the nub of important matters and showed a precision of logic that gave force to his arguments. As one admiring newspaper would later put it, "His preference for the useful and substantial . . . has made him select a style of elocution which would, perhaps, be deemed too plain by the shallow admirers of flashy declamation. The worst of all styles is the florid and exaggerated!" Besides, no one would demonstrate greater discipline or put in longer hours. Few could match Polk's analytical skill in assessing the meaning of political events. And he was utterly loyal. Not only did he share Jackson's broad political philosophy, bequeathed through their shared family and ethnic heritage, but he would avidly embrace any tasks placed before him. Thus, as the struggle between Jackson and Clay intensified to an ever greater pitch of emotion and risk, young Polk would find himself with ever greater political tasks.

2 · TENNESSEE AND WASHINGTON

The Rise and Fall of a Presidential Loyalist

ON MAY 27, 1830, President Jackson shocked official Washington by stamping his veto upon a piece of legislation that most politicians had considered routine. It was a measure to extend the so-called National Road from Maysville to Lexington, Kentucky. The National Road project had begun back in 1811 in Cumberland, Maryland, and extended west in stages over the succeeding years. It was just the kind of public works that fit neatly under Clay's American System. But Jackson had always opposed the idea of Congress appropriating federal money for local projects. Now, as president, he knew his veto would generate anger among westerners even within his own party. But he sent it up anyway, along with an extensive rationale aimed not at legislators but at voters. The people, he said, had a right to expect a "prudent system of expenditure" that would allow the government to "pay the debts of the union and authorize the reduction of every tax to as low a point as . . . our national safety and independence will allow." Once the national debt left over from the War of 1812 was repaid, he promised, the government would make surplus resources available to the states for internal improvements. But direct expenditures for projects that went beyond purposes of defense and national benefit struck Jackson as constitutionally suspect.

Characteristically, the president feared that such power in the hands of federal officials would lead inevitably to "a corrupting influence upon the elections" by giving people a sense that their votes

31

could purchase beneficial governmental actions to "make navigable their neighboring creek or river, bring commerce to their doors, and increase the value of their property." This, he said in a series of "notes" on the issue, would prove "fatal to just legislation" and the "purity of public men."

This was all too much for Henry Clay. Following events from his Ashland estate near Lexington, Prince Hal promptly heeded Webster's call and got himself elected to the Senate in November 1831. He would take the reins of leadership in the struggle to thwart and destroy this dangerous administration. From that moment, Clay would be, as historian Claude G. Bowers put it, "the brilliant, resourceful, bitter, and unscrupulous leader of the Opposition."

Young James Polk, emerging by now as a skilled legislator, was thrilled to be in the thick of these fights. A publication known as the *Democratic Review* identified him as one of the administration's leading supporters "and at times, and on certain questions of paramount importance, its chief reliance." Polk also enjoyed having Sarah with him during the congressional sessions. The couple settled into a pleasant routine during their Washington stays. Each session they would join a small group of other couples who lived together, according to the custom of the day, in a boardinghouse, with private apartments upstairs and a common dining room and parlor downstairs. Among their early housemates were Tennessee senator Hugh Lawson White, Maine congressman Leonard Jarvis, and South Carolina's John C. Calhoun. Sarah enjoyed the capital's social scene and developed friendships with the wives of numerous major players in Congress and the president's cabinet. She acquired a reputation as a lively conversationalist who nevertheless avoided expressions that could raise questions of any kind of impropriety. She eschewed any hint of gossip or mirth at the expense of others, in part because it was against her nature but also because the priggish James considered such conversational habits to be particularly discreditable. If, in her social exuberance, she slipped into a hasty observation that nobody else would question, James nevertheless might direct toward her a particular smile that she came to interpret as a gentle hint that she may be close to the line.

Later he might say, "Sarah, I wish you would not say that. I understand you, but others might not, and a wrong impression might be made." For her part, she felt such nudges reflected his essential gentleness. "That was the strongest rebuke he ever gave me," she once said. "When persons speak of my strict ideas of propriety, I think of my husband's circumspection, and reply, 'You were not brought up in so strict a school as I was.'"

But her own social standards were just as strict. When the wife of a cabinet secretary invited her on an afternoon outing to the horse races, she declined. Later that evening, she encountered the woman at a social event.

"Oh, why did you not go with me to-day?" she asked, adding that many members of Congress and their wives had attended the exciting event, featuring a race between the thoroughbreds of two prominent Tennesseans. Sarah replied pleasantly that she never attended the races and didn't wish to violate her rule.

"Well," said the woman with a smile, "that is a reflection on me."

"Oh, no," replied Sarah tactfully, "not at all. You are in the habit of going. I am not." She avoided horse races throughout her life.

Polk never allowed his social obligations to interfere with his defense of the Jackson agenda. When the Maysville Road bill arrived on the floor, with clear majority sentiment behind it, he tied it up for three days of debate. He disputed its constitutionality, since it benefited but a single state, and accused members of Congress of labeling as "national" any project that sent federal dollars to their particular districts. After the bill cleared Congress, Polk helped Jackson and his speechwriter, Amos Kendall, draft the veto message. And, when the veto was sustained, he joined his administration friends in rejoicing.

Jackson and Polk viewed such issues as reflecting a wide philosophical chasm over the very essence of American democracy. Though Clay had never embraced the concept of an entrenched aristocracy of the kind that captivated some members of the dying Federalist Party, he nonetheless believed in an office-holding class that would emerge through a system of indirect democracy and serve the country by running it. In this view, no one should be born to power; it should be earned through meritorious service. But, having earned it, national leaders should be allowed to manage affairs of state without undue interference from the masses. Leadership—and power—should come from landed interests, business and financial interests, the intellectual classes. Clay had in mind men rather like himself who possessed sufficient brilliance and understanding to know what was best for the nation. This was precisely the concept of government that Jackson despised. With Thomas Jefferson, he distrusted any elites or concentrations of power, particularly if they were insulated from the reach and passions of the broad electorate. Power corrupts, he believed, and the best protection against tyranny was to bring the masses into the process to the fullest extent possible. In this view, the people possessed a collective judgment and wisdom that would guide the nation to its destiny in a manner that would be appropriate and just. Jackson believed his own election, by repudiating the "corrupt bargain" of Adams-Clay elitism, made the point. Providence, he said, had "pronounced . . . that the people are virtuous and capable of self-government."

This conflict of politics and philosophy was reflected in an issue that emerged following Clay's return to Washington—disposition of more than a billion acres of federal lands in the West and South. Clay and his allies saw this acreage as a vast governmental revenue source that could be poured back into the nation in the form of internal improvements. Jackson and Thomas Benton, on the other hand, favored a system of graduated prices, with free grants to actual settlers who would promise to develop the land. Benton argued the country could benefit most by making these lands readily available to ordinary citizens who would raze the foliage, till the soil, build wealth through hard work, establish communities, and, in the process, expand the culture of American democracy. Elites weren't needed, in this view, because the people themselves would build up the nation from below.

Clay employed his brilliant oratory to get his version through the Senate, but it died in the House. Still, he and his allies celebrated what they considered a notable senatorial victory, unmindful that most voters viewed their Senate triumph as added impetus for supporting Jackson over Clay in the 1832 election. With that election approaching, the Kentuckian needed a big issue to cut into Jackson's popularity. The internal improvements issue didn't work because most voters actually approved the Maysville Road veto. The lands issue, Clay eventually realized, was actually hurting the cause. The tariff didn't work because the president cleverly had crafted a compromise approach designed to capture majority sentiment—bringing down the so-called Tariff of Abominations enacted in the John Quincy Adams administration while leaving in place sufficient duties to placate northern industrialists. So he would make his stand on the Second Bank of the United States.

The First Bank of the United States, chartered during the country's early Federalist period, was the brainchild of Alexander Hamilton, who saw the bank as a means of giving the economy sufficient liquidity, maintaining currency stability, and ensuring economic efficiency. Jefferson and his Republican allies had attacked the bank as a dangerous concentration of financial power, and in 1811 the bank's charter had been allowed to expire. However, with the outbreak of the War of 1812 it became clear the country needed a central banking authority. State banks in the Northeast, where the war was unpopular, were hoarding the country's meager reserves of specie (gold and silver), and banks in other regions were forced to rely solely on printed money. The result was a menacing wave of inflation and considerable economic dislocation. Thus, the Second Bank of the United States, patterned on the first, was established in 1816 and set up shop in the nation's financial center of Philadelphia. Immediately it slipped into corruption as its first president, William Jones, promiscuously violated terms of the charter, speculated in the bank's stock, and exploited the venal practices of the bank's branch members. Jones was forced out, and his successor sought to clean up the mess by calling in unsound loans, foreclosing on overdue mortgages, and redeeming overextended notes from state banks. The result was the Panic of 1819 as local banks slipped into bankruptcy, prices collapsed, unemployment soared, and a general economic malaise gripped the country.

Inevitably the bank became the focus of intense political passions.

Not surprisingly, Jackson abhorred this concentration of economic power in what he called a "hydra-headed monster" that eastern elites inevitably would exploit for their own corrupt ends. But he wasn't inclined to force the issue, as the bank charter was not due to expire until 1836. Clay had other ideas. Looking ahead to the 1832 election, when he fully expected to get the presidential nomination of the opposition party, he settled upon a simple political calculus: If Jackson were forced to attack the bank, he would lose Pennsylvania; if he lost Pennsylvania, he would lose the election. Clay sought to get the bank's young president, Nicholas Biddle, to seek an immediate charter renewal from Congress.

Biddle was the picture of the educated eastern establishment of his day—dapper, smooth of manner, highly literate, widely schooled. Though he professed no interest in politics, he maintained a wide network of political friendships that practically constituted a pro-bank political faction encompassing elements of both political parties. Arrogant to a fault, he had cultivated a reputation as a man of power and influence beyond what was prudent. When addressed as "Emperor Nicholas," he would smile approvingly, unmindful of the political hostility generated by such personal grandiosity. On January 6, 1832, Biddle complied with Clay's request by submitting to Congress a request for renewal of the bank. What followed was an epic political struggle that would reverberate throughout the remainder of Jackson's presidency and beyond.

Clay knew the bank enjoyed sufficient congressional support, even among Democrats, to ensure victory for the new charter. The only question was whether Jackson would veto that bill and invite a political backlash in an election year. "Should Jackson veto it," the Kentuckian declared, "I shall veto him." Jackson's anti-bank forces developed a strategy best described by Thomas Benton: "attack incessantly, assail at all points, display the evil of the institution, rouse the people—and prepare them to sustain the veto." Benton took command of the anti-bank effort in Congress, but Polk wasn't far behind. When the recharter memorial was assigned to the Ways and Means Committee, chaired by the implacably pro-bank and anti-Jackson

George McDuffie of South Carolina, Benton got Georgia's neophyte Representative Augustin Clayton to introduce a resolution calling for an investigation of the bank's condition and methods. When the pro-bank forces fought back, Polk led the opposition with what historian Claude Bowers called "the strongest speech of his congressional career." He attacked the bank for requesting a recharter while opposing the kind of scrutiny needed to justify voting for it. It all raised suspicions, he said, that there was something "rotten in the state of Denmark." The investigation was approved, in part because many pro-bank members feared their opposition would raise questions about the favorable loans and other financial beneficence bestowed upon them by bank president Biddle.

The investigations committee brought forth three reports. The majority issued allegations of wrongdoing and corruption while two minority reports exonerated the bank. There wasn't much definitive proof in any of them, but the majority report gave Jackson the fodder he needed for his planned veto, while the pro-bank forces seized the minority tracts to bolster their anti-Jackson campaign rhetoric. In the summer of 1832 both houses of Congress approved Biddle's bill. "I congratulate our friends most cordially upon this most satisfactory result," wrote the egotistical banker. "Now for the President."

The president promptly brought in Kendall and nephew Andrew Jackson Donelson to draft a veto message, then got Attorney General Roger Taney's guidance. He sent the completed political manifesto to Congress with full awareness that it would hit political Washington—indeed the country—like a boulder thrown atop an anthill. For it turned out to be a turning point in the rise of American democracy, a quantum leap in the emergence of the mass electorate. Thenceforth, any politician desiring to lead the nation would have to go beyond expressing merely what was best for the people. He would have to speak in the *name* of the people.

In measured and detailed language, Jackson's veto message portrayed the bank as a government-sponsored monopoly that employed the money of taxpayers to enhance the power, privileges, and wealth of a very few Americans and foreigners—"chiefly the richest class"—

who owned stock in the bank. If government is to grant such gratu-
ities, he said, "let them not be bestowed on the subjects of a foreign
government nor upon a designated and favored class of men in our
own country." Rather, he added, such favors should be confined "to
our own fellow-citizens, and let each in his turn enjoy the opportunity
to profit by our bounty." Jackson made it clear he harbored no impulse
toward economic equality or societal leveling, but wished merely to
ensure that the levers of government were not used to bestow special
beneficence upon a well-positioned few. He explained:

> Distinctions in society will always exist under every just govern-
> ment. Equality of talents, of education, or of wealth can not be pro-
> duced by human institutions. In the full enjoyment of the gifts of
> Heaven and the fruits of superior industry, economy, and virtue,
> every man is equally entitled to protection by law; but when the
> laws undertake to add to these natural and just advantages arti-
> ficial distinctions, to grant titles, gratuities, and exclusive privi-
> leges, to make the rich richer and the potent more powerful, the
> humble members of society—the farmers, mechanics, and labor-
> ers—who have neither the time nor the means of securing like
> favors to themselves, have a right to complain of the injustice of
> their Government. . . . If it would confine itself to equal protec-
> tion, and, as Heaven does its rains, shower its favors alike on the
> high and the low, the rich and the poor, [government] would be
> an unqualified blessing.

With such language did the Old General once again outmaneuver his great rival Clay, whose political power had been accumulated
through alliances with the wealthy, the influential, and the educated.
Now Clay, having induced a powerful moneyed institution of the East
to seek the humiliation of a beloved president, had instead fostered a
new political force comprised of the mechanics of the cities, the farmers of the plains, and the pioneers of the frontier. "Clay," wrote historian Bowers, "had unwittingly intrigued the Jacksonians into the
advantage." As Jackson himself put it to Van Buren, "The bank . . . is

trying to kill me, but I will kill it!" Neither Clay nor Biddle understood the significance of the message. Clay called Jackson's action "a perversion of the veto power." Biddle, presuming incorrectly that the electorate would recoil at Jackson's message, had thirty thousand copies distributed as a campaign document. "It has all the fury of the unchained panther," he declared, "biting the bars of his cage."

But in the November elections Jackson brushed aside Clay with 54 percent of the popular vote and 219 electoral ballots to Clay's mere 49. Elated with Polk's dedication and effectiveness on the bank issue, the energized Jackson forces promptly got him assigned to Ways and Means, the epicenter of the next big bank controversy. With four more years on his political lease, Jackson now vowed to destroy the bank by withdrawing federal funds from its vaults and depositing them in various state banks, quickly dubbed "pet banks" by his detractors. Biddle, consumed with rage, responded by constricting the money supply in an effort to induce a recession and bring the wrath of voters down upon Jackson. "The Bank feels no vocation to redress the wrongs of these miserable people," declared Biddle. "This worthy President thinks that because he has scalped Indians and imprisoned Judges, he is to have his way with the Bank. He is mistaken."

The second bank battle began on December 4, 1832, when Jackson's annual message urged an investigation into the soundness of the U.S. Bank. The new Ways and Means chairman, Gulian Verplanck of New York, initiated a committee inquiry. But Jackson didn't trust Verplanck and turned instead to Polk. On December 16 he sent his protégé information to show, as he put it, "the hydra of corruption is only *scotched, not dead,* and that the intent is . . . to destroy the vote of the people lately given at the ballot boxes." He added: "An investigation kills it and its supporters dead. Let this be had." He urged Polk to get the treasury secretary involved and then issued a peremptory command: "Attend to this."

Polk dutifully complied. Throughout the subsequent investigation, which included testimony under oath by bank directors and others, Polk served as a leading administration functionary in the maneuvering, intrigue, and power politics that ensued. His job was to ensure that Verplanck's investigation turned up plenty of dirt on the bank. In early January 1833, Treasury Secretary Roger Taney forwarded to Polk a document calling into question certain bank actions, and later he found himself frequently cajoled by Jackson's excitable ally, Reuben Whitney, a Philadelphia businessman and former bank director. "It is of the utmost importance," Whitney wrote Polk, "that while the investigation is undertaken, it should be as thorough as possible, and the exposures as complete. . . . I beg of you to see the Secy. and the President both, *tomorrow morning* upon the subject." On a mission to Philadelphia, Whitney discovered that bank partisans planned delaying tactics until Congress adjourned. He also learned that pro-bank forces viewed Verplanck as their leading congressional ally and expected help also from John Gilmore of Pennsylvania, a Ways and Means member considered a Jackson loyalist. "I communicate to you these facts," Whitney told Polk, "to show you the importance of hastening the examination, and of our taking care that Gilmore is not tampered with." He added, "I beg of you to guard against the secret machinations of our adversaries."

Throughout these weeks Polk worked behind the scenes. But in March, Verplanck issued a Ways and Means report declaring the bank to be financially sound. The House promptly accepted Verplanck's interpretation. Polk issued a Ways and Means minority report, centering his critique on the "three percents"—securities bearing 3 percent interest that had been issued by the government some forty years before. When the government in March 1832 sought to pay off $6.5 million of these, Biddle sought a delay, citing routine timing reasons. But then the bank frantically and secretly sought to unload some of its own debt on unfavorable terms—apparently to make good on the three percents. The Verplanck report had criticized these questionable maneuverings but raised no connection between them and the bank's fiscal health.

That was too much for Polk. He rose on the House floor to deliver a scathing speech drawing a direct link. Practically the entire Jackson cabinet traveled to the Capitol to hear his rhetoric, along with that of Thomas Benton, who on the same day excoriated Clay on the

Senate floor. Polk accused Biddle of dissembling on the 3 percent matter and suggested the bank had needed the delay to shroud its own financial woes. All of Polk's fundamental political traits emerged in the speech—his exhaustive study of the issues, his capacity for clearheaded argumentation, his demeanor of dignity mixed with an instinct for partisan pugilism. "When the President of the Bank not only induces the board to act for reasons unknown to themselves," said Polk, "but conceals even from the committees acts done in their names, something stronger than doubt almost seizes on the mind." He added that given the actions of Biddle and his bank, "there is just ground to doubt whether there be soundness in the institution, or proper precaution and responsibility in its management."

Polk also argued that the president alone had jurisdiction over questions of whether the bank had violated its charter or been guilty of mismanagement. Congressional action on the matter, he declared, was "unauthorized and improper." Jackson quickly incorporated many of Polk's arguments into his bank speeches.

Biddle was outraged. He personally sought to get Polk defeated at his next election in August by funneling bank money to the anti-Polk newspaper in Nashville, while other bank proponents joined in the assault. Polk's friend Andrew Donelson wrote to say his supporters "are well apprised of the instruments which are employed to defeat you." And Polk himself described his race as "an angry and most violent contest. I am assailed from all quarters." But he won easily with 70 percent of the vote—just as the next and final battle in the long bank struggle was about to begin.

On August 31, 1833, Jackson wrote Polk saying he had managed to get a *"small peep"* at the bank's financial records and thus discovered that Biddle had funneled $80,000 into political activity aimed at getting his recharter. "Can anyone really say, from this expose that the U.S. Bank is a safe deposit for the peoples mony?" he asked, adding Polk could use the information as he wished so long as he kept the president's name out of it. Already Jackson was clearing the way for his next bold move—withdrawal of federal funds from the bank. He wanted Polk to be fortified for that battle and also for the next assignment Jackson had in mind for him—Ways and Means chairman. Not only did the Jackson men install Polk as head of the committee when Congress convened in December but also assigned to the panel enough Jackson loyalists to ensure its fealty. At the same time, Jackson sent to Congress two powerful documents—a presidential message outlining his decision to remove federal deposits from the bank; and a report from Treasury Secretary Taney defending the action.

An intense parliamentary battle ensued over which committee would get the assignment—Polk's pro-Jackson Ways and Means or the Committee of the Whole House, which could open up endless debate on the matter. Through some deft legislative maneuvering Polk outflanked the relentlessly anti-Jackson George McDuffie, but when McDuffie counterattacked the chairman faltered. He missed a chance to call for the "previous question," which would have ended floor debate and assigned the matter to his committee. Thus, the debate raged on for another two months. But throughout the subsequent floor debate, Polk thoroughly dominated the chamber, eventually getting full jurisdiction for his committee. In the meantime, on February 11, 1834, the panel had issued a report scoring the bank for its handling of certain pension matters. "The committee cannot condemn, in terms too strong, the conduct of the bank in this transaction," stated the report. A month later the committee issued a broader report upholding all of Jackson's actions related to the bank. And on April 22, Polk reported out a bill to regulate state deposit banks, thus authorizing the president's action. The full House passed the measure on June 24.

The Senate refused to go along and, in fact, under Clay's leadership, assaulted the president with a resolution censuring his bank actions. But Polk had emerged as something of a national figure for his brilliant legislative success in the House. The *Daily Globe* of Washington, the country's leading Democratic newspaper, called one of his floor speeches "perfectly irresistible" in fact and reasoning. Speaking in Tennessee, Jackson praised the chairman's performance and added, "Polk for the hard service done in the cause deserves a Medal from the American people." So pleased was the president that when Stevenson resigned as House speaker in June 1834 Jackson favored Polk for the job. But it went to fellow Tennessean John Bell, who had been emerging as a rival to Polk and a critic of Jackson. Bell promptly leveraged his new position to gain control over the Nashville newspapers and to establish a Democratic alternative to Jacksonism in Tennessee. It began to appear that Jackson could lose his longtime dominance over Tennessee politics.

The following year, when the new Congress convened in December, Polk marshaled his political resources and ousted Bell from the speakership, getting 132 votes to Bell's 84. Now he held a constitutional office and considerable sway over national politics. It was a triumph for Jackson as well. Thomas Benton called it "a test of the administration strength, Mr. Polk being supported by that party." Sarah believed her husband's new position, if held by the right kind of leader, could rival the presidency in power and influence. She had no doubt the new speaker would be the right kind of leader. The new position also required that the couple secure larger living quarters away from the common-mess boardinghouses. Political protocol dictated that the speaker shouldn't dine regularly with other members.

"The principal reason for this," James explained to Sarah, "is that awkward positions might ensue when the affairs and measures of Congress are discussed at meals."

"As would inevitably happen," she replied with a smile, "and if you were there they couldn't openly criticize the Speaker, could they?"

"Hardly," said James in an affectionate retort, "neither do I want to be subject to a charge of overintimacy by a small group of congressmen to continue to share a house with them."

But Polk's election as speaker widened Tennessee's Democratic Party split, which now threatened to go national. In 1836, Bell persuaded Tennessee's Senator Hugh Lawson White to run for president against Jackson's chosen successor, Vice President Martin Van Buren. Jackson may have overreached by forcing Van Buren on the party. A brilliant lawyer, the New Yorker had a reputation for letting his famous cleverness and zest for intrigue supersede his statesmanship and intellectualism. In fact he possessed both intellectual depth and an unerring instinct for assessing political events. But his smooth demeanor, persistent drollery, and courtly manner generated suspicion among some, particularly southerners, and his political wiles earned for him the nickname "the Magician." From the beginning Jackson could see the full measure of the man and came to revere his manifold talents. But not all of the president's followers were so inclined. Hence an intraparty challenge was probably inevitable.

Few would have predicted it would come from White, a loyal Jackson ally for years. In temperament and political approach he was the anti-Jackson. Tall, well proportioned, with kindly blue eyes and long flowing hair, he both looked and acted the part of the dignified senatorial statesman. Often viewed as a throwback to the glory days of Rome, he spoke softly, without fire or eloquence but with a clarity and common sense that elevated him above his peers. In the Senate he commanded respect, and in Tennessee he was beloved. Jackson, enraged to see this old friend trying to thwart his plans, fostered a steady attack on the senator by the *Globe* and other Democratic organs. It was a mistake. The attacks caused White's popularity to soar among protective Tennesseans.

When the votes were counted in November, Van Buren won easily, carrying fifteen states with 170 electoral votes. It was clear Jackson's populist convictions still held sway over the new Whig Party that Clay had forged in 1834 upon the foundation of his American System. For Clay, it was the final blow from his old rival. He vowed to escape Washington as soon as possible. "Jackson played the tyrant to the last," he complained, adding he now felt little enthusiasm for the trials of the Senate. "I shall escape from it as soon as I decently can," he declared, "with the same pleasure that one would fly from a charnel-house."

But the Jackson–Van Buren victory brought with it a troubling development. Tennessee shunned Van Buren and gave its electoral votes to White, who also carried Georgia. Worse, White's Tennessee supporters, combined with the state's new Whig contingent, now formed the foundation of a strong Whig Party in Tennessee, capable of commanding close to half the electorate. Jackson's dominance over the state was now lost.

Soon he lost his dominance over the nation as well. Within nine weeks of Van Buren's inauguration, economic collapse swept the country. It began when New York banks suspended specie payments, causing widespread alarm and setting in motion a deflationary spiral as credit dried up, loans were called in, and prices plunged. The Panic of 1837 ushered in "a cycle of recession, recovery, and depression" that would dominate American politics for the next seven years. Suddenly the Democratic ethos lost much of its luster, and Van Buren lost much of his popularity. With people in financial anguish, they wanted action at the national level—the kind of action that Clay and his allies had been advocating for years. Van Buren, clinging to his Jacksonian heritage, seemed out of touch with the needs of his constituents.

The political focus centered on the Specie Circular, Jackson's departing executive order that had been designed to curb a dangerous inflationary wave sweeping the country in the wake of wild land speculations in the West. Prices had skyrocketed across the board, leading Jackson to require future purchases of government property to be transacted in gold or silver. But now, with prices plummeting and liquidity scarce, the call went up to rescind the Specie Circular. Neither Jackson, Van Buren, nor Polk would hear of it. The result was that Democrats found themselves utterly on the defensive. Polk, true to his political convictions and his sense of loyalty, remained a stalwart floor leader for Van Buren's agenda, but the tide had turned against his party. Worse, the fissures in Tennessee politics had taken on the appearance of a blood feud. Two fervent politicians—Tennessee's bellicose Balie Peyton and Virginia's fiery Henry Wise—let it be known they planned to insult Polk incessantly and draw him into a duel with Wise, known as a "dead shot" with a pistol. They showered Polk with invective, calling him, among other things, "a cancer on the body politic," "a petty tyrant," and "as destitute of private honor as he was of private virtue." The disciplined Polk refused to respond, proving that in this one respect he didn't aspire to be like his great mentor. Eventually, the storm passed, but the spectacle would linger in people's minds for years.

In summer 1838, Polk announced his intention to leave the House and run for Tennessee governor the next year. It wasn't the career path he desired, but Tennessee Democrats had implored him to return home and oust the Whig governor, Newton Cannon, elected in 1835 and reelected handily two years later. Only Polk could restore Democratic hegemony, they argued. Besides, with the Democrats' House dominance also threatened by economic travail, it wasn't clear Polk could hold on to the speakership. Upon his departure from the House after fourteen years, his adversaries contrived one last humiliation. When a routine resolution was brought up thanking him for his service, some Whigs quibbled with the wording, and fifty-seven members actually voted against the customary measure. Ignoring the slight, Polk responded with dignity, adroitly characterizing the vote, because of the opposition, as more than a mere formality and hence "the highest and most valued testimony I have ever received from this House."

Polk brought to the gubernatorial campaign his characteristic analytical acumen, attention to detail, and debating skill. He honed a campaign style that included repartee and ridicule in sufficient abundance that the stolid Cannon soon announced the duties of his office precluded further joint appearances. When the votes were counted, Polk had a narrow victory margin of 2,616 ballots out of more than 105,000 cast. Democrats rejoiced at the outcome.

Monday, October 14, 1839, in Nashville was a day of raucous political celebration mixed with a certain religious solemnity. Amid two church conventions that drew hundreds of Baptists and Methodists from around the region, the city also that day witnessed the inauguration of its new governor. To top it off, Nashville's fall horse races had drawn a contingent of "genteel horse fanciers and rakish gamblers." It seemed to some that just about every Democrat from the state had made it to Nashville for the political festivities, some to celebrate the return of their party to the statehouse but many to seek patronage jobs in the new administration of James Polk. At eleven o'clock, the state's legislators formed up at the courthouse and began a procession to the Presbyterian Church, site of the inaugural ceremonies. There the Baptists and Methodists already had congregated, along with the man whose presence drew the eyes of everyone on the scene—Andrew

Jackson, looking a bit infirm but proud as he strolled through the throng, directing courtly nods here and there and pronouncing himself to be *"mighty happy"* with his party's political restoration. When it came time for the new governor to speak, Polk stepped forward to proclaim his resolve to regulate state banks, bolster education, foster internal improvements with state funds, and align corporate power with the interests of ordinary citizens.

That day turned out to be the high point of his political career for a considerable time. As governor, Polk confronted the same economic blight that buffeted Van Buren and eventually forced him out of the presidency in the 1840 elections. That economic environment also rendered a successful governorship impossible. Polk's adversity was compounded by the nature of his opponent when he sought reelection in 1841. This was James C. Jones, a thirty-year-old freshman legislator from the outlands of Wilson County. Tall, thin, ungainly, with an audacious wit and a lighthearted air, he went by the name of Lean Jimmy, and in the legislature he had emerged as the governor's most nettlesome political pest. Now the Whigs turned to him to disorient Polk and blunt his campaign repartee. Lean Jimmy did it with aplomb. Lacking Polk's conventional debating skills and expansive knowledge of the issues, he brought to the campaign "ridicule, sarcasm, wit, buffoonery, and a deluge of epithets." When Polk, struggling to puncture this irrepressible jester, suggested Lean Jimmy's style was less suited to a gubernatorial campaign than to a circus, the challenger retorted that they both belonged in the circus—himself as the clown and Polk "as the little fellow that is dressed up in a red cap and jacket and who rides around on a poney." Their joint appearances generated huge crowds, and Polk could see many of those in attendance had come specifically to see Jimmy.

Whether it was the depression or Lean Jimmy or Polk's continued devotion to the discredited Van Buren, the governor lost his reelection bid by 3,243 votes out of 103,000 cast. Never before had Polk experienced such a defeat. Throughout his career he had been buoyed by the Jacksonian wave, that great political force that had dominated Tennessee and the nation for nearly two decades. This potent wave had shaped him and guided him through countless political struggles during a particularly intense time of civic combat. It had incubated his congressional career and sustained it through seven terms in the House. It had propelled him to positions of influence in that chamber, then to its highest station. It had swept him into his state's premier political office. And throughout his adulthood it had instilled in his consciousness a sense that his career was moving always in tandem with history. Now it had failed him.

But not for long, he vowed. He would return to the fray two years hence, oust Lean Jimmy from the governor's chair, and restore his self-identity as a man of destiny. The rematch proved unavailing. Jones outpolled him by 3,833 votes out of some 110,000 cast—hardly a change from the previous tabulation. Now he was a two-time loser in his own state. At forty-seven, he knew he looked washed up, and it wasn't clear what he could do to restore his political standing. Stung and depressed, he lingered in Columbia pondering his fate.

3 · THE 1844 ELECTION

Searching for a Means of Political Recovery

FOR JAMES POLK, the 1844 presidential campaign began on August 14, 1843, precisely two weeks after his second gubernatorial humiliation. On that day he ordered the family buggy hitched up for the forty-five-mile ride north to Nashville, where he planned to assess his political circumstances and craft a strategy to rekindle his career. For two weeks he had sat in his comfortable but modest home on a wide, tree-lined avenue in Columbia, contemplating the wreckage of his political standing. One biographer later would conjure up a picture of the former governor sitting in retreat, saying little, stirring little, just thinking—as Sarah sat nearby sewing or knitting with Presbyterian devotion.

Neither was given to deep introspection; neither had much tolerance for expressions of self-pity or even words of sympathy if offered with any degree of effusiveness. But they shared a deep devotion to the husband's career. For James, political success was the only kind worth striving for. He was a man of conviction, driven by ideology, and passionate in his love of the political game. If he wasn't devoting his life to his vision for America nothing else mattered.

For Sarah, her steely dedication to her husband's political success may have emerged in part from her childless marriage. Without children to occupy her daily existence, she found her greatest enjoyment in serving as political counselor to her ambitious husband and mixing in the company of the nation's most powerful men. She thrived in this environment and derived pleasure in her success. She was proud of her Washington reputation as an independent-minded woman, reflected in one instance when she resisted her husband's anti-banking convictions and his consequent aversion to paper money. "Mr. Polk," she said to him jocularly in the company of some of his political allies, "you and your friends certainly are mistaken about the bank question. Why if we must use gold and silver all the time, a lady can scarcely carry enough money with her." On another occasion, when he extolled the steamboat as having outdated all other means of transportation, she demonstrated a clearer vision of the future. "What about the steam-car?" she asked. Clearly she possessed special attributes as a political helpmate.

And so it was probably inevitable that this marital partnership—the introverted, driven politician and his only true confidante—would quietly reach a mutual resolve to shake off the despondency of defeat and revive the White House dream. The eclipsed politician set his consciousness on two immediate goals—rising from the ashes of his career by capturing his party's vice presidential nomination and reclaiming control over Tennessee politics from his rivals. He had plenty of time to contemplate both during his four-hour ride to Nashville.

Any serious analysis would begin with the national party. It was widely assumed the Democrats' presidential nomination would go to Van Buren, who hankered to challenge Whig president John Tyler, vice president under William Henry Harrison and president since Harrison's death in 1841. Many Democrats chafed at the thought of Van Buren at the head of their ticket in 1844. New political and economic developments were driving a wedge through the party. True, the fires of passion surrounding the national bank issue were now mere embers of political sentiment. Most Americans accepted the death of the Bank of the United States and appreciated the growing paper money state banks now operating under various regulatory safeguards. But this emerging consensus unleashed its own divisiveness. As many Democrats retreated from the ideological commitment to hard money, the hard money men dug in to defend the old orthodoxy. The new entrepreneurial "conservatives" had seen how Van Buren's rigid adherence to the hard money doctrine had squelched needed liquidity and thus lengthened the economic depression. With recovery now in serious prospect, they feared a second Van Buren administration would further restrict liquidity and kill the recovery. For their part, the Van Buren partisans viewed these conservatives as party traitors whose disloyalty had cost their man his reelection in 1840. They vowed to purge the party of these perfidious rebels and redeem the Magician's national standing through a glorious 1844 victory.

Van Buren faced opposition also from southern Democrats under the considerable sway of that irrepressible orator, John C. Calhoun. With his penetrating yellow-brown eyes set into deep sockets, his raven black hair, chiseled face, and captivating fluency of speech, the South Carolinian loomed large over American politics. He was one of the most brilliant politicians of his era and one of the most erratic; one of its most mesmerizing figures and one of its most polarizing; a man who could give expression to hallowed causes with unmatched eloquence and then alter his causes with apparent ease. He was much enamored of his own manifest talents. John Tyler called him "the great 'I am,'" and one devoted follower observed: "He liked very much to talk of himself, and he always had the good fortune to make the subject exceedingly interesting."

Calhoun wanted to be president, and his desire for the office took on added intensity through his hatred of Van Buren. The two had been rivals since their days together in the Jackson administration. Aside from the tariff issue, which had set southerners against their northern brethren for decades, there was also the lingering slavery issue. As the country's premier defender of the South's slave culture, Calhoun had developed a fervent distrust of the New Yorker. With abolitionism gaining force in the North, many southerners feared that even states'-rights northerners eventually would abandon the South. As one Richmond editor warned, "Vote for a Northern President from a free state, and when the test comes he will support the abolitionists." So Calhoun now had his sights focused on his party's nomination. Barring that, he would settle for destroying Van Buren.

Among the other contenders circling the nomination, two stood out. One was Richard M. Johnson of Kentucky, former vice president during Van Buren's presidential term, whose national reputation had begun with news that he had personally killed the famous Shawnee

Indian leader Tecumseh at the battle of the Thames in 1813. It was never established definitively that he had done so, but Old Dick, as Johnson was often called, had been dining out on reports of it throughout his life—traveling across the land; visiting churches, schools, and town meetings; insisting he had no wish to dredge up once again the famous story and then regaling audiences with every detail, as well as a furtive display of the mutilated finger he had acquired in the battle. He was a man of no fixed opinions—"the damndest political whore in the country," as Thomas Hart Benton described him. Johnson let it be known that, while he aspired to the presidential nomination, he would just as avidly accept the ticket's second spot.

To the anti–Van Buren forces looking for an entrepreneurial conservative to supplant the rigidly hard-money Van Buren, Old Dick didn't measure up. They favored Lewis Cass of Michigan, a rich and erudite frontier empire builder with a wide girth, weary eyes, and demeanor that suggested he was not to be trifled with. Barely past sixty, he had a long history of service to his country—as Ohio legislator, Indian fighter, army general against the British, governor of Michigan Territory, secretary of war, and minister to France. Yet, throughout that protracted career, he had somehow managed to avoid being identified with one side or the other in any of the truly contentious issues of his day.

The political calculus facing Polk as he headed north was simple: Van Buren, despite the pockets of opposition and the determined rivals, would be the nominee, and Polk's chance of being the running mate depended entirely on his ability to unite Tennessee Democrats behind the New Yorker. It wouldn't be easy. Many Tennessee Democrats disliked Van Buren, and some didn't care much for Polk either. The challenge loomed before him most starkly in the person of Alfred O. P. Nicholson, a tall, oblong-faced lawyer with a knack for powerful eloquence and an endless capacity for political mischief. He had proved troublesome to the party establishment since the day he emerged on the scene and promptly began promoting Hugh Lawson White over Van Buren for the 1836 presidential nomination. "A hypocritical friend in disguise"—that's how Polk described Nicholson.

As governor, Polk had once given the man an interim appointment to the U.S. Senate—and later regretted this "capital error of my political life." It was clear to Polk that Nicholson wanted to replace him as the state's party leader.

His method of doing so was clever in the extreme. Shortly after Polk's second gubernatorial defeat, Nicholson publicly blamed Van Buren's unpopularity for the unfortunate outcome and endorsed Cass as a stronger presidential candidate for the Democrats. The state's pro-Polk newspapers naively echoed this assessment, and soon the Cass boomlet was in full cry. The irrepressible Nicholson had set in motion a chain of events designed to destroy Polk's career, and he had done so under the guise of professing friendship for the man. Polk wasn't fooled, but he couldn't be sure about Van Buren. The New Yorker would be forced to conclude Polk either wished to do him in or else had lost control of his own state party. Either way, it wasn't much of a recommendation.

Arriving in Nashville, Polk promptly turned to the political tasks at hand—galvanizing his troops; organizing letter-writing campaigns to get his name into the party consciousness; reaching out to Van Buren. He would rely primarily on three loyal associates. One was Cave Johnson, then serving his seventh term in the U.S. House. The tireless and unassuming Johnson could be counted on to be precisely where needed to serve Polk's interests at any given time. His constancy was unquestioned. As a young man in 1815 he courted a woman named Elizabeth Dortch, who rejected him for another. He vowed never to marry and didn't—until Elizabeth was widowed some twenty years later and he courted her again, this time successfully. Johnson's devotion to the politics of Andrew Jackson stirred Quincy Adams to label him "the nuisance of the House."

Then there was Aaron V. Brown, son of a Virginia preacher, who had practiced law with Polk in their early manhood and who had developed a deep friendship with Sarah as well as with James. More ambitious than Johnson, he also was more demanding. His availability for service emerged largely "when tangible rewards were in view," as one Polk biographer put it. As a Tennessee congressman, he was showing signs of sympathy toward the southern Democrats then angling to thwart Van Buren. And finally there was Samuel H. Laughlin, a generous-spirited and highly literate writer and political organizer whose intermittent weakness for spirituous liquors rendered him often in need of cash—and hence available for whatever tasks Polk placed before him. His affection for his ambitious friend was requited with a high degree of regard and friendship from the normally aloof Polk.

Having assigned various political tasks, Polk returned to Columbia and sought to assure Van Buren that Tennessee remained a Democratic state despite his own unfortunate defeats. This was crucial. Polk had value as a potential vice presidential candidate only if Tennessee remained in play. If the state had been captured by Whiggery, as many suspected, then Polk was essentially worthless to Van Buren. In a letter to the New Yorker, Polk assured him Tennessee would rise above the local causes that had upended his own candidacy and would give full support to Van Buren. Andrew Jackson added his own assurance—particularly, he noted, if Polk were on the ticket.

In early October Polk returned to Nashville and spent a week seeking to solidify his standing among state Democrats through cajolery, entreaty, and old-fashioned political horse-trading. Polk and his top lieutenants also crafted their strategy for the Tennessee Democratic convention, set for November 23 at Nashville. It had three elements: control the selection of Tennessee delegates to the national convention at Baltimore; instruct the delegates to support Polk for vice president; and keep the delegation neutral on the presidential outcome while pledging support for the eventual nominee. This was risky. Van Buren might view it as an effort by Polk and his allies to thwart his presidential ambition. But Polk concluded he could manage that more easily than the two risks inherent in a Van Buren endorsement. First, with Tennessee delegates so intensely divided on the presidential succession, an effort to force the issue could split the party and destroy Polk's ability to dominate events. Secondly, as soon as Van Buren had Tennessee's delegates safely secured, he no longer had any incentive to deal with Polk.

With characteristic candor, Aaron Brown explained the concept: "If V. Buren, or his folks intend to give Polk the *go by* . . . we must then . . . just let them know, that if they will take Polk for Vice President, we will take Van Buren; if not, and they go for Col. Johnson, that then we will go for Cass." With the convention strategy settled and his allies thoroughly briefed on what to do, Polk left for a three-week inspection visit at his Mississippi plantation. Immediately the politically rebellious Alfred Nicholson initiated an effort to gain dominance over the Nashville Democratic Association. His plan was to use that dominance as leverage to force the state convention to endorse Cass for president. The Polk forces suppressed the rebellion but enjoined their leader to rush to Nashville upon his return from Mississippi in order to quash any lingering Cass sentiment.

Polk got to Nashville three days before the convention and almost immediately reestablished his party leadership. On November 23, the convention strongly endorsed Polk for vice president while avoiding a presidential endorsement. What's more, of the thirteen Tennessee delegates to Baltimore, at least ten and perhaps a dozen were Polk loyalists. Polk had accomplished his first big goal of consolidating power within the Tennessee Democratic Party. But now he faced the challenge of assuaging any resulting Van Buren anger. In a November 30 letter to the New Yorker, he blamed the outcome on "a few discontented members of our party" who had agitated for Cass, thus necessitating a compromise whereby no candidate was endorsed. Polk assured the New Yorker he would control up to twelve of the thirteen delegates, and all would support Van Buren at Baltimore.

Van Buren did not rush to reply, nor did his response, though cordial, offer any assurances of support. "No explanations were necessary to satisfy me of the goodness of the motives of my friends in Tenn.," he wrote on December 27. But he expressed puzzlement over the political situation there and slyly lamented the impact of this Democratic decline on poor Andy Jackson. "It is not to be endured that the Old Chief should go out of the world with his favorite Tenn. in Whig Hands," he wrote. The message was clear: Polk could not look to Van Buren to help him capture the vice presidential slot.

But, with the state party under control and Van Buren at least neutral, Polk and his lieutenants turned their attention to the national scene. In early December, Cave Johnson and Aaron Brown arrived in Washington for the new session of Congress and began collecting intelligence on the forthcoming state conventions. Johnson established ongoing contact with New York's veteran senator Silas Wright, a strong Van Buren associate and Polk friend, who might keep the Polk men apprised of thinking within the Van Buren camp. And on December 9 he reported some good news. Prominent politicians from Missouri, Kentucky, and Ohio all predicted their states would support Polk. Johnson promised to mingle with other colleagues "as if by accident . . . & bring up the subject & try what I can hear." He also shared some bad news—rumblings that Tennessee's refusal to support a presidential candidate had angered some Democrats. With many, it had a "bad aspect on paper. It seems to say, that we hold ourselves in readiness to take part with the man which will take our Vice president."

Shortly after Congress convened, Van Buren scored a triumph. Anti–Van Buren members of the House Democratic caucus sought to thwart the New Yorker's followers by imposing a two-thirds rule for selecting various House officers. The Van Buren men readily accepted the supermajority rule and promptly rolled over the opposition in placing their chosen candidates in each position. This remarkable show of strength gave Van Buren an appearance of inevitability, and many opposition forces quickly fell into line. Pennsylvania's Senator James Buchanan, who had allowed his friends to submit his name as a longshot presidential candidate, withdrew. Johnson reiterated his secondary interest in the vice presidency. And John C. Calhoun pondered the hopelessness of his presidential ambitions and withdrew from the race.

Cave Johnson observed to Polk that "all the fragments of our party seem likely to unite upon Van Buren, make his nomination unanimous & each party seek the succession by distinguished services in his behalf." In other words, party members harboring presidential ambition would begin maneuvering for future presidential elections by outdoing each other in supporting the Magician. Thus, the party likely would get through the nomination process without any threat

of splitting and thus would present a united front against the Whigs'
Henry Clay in the fall election.

Still, it posed a danger to Polk. Some of those presidential aspirants now falling into line would oppose any vice presidential prospect with presidential stature. This was particularly true of the men
Cave Johnson called "the B's"—Buchanan and Benton. He wrote: "I
think both the B's are afraid to yield to your nomination lest you
should be in the way in 1848 & I fear may be inclined to throw their
weight for Col. K," meaning Senator William R. King of Alabama,
longtime legislator with a distinguished public record but insufficient gravitas for the presidency.

Sure enough, Benton and his allies began agitating against Polk
on the basis of the Tennessee party's refusal to back Van Buren. Johnson encountered Benton in late December and received an earful from
the cantankerous lawmaker. "He regretted the position of Ten. . . . ,"
Johnson wrote to Polk, "& *feared* it would loose you the nomination
& seemed full of wrath that *Jacksons State* should have taken such a
course." Ohio's Senator William Allen echoed the sentiment in a separate conversation. This was particularly ominous as Ohio was a crucial
state in Polk's calculus. As Polk wrote to Jackson on Christmas Day,
"*Ohio* I regard to be the *pivot,* upon which the question of the Vice
Presidential nomination will turn." Jackson promptly wrote a strong
Polk endorsement letter to the state's most prominent Democratic
editor—"modestly couched, so as to be disarmed of all appearance of
dictation . . . with proper deference to the judgment of the democracy
and the claims of others," as Samuel Laughlin described it to Polk.

But on January 8, Ohio Democrats instructed the state's Baltimore
delegates to support Van Buren for president and Richard M. Johnson for vice president. This bad news stirred Polk to indulge himself a
flight of self-pity. "It will not be the first time," he wrote to Laughlin,
"that I have performed *hard service* & made immense sacrafices in the
cause, whilst others who have enjoyed their ease have been rewarded
with the *Honours*." He added he would never retreat and, if rejected by
the convention, would fight in the ranks.

Throughout January, Polk's prospects declined further as an exchange of correspondence in Washington's leading Democratic newspaper, the *Daily Globe,* raised eyebrows among party officials. It began on January 8, when the *Globe* ran a letter from an anonymous writer calling himself "Amicus." It praised both Polk and Alabama's King as vice presidential nominees but ultimately favored King based on his longer and more varied public record. Then the letter pointedly noted that Democrats in King's Alabama had endorsed Van Buren for president while Tennessee Democrats had passed over a Van Buren endorsement. The letter added that Alabama was firmly Democratic "and can help the cause," whereas Tennessee remained politically unreliable.

This was a serious blow, striking Polk where he was most vulnerable. Polk immediately saw the hand of Thomas Benton in the letter and moved quickly to respond. On January 15 the *Globe* ran a letter from "A Tennessee Democrat"—actually Aaron Brown—that disputed "Amicus" on all points. It dismissed King's record as being that of a backbencher whereas Polk had been at the center of the major storms of the Jackson era. It noted that King had voted for the Bank of the United States in 1816 and asked, "How *could* Col. King be conspicuous on these subjects, when he had voted for that very bank in 1816." "A Tennessee Democrat" went on to direct his most vitriolic language at the allegations regarding Tennessee's Democratic constancy. The letter said Jackson himself concurred in the decision to avoid a presidential nomination. "And is it possible, after all that General Jackson has done, and all the Jackson party in Tennessee has done and suffered, in the support of Mr. Van Buren, that he and they cannot now be permitted to take a course of forbearance, for the sake of union and harmony in the State, without subjecting themselves to the wanton and unjust suspicion of being indifferent or unfriendly to the election of Mr. Van Buren?" Three more entries rounded out the exchange, each more pungent than the last. It had all the appearance of a three-ring circus.

Almost immediately Democrats in Washington, perhaps spurred on by Benton, began discussing ways of defusing the unseemly Polk-King controversy. As Cave Johnson wrote to Polk, "There is already a good deal of talk of settling the controversy between you & King by giving it to R.M.J.," meaning Richard Johnson. As the letter exchange unfolded, Polk found himself in a delicate position. He couldn't let the "Amicus" assault go unanswered, and yet he couldn't afford to alienate King because it would take a united Polk-King effort to stop the accelerating Johnson bandwagon. Polk wanted the letters in his behalf to be measured and "in good temper," as Aaron Brown put it, but he also wanted them to state his case powerfully, as he intended to have them printed up and distributed widely to Democrats throughout the country. "I deem this of such vital importance at this moment," he wrote to Cave Johnson, "that I hope you will not fail to attend to it."

In mid-January word arrived in Columbia that Mississippi Democrats had endorsed a Van Buren–Polk ticket, with Polk beating Johnson two to one in the convention balloting. Yet bad news always seemed to follow the good. Back in November the Tennessee Democratic convention had named a group to produce a statement of Democratic purpose for wide distribution throughout the state, and Polk had wanted it to include a strong Van Buren endorsement. This could serve as an antidote to party rancor over the lack of a convention stand for president. But then came that persistent irritant, Alfred Nicholson, who gained sway over the drafting committee and worked stealthily to excise the pro–Van Buren language. Thus watered down, the statement proved worthless to Polk's designs.

Polk decided to write a carefully crafted letter to Van Buren's friend Silas Wright designed to clarify his complex circumstances. He detailed at length the maneuverings of Nicholson, who "has given us much trouble, and yet claims to be one of us." He offered absolute assurance that Tennessee would go for Van Buren at the convention. He expressed "regret" at the recent letter exchange in the *Globe*, which Wright himself had lamented in a previous letter. "I of course could have had no agency, and at this distance knew nothing of them, until they appeared in the *Globe*," wrote Polk in one of his more conspicuous lies. And he counseled Wright that his friends would never consent to withdrawing his name from the convention even if he wanted them to. But of course he would cheerfully accept any convention outcome that emerged.

Wright, who liked Polk and favored him for the vice presidential nomination, responded with words of appreciation for Polk's "frankness and confidence" and for the "manly and patriotic manner" with which he had comported himself in the recent political battles. Wright also gave vent to an emerging development on the political scene— a growing expectation by the party's anti–Van Buren forces that they might actually manage to upend the New Yorker at Baltimore. "It is said that new hope has spring up . . . ," wrote Wright, "that there is yet a possibility of defeating the nomination of Mr. V.B." He speculated that these "base feelings," by crystallizing the need for a quick and clean compromise on the vice presidency, were serving to solidify the nomination efforts of Old Dick Johnson over Polk, particularly in Pennsylvania.

This negative assessment was echoed by Cave Johnson. "A serious & earnest movement secretly to supplant Van & nominate Cass is now on hand & is injuring us now by producing despondency among our friends in the country," wrote Johnson. Polk chose to ignore the warnings. Writing to Laughlin, he noted receiving Wright's letter, then added, "My own opinion is that Col. J cannot get the nomination." This confidence remained intact even after word reached Polk that the Pennsylvania convention had endorsed a Van Buren–Johnson ticket by acclamation. William King promptly accepted a post as minister to France, thus further solidifying Johnson's position in the vice presidential competition. Polk told Cave Johnson he had expected Old Dick's Pennsylvania victory and King's exit. "Still it can scarcely be possible that [Old Dick] can receive the nomination at Baltimore." It would destroy the party, he said, so it could not happen.

What accounts for this persistent optimism in the face of these defeats? History offers no definitive answer. Perhaps the shrewd and ambitious Tennessean was operating from an analytical framework rather like the one posed by Aaron Brown in a letter to Sarah Polk back in January. Seeing the forces converging against his patron, Brown had suggested that perhaps his man was shooting too low. "Colo Polk is now encountering the very identical difficulties as to the *vice*," Brown had written, "that he would do for the first office of the government, & if he can overcome the one he could have done the other." Given his lingering discomfort with Van Buren's policy outlook on hard money and his sympathy for the Calhoun southerners, Brown may have been quicker than other Polk loyalists to see the New Yorker's inherent vulnerabilities. It was clear even in January that the party in Congress was moving into a period of regional divisiveness over slavery and tariff issues, and this in turn was generating intraparty animosities against Van Buren. "There is a good deal of submission or acquiescence in what is inevitable, without being satisfied with it," Brown had written to Sarah. "Our friends are really doubtful not of the nomination but of success under it."

Cave Johnson warned Polk that he must stand aloof from all this anti–Van Buren agitation. "If Van was withdrawn or declined our party would be irretrievably lost," wrote Johnson, because the party's big guns—Benton, Calhoun, Buchanan—would never go for Cass. "Our unity, our safety depends upon Van." Polk agreed and made clear he would take not the slightest action against Van Buren's interests.

But a new issue was brewing that could throw the entire party instantly into chaos, and Polk was watching this development closely. As winter gave way to spring, rumors began circulating throughout official Washington that President Tyler secretly was negotiating an annexation treaty with the Republic of Texas. If true this would create new political fault lines in the party and introduce powerful new emotions. It could give new impetus and force to the anti–Van Buren elements. Whether Polk had incorporated this possibility into his thinking is unknown. But it wasn't long before events would force it into his thinking, along with that of everyone else playing any major role in American politics in that fateful year—including the nation's leading Whig, Henry Clay.

CLAY HAD NOT enjoyed the career trajectory he might have anticipated upon the departure of his old nemesis, Andrew Jackson. Although he hungered for the Whigs' 1836 nomination against Van Buren, it was clear he didn't enjoy the party's confidence. But no one else did either, and so the Whigs limped into the contest without much expectation of victory. Shortly after Van Buren's inauguration, Clay wrote a friend: Can I offer "any consolation . . . for the future, as to public affairs? I regret to say not much." But then the Panic of 1837 abruptly turned the Democrats into a beleaguered party. The Whigs' enthusiasm for using federal power to promote public works and economic expansion now found resonance with the electorate, and the result was that just about any Whig could win the presidency in 1840. Clay thought this would be his year. "There is everywhere," he wrote with characteristic self-absorption, "an irresistible current setting in towards me." But the party rejected him in favor of William Henry Harrison, an aging and colorless military hero. Party elders simply viewed Prince Hal as too much of a liability. He had sliced up too many rivals with his rapier wit, had made too many enemies. And that old "corrupt bargain" charge that Jackson had pasted upon him twenty years earlier still lingered as a mark of opprobrium.

Harrison won the election, as just about everyone had anticipated, and then he died a month into his presidency. The new president would be the rigid and self-confident John Tyler, an angular-faced former governor and senator who prided himself on his defiant adherence to principle. He had been a Democrat until breaking with that party over Jackson's policies, and he had brought to his new Whig home many of his old Democratic leanings. Soon it was clear that this particular Whig had no intention of embracing the Henry Clay agenda. He opposed the national bank, protective tariffs, and just about the entire American System. Clay was incensed. From his position as leader of Senate Whigs, he declared war on Tyler, but it didn't avail him much beyond a protectionist tariff bill enacted in 1842. His frustrations became visible in his political demeanor.

Sometimes the old Henry Clay of scintillating good humor remained much in evidence, as when he greeted a Tennessee audience by asking where their old friend Felix Grundy was. "Off in East Tennessee," someone shouted from the crowd, "stumping for Mr. Van Buren." Replied Clay with a smile, "Ah, at his old occupation, defending criminals." The crowd roared. But at another occasion in Indiana he responded with high dudgeon when someone yelled, "Hurra for Jackson." "Hurra for Jackson, you say," he bellowed. "Where is your country? I say hurra for my country, and the man that says hurra for Jackson, deserves not the name of a freeman, but he ought to be a subject of the autocrat of Russia, and have the yoke of tyranny placed upon his neck till he was bowed down, down to the very dust." And with that outburst he terminated his speaking tour. It was not the performance of the old Henry Clay.

More significantly, Clay seemed unmindful of a fundamental reality of democratic politics: It's always about the future, not the past. Clay seemed stuck in the past, fervently pressing issues that no longer had the same resonance as when he had brilliantly interjected them into the American consciousness so many years before. The bank issue had lost its sting through compromise and a salutary evolution toward constructive state banks. Yet Clay still flogged the issue. The same could be said about tariffs. Jackson had demonstrated how anti-tariff Democrats could effectively finesse the issue by accepting "incidental" protection within tariff systems designed solely to raise revenue. One could label this as cynicism, which to some extent it was, but its political effectiveness was beyond dispute. And on the matter of American expansionism he seemed deaf to the rumblings of enthusiasm emanating from the electorate. The question of Oregon Territory was a good example. Britain and the United States administered those vast lands jointly, but pressures were mounting for a negotiated solution, and most Americans wanted at least most of that expanse. Not Clay. He argued for confining American settlement to lands east of the Rocky Mountains and postponing "the occupation of Oregon some thirty or forty years."

It was as if Clay didn't want these new issues or developments to intrude into American politics lest they negate his own brilliance in crafting his American System and impede his ability to control the national debate. But he no longer controlled the debate anyway. On the campaign stump he actually took to apologizing to his audiences for haranguing them with the same old dialectic. But he persisted in doing so.

Still, Clay remained supremely confident as he watched events converging upon the Democrats. If the rival party could avoid an implosion, given all the frictions and animosities surrounding the Van Buren candidacy, it would be a miracle. Meanwhile, he had a lock on the nomination of his own party, which remained united and serene. Maybe 1844 was destined to be his year. Perhaps his third try would be the charm. Still, if so, he would have to be more politically dexterous and flexible than he had demonstrated in recent years.

4 · TEXAS

Dawn of a New Era

O N FEBRUARY 14, 1844, Washington's *Daily Globe* ran a letter from Navy Captain Robert F. Stockton, a rich adventurer with a flair for the dramatic and an instinct for the main chance. Stockton announced the arrival of his new warship, the USS *Princeton*, to the waters of the Potomac, just off the capital. In orotund language the captain expressed pride in his vessel's two unique characteristics—its capacity to run under either wind or steam power; and its two wrought iron guns, larger than any naval cannon ever before built and capable of throwing immense shot nearly six hundred yards with unprecedented accuracy.

Stockton's ship was in fact a marvel of naval architecture. Its steam engines powered not the traditional cumbersome side wheels but underwater screw propellers that generated greater speed and mobility than that of any other naval vessel. "The advantages of the *Princeton* over both sailing ships and steamers . . . are great and obvious," wrote Stockton. "These advantages make the Princeton . . . the cheapest, fastest, and most certain ship of war in the world." He added that the *Princeton*'s martial attributes could presage "more important results than anything that has occurred since the invention of gunpowder."

Always alert to political opportunity, Stockton invited a bevy of Washington bigwigs aboard his ship for an afternoon inspection cruise. It had the desired effect. One Ohio reporter later gushed in print: "A nobler and a hardier man—a man whose appearance more favorably impresses you with his qualifications as a man and a sailor— is not to be found than Captain Stockton." So successful was this public relations cruise that Stockton scheduled another for February 28.

This time his guests would include President Tyler himself; numerous senators and congressmen of prominence; just about the entire cabinet, including the new secretary of state, Abel Upshur, and the new navy secretary, Thomas Gilmer; and a "great number of ladies," as Thomas Hart Benton noted, including presidential widow Dolley Madison. In all, some four hundred guests boarded the warship and headed downriver toward Mount Vernon under a cloudless sky. The mild air of an early-spring afternoon enveloped the entourage as Stockton's crew maintained a steady flow of libation and the guests noted the smoothness of the ride and the quiet of the ship's machinery. They brightened with excitement when Stockton ordered his gunnery crew to demonstrate the *Princeton*'s firepower.

After the crew served what Benton called a "sumptuous collation" belowdecks, word arrived that the captain planned another cannon demonstration. A dining room exodus ensued as guests clambered up to the deck to witness the spectacle.

Upshur, Gilmer, and Benton took position to the gun's left, but Benton decided to reposition himself directly behind the armament, the better to see the 225-pound ball's trajectory. The senator opened his mouth wide so his eardrums might better absorb the shock of the powerful noise. Then the big gun was ignited.

Suddenly everything went awry. At ignition, the huge gun disintegrated with an ear-splitting blast. Huge chunks of shrapnel swept into the unsuspecting crowd, spilling blood and mutilating human bodies. Benton was knocked several feet inward, as if into a vacuum, landing facedown, unconscious. He was not seriously injured, but Stockton, standing next to the faulty armament, was singed by burning powder. Secretary of State Upshur and Navy Secretary Gilmer were killed outright. So were a naval officer, a diplomat, the father of the young woman whom President Tyler planned to marry, a presidential servant, and two sailors. Some nine other seamen were wounded seriously. The president had been out of harm's way belowdecks. Nevertheless, it was a stunning and tragic turn of events that would cast a pall over official Washington as survivors of the deceased grappled with the ache of sudden loss and people generally contemplated the vagaries of fate.

The *Princeton* incident also unleashed new vagaries of political fate. For months Tyler secretly had been pursuing a plan to bring Texas into the United States through an annexation treaty, and Upshur had been his lead negotiator on this weighty initiative. Now Tyler offered the State Department portfolio to John C. Calhoun, who would place the issue of Texas annexation before official Washington with an aggressiveness guaranteed to generate controversy and disruption. Upshur also had favored annexation, but he hadn't possessed Calhoun's stature or wiles. Thus the bloody event aboard the *Princeton* would redirect history. The emergence of the Texas issue would mark the dawn of a new political era.

The ascendancy of Texas is best understood through the aims and ambitions of seven influential Americans, beginning with the president. It wasn't surprising that Tyler, an ardent expansionist, would set in motion the powerful chain of events leading to annexation. But, by the time he actually moved on the issue, Tyler had other reasons in mind besides his vision of an expansive America. In his early career, he had been a Democrat, and his party had been good to him, sending him to the Senate at age thirty-seven. Then in the Jackson years he had switched to the Whigs, and his new party had been even better to him, making him vice president and, with fate's intervention, president. But, refusing to embrace the Whig agenda, he had essentially become a president without a party, and a president without a party couldn't govern effectively. Neither could he get the voters to retain him in office. Tyler decided to shake things up. Perhaps, he mused, by introducing the powerful Texas issue into American politics he could ride the resulting political wave and win a presidential term in his own right.

John C. Calhoun was happy to oblige, but for different reasons. He wanted to expand the country's slave territory and thus retain the South's numerical and political advantage in regional disputes. He also wanted to force a slave issue confrontation within the country, which he knew would enflame the South and ensure his status as the country's leading exponent of the southern cause. Besides, if that confrontation should split the union, Texas would add luster and power to an independent South. Already many southerners were making the point. The *Madisonian*, a Tyler-Calhoun newspaper, had declared the South's defense required either secession or annexation. And South Carolina's governor, James Hammond, had written, "If the Union is to break there could not be a better pretext. With Texas the slave states would form a territory large enough for a *first rate power* and one . . . that would flourish beyond any on the Globe."

For Thomas Hart Benton, such sentiments turned his normal flows of outrage into gushers of indignation. As a Jackson Democrat and fervent expansionist, he wanted Texas in the union. And he fully expected "the ripened pear to fall of itself into our hands" at some appropriate future time. But now wasn't that time, and behind this cheap maneuver he saw a conspiracy of unsavory politics and unpalatable greed—"on the part of some," as he expressed it, "an intrigue for the presidency and a plot to dissolve the union; on the part of others, a Texas scrip and land speculation." He vowed to fight this unholy movement—and perhaps, in the process, cleanse his party of the nettlesome Calhoun.

Up at Lindenwald, in Kinderhook, New York, where Martin Van Buren resided on his expansive estate, the former president watched events with concern. He knew the Texas issue would drive a wedge through his party and perhaps through his own presidential ambition. Southern and western Democrats, those in the regions of his greatest vulnerability, would rally excitedly to annexation, while northerners would remain wary. The Magician had a reputation as a bloodless politician whose lack of deep conviction enabled him to navigate the shoals of politics with smooth efficiency. If true to that reputation, he would simply embrace annexation and go with the crowd. But he found this development bothersome for many of the same reasons that animated Benton. Besides, he had reason to believe Henry Clay, his likely opponent in the fall election, opposed annexation also, so perhaps the issue could be neutralized and relieved of its sting.

Out at his Ashland estate near Lexington, Clay followed the issue with irritation. At age sixty-seven, he knew 1844 represented his last good chance for the presidency, and he would exploit that opportunity by leveraging the political framework that had guided him for decades. He would run on his trademark American System or not at all. If other issues emerged, he would finesse or attack them. This included Texas. His good friend John Crittenden, the Kentucky senator, had warned him about the impending issue, but Clay had ignored the alarm. He deemed it unimportant and considered himself the arbiter of what *was* important. He would take a leaf from the Democrats' book: Just as they always sought to mute the slavery issue, he would seek to mute the expansion issue.

Andrew Jackson had devoted much of his career to outmaneuvering Clay, and now Texas was giving him one last chance. At seventy-six, Jackson was near death and knew it. His physical frame, once so commanding, was withering, and seldom could he venture comfortably beyond his bed. But his mind remained sharp, his spirit robust. He set his consciousness to what he considered his country's next big issue—territorial expansion. Even wracked by pain, he thrilled to the dream of a transcontinental nation facing both Atlantic and Pacific, positioned to become one of the great powers of the world. But he feared this dream would be destroyed by the hated British, who were meddling in Texas politics and retaining their claim to vast portions of Oregon. The country must seize the moment, pull Texas to her bosom and take possession of Oregon. The vehicle for accomplishing this would be his beloved Democratic Party, under the leadership of his protégé Van Buren. If the Magician wouldn't do it, he would find someone else.

That someone else most likely would be James Polk. His struggle to cadge his party's vice presidential nomination wasn't going well, but perhaps the Texas issue would improve his prospects. He had hitched his ambition to that of Van Buren, and by every outward action he would remain loyal to that plan and that man. But, should Van Buren falter, perhaps Polk's vice presidential quest could turn into something more lofty.

THESE AIMS AND ambitions emerged atop a history stretching back to 1803 and Thomas Jefferson's celebrated purchase of the Louisiana

Territory from France. One problem was that the precise boundaries of these vast lands were unknown. Thus, Spain and the United States found themselves in dispute over Louisiana's western border and the extent to which Jefferson's purchase had included portions of Texas. The United States argued the border stretched to the Rio Grande River; Spain contended it was far to the east of that. Efforts to negotiate a settlement failed, and the countries agreed to an interim solution—a ten-year "neutral strip" encompassing the disputed lands.

Then in 1819 the matter was incorporated into the two countries' effort to settle the status of Florida. John Quincy Adams, then secretary of state, negotiated an agreement with Spain awarding Florida to the United States and establishing all of Mexico west of the Sabine River as Spanish territory. This enraged many U.S. expansionists, not least Thomas Benton, who called the concession "a gratuitous and unaccountable sacrifice" that had "dismembered the valley of the Mississippi, mutilated two of our noblest rivers, [and] brought a foreign boundary to the neighborhood of New Orleans." Anger over the treaty lingered for decades.

In the meantime, Mexico established its independence from Spain in 1821 and set about to address a problem that had plagued the Spanish overlords for generations—the dearth of settlement in Texas and California and a consequent inability to establish dominion over those lands. Unlike the robust Anglo-Saxon migrations to the New World, the Spanish influx had not encompassed large numbers of families seeking land for cultivation and settlement. The Spanish migrants had been bent more on establishing themselves as a societal elite superimposed over the established Indian societies. This worked in the New Spain heartland, where the populous Indians had established a high degree of civilization. But in areas such as Texas, where the landscape was forbidding and Apache and Comanche Indians posed a brutal threat, it faltered. To address this problem, Spain had granted large tracts of Texas land to an American group headed by Moses Austin. His son Stephen arrived in 1821 and established sway over 100,000 acres of arable land. He set about to sell it to American settlers willing to brave the hardships of weather and Indian attack.

They arrived in a torrent, reaching nearly forty thousand inhabitants by 1835 and nearly 150,000 a decade later. Down in Mexico City, the new independent government watched all this with growing alarm. The nation's leaders foresaw a burgeoning cultural chasm as the newcomers rejected loyalty to Mexico and cast their devotion to their ethnic brethren in the United States. In 1830, Mexico outlawed this immigration wave, but it proved inexorable. As Mexican officials had feared, in March 1836 the tough-minded migrants of Texas declared their independence and repulsed efforts by Mexican president Antonio López de Santa Anna to bring them to heel. Three battle names—the Alamo, Goliad, and San Jacinto—etched the cultural struggle into the consciousness of two peoples on either side of the Rio Grande.

There matters stood for the better part of a decade. Mexico never recognized the Texans' right to split off and vowed to retake the territory. Hence, an official state of war existed between the two entities, although it never erupted into full-scale fighting. In Washington, many expansionists advocated bringing the new republic into the Union, but the country's leaders remained wary. Jackson, who wanted the territory as much as anyone and who had sought to purchase the province from Mexico before Texas independence, concluded any annexation effort would overwhelm his other domestic and foreign initiatives. His only concession was a formal recognition of the defiant new nation, extended just before he left office. Van Buren, cautious by nature and highly conscious of his northern political base, followed suit. He particularly feared any sectional flare-ups over slavery that could ensue from an annexation effort.

Tyler had other ideas. The Texas republic was in financial distress, and the always meddlesome British were hovering over it with an aim of establishing an alliance of mutual convenience with the struggling republic. In exchange for financial help and military protection, Britain would be positioned to undermine the United States's supremacy over the Gulf of Mexico and to menace its dominion over New Orleans, gateway to the strategically crucial Mississippi River. Besides, if Britain could dominate this southwestern territory, it would have the United States neatly hemmed in between that region and its Canadian possessions to the north. Britain's premier New World aim was to thwart the American dream of a burgeoning power stretching from sea to sea.

Then there was slavery. As an antislave power, Britain sought to end the institution wherever it could. Thus, many southerners feared a British-Texas alliance could lead to the abolition of Texas slavery, which in turn would threaten slaveholders in the southern states. Fugitive slaves would have a new and relatively easy route to freedom, which would encourage escapes and complicate southern relations with a free Texas and its British protectors. The British minister to Mexico, an ambitious and scheming naval captain named Charles Elliot, had actually formulated a plan for extensive British loans to Texas in exchange for abolition and a free trade policy between the two countries. His clear aim was to detach Texas completely from United States influence. The plan quickly generated agitation in the American South and diplomatic concern in London. Lord Aberdeen, the British foreign secretary, on three occasions sought to assure America that Britain harbored no such ambitions. Although his country would continue its "open and honest efforts" in behalf of worldwide abolition, said Aberdeen, his government "shall neither openly nor secretly resort to any measures which can tend to disturb [the slave states'] internal tranquility, or thereby to affect the prosperity of the American Union."

But a Virginian named Duff Green, Tyler's man in London, chose to ignore Aberdeen's assurances. His motive is discernible in his private warning to his friend Calhoun that, without the Texas issue, the Calhoun forces would be overwhelmed by the presidential momentum of their rival Van Buren. More publicly, Green wrote a warning letter that made its way into a Baltimore newspaper. It alleged that Aberdeen himself had earmarked the Texas loans "as an indemnity for the abolition of slavery." Though false, this was highly incendiary throughout the South—and also in a White House occupied by a Virginia slaveholder and longtime Calhoun confidant. By fall 1843, Tyler had decided to go for annexation with full force and inject the issue into the 1844 campaign. His Annual Message to Congress in December 1843 hinted at his intentions.

Aaron Brown, Polk's congressional ally, perked up at the president's hint. Running into Benton outside the Capitol, he suggested that the Missourian, as an early and powerful voice against the U.S. loss of Texas in 1819, should take the lead in getting it back. Benton "took fire at his words," rebuked Brown, and attacked Tyler's move as part of a nasty intrigue likely to get the United States into war with Mexico. Brown, taken aback, responded with some heat of his own. That exchange signified the emergence of the Texas rupture within the Democratic Party.

When Upshur, at Tyler's instruction, opened annexation discussions with Texas president Sam Houston, the result was a Houston rebuff. Weary of having his own annexation overtures rejected by the United States and skeptical of Democratic support, Houston had allowed Britain and France to become interlocutors in a plan to grant Texas peaceful recognition from Mexico in exchange for Texas assurances it would not join the American union. Undeterred, Upshur conducted a private survey of congressional sentiment on the matter and reported to Houston widespread enthusiasm. But the key was Old Hickory, Houston's friend and mentor from earlier days, who dispatched a series of letters extolling his protégé's opportunity to ensure "the prosperity & permanent happiness of Texas." Jackson's influence proved decisive. In February Houston sent an emissary to Washington to negotiate a treaty. By then Upshur was dead, but Calhoun was positioned to proceed. By April 12 the treaty was signed, and ten days later it was submitted to the Senate for ratification.

But in the process Calhoun had added a powerful twist to the issue. Attached was a Calhoun letter to British minister Richard Pakenham that contained language so incendiary and politically audacious that it would render Senate ratification nearly impossible. In his letter—which Benton quickly labeled Calhoun's "Texas bombshell"—the secretary of state declared the actual rationale for the U.S. annexation initiative was strictly to protect southern slavery from British meddling. He praised slavery as beneficial to mankind, slave and freeman alike. And he piled up extensive statistics purporting to demonstrate the South's slaves were better off than the North's free blacks—and Britain's white industrial workers. Whatever his motive, Calhoun rendered it impossible for most northern politicians to support a treaty billed as a pro-slavery document. Among those northern politicians was New York's Martin Van Buren.

Before the treaty or Calhoun's Pakenham letter actually materialized, however, rumors of the secret negotiations circulated through Washington. And it became increasingly clear that all other issues—the tariff, Clay's American System, currency matters—instantly took a secondary position. On March 19 numerous newspapers throughout the East published a letter by Daniel Webster, a leading voice of New England morality, expressing vehement opposition to annexation, largely on the ground that the country should not allow any extension of slavery within its territory. "I regard slavery . . . as a great moral, social, and political evil," wrote Webster, who added that the country should abandon its push for ever greater territorial aggrandizement and concentrate on internal matters. That stirred Aaron Brown to publish in the *Globe* a letter from Andrew Jackson that had been in his possession for a year. The Old General crystallized the strategic rationale for annexation by arguing that British dominance over Texas would threaten the entire U.S. position on the continent. From Texas, the British could plant up to thirty thousand troops on the country's doorstep before the United States could do a thing about it; threaten the Mississippi River and, with it, New Orleans; stir slave insurrections in the South; and tie down the U.S. military in the Southwest while fortifying its position in Oregon. Remember, wrote Jackson, that with Texas the U.S. western boundary would be the Rio Grande, a powerful fortification due to its extensive barren plains. "With such a barrier on our west," wrote Jackson, "we are invincible." He endorsed the idea of the United States positioning itself to "enlarge the circle of free institutions" and having "greater efficiency in spreading the blessings of peace."

In early April, Polk received a letter from an Ohio politician named Salmon P. Chase, who sought to learn, on behalf of a group of anti-annexation citizens, the Tennessean's annexation views. Polk immediately placed himself foursquare with Jackson. "I have no hesitation," he wrote, "in declaring that I am in favour of the immediate re-annexation of Texas." Polk's use of the term "re-annexation" represented a not-too-subtle suggestion that Texas once had been part of the United States and never should have been relinquished. Hence, in this view, there was ample justification now for the country to get it back through "re-annexation." He added that the strategic threat of British meddling was too grave to ignore.

Clay and Van Buren received similar letters from inquisitive citizens. By chance their replies ran the same day, April 27, in their respective party newspapers, the *National Intelligencer* for Clay and the *Globe* for Van Buren. Clay's was eloquent and relatively brief, Van Buren's considerably longer and a bit ponderous in the nature of a legal brief. But they took precisely the same position—opposition to immediate annexation. Clay's letter, written from North Carolina and quickly dubbed his "Raleigh letter," explained that he had remained silent on the issue, despite entreaties that he speak up, because he hadn't seen any reason to introduce "a new element among the other exciting subjects which agitate and engross the public mind." And he saw no evidence the American people cared particularly about the annexation question. But the president had forced the issue, so he would speak.

He said he would embrace annexation if it could be effected "without the loss of national character, without the hazard of foreign war, with the general concurrence of the nation, without any danger to the integrity of the Union, and without giving an unreasonable price for Texas." Unfortunately, he averred, none of those conditions could be met. The United States had forfeited Texas in a previous era, he argued, as France had forfeited Louisiana and Spain had Florida. And, just as the United States would not relinquish those valuable territories, so would Mexico not relinquish Texas. "Mexico has not abandoned, but perseveres in, the assertion of her rights by actual force of arms, which, if suspended, are intended to be renewed." Hence, if the United States acquired Texas, it would also acquire its war with Mexico. "Annexation and war with Mexico are identical." And, asked

Clay, was it wise to assume Mexico would acquire no allies in her effort to thwart U.S. annexation? Suppose Britain or France, or both, were to enter the fray, arguing that such intervention was necessary to protect a weak and helpless nation at risk of dismemberment from an increasingly expansive American power. Not only would that subject the Union to a much greater military challenge than anticipated but also would subject the American nation to the opprobrium of "an impartial and enlightened world."

Clay then introduced the fearsome implications of the slavery question without putting to paper the politically charged word. There were those, he said, who favored annexation and those who opposed it "on the ground of the influence which it would exert in the balance of political power between two great sections of the Union." This was ominous, he argued, for "such a principle, put into practical operation, would menace the existence . . . of the Union. It would proclaim to the world an insatiable and unquenchable thirst for foreign conquest or acquisition of territory." That's because if Texas were acquired to further the internal ambitions of one region, then the opposing region could just as appropriately argue for the acquisition of, say, Canada to redress the imbalance. The logic leads inexorably to an ideology of conquest and hence to the destruction of fundamental principles underlying the republic.

No, said Clay, it would be better for the American republic to forgo such territorial ambitions. "I think it far more wise and important," he wrote, "to compose and harmonize the present confederacy, as it now exists, than to introduce a new element of discord and distraction into it."

Van Buren offered legalistic arguments on the constitutionality of territorial purchases, on the boundary issues underlying the matter, and on the legal question of whether U.S. recognition of Texas independence implied Texas's international right to that independence (it didn't, said Van Buren). He dismissed the notion that the Texas people—"so many of whom carry in their veins the blood of our revolutionary ancestors . . . [and] are thoroughly imbued with democratic principles"—would invite into the hemisphere the armies of Europe's crowned heads. And he agreed with Clay that Mexico would view annexation as an act of war and hence would embroil the U.S. republic in a military conflict with unpredictable consequences. He also agreed that such an action would violate fundamental principles of the nation. "It has hitherto been our pride and our boast," he wrote, "that, whilst the lust of power . . . has led other and differently constituted governments to aggression and conquest, our movements in these respects have always been regulated by reason and justice."

Whatever might be said about the eloquence and soundness of these arguments, their underlying significance was clear: The political establishment of both parties had taken a position at variance with the strong sentiment of the broad electorate. Clay held such dominance over his Whig Party that the impact of his Texas position would not be immediately discernible. He would be nominated as the Whig presidential candidate, as expected, at the party convention in Baltimore on May 1. But for Van Buren the impact was more immediate and more ominous. Already he had faced considerable opposition within his party, particularly from southern slaveholders and western entrepreneurs. In the best of circumstances it would not have been easy getting the nomination while avoiding a party rupture. Now that rupture was unavoidable.

Out in Columbia, James Polk followed developments with near disbelief. The day after Van Buren's letter appeared in the *Globe*, Polk's ever-loyal friend Cave Johnson wrote an anguished letter to his patron. Democratic spirits had been sinking to a new ebb, he reported from Washington, and party discontents now had strong new leverage to work against Van Buren. He speculated that they likely would take up the cause of Lewis Cass as their best chance of thwarting the Magician. Two days later he returned to his writing desk with more news, none of it good. The discontents had mobilized, held meetings, apparently planned letter-writing campaigns aimed at generating anti–Van Buren sentiment from around the nation to exhibit at the Baltimore convention. "If Van Buren is to be thrown over which I do not believe possible we must have an *entirely new man*," wrote Johnson, adding he saw little hope for Democrats in the fall election.

"We are broke up *here* & I see *no hope* of mending matters." A few days later the picture looked even worse: "Vans opponents & the friends of Texas are outrageous & the chances now seem to be, that his nomination will be defeated." Van Buren's position within the Democratic Party was unraveling.

But he had defenders too, and their growing anger at the turn of events was fomenting further intraparty dissension. Particularly vengeful was Thomas Benton, who published a vehement letter in the *Globe* defending Van Buren and attacking the advocates of immediate annexation. In private he hurled allegations of treason at his adversaries. "Texas is all now—," he wrote a friend, "tariff nothing—Van Buren & his friends are kicked off—Tyler and Texas is the word—and all the rest may go to the devil." Amos Kendall said Benton "roars like a madman," and the Old General wondered aloud whether perhaps the Missourian's experience aboard the *Princeton* may have affected his ability to think clearly.

When Clay's *Intelligencer* letter reached the Hermitage, the Old General practically whooped for joy and pronounced his enemy "a dead political Duck." Van Buren, he surmised, now only had to embrace annexation and he was home free. The next day, when his friends Willoughby Williams and Robert Armstrong stopped by, he was still spouting enthusiasm at the turn of events.

"I knew Clay would not be President," he exclaimed. "[I knew] he would commit some indiscretion."

"General," replied Williams, "we came to submit other developments to you. The late mail brought a letter from Mr. Van Buren in which he takes the same ground that Mr. Clay has taken."

"It's a forgery!" roared the General. "Mr. Van Buren never wrote such a letter."

Williams placed the *Globe* in the General's hands and then the two retreated to give him time to read it alone. When they returned, Jackson was subdued and crestfallen. Perhaps, he mused aloud, Van Buren could find some way to reverse his position. Too late, said his friends. There wasn't time to repair the damage before the Baltimore convention. The General sat wordless, his eyes moist, shaking his head in silence. As he saw it, the New Yorker could simply have said he had no way of assessing the rumors about British interference in Texas and hence favored annexation. Had he done so, his election would have been assured. "I have shed tears of regret," he wrote a friend. To Van Buren he wrote with deep sorrow that it now seemed "impossible" to elect him. His chances, said the General, were roughly equivalent to turning the current of the Mississippi. Then, never one to sit back passively, Jackson took action.

On May 10, Polk received letters from Armstrong and Andrew J. Donelson, summoning him to the Hermitage for a talk with the General. "I am particularly anxious," wrote Donelson, "that the ground occupied by the Genl should be thoroughly understood by you." Polk immediately rode to Nashville, where he spent the evening in discussion with Armstrong. The next morning the two rode out to the Hermitage. Along the way they encountered Donelson, riding to Nashville to deliver a Jackson letter to the *Nashville Union*. It would be the General's first public pronouncement upon the Van Buren letter, which he picked apart with merciless precision. Although "no difference on this subject can change my opinion of his character," Jackson wrote of Van Buren, the New Yorker was wrong to ignore the possibility that Texas could be "inevitably driven into alliances and commercial regulations with the European powers, of a character highly injurious and probably hostile to this country." Polk considered it stunning that the General would take such potentially devastating steps against his old protégé.

Donelson decided to return to the Hermitage with Polk and Armstrong, and upon arriving at the Jackson home the three immediately engaged the General about the situation. Jackson expressed both sadness and anger at Van Buren's letter and noted ruefully that the New Yorker had had the General's views before him as he wrote. He added that he considered Van Buren "ruined" unless he could find some plausible way to modify his opinions, which didn't seem likely. Hence he believed Van Buren should withdraw from the presidential race and had suggested as much in his private letter. The Democratic nominee, said Jackson, must be an annexation man from the Southwest.

Then, turning to Polk, he identified his Tennessee protégé as the most available man for the job. If Polk could be nominated, he added, then the party could take a northern man for vice president. And perhaps a fatal party split could be avoided.

Writing to Cave Johnson shortly afterward, Polk expressed skepticism. "This I do not expect to be effected," he wrote. He added a more likely outcome would be that the Van Buren partisans, following a Van Buren withdrawal, would hold the balance of power in the party and select a northern man for the top slot and then look south for a vice presidential candidate. Hence, his best hope still seemed to be the ticket's second spot, which would continue to require cordial relations with the Van Buren people. And yet the Jackson formulation was intriguing—all the more so following a conversation in Washington between Cave Johnson and New York's Silas Wright, Van Buren's close confidant. Johnson had suggested that if Van Buren failed to get the nomination at Baltimore, perhaps Wright should step forward in the interest of party unity. The New York senator firmly had demurred, in part because he shared Van Buren's views on immediate annexation and also because he would never tarnish his relationship with his New York friend. Then he had identified Polk as the only new man acceptable to northern Democrats "because you was known to be *firm & true* to the cause," as Johnson expressed it to Polk.

Polk began to think that perhaps the Jackson formulation wasn't so fanciful after all. Jackson's devastating letter would run in the *Globe* a few days before the nominating convention—and at a time when most delegates would be clustered in Washington on their way to Baltimore. So long as the New Yorker remained in the game, Polk would profess utter loyalty. But he knew the party was doomed unless it bypassed the Magician and united behind a pro-annexation man. The party and the country were in flux, and nobody could predict what would emerge out of it.

5 · BALTIMORE

America's First Political Dark Horse

O N MAY 4, 1844, James Polk crafted a letter to Cave Johnson in Washington instructing him to establish a close working association with a Polk confidant named Gideon J. Pillow, soon to arrive in the capital on his way to the Baltimore convention. "You will find Pillow . . . a most efficient and energetic man," wrote Polk from Columbia. Eleven days later he returned to the theme: "Whatever is desired to be done, communicate to *Genl. Pillow*. He is one of the shrewdest men you ever knew, and can *execute* whatever is resolved on with as much success as any man who will be at Baltimore. . . . He is perfectly *reliable*, is a warm friend of V.B.'s, and is my friend, and you can do so with entire safety."

Gideon Pillow would be Polk's pivot man in Baltimore, the Tennessee delegate who would assess the scene, size up the players, identify the opportunities, and execute the plans that emerged from the chaos. Cave Johnson, also a delegate, would be well positioned to support the cause with his characteristic loyalty. Samuel Laughlin and Aaron Brown would be on the scene as well, gathering intelligence and helping in the effort. But Pillow would be the field commander.

He was thirty-seven at the time and a man of considerable distinction. A graduate of the University of Nashville, he became a lawyer in 1830 and soon emerged as one of Tennessee's most brilliant legal practitioners. He was brilliant enough, in fact, to save Polk's brother William from an extensive prison term in a celebrated Columbia criminal case in 1838. William, a troubled and troublesome lad with a wild streak and weakness for alcohol, had killed a man in Columbia's public square during an impromptu gun duel that followed an altercation

81

some days earlier in a local tavern. Pillow got him off with a $750 fine and six months in jail—an outcome that cemented a bond between Polk and Pillow that would last throughout their lives.

Pillow's abundant wealth, accumulated through his law practice, enabled him to maintain what was widely considered one of his state's most splendid estates—Clifton Place, near Columbia. He also was known as an accomplished farmer who employed the latest and most sophisticated agricultural methods on his far-flung landholdings in Tennessee, Mississippi, and Arkansas. At age twenty-seven he had become adjutant general in the Tennessee militia. With his unruly shock of dark hair over a broad forehead, deep-set eyes, a prominent Roman nose, and thin lips, he had the look of confidence and displayed a knack for establishing rapport quickly with other men. Less visible was an underlying self-absorption that could cloud his judgment, but his devotion to Polk's success in Baltimore now shrouded that character weakness.

In Columbia, James and Sarah Polk conducted life according to their normal habits and routines. By mid-May he had done just about everything he could to squeeze a political rehabilitation out of the Baltimore convention, and his own ability to influence the outcome now had expired. On May 15 he penned his letter to Cave Johnson that included his final words seeking to analyze or affect the coming Baltimore events. He spun out a scenario by which his name might actually emerge—with considerable help from his friends—at the top of the ticket but allowed as how this speculation might in fact be "ridiculous." He added, "I think it probable that my chief hope will be for the second office, and if so, I wish my name to go before the Convention at all events." In the meantime he would get letters from Johnson, Brown, and Pillow, but they would all arrive at least a week after being sent, and so he wouldn't know his fate until the eighth or ninth of June. There wasn't anything he and Sarah could do now but wait.

Pillow arrived in Washington on May 21 with Laughlin, and the two immediately sought out Cave Johnson for an evening of information-sharing and strategic-planning. From Johnson they learned the bitterness and distraction within the party was even more intense than they had anticipated, and Van Buren's position was even more tenuous. The next day Pillow encountered Silas Wright and Alabama senator Arthur Bagby, Van Buren's top convention operatives. They expressed near despair at the state of things and confessed being at a loss as to how to deal with it. But they insisted northern Democrats would never abandon Van, and his name would never be withdrawn.

Meanwhile, Pillow learned that delegates from the Southwest and West were threatening to bolt the convention if Van Buren were nominated over Cass. "If they continue to occupy that ground," Pillow wrote to Polk, "they will breake up *the* party & will leave no hope of reconciliation." He immediately set out to foster a series of conciliation meetings to get northern and southern factions to accept the final convention judgment. He also met with members of the Tennessee delegation to bring some discipline to the contingent and craft a plan for getting Polk the vice presidential nomination. "My great effort," he wrote his friend, "shall be to *conciliate* & to hold things in attitude to secure your nomination no matter which party may succeed."

The first Tennessee delegation meeting, on May 22, didn't go well. Two congressmen from the state, George Jones and Andrew Johnson, transferred their rabid anti–Van Buren sentiment to Polk, vowing to thwart his vice presidential ambitions if he continued to support the New Yorker. Pillow later received a similar message from several Mississippi and North Carolina delegates. "They . . . said that if Polks friends voted for V. they would not vote for P.," Pillow reported. And there was a new complication. The southern delegations seemed bent on instituting a convention rule requiring a two-thirds vote for the nomination. This could destroy Van Buren. "I do not think V. will get the nomination," wrote Pillow. "I think he will be cut off under the 2/3 rule." He feared Polk's standing could slip badly among southern delegates if he continued to support the fading New Yorker.

But perhaps, mused Pillow, some good could emerge from the chaos. If Van Buren faded rapidly enough, Polk might avoid going down with him. Then he might even emerge at the top of the ticket. "I would not still be surprised if a compromise were finally made by both parties taking you up for the P," he wrote on May 24. The next day, just before heading to Baltimore, he reiterated the thought, noting his friend's stature seemed to be rising amid the chaos. "I am satisfied," he wrote, "you are the choice of 2/3 of the convention for the Vice, & almost every one of your friends say they would prefer you for the Presidency." Pillow posed the tactical notion that such a turn of events would have to be initiated by northern delegates. "We of the south cannot bring *that* matter up," he emphasized. "If it should be done by the north it will all work *right,* but if we were to make such a move it would in all probability injure your prospect for the Vice." Gideon Pillow was piecing together a strategy to position his man for ultimate success while avoiding actions that could harm his chances for secondary success.

SHORTLY AFTER NOON on Monday, May 27, the Democratic National Convention assembled in the ornate but cramped Egyptian Saloon of the Odd Fellows' Hall on Baltimore's Gay Street. The first order of business was selection of a chairman, a designation quickly conferred upon Hendrick Wright of Pennsylvania, a thirty-six-year-old former prosecutor and state legislator. Hardly had Wright taken the gavel when Romulus Mitchell Saunders of North Carolina rose to move a simple procedural resolution: "*Resolved,* That the rules and regulations, as adopted by the national convention of May, 1832, and as adopted by the national convention of May, 1835, be the rules and regulations for the government of this convention." Those two previous conventions had required a supermajority for nomination, and thus adherence to precedent meant Van Buren would need a two-thirds vote to get the party's nod. No one thought he could get two thirds, and thus his people faced the need to kill this motion.

Following nearly three hours of procedural fits and starts on such matters as the credentials process and a means of naming convention officers, the delegates finally proceeded to Saunders's two-thirds motion. The debate began with Robert J. Walker of Mississippi, a wisp of a man weighing barely a hundred pounds and beset by chronic ill health. Walker was one of his generation's most cunning political operatives. Born to wealth and prominence in Pennsylvania, he had fled his state's sluggish elite to embrace the more open and raucous society of Mississippi, where he had emerged as a brilliant and successful lawyer, planter, and land speculator. Elected to the Senate in 1835, he had developed a stealthy knack for leveraging his position and wiles to direct events in favored directions. Lately he had been seeking to direct events toward Texas annexation. In 1843 he had slyly persuaded the Van Buren people to schedule the Democratic convention in spring 1844 rather than the fall of 1843. Had the earlier schedule been adopted, Van Buren would have secured his party's nomination with ease before the Texas issue could have intervened to complicate his ambitions. Later Walker successfully had prodded Jackson to press the annexation matter with Texas president Houston and had helped Secretary of State Upshur marshal arguments for convincing Houston that Congress would embrace Texas statehood. He also had published a long pro-annexation treatise that had helped galvanize the issue and get it into the public consciousness.

Now the diminutive politician rose to project his "wheezy voice" across a silent hall in behalf of the two-thirds principle. "We were successful in both the nominations made in pursuance of this rule," he said, "because it produced that union and harmony which are indispensable to success." The convention, he argued, must produce a nominee who enjoyed not just majority support but a broad following of consensus that ensured political strength in the general election. "If the candidate proposed to be nominated . . . can never receive the vote of two-thirds of the convention," he asked, "what hope is presented of electing such a candidate to the presidency of the Union?"

Walker cleverly suggested the majority rule actually worked against the majority in a paradoxical way. Suppose, he said, one candidate should get the first-ballot votes of New England, New York, Pennsylvania, Ohio, Delaware, and New Jersey. That would be 138 votes and a majority, and thus that candidate would get the nomination. And yet in 1840 those particular states had given only seven electoral votes to the Democratic ticket. And, looking back as far as 1801, those states had never constituted a majority of the national Democratic Party in any election. "This rule, then," he said, "which is called the majority rule, ought to be called the minority rule; for it enables a small . . . minority of the democratic party to control, and force their nominee upon the majority."

North Carolina's Saunders then warned against violating "the well established usages of our party—usages to which the democratic faith is pledged; and that is, we go for principles, not men." The only reason this was contentious now, he suggested, was because a particular presidential aspirant—Van Buren—couldn't get support from two thirds of the delegates. "How dare we, then," he demanded, "do what we would not do but to advance the success of particular men?" He noted that a vote had occurred on the matter also at the 1835 convention. Then, directing his words to Benjamin F. Butler of New York, he added, "And, let me tell the gentleman from New York, the delegation of that great State—then having forty votes—cast their votes unanimously for the rule. Is that great State so selfish as to contend for and support a measure as right, when it is to her advantage, but wrong when against her?"

There was a reason why Saunders directed his question to Butler, Van Buren's former law partner and also former war secretary under Jackson and attorney general under Van Buren. Everyone in the hall knew Butler would be the most formidable advocate for majority rule. And, upon Saunders's conclusion, he rose with solemnity to assault the two-thirds requirement and the idea that precedent should prevail. What if Andrew Jackson had been guided by precedent when he confronted the evil Bank of the United States? Wouldn't he have been forced to accept the bank as the product of his predecessors, including the great Washington himself? Where, he asked, was the precedence for the Declaration of Independence? Principle trumped precedence, said Butler, and the principle was best articulated by Thomas Jefferson. With a flourish Butler went on: "Mr. Jefferson said that absolute acquiescence in the will of the majority was the principle of republicanism, and that a departure from it was a return to the rule of force, which was next to despotism."

Butler challenged Walker's complaint that majority rule would place the nomination decision in the hands of a few states that did not vote for Democrats in general elections. He said he would give to the true Democrats of Massachusetts, Kentucky, and Delaware "an equal voice with my own proud state; and I consider them as truly the representatives of democratic principles . . . as any State in which the baleful star of federalism never was in the ascendant." After all, he said, Democrats in those Whig states had labored just as hard for their shared principles as those in Democratic states—and with fewer prospects for political reward in the form of state offices.

Butler then took aim at the allegation that New Yorkers were somehow selfish for wanting a rule that would benefit their preferred candidate. Remember, he said, that they were all there under instructions from state conventions "to vote for a particular individual and not only to vote for him, but to use our best expertise to secure his nomination." How, he asked, could he honor his pledge to secure the nomination for Van Buren if he were to vote for a rule that would destroy Van Buren's prospects for getting the nomination? Suppose a delegate voted for the rule, and suppose his candidate then got a simple majority but not a two-thirds majority. Wouldn't his constituents legitimately question whether he had actually honored his pledge? Why, they might ask, had he voted for the two-thirds rule knowing it would militate against his own pledged candidate.

"We have no discretion," he said. "We are sent here to act; and if we are satisfied, as all candid men must be, that there are not two-thirds in favor of any one individual for either of the offices in question, then, by adopting a rule which requires an impossibility, or which requires, contrary to the doctrines laid down by Mr. Jefferson, the majority to yield to the minority, we say, at the outset, that we have determined not to accomplish the object for which we were sent here."

By the time Butler finished speaking, it was nearly nine o'clock, and the convention soon adjourned until the next morning. That evening Cave Johnson wrote to Polk describing the two-thirds debate and predicting the rule would pass the next day, with the full support of the increasingly anti–Van Buren Tennessee delegation. "From what we can learn," he said, "public opinion [within the delegation] will not justify us in giving our vote to Van." As for the presidential outcome, he added, "everything is in doubt."

When the two-thirds debate resumed Tuesday morning, particularly notable was John W. Tibbatts's reply to Butler's powerful speech of the previous day. The Kentucky congressman dismissed Butler's explanation of why he must oppose the two-thirds rule in order to fulfill his convention pledge to Van Buren. After all, he emphasized, Kentucky's delegation was equally devoted to the nomination of its favorite son, Richard M. Johnson. But, said he, "so soon as we ascertain that we cannot procure the nomination of the favorite son of the democracy of Kentucky, with the sanction of the whole democratic party, just so freely are we ready to offer him up as a willing sacrifice to the harmony of the democratic party, and the success of the principles we advocate." This was greeted by "great applause" from the anti–Van Buren delegates.

Finally the question was called and the vote commenced. Maine and New Hampshire, the first states on the roll call, went against the two-thirds rule, but the rest of New England split on the issue. New York cast its full 36 votes against, but Pennsylvania split 12 for and 13 against. Then came a cluster of southern states in succession—Virginia, North Carolina, Georgia, Alabama, Mississippi, Tennessee, and Kentucky: 78 votes in favor, none against. The two-thirds rule was adopted. Many Van Buren partisans may have resisted the reality unleashed by the vote, but their man was finished. The convention recessed until three o'clock, when the roll would be called for the presidential nomination.

As the nomination balloting unfolded, Van Buren showed his strength, retaining a commanding lead over his nearest rival, Cass. Three big states—New York, Pennsylvania, and Ohio—together gave him 85 votes out of the 177 needed to capture the nomination. But, when the voting ended, Van Buren had only 146 votes, to 83 for Cass and 24 for Old Dick Johnson. Calhoun captured 6 votes, while Pennsylvania's James Buchanan got 4. As Butler had predicted, Van Buren commanded a majority but not the requisite two thirds.

In subsequent votes, ordered in rapid succession, Van Buren's standing steadily fell as tensions within the Egyptian Saloon steadily rose. In the second balloting, Van Buren lost 19 votes, while Cass and

Johnson each gained 11. Buchanan gained 5. Van Buren's erosion continued in the third balloting, when he dropped another 6 votes while Cass lost 2 and Johnson gained 5. On the fourth ballot, Van Buren's total dropped to 111 votes, only 6 ahead of a resurgent Cass. Johnson dropped slightly to 32 votes, while Buchanan rose slightly to 17. Van Buren's position looked precarious. It now seemed apparent that Cass had a realistic chance of capturing the nomination if Van Buren's support continued to erode or if Johnson and Buchanan delegates suddenly switched to Cass. On the fifth ballot Van Buren lost another 8 votes while Cass picked up 2. It was a slow transfer, but Cass now possessed 107 votes, 4 more than Van Buren, while Buchanan and Johnson hovered in the 20s.

A Pennsylvania delegate, apparently fearing more Van Buren erosion, moved adjournment until the next morning, but the delegates defeated the motion and headed to a sixth ballot. It ended with Cass at 116 votes to Van Buren's 101, with Buchanan and Johnson holding steady. A seventh balloting yielded 123 votes for Cass to Van Buren's 99. The transfer of Van Buren delegates to Cass now was accelerating. The Pennsylvania delegation, which had given Van Buren 17 votes on the sixth ballot and only 12 on the seventh, was on the verge of abandoning him altogether, and it now seemed likely that Cass could get over the top within the next two or three ballots. If that happened the party would be hopelessly split, as Van Buren's residual support throughout the party would never accept the triumph of what one Van Buren partisan called "the *damned rotten corrupt venal* Cass cliques."

Then Ohio's John Miller rose to submit a motion, which, he said, if voted down, would lead to his likely departure from the convention. The motion declared Van Buren the nominee based on his majority standing on the first ballot. Pandemonium spread across the convention floor, with Miller demanding to speak over a steady din while several delegates attempted to call for a point of order. Miller's aim was twofold: first, to thwart another Tuesday ballot that would lead to further Van Buren erosion and further Cass strength; and, secondly, to get Hendrick Wright to rule the motion out of order. Then Miller and his Ohio colleagues would challenge the ruling—which, they surmised, could be overturned with a majority vote. Hence the two-thirds rule, instituted with a majority vote, would be rescinded with a majority vote. But Wright thwarted them at every turn, first demanding the motion be sent up in writing, then ruling it must be submitted twenty-four hours before a vote could be taken, finally insisting that it would take a two-thirds vote to amend the convention rules. Various Ohio delegates attacked the chair's rulings, their fiery rhetoric frequently interrupted by emotional points of order. Valuable time was consumed as the Ohio delegates argued with the chair until seven o'clock, at which point a motion was made, and carried, to adjourn until the next morning at nine.

As ALL THIS unfolded, Gideon Pillow sat on the convention floor and calmly wrote a letter to James Polk in Tennessee. The letter wouldn't arrive until after the outcome was known, but such were the protocols of communication that it was deemed important to maintain a steady flow of news. Pillow reported that he had been working the floor all day in behalf of his friend, approaching well-chosen delegates, always focusing on Polk's vice presidential ambitions but subtly interjecting hints of his availability for the top spot should the convention wish to pursue such a course. Perhaps some of the seeds he had cast upon the soil were now beginning to germinate. Just a few minutes before, he revealed in his letter, he had been approached by leading delegates from Pennsylvania and Massachusetts with the idea of putting Polk before the convention as a compromise candidate. He had replied that Polk's name certainly was subject to the will of the convention, that he would not at the present time bring it forward, and that, should such a development occur, it would have to be at the instigation of northern delegates. "There is, I think," he wrote to Polk, "a strong probability of your name ultimately coming up for President. I do not think it prudent to move in *that* matter now. I want the North to bring you forward, as a *compromise* of all interests." Pillow would have a long night ahead of him, much of it in league with George Bancroft of Massachusetts, a kindly and erudite poet and historian whose work had brought him national fame. Bancroft, a convention delegate and longtime Polk admirer, had decided the time had come to thwart Cass by inserting Polk into the proceedings.

Upon his arrival in Baltimore, Bancroft had sought out Pillow and Andrew Donelson to assure them that his state would cast at least ten and perhaps twelve votes for Polk in the vice presidential balloting. Thus the connection had been established at the beginning of the convention. On Tuesday, as the convention broke into near chaos and Cass kept rising in the voting, "it flashed on my mind," Bancroft later told Polk, "that it would be alone safe to rally on you." He approached New Hampshire delegate Henry Carroll, editor of the Concord *New Hampshire Patriot and State Gazette* and a convention secretary. When he proposed Polk as compromise candidate, Carroll "fell in to it heartily," as Bancroft later put it. The two then went to New Hampshire governor Henry Hubbard, head of that state's delegation, and he also embraced the idea. Now Bancroft had New Hampshire, not a large state but pivotally located in the North, whence a Polk boomlet must come. Next Bancroft brought into the plan his good friend Marcus Morton, former Massachusetts governor and head of that state's delegation. He signed up immediately.

That's when Bancroft went to Pillow and got word that, if the Polk initiative began in the North, Polk's friends would immediately set to work on the southern delegations. Pillow mentioned specifically Mississippi, Alabama, and of course Tennessee. This was precisely the circumstance Pillow had anticipated, and he now moved with passion and energy to exploit the opportunity. He found Bancroft equally enthusiastic and ready for a long night of heavy political exertions. Pillow possessed complete faith in his reading of the opportunity and thus devoted nearly the entire night to swaying southern delegates toward Polk.

Meanwhile, Bancroft and Donelson showed up at the residence of the New York and Ohio delegations and argued with delegates there for hours. Samuel Medary, head of the Ohio delegation, listened intently and seemed to grasp the dual reality that Van Buren was gone and only Polk could stop Cass. He said he anticipated that his state eventually would go for Polk. New York was tougher. Its delegates naturally were in "a great state of agitation," as Bancroft later recalled, and hardly open to entreaties that they abandon their man. But Bancroft found a receptive audience in Gouverneur Kemble, industrialist and former congressman, who suggested his delegation needed to move decisively and not simply drift into the vortex of convention confusion. He agreed that Polk would make a sound compromise and suggested he was prepared to take a lead in getting his delegation to act assertively. Bancroft returned to his lodgings near midnight "tranquil & happy." Next morning the relentless Bancroft enlisted Maryland's William Frick in the scheme and also confirmed Louisiana's enthusiasm.

The convention reconvened at nine o'clock and devoted a good portion of the morning to the Ohio delegation's protest motion to declare Van Buren the majority nominee. This gave Pillow, Bancroft, and others valuable time to work the floor in behalf of their scheme. When the eighth ballot finally commenced, a new political dynamic emerged. New Hampshire, the second state to be called, awarded its six votes to James K. Polk. The Egyptian Saloon erupted in cheers, repeated two states down the register when Bancroft called out seven Massachusetts votes for Polk. As the balloting continued, it became clear that Van Buren and Cass were largely holding their ground while support for Johnson and Buchanan had evaporated. When the roll call reached Tennessee, Cave Johnson rose to say his delegation had not traveled to Baltimore to press the nomination of Tennessee's Polk. Yet, he said, the delegation felt the same warmth toward its favorite son as did the other states for their favored candidates. And, now that other states had voted for Polk, Tennessee would do the same. The hall erupted in cheers. With Alabama's 9 votes and a scattering of others, Polk ended the ballot with 44 votes.

As delegates on the floor pondered the significance of what had just happened, Pennsylvania's Reah Frazer moved that the assemblage proceed to a ninth ballot. In doing so, he noted that he had followed party instructions to vote for Van Buren three times, only to see him sink with every vote. Then he had supported his state's own James Buchanan, who clearly couldn't emerge. So now, said Frazer, he was going for Polk—"the bosom friend of Old Hickory . . . the man who stood up in defence of the old hero during the panic session . . . the man who fought so bravely and so undauntingly the whigs of Tennessee—the pure, whole hog, locofoco democrat, who goes against . . . the ring-streaked and speckled whig party, with all its odious, abominable measures."

There followed a series of testimonials from the floor on Polk's behalf, including one from Ohio's influential Samuel Medary, who said they all must now be willing to sacrifice their first-choice candidates in the interest of "brotherly affection." When the ninth roll call unfolded, it soon became apparent it would be the final ballot. As the *Daily Globe* later reported, "The enthusiasm and perfect harmony that now prevailed in the convention was in striking contrast with the proceedings of an hour previous. The delegation from each State appeared to be firm and undivided in their support of Mr. Polk."

But the drama was not yet over. The New York delegation had left the floor for caucus discussions following the eighth ballot, and Virginia followed upon seeing the rush to Polk in the early ninth-ballot voting. Other delegations asked to be passed over in the roll call so they could discuss the sudden turn of fortunes. When Virginia returned, William Roane of that state rose to say that, after the Texas issue had emerged, Virginia had abandoned Mr. Van Buren "with a bleeding heart," for Virginians "loved and admired Mr. Van Buren as a patriot and statesman." Virginia's delegation had been for Cass through eight ballots, and Roane's kindly words for Van Buren now represented a significant effort to foster that "brotherly affection" throughout the hall that Medary had advocated. Now, said the Virginian, they all had a "higher duty to perform," necessitated by "the arch apostate Henry Clay, who, for twenty years, has been . . . stimulating every vindictive feeling of his heart against the democracy of the country." It was to defeat Clay, said Roane, that Virginia now extended its seventeen votes to James Polk. "Thunders of applause," reported the *Globe*.

New York had returned to the hall during Roane's remarks, and now Benjamin Butler rose to the rapt attention of the assemblage. The New York delegates, he explained, had been discussing whether they had fulfilled their pledge and could now in conscience withdraw Mr. Van Buren's name from convention consideration. It touched the hearts of them all, he said, but perhaps none so much as his own. From his earliest youth Van Buren had been his friend, protector, and teacher, with "ties equal to those of father and son." He had brought to Baltimore, he revealed, a letter from Van Buren authorizing him to withdraw the New Yorker's name if he concluded Van's continued participation could harm the party. Statesman to the last, Van Buren had taken steps to ensure his ambition wouldn't precipitate a convention breakup.

Butler then said he had told his New York colleagues in caucus that he reluctantly would exercise the sad duty of pulling Van Buren's name from the roll call. He added he would cast his vote for Polk, who fully met "the Jeffersonian standard of qualification, being both capable, honest, and faithful to all his trusts." When all but one of New York's thirty-six delegates also went for Polk, the rush was on. One after another, delegation leaders rose to cast full delegation support to James K. Polk, often adding warm praise for the man or directing piquant invective at Henry Clay. By the time it was over, around two o'clock that afternoon, every delegate had cast his vote for James Polk, and the Tennessean was declared the unanimous choice of the Democratic convention. The result, said Mississippi delegate Williamson Smith in a letter to Polk, was "a continued and heartfelt burst of enthusiasm of gratulations and heart cheering speeches I have never before witness in any assemblage of People."

That left two outstanding matters of business—the vice presidential nomination and approval of the platform. The delegates moved with dispatch to give the ticket's second spot to Silas Wright, the New York senator and Van Buren confidant. When he declined the honor out of devotion to his New York friend, the convention turned to Pennsylvania's George Dallas. The party platform consisted of standard Democratic fare praising strict construction of the Constitution and states' rights while opposing any national bank, all high tariffs, and Clay's federal system of internal improvements. On foreign policy, it resolved: "that our title to the whole of the Territory of Oregon is clear and unquestionable; that no portion of the same ought to be ceded to England or any other power, and that the reoccupation of Oregon and the reannexation of Texas, at the earliest practicable period, are great American measures, which this convention recommends to the cordial support of the democracy of the Union." The convention, boisterous to the end but serene now in the harmony that had descended upon it so unexpectedly, adjourned *sine die* at one o'clock in the morning of June 1.

6 · POLK VS. CLAY

Answering the Question, "Who Is James K. Polk?"

NEWS OF JAMES Polk's nomination crept across the land, reaching the nominee as mere rumor a full nine days after the event. The next day, June 10, brought confirmation in the form of newspaper accounts and congratulatory letters. Polk responded with characteristic matter-of-factness. "I need scarcely say to you," he wrote to Robert Walker, "that the nomination was not anticipated or expected by me." At no time did he allow his correspondence to betray any hint of excitement or even surprise. The closest he came was an expression to a Philadelphia lawyer and staunch Jacksonian named John K. Kane. "If the nomination made at Baltimore shall have the effect of restoring harmony to our party," he wrote, "I shall be heartily rejoiced." But to Cave Johnson he extended a rare expression of appreciation: "I am under many personal obligations to my friends—and to yourself especially—for the agency which I know you had in bringing about the result."

At his Ashland estate outside Lexington, Henry Clay responded with typical scorn. "Are our Democratic friends serious in the nominations which they have made at Baltimore?" he asked his friend Willie Mangum, the North Carolina senator. "We must beat them with ease if we do one half of our duty." Mangum agreed. "It is a *literal disbanding of the party* for this Campaign," he said. "We will literally crush the ticket." New York's Francis Granger labeled the nomination "a farce," and a Whig senator from Louisiana named Alexander Barrow declared, "I hardly believe such a ridiculous thing." Whigs across the land delightedly took up the chant, "Who is James K. Polk?"—a sneer at the candidate's relative obscurity and lack of political stature.

But astute Whigs, including Clay, privately knew this was not good news. A Van Buren nomination would have sliced up the Democratic Party and left the South and West ripe for Whig capture. It also would have neutralized the powerful Texas issue. Now the Democrats appeared at least temporarily unified, and the Texas issue was unavoidable. For Whigs, capturing the crucial southern and western states now would be more difficult.

Still, Polk nervously identified four looming impediments to victory. First was the tariff issue, which lingered as a serious regional threat, particularly in industrial Pennsylvania. Next was the prospect that John Tyler would run for president under some kind of new party label, thus siphoning away votes that otherwise would go to Polk. The New York political situation posed another danger. The nation's largest state teetered precariously between Democrats and Whigs, and a strong Democratic candidate in the coming gubernatorial race was needed to quell intraparty frictions and bring victory in November. No such candidate had been recruited, and none appeared willing to step forward. Finally, there was the ever-threatening specter of Benton's angry northerners and Calhoun's rebellious southerners squaring off in a spasm of intraparty belligerency.

Then there was the Texas issue, generally a political boon to Polk given the country's growing expansionist sentiment but complicated by Calhoun's provocative linkage of annexation and slavery in his famous letter to Ambassador Pakenham. The Senate was about to vote on the annexation treaty, and everyone anticipated its defeat. In the wake of that, Polk would have to decouple the two issues in order to get the full benefit from the annexation emotions emerging within the country.

The tariff issue presented itself immediately. In his first batch of post-convention letters, Polk received earnest agitations on the matter from Robert Walker and Andrew Donelson. Walker considered this the "one question which can by any possibility defeat your election." Without Pennsylvania, the election would be lost, he said; and, without a flexible tariff position, Pennsylvania would be lost. Donelson advised Polk to embrace the deftly crafted positions and language of Andrew Jackson. "He stood up all the time against Clay," wrote Donelson, "and yet conciliated the good feeling of both sections of the union." It was, however, he added, "the most difficult task of his administration."

Pennsylvania long had been the hotbed of pro-tariff sentiment, rendered all the more intense with the Panic of 1837 and the succeeding depression years. The shift to anthracite coal from charcoal in the production of iron was generating even greater distress among owners and workers at iron companies that had been slow in making the conversion. The result was that coal producers now were joined with iron producers in demanding strong protective tariffs to indemnify themselves against foreign competition, and this combination constituted a powerful political force. It had captured Pennsylvania's newspapers and its entire congressional delegation, including its Democrats. It had fostered passage of the protectionist Tariff of 1842 and stood ready to defend that legislation at all costs. Polk had opposed the Tariff of 1842 and now had to determine just what he would—or could—say about it.

On June 18, Walker offered further counsel, noting it wasn't simply the South and West that had abandoned Van Buren in 1840 but also northern entrepreneurial conservatives who chafed under the Magician's rigid economic constrictions. These "wanderers of 1840" would never again vote for Van Buren, but they could be lured back to the party if Polk could "harmonize, as far as possible, all conflicting interests on this dangerous and difficult question." To do that, said Walker, Polk should build his position upon two foundations: first, that tariff rates should not exceed levels needed to run the government, as administered according to "a spirit of republican simplicity & economy"; and, second, that within that range it would be acceptable for the government to impose particular duties to benefit specific industries in need of protection.

Walker added that Polk's friends in Washington urged that he use the word *"aid"* in place of *"protection"* and suggested Polk should hark back to his consistent support of Jackson's tariff policies during the Old General's popular presidency.

Polk promptly drafted a letter to John Kane in Philadelphia outlining his tariff position, with a cover letter authorizing Kane to
publish the document if Polk's Pennsylvania friends deemed it beneficial. He took his language almost entirely from Walker: "I am in
favour of a tariff for revenue, such an one as will yield a sufficient
amount to the Treasury to defray the expenses of the Government
economically administered. In adjusting the detail of a revenue tariff,
I have heretofore sanctioned such moderate discriminating duties as
would produce the amount of revenue needed, and at the same time
afford reasonable incidental protection to our home industry." As
Walker had suggested, Polk noted his previous support of Jackson,
but he opted for the bold use of the word "protection" over "aid."
And he added this deftly crafted sentence: "In my judgment it is the
duty of the Government, to extend as far as it may be practicable
to do so, by its revenue laws, and all other means within its power,
fair and just protection to all the great interests of the whole Union,
embracing agriculture, manufactures, the mechanic arts, commerce
and navigation."

It was a brilliant stroke. By twice inserting the word "protection,"
Polk gave Pennsylvania's Democratic protectionists plenty of room to
maneuver. They promptly distributed the statement widely, suggest-
ing they had nothing to fear from this southern Democrat. As James
Buchanan later told Polk, "Your discreet & well advised letter to Mr.
Kane . . . has been used by us, with great effect."

Of course, Whigs everywhere correctly pointed out that Polk had
ignored the most important question: whether he would repeal or
modify the Tariff of 1842. It was all essentially duplicitous, they
argued, bolstering their case with past Polk statements such as, "I
have at all times been *opposed to the protective policy*." But Polk successfully had finessed the issue. All he needed now was the discipline
of silence; the statement must speak for itself. This proved difficult
in late September when a group of Whigs from neighboring Giles
County arrived in Columbia with a set of questions probing Polk's
specific views on the 1842 tariff. The group expressed a resolve to
remain in Columbia pending Polk's reply and reminded the candidate

of his lifelong advocacy of open political dialogue. Polk fretted over the matter for nearly a week and drafted six possible replies. In the end he opted to brush aside the interrogatories. "Having declared the general principles which I entertain, and to which I would conform in the event of my election to the Presidency," he wrote, "it cannot be expected that I should do more." His reticence generated widespread Whig criticism, but his tariff finesse remained intact. Pennsylvania looked safe.

The New York problem solved itself when the highly popular Silas Wright accepted the mantle of Democratic gubernatorial candidate. He had wished to avoid the call and remain in the Senate, which he loved. But there wasn't anyone else who could carry the banner with sufficient weight in that crucial swing state. Writing to Jackson, Polk had reported that former New York governor William Marcy had despaired of finding a "satisfactory nomination." Polk had added it would be "most unfortunate" if the state party's internal difficulties "shall have the effect to weaken our cause, as I think there is some reason to fear they may." But Wright, one of the true statesmen of his time, had seen the political imperatives facing his party and stepped up to the need. "The Whigs are aghast at the nomination," a Polk ally named Albert Gallup wrote from Albany. "You can put us down for 20,000"—meaning a New York victory margin of that magnitude in the presidential race.

The Tyler problem proved more nettlesome. The stubborn president had never expected his third-party effort to keep him in the White House, but he did think he could craft a distinctive brand of politics encompassing states' rights Whigs, expansionists, and Jacksonian populists. He estimated his core supporters as numbering some 150,000 men, mostly business-minded Democrats, a few influential newspaper editors, and beneficiaries of his own expansive use of presidential patronage. His aim was to marshal these followers into a knot of political sentiment with enough clout to hold the balance of power in the presidential campaign. Polk quickly concluded that only Andy Jackson possessed sufficient stature to nudge Tyler out of the race.

In early July Jackson wrote John Y. Mason, former congressman from Virginia and a Tyler intimate. Now that the Democrats had nominated a pro-annexation candidate, he argued, there was no need for Tyler to press his cause. Then that dexterous behind-the-scenes operator, Robert Walker, paid a visit to Tyler at the White House. Over several hours of conversation—"a most disagreeable duty," as Walker later wrote—the president rambled at considerable length about what he considered his unfortunate situation. First, said Tyler, his sentiments now rested firmly with the Democrats, and he fervently wished for Polk's election. His followers also tended toward the Democrats. But the Democrats had been attacking Tyler and his followers so vociferously, said the president, that his withdrawal could only benefit Clay. Stung by these Democratic attacks, particularly from the Democrats' official Washington newspaper, the *Globe*, the Tyler men considered themselves proscribed from the Democratic Party and thus would vote Whig or withdraw from the race altogether if Tyler exited the campaign. On the other hand, the president continued, if the Democrats would signal that his followers would be welcomed back into the party—treated with respect and considered for future patronage jobs—then he would gladly withdraw and cast his support to Polk and Dallas.

Walker replied, as he later wrote Polk, that "no effort would be omitted on my part, to produce an honourable & cordial union between the democratic party & himself & his friends." To Polk he added: "I think that the importance of this union & cooperation *cannot be overrated*." He urged the candidate to write a private letter to a friend, to be shown confidentially to Tyler, expressing devotion to the president and his friends. He also urged Polk to enlist Jackson to write a similar letter, which might find its way into print. Stirred by this turn of events, Polk moved to action.

First, he had to do something about the *Globe*, run by the brilliant and cantankerous Jackson ally, Francis P. Blair. Blair was an unabashed Van Buren man and close friend of Thomas Hart Benton, and he wasn't happy about what had happened at Baltimore. He also delighted in directing his famous bellicosity at President Tyler, whom he considered a menace for having derailed his favorite Democrat by forcing the Texas issue. Now, in the wake of the Baltimore outcome, he not only continued his assault on Tyler but displayed a visible coolness toward his party's own standard-bearer, Polk. George Dallas, writing from Philadelphia, had complained that "*Mr Blair's* columns are exceedingly cold," and this frostiness was confusing Democratic activists in his state and undermining the Polk-Dallas candidacy.

Polk wrote to Andrew Donelson, never far from Jackson in proximity or friendship, and urged him to get two letters off to Blair, one from himself and one from Jackson. "I know of none," wrote Polk, "unless your intimacy with Blair would authorize you to write him, a plain, but at the same time friendly and conciliatory letter, urging him as a matter of duty to the party to take stronger ground than he has yet done." As for Jackson, he suggested "one of his strong letters in his own hand-writing." The same day he wrote to Jackson. "I wish the tone of the Globe was more cordial," he said, adding the paper's "transparent coldness and indifference" had been attracting attention in the country.

The next day Polk wrote again to both men, this time enclosing Walker's letter describing his session with Tyler. "I believe," Polk wrote to Donelson, "Gen. Jackson is the only man in the country whose advice Mr Tyler would take." He doubted the propriety of making public any Jackson letter but suggested a private correspondence to some friend that then could be shown confidentially to the president. Returning to his previous complaint, he added: "The Genl. can certainly induce Blair of the Globe to change his course. To continue his attacks on Tyler can do no good." To Jackson, he diplomatically suggested he would defer to the General's judgment on what should be done in the way of a Jackson letter, but he left no doubt that he desired some kind of action designed to assuage Tyler. He added the main impediment to Tyler's withdrawal seemed to be Blair's sustained attacks in the *Globe.* "There is certainly no necessity," he wrote, "for the *Globe* to continue its attacks upon him or his administration," particularly since a full-blown Tyler candidacy could "put in jeopardy the vote of several closely contested States."

Jackson responded on July 26 as Polk's stern mentor. He was taken aback, he suggested, at Walker's "great want of common sense" in suggesting Jackson should express himself publicly on what the Tyler men would get from Polk if their man would withdraw from the race. "Why my dear friend," he lectured Polk, "such a letter from me or any other of your conspicuous friends would be seized upon as a bargain & intrigue for the presidency"—rather like Clay's "corrupt bargain" of 1825. "Let me say to you," wrote the General, "that such a letter . . . would damn you & destroy your election." But Jackson had no intention of ignoring the problem. He sent a carefully worded letter to his old friend William B. Lewis, also a confidant of Tyler, in which he sought to assure the president that his friends would be *received as brethren . . . all former differences forgotten.*" He authorized Lewis to show the letter to Tyler but refused to allow its publication and steadfastly avoided any specific promises or any suggestion that his expressed spirit of generosity was predicated upon any Tyler action.

It worked. Within three weeks Tyler wrote to Jackson saying the General's expressions "as to the proper course for me to pursue in the present emergency of public affairs" had prompted him to withdraw. He said he would seek to get his friends to support Polk but added that might prove difficult in the current climate of attack from Blair's *Globe.* Jackson promptly wrote to Blair. "I pray you," he said, "to desist from the abuse of Tyler or his supporters, but treat them as brethren in democracy and hail them welcome to the support of the great democratic cause to aid in the defeat of Clay and Whiggery." Blair eased up, and on August 20, Tyler published in the *Madisonian* a letter of withdrawal. Another potential impediment to Polk's victory was gone.

But the frictions within the party still posed an ongoing threat. Polk's first move was to neutralize any hostility that might arise from Democrats inclined against him because he stood in the way of their own aspirations. He knew he would be more likely to get enthusiastic backing from ambitious party leaders such as Cass, Benton, Wright, Buchanan, and Calhoun if he promised not to seek a second term. As Aaron Brown had expressed it to Polk, "I need not say who & how many of our friends expect it. The thing is right *per se* & under all the circumstances I think you ought not to hesitate to do it." Polk didn't. In officially accepting the nomination by letter on June 12, he wrote that, if elected, "I shall enter upon the discharge of the high and solemn duties of the office, with the settled purpose of not being a candidate for re-election." He added this promise not only imposed "a salutary restraint" upon himself but also allowed the party to select a successor "who may be best calculated to give effect to their will, and guard all the interests of our beloved country."

That done, Polk turned to the lingering angers among the New Yorkers. This was delicate, as reflected in a letter from Silas Wright written two days after the nomination. Ostensibly a courtesy letter outlining his reasons for declining the vice presidential nomination, the missive also was laced with expressions of resentment at the Baltimore outcome, including a jibe at Tennessee for having voted for the two-thirds rule. "Upon every principle of democracy," he wrote, "Mr. Van Buren was nominated upon the first ballot." The country, said Wright, "was never so much in danger as at this moment." This he attributed to "Mr. Calhoun and his clique in all the Southern states, and the success they have had upon this occasion, together with . . . the Course of the Southern delegations in the late convention." The Democrats could lose the election, he warned, if the North abandoned the party due to the South's "sectional issues, mischievous intrigues, and sudden excitements." He wanted the candidate to get his complete support and that of New York, but that would be impossible if Polk became captive of the Calhoun forces.

Polk took pains in response to emphasize his long-standing support for Van Buren and his happy anticipation, prior to the "Texas excitement," that the New Yorker would be the party's nominee. "I need scarcely assure you," he wrote, with something less than complete ingenuousness, "that my nomination . . . was not only not anticipated, but was wholly unexpected by me." He stressed that, when he had publicly expressed support for Texas annexation, he had not yet seen Van Buren's opposition letter and had fully expected the New Yorker to embrace the same sentiment. Wright's immediate reaction was to declare publicly—"cheerfully and proudly"—that next to Van Buren he considered Polk the country's best qualified man for president. Van Buren added his own warm endorsement shortly thereafter.

But intraparty tensions continued to pose a grave threat to Polk's election. On June 10, two days after the annexation treaty died on the Senate floor, Cave Johnson wrote from Washington to say Benton was making considerable mischief on the issue. He had voted against the treaty, along with Wright and a number of other northern Democrats, and now he was proposing his own annexation approach designed to assuage Mexican angers and bar slavery from Texas's northern portions. He wrapped his compromise effort in rhetoric so bellicose as to enflame southern Democrats. Now, said Johnson, some southern hotheads were proposing a southern convention to air the issue—"a sort of rally upon Southern principles agt Northern principles." This could prove very troublesome.

Two days later Johnson related what had happened in Washington when he called a meeting of Democrats to craft a campaign fundraising strategy. The sectional tensions were so intense that he had to adjourn the session just to avoid an explosion. Southerners, he said, were bent on expropriating Polk as an ally in their war against the North, and northerners were equally bent on making sure that didn't happen. Johnson expressed fears that "the war will go on between C——n & B——on [Calhoun and Benton], to extermination." He had gone to see Wright with hopes he would somehow intervene, only to discover this normally dispassionate politician too angry at Calhoun to be of any help. "He is furious and I think determined to push C. & his clique to the wall or perish."

A week later the fretful Johnson warned Polk that the southern convention idea was gaining force, and now the Calhoun men wanted to stage it at Nashville, bringing southern agitation right to Polk's backyard, complete with pugnacious threats of secession if annexation dies. Meanwhile, Wright suggested that, if Polk were identified with the southern agitators, his cause in the North would be ruined. The northerners feared, said Johnson, that Jackson might somehow get drawn into the mess, perhaps induced by his southern friends to bless the southern convention idea without weighing the consequences. Asked Johnson: "Can not you see him & have a free conversation as to the Southern movement & put him on his guard?" Polk promptly dispatched the Johnson letter to Jackson.

The Old General was in a sad state of health, but he bestirred himself to reply. "I assure you it was not necessary to put me upon my guard," he wrote. He had been in correspondence with Benton and had assured him that Polk fully embraced the sentiments of Jackson's famous toast of many years before: *"The Federal Union must be preserved."* He added: "You will perceived I have estoped Benton or any others from believing that you or I could countenance nullification or disunion." Still, Jackson harbored no illusions about Benton. "I found from his letter, that his hatred to Calhoun & his Jealousy of the growing popularity of Tyler had deranged him." He speculated that it had been Benton who had induced Van Buren to take his fatal annexation stand in May. And, no, he would never countenance a southern convention, though he favored the emerging idea of a broad Democratic meeting at Nashville in mid-August to blunt the southern initiative and bring the entire party together. "Nothing but a Mass meeting should be held," the General declared.

Polk knew he must squelch the southern convention. Most of the agitation was coming from South Carolina—but not, Polk noted, from Calhoun. The most vociferous agitator was Robert Barnwell Rhett, the congressman from Beaufort. Born 1800 as Robert Barnwell Smith, he had changed his name in 1838 as he was rising through South Carolina politics. Senator George McDuffie, no appeaser on issues of importance to South Carolina, considered Rhett "vain, self conceited, impracticable and selfish in the extreme." Unfortunately for Polk—and for Calhoun and McDuffie—Rhett had a large following among young political fire-eaters in the state. Now he was seeking to destroy Polk's presidential bid and precipitate a crisis, with the eventual aim of national disintegration. He railed against Polk's Kane letter on the tariff, attacked Calhoun as a cynical political manipulator, and declared himself the last great defender of South Carolinian honor. Soon others felt obliged to echo these sentiments lest they appear unsteady in protecting their state from nefarious north-ern threats. Even McDuffie sought political cover in his famous query whether his constituents were true South Carolinians or curs habitu-ally kicked by the Washington enemy but always returning to lick the boots that inflicted the blow.

Polk's opportunity came when Calhoun sent a confidant and former congressman named Francis Pickens to the national party meeting at Nashville on August 15. Polk promptly invited Pickens to Columbia for two days of conversation, then fostered a day-long meeting with the increasingly infirm Jackson. Polk showered the Calhoun emissary with cordial hospitality, demonstrated robust respect for Calhoun and the politics of South Carolina, digressed candidly about prominent northern Democrats, including Benton, Wright, and Blair. Calhoun wanted assurances that Polk would liquidate the *Globe* as the Demo-crats' leading newspaper and would attack the Tariff of 1842. Appar-ently the assurances were forthcoming. Retreating to Polk's library, Pickens dashed off a letter to his patron, then showed it to Polk before sending it. *"Everything is completely satisfactory,"* he reported, adding the nominee was engaging in *"no correspondence even"* with the Van Burenites (not entirely true, but no doubt an accurate rendition of what he had been told). He added Polk "is determined to do all he can to reform the gov; and the 1st thing is to reduce the Tariff of 1842 to a revenue measure entirely . . . , 2d. to introduce strict economy, 3d, acquire Texas at all hazards."

That was all Calhoun needed. Not only had Polk promised to pursue policies favored by the South Carolinian, but his one-term pledge also kept alive the man's lingering presidential ambitions. He instantly became an ardent Polk supporter and intensified his efforts to thwart the Democratic meeting at Nashville. The prospect was now brighter, declared the great orator, that the region could "throw off the burthen, which has been weighing down the South, exhaust-ing her means & debasing her spirit, than it has been since 1828." The great South Carolina rebellion had been neutralized, and another impediment to Polk's election greatly diminished.

But Benton and his allies continued their belligerent ways. The

Whig Central Committee appreciated Benton's anti-annexation fulminations so much, according to reports of the day, that it bundled
his Texas speeches into a pamphlet, along with Van Buren's Texas letter, and printed 500,000 copies for distribution. The problem was
that Benton's emotional intensity outstripped the actual differences
that separated him from the more aggressive annexationists. His
actual legislative activities on the issue reflected a creative approach
to a complex issue and a devotion to the eventual American incorporation of both Texas and Oregon. Silas Wright, in crafting his message for the New York gubernatorial campaign, took essentially the
same position. But Benton's angry rhetoric was confusing the electorate and undermining Democratic unity.

As the campaign unfolded, however, it became increasingly clear
the broad electorate favored annexation, and this served to dampen
Benton's influence. News reports and local political analyses suggested widespread support for annexation in Pennsylvania, New
England, Indiana, Illinois, and elsewhere, while in the avidly pro-
Texas South several leading Whigs were bolting the Clay party to
support the annexationist Polk. "From all quarters reports are gratify-
ing," the well-informed Jackson wrote Polk in early September. "Let
the Texean question be kept up." Though "quite low . . . and debile-
tated" and hardly able to walk across the hall without "great oppression," he retained his feisty spirit and mental acuity. He suggested in
his letter that the treaty's demise in the Senate would serve merely to
agitate the electorate. *There never was such treachery to the laborer of the
South & west, as the rejection of this treaty. . . .* It must, when explained
to our farmers, arouse them against Whigery. Have it laid before the
people."

OUT AT ASHLAND, Henry Clay also could see that his now famous
Raleigh letter had placed him athwart national sentiment on the
Texas issue. He desperately needed to maneuver himself into a better
position in order to redeem his lifelong presidential dream. In June
an opportunity arrived in the form of a letter from the editor of the

Tuscaloosa, Alabama, *Monitor*. Clay's Raleigh letter, said the editor, had fostered an abandonment of his candidacy by many state Whigs, and now Alabama Democrats were boasting that "Polk and Texas will sweep the state." Clay seized the chance to clarify his Raleigh stand on annexation. "Personally," he wrote, "I could have no objection to the annexation of Texas, but I certainly would be unwilling to see the existing Union dissolved or seriously jeoparded for the sake of acquiring Texas." Clay's aim was to dig himself out of a political hole, but it served to dig him further into it. Northerners complained that he was retreating from what he had hailed as sacred principle while southerners saw it as an insincere effort to patronize them.

The howls of protest from both sides stirred Clay once again to recalibrate his Texas position, this time with a letter—soon labeled the "second Alabama letter"—published in the Tuscumbia, Alabama, newspaper. He had always wanted Texas in the Union, he said, and had sought to reacquire it during his years as secretary of state. But he backed off when Mexico declared it would consider annexation an act of war. He concluded it wasn't worth the price in "national dishonor, foreign war, and distraction and division at home." But, as president, he would promote annexation so long as it wasn't accompanied by dishonor or war. Regarding the increasingly inflammatory slavery question, he expressed doubt that annexation would affect slavery in any serious way, as American slavery was destined to fade away eventually anyway. Hence, he would simply be guided by public opinion on the matter and his "paramount duty of preserving the Union entire, and in harmony." This was a remarkable document, almost guaranteed to undermine his traditional support without adding any new voters. Not surprisingly, anti-slavery northerners reacted with acrimony.

Now Clay was in an even deeper hole, and prospects for getting out appeared slim. Thurlow Weed of New York, a stalwart Whig and one of the nation's most astute political observers, pronounced Clay's document "an ugly letter" and added, "Things look blue." Daniel Webster wrote a friend, "I feel pretty tolerably angry." Throughout the country Clay was seen once again as a master of cunning and duplicity. This wasn't entirely fair. He had intended his Alabama letters to be clarifications of his Raleigh position, not a retreat. But an astute politician would have seen the futility as well as the danger in attempting such a clarification at this stage of a campaign. Though Clay viewed himself as infinitely more brilliant and politically dexterous than the stolid and sober-sided Polk, he lacked a crucial political attribute that Polk had in abundance: discipline. Had Polk sought to clarify his Kane letter under pressure from voters, he would have experienced the same whipsaw response. He knew better and managed to resist the temptation.

But something else was at work here that went beyond late-campaign rhetorical tactics. Clay's underlying problem was that he had taken a position at variance with the preponderance of voter sentiment on the most powerful issue of the day: American expansion. For whatever reason—stubbornness, ideology, ego, nostalgia—he had not sufficiently plumbed the depths of public opinion on the emerging vision of a transcontinental nation before rushing to his political stand on the issue. He remained stuck in the politics of the past, clinging to the perceptions, philosophies, and principles that had guided him ever since he brilliantly had bundled them all up into his famous American System. This outlook never fully had captured the imagination of the American electorate, though it had fueled the Whig Party and been an integral part of the national debate for more than a quarter century. But nearly always it had been thwarted by the more popular perceptions, philosophies, and principles of Jackson and his Democratic adherents. Now the country was moving into a new era, and once again the Jacksonians had moved quickly to align themselves with the country's majority sentiment. They had seized the new force of expansionism, and it would sweep them back into power.

When the votes were counted, Polk was elected the country's eleventh president by a slim margin of 39,490 votes out of 2,703,659 cast—49.5 percent to Clay's 48.1 percent. Polk captured fifteen states for 170 electoral votes, while Clay pulled eleven for 105 electoral votes. But it was actually much closer than it might appear. The antislavery Liberty Party, led by James G. Birney of Michigan, a former Alabama slaveholder who had become a fervent enemy of slavery, amassed

62,103 votes, including enough ballots in Michigan, New York, and Ohio to have possibly captured the balance of power in those three states. Had he not been on the ballot, it is likely Clay would have carried all three and thus the election. Although slavery in itself galvanized only a small proportion of the electorate, it now was gaining force as an issue and on the margin could affect the course of political events. Nevertheless, history does not linger over such electoral speculations, and the country quickly absorbed the reality that Henry Clay's White House claim had been rejected yet again, and probably for the last time, while the new president would be that colorless but cagy and relentless expansionist from Tennessee. The Whigs' snide question, "Who is James K. Polk?," had been answered.

7 · THE VICTOR

Preparing for the Mantle of Leadership

JUST BEFORE SIX o'clock on the evening of November 15, 1844, Nashville's postmaster, Robert Armstrong, Andrew Jackson's close friend and also a close friend of James Polk, received the information he had been anticipating with coiled anxiety: His friend Polk had captured the presidency. He sent the news on through the mail and then dispatched a fast horseman to Columbia to inform the new president-elect. The messenger arrived at Polk's doorstep at daybreak, and the triumphant politician was awakened to receive Armstrong's message: "Reid of Louisville sends me an Express with the *Glorious* News that New York is Yours. . . . This settles the matter and put Whiggery & Mr Clay to *rest*. . . . Our friends are *happy* and rejoicing."

Never one to inform others of his own good fortune, Polk spent the day wandering around Columbia, nodding at friends' speculations on the electoral result. He accepted the congratulations of his community the next day, after the regular mails arrived and the news swept through town. At the Hermitage, the Old General exulted in what he knew would be his last opportunity to savor a Democratic triumph. "I can say in the language of Simeon of old 'Now let thy servant depart in peace,' for I have seen the solution of the liberty of my country and the perpetuity of our Glorious Union," Andrew Jackson wrote with stoic acceptance of his looming death.

Across America, people of all persuasions adjusted to the next four-year installment in the ongoing chain of democracy set in motion fifty-five years before. Democrats basked in their majority status while Whigs struggled to put a sheen of optimism on a miserable

112

outcome. The *Daily Globe* noted that generations had come and gone since Clay's political emergence "and again and again and again sealed their verdict of condemnation on Mr. Clay and all his measures." The paper quoted an old saying that when the brains were out the man would die. "And this we take to be Mr. Clay's case at present."

The Whigs' *National Intelligencer* acknowledged complete surprise, adding "the blow came upon us with a staggering force." The journal consoled itself with the observation that "the larger portion of the educated and informed people of the land voted for Clay [and his running mate], and much the larger portion of those neither educated nor well-informed voted for their successful opponents." Thus did the *Intelligencer* express the elitist outlook that had contributed to the Whigs' wilderness existence for most of two decades. At Ashland, Clay pondered "the general wreck of our Cause" and said he felt "the severity of the blow most intensely."

At Columbia, Polk received bundles of congratulatory letters. Never inclined to bask in glory, or even acknowledge it, he turned his mind to two key challenges. The first was creation of a cabinet to serve his national stewardship. All the conflicts, animosities, and furies welling up within the party had to be weighed and pacified, and somehow he had to craft an inner circle that could gain acceptance from both Benton and Calhoun. There had to be balance in geography, ideology, and personal temperament. And of course he must ensure loyalty to himself and his policies.

Next, he had to monitor events related to Texas annexation. When the Tyler treaty, wrapped in the infamous Calhoun letter to British ambassador Pakenham, had failed to gain Senate ratification the previous June, thirty-five senators opposed it while only fourteen voted in favor. Whigs remained largely united, with fourteen against and only one for it. But the wily Calhoun, even in defeat, scored a political triumph. Not only did he destroy the political career of the despised Van Buren but he also split the Democrats along North–South lines. Seven northern Democrats, led by the outraged Benton, joined the Whig majority in opposing the treaty on the Senate floor. Now this party fissure lingered as a major headache for Polk.

Following the Senate vote, Whigs naturally hoped the issue would go away. But Tyler sent a message to the House urging annexation through a different means: a joint resolution, to be passed by both congressional chambers according to the legislature's constitutional right to admit new states into the Union. This would be unprecedented. Never before had Congress admitted any state not carved from U.S. territories. But pro-annexationists promptly embraced the concept as a more effective and perhaps even more appropriate approach to bringing Texas into the Union. As Cave Johnson had expressed it to Polk the previous spring: "We should . . . carefully distinguish between *the treaty & annexation*. The treaty *is dead*, but *annexation* as soon as *practicable*." Now annexation would dominate the congressional session scheduled to convene in early December. Polk would have to watch these unfolding developments carefully.

POLK'S CABINET PLANNING began with two competing imperatives: dealing with John C. Calhoun and maintaining cordial relations with Van Buren. These dominated the discussions in late November when Polk and Aaron Brown spent two days with Jackson at the Hermitage. It was agreed that Calhoun would not be retained as secretary of state. This would gratify northern Calhoun haters, particularly Benton. The thunderous Missourian had warned that Calhoun's retention would make for Polk "a hotter bed than Tyler ever lay on." He told Blair, as the editor later recounted to Jackson, that "if a 'rotten egg' were left he would fire at it." But how could Polk exclude Calhoun without stirring the animosity of his mercurial southern supporters? Perhaps, the three men pondered, Calhoun would go quietly if offered the ambassadorship to London.

They agreed further that Polk should reach out to Silas Wright in a confidential letter offering him a top cabinet slot. And they resolved that Polk's cabinet should include no presidential aspirants. The virus of competing presidential ambitions must not be allowed to infect Polk's inner circle. Hence there would be no offers to Van Buren, Benton, Cass, Old Dick Johnson, or Calhoun. Buchanan, maybe.

After the Hermitage discussions, Brown traveled on to Washington, where he and Cave Johnson would assess party sentiment and monitor rumors. Meanwhile, the president-elect sat down on December 7 to write a long and cordial letter—labeled *"Strictly Confidential"*—to the freshly elected governor of New York, Silas Wright. "I desire that you will accept a place in my Cabinet," he wrote, adding he considered Treasury to be the most important of the executive departments. "If you are at the head of the Treasury Department the whole country will feel and know that it is in able and safe hands." Polk considered it unlikely Wright would accept the offer, but he wanted the New York party to see it as a friendly overture.

Upon arriving in Washington, Brown called on Calhoun and enjoyed a cordial conversation with the secretary. While avoiding any discussion of his own ambitions, the South Carolinian offered solicitous counsel, suggesting the government should be essentially southern in its policies "but tempered with moderation & justice as to create no northern aversions." Calhoun's amicable demeanor gave hope that perhaps he would not cling unduly to his cabinet post. Brown also talked with Fernando Wood, a prominent New York City shipping merchant and former congressman. He said Polk should offer a cabinet post to Wright but predicted there was "no earthly probability of its acceptance," as Brown later reported to Polk. But New York would expect a prominent position in the cabinet, said Wood, who offered a number of recommendations, including Churchill Cambreleng, former congressman and minister to Russia; Azariah Flagg, steadfast machine politician, state comptroller, and leader of the so-called Barnburners, the most staunch of the Van Burenites; and William Marcy, former senator and governor. All were names on Polk's list, along with that powerful figure with extensive Washington experience, Benjamin Butler.

Toward the end of December, Polk received Wright's reply. "I am not at liberty," he wrote, "either as a matter of public duty, of party obligation, or of personal justice, to accept of your offer." Along with fulsome expressions of esteem for Polk, Wright outlined the complex and disturbing political situation in New York. The state's Demo-

cratic Party was hopelessly split between Van Buren's Barnburners
and an opposition group known as the Hunkers. The Barnburners professed strict adherence to sound borrowing policies and firm
opposition to most publicly financed improvement projects. In short,
they were traditional Jacksonians, full of skepticism toward banking
interests and government intrusion into the economy. The Hunkers
sought a more flexible approach somewhere between the Barnburners'
rigidity and the more freewheeling policies of the state's Whigs. They
favored some government financing of public improvement projects—"almost irrespective of the consideration of debt," as Wright
put it—as a necessary spur to prosperity and civic harmony. This fissure threatened the New York party so severely, wrote Wright, that it
had necessitated his reluctant run for governor and now his ongoing
commitment to remaining in the state.

Upon receiving Wright's letter, Polk wrote to Van Buren. He
recalled their last meeting in spring 1842 as a time when he had
"confidently anticipated, that you would now occupy the position, in
which I have been placed." He added his "personal thanks" for Van
Buren's generous support following the Baltimore convention. Then,
getting down to business, Polk solicited the New Yorker's counsel
on possible cabinet appointments from New York. He particularly
wanted recommendations for State and Treasury, "as I think it probable that I will desire to take some one from New York to fill one
of these important places." But he wanted to hear from Van Buren
on any or all of the positions to be filled. The same day he wrote to
Wright seeking similar counsel. In both letters, Polk expressed an element of urgency: He expected to leave Columbia at the end of January, with hopes of reaching Washington around February 20. He
wished to hear back before his departure, since the March 4 inauguration would arrive quickly and communication was slow.

Throughout December and January, the solitary Polk sat in
his study at Columbia and pondered the calculus of his cabinet decisions. Early on he fixed on Pennsylvania's senator James Buchanan

as his first choice for State. Son of an Irish immigrant storekeeper, Buchanan had made a fortune in the law and then gone on to a successful congressional career. He had impressed Polk with his steadfast loyalty to the Democratic cause and, more recently, his eloquent support of Texas annexation. He was a cautious man, unlikely to rebel against Polk's policy prescriptions. And Polk calculated that having a Pennsylvanian at the top of his cabinet would prove helpful when he initiated his planned assault on the Tariff of 1842. But he couldn't move on this nomination until he disposed of the Calhoun question, and it still wasn't clear how tenaciously the South Carolinian would cling to the job at State.

Soon a letter arrived from Aaron Brown relating a recent conversation with Calhoun intimate William Gwin. Calhoun, said Gwin, would be pleased to remain in the cabinet under Polk. But, should the new president prefer someone else, "he will retire without the slightest possible dissatisfaction." Further, said Gwin, Calhoun expected to support Polk's presidency fully, even on the tariff issue should Polk feel compelled to trim his views somewhat to mollify his Pennsylvania constituency.

This was excellent news. Polk promptly reserved State for Buchanan. That meant Treasury must go to New York, but he wouldn't decide on who should get it until after hearing from Van Buren and Wright. Now, with Pennsylvania and New York represented and Calhoun gone, another slot would have to go to someone from the lower South. The choice was obvious: Senator Robert Walker, the diminutive Mississippian whose qualifications included his unquestioned brilliance, undoubted loyalty, and chess master's instinct for stealthy political maneuver. He slotted Walker in as attorney general.

That left the War and Navy secretaries and postmaster general. The latter by tradition went to a close associate of the incoming president, and Polk had no difficulty in selecting Cave Johnson. The only other possibility would have been Aaron Brown. Both men wanted the job, perhaps Brown with greater intensity. In early January he had sent Polk a poignant letter outlining his career thinking in light of his wife's death the previous May and his "solemn pledge" to see his five motherless children cared for and educated. Hence he really wished to resist pressures from Tennessee party regulars that he run for governor. He would rather, he said, "rent a brickyard in this or some other Town than to go through the vituperation & abuse of another campaign." Perhaps, he suggested, he might be useful as the next editor of the *Globe*. He quickly described this as a "mere notion" that he would abandon instantly "if you can think of a better arrangement." Polk brushed aside these heartfelt musings, and soon thereafter Brown announced his candidacy for governor. Johnson would get the post office job. Though a bit limited in imagination and occasionally hampered by his habitual fretfulness, Johnson always put Polk's interests above his own and hence held a powerful lien on the president-elect's affections.

The final two slots posed a dilemma. Tyler's Navy secretary was John Mason of Virginia, a congenial politician who pursued his public duties without much intensity and displayed an instinct for landing jobs that many considered a bit beyond his talents. One wit described his career as "a marvel to every one who knew him well, and a piece of good luck at which he himself was much astonished." But he and Polk had been close friends since their days together at the University of North Carolina, and in the 1830s, as a House member, Mason had stepped aside to pave the way for Polk's elevation to speaker. Thus Polk felt immense loyalty to the man, and he initially resisted Jackson's insistence that he pass over Mason along with the rest of Tyler's cabinet. But ultimately he gave in. That brought to the fore another Virginian, former House speaker Andrew Stevenson, slotted in by Polk as his new War secretary. That in turn meant the Navy job would go to a New Englander, and the president-elect leaned toward George Bancroft of Massachusetts, the historian who had served Polk so well at Baltimore the previous May.

It all came together when he received Van Buren's reply just before setting out for Washington. The New Yorker issued a strong endorsement for Azariah Flagg, whose "reputation in this State stands higher I think as financier than that of any man who has gone before him." Not surprisingly, the former president expressed enthusiastic praise for Ben Butler. But he added strong doubts that the man would leave his lucrative law practice for a return to government service. And Van Buren warned that only the State Department could possibly beguile Butler. "If therefore you for any reason decide to go elsewhere for a Secy of State he will be out of the question & I am sure very happy to be so." As for Bancroft, "I have tried him & know him to be fit for any thing, & . . . you never would regret having taken him."

That settled it. James and Sarah Polk stayed with Jackson at the Hermitage on the night before setting out for Washington, and that evening Polk presented to the General his thoughts: for State, Buchanan of Pennsylvania; for Treasury, Flagg of New York; for attorney general, Walker of Mississippi; for War, Stevenson of Virginia; for Navy, Bancroft of Massachusetts; and for postmaster general, Johnson of Tennessee. It was an excellent list with regional balance (three slave states and three free states represented), with a tilt toward Van Buren over Calhoun, with no Tyler holdovers, and with undisputed men of stature in every slot. The only question was whether Buchanan would forswear any presidential ambition. Jackson pronounced himself highly pleased and promised to write letters to Washington friends predicting acclaim for the lineup.

The next morning, January 31, James and Sarah Polk stood on the steps of the Hermitage and shook hands for the last time with Andrew Jackson, who barely managed to get himself so far from his bed. It must have been an emotional moment as the younger man set off to assume the mantle of power once so effectively shouldered by the older. Jackson expressed his conviction, as he later expressed it to a friend, that Polk would "fearlessly carry out all his principles heretofore acted upon neither turning to the right or to the left." After an all-day open house at Nashville for supporters and well-wishers, Polk and his party embarked upon a chartered steamboat called the *China* that took them to the wide Ohio River via the smaller, winding Cumberland. From there the little boat chugged its way north and east, past Louisville and Cincinnati and finally to Wheeling, West Virginia. The president-elect avoided all fanfare and, when pressed for some public remarks at Cincinnati, simply expressed a conviction that he represented not a single party but the whole country. Reaching Wheeling on February 9, the party departed the river and joined a procession of lavish carriages that transported the dignitaries over the mountains to Cumberland, Maryland. There a private railroad train was waiting to whisk the presidential party to Washington in a single day.

As Polk was making his way to Washington, Washington was grappling with the country's most divisive issue, Texas. When the lame-duck second session of the Twenty-eighth Congress convened on December 2, Tyler was waiting with a presidential call to action based on his reading of the recent electoral results. "A controlling majority of the people, and a large majority of the States," he declared in a presidential message, had expressed support for annexation "in terms most emphatic." In extensive language Tyler outlined his policy rationale and dismissed his critics' objections. Mexico and Texas had been in a state of war for nearly a decade, he said, because of Mexico's unwillingness to accept the reality of Texas independence. "Mexico has no right," declared the president, "to jeopard the peace of the world, by urging any longer a useless and fruitless contest." And any effort to do so would inevitably arouse the American people, who after all shared with the Texans an affinity of race and culture. The country was settled by immigrants from the United States, noted Tyler, whose friends and relatives "would not fail to sympathize with them in their difficulties, and who would be led by those sympathies to participate in their struggles." Far better, he suggested, to bring Texas under United States protection and then establish a clear and reasonable boundary between the two countries. Besides, added the president, the ongoing hostilities between Mexico and Texas threatened to weaken both to such an extent as to invite foreign powers into the region, which could "eventuate in the most serious injury to the United States."

For all these reasons, suggested Tyler, Congress should resurrect the rejected treaty language as a resolution. Seven annexation resolutions quickly emerged in the Senate, another ten in the House. Throughout late December and into January, the House grappled with the issue until Democratic leaders finally embraced the resolution language of a Tennessee Whig named Milton Brown, whose fears of a voter backlash had compelled him to break with Whig doctrine and embrace annexation. Brown's resolution envisioned Texas joining the Union as a single slave state, not a territory, with the United States taking responsibility for settling final boundaries with Mexico. The republic's debt would remain with the new state, which also would retain its public lands. But the Brown resolution also provided that Texans could carve out an additional four states from the territory, meaning there could be five new slave states in the Union represented in Washington by ten new senators. To soften northern opposition to this bold assault, Brown embraced the compromise language of Illinois representative Stephen A. Douglas, which would extend the Missouri Compromise line westward through Texas. This meant slavery would be permitted below the line 36°30' but proscribed north of that latitude. No one missed the point, however, that there wasn't much Texas territory above that line.

On January 25, the House approved the Brown resolution 120 to 98, largely along party lines. Only eight Whigs, all from the South, joined 112 Democrats in supporting the measure, while 26 northern Democrats aligned themselves with the Whig opposition. The *Daily Globe* crowed: "We congratulate the democracy on the vote of the popular branch of Congress. It is auspicious to the peace, prosperity, and happiness of the whole continent." The measure then went to the Whig-controlled Senate, where hardly anyone gave it much prospect of success. In the way stood that force of nature, Thomas Hart Benton.

Benton had contributed mightily to the defeat of the Calhoun treaty the previous June with a stream of harsh invective and eloquent entreaty. He could never, he declared, sanction annexation on "weak and groundless pretexts, discreditable to ourselves, offensive to others, too thin and shallow not to be seen through by every beholder and merely invented to cover unworthy purposes." He could only support annexation, he said, if Mexico first gave its assent. And, though a southerner and slaveholder who would resist all assaults on slavery, he added, "I shall not engage in schemes for its extension into regions where it was never known." Now, with the new Tyler initiative before Congress, he still opposed any annexation initiative that ignored Mexico's interests, that mixed slavery with expansionism, or that skirted the Constitution through mere legislation rather than Senate ratification of a treaty. Aaron Brown reported to Polk that many of Benton's western friends expected him to be "antagonistical" to the incoming administration. "He shews no mitigation of his opposition & nothing but instructions plain & powerful can subdue him," wrote Brown. Then the Missouri General Assembly issued plain and powerful instructions to its senators, suggesting boundary questions be left to future negotiations and advocating considerable leeway for compromise on key issues by the executive branch (meaning, presumably, the Polk administration).

On February 5, Benton surprised his colleagues by introducing new legislation without any reference to Mexican assent or slavery. It called simply for an appropriately sized state to be carved out of the Texas expanse, with the rest to be incorporated into the United States as a territory. Other issues, including those related to slavery, would be negotiated by a five-man commission appointed by the president. Benton said his new approach reflected his faith in the incoming Polk administration to negotiate the remaining issues with judgment and wisdom, and he believed particularly the slavery questions and the needed negotiations with Mexico were "just as fully in the mind of the President as if submitted to him in a bill."

This was a major breakthrough. The *Globe* endorsed the Benton formula. The Texas representative in Washington declared it the best approach. Even South Carolina's George McDuffie embraced it. Polk, arriving in Washington just as these developments unfolded, quickly concluded the issue had been resolved and he would avoid its sting. But then John C. Calhoun declared his opposition, and considerable southern support evaporated. Now the issue appeared hopelessly deadlocked, with the Senate clearly unwilling to accept the House version and the House equally unwilling to accept the Benton approach, which didn't seem to have enough Senate votes anyway. That's when the politically adroit Robert Walker proposed a compromise: Combine the two versions into one and pass it with a proviso that Texas could choose whichever approach it deemed most appropriate. This seemed promising but ultimately proved insufficient. Benton and his allies pronounced themselves unwilling to give Texas such a prerogative while many southerners insisted on the House bill's Missouri Compromise line on slavery.

Polk, now comfortably ensconced at Coleman's hotel, found himself increasingly involved in behind-the-scenes maneuverings. "He is for Texas, Texas, Texas; & talks of but little else," North Carolina's Senator Willie Mangum wrote a friend. By assiduously avoiding all leaks on his cabinet musings, he kept the pressure on office aspirants to find a solution. Benjamin Butler persistently worked New York's Senator John Dix, newly appointed to fill Silas Wright's seat, trying to get him to accept the House resolution if Benton's bill failed. With Walker's combination idea seemingly stalled, Polk pursued the idea of forcing the House version to a Senate vote on the theory that, with a week left before adjournment, Benton and his allies wouldn't dare vote against the session's last hope for annexation. By Sunday, February 23, however, it was clear this wouldn't work; Benton's allies, particularly Dix, remained adamantly opposed to the House version and its presumed extension of slavery. That's when Polk, in discussions with key Democrats, apparently hit upon a variation on the Walker approach: combine the two versions but leave it to the president, not Texas, to decide which one to embrace. According to numerous accounts, Polk added his strong inclination to embrace the Benton approach should the choice fall to him.

The Bentonites leaned toward acceptance but expressed reluctance to extend the prerogative of action to the outgoing president. McDuffie quickly assuaged those concerns by dismissing any prospect that the Tyler team would "have the audacity to meddle with it." Thus, the Bentonites quickly fell into line when Walker introduced the new version on the Senate floor on Thursday evening, February 27. Calhoun continued his opposition, but it cleared the Senate 27 to 25, with three southern Whigs joining a united Democratic Party to seal a victory without a vote to spare. The next day the House approved the amended version. Polk's late interventions had proved deft and successful.

MEANWHILE, HOWEVER, THE president-elect's carefully crafted effort to forge a cabinet was unraveling. It began when word spread through official Washington that Polk had offered State to Buchanan. The negotiations preceding the offer had been extensive, with Polk insisting that Buchanan, in accepting the job, must forswear participation in the party's succession battles as either partisan or candidate. Buchanan accepted the conditions but added he "could not . . . accept the high & honorable station to which you have called me at the expense of self-ostracism." Hence, he could not proclaim that he would never vie for the 1848 Democratic nomination, only that, should he do so, he would resign from the cabinet if Polk so wished. Polk accepted Buchanan's proviso, and the deal was struck. Around the same time Cave Johnson accepted the postmaster job on the same terms.

But hints of the Buchanan appointment stirred Vice President–elect George Dallas into a frenzy of activity aimed at getting Robert Walker appointed to the Treasury job, where he could serve as a counterweight to Buchanan, Dallas's Pennsylvania rival. Dallas and Walker were blood relatives, born into the same upper-crust Pennsylvania family, and Dallas wanted his kinsman well positioned to help fend off Buchanan on major patronage decisions within the administration. Soon intense pressures converged on Polk from the Cass contingent, from the Calhounites, from Dallas's Northeast friends. All insisted Polk's plan to make Walker attorney general was insufficient; the Mississippian must be elevated to Treasury.

Polk initially resisted this pressure, though it seemed to encompass a preponderance of party sentiment. On February 19, the day after the Buchanan deal was struck, he drafted a letter to Walker offering him the Justice Department. But he didn't send it. Instead he began pondering a revised lineup. He recalled Van Buren's warm praise for Bancroft and his suggestion that the Massachusetts intellectual could serve in any cabinet capacity. Why not shift him from the Navy Department to Treasury? A strong Van Buren man whose pro-Texas sentiments matched Walker's in intensity, he might serve as a compromise choice that could mollify both party factions. Then his old friend John Mason, who had been displaying a hangdog demeanor as it became clear he would be passed over, could be resurrected as navy secretary. That left only the War Department for New York. This was tricky. Van Buren and Wright had come to expect a New York appointment of greater stature, based in large measure on Polk's own representations. Now he was about to deliver to them a serious disappointment.

Confident he could justify his new thinking, he wrote to Van Buren describing the "great difficulties interposed" upon him—the intense pressures on behalf of a "distinguished individual" from the South getting the Treasury slot and his conclusion that a satisfactory compromise choice might be Bancroft of Massachusetts. He explained his desire to appoint a New Yorker as war secretary and expressed entire satisfaction, in confidence, with either Butler or William Marcy, the former governor and senator. "Would you give your advice in like confidence?" he asked. "Who ought to be selected?"

Polk was running out of time, and the mails were slow. Thus, before hearing back from Van Buren, he dispatched a warm letter to Butler offering him the War Department: "I most sincerely hope that you will not hesitate to accept the office which I now tender to you." Butler quickly replied that he would have to decline the offer because of "domestic and prudential considerations which forbid (except in a case of duty too clear and imperative to be mistaken) my removal to the seat of Government." But, he added with a touch of malice, he would have felt compelled to accept either State or Treasury notwithstanding those domestic and prudential considerations.

From this point things went seriously awry. On February 26, Van Buren received Polk's letter. He was shocked. Not only had New York lost a chance at one of the top cabinet slots but it had all happened under pressure from the same culprits who had destroyed Van Buren's career at Baltimore. The New Yorker took time in crafting a reply, traveling to Albany to consult with Wright. When he finally put his thoughts to paper, he did not stint on bluntness. Polk's decision, he wrote, "has caused me considerable embarrassment, and not a little pain." He added that Democrats of his state "will feel their pride severely wounded, & the recollection of past events painfully revived." Worse, Van Buren considered Marcy a political enemy, increasingly inclined to join the Hunkers in their intensifying battles with Van Buren's rigid Barnburners. He couldn't believe Polk didn't know this, and he was enraged that the president-elect would consider appointing one of his most nettlesome opponents to the cabinet. In dispatching his reply to Polk by hand of his son, Smith Van Buren, he gave Smith also a letter to be delivered to Butler in New York City. In it he implored his friend to take the War Department lest it fall into the hands of their New York nemesis.

Too late. Butler already had sent his letter of decline. Smith Van Buren continued on to Washington but found himself delayed by a railroad mishap. Hence he didn't get to Polk until Sunday afternoon. Again, too late. The previous evening, desperate to get news from Van Buren but fearful he would miss his chance to have a cabinet in place for the inauguration four days hence, Polk had sent off a letter to Marcy offering him the War Department. At the same time he had dashed off to Van Buren an explanation of his action and its rationale. "I hope this appointment may be satisfactory to you," he wrote, clearly unmindful of the feud that had emerged between the two New Yorkers.

When Smith Van Buren arrived with his father's harsh letter, Polk was crestfallen. The president-elect held the letter, according to the younger Van Buren, "as nervously as if it had been a pet snake, which he was half disposed to hold on to & half disposed to throw out of the window." There wasn't much he could do, except endure the haughty outrage of Van Buren's impudent son. In a later conversation, young Van Buren denigrated Marcy mercilessly and warned Polk that his elevation to war secretary would "utterly paralyze the party in our state & prostrate the administration & its friends." Polk expressed surprise to learn of the Van Buren–Marcy feud and asked the young man to convey to his father that as president he would, as Smith Van Buren later recounted to his father, "endeavor to rectify the bad effects of it &c & that Mr Wright & yourself should have the patronage for New York, & that a foreign mission was one of the plums which he had in store for New York . . . & such fol-de-rol."

It was a serious political setback on the eve of the Polk presidency. He had begun the exercise of crafting a cabinet with the primary goal of ensuring the satisfaction and support of Van Buren and his New York Barnburners. Now, at the end of the process, he had ensured their anger and enmity. Three days later, under pressure from the usual southern and western interests and still smarting from Smith Van Buren's display of disrespect, Polk abandoned the notion of giving Treasury to Bancroft and offered it instead to Robert Walker. That left open the Justice Department, which he promptly offered to his old friend John Mason. Thus the final cabinet selections were: Buchanan at State; Walker at Treasury; Mason at Justice; Bancroft at Navy; Marcy at War; Johnson at the post office. This new lineup enraged Van Buren and his partisans all the more. "It is an evil which neither civil words nor the disposition of patronage can repair," the ex-president later declared to Bancroft, "& which, under the circumstances, nothing can justify." Both Van Buren and Wright vowed to have nothing to do with the new Polk government.

As this was unfolding, a new development of politics and diplomacy emerged from the twilight of the Tyler presidency. On Sunday, March 2—two days after Congress passed the dual resolution on Texas annexation and two days before the Polk inauguration—Tyler convened his cabinet and rushed to Texas a courier bearing an offer of annexation under terms of the House resolution. As word of Tyler's action spread through official Washington, outrage erupted among the Benton followers, not to mention the Missourian himself. "It was not a barren fraud, but one prolific of evil, and pregnant with bloody fruit," Benton wrote later. He argued that at least five senators had voted for the dual resolution upon getting assurances the matter would be left to Polk and dealt with according to the Benton formula. Any two of those five senators, voting against the resolution, would have killed it. "Thus was Texas incorporated into the Union," said Benton, "by a deception, and by deluding five senators out of their votes." With Tyler's eleventh-hour move, Polk escaped the need to initiate action on Texas, but he would not escape the passions engendered by the issue.

As JAMES POLK prepared to assume national leadership, he stood before a nation in transformation. Of course many of the old passions remained that had stirred that long and bitter rivalry between Old Hickory and Prince Hal. There still would be tensions over the definition of America in economic terms: whether the country should be guided by those who sought to generate progress through governmental projects and good works, through protective tariffs and the concentration of economic power in a federal bank; or whether the country should avoid concentrations of power, either economic or political, and distribute it as widely through the polity as possible. But these frictions were less intense now. They had been superseded by a new political development—the explosive emergence of the expansionist impulse. Soon a New York editor named John O'Sullivan would codify this powerful sentiment in a catch phrase that would last as long as the nation—Manifest Destiny. In doing so, he would bring a powerful sense of justification to the country's territorial aims and implant the new impulse into the framework of the Democratic Party. A new dream had taken hold, of a vast and bountiful nation stretching from the Atlantic to the Pacific, with ports and commerce and naval fleets on both oceans and a burgeoning and productive population in between.

As a product of the old politics, Polk took pride in his lifelong attachment to Jackson and his relentless opposition to Clay. And, with his surprise presidential victory, he not only had regained his own sense of personal destiny but also had reestablished his party's sense of national destiny. His November triumph ensured that his party would dominate American politics for sixteen of the twenty years between 1829 to 1849, interrupted only by the aberrational tenure of Harrison and Tyler. But Polk was not a man to get stuck in the past, and he thoroughly embraced the new expansionist impulse that was capturing the national consciousness. With his limited imagination tied to a propulsive ambition and an unceasing tenacity, he embraced this new outlook without thought of nuance or ramification. On this issue, he had little time or regard for the opposition, whether expressed in the elegant phrases of Clay, the stolid legalisms of Van Buren, or the outraged fulminations of Benton. His mind enveloped the simplicity of the concept, and that is what would propel him through four years of national leadership.

But this simplicity of outlook shrouded from his thinking an ominous new political reality unleashed by the expansionist impulse—the growing intensity of the slavery issue. The force and danger of that sectional fissure had struck many Americans over the years. Thomas Jefferson had recalled famously that the perils of the issue had hit him "like a fire bell in the night." But the nation at large had managed again and again to shake off the intermittent eruptions of the issue and keep it from getting embedded at the center of the nation's politics. Now that was changing. Northern Whigs, outraged by Calhoun's insistence on tying Texas annexation to slavery and the prospect of five new slave states along the Rio Grande, increasingly coalesced behind the politics of abolitionism. This put immense pressure on northern Democrats, who couldn't ignore this growing voter sentiment without risking the loss of political standing. The first test case was New York, where antislavery Whigs held the balance of power in ten upstate congressional districts and where many Democratic voters remained outraged over the outcome at Baltimore. Democratic dominance was so thin, remarked Senator John Niles from neighboring Connecticut, that the abolitionists could capture the state for the Whigs by luring away a mere one percent of the state's Democrats.

Meanwhile, many southern politicians grew increasingly alarmed at these developments. With more and more northern Whigs demonstrating abolitionist sentiments and the Democrats split over annexation, they foresaw a coming assault on their culture, their economy, and their way of life. The cry, "annexation or secession," heard with growing frequency among southern politicians, reflected the deeply embraced feelings on the slavery issue among large numbers of southerners.

There is no evidence Polk took serious note of these developments. Like most Democrats throughout the Jacksonian ascendancy, he considered slavery a side issue, something that just got in the way of the important political objectives—such as preventing concentrations of power in government and commerce, keeping tariff rates just high enough to sustain a prudent national government, finding some means of maintaining currency stability without resorting to a nefarious national bank. And now, in the glorious dawn of expansionism, he added consolidation of the nation's position on the North American landmass from sea to sea.

That's where he would direct his concentration, and nothing would deflect him from those ambitious objectives. There might be setbacks along the way, such as the cabinet fiasco with Van Buren and his New York allies. Such things might give momentary pain. But never would they induce him to slow or alter his course. And ultimately even the cabinet makeup wasn't paramount in his thinking. As he had written Cave Johnson back in December, "I will if I can have a united and harmonious set of cabinet counselors, who will have the existing administration and the good of the country more at heart than the question of who shall succeed me, [but] . . . in any event I intend to be *myself* President of the U.S." No one could know, as James Polk began his presidency, just how much that sentiment would guide his actions.

8 · TAKING CHARGE

America's Zest for Grand Ambitions

AROUND THE TIME of Polk's inauguration, the Tennessean sat down for a private chat with his new navy secretary, George Bancroft. Polk liked Bancroft, respected his intellect, and trusted his loyalty. Thus he indulged himself a rare bit of candor. Speaking with a degree of animation seldom seen in the man, he slapped his hand upon his thigh and laid out the four central elements of his presidential ambition.

First, he said, he planned to settle the Oregon question with Great Britain and extend America to the Pacific Ocean. Second, he would acquire California from Mexico and secure for his country an additional broad expanse of coastal territory. Third, he would reduce the Tariff of 1842 and replace its overt protectionism with a pure revenue rationale. And finally he would revive Martin Van Buren's "independent treasury" designed to protect federal monies and ensure currency stability.

The two domestic aims, representing standard Democratic doctrine, were predictable enough. The foreign policy goals were of a different cast—almost breathtaking, a bold extension of the expansionism that had burst upon the scene with John Tyler's effort to bring Texas into the Union.

What was remarkable about them collectively, aside from the Jacksonian audacity they represented, was that Polk never went beyond Bancroft in discussing the daring goals he set for himself and his country. He was in many ways a smaller-than-life figure, but he harbored larger-than-life ambitions. This dual reality was to shape his presidency, bringing forth both his success and the high price he would pay for his success.

Particularly intriguing was Polk's resolve to acquire California. How, as he sat there with Bancroft on the threshold of his presidency, did he intend to accomplish this? Polk didn't say, and apparently Bancroft didn't ask. But both men were wise in the ways of diplomacy; both knew every previous effort to broach the subject with Mexico had been firmly rebuffed. Hence, both had to realize that any such resolve would be frivolous without a corollary willingness to force the issue through war.

Beyond Polk's four bold ambitions were two challenges of more immediate urgency—completing the annexation of Texas and shoring up his political standing within a fractious Democratic Party. The first would require decisive moves likely to generate intraparty frictions. The latter would require that he get rid of Francis Blair as editor of the *Daily Globe*. This wouldn't go down easily. Blair was a Jackson protégé and close friend to both Van Buren and Benton. Clearly, Polk's presidency would traverse some treacherous territory.

THE UNITED STATES that accepted James Polk's leadership in March 1845 was a nation on the move, animated by an exuberance of spirit. The population, having roughly doubled every twenty years since the Revolution, now stood at seventeen million, equivalent to that of Great Britain. The national economy had been expanding at an average annual rate of 3.9 percent. Not even the Panic of 1837, for all of its destructive force, could forestall for long this creation of wealth. And throughout the land could be seen a confidence that fueled national success. "We are now reaching the very height, perhaps, to which we can expect to ascend," declared the Democratic *Wilmington Gazette* of Delaware. "Every branch of industry is receiving its reward, and a just, settled policy . . . is all that is required to prolong, if not perpetuate, such blessings."

This faith in the future produced an explosion of new technological developments, most notably steam power and Samuel F. B. Morse's magnetic telegraph. Steam was propelling people and goods across the country at speeds never before imagined—over rails connecting more and more cities and through the waters of America's many navigable rivers and man-made canals. By the 1830s, during Jackson's presidency, the country had 450 locomotives pulling trains over 3,200 miles of track. Now the country's track mileage exceeded seven thousand, and train travel over vast distances had become routine. Henry Clay's first trip to Washington from Lexington, Kentucky, in 1806 had taken three weeks; now he could make the journey by rail in four days—and with much greater comfort.

As remarkable as this was, it seemed almost commonplace alongside Morse's ability to send information across vast expanses almost instantaneously—"the improvement that annihilates distance," as Thomas Benton put it. Morse had strung his famous wires from Baltimore to Washington in time for the Democrats' nominating convention the previous May, and had thrilled Washingtonians with the latest news of developments there. On that rain-soaked day of Polk's inauguration, Morse had been on the platform, hunched over his little gadget, clanking out detailed descriptions of the inaugural events for an expectant crowd in Baltimore and for subsequent readers of newspaper extras rushed to the streets with unprecedented immediacy.

Now the idea was emerging of those wires crisscrossing America along with the expanding ribbons of locomotive transport—connecting North and South and stretching westward with the human migrations then becoming an increasingly powerful element of the American story. All this served as a resounding reply to hidebound skeptics who asked whether America's expansionist impulse would eventually outstrip the country's ability to govern itself. The answer was no: Just as America was encompassing ever greater distances, technology was obliterating the sluggishness of distance.

And so the impulse of exuberant expansionism continued—sending more and more citizens westward and into ever greater cities; fueling an entrepreneurial spirit and technological inventiveness that in turn generated ongoing economic expansion; spreading a sense of national destiny. "America is the country of the Future," declared Ralph Waldo Emerson in 1844. "It is a country of beginnings, of projects, of vast designs and expectations."

Polk shared this American vision. But he never allowed his mind to wander far from the details of everyday toil. And so he set about organizing his government and establishing its routines. One of his first actions was to place in his White House office Thomas Sully's famous portrait of Jackson—a huge likeness of the man in full military regalia. "The contrast between your appearance then and now is very great," Polk wrote the General.

Early on he had resolved to govern largely through his cabinet, which would meet in private sessions twice a week—on Tuesdays and Saturdays at noon. All issues of consequence would be aired at those meetings, or at irregular sessions called at other times of necessity, and he would assess the collective judgment of the six cabinet members before rendering major decisions.

The cabinet could be divided into three categories—the loyal friends, the newcomers, and the men of stature. The loyal friends were Cave Johnson and John Mason. As postmaster general, Johnson held the least imposing cabinet portfolio, which he seemed to acknowledge by remaining relatively quiet in cabinet meetings. But, when he did speak up, he nearly always supported the president's favored direction, and he extended to Polk quiet counsel in private conversations. Attorney General Mason, Polk's friend since college, proved to be something of a surprise—more sound in his judgments than one might have anticipated and more effective in his decisions and actions. Like Johnson, Mason made clear in word and deed that his highest priority was serving the president's interests.

The newcomers were Navy Secretary Bancroft and Army Secretary William Marcy. Though Polk had not known Bancroft well, he had esteemed the man's famous histories of the American experience. Now this presidential respect was fostering a mutually comfortable association that included quiet conversations on matters of state, much like the revealing discussion involving Polk's presidential ambitions. But Polk knew Bancroft hankered for an eventual ambassadorial post in Europe. Marcy, the New Yorker whose elevation had nettled the Van Buren forces, emerged as able, sagacious, and loyal—in short, a highly valuable lieutenant.

The men of stature were Treasury Secretary Robert Walker and Secretary of State James Buchanan. Walker's audacious temperament was brought to bear most often in behalf of Polk's aims, but occasionally he would set his own goals at a higher plane. More troubling was a suggestion, sent from a concerned Jackson, that Walker, well known for his land speculations, might fall under the sway of a coterie of "corrupt speculators" who had bought up Indian lands in Mississippi, then issued scrip upon those lands worth some $1.5 million in the hope the U.S. government would buy it at elevated prices. The scrip now was worth only fifty cents on the dollar, and Jackson anticipated pressures emerging on the secretary to bail out the investors.

"There never was a greater fraud attempted & committed than in these claims and when properly investegated will throw shame & disgrace upon all concerned," wrote the General. "Look to this my friend, let the scrip rest on its own basis. . . . Do you not believe that such an act in the Secretary of your Treasury would blow you & your administration sky high." Despite this troubling warning, Polk remained appreciative of Walker's talents and contributions.

Buchanan soon emerged as Polk's most nettlesome adviser. Bright enough and willing to work hard, he was a man of stubborn whims, puzzling inconsistencies, and self-interested maneuvers. With his six-foot frame, unruly white hair, high forehead, and large jutting chin, the humorless Buchanan brought instant attention to himself when he entered a room. But closer inspection revealed a certain effeminacy in his demeanor, accentuated by soft features and a beardless face. Andrew Jackson considered him "an inept busybody" and once referred to him derisively as an "Aunt Nancy"—hinting at possible homosexuality. Indeed, Buchanan's longtime friendship with the handsome and foppish Senator William King of Alabama, known as an "Aunt Fancy" among colleagues, was so intimate as to stir whisperings around Washington. One congressman referred to the two as "Buchanan & his wife."

It soon became clear that, in naming Buchanan to his cabinet, Polk failed in his resolve to keep presidential ambitions away from his inner circle. Buchanan's presidential aspirations were so raw that he seldom managed to keep them hidden. This ambition, combined with an erratic temperament and a proclivity to stir things up almost for sport, rendered him a sometimes disruptive force. But Polk accepted Buchanan's occasionally irritating cabinet machinations and even seemed to harbor a grudging respect for him.

THE NEW PRESIDENT wasted no time in taking charge of the complex Texas issue. His first decision was whether to dispatch a fast horse to overtake Tyler's March 3 annexation message to Andrew Donelson—the one instructing the U.S. emissary in Texas to press the take-it-or-leave-it House approach as opposed to the Senate's Benton formula, which had envisioned greater negotiation over key issues such as slavery and boundaries. After studying the Tyler dispatches, Polk on March 7 instructed Donelson to disregard the Tyler message until he heard subsequently from the secretary of state.

Three days later Buchanan dispatched a message to Donelson confirming Polk's decision to follow the Tyler approach. This, he said, would "most speedily and certainly secure the admission of Texas into the Union." He instructed Donelson to assure Texans that, if the republic accepted that approach, Texas could rely on "the well-known justice and liberality of her sister States" to ensure good-faith negotiations on the terms of admission. But he added: "Should Texas refuse her assent to the terms . . . or present new conditions for the acceptance of Congress, we are then again at sea, and the success of the great measure may be placed in jeopardy."

This was a momentous first decision by the new president, and it would have lingering political consequences. Benton and his allies felt they had received a commitment from Polk to choose the Senate version over the more austere House approach, and now some felt betrayed. Polk later would deny that he had made any such commitment, and anyway he was merely following a last-moment presidential decision made by Tyler. Polk would write years later that, while he had suggested he would *endeavor* to follow the Benton course, he had never promised to do so. But many Democrats, particularly the Silas Wright contingent, chalked it up to a tendency by Polk to deceive and dissemble.

Over the next two weeks Polk received two Donelson letters and two from Archibald Yell, a flamboyant Arkansas politician and long-time Polk friend who had been sent to help Donelson secure annexation. Taken together they painted a mixed picture of the Texas situation.

There was no question, they said, that public sentiment throughout Texas favored annexation. But the republic's leadership viewed the question differently. Even those who generally favored annexation disliked the House version, which deprived them of the opportunity to negotiate favored terms before accepting annexation. Writing from New Orleans, Donelson said the government's official newspaper, the *National Register,* opposed the House version "with a great deal of feeling." Yell called its editorials "very indignant and abusive." Even Sam Houston, the republic's most prominent and beloved citizen and an old friend of both Andrew Jackson and James Polk, seemed lukewarm on the matter. Meanwhile, other leaders, including Texas president Anson Jones, seemed opposed altogether. There were rumors Jones's administration had approached Mexico with promises of remaining out of the United States if Mexico would recognize Texas independence.

It was clear that most Texas leaders wanted Polk to revert to the Senate version, but Donelson and Yell both believed that approach would introduce so much complexity into the process that annexation could ultimately be defeated. Writing from Galveston, Yell said Houston was viewed as "occupying a doubtful position," although Yell hoped Houston would be swayed by recent correspondence from Jackson urging his old friend to embrace the annexation movement. If Houston got on board, so would Jones, Yell speculated, but "if H. doubts, Jones will be against it" and likely would refuse to call a special session of the Texas Congress to consider the matter. Thus he added that "the thousand difficulties that the Admn. can throw in the way may finally defeat us if it should be attempted, which I hope, & rather believe will not be the case."

Meanwhile, reports reached Washington that the British minister to Texas and other agents of that sprawling empire were locked in a fierce struggle to induce Texas leaders to reject annexation. One anonymous insider was quoted in the *Richmond Enquirer* as saying, "every possible inducement is held out by the English minister and agents, to the people of Texas, to reject the proffered terms. Magnificent offers are made, a reaction has taken place, and I feel warranted in saying that the issue is *doubtful*."

As Polk awaited further Texas developments, he turned his attention to the problem of Francis Blair and his *Daily Globe*. Born and raised in Kentucky, the intellectually feisty Blair had emerged as a prominent newspaper editor in Frankfort, then moved to Washington near the beginning of the Jackson presidency to found the *Globe* as the administration's "court journal." He quickly became a Jackson favorite and one of the country's most influential journalists.

But, as fissures emerged in the party during the 1840s, Blair took sides, aligning himself with Van Buren, Benton, and Wright against Calhoun's southern politics and Cass's western outlook. This proved foolhardy after Van Buren published his famous letter in April 1844 opposing immediate Texas annexation. Blair stayed with Van Buren, setting himself against his party's majority sentiment and then becoming enraged when that sentiment prevailed at the Baltimore convention. "The corrupted intriguers," he wrote to Van Buren, "have succeeded so far as to defect [defeat] us but it will only be temporary chagrin we suffer while immediate disappointment and lasting anathema & disgrace is all they have gained."

As for Polk, Blair's letter to Van Buren portrayed him as merely a shill for the "corrupted intriguers." Blair never truly respected Polk, which was discernible to close readers of the *Globe,* including Polk himself. The Tennessean was stung by the anti-Polk letters of early 1844, appearing in the *Globe* under the pseudonym "Amicus," that had favored Alabama's William King over him for the Democratic vice presidential nomination. Then there were those rabid attacks on Tyler during the general election campaign that Polk viewed as harmful to his electoral prospects. And, as George Dallas had noted, the paper just seemed lukewarm toward Polk, extending to him what seemed like the bare minimum of support needed for appearances' sake. Seldom was he mentioned with any prominence and never did he receive the kind of praise routinely heaped upon Jackson, Van Buren, Benton, and Wright.

Polk viewed the situation as untenable. His entire aim as Democratic leader was to avoid aligning himself with any party factions. That's why he had resolved to exclude presidential aspirants from his cabinet. That's why as a candidate he had so carefully avoided any campaign promises that would tie himself to any party factions. And now he faced the prospect of an official newspaper fervently embracing a favored faction against other Democrats. Polk's course was clear: Either Blair would have to yield his *Globe* editorship or Polk would foster creation of a new official organ.

But there was a difficulty: Blair's close friendship with Jackson. Already Jackson had become disturbed by rumors that Polk planned to take charge of Calhoun's *Madisonian* and make it the official paper. This was entirely false, the result of intrigues by various party functionaries bent on enhancing their own party influence through a new official newspaper. But in responding to his mentor Polk took the occasion to outline his concerns. The problem, he wrote on March 17, was that Blair had become so identified with "certain prominent men of the party" and so hostile to other party leaders that he could not possibly command the support of the entire democracy. Thus, he would stimulate party squabbles and harm Polk's ability to govern effectively.

Worse, the *Globe* "manifestly does not look to the success or the glory of my administration" because it already was preoccupied with the question of who would succeed Polk in 1848. "I feel," said Polk, "that my administration is at this moment defenseless so far as the public press here is concerned." To address this state of affairs, Polk proposed that Blair and his partner, John Rives, maintain ownership while letting Polk name an interim editor who would hold the title during his presidency. "If Blair continues at the head of the Globe," wrote Polk, "and it shall be understood to be the Government organ it is certain that the administration will be in a minority from that moment."

Polk knew this unfortunate turn of events would place a burden upon the ailing Jackson, and so he tossed out the possibility that Andrew Donelson, the General's nephew and namesake, would perhaps assume the editorship. Barring that, he thought the best prospect would be Thomas Ritchie, longtime editor of the *Richmond Enquirer* and a strong Polk advocate.

Jackson's initial reaction was highly negative. The General couldn't bring himself to accept the Polk-Blair split, and objected with such vigor that Polk apparently destroyed his letter. But a flavor of his tone was preserved in a Jackson letter to Blair. "I am sick exausted by writing to Polk," he told Blair, adding he had asked the president "what excuse can he give . . . for not letting you [Blair] & your paper go on as his organ. . . . I ask, have you (the Col) any new principles, other than those you have always advocated & set forth in yr. inaugural, to bring before the people, that you think Mr Blair will oppose."

But Polk was unmoved even by his mentor's anguish. On March 24, Blair called at the White House to inquire whether the *Globe* was to be considered the administration paper. Polk candidly outlined his concerns and aims. He said Blair had rendered himself unacceptable to a large portion of the party, and if he were to remain as the administration's official editor it was likely the Democrats would find themselves in the congressional minority at the next election. The president noted their party didn't enjoy much of a numerical advantage over the Whigs, and hence Democratic unity was all the more imperative. Then Polk proposed his solution: Blair should relinquish the *Globe*'s editorship for the duration of Polk's presidency.

"All I said to him was in a friendly spirit," Polk assured Jackson, adding: "He would not yield to any of my suggestions, and separated from me with the distinct understanding, that if the Globe was my organ, I must take it just as it was, and if I did not choose to that, I must take my own course."

That evening the *Globe* arrived at the White House with a Blair editorial that enraged the president. It was a spirited defense of Ben-

ton's actions on Texas annexation, with an implication that his outlook was now the party's leadership position. "This," declared Polk
to his mentor in Nashville, "is placing me in a false position and one
which I am unwilling to occupy." He added:

> The truth is, Blair is more devoted to *Col. Benton* than to the suc-
> cess of my administration, and his Editorial articles have already
> shown this, and will I doubt not continue to shew it, upon the
> greatest question, (the Texas question) now before the country.
> To be plain with you, I have a very strong impression, that *Mr.
> Blair* expected to control me and the policy of my administra-
> tion. . . . The inference I drew from the tone of Blair's conversa-
> tion was, that he was acting on the belief, that I was helpless and
> defenseless without the Globe. I feel this, and am unwilling to
> remain in so defenseless a position.

Jackson could see there wasn't any point in protesting further.
Clearly, his own powerful mentorship of these two men wasn't sufficient to keep them in harmony as he lay dying. But he wasn't happy
about it. "How loathsome it is to me to see an old friend laid aside,"
he wrote to Blair in a letter advising him to sell. "I cannot reflect upon
it with any calmness."

Blair, seeing no avenue of victory, told Buchanan he might be willing to sell out and retire. Polk was elated. "If he will do this," he
wrote to Jackson, "and a proper man could take hold of it, the whole
party would be united, and I would have a bright prospect of having
a successful administration." The president immediately set about the
task of making it work.

Donelson removed himself from consideration as editor or publisher, but John Heiss, publisher of the *Nashville Union,* strongly
desired a similar role in Washington, and he traveled to Richmond
to persuade a reluctant Ritchie to join him in the new venture. The
financial arrangements, involving Pennsylvania banking and political
interests, were complex and remained cloaked in mystery. Heiss and
Ritchie paid $35,000 for the business, a third up front and the rest

in two yearly installments. The purchase capital came from other parties, who later were repaid from the proceeds of the lucrative printing contracts the *Globe* enjoyed with the federal government. Indeed, it has been suggested that federal funds actually made their way into the Pennsylvania banks that facilitated the purchase as a kind of advance on those printing contracts. One Polk biographer speculated that the president probably shrouded himself from any detailed knowledge of these financial maneuvers, which likely would have raised eyebrows had they become public at the time.

In any event, Blair retired to his Maryland mansion a rich and by all accounts happy man. And Polk got the official newspaper he wanted, though he couldn't escape the lingering irritation of his mentor. "But my dear friend," lectured the General when it was all over, "this movement was hasty, and as I think badly advised and I pray my god that it may not result in injury to the perfect unity of the democracy." In his usual suspicious way, he warned Polk to keep an eye on those who crafted the financial transaction.

On April 14, Blair and Rives announced the sale of the *Globe*. It had been the paper's misfortune, they wrote, "to make enemies of some who united with the democracy in its last struggle," while the new owners had the good fortune "not to have offended any portion of those whose adhesion to the party is necessary to its safety and success." And on May 1 the new publication arrived on the streets under new management and a new name—the *Union*. Its motto: "Liberty, the Union, and our Country." Ritchie wrote: "Pledged to no candidate, committed to no clique, prejudiced against no portion of our party, anxious to extend the right hand of fellowship to every section, and to every honest republican, we go to our post of duty not to disturb, but to unite."

That was precisely what Polk wanted to see as the guiding principle of his official newspaper. He had paid a price for his resolve to take control of the newspaper that had begun fifteen years earlier under the auspices of his beloved mentor. No doubt it was painful to stir up so much anguish and anger in the failing old man. But in doing so he demonstrated his hallmark tenacity and political willfulness.

Barely six weeks after the demise of the *Globe,* Jackson's life ended. On June 6, his bowels dissolved, and he knew his long agony of decline was nearly over. "It must soon take me off," he told his adopted son, Andrew Jackson, Jr. He asked for pen and paper so he could write a final letter to his protégé in the White House. He was urged to wait until he felt stronger, but he insisted. It required two hours of effort to produce his final missive, which was that anxious warning about the dangers lurking in that Mississippi land speculation.

Then he called his family and household to his bedside for final farewells and admonitions. He urged the grandchildren to be always obedient, to keep holy the Sabbath, and read the New Testament. He expressed confidence that he would see them all again in heaven, "both white & black," as Jackson Jr. recalled later. Putting on his spectacles and seeing tears in their eyes, he drew back.

"Oh! do not cry—be good children & we will all meet in heaven," he said. Then he dozed off, "with perfect serenity of mind," said Sam Houston, who arrived at the Hermitage just after the General's end. It came the afternoon of June 8.

"His life is a volume of his country's history," wrote the *Union* in a heartfelt obituary on June 16. As news spread across the land, citizens of all political convictions paused to reflect upon "the death of a great man," as the *Union* expressed it. June 27 was designated Washington's official day of mourning. "There was an almost total suspension of business," reported the *National Intelligencer*. The observance included cannon salutes, the tolling of church and engine bells, the appearance of numerous military honor guards, a procession to the Capitol, and a subsequent reception at the White House. At the Capitol, those assembled heard a speech by the "orator of the day," George Bancroft. He spoke for nearly two hours—placing Jackson, said the *Intelligencer,* "on the most exalted ground both as a hero and a statesman."

It was of course an occasion dominated by Democratic sensibilities, as indeed the Democrats had dominated American politics for most of twenty years under the Jacksonian banner. President Polk's statement was properly simple: "Andrew Jackson is no more!" he said. "His country deplores his loss, and will ever cherish his memory." In a private letter to a friend, he expressed himself with more anguish, calling Jackson "the greatest man of the age in which he lived, a man whose confidence and friendship I was so happy as to have enjoyed from my youth to the latest hour of his life."

But Whig politicians and institutions had their say as well, though generally expressed more cautiously. "There is no doubt," said Daniel Webster, "that he sought to distinguish himself by exalting the character and honor of his country." Noting Jackson's famous declaration that the Union must be preserved, Webster added, "I believe he felt the sentiment with the utmost sincerity."

Less inclined toward polemical charity was the *Intelligencer*, which offered to refrain from raising old animosities in exchange for a corollary forbearance on the part of his admirers. But even this grudging expression was an indirect testament to the Jackson legacy. The editors wrote:

> He has occupied a large space in the history of his country during the greater part of the last thirty years, and, for good or for evil, has exercised an irresistible influence on public affairs. Grateful for the good that he has done, and willing to allow him credit for patriotic motives for such acts of his as we have most disapproved, we have no disposition . . . to pronounce a discourse upon the merits of his public life. That duty we shall leave to his friends; trusting that it will be discharged . . . with such delicacy and such respect for opinions differing from theirs as to leave no ground for controversy over his grave.

9 · ANNEXATION COMPLETE

Diplomacy, Intrigue, and the Force of Politics

O N APRIL 2, 1845, Navy Commodore Robert Stockton received orders to join the fleet of Commodore David Conner, then hanging off the Mexican coast near Veracruz. Stockton never arrived. Instead, he set out for Galveston, Texas, where he appeared on May 12 with four ships, including the ill-fated *Princeton*, vessel of that bloody cannon explosion the previous year. He entered Galveston harbor aboard his brig the *Porpoise* and fired off a twenty-one-gun salute to announce his arrival. Then he went ashore amid much fanfare and quickly embroiled himself in a complex intrigue to foment a war between Texas and the Republic of Mexico.

Of all the bizarre twists in the story of America's expansionist surge of the 1840s, nothing quite matches the Stockton intrigue. It unfolded against a backdrop of the final annexation maneuverings, and it ensnarled those events in mysteries that history has never fully unraveled. One of the biggest mysteries was the level of involvement by President Polk. What we know is that Stockton joined up with Charles A. Wickliffe, a Kentucky politician and former U.S. postmaster general, who had been sent to Galveston by Polk. Together, they aligned with Major General Sidney Sherman of the Texas militia in a plan to attack Mexico. The concept was that, in the ensuing war between Texas and Mexico, the United States would be drawn in to protect Texas, and the result would be U.S. acquisition of California.

The story of the final weeks of the annexation issue, including the Stockton subplot, is best told through the personalities and machinations of the outsized figures involved—Stockton, Wickliffe, Sherman, Texas president Anson Jones, Sam Houston, and U.S. Minister Donelson. In the end, the Stockton-Wickliffe-Sherman plot failed, due largely to Jones, Houston, and Donelson.

For audacity or dash, few men of the era could match Stockton, who displayed piercing eyes and a defiant mouth under a thatch of thick, dark hair. Born into one of New Jersey's most prominent families, he had leveraged his filial connections and bustling intellect into success as both naval officer and business entrepreneur. Just thirteen when he entered the College of New Jersey, he left without a degree to become a naval midshipman. He thrived in the navy, serving in the Mediterranean, the Caribbean, and off the coast of West Africa. He saw action in the War of 1812 and the war with Algiers, intercepted slave ships, helped negotiate a treaty that led to the founding of the African nation of Liberia. Then for fifteen years beginning in 1823 he assumed furlough status, returned to New Jersey, and made a fortune in canals and railroads.

Now he was back in the military, demonstrating his irrepressible nature. Not even that February 1844 *Princeton* explosion, which had killed the secretaries of state and war, among others, could arrest his ascension. A court of inquiry absolved him entirely. "He appears to have been animated by motives the most patriotic," said the court, and "stimulated by the laudable desire of being himself instrumental in promoting the honor of his country."

A nationalist of rare ideological fervor, he fought a number of duels with British officers during his Mediterranean service—initiated, it was reported, because they had expressed contempt for the United States. "God and nature, and inevitable circumstances," he declared in an 1844 political speech, "destine the United States to be the only curb or check upon the ambition of Great Britain to rule the world." Should the United States, he asked, stand by and forgo expansion opportunities while Great Britain increased its global dominance? This question, he announced, "affects the progress, the glory, the grandeur, and the ultimate importance of our country."

Charles Anderson Wickliffe was a broad-faced lawyer known for his wealth, aristocratic mien, and disdain for society's lower classes. In Kentucky they called him "the Duke," and he enjoyed considerable success as office seeker there following combat experience in the War of 1812. He served in the state legislature, the U.S. House, as Kentucky lieutenant governor, and briefly as governor. National prominence came when Tyler named him postmaster general in 1841.

General Sidney Sherman emerged a hero in the war for Texas independence, when he served under Sam Houston as a colonel and played a decisive role at the Battle of San Jacinto. Born in Massachusetts, he eventually settled in Newport, Kentucky, then formed a rifle company that joined the Texas fight in 1836. After independence, he became a Texas landowner and member of the republic's House of Representatives. As legislator, he fostered a bill to create a major general of the Texas militia and then, of course, captured the job. He had always been considered something of a Houston rival, and Houston never fully trusted him.

Anson Jones brought to his Texas presidency a natural shyness, unprepossessing demeanor, and a troubled past. Born into a destitute Massachusetts family, he had become a doctor at age twenty-two and then spent a dozen years in failure at the profession. In 1832 he moved to New Orleans to try his hand in business. Again, he failed. That led him to Brazoria, Texas, where he again took up medicine. "I had struggled almost in vain against innumerable obstacles," he wrote, "and finally abandoning myself to a fate which it appeared I could not control or direct, I passively floated . . . upon the tide which bore me to Texas."

From that point forward, he thrived—first in his medical practice, then in military and political service. He joined the Texas revolutionary army as a private and quickly became surgeon in the San Jacinto campaign. After independence, he served as Texas congressman, minister to the United States, secretary of state, then president. Still shy and unimposing, he developed a reputation as a modest and congenial man with strong convictions, a resolute temperament, and a capacity to master the minute details of any problem. He also enjoyed a marked identity with the republic's premier figure, Sam Houston.

Houston was the Andrew Jackson of Texas. Like his Tennessee mentor, he was tall, manly, dashing, impetuous, highly intelligent in a rough-hewn way, and fearless in battle. Born in Virginia of Scotch-Irish ancestry, he moved as an adolescent to eastern Tennessee. A congenital rebel, he fled frontier life at sixteen and went to live with the Cherokee Indians, who adopted him and gave him the name Colonneh, "the Raven." He returned to Anglo-Saxon life in time for the War of 1812.

He excelled as an infantryman, became an officer, got wounded three times, and won the attention of Jackson. After the war, with Jackson's patronage, he emerged as a leading Tennessee citizen—lawyer, major general of the state militia, prosecutor, U.S. congressman, and governor at age thirty-four. It appeared he might follow his mentor into the White House.

Then came a series of setbacks. His marriage to a young Tennessee beauty fell apart after eleven weeks. He took to drink, resigned the governorship, and returned to the Cherokees. During one foray back among his own people, he responded to an insult in Washington by thrashing an Ohio congressman with a cane. He was arrested, tried, and fined. He set out for Texas in search of fame, land, wealth—and perhaps himself. He quickly became a leader of the Texas independence movement and its top general. With his victory over Santa Anna at San Jacinto, he acquired the stature and acclaim in Texas that Old Hickory enjoyed in the United States. Like Jackson, he served two terms as his country's president.

Finally, there was Andrew Jackson Donelson, Jackson's nephew, who had grown up at the Hermitage after the death of his father. Throughout his young life he was thoroughly under the sway of his beloved uncle, who showered him with encouragement. "So long as you continue in that virtuous path, you have had from your infancy, so long will my thoughts delight to dwell upon you," the General wrote him during his college years. He extolled the young man's "genius and application."

Donelson graduated from West Point, second in his class, then served his uncle as aide-de-camp during the Seminole campaign and as private secretary during the Jackson presidency. Afterward he practiced law in Nashville, built a grand home near the Hermitage, and enjoyed the life of a country squire. When President Tyler appointed him minister to Texas, with instructions to bring about annexation, everyone felt Tyler was seeking to capitalize on Donelson's connection to Old Hickory. But he brought his own traits to the challenge—solid judgment, quickness of mind, and a congenial but firm negotiating style.

THE STORY OF the final annexation events begins in early March 1845, at the republic's main port of Galveston. There Texas secretary of state Ashbel Smith initiated a private conversation with the British chargé and consul general, Captain Charles Elliot. America's annexation proposal was coming, warned Smith, and Anson Jones's government wished to get a credible independence option on the table as a counterweight. Jones, he added, would appreciate Britain's good offices in behalf of a settlement with Mexico that would bring Mexican recognition of Texas independence in exchange for Texas renunciation of U.S. annexation. On March 6 Elliot dispatched a message to London asking for instructions. He asked his French counterpart, Count Alphonse de Saligny, to get Paris involved as well.

In New Orleans, Donelson heard reports of the maneuver and rushed to Galveston to head it off. He carried with him official word of the congressional resolution and his government's decision to press the House annexation approach rather than the Senate's Benton option. He left New Orleans on March 24 and arrived at Galveston on March 27. He arrived too late.

On March 24, Her Majesty's warship *Electra* docked at Galveston with the instructions Elliot had been waiting for—and also Paris instructions for Saligny. Proceed to broker a deal between Mexico and Texas under British and French guarantees, the two diplomats were told, and do all you can to prevent annexation. They hurried overland some fifty miles to the Texas capital, Washington-on-the-Brazos, to confer with Jones.

Jones was waiting with anticipation. For years he had sought a simultaneous two-way choice for Texas—independence with Mexican recognition or annexation to the United States. If that could be arranged, he argued, then Texans could make a reasoned and sound decision. He professed not to care about the eventual outcome, but in truth he favored independence and everyone knew it.

Elliot and Saligny began to press their case with great elaboration, but Jones wearily waved them off. He knew the arguments, he said, and they should bear in mind he was "but the agent of the people." Twice he conferred with his cabinet, once bringing the two diplomats with him. Finally he agreed. They must move quickly, he said, and produce proof that Mexico would accept Texas independence. In the meantime, he would delay any official annexation action for ninety days. But he emphasized that an eventual decision favoring annexation, should it emerge, would not constitute any "breach of faith."

Elliot and Saligny set out for Mexico City, while Jones dispatched Ashbel Smith to Europe to deal with any diplomatic necessities arising from either decision. Then Jones sat back and waited for the imminent arrival of Donelson. Upon reaching Washington City, Donelson rushed first to see Secretary of State Smith, who was preparing for his European voyage. Smith received him cordially but offered no assurances as to his intentions. The secretary rambled on about what a momentous decision this was—not one to be taken lightly or hurriedly. He would have to confer with his subordinates, he said, and give it appropriate time and thought. Donelson wasn't fooled. He sensed "some settled scheme of delay" and quickly concluded there wasn't much point in dealing with Smith.

He penned an official letter to Texas attorney general Ebenezer Allen, interim head of foreign affairs in Smith's absence, giving a detailed explanation for President Polk's insistence on the streamlined House approach. "If annexation should now be lost," Donelson wrote to Allen, "it may never be recovered."

Then he turned his attention to Houston. On April 2 he wrote asking for a meeting. The former president, traveling in East Texas, demurred. He would say only that he considered the U.S. annexation approach to be faulty. Then on April 9, Houston crafted an extensive letter to Donelson outlining his concerns. "I am in favor of annexation," he wrote, "if it can take place on terms mutually beneficial to both countries." But he expressed serious misgivings about whether that was possible under the House approach.

"The terms are dictated and the conditions absolute," he complained, adding the House version would cede to the United States all public lands and other property without payment. This, he said, "can only be regarded in the light of . . . tribute." And he outlined two further objections—first, should Texas accept the House terms, the outcome could still be rejected by the U.S. Congress; and, secondly, that U.S. anti-annexationists could come to power following annexation and meddle in Texas's internal affairs (meaning, presumably, Texas slavery). Houston confessed to some conflicted emotions on the subject. "I have felt so deeply for my venerated and highly valued friend, the sage of the Hermitage," he wrote, "that nothing but a most sacred regard for my adopted country could have induced me again to thus express my opinions upon this subject."

Houston's uncooperative approach was bad news for Donelson, who now would have to call in the big gun, the sage of the Hermitage. "Tell Uncle," he wrote his wife on April 16, "Houston has disappointed me and has not given me the support I expected." But it turned out Jackson's lingering magnetism already was having its effect upon Houston. Soon the Texan was not only coming around on annexation but also making plans to visit his old mentor at the Hermitage one last time.

As THIS WAS unfolding, the corollary Stockton drama was beginning. On April 22, the commodore received private instructions countermanding his previous April 2 orders to proceed to the Conner fleet. The new orders, straight from Navy Secretary Bancroft, instructed Stockton to proceed to Galveston, enter the harbor with one of his ships, then "go on shore and make yourself acquainted with the disposition of the people of Texas, and their relations with Mexico, of which you make report to this Department." He was to remain "as long as in your judgment may seem necessary" and then proceed to join Conner.

On May 2, Wickliffe arrived in Galveston, preceded by a letter of introduction to Donelson from Polk. "He has my confidence and will be entitled to yours," wrote the president. Wickliffe sought out Archibald Yell, who reported the Kentuckian's arrival to Polk. Then Houston arrived on his journey to the Hermitage. Yell saw immediately that Donelson's entreaties and Jackson's hold on his protégé had had the desired effect. Houston, Yell reported to Polk, "is now safe, and no apprehensions need be feared from that quarter." Donelson, after much frustration, was getting the same signals. On May 11 he had written to Polk, "I have been greatly vexed by the course of Houston who has controlled the president and all his cabinet." But by May 14 the picture had brightened. He received a letter from Houston, reported Donelson, that "authorizes the declaration that he will not be an opponent of the measure."

During a subsequent stopover in New Orleans, Houston publicly confirmed this position. Looking "wonderfully preserved," as a dispatch in the *Union* put it, he spoke to an overflow crowd at the New Orleans Arcade and noted his repeated, and always unsuccessful, efforts during his two presidencies to get the United States interested in Texas statehood. It was that frustration, he said, that explained why he had "coquetted a little with Great Britain" to stir U.S. jealousy and enhance the prospect of annexation—which now, he added, was at hand. "He said," reported the *New Orleans Commercial Bulletin,* "there was no opposition among the people; he was sure the President would not, nor would he himself, interpose one breath in its way."

Meanwhile, Stockton had made his dramatic entrance into Galveston Bay on May 12, then entered into extensive private discussions with Wickliffe. At some point General Sherman was brought into the talks. On May 21, Stockton sent a dispatch to Bancroft reporting that annexation appeared safe. But he conveyed reports—erroneous, as it turned out—that Mexican troops were crossing the Rio Grande and taking possession of a large swath of disputed territory east of the river. He said Donelson was away at New Orleans and President Jones couldn't be trusted to handle the crisis. "I will do the best I can," wrote the self-important military man.

That night Galveston held a grand ball in Stockton's honor at the Tremont House—"far superior," reported the *Galveston News,* "to anything of the kind ever before exhibited in this city." Nearly 350 dignitaries—officers of the squadron, foreign functionaries, Texas notables from throughout the state—attended, including, said the *News,* "more than a hundred ladies of the first respectability, embracing all the elegance, beauty and fashion of our city." Galveston's mayor intoned a toast: "Commodore Stockton, our guest, the friend of Texas: May his life be as long and happy, as it has been patriotic and honorable." Stockton proposed a toast to Texas: "free and independent: Annexed or not annexed . . . she will command the admiration of the world." Then a Texas colonel proposed a toast to Wickliffe: "the early, steadfast, and undeviating friend of this republic." Wickliffe returned the favor with an extended speech extolling the virtues of Texas, and then a city official proposed a toast to Stockton's squadron. That prompted Stockton to accept the gesture with a fifteen-minute speech delivered "in an eloquent and soul-stirring manner." A tear glistened his eye as he recalled "the soulless butcheries of Goliad and the Alamo," as the *News* expressed it. This spree of congratulatory expression ended with nine cheers for the commodore, and then the party retired to the ballroom for dancing until 3 A.M.

The next day Stockton sent another letter to Bancroft. He said he had sent for General Sherman, who had "consented to call out the troops, to clear and protect the boundary." Stockton said he planned a naval expedition to the mouth of the Rio Grande to ascertain the military situation there, and during his absence Sherman would meet with President Jones to apprise him "of the probable danger and obtain if possible his cooperation in any measure which it may be precedent to adopt if Mexico contemplates an invasion." He added he might need more provisions and gunpowder and hoped he could find them available at Pensacola. Upon receiving the request, Bancroft replied, "Orders will be given to furnish powder and supplies at Pensacola on your requisitions."

A week later, Stockton sent an update to Bancroft:

My Dear Sir

Since my last letter I have seen Mr. Mayfield late Secretary of State—who says that if the people here did not feel assured that the Boundary line would be the Rio Grande three fourths and himself amongst the number would oppose the annexation— But I need hardly say another word on that subject; its importance is apparent—But it may perhaps be as well for me *in this way* to let you know how I propose to settle the matter without committing the U. States—The major Genl [Sherman] will call out three thousand men & "R. F. Stockton Esq" will supply them in a private way with provisions & ammunition—

Yours
[Signed] R. F. Stockton

So Stockton was planning to establish a private army to fight Mexican troops on the Rio Grande. On May 28 the commodore set out on his naval reconnaissance mission, with Wickliffe aboard the *Princeton*. Bad weather and Wickliffe's subsequent seasickness prompted Stockton to turn back without reaching the Rio Grande. In the meantime, Sherman called on Jones, bringing with him Dr. John Wright, Stockton's squadron surgeon and private secretary. After pleasantries, Wright told the president he had been sent by Stockton to get Jones's authorization for a military action against Mexico. Sherman, as militia commander, would raise two thousand troops or more, he said, and with Stockton's naval support would take the Mexican town of Matamoros, just west of the Rio Grande at its mouth. Further, said Wright, Stockton would supply the expedition and pay the men and officers to be deployed. Sherman assured Jones that Wright did indeed speak for Stockton. He urged approval.

Stung by the audacity of this scheme but wishing to appear businesslike, Jones replied that this was a serious affair and he would need some kind of documentation that Wright actually spoke for the commodore. Had Stockton, asked Jones, sent along any communication for the president's inspection? The reply: No. But Stockton would be willing to visit the president in person to relay his interest in the plan.

Jones asked if Donelson was aware of the scheme. The plan, replied Wright, was rather "a confidential and secret one." Then, according to Jones's memoir, published posthumously in 1859, Wright said Stockton was operating under sanction of the U.S. government, with presidential knowledge, but that Polk didn't want to be known in the matter. But, he added, Wickliffe, a close associate of the president, was working with Stockton on the plan, and Stockton possessed the means to support the expedition while giving it an appearance of a private effort. The aim, he explained, was to place Texas in a position of active hostility with Mexico so that, when Texas came into the Union, she would bring that war with her.

Jones smiled through his growing anger.

"So, gentlemen," he asked, "the Commodore, on the part of the United States, wishes me *to manufacture a war* for them[?]" According to Jones's memoir, they replied affirmatively.

Jones politely demurred. He said the Texas Congress would convene on June 16, and he couldn't sanction any such activity without congressional consent. Besides, he added, he was waiting for the return of the British chargé, Charles Elliot, with an anticipated Mexican offer of recognition for an independent Texas. He couldn't approve any such military plan without violating commitments he had made to Elliot before his departure. Privately, Jones viewed Elliot's return as an opportunity to thwart Stockton—and, as he put it in his memoir, "declare *my* independence of Com. Stockton, and Mr. Wright, Gov. Yell, Major Donelson, Mr. Polk, and Mr. Buchanan."

Meanwhile, the *New Orleans Republican* published a letter from an anonymous observer at Galveston. "The important event of the day," the letter said, "is the arrival of Com. Stockton, with his fleet." It added Texas officials had received word that Mexico planned to capture disputed territory east of the Rio Grande, all the way to the Nueces River. The letter continued:

> This news [was] communicated to the Commodore, who advised an immediate occupation of the line by the Texan troops, offering his cooperation by sea. The Commodore . . . will sail to-morrow to obtain intelligence, and will return in a week. In the mean time, Major General Sherman is to visit the Executive and ask his approval and co-operation. Should he refuse, Sherman contends that he is empowered by the general terms of an existing law to act independently of the President, *and he will do so*. He will call three thousand men into immediate service to rendezvous at Corpus Christi, *and the call will be promptly obeyed*. Things here are in a great ferment.

History does not record whether Donelson, during his New Orleans visit, read this provocative item in the *Republican*. History does record that Donelson moved aggressively about this time to rein in Stockton. On June 2, writing to Buchanan from Galveston, he corrected an impression left in his previous dispatch, in which he suggested that Stockton had joined up with General Sherman to protect the Rio Grande region. "This was not correct," he now explained. Since Stockton's return from his recent cruise, he said, the commodore "has taken no step susceptible of construction as one of aggression upon Mexico, nor will he take any unless ordered to do so." Though Donelson expressed skepticism that Mexican troops were poised to cross the Rio Grande, he said Texas was prepared to thwart any such move, but without U.S. assistance. "Captain Stockton will not cooperate with it," he emphasized, so long as Texas remained officially an independent republic.

Wickliffe too could see the grand scheme beginning to deflate. On June 3 he wrote to Polk saying he soon expected "to hear through Genl Sherman the views and wishes of President Jones." He predicted Jones would "discountenance the movement under the impression that the United States will have the right, and will be bound to remove the Mexican military from east of the Rio Grande after annex- ation." He asked, "Would not this be an act of War upon Mexico by the United States?"

The next day Wickliffe dashed off another letter to Polk with the news, through Sherman, that Jones had indeed discountenanced the plan. In the meantime, Elliot had returned with the Mexican offer: acceptance of Texas independence if the Lone Star republic would forswear any intention to join the United States. Jones immediately issued a proclamation announcing the development and adding: "I do hereby declare and proclaim a cessation of hostilities by land and by sea against the Republic of Mexico." For the first time in a decade, the two states were in an official state of peace—and the Stockton-Wickliffe-Sherman war scheme was dead.

Jones now had the simultaneous dual choice he wanted. The Texas Congress was set to convene on June 16, and he would place before the members the two options—independence under terms of peace with Mexico; or statehood within the United States. His apparent aim was to get Congress to place the Mexican treaty on hold and then use it as leverage to extract from Polk better terms than the president was willing to grant under the House annexation approach. Meanwhile, Jones issued a second proclamation calling for a state convention to ratify whichever action Congress adopted. Delegates to this conven- tion would convene on July 4. The president took pride in his success in maneuvering his country into position to decide its destiny.

But from this point forward things began to go awry for Jones. He had not taken sufficient account of his constituency's overwhelming enthusiasm for annexation, and now his well-meaning machinations simply struck most Texans as a clever conspiracy designed to thwart their wishes. "Public sentiment," declared the *Union*, "is rushing on with the impetuosity of a mountain torrent." The *Galveston News* accused Jones of seeking to kill annexation through a triple alliance among Texas, England, and Mexico. And a town meeting in Bastrop, Texas, dismissed his convention proclamation, which placed indepen- dence on an equal footing with annexation, as "dictatorial and designed to frustrate the anticipated action of Congress." Angry crowds gathered in the streets to protest the president's actions; throughout the state he was "pilloried as a villain" and labeled a traitor.

When the Texas Congress convened on June 16, Jones beheld the assembled politicians as "demagogues, emissaries, factionists, disorganizers, and personal and political enemies, all, all united against me." The members of both Senate and House promptly brushed aside Jones's complex maneuver and unanimously embraced annexation. Then the Senate, voting to a man in executive session, killed the Mexican treaty. Sighed Jones, "The Senate are so much afraid of the people, they dare not do right." The legislators also approved a resolution asking the United States to send troops to the Texas frontier to repel any Mexican hostilities that might materialize there.

Nineteen days later in Austin, at the old capitol now used as a schoolhouse, delegates assembled for the state convention established to consider the congressional actions of June 16. "Our duties," declared convention president Thomas Rusk (soon to be a United States senator), "are plain and easy . . . to enter the great American Confederacy with becoming dignity and self-respect." The convention promptly ratified annexation with a single dissenting vote. News of the decisive congressional action was rushed to Washington by Stockton, whose warship *Princeton* made the sea journey to Annapolis in nine days.

"The act," pronounced the *Union,* ". . . was one of great solemnity, marked by that quiet dignity of manner which is most expressive of the decision and firmness of a free people." The paper added the Texas decisions gave "unqualified assent to the reunion of that fair country to the parent stem, from which, in an unguarded moment, it had been rudely torn." The Texas convention spent most of the next two months crafting a state constitution to be presented to the United States Congress by the new state's elected representatives. And throughout Texas, and throughout the United States, there was much celebration.

TEXAS ANNEXATION WAS not listed among Polk's two great expansionist ambitions—settling the Oregon question with Great Britain and acquiring California from Mexico. No doubt this was because the Texas matter had been set in motion a year earlier by John Tyler, who inevitably would garner a substantial share of the credit. But the issue obsessed Polk and filled him with an intense sense of urgency during his first months in office. The president's approach reflected traits that were gaining notice throughout official Washington—impatience, a penchant for intrigue, a willingness to stir political animosities, a focus on large ambitions. By insisting on the House version, Polk risked not only the enmity of Benton, a man whose Senate voice and influence he would need in coming political battles, but also the adversity of Sam Houston, the one man in Texas he couldn't afford to antagonize. And yet the prize before him, by his calculation, was so alluring, so grand and consequential, that he would pay the political price necessary to secure it. Few other presidents had been willing to operate on the basis of quite so bold—or reckless—a political calculus.

Did this include a willingess to manufacture a war with Mexico to advance another of his grand goals, acquisition of California? Perhaps, but the historical record provides no clear evidence that he did. Clearly, Stockton and Wickliffe were sent to Texas with instructions that went beyond those officially recorded, and clearly Polk and Bancroft monitored their activities in nuanced terms not fully captured in the official correspondence. But the only direct allegation that Polk involved himself in a plan to invade Mexico came from Anson Jones. This was written some fifteen years after the fact—and shortly before Jones, despondent over his reduced circumstances and the course of his life since becoming a national villain at the time of annexation, killed himself. Even assuming Jones accurately portrayed his sessions with Wright and Sherman, there is no historical confirmation that Wright accurately portrayed the president's wishes or that Stockton was acting explicitly on orders from Washington.

But the Stockton intrigue did not escape notice among prominent Texans. Particularly vexed was Houston, who sent Donelson a letter extolling his diplomatic success and expressing opprobrium for Stockton and Wickliffe. The two, he wrote, "stood forth, in the first ranks of [the] political menagerie! They were the 'big beasts.' . . . Such men, such scoundrels, ought to be repudiated, or abated as nuisances. Nothing but respect for the President Polk has prevented the exposure of their conduct."

Later historians, to the extent they paid much attention to the Stockton intrigue, generally portrayed it as a rogue operation by an expansionist zealot given to manipulating people and facts. One academic, Glenn W. Price, sought to prove presidential complicity in the intrigue, but his effort is marred by ideological fervor and historical conjecture. We simply don't know precisely the extent of presidential interest in an invasion of Mexico, as opposed to a resolve to protect Texas from an invasion from Mexico.

What we do know is this was a time of abundant American adventurism and unbridled adventures. In most instances, these adventurers were driven by an overarching sentiment that animated the national consciousness of the day—the dream of expanding America's territorial reach to the Pacific, then as far north and south as possible along that coastline. Texas represented a large chunk of that dream.

10 · THE UNITED STATES AND OREGON

"The People Here Are Worn Out by Delay"

O N APRIL 29, 1845, Washington's two rival political newspapers—the *Globe* and *National Intelligencer*—carried editorials on the often troubled relationship between the United States and Great Britain. Reflecting two distinct perspectives, the editorials framed a debate that would rage throughout America over the next year. At stake was nothing less than whether the American people would once again go to war with their mother country—for the third time in seventy years. The flash point in this instance was Oregon Territory.

Francis Blair's *Globe*—like its successor, Thomas Ritchie's *Union*—extolled with utter consistency the Democratic Party philosophy. And on April 29, in one of its last expressions before ceasing publication, the *Globe* waxed bellicose, almost dismissive of British world power. Without discussing Oregon specifically, it defined the issue as one involving an epic struggle between two world outlooks—and two competing ambitions for global influence. What, asked the *Globe,* can explain Britain's seemingly obsessive preoccupation with America's continental aims? It was, the paper answered, that nation's passion for global dominance:

> We are beginning sensibly to interfere with their pursuit of wealth, and they have the sagacity to perceive that a continuance of peace, and commercial and mechanical activity, will, in the end, give us the trident of the seas; that free government, freedom

161

from national debt, fertile soil, and various climate, are elements
of national greatness and commercial prosperity which the mere
concentration of money capital in England cannot withstand; that
the bare prospect of the supplanting of their trade draws with it
their capital and population; and, finally, that successful competition with us involves a change of the form of government itself:
so that, to keep pace with us in commerce and the arts, they must
keep pace with us in the march of freedom, which imparts the
energy, ingenuity, and activity to our pursuits.

The Whig *Intelligencer*, run with feisty conviction by Joseph Gales
and William Winston Seaton, viewed such thinking as dangerous,
a spur to American hostility toward Britain that almost inevitably
would lead to war. Consider, said the paper, the question of Oregon,
jointly occupied by the United States and Britain. Nearly everyone
agreed the current joint occupancy could not continue indefinitely.
But why take a belligerent tone now when all the realities surrounding the issue favored America in the long term? "We run the hazards
of war, and all the miseries which war brings with it, to get immediate possession of that which time must inevitably make ours," said
the *Intelligencer*.

The key was immigration. The Oregon settlement ratio between
the two nations was nine or ten Americans to one Englishman. Thus,
when Oregon's white population reached a hundred thousand, there
would be only ten thousand Englishmen. "Now," asked the *Intelligencer*, "does any man in his sober senses believe that these ninety
thousand are going to take their notions of civil freedom and of civil
government from the remaining ten thousand? Does any man believe
that these ninety thousand will forget their lineage, lose their sympathy with republican institutions, and swear allegiance to the British
Crown?" No, said the paper, Oregon "is bound to us by the great laws
of affinity and sympathy, laws which can be defeated only by rashness
and folly." In short, all the country needed was patience.

Patience was not a trait to be found in the personality of James
Polk. He had promised to invest his national ambitions in a sin-

gle presidential term, and he wasn't about to leave to successors the accomplishments he could himself obtain. Oregon loomed among his four central goals, and he would bring it into the American union at all costs.

The Oregon story is one of intertwined geography and history. The geography was relatively straightforward, although the region's remoteness led some easterners to underestimate its richness and value. The history was another matter. It stretched back centuries into reaches of the past only sketchily recorded and dimly understood, offering shards of knowledge that could be pieced together coherently only with great difficulty—and then with little definitiveness. Yet this fragmented narrative, subject to all manner of interpretation, formed the basis for both the British and American claims upon those mysterious lands.

The prize was immense—360,000 square miles stretching from the Rocky Mountains to the Pacific Ocean, and from the California border to the frosty frontiers of "Russian America," later known as Alaska. The region was rich in water, supplied by the mighty Columbia and Fraser rivers and their tributaries, as well as myriad other streams fed by winter snows in the Cascade and Olympic mountains; in navigable harbors within that maritime jewel, Puget Sound, and points north; in sturdy evergreen timber for structures, ships, and bridges; and in fertile agricultural valleys and plains. The regions west of the Cascades enjoyed an equable climate, seldom reaching extremes of cold or heat, and were cleansed frequently by gentle rains. East of the mountains could be found excellent conditions for growing wheat and apples.

Although Spanish and British adventurers had arrived at the remote coastline as early as the sixteenth century, no real settlements emerged until the early 1800s. Even then, settlements remained few and sparse. The white population consisted mostly of a few missionaries and a collection of rough fur trappers and traders associated with two big companies—John Jacob Astor's American-chartered Pacific

Fur Company, at the mouth of the Columbia River; and Britain's Hudson's Bay Company, headquartered upriver at Fort Vancouver. At one point the Hudson's Bay Company administered lands that encompassed nearly the entire Columbia River watershed. But the aim was pelts, not people.

Now people were arriving in ever greater numbers. Most came overland in covered wagons, starting off in Missouri and proceeding via numerous routes jointly dubbed the Oregon Trail. By the time of Polk's inauguration, there were some seven thousand American whites in the region, mostly in the rich Willamette Valley, and their numbers were growing by the month. One settler sent a letter from his new home of Oregon City, near Willamette Falls, that made it into the pages of Blair's *Globe*. The town, he reported, "contains a population of several hundreds, four respectable stores, three saw-mills, two flour-mills, one of which has five run of stone, and is worth at least $15,000."

In the surrounding area, he added, "we have now a regular colonial form of government, well administered—five district counties, represented by thirteen members." The little legislature established by these civic-minded folk recently had conducted a "quiet but effective" session that resulted in passage of twenty-five bills—"all in due form, and several of them of considerable length and much importance." He concluded: "Crops of all kinds come in favorably this season, and the late emigrants are delighted with the country."

But a certain political impatience was emerging. The settlers wanted full U.S. government protection—and soon. Another letter writer, to the *Platte Argus* in Missouri, reported that Oregonians were waiting anxiously for word of a U.S.-British resolution on the region, but if no resolution emerged they likely would go their own way. "A regular convention will be held," he warned, "and a constitution adopted . . . and an independent government put in operation at once." He added that his neighbors wished to be citizens of the United States, "but if she will never do anything for us, we must and will do it for ourselves. The people here are worn out by delay, and their condition becomes every day more intolerable."

But which nation would gain sway over the region and take jurisdiction over these people? At the heart of that question was the sketchy
history stretching back three centuries—a history of exploration, territorial claims, the fur trade, land skirmishes, treaties, failed negotiations, and endless confusion. No one on either side of the Atlantic
could ignore that history, and neither could anyone later who wished
to understand how the issue unfolded during the Polk years.

THROUGH CENTURIES OF New World maneuverings and wars over
territory following the European discovery of America, certain conventions emerged for resolving land disputes. Though vague, they
boiled down to four principles: exploration; cession, or transfer by
treaty; contiguity, meaning a nation's right to claim territory necessary to protect adjacent undisputed lands; and settlement. Ultimately,
no country could maintain a claim to any lands indefinitely if it didn't
send its people there to take jurisdiction through settlement.

Four nations claimed parts of Oregon based on exploration—Spain,
Britain, Russia, and the United States. Various Spanish adventurers
explored the region's coastline between 1543 and the late eighteenth
century, reaching as far north as latitude 53 degrees. One, Juan de
Fuca, sailed into the strait that was to bear his name—the gateway
to Puget Sound. Another, Juan Pérez, reached the 54th parallel, dis-
covering Nootka Sound on Vancouver Island and, further north, the
Queen Charlotte Islands. In 1775, Bruno Heceta also reached Vancouver Island and later spotted the mouth of what would be called
the Columbia River, although he didn't realize the magnitude of the
waterway and didn't explore it. These wanderings, all catalogued in
fragmentary records maintained in dusty archives in Mexico City and
Madrid, bolstered Spain's claim to the region, although it fostered no
lasting settlements north of latitude 42 degrees.

The British claimed a record of discovery stretching back to 1579
and the arrival of Sir Francis Drake, who explored the coastline as far
north as latitude 43 degrees or 48 degrees—his ship logs were ambiguous on the question. In 1778 Captain James Cook of the Royal Navy

conducted a careful exploration of the coastline, including a thorough inspection of the inviting Nootka Sound, previously discovered but never settled by Spain.

In the early 1790s two explorers—one an American private citizen, the other a British naval officer—found themselves in the region at the same time. Captain Robert Gray, the American, commanded a merchant ship, the *Columbia,* on a mission to acquire Indian otter pelts and transport them to China for sale. In the course of his explorations he found the mouth of the great Northwest river, sailed some fifteen miles into the interior, named the river after his ship, and claimed its headwaters for the United States (although there was some question whether a private citizen could legitimately make such a claim). Some months later he encountered the British captain, George Vancouver, and told him of his discovery. Vancouver proceeded to the Columbia and sailed upriver some 150 miles in a small craft.

Vancouver's primary mission was to accept the Spanish surrender of Nootka Sound following resolution of a land dispute that almost led to war between Britain and Spain. It began when Lieutenant John Meares, a Briton leading a mercantile mission under the Portuguese flag (to evade Spain's resolve to thwart British trade in the region), landed at Nootka Sound, erected some buildings, built a ship or two, and utilized the protected waters as a staging area for coastal trading expeditions. The viceroy of Mexico, agitated at this encroachment, dispatched an armed force that seized Meares's ships and destroyed his business. Britain responded by disputing Spain's Nootka claim and demanding reparation. Both countries armed for war, but ultimately the dispute was settled by what became known as the Nootka Sound Convention.

This treaty restored Meares's settlement and trading enterprise. More important, it gave citizens of each nation free access to areas of the territory not already settled by citizens of the other. In other words, the two nations accepted joint occupation. Ultimately the dispute was settled not through any careful study of the historical record but by perceptions of power: Spain knew the British navy possessed the might to cancel out Spain's sole Nootka claim, so it settled for a shared arrangement.

But soon overland explorations were adding to the cumulative history. In 1805 the Lewis and Clark expedition traversed the Rocky Mountains, reached a tributary of the Columbia River and navigated that great waterway some three hundred miles to the Pacific. Around the same time, the British explorer Simon Fraser traveled some eight hundred miles down the river that was to bear his name. The two expeditions claimed for their respective countries these rivers, their tributaries, and their watershed lands.

Thus by the second decade of the nineteenth century, the record of exploration generated more confusion than clarity—and plenty of agitation. The matter was complicated further by Russian claims based on coastal explorations from the Arctic Circle down to about latitude 56 degrees. Based on the contiguity doctrine, Russia declared coastline rights well south of that to ensure security for its northern lands.

But slowly a series of treaties brought a measure of clarity to the matter. First, President Jefferson's Louisiana Purchase gave the United States a vast new frontier to the west, thus providing a contiguity argument for adjacent Oregon territory even further west—subject, however, to other claims and rights. Then in 1819 came the U.S.-Spanish Florida treaty—formally called the Adams-Onís Treaty—ceding all of Florida to the United States in exchange for clear Spanish title to Texas and all western lands below latitude 42 degrees. As for lands north of that latitude, Spain ceded all "rights, claims, and pretensions," whatever they might be, to the United States. After Mexican independence in 1821, the two republics renewed that agreement.

This was big. The United States now held four titles to Oregon—her own by discovery and contiguity; and those of Spain by discovery and contiguity. Whatever merits these claims might have, they were nonetheless subject to the claims and interpretations of other nations—including, Britain maintained, the joint occupancy provisions of the Nootka Sound Convention.

But there also remained the Russian question. That was resolved in separate treaties the czarist empire signed with the United States and Britain around 1825. The three nations agreed on a boundary at latitude 54°40'. Russia's claims were contained.

So now only the United States and Britain vied for the vast lands between latitudes 42 degrees on the south and 54°40' on the north. Even before the Russian treaties, back in 1818, the two English-speaking nations had sought to settle the Oregon question in conjunction with a negotiation in London over a number of contentious issues left over from the War of 1812, including the U.S.-Canadian boundary east of the Rocky Mountains. Those talks, led on the American side by Secretary of State John Quincy Adams, established a boundary line of latitude 49 degrees from Minnesota's Lake of the Woods to the crest of the Rocky Mountains. The American negotiators offered to extend the 49 degree boundary to the Pacific, thus giving Britain clear title to all lands north of that line. Britain countered with a proposal to extend the 49 degree line west to the Columbia River, then down that waterway to the ocean. This the Americans rejected outright because it would have meant relinquishing full dominion over the Columbia and the harbors of Puget Sound.

The final Treaty of 1818 fell back on the joint occupancy concept of the Nootka Convention. The full territory would be left "free and open, for the term of ten years . . . to the Vessels, Citizens and Subjects of the Two Powers," without mitigating territorial claims of either country or any other nation. Thus, the two powers opted for the status quo and avoidance of a nettlesome territorial confrontation. "It will certainly come upon us again," predicted Quincy Adams, "for which I ought to be prepared."

It came upon him during his presidency when the countries in 1826 sought to settle the matter before expiration of the 1818 treaty. America put forth the same offer—extension of the 49 degree line to the Pacific. Britain extended the same counteroffer—all lands north of the Columbia River, including Puget Sound, ceded to Britain. The two powers finally agreed, in what became known as the Convention of 1827, to extend the joint occupancy formula indefinitely into the future, subject to abrogation by either party with a year's notice. There the matter rested for the next nineteen years.

But through those years the points of dispute took on greater emotion and edge. Every rationale put forth by one nation was reflexively countered. America said Gray's exploration of the Columbia River gave it clear title to that waterway and its drainage lands; Britain dismissed Gray as a private citizen whose exploration didn't count. Britain said Drake's voyage bolstered its claims; America argued he never got above latitude 43 degrees. Britain said the Nootka Sound Convention nullified Spanish title to any lands claimed by America through the Florida treaty; the United States vehemently disagreed, but argued in any event this agreement was vitiated by a doctrine of international law that Britain championed whenever it served its interests—namely, that wars between nations nullified all treaties between those nations. Britain and Spain had fought a war following the Nootka agreement. And anyway, said America, John Meares had been operating under Portuguese colors, so his ordeal had little relevance to the question. Britain argued its Hudson's Bay enterprise constituted a claim by settlement; America said its citizen migration trumped Britain's collection of trappers.

And on it went. Both sides genuinely wished to settle the matter and bind up the festering sore in their relations. But neither would relinquish the strategic imperatives driving its stance. For America, it was that vision of a transcontinental power facing both east and west across two oceans, unmatched in naval and commercial prowess. For Britain it was the geopolitical imperative of thwarting that vision and becoming itself the dominant North American power, with possessions encompassing Canada to the Pacific, large stretches of Oregon, and perhaps even the vast Mexican lands to the south that seemed ripe for the picking.

DURING JOHN TYLER'S presidency the two nations tried afresh to negotiate a settlement but couldn't get past the old arguments. British ambassador Richard Pakenham contended anew that Nootka Sound nullified any exclusive claim America wished to assert, particularly those derived from the 1819 Adams-Onís Treaty with Spain. "If Spain could not make good her own right of exclusive dominion over those regions," he wrote, "still less could she confer such a right on another power."

John C. Calhoun, then secretary of state, countered that Nootka Sound was vastly overblown in Britain's assumption of rights. There was, he said, "nothing in the Nootka Sound convention, or in the transactions which led to it, or in the circumstances attending it, to warrant the assumption." With this and other arguments, Calhoun claimed for the United States "a clear title . . . to the whole region drained by the Columbia." Calhoun said his government would offer no counterproposal in light of Britain's hard stance.

These failed efforts seemed all the more frustrating to insiders in light of some enticing behind-the-scenes diplomacy in London. Tyler's minister to Great Britain, Edward Everett, had been working the issue for some time with Britain's peace-minded foreign minister, the Earl of Aberdeen, and had come up with a solution to what seemed like a hopeless snag. The snag stemmed from each side having repeatedly rejected the compromise proposal of the other without offering any further compromise. Now, in light of all that past rigidity, any movement by either side would constitute an untenable diplomatic defeat. There had to be some further compromise that could pass muster with both sides. Everett's formula was simple and modest, yet perhaps just enough to break the impasse. He proposed extending the 49th-parallel line to the Strait of Juan de Fuca, then south and west in order to skirt the southern tip of Vancouver Island. This would give Britain full possession of that large and strategically placed island while preserving Puget Sound for the United States.

Aberdeen responded warmly to the concept, and Everett, before returning home to make way for his successor, informed Washington that his formula might constitute a framework for breaking the deadlock.

And there matters stood on inauguration day, March 4, 1845, when James Polk, covered under that umbrella in a driving rain, declared: "Our title to the country of Oregon is 'clear and unquestionable,' and already are our people preparing to perfect that title by occupying it with their wives and children." This was audacious diplomacy by any reckoning. It was true the Democratic platform had declared the same "clear and unquestionable" title, and thus Polk was merely expressing a party policy he had no role in creating. But his provocative statement set off firestorms of protest throughout America—and in London.

In April, Her Majesty's Government ordered a thirty-six-hour delay in the departure for Boston of the steam packet *Caledonia* so the mail it carried could include news of a forthcoming parliamentary debate. In that debate, Prime Minister Sir Robert Peel, saying he wished to state his case in language "the most temperate, but at the same time the most decisive," declared it was Britain that held "clear and unquestionable" rights to Oregon. He said he desired "an amicable adjustment" of the issue, but "having exhausted every effort to obtain it, if our rights are invaded, we are resolved and prepared to maintain them." Lord John Russell, the opposition leader, denounced Polk's "blustering announcement" and America's efforts at "territorial aggrandizement." He too hinted at war if Polk insisted on clinging to his inaugural formulation.

News of the debate reached Washington on April 23, along with copies of the *Times* of London, which bared a bellicosity reminiscent of Ritchie's *Union*. Americans, said the *Times,* should be warned "in the most explicit manner that their pretensions amount, if acted upon, to the clearest casus belli which has ever yet arisen between Great Britain and the American Union." The London paper added: "The same democratic folly which makes [Americans] arrogant in the Cabinet, makes them habitually feeble in all that constitutes a nation's strength in the field." For good measure, the British government ordered the Admiralty to keep frigates in the vicinity of Oregon and asked the Colonial Office to assess the country's military prospects in Oregon should war break out.

Much of America reacted with outrage. Democratic sentiment was led inevitably by Ritchie's *Union*, which castigated the "insolent tone of the British public," and its supposition that "we are weak and cowardly; devoid of public spirit and patriotism." But, said Ritchie three days later, "England cannot be serious in her menace. . . . The expansive power of popular freedom cannot be restrained." Not surprisingly, the *Intelligencer* took a different line, rebuking Polk for setting off the controversy with "an indiscreet, but irregular and ineffective declaration." Whatever America's rights to Oregon, the *Intelligencer* said, it was "entirely wrong and unpardonably imprudent" to assert them in Polk's "extreme and violent" manner. The more blunt-spoken Horace Greeley of the *New York Tribune* called Polk's declaration "palpable knavery and babbling folly." The political temperature in America was rising.

This was bad news for Polk, who had resolved to settle the Oregon question amicably if possible by pressing once again the 49th parallel as the natural compromise, with perhaps a nod toward the Everett formula to loosen the logjam. Although firmly believing in America's right to all of Oregon, he felt constrained, given previous U.S. compromise proposals, to seek a resolution along the same lines. But the raging controversy increased his political difficulties in taking that tack. Particularly intense was expansionist sentiment in the old Northwest—the area encompassing Michigan, Illinois, Indiana, Wisconsin, and Minnesota—where frontier Americans felt a kindred spirit with the settlers of Oregon and foresaw ripening trade opportunities with the region.

The new president also couldn't ignore the ire of his dying mentor. "This is the rattling of British drums," wrote Andrew Jackson on May 2, "to alarm . . . the timid, & give strength to the traitors in our country, against our best interests & growing prosperity." The General reminded his protégé "that during the canvass, I gave a thousand pledges for your energy & firmness, both in war & in peace, to carry on the administration of our government." He concluded: "No temporising with Britain on this subject now. . . . War is a blessing compared to national degradation."

Even before getting this admonition, Polk had written to assuage any Jackson concerns. "The arrogant tone of defiance, and of menace" of the British press and government, he wrote, "has not disturbed my nerves." He promised to pursue the matter "firmly and boldly, but at the same time, prudently." But Polk didn't want war, and he instructed Secretary of State Buchanan to pursue serious negotiations with Pakenham aimed at a compromise at the 49th parallel, perhaps with the Everett formula attached.

Buchanan found Pakenham coy, unwilling to commit to a position and pushing for arbitration. The British minister was aware of Aberdeen's interest in a new compromise, but he feared a British offer along the Everett lines would be rejected summarily by the United States, at which point the impasse would simply be extended. Pakenham said if negotiations were to be revived, the United States would have to make the first move.

Thus on July 16, Buchanan delivered to the British minister a letter that can only be described as diplomatically inelegant. It declared America's right to the whole of Oregon, dismissed the Nootka Sound Convention as irrelevant, and added that, anyway, America's claim to the Columbia River Valley predated its 1818 treaty with Spain and was controlling. Thus, said Buchanan, America's own legitimate claims gave it rights to the Columbia River Basin, while its 1818 treaty with Spain provided title to the rest of Oregon. Britain had no permanent right to any of it.

Then he eased up. Buchanan's letter said President Polk found himself "embarrassed, if not committed, by the acts of his predecessors," who had uniformly pursued the compromise line at the 49th parallel. Thus the president was willing to pursue a similar compromise. "In this determination," wrote the secretary, "he trusts that the British government will recognize his sincere and anxious desire to cultivate the most friendly relations between the two countries, and to manifest to the world that he is actuated by a spirit of moderation." He added the United States was willing to give Britain free access to harbors on Vancouver Island that dipped below the 49th parallel. But he didn't include British navigation rights on the Columbia, something previous U.S. presidents had offered.

Though stark in its claim to all of Oregon, the Buchanan letter, written with Polk's close supervision, was designed to offer the British an opportunity to put forth a counterproposal more along the lines of the Everett formula. Through some recent backchannel communications to Bancroft from an American businessman in London, Polk and Buchanan had reason to believe Aberdeen genuinely wished for such a solution. The letter was designed to leave some negotiating room for getting there.

Meanwhile, Polk sought to ease the way politically for his likely retreat from his inaugural pronouncement. On May 2, the *Union* offered a historical analysis that seemed remarkably passive given the paper's past expressions. It noted that the United States had been pressing its claim to all of Oregon for thirty years and had been, throughout that time, willing to compromise at the 49th parallel. Conversely, Britain had been declaring its right to the whole of Oregon while also offering to compromise. Thus, suggested the *Union,* there was nothing wrong with either country demanding its perceived rights while offering to give up a portion of them.

Such expressions in the *Union* and elsewhere diminished the war fevers in Washington and generated a mood of peace—along with jeers from the Whig press. In Maine, the *Portland Advertiser* proclaimed, "Mr. Polk will not fight for Oregon" and thus his inaugural pronouncement was "mere clap-trap."

Indeed, this surge of optimism turned out to be ill-timed. Less than two weeks after receiving Buchanan's letter, Pakenham rejected the proposal outright and declined to submit a counterproposal. He didn't even send the American offer to London, leaving Polk with the impression that Pakenham had operated under instructions to adhere strenuously to his government's previous position, irrespective of what Polk proposed. Pakenham said he hoped the United States would "be prepared to offer some further proposal for the settlement . . . more consistent with fairness and equity, and with the reasonable expectations of the British government."

Polk was stung—and furious. He had no way of knowing Pakenham's superiors in London also would be upset that the minister hadn't submitted the Polk formulation to them for consultations on how they might respond. Neither would he concede that Pakenham's response was dictated at least in part by his own diplomatic lapse in sheathing his letter of compromise in a querulous argument for the extreme U.S. claim to all of Oregon. Now the negotiation, which had appeared so close to resolution, was close to death. Those who knew Polk weren't surprised that his response was one of pique mixed with a cold calculation on how he could exploit the situation through toughness and guile. He withdrew his compromise offer, refused to extend another, and resolved to make his stand upon what he considered America's rightful claim to the entire territory of Oregon. There would be, as Andrew Jackson had insisted, no temporizing.

11 · THE UNITED STATES AND MEXICO

Divergent New World Cultures on a Path to War

THE REPUBLIC OF Mexico didn't wait to see what Texas would do about the U.S. annexation resolution before making its move. On March 28, 1845, Foreign Minister Luis G. Cuevas addressed a letter to U.S. ambassador Wilson Shannon, protesting America's annexation action and calling it "as offensive to Mexico as it is derogatory to the honor of the American Union." He added that "diplomatic relations between the two countries cannot be continued."

Shannon replied in measured terms that he had hoped differences between the countries "could be arranged amicably, upon terms just and honorable to both." But, he added, it appeared "Mexico declines to adjust these differences in this manner, and thus preserve the peace." The United States didn't pursue annexation "in any spirit of hostility," he said, and Mexico must decide whether the countries' peaceful relations would be severed "by a conflict equally injurious to both."

Cuevas rejected the ambassador's note, saying Mexico could not maintain friendship with a country "which has . . . usurped a portion of territory which belongs to Mexico by a right which she will maintain at whatever cost." Then he cut off further communication.

It wasn't surprising that once Texas embraced annexation on July 4 a war spirit would emerge within both countries. On July 15 the *New Orleans Jeffersonian Republican* reported that "the probabilities of a war . . . grow more and more likely." The paper reported Mexico was marching troops into its interior "no doubt destined for Texas."

176

The *Baltimore American* ran a letter from a U.S. businessman in Veracruz saying, "War between this country and the United States appears inevitable." Ritchie's *Union* considered it "probable that Mexico will declare war."

If the two countries were indeed on a path to war, it was a path that stretched far into each nation's history, accentuating profound differences between Anglo-Saxon and Spanish-Indian outlooks, attitudes, religious sensibilities, and governance. Those differences would complicate all efforts at post-annexation conciliation.

The Anglo-Saxon migrants to the New World arrived bent on perpetuating the folkways and mores of the Old Country. The menfolk brought their own women and generally refused to mix with the Native Americans, whom they pushed aside brutally to make way for the preservation of their own culture. That culture included powerful new concepts of the Enlightenment, incubated through centuries of English history and reflected in Anglo-Saxon jurisprudence and such profound civic principles as freedom of speech and conscience, popular sovereignty, governmental checks and balances, a degree of social and political equality, and free enterprise.

Eventually, many of these concepts were codified in the U.S. Constitution, considered by citizens of the new nation to be a quantum leap forward in the development of human freedom and progress. Alexis de Tocqueville agreed. The famous French intellectual called the Constitution "one of those beautiful creations of human diligence which give their inventors glory and riches but remain sterile in other hands." An example of "other hands," he said, was Mexico, beset by "anarchy" and "military despotism."

Unlike the early Anglo-Saxons who ventured to America as families to create communities, commerce, and wealth born of toil, the early Spaniards came as conquerors and plunderers. They mixed freely with indigenous women—beginning with Hernán Cortés himself, who, upon arriving, promptly took a mistress, the lovely Princess Malintzin. They wanted quick riches, preferably in the form of gold and rare gems stored away by leaders of the highly developed civilizations of central Mexico, Peru, and elsewhere.

The story is well known of the Spanish conquest of Mexico, particularly the bloody 1521 victory of Cortés over the Aztec civilization and its capital, Tenochtítlan, as refined and exquisite a city as could be found anywhere in Europe. It contained nearly 300,000 inhabitants and presided over a sprawling empire of several millions. In a few months the Castilian conquistador and his hearty band of adventurers, in one of the greatest exploits of derring-do in the history of the European explorations, laid waste to the entire place. The empire, as Oswald Spengler would lament centuries later, "was destroyed like a sunflower whose head is struck off by one passing." Soon the population was decimated by waves of European diseases for which the Indians had no immunity, and a once proud people were reduced to degradation.

Modern Mexico was thus born in blood but born also with a dual legend. The first was that of Tenochtítlan and its fallen heroes—the last emperor, Moctezuma, and the martyred resistance fighter, Cuauhtémoc. The other legend was that of Cortés, the military genius who brought the Spanish culture and Catholic religion to these New World lands. The two intertwined legends framed centuries of subsequent history marked by ongoing tensions between the heirs of Tenochtítlan and the heirs of Castile. Three primary forces would be embedded in this history—the dynamic of ethnicity, the Spanish Crown, and the Catholic Church.

Ethnicity was a particularly perplexing issue in the lands of New Spain. Unlike the Anglo-Saxons to the north, who could subjugate with relative ease the weak and scattered Indian tribes whose lands they wished to confiscate, the descendants of Cortés had to live with the much more numerous Indians of the Mexican plateau. They lived with them by assigning them a second-class social status but also— over time—by mixing with them. Both added delicate complexities to the social fabric and political framework of the Spanish colony.

Cortés's military conquest soon gave way to what was called the "spiritual conquest"—the conversion of millions of Mexicans to Catholicism. From Old Spain to New Spain thousands of friars flocked. They became known among the indigenous peoples as *padrecitos*, or beloved fathers. The appellation was well earned, for the priests showered affection as well as instruction upon the Indians, who embraced the teachings of Christ at least in part to fill a gap created by the utter destruction of their own religious structures, which included the worship of many gods and elaborate ceremonies marked by human sacrifice and, sometimes, cannibalism.

The *padrecitos* also fostered what was called the New Laws of the Indies for the Good Treatment and Preservation of the Indians, promulgated by the Spanish Crown in 1542. Put forth with compassionate intent and designed as protection for the Indians, this charter locked them into a perpetual state of paternalistic servitude. There were rules for proper treatment of the Indians by the Spanish, and to ensure their observance the Indians were kept apart, in their own communal lands and separatist societies, with little education, few economic opportunities, and no political sway. New Spain would be run by the heirs of Castile.

Such was the Castilian dominance of New Spain's society and government that even colonists of Spanish blood but born in New Spain—the creoles—were considered second-class citizens. In theory they enjoyed full rights, but in practice they never seemed to rise very high in governmental or church hierarchies. Over the three centuries of colonial New Spain there emerged a new class, the mestizos, persons of mixed Spanish and Indian blood. Initially, they were almost universally despised by Indian and Spaniard alike, in part because they invariably were of questionable legitimacy. But the intermixture soon absorbed a substantial part of the population, approaching 40 percent by 1803 and likely constituting a national majority by the time of Mexican independence in 1821. They constituted also a large reservoir of political and social resentment directed at the European elites who kept them locked in working-class status.

The elites turned avidly to Old Country customs of autocracy to preserve their standing. Societal structures were based rigidly on inherited privilege. Rights were bestowed from above, notably from the king of Spain, rather than proclaimed from the people, who were given no avenue for demanding prerogatives of citizenship. Social inequalities were considered part of God's plan, a blessing to ensure social stability. Commerce was firmly controlled through a mercantilist system that included no concept of wealth creation, the central idea of Anglo-Saxon capitalism. In the Spanish mind, wealth was finite, and thus the elites must ensure dominion over their share. The government controlled the means of production, the distribution of goods, the development of natural resources. The result was economic stagnation, masked only slightly by the rich seams of silver and other minerals extracted from the ground of New Spain and transported to Old Spain in monopoly ships.

New Spain's powerful priesthood embraced this system, which bestowed upon the Church immense benefits—huge landholdings, its own tax system, an opulent way of life, even immunity from prosecution under civil law. One Mexican historian would write that Mexico had been conquered by "the Spanish sword," then held in check by "the cross on that sword."

In short, Mexico was a place of social and economic rigidities, governmental despotism, massive illiteracy, and high mortality. The German scientist Alexander von Humboldt, after traveling through Mexico in 1803, called it "the country of inequality. Nowhere does there exist such a fearful difference in the distribution of fortune, civilization, cultivation of the soil and population."

This generated two political realities—a rumbling discontent among the masses and feelings of hostility toward the Anglo-Saxons to the north, viewed as a gathering threat. In 1800 total income in the United States was about twice that of Mexico's; half a century later it was thirteen times greater. In 1790, Mexico's population approached five million compared to fewer than four million in the United States. By 1840, the U.S. population had soared to seventeen million while Mexico's had reached just seven million.

Among Mexico's white creoles, there was no shortage of hostility toward their Spanish overlords, but a move toward independence seemed risky, likely to unleash the wrath of the country's impoverished Indian and mixed masses. This was confirmed in 1810 when a fifty-seven-year-old priest named Miguel Hidalgo, dedicated to the liberal ideals of democracy, equality, and liberty, initiated a rebellion against the government and enlisted the masses in his movement. The result was a spree of looting and killing in two major cities that left hundreds dead, their bodies mutilated and decapitated in the streets.

Hidalgo was captured and executed a year later, but the white population embraced a renewed conviction that dangerous liberal ideals must be suppressed at all costs. Political power would be the domain of the conservatives, who styled themselves *hombres de bien*—men of goodness—who would protect the nation from the violent passions of the masses.

Indeed, when the break with Spain did materialize in 1821, it came through the agency of an archconservative royalist army officer, Agustin de Iturbide, who brought together his fellow *hombres de bien* with remnants of the Hidalgo rebellion in support of a new nation based upon three general ideals they could all embrace. Mexico would be independent; it would be Roman Catholic; and it would be a constitutional monarchy. Once established, Iturbide brushed aside his former allies among the liberals and crafted a system of centralized power in Mexico City controlled by the white autocracy, with himself as emperor. Thus did he establish the political fault lines that would shape Mexican history for decades.

That history, which now converged with that of the United States, is best seen through the life and exploits of one man, Antonio López de Santa Anna. For twenty-five years, from independence to the time of the Polk presidency, he managed to insert himself into nearly every military and political development of his country, often rising to the pinnacle of the nation and then thrust to the depths of misfortune. He was Mexico's irrepressible man.

Born without advantage in Veracruz, he amassed considerable local influence in his native region through his wiles and force of personality. One newspaper described him as standing six feet tall, dark of complexion, "well made and of graceful bearing," with a showman's flair, a gambler's temperament, and a military man's resolve—but without any discernible conviction about the issues then roiling his country. He attached himself to Iturbide in the early years of independence, expelled the Spanish from Veracruz, and was awarded the governorship of his home region. But, when Iturbide sought to remove him from his command, Santa Anna took up arms against the emperor, attached himself to the rising republican forces, and helped overthrow the fledgling Mexican monarchy.

The result in 1824 was a new constitution patterned after the U.S. document and encompassing a greater degree of liberal values. In place of Iturbide's centralized authority, the new federalist approach granted far more autonomy to the various Mexican states. But Santa Anna felt the new leader, Guadalupe Victoria, hadn't sufficiently rewarded him for his exertions. Soon he took up arms against Victoria. Failing to dislodge the president, he retreated to one of his intermittent retirements at his vast estate at Manga de Clavo in the Veracruz region.

Subsequently he initiated a new assault on Victoria's successor, with similar results. He fled to the mountains, "to all appearance an outlaw and a ruined man," as the *Union* described it in an 1845 profile. Ultimately, however, that revolt, under other leadership, succeeded, and Santa Anna found himself secretary of war under the new president, Vicente Guerrero. He took command of the forces sent to repel the last Spanish effort to retake Mexico. He succeeded and became a national hero, finally enjoying a level of national acclaim to match his own extravagant self-regard. Alas, within a few months Guerrero was deposed by his vice president, Carlos María de Bustamante, and Santa Anna again found himself tending his cattle and orchards at Manga de Clavo.

Bustamante brought back centralized authority, turned the autonomous states into "departments" of the Mexican government, and generated angry opposition in many outlying regions. Among them was the northern department of Texas with its large population of U.S. migrants who had no intention of submitting to the overthrow of the 1824 constitution and the suppression of their own previous grants of authority.

Bent on getting back into action, Santa Anna soon initiated a movement against Bustamante, forced him to flee, installed a new president, and placed himself in position to succeed to national leadership. Though he had fought on the side of both autocratic centralizers and democratic federalists and had deposed the latest centralizer, he now embraced Bustamante's governmental philosophy and fostered a new constitution to replace the 1824 document. Then he took an army north to subdue the rebellious Texans.

He fell upon the hapless rebels of the Alamo and Goliad with a bloodlust that would live in the American consciousness for generations. But he succumbed to the far greater military acumen of Sam Houston, who annihilated Santa Anna's army at San Jacinto on April 21, 1836. Hunted down and forced to sign a Texas independence treaty upon pain of death, he did so, then returned to Mexico once again a broken man. Mexico declared the treaty null and void, and Santa Anna again returned to Manga de Clavo.

In the resulting power vacuum Bustamante returned to the presidency. But Santa Anna was called back to service when France invaded Mexico at Veracruz to force reparations for French citizens whose rights had been trampled by Mexicans in and around the country. France got the reparations, but in the course of the fighting Santa Anna lost a leg, which endeared him once again to the Mexican populace. In typically grandiloquent fashion, he held a solemn burial ceremony at Veracruz for the severed limb.

In 1841, upon efforts by General Mariano Paredes y Arrillaga to overthrow Bustamante once again, Santa Anna returned from retirement and threw himself into Paredes's campaign. It succeeded, and Santa Anna fostered a movement to cast aside the constitution of 1836. He was invested with the powers of dictator, with a mandate to reconstitute the republic under yet another constitution. In 1843 that new constitution, called the Basis of Political Organization of the Mexican Republic, was promulgated by a committee under the dominance of Santa Anna. One historian later would call it "a most cynical attack on popular rights under an assumption of the form of democracy." Its creation was essentially a "constitutional despotism," with Santa Anna at its center. Liberalism and federalism were cast aside.

In January 1844, Santa Anna resigned his position as dictator and assumed presidential powers. But before the year was out Paredes was at it again, organizing an army for the overthrow of Santa Anna on allegations of administrative abuses. When the president raised his own army to defend his government, a series of revolts broke out in the departments. His government collapsed. Routed on the battlefield, he submitted to the new regime, installed by Paredes and headed by José Joaquín de Herrera. He was, said the *Union,* "forced to yield to the common fate of eminence in Mexico—that is, exile or the scaffold." He chose exile and retreated to Cuba on orders to remain out of the country for ten years.

WHAT THIS STORY reflects, aside from the extraordinary resilience, trickery, and force of Santa Anna, was the unfortunate reality discerned by Tocqueville: Mexico, despite its pretense to constitutional government, was a dysfunctional country.

Throughout the 1830s and into the 1840s, officials and citizens of the United States watched these developments with sympathy mixed with growing contempt. The United States had been the first nation to recognize Mexican independence, had befriended its sister republic, had signed treaties of territorial limits and mutual friendship with Mexico. And the United States also sought to settle peacefully a reparations issue similar to that which had stirred the French to military action. Britain also had threatened a military assault if Mexico wouldn't pay reparations to British subjects abused by Mexican officials and citizens, and the threat had led to a settlement. The United States had confined itself to diplomacy, with little to show for it. Now U.S. patience was running out.

By the end of Andrew Jackson's presidency, the reparations issue had become a serious point of contention between the two nations. For years American citizens who had ventured in or near Mexico had experienced abuses at the hands of Mexican officials and citizens. U.S. ships were seized in Mexican ports by government officials or upon the high seas by rogue Mexican vessels. U.S. businessmen operating in the fledgling republic were abducted and impressed into servitude or thrown into jails without benefit of jurisprudence. An American merchant ship captain, transporting Mexican soldiers on a government contract, was killed en route, along with his mate. The soldiers forced his crew into servitude for three years. Ship cargoes were stolen at gunpoint in Mexican waters. In all there were some ninety-five episodes of such abuses recorded by U.S. officials; they added up to millions of dollars in reparation claims.

When the United States protested, the Mexican government, preoccupied with its internal strife, generally ignored the protests. That led President Jackson, just before leaving office, to send the matter to Congress, along with a suggestion that these "wanton . . . outrages," and Mexico's refusal to offer redress, "would justify, in the eyes of all nations, immediate war." Yet even this impetuous warrior urged a more measured response based on a national desire to treat the sister republic with particular courtesy. "We should act," he said, "with both wisdom and moderation by giving to Mexico one more opportunity to atone for the past, before we take redress into our own hands."

Congress agreed. The Senate Foreign Relations Committee submitted a report saying it could, "with justice, recommend an immediate resort to war or reprisals." The corollary House committee suggested Mexico's refusal to redress these wrongs stemmed from its assumption that the United States, unlike France and Britain, would refrain from military action. It added that "ample cause exists for taking redress into our own hands." Both committees recommended, however, one last effort to secure an appropriate Mexican response.

The matter wasn't quite as simple as this rhetoric suggested. First, while international law at the time accorded foreigners in Mexico all the rights they would enjoy in their home countries, it could be argued that U.S. citizens in Mexico were subject instead to the 1831 U.S.-Mexican friendship treaty, which seemed to specify that the countries' citizens should be subject to the laws of the country they were visiting. Mexico thus argued that U.S. citizens should seek redress through Mexican courts. Mexican citizens couldn't easily swallow the idea that U.S. visitors should get legal rights they themselves didn't enjoy. Secondly, Mexican officials believed many U.S. citizens, seeing financial opportunity in the controversy, had filed inflated or specious claims.

Moreover, Mexico simply didn't have the resources to make payment on even legitimate claims. Indeed, portions of the British claims had been settled with grants of California land rather than cash. And Mexican officials harbored suspicions that the United States, knowing Mexico couldn't make payment, pressed the issue to secure Mexican land through ultimate negotiation. Thus, some Mexican leaders felt justified in doing whatever they could to nullify or minimize the U.S. claims.

But they could not resist the issue entirely, and in 1839 a U.S.-Mexican negotiation yielded a method for resolving the multiple disputes. The two countries agreed to empanel a joint board to identify the various claims and specify the information needed to assess each. Then, when all the information had been collected, it would be submitted to an independent arbitrator for final disposition. After numerous delays, which the Americans attributed to Mexican intransigence, the board finally met in Washington in August 1840, with an eighteen-month timetable for transfer to the arbitrator.

Immediately the Americans perceived Mexican bad faith. Requested information was presented in sketchy form or not at all. False documents found their way to the table. Delays threatened to push some cases beyond the deadline. Mexico, declared U.S. secretary of state Abel Upshur in a letter to his ambassador at Mexico City, "has rendered herself liable to the charge of having . . . disregarded her obligations. She has not complied with a single stipulation of the convention of 1839." Thus, the information ultimately submitted to the arbitrator hardly constituted a complete rendition of the facts.

With the information at hand, the arbitrator certified claims of some $2 million out of $6.5 million originally submitted, and Mexico accepted an obligation to pay these in twenty installments. By the time of Polk's inauguration, however, only three payments had been made. And new claims were piling up. Mexico was stuck with a monetary obligation it could not meet.

No doubt Polk had this in mind when he listed the acquisition of California among his top four presidential goals. A grant of rich Mexican territory could serve as a tidy bit of recompense for those American claims, with the U.S. government then paying off the claimants in cash. And California was the ideal territory—lightly populated, beyond Mexico's ability to govern anyway, a perfect adjunct to the coveted Oregon territory to the north. John Tyler's ambassador to Mexico, Waddy Thompson, had suggested such a settlement as early as 1842.

But now, as Polk contemplated the impending annexation of Texas and its diplomatic aftermath, this nettlesome issue was only one of three incendiary conflicts between his country and Mexico. Another was the annexation itself, which Mexico considered an act of war. And the third was the boundary question between Mexico and Texas—whether the border rightfully was the Río Bravo del Norte (as the Rio Grande was often called) or the Nueces River to the east. Although only about two hundred miles separated the rivers, Texas's Rio Grande claim encompassed a huge tract of land to the north and west, beyond both rivers, stretching all the way to the 42nd parallel. This disputed land now loomed as a major flash point between the two countries.

Polk justified the Rio Grande claim on a number of counts. It had been the U.S. claim when it possessed Texas as a result of the 1803 Louisiana Purchase. Texas had stipulated the claim in declaring its independence, had forced the claim upon Santa Anna in its 1836 treaty with the defeated Mexican, and had declared it formally in legislative action in December 1836. Besides, Mexico had been unable to reverse those actions militarily for some ten years. On the other hand, Mexico could argue that Texas, as a Mexican state or department, had never extended west of the Nueces, and hence no land claim beyond that river could be justified. The problem with this argument, noted repeatedly by Democratic politicians and newspapers in the United States, was that Mexico made no distinction between lesser Texas and greater Texas; it insisted the entire territory rightfully belonged to Mexico, and U.S. presence on any portion of it constituted an invasion.

As Texas's July 4 annexation approval approached, President Polk grappled with the delicate territorial challenge before him. As soon as Texas became part of the United States, he would be charged with the military protection of its territory. He had no intention of ceding the disputed lands beyond the Nueces, and hence he would have to defend all of greater Texas. And yet he wished to avoid war if possible and settle the matter diplomatically.

But he would need an army at the ready. And perhaps, he thought, a show of force would stave off hostilities from the agitated Mexicans. The man chosen to field this army was Brevet Brigadier General Zachary Taylor, then sixty-one years old and a veteran of every American war since 1812. An angular-faced man with a rugged countenance and air of confidence, he came from a wealthy family that had amassed large landholdings in Virginia and Kentucky. He himself had purchased two extensive southern plantations during his military career. A figure of little spark or imagination, he showed almost no curiosity about subjects beyond his immediate involvement. In settings of peace, he seemed aloof, even languid, perhaps a bit cynical about the machinations of civilian leaders. In war he manifested an instinct for action that had served him well in the few combat episodes he had experienced in his long career.

On May 28, War Secretary William Marcy sent a letter to Taylor, then commanding a force at Fort Jesup, Louisiana, on the Texas border. The general was instructed to prepare for a march to the Texas frontier. With annexation, said Marcy, would come the government's responsibility to protect and defend Texas. Taylor's troops were to be "placed and kept in readiness to perform this duty." Marcy also authorized Taylor to draw upon state governors for additional troops.

A few days later Taylor was ordered to gather two thousand soldiers. And on June 15 he received War Department orders, pending Texas acceptance of annexation, to march his troops to Texas's western frontier, all the way eventually to the Rio Grande. But on July 8, Marcy added a clarification, saying Taylor was not to disturb any Mexican military outposts on the east side of the Rio Grande "unless an actual state of war should exist." Around the same time Navy Secretary George Bancroft sent similar instructions to Commodore David Conner urging him to position himself for war but avoid all actions that could lead to it. "That you may precisely understand what is meant by aggression you are instructed to avoid," wrote Bancroft. "I will add, that while the annexation of Texas extends our boundary to the Del Norte, the President reserves the vindication of our boundary, if possible, to methods of peace."

On the other hand, both Taylor and Conner were instructed by Washington to respond to any breach of peace with highly aggressive tactics—"it being the determination of the President," as Bancroft put it to Conner, "to preserve peace, if possible; and, if war comes, to recover peace by adopting the most prompt and energetic measures."

Polk found himself well pleased by these show-of-force maneuvers, which he thought had staved off any hostile action by Mexico. In late July he wrote to Alfred O. P. Nicholson, the prominent Nashville politician, saying he suspected Mexico would have declared war "but for the appearance of a strong naval force in the Gulf and our army moving in the direction of her frontier on land." Now if these actions could ensure stability at the border, Polk surmised, then perhaps he could settle the matter through negotiation and satisfy his aims without war.

As measured as he considered his actions to be, Polk nevertheless set off a powerful political debate. The question involved America's proper policy with regard to Texas's expansive land claim to the Rio Grande—and prospects for war unleashed by that claim. As usual, the debate was crystallized in the rival polemical writings of the *Union* and the *Intelligencer*. If America allowed a Mexican invasion of any territory claimed by Texas, said Ritchie's *Union*, "we should sacrifice our own rights, disregard our obligations to Texas, violate our honor, and cast a stain upon the American escutcheon." Gales's *Intelligencer* decried such bellicosity: "But it is apparent that Texas has claimed, and we fear it is equally apparent that the Executive has granted, the occupation of everything up to the Rio Bravo; which occupation is nothing short . . . of an invasion of Mexico. It is *offensive war*, and *not* the necessary defence of Texas." This debate, beginning as small rivulets of sentiment in these rival newspapers, would grow through the Polk presidency to become a rushing river of political contention.

12 · BRITAIN AND MEXICO

Playing with Prospects of a Dual War

THE POLK ADMINISTRATION was barely six months old when the president discovered the extent of James Buchanan's penchant for generating presidential irritation. A pivotal episode occurred on Tuesday, August 26, as the cabinet discussed the U.S. government's reply to Richard Pakenham's stern rebuke over the Oregon question. Buchanan, at Polk's direction, had drafted the reply, a lengthy exposition of the American stance and a firm rejection of the Pakenham critique. But now he wished to soften the language and undermine Polk's resolve to place the onus for further negotiations squarely on the British.

Buchanan proposed a paragraph inviting Britain to make a counterproposal. Polk instantly rejected the idea. It would mean, he said, they soon would be haggling over a line between the 49th parallel and the 42nd. He would never settle for less than the 49th, he insisted, and actually wanted more. That was the point of his decision to withdraw the U.S. proposition and refuse to submit another. That was why, he added, he was glad Pakenham had rejected his proposal.

"Let the British minister take his own course," said the president. "If he chooses to close the negotiation he can do so. If he chooses to make a proposition he can as well do it without our invitation as with it."

Buchanan, unmoved by these presidential words, said the president's approach could lead to war. The rest of the cabinet listened with some disbelief at Buchanan's obstinacy.

"If we do have war," replied Polk, reflecting his own stubbornness and sanctimony, "it will not be our fault."

Buchanan said the American people would not sustain such a war. Polk disagreed.

Buchanan then suggested the administration should hold off sending the letter until it could be discerned what would happen with Mexico. Polk said he didn't see any connection between the two issues.

"We should do our duty to both Mexico and Great Britain and firmly maintain our rights," said the president, "and leave the rest to God and country."

"God won't have much to do in justifying us in a war for a country north of 49°," said Buchanan. He proposed withholding the letter until the following month. Polk said absolutely not. That would show "hesitancy and indecision." Already the reply was tardy, he said. He asked when the final draft could be completed. Buchanan said Thursday, two days hence. Polk said he wanted it the following day and announced a special cabinet meeting to discuss it.

This sparring reflected two distinct personalities. Polk prided himself on his boldness and resolve, traits that now would be bundled into a bargaining stratagem designed to place the British adversary off balance. Buchanan had no stomach for such stratagems. His instinct for accommodation didn't mix easily with Polk's Jacksonian impulses. Yet, in a kind of paradox of personality, he was perfectly willing to forgo accommodation at cabinet meetings and challenge the president with numbing persistence. And Polk, who took pride in his decisiveness and policy-making audacity, accepted Buchanan's argumentative demeanor despite the annoyance it generated.

Yet Polk was sufficiently angered by Buchanan's obstinacy that he went to his writing table that evening and summarized the episode for posterity. Thus began, on that contentious day, Polk's presidential diary, a daily rendition of events, conversations, thoughts, and complaints that would illuminate the remainder of his presidency.

Polk's opening ploy was clever and bold. In withdrawing his offer and refusing to submit another to the British, Polk had in fact placed them in a seriously awkward position and removed prospects for a compromise below the 49th parallel. On the other hand, Buchanan had identified an ominous flaw in the president's approach—the prospect that his aggressiveness could lead to war with Britain at a time when war with Mexico also loomed. A disastrous scenario for Polk—and for America—would be a dual war with two continental powers acting in concert to attack the United States wherever it was most vulnerable. Yet Polk seemed unmindful of any risk.

The next day the cabinet met to discuss the final draft, and Polk pronounced it "able and admirable." Everyone agreed—except Buchanan, who again suggested postponement. Polk, finding his secretary of state increasingly tiresome, again rejected the notion. But the specter of dual war emerged within twenty-four hours when the cabinet took up the threat of a Mexican invasion of Texas. Polk submitted a number of propositions, which were quickly embraced by his team. First, if Mexico should declare war or otherwise commence hostilities, General Taylor should attack and drive the Mexican forces back across the Rio Grande. Second, even if Mexico simply crossed the Rio Grande into what Texas considered its territory, that in itself would be considered an act of war, and Taylor's orders would include a counterattack. Finally, Taylor would be authorized, in the event of hostilities, to push far enough into Mexican territory to take the town of Matamoros and any other strategic towns west of the river—but not to penetrate any great distance into enemy lands.

Meanwhile, Commodore Conner, commanding the U.S. naval squadron in the Gulf of Mexico, would be ordered to blockade all Mexican ports on the Gulf if war broke out; then he was to seize them if possible.

At the next day's meeting, Buchanan arrived late, as he had been at the British embassy to deliver his letter.

"Well, the deed is done," said the secretary as he strode into the Cabinet Room. He couldn't help adding, with a touch of petulance, he didn't consider it wise statesmanship given the state of Mexican relations.

"I'm glad it was delivered," replied the president. Then the cabinet approved the formal language of the orders to Taylor and Conner, which were dispatched the next day via an express messenger.

Polk's hope, as those dispatches went out, was that the military maneuvers of his land and naval forces would inhibit Mexico from any belligerence. As he remarked to Senator William Archer of Virginia during a courtesy call by the senator on September 1, he felt those maneuvers would "deter and prevent" Mexico from either declaring war or crossing the Rio Grande. Archer agreed.

By September 16 it seemed Polk had made the right moves. At the noon cabinet meeting that day, the president's men discussed three dispatches just arrived from Mexico, suggesting an opportunity had emerged for negotiations. The most significant came from a former Mexico City dentist named William S. Parrott, an American whose reparation claim against Mexico—$690,000 for the illegal seizure of a large shipment of port wine he had ordered—constituted the single largest American claim against the Mexican government. The episode had thrown him into personal bankruptcy, but Mexico insisted Parrott's claim was wildly inflated and labeled him untrustworthy. Some of Parrott's countrymen shared that view.

Despite Parrott's history, Polk had sent him to Mexico City as a confidential agent to inform the president on developments there. By mid-September, Parrott had dispatched nearly thirty reports tracing political, military, and diplomatic activities within the country. Buchanan never quite trusted the man and asked two U.S. consuls in Mexico to evaluate his dispatches. They generally verified his interpretations.

Now Parrott was reporting Mexican willingness to receive a U.S. envoy charged with negotiating a settlement between the countries. The republic unrealistically wanted payment for the loss of Texas, said Parrott, and he had sought to disabuse its officials of any prospect of that. But, despite that issue, he wrote, an envoy from the United States "might, with comparative ease, settle, *over a breakfast*, the most important national questions." U.S. consul John Black, writing from Mexico City, corroborated Parrott's favorable perception, as did the U.S. consul in Veracruz, F. M. Dimond. Black added, however, that Mexico's foreign minister, Manuel de la Peña y Peña, would not deal with Parrott. "The prejudices existing against him cannot easily be removed," he wrote.

Discussing all this on September 16, Polk's cabinet decided to send Louisiana representative John Slidell, who was fluent in Spanish, to Mexico as envoy. Then the president digressed a bit on what he called "one great object of the Mission"—the acquisition of substantial portions of Mexican territory in exchange for a "pecuniary consideration." He wanted, he said, Upper California and New Mexico. But he added a better boundary would be the Rio Grande to El Paso, near the 32nd parallel, and then west to the Pacific, with the United States getting all the country east and north of these lines. Such territory, combined with the greater Texas demands embraced by Polk, would encompass all of present-day Texas, New Mexico, Arizona, Utah, Nevada, and California, as well as parts of present-day Kansas, Oklahoma, Colorado, and Wyoming. It was a huge swath of land that, combined with Oregon territory, would expand the United States by more than a third and secure its dominance of western North America and the Pacific Coast from Juan de Fuca to San Diego.

"For such a boundary the amt. of pecuniary consideration to be paid would be of small importance," the president said, adding it might be available for $15 million or $20 million. But he gladly would pay $40 million, and his cabinet colleagues agreed.

The next day, alas, this excitement dissipated. Polk called another cabinet meeting to discuss new developments conveyed in New Orleans newspapers reaching Washington the previous evening. On August 21, Mexican president Herrera had issued a military circular "breathing a war spirit," as Polk put it in his diary. Herrera also had appointed the fiery Anastasio Bustamante commander-in-chief of the Mexican army. This raised questions about Mexico's true intentions. Polk wished to avoid the embarrassment of sending an American minister to Mexico City and having him rejected by authorities there.

The cabinet members decided to proceed more cautiously: They would wait for further dispatches before assessing the climate for negotiations. Buchanan would ask Consul Black to ascertain officially whether a minister would be received, with the answer to be whisked back to Washington in a fast military ship. And Polk would write to

Slidell asking him to take on the diplomatic mission and, if he consented, to stand by for further instructions. The letters went out that evening.

In his letter to Black, Buchanan suggested that, were the president "disposed to stand upon a mere question of etiquette," he would wait for the Mexican government to request a restoration of relations, since it was Mexico that had severed contact between the two countries. "But his desire is so strong to terminate the present unfortunate state of our relations with that republic, that he has consented to waive all ceremony and take the initiative."

No doubt this was a sincere expression of administration sentiment. Polk genuinely wanted to avoid war. But he wanted Mexican territory more, and it wasn't clear he could get it peacefully. Parrott had written back in July that "it would be far better that Mexico should declare war now, than that she should propose to open negotiations for the settlement of pending differences." That was because a territorial settlement might be possible following a war, he explained, "but not in negotiation, now, nor at any future period." He added, "I am fully persuaded, they never can love or respect us . . . until after we shall have given them a positive proof of our superiority." Hence, he advocated that Mexico should be "well flogged by Uncle Sam's boys, ere we enter upon negotiation."

But Polk reversed the Parrott formula and sought negotiation first. His calculation was that Mexico was too weak and chaotic to confront the United States, however intense the anti-American sentiments then flowing through the body politic. The cabinet was weak. Herrera seemed beleaguered. General Paredes had refused to march to the Rio Grande with his army of seven thousand men and now threatened a return to Mexico City to depose Herrera. The populace was livid over the loss of Texas and the failure of the Elliot mission but didn't know what could be done about it. Mexico hardly seemed in position to wage war against the United States, and hence the time seemed perfect for negotiation.

As Polk waited for word from Black, another political drama emerged with the death of Supreme Court Justice Henry Baldwin

of Connecticut, named to the bench by Jackson in 1830. Buchanan
called on the president one evening in late September to say he wished
to discuss rumors that he wanted Baldwin's seat. First, he said, it
might be best to remove him from the cabinet because his political colleagues in Pennsylvania were certain to oppose Polk's plan to
reduce tariffs, and his presence in the cabinet thus might prove awkward for the president (not to mention, though he didn't say it, awkward for himself). On the other hand, he said, should war come with
Mexico or England, he would wish to remain in his current pivotal
position. But Buchanan wanted the president to know he had harbored for years a strong desire to become a High Court justice, and he
wondered whether, should he remain in the cabinet, he might be considered for some future court vacancy. Polk expressed complete satisfaction with Buchanan at State and noted the difficulties he would
face in seeking a replacement. He suggested they let the matter ride
until Congress convened in December, and Buchanan agreed.

Two weeks later Buchanan reported to the president on a shrewd
bit of politicking he had undertaken at Polk's behest. The secretary
had conversed at length with Senator Benton and had submitted to
him large portions of the official correspondence on the Oregon question. Benton had seemed pleased with this display of confidence and
responded favorably when Buchanan suggested the president would
enjoy talking with him directly. Benton said he would make himself
available at the president's pleasure.

The timing was good, for the Oregon issue was heating up. On
October 21 the cabinet took up a dispatch from Polk's ambassador to
London, Louis McLane, who reported an intriguing conversation with
British foreign minister Lord Aberdeen. Aberdeen expressed regret at
Pakenham's rejection of Polk's compromise proposal and suggested a
willingness to accept a modified version of that proposal. Would the
president, asked Aberdeen, negotiate further on the subject?

Buchanan, visibly excited, said he expected Pakenham had received
new instructions by the same ship that had brought the McLane dispatch. No doubt, he said, the British minister would call on Buchanan
to inquire whether the U.S. government would receive another prop-

osition. If so, what modifications would be acceptable? He turned to Polk for the answer.

The president offered nothing. His proposal, he said, had been rejected "in terms not very courteous." Thereafter, the United States had withdrawn its offer and vowed to extend no other. However, America remained open to further negotiation—if the British wished to put forth a proposal. Hence, Buchanan could say only that the United States would consider any British proposal. He was instructed to say nothing as to what the United States would or would not accept.

This did not please Buchanan, who repeated his earlier suggestion that the president's approach would "inevitably lead to war." Polk expressed satisfaction with his country's position and digressed at length on why he had never wished to pose the 49th parallel in the first place and why he was pleased it had been rejected. Now he was free to spurn that compromise line altogether and hold out for more. He doubted, added the president, that the British minister could propose anything he would accept, although he might submit the proposal to the Senate for its judgment prior to his taking action.

Seizing on that concept, Buchanan asked if he could tell Pakenham that Polk would submit a British offer to the Senate for its prior advice. That would be "improper," said Polk. The British minister had no right to know U.S. intentions. Polk emphasized that he had not closed the door to further negotiations, and that was all the British needed to know.

On October 23, Buchanan reported to Polk the substance of a two-hour conversation between himself and Pakenham at the State Department. Pakenham clearly was feeling the heat, seemed troubled, and expressed regret the American proposition had been withdrawn. Following his instructions carefully, Buchanan said simply his government would consider any proposition put forth by the British minister. After hearing Buchanan's report, Polk reiterated he was unlikely to accept any Pakenham proposal.

The next morning Polk sent a message to Thomas Benton: The president would receive the senator that afternoon if he was available. Benton arrived at one o'clock, and the two men held a long conversation, focusing particularly on Oregon. This was important political outreach. The maverick from Missouri was well positioned to help or thwart the president's aims in the Senate according to his latest whim, and it was always best to control his whims if possible.

Benton entered the discussion "very cheerfully," as Polk put it to his diary, and expressed support for administration policy up to that point. He noted an earlier promise to Buchanan to support the 49th parallel as a compromise line. Polk carefully walked through his own thinking—that he had offered the 49th only in deference to actions of his predecessors and that now, in the wake of British rejection, he was inclined to press for the whole territory all the way to 54°40'. Despite a brewing disagreement on this question, the two men found common ground on a number of items. Benton agreed Polk should give the twelve-month notice for abrogation allowed under the Convention of 1827; that U.S. laws and jurisdiction should be extended to American citizens in Oregon in the same way that British laws had been extended to British subjects; that the U.S. government should establish forts and other means of protection for Americans traveling to Oregon; and that U.S. Indian policy should be extended to the territory.

The two felt none of these issues would violate the current treaty. Polk added he was "strongly inclined" to reaffirm the Monroe Doctrine against permitting foreign colonization in North America, including Mexican lands that weren't being seriously administered, such as California. Benton, without taking issue with that, then remarked that Britain's claim to the Fraser River Valley in the north of Oregon was every bit as strong as America's claim to the Columbia River Valley in the south. A bit of wary sparring on the question revealed a possibly serious disagreement on this point. Benton did agree that the United States could permit no European power to colonize California, particularly the maritime jewel in that territorial crown, San Francisco harbor.

The senator then mentioned his son-in-law, John C. Frémont, the army's famous scientific explorer and topographer then on his third expedition into the wilds of the western lands only vaguely mapped and catalogued for civilized eastern folks who might want to make their way there. Frémont, then in his early thirties, was a man to stir the nation's imagination. Handsome and imposing, with a luxuriant black beard, fiery eyes, and a messianic mode of expression, Frémont was a man on the make. The bastard son of a penniless French vagabond and a fallen woman of Virginia society, he seemed driven to attain fame and glory. He had his fame; now he was looking for the glory.

The fame had materialized through his first two remarkable western expeditions—an 1842 journey to chart and depict the Oregon Trail and a later 1843–1844 trek that had wound its way extensively throughout much of the West, including California, Oregon, and vast expanses of the Rocky Mountains. The third voyage, which had commenced the previous June from St. Louis, was ostensibly a mere six-month affair focused on the exploration of the southern Rockies and the upper Arkansas River. But now the explorer's devoted father-in-law was telling the president he expected Frémont to go beyond his precise orders and veer into California before returning to St. Louis.

"Col. B," Polk later reported to his diary, "expressed the opinion that Americans would settle on the Sacraminto River and ultimately hold the country." Indeed, this process was already well in progress. Like Texas before it, California was a land that Mexico could not adequately govern or control. Mexico had neither the population to stock it nor the military reach to protect it. And, again like Texas, it was now in receipt of growing numbers of U.S. citizens making their way there for land and opportunity. Particularly receptive was the Sacramento Valley and the protective harbor at Monterey, operational base of U.S. whaling enterprises for a generation. Polk and Benton shared the same view about California—namely, it would fall into U.S. hands eventually and there was no reason not to accelerate the process. Besides, for Benton the added incentive was that in California John C. Frémont might find his glory.

On October 27, Pakenham delivered to Buchanan a letter designed to seek progress in negotiations, and the next day's cabinet meeting was devoted to the proper U.S. response. The members began with a draft prepared by Buchanan—and unpalatable to his colleagues. There ensued the same old argument between the president and his secretary of state. Finally Polk suggested the reply language was too important to craft in the heat of debate, and so they should sleep on it and resume the discussion at nine the next morning.

But Polk didn't sleep on it. Instead he asked Treasury Secretary Robert Walker to come by the White House at six and help him restructure the Buchanan draft. With a brief interruption for the president to greet White House visitors, they worked until ten o'clock to fashion a final product. Gone were Buchanan's passages of accommodation and signals of U.S. flexibility. In their place was the austere Polk language: We have nothing to say, but go ahead and make an offer and we will consider it when we see it. The revised letter was presented to the cabinet at the next morning's meeting and accepted.

Outmaneuvered, Buchanan took a new approach. Noting that Pakenham had suggested he might not declare his letter to be official until after he heard the response, Buchanan proposed that he read the reply and then let the British minister decide whether his letter was official. If not, he could withdraw it. Polk soundly rejected this approach. Pakenham, he said, must declare whether his letter was official before he could know the U.S. response. Buchanan protested "with some earnestness" that his honor was at stake, as Pakenham had indicated earlier he might reserve the right to withdraw the letter. Polk sternly issued instructions as to how Buchanan must approach the impending Pakenham meeting. He must force the minister to declare whether his letter was official; if so, he could release the reply. If not, no U.S. communication would be forthcoming. Buchanan accepted the instruction and retired.

An hour later he returned to report on his meeting with Pakenham. He did as instructed, said Buchanan, and the British minister had responded with apparent anguish and indecision. Buchanan then remarked that Pakenham could not expect the United States to abandon the ground it had taken in the negotiations, whereupon Pakenham withdrew his letter, and the interview ended.

Polk was furious, certain the secretary's remark had generated Pakenham's response. He said as much to Buchanan. "The result of the whole," he later complained to his diary, "is that after two Cabinet meetings and much anxious discussion the matter ended where it began." It was clear, he added, that Buchanan disapproved the president's approach and was "laboring to prevent it." Polk had hoped his bold stratagem on Oregon would accelerate events and lead to a quick settlement, but now events were in suspension.

They were, however, heating up elsewhere. On October 30, Polk initiated a "confidential conversation" with a young marine lieutenant named Archibald Gillespie, about to embark on a secret presidential mission to California. He was to deliver confidential messages to the U.S. consul in Monterey, Thomas O. Larkin, and to John C. Frémont, wherever he might be found.

Then on November 7, at ten o'clock in the evening, Bancroft arrived at the White House with the reply from John Black, the U.S. consul at Mexico City. The dispatch had been conveyed by William Parrott in one of Commodore Conner's fast ships, and it reported Mexico's willingness to accept an American envoy. Specifically, Black had inquired in writing whether Mexico "would receive an envoy from the United States, intrusted with full power to adjust all the questions in dispute between the two governments." The Mexican foreign minister, Peña y Peña, had replied that his government was "disposed to receive the commissioner of the United States who may come to this capital with full powers from his government to settle the present dispute in a peaceful, reasonable, and honorable manner."

Peña had requested that the United States remove its fleet from the waters around Veracruz as a sign of good faith and a signal that no coercion was intended or implied by the Americans. Polk promptly complied as he unleashed a flurry of activity designed to set in motion the crucial negotiations. Instructions were drafted for John Slidell, who was invested with full powers as "envoy extraordinary and minister plenipotentiary." Strict secrecy regarding the entire mission was ordered, lest Britain or France find out about it and try to thwart the negotiations. Then Polk did a curious thing. He asked Parrott to return to Mexico as secretary to the Slidell legation. Polk knew from

Black's earlier dispatch that Peña and other Mexican authorities considered Parrott untrustworthy and wished never to treat with him. Yet he urged the man nonetheless to take the assignment. Parrott reluctantly agreed.

With Slidell organizing his trip to Mexico, Polk turned his attention to other matters, particularly the production of his extensive Annual Message to the new Twenty-ninth Congress, which he intended to flood with major presidential initiatives. On November 17, he met with Senator William Allen of Ohio, chairman of the Foreign Relations Committee. Then only forty-one, the earnest and easily agitated Allen was an ardent Polk ally, and he gave full assent to the president's decision-making, including his actions on Oregon.

Buchanan came by on November 19 to say he had decided against asking for the vacant Supreme Court position. Polk expressed gratitude, adding he was "entirely satisfied" with Buchanan's cabinet performance. To his diary, the president confided that, although the secretary had differed with him on Oregon and tariffs, he had never caused embarrassment and had ultimately carried out presidential policies. The two men digressed a bit on Buchanan's political ambitions. The secretary said he aspired ultimately to a court seat and desired that position more than the presidency itself—particularly since his cabinet duties had given him a window on that difficult job. But some of his Pennsylvania friends harbored presidential ambitions for him, he confessed, and he hoped Polk would know that their agitations didn't have the secretary's sanction.

Polk replied in avuncular fashion that history indicated presidential aspirants who were prominently before the electorate for too long a period often found their ambitions thwarted. He cited Henry Clay among others. Hence, if Buchanan ever did want the presidency, the president counseled, he should do everything possible to curtail his friends' activity in his behalf. Polk then assured his friend that he would be happy to consider Buchanan for future Supreme Court vacancies, and the secretary departed "well satisfied," as it appeared to Polk.

Yet within ten days the cabinet sparring between the president and his secretary resumed. The topic, as usual, was Oregon, specifically the president's Annual Message language suggesting a desire to obtain all of Oregon. With congressional members flocking to Washington, said Buchanan, he had divined that many wished for a speedy compromise at the 49th parallel.

Buchanan's "channels of information," said Polk, were "very different from mine." He added he had conversed with many members who were roused on the issue and wanted "the whole length."

Buchanan contended the country would not justify a war for territory north of 49 degrees, and Polk's greatest political danger was that he would be attacked for his "warlike tone," as Polk put it to his diary.

Polk said his greatest danger was opposition within his own party to any compromise at the 49th parallel. Had Britain accepted that compromise, he added, he would have sustained much anger from western Democrats. It could have upended his entire administration, he argued.

Later Attorney General John Mason took Polk aside to report rumors that Buchanan had been promoting the 49th parallel with congressional members. "The truth is," reported the president to his diary, "Mr. Buchanan has from the beginning been, as I think, too timid and too fearful of War on the Oregon question."

Around the same time Polk received an evening visit from Representative Robert McLane of Baltimore, son of Polk's ambassador at London, Louis McLane. Young McLane wished to impart to the president the substance of an hour-long train conversation he had shared with John Van Buren, son of the former president. Van Buren disparaged the president bitterly, said he was setting himself against his former New York friends on patronage matters, seemed intent on running for a second term, and was ill-treating Silas Wright. McLane said the younger Van Buren was emotionally opposed to the administration, and he speculated that he was visiting Washington to ascertain the tone of public sentiment toward the president. Polk himself speculated that if the administration were adjudged to be weak with the public, the New York Barnburners would go public with their opposition.

Polk didn't note to his diary his extensive and ardent efforts to ingratiate himself with the Van Buren faction during the long run-up to the 1844 election. The vice presidency had been his only request, which Van Buren had brushed aside with the barest minimum of politeness—while his good friend Francis Blair had used his *Globe* to put forth a barely credible opponent. It all reflected the tenuous nature of politics, the shifting winds and fortunes of the game. Such slights and injustices of political life weighed heavily upon the consciousness of James Polk, as his diary revealed. But they never seemed to deflect him from his chosen course.

13 · THE TWENTY-NINTH CONGRESS

Polk Takes Command of the National Agenda

THE TWENTY-NINTH CONGRESS of the United States opened its first session on December 2, 1845. At two o'clock that afternoon members received at their desks the president's first Annual Message. It was a manifesto of presidential resolve. James Polk intended to seize the national agenda.

Running to more than sixteen thousand words, the message laid out in crisp and lucid prose the background of the major issues facing the country and presented the outcomes Polk wanted. Its tone reflected firm reasonableness, but there was an undercurrent of the self-righteousness that so often crept into the man's demeanor to the indignation of his critics—and sometimes the consternation of his allies.

He extolled Texas annexation, soon to be consummated with congressional approval, and proudly noted that "the sword has had no part in the victory." But he acknowledged with "regret" that U.S. relations with Mexico "have not been of the amicable character which it is our desire to cultivate with all foreign nations." He attributed this in part to the long reparations history and Mexico's intransigence on that issue. Contributing also was that country's angry response to annexation. So far, the message said, he had managed to avoid hostilities by demonstrating America's military might on the Texas frontier and in the Gulf of Mexico. But he revealed he had sent "a distinguished citizen of Louisiana" to Mexico City with a mandate "to adjust and definitively settle all pending differences between the two countries." He hoped for a peaceful resolution before Congress adjourned and said he would recommend no legislative action on the matter until completion of the negotiations.

On Oregon, Polk boldly dismissed "British pretensions of title . . . to any portion of the Oregon Territory upon any principle of public law recognized by nations." He had proposed his 49th parallel compromise, he said, only out of deference to his predecessors and in a "spirit of moderation." Now that it had been rudely rejected, he told Congress, he asserted U.S. rights to the whole territory. He added: "The civilized world will see in these proceedings a spirit of liberal concession on the part of the United States, and this Government will be relieved from all responsibility which may follow the failure to settle the controversy."

He asked Congress to approve giving Britain notice of U.S. intent to abrogate the 1827 treaty of joint occupation so the matter could be settled after a year's time. And he recommended legislation extending the jurisdiction of U.S. law and the protection of U.S. force to Americans in Oregon or on their way there. He invited other approaches from members of Congress but emphasized the British insistence on getting all territory north of the Columbia "can never for a moment be entertained by the United States without an abandonment of their just and dear territorial rights, their own self-respect, and the national honor."

On domestic issues, Polk pressed Congress to reduce the nation's import taxes under the Whigs' Tariff of 1842 and to create the "independent treasury" that had been a hallmark of his presidential campaign. The only legitimate object of import duties, Polk declared, was to raise federal revenue; discriminatory rates on various imported articles to help U.S. manufacturers could be justified only within a context of raising just enough revenue to sustain the government. He advocated modest "ad valorem" tariffs that taxed imports on a percentage basis so the "articles consumed by all are taxed at the same rate."

Recalling the furious battles over the Bank of the United States, Polk expressed his resolve to ensure that federal funds would never again fall under the sway of private moneymen untethered from the popular will. "The safe-keeping of the public money," he wrote, "should be confided to a public treasury created by law and under like responsibility and control."

He ended his message with the hope that "it may not be deemed inappropriate" to memorialize "the most eminent citizen of our country who during the summer . . . has descended to the tomb." Andrew Jackson, said Polk, "had an unfaltering confidence in the virtue and capacity of the people and in the permanence of that free Government which he had largely contributed to establish and defend."

JOURNALISTS AND POLITICIANS alike reacted favorably to Polk's extensive message. "Never, in the period of our existence as a nation," gushed the *Union*, "has a document appeared which could announce to the world a more prosperous state of affairs, or which is more imbued with the spirit of justice and nationality." Lewis Cass, now a Michigan senator, told Polk: "You have struck out the true doctrine." Even Pennsylvania politicians seemed pleased. "We Pennsylvanians may scratch a little about the tariff," said Senator Simon Cameron, "but we will not quarrel about it."

More important perhaps than Democratic enthusiasm was the muted response from Whigs. The *National Intelligencer* pronounced itself pleased with the president's "moderation," though the compliment was extended, said the *Union*, with the "appearance of a charitable donation."

Everyone knew, though, that serious debates would ensue shortly. On December 9, as the cabinet mulled a forthcoming meeting between Buchanan and Pakenham, the secretary asked what he could say to the minister. Polk said he could say nothing beyond what was in his message.

"But," Buchanan protested, "suppose Mr. Pakenham inquires whether any further proposition which the British Government might make would be received, what shall I say to him?" Polk replied the British government had no right to ask such a question. He repeated his oft-stated position that the onus for action rested entirely with the British.

Polk, however, did modify his position slightly. In a draft letter of instruction to U.S. ambassador Louis McLane, Buchanan had suggested Polk would send to the Senate, for prior advice, a British compromise proposal at the 49th parallel. Polk scratched out Buchanan's language and substituted his own: "Should that Government [Britain] take any further step with a view to settle the controversy, the President would judge of the character of any new proposition when made, and if in his opinion it was such as to justify it, would feel inclined to submit it to the Senate for their previous advice before he would take any action upon it." Buchanan deemed this an insufficient gesture and warned once again the country "had better prepare for war."

A few days later this debate spilled onto the Senate floor when Cass introduced a resolution calling for executive branch reports on the country's military readiness to fight Britain. "A crisis is fast approaching in the intercourse between that country and ours," said Cass.

Colleagues noted with interest Cass's leadership on the issue. They appreciated his immense stature, purchased over decades of public service as military leader, territorial governor, cabinet secretary, and diplomat. But they also had come to expect cautious circumspection from him on controversial issues. Now, having narrowly missed his party's presidential nomination the previous year, Cass appeared to have contracted the presidential bug and seemed bent on positioning himself for another try in 1848. That might explain this bold position on the superheated Oregon question.

"I have said elsewhere what I will repeat here," declared Cass on the Senate floor, speaking for his midwestern constituency, "that it is better to fight for the first inch of national territory than for the last. It is better to defend the door sill, than the hearth stone—the porch, than the altar." The current system of joint occupation, said Cass, was becoming untenable as Americans flooded into Oregon in search of opportunity and betterment. He added:

> England has placed herself in the path that is before us; and if she
> retain her position, we must meet her. If the last proposition she
> has submitted is her ultimatum, it is effectively a declaration of

war. . . . I hope—or I ought rather to say I wish—that England would awaken to a sense of her injustice, and would yield where she could yield honorably. . . . But will she do so? It is safest to believe she will not, and this dictate of prudence is fortified by every page of her history. When did she voluntarily surrender a territory she had once acquired, or abandon a pretension she had once advanced?

William Archer of Virginia attacked the Cass resolution, deriding the country's war fever and asserting urgently the concerns that Buchanan expressed more mildly in cabinet meetings. "Could any man calculate," he asked, "the evil which would be conveyed to hundreds and thousands of bosoms by the mere intimation that we were to have war?" He decried the "overboiling patriotism" guiding the debate. And for what? He answered: "a small strip of territory, almost valueless, and barren, beyond the reach of human comprehension, and so distant that it might not be found out—for an object so absolutely valueless" that to fight a war for it would reflect "criminality and venality."

The next day, after further debate, the Senate passed the Cass resolution unanimously. No one felt comfortable opposing a measure that appeared so innocuous on its face even if it carried ominous implications underneath. The debate had been the opening salvo in what would become a national preoccupation in the coming months.

But American foreign policy ran on two tracks, and the Mexico track was rumbling with powerful events. John Slidell reached Mexico City on December 6. When U.S. consul Black informed Peña y Peña of Slidell's arrival, the foreign minister "manifested great surprise" at his speedy appearance and indicated a delayed schedule would have been better. Then when Slidell sought to present his credentials to President Herrera, the response was vague. Word arrived the matter would be submitted to the "council of government," an official advisory body of indeterminate standing but well-known capacity for mischief.

The council, Slidell reported to Washington, was dominated by

men "not only in open and violent opposition to the present administration but . . . endeavoring to get up a revolutionary movement to
overthrow it." It seemed the body had not been consulted when Herrera had opted for the negotiation, and now it was seeking to use the
issue as leverage to bring down the president, whose cooperative spirit
toward the United States was a minority sentiment in the country. As
for Herrera, Slidell suspected he was desperately trying to fend off the
opposition by cooperating with it. Mexican officials, Slidell wrote to
Washington, "in referring a matter entirely within their own competence to a body whose decision they cannot control, and upon whose
sympathies they cannot rely, manifest either a weakness or a bad faith,
which renders the prospect of any favorable issue to negotiations with
them at best very problematical."

On December 20 came word the council had rejected Slidell on the
ground that Mexico could not accept any U.S. envoy with full diplomatic powers. When Mexico had accepted the U.S. offer to send an
emissary, wrote Peña to Slidell, it had not anticipated he would arrive
with the presumptuous status of "envoy extraordinary and minister
plenipotentiary"—which implied the two countries enjoyed normal
relations. They didn't, said Peña, and they couldn't while the Texas
issue remained unresolved. Hence the United States needed to send an
ad hoc minister whose negotiating portfolio was confined to the nettlesome issue of Texas. "Mr. Slidell cannot be admitted in the character with which he appears invested," wrote Peña, "as the honor, the
dignity, and the interest of the Mexican republic would thereby be
placed in jeopardy."

Slidell was livid. In replying to Peña on Christmas Eve, the envoy
said he would "abstain from the full expression of the feelings of
astonishment and dissatisfaction . . . fearful that, if he did not do so,
he might overstep the bounds which courtesy and the usages of diplomatic intercourse prescribe." He traced the correspondence that had
brought him there and found no suggestion that Mexico would reject
an envoy with full diplomatic powers. Besides, he added, without
such status he could not treat on all the issues separating the two
countries. He described his country's good-faith gestures, including

the removal of Commodore Conner's naval forces from the vicinity of Veracruz.

Then he turned menacing. Recounting the reparation history, he said the "annals of no civilized nation present, in so short a period of time, so many wonton attacks upon the rights of persons and property as have been endured by citizens of the United States from the Mexican authorities." Failure to resolve the countries' differences, said Slidell, would lead inevitably to war, as Peña himself had suggested. "If this, unfortunately, should be the result," warned the U.S. envoy, "the fault will not be with the United States; the sole responsibility of such a calamity, with all its consequences, must rest with the Mexican republic." With that broadside Slidell left Mexico City for Jalapa, nearer the coast, where he planned to await further instructions from Washington.

NEWS OF THESE developments didn't reach Washington until well into the new year, and in the meantime Polk's attention remained fixed on Oregon. On December 22 he received a visit from John C. Calhoun, who arrived in "a fine humor" but promptly expressed opposition to the one-year abrogation notice. He said he feared peace would be destroyed by an emotional congressional debate on the issue that could lock the country into a position of hostility toward Britain. Even on the tariff the free trader Calhoun was petulant. He supported the president's position generally, but complained it didn't go far enough. After the session Polk predicted to his diary that Calhoun "will be very soon in opposition to my administration."

At the next day's cabinet meeting the relentless Buchanan won a concession of sorts from the president on Oregon. Peppering Polk with questions on how he would react to particular contingencies, the secretary posed a hypothetical: If Britain proposed a compromise at the 49th parallel, leaving the southern tip of Vancouver Island to Britain but giving the United States full rights to the Columbia, would the president submit the proposal to the Senate for its prior counsel before responding?

Polk replied he would consult three or four senators from different regions of the country and, if they agreed, he *might* submit the
proposal formally for a senatorial judgment before acting. It was a
small concession, but it pleased Buchanan, who reduced the proposition to writing in order to lock the president to it. The next day
Senator Allen called and bolstered Buchanan's position that a British offer at the 49th parallel should be submitted to the Senate for its
prior advice. Polk replied that he thought that would be an appropriate course.

Polk clearly was softening on Oregon as it became clear he could
find himself in a political vise on the issue—caught between southern senators fearful that war with Britain would destroy their cotton
trade and hawkish western senators bent on coupling all of Oregon
with their own territory. The westerners, Tennessee senator Hopkins
Turney told Polk, were "almost mad on the subject." Turney warned
of a brewing alliance between Calhoun and Benton to oppose Polk.
Benton still harbored animosities over Van Buren's fate at the Baltimore convention and would break with the administration as soon
as he thought he could do so safely, said Turney, while Calhoun was
almost sure to organize a southern spearhead of opposition. He counseled a quick compromise on Oregon to forestall this political threat.
When Polk candidly revealed his inclination to seek prior senatorial
advice on any British compromise at the 49th parallel, Turney "heartily approved."

James and Sarah Polk enjoyed a rare time of relaxation on Christmas Day. Few visitors called, and those who did stayed only briefly.
Congress was out of session, and no public business was transacted in
the city. But the president, never able to stay away from his toil for
long, wrote an urgent letter to Vice President Dallas in Philadelphia,
imploring him to return to Washington so he could sign, on behalf
of the Senate, the joint congressional resolution admitting Texas into
the Union. When Polk himself got a chance to sign the resolution a
few days later, he used a quill pen made from an eagle feather sent him
by a friend, Elizabeth Curtis of Virginia. Mrs. Curtis said the feather
had dropped from an eagle flying overhead on the day Henry Clay got

the Whig presidential nomination, and hence she considered it a welcome omen of Clay's inevitable defeat. Polk enjoyed a rare feeling of mirth over this little joke.

Late on Christmas evening Buchanan called at the White House in a mood of severe agitation. The issue was Polk's decision to nominate Judge George Woodward to the vacant Supreme Court seat. Polk considered the bright, young Pennsylvanian to be "a sound, original, & consistent democrat, of the strict construction school." But Pennsylvania's Buchanan-Cameron faction considered him a rival, and Buchanan viewed his nomination as a personal affront. The secretary complained bitterly that Polk had not alerted him in advance and accused Polk of undermining his political standing in Pennsylvania with numerous adverse patronage decisions. Polk vehemently denied this and walked through his many appointments to bolster his defense. He said he wished his cabinet could accept his personnel decisions, but he must "act on my own convictions" on such matters. "It was a painful conversation," Polk confided to his diary afterward, "but Mr. Buchanan finally retired, expressing himself to be satisfied."

Two days later Buchanan arrived at the regular Saturday cabinet meeting in apparent high spirits. On the question of soliciting prior Senate advice on a 49th parallel compromise, Polk went around the room to get the counsel of each member. Cave Johnson initially balked at the idea, but eventually all agreed it must be done. They also agreed to reject any British proposal to submit the matter to arbitration, in which a mutually acceptable third-party nation would determine the appropriate outcome. Pakenham had indicated an interest in an arbitration approach.

As Polk inched toward a compromise position on Oregon, the debate intensified in Congress. On December 30, Senator Edward Hannegan of Indiana expressed the fiery western sentiment with a resolution demanding all of Oregon as "part and parcel" of the United States and declaring the government had "no power . . . to transfer its soil, and the allegiance of its citizens to the dominion, authority, control, and subjection of any foreign prince, state, or sovereignty." Not surprisingly, the Senate erupted into a frenzy of political agitation.

Calhoun promptly introduced a counterresolution affirming the president's right to negotiate an Oregon settlement and pointedly declaring a compromise at the 49th parallel would "not abandon the honor, the character, or the best interests of the American people." If the country could not avoid war on the issue, said Calhoun, he would support his country in war. But, he added, the "war would be one of no ordinary character," and he "would hold those responsible who rashly rushed us into it."

Hannegan responded: "If it is rashness in the representatives of the people to assert the rights of the country, and if this rashness should produce war, and for which we shall be held responsible, I, for one, do not fear the responsibility." All Democrats, said Hannegan, must adhere to the "declaration of party, made in solemn convention." By this, he added, he was "willing to live or die. No compromise at forty-nine; the people in this country would never consent to such a surrender." The resolutions were then placed on hold, to be brought up at a later time.

A few days later the issue kicked up even more emotion in the House when Georgia's Democratic representative Hugh Haralson introduced a bill to raise two regiments of dragoons. The military debate quickly spilled over into an Oregon debate. Charles Ingersoll of Pennsylvania, Democratic chairman of the Foreign Affairs Committee, urged calm and patience by arguing Oregon would fall into American hands peacefully in time based on demographics. He noted Benjamin Franklin's famous admonition to American colonists facing the prospect of war with Great Britain. "Get children as fast as possible," Franklin had said. Added Ingersoll: "That is precisely what we have to do now." The House erupted in "tokens of assent" that were "loud and numerous," reported the *Union*.

Preston King of New York believed the situation required more immediate action. Polk was wrong to propose the 49th parallel as a compromise, said King, because the British would use Oregon as a staging ground for attacks on U.S. western lands. What, he asked, was the purpose of such diplomacy—"that it should demonstrate to ourselves and to the world that a territory was ours that we may then be enabled to show our magnanimity by surrendering it to our enemy?" He warned that the British had but one purpose for that territory—"a road on which she might send her powder, her balls, ay, and her scalping knives to her northwestern allies [Indian tribes]."

Robert Winthrop of Massachusetts rose to declare his absolute enmity toward all war generally and warlike talk regarding Oregon specifically. Everyone favored peace, he said, but everyone qualified it by saying it must be an "honorable" peace. Well, he wished to announce that he viewed peace as "in its own nature, and in its own simple essence, the highest of all honor, and war . . . the deepest of all disgraces." That's why he vehemently opposed giving Britain notice of America's intent to abrogate the joint occupation treaty. Such an action, he declared, "would almost unavoidably terminate in war, followed up as it would probably be by an immediate occupation of the whole territory" by Britain. To those who cried, "the whole of Oregon or none," he would reply, "none."

The House debate became even more fiery two days later when Ingersoll introduced a resolution effectuating the twelve-month notice for U.S. abrogation of the 1827 treaty. That stirred Joshua Giddings of Ohio to deliver unto the House his usual brand of incendiary political prose. Giddings was a courtly and generous-spirited Whig who nonetheless projected himself in political discourse as a savage warrior against the ideas he hated. What he hated most was slavery and the "slave-holding oligarchy" of the South, and he viewed just about every issue before the House through the prism of human bondage. He had been livid when it became clear that Texas would enter the Union as a slave state, and now he wanted to redress that wrong through a war with Britain that would very likely, he believed, destroy the slave power forever.

"I am led to the conclusion . . . ," he declared, "that war, with all its horrors and its devastation of public morals, is infinitely preferable to a supine, inactive submission to the slaveholding power that is to control this nation if left in its present situation." The North and West would survive the devastation, he said, but the greatest burden would fall upon "the weak, helpless, slaveholding South," which

now saw before it "servile insurrections which torment their imagina-
tions." He added:

> Murder, rapine, and bloodshed, now dance before their affrighted
> visions. Well, sir, I say to them, this is your policy—not mine.
> You have prepared the cup, and I will press it to your lips until
> the very dregs shall be drained. . . . Let no one say that I desire
> a slave insurrection; but, sir, I doubt not that hundreds of thou-
> sands of honest and patriotic hearts will "laugh at your calamity,
> and mock when your fear cometh." No, sir; should a servile insur-
> rection take place—should massacre and blood mark the foot-
> steps of those who have for ages been oppressed—my prayer to
> God shall be that *justice*—stern, unyielding, and unalterable *jus-
> tice*—may be awarded to the master and to the slave.

But, added Giddings, he didn't expect that war to come, even after
treaty abrogation, because the Democratic executive would save the
South with a compromise. "Yes, sir, I verily believe that he will surrender up all that portion of Oregon lying north of the 49th parallel."
Thus, Giddings vowed to vote for abrogation so the slave oligarchy
would be destroyed, but he would do so knowing the president would
never permit the war that would destroy the slave oligarchy.

Virginia's James McDowell pounced on the inconsistency. "In one
breath," he pointed out, "the gentleman has declared that the notice
to Great Britain would be inevitable war; and in the next breath, that
there will be no war and that he would vote for the notice."

Giddings's rhetorical aim was never logical coherence or arguments designed to persuade. He wanted to insert the slavery issue
into the consciousness of an institution that wished at all costs to
avoid that damnable subject. His tool was outrageous rhetoric that
stirred outrage—but stirred also a focus on the profound implications of slavery. A couple of years before he had been forced to resign
from the House under censure for defending a murder that occurred
during a slave revolt aboard a ship called the *Creole*. Arguing this
could not be murder because the slaves were merely pursuing "their

natural rights of personal liberty," Giddings effectively advocated the lawless and violent overthrow of slavery. His constituents in Ohio's Western Reserve promptly sent him back to the chamber that had reproved him.

The debate raged on that day and in many days to come. Southerners decried the notice resolution as leading inevitably to "plain, unequivocal war," as Democrat Robert Barnwell Rhett of South Carolina put it. Midwesterners, alternatively dismissing prospects of war and welcoming it, demanded the full territory upon pain of national degradation. "I am for the whole of Oregon . . . ," declared Democrat Leonard Sims of Missouri, "and in defense of it I will willingly see every river, from its mountain source to the ocean, reddened with the blood of the contest." Others supported the notice resolution on the grounds it would lead to a prudent middle-course compromise at the 49th parallel.

James Polk followed the debate with one thing firmly in mind: Whatever the outcome, he would not show weakness. As he told South Carolina's Democratic representative James Black, who called at the White House on January 4 to urge compromise: "The only way to treat John Bull [is] to look him straight in the eye." Thus, he said, "a bold and firm course on our part" was the more pacific approach, and if Congress faltered or hesitated, John Bull would "immediately become arrogant and more grasping in his demands."

On January 10, Calhoun called again for what was a congenial conversation on Oregon, though the two men clearly saw the matter through different eyes. Calhoun urgently argued the president's notice policy was a recipe for war. He asked if Polk had any new information on what Britain might do. The president replied there had been no new compromise proposal, but signals from London indicated Britain was anxious to avoid war. He added his strong conviction that a compromise would be possible only after the treaty had been abrogated.

Calhoun then offered a dosage of his characteristically insightful and well-grounded political analysis. Those favoring notice brought different considerations to the question, he said. Most did so in hopes it would foreclose any compromise—in which case, Calhoun feared, war would be inevitable. A few favored notice in hopes it would foster compromise. Calhoun feared the influence of the first group and revealed that two moderate midwestern senators had offered Calhoun a deal: They would vote against the notice resolution if the South Carolinian and his southern friends would promise to oppose any subsequent compromise. Calhoun, echoing Benton, emphasized he felt the United States held no legitimate title to any Oregon lands north of latitude 49.

Two days later Ritchie's *Union* ran an editorial that reflected Polk's emerging flexibility on the issue. Noting the paper had always advocated a peaceful resolution, it now argued that such a resolution was possible only after treaty abrogation. Under joint occupation, argued Ritchie, Britain had no incentive to adjust the arrangement because it had never claimed an exclusive right to any territory below the 49th parallel. Thus, the current arrangement gave Britain cover for extending its administrative reach over the entire expanse in a way that never would be possible under any compromise. "Notice to terminate this state of things must be given," said the *Union,* "before a settlement of the question, by negotiation, can be hoped for." This was a strong signal that Polk was moving toward a compromise at the 49th parallel.

EVENTS IN MEXICO were proving more nettlesome, however. In early January, Polk received word from Slidell that his mission had been rejected by Herrera. By this time word also had reached Washington that Herrera's government was in danger of collapse as General Paredes was moving toward the capital with his army, now approaching nine thousand men. In a letter to Slidell, Buchanan praised the envoy's actions up to that time and urged a three-pronged approach. First, he should conduct himself "as to throw the whole odium of the failure of the negotiation upon the Mexican government." Secondly, he should declare his intention of staying in Mexico pending receipt of instructions from Washington. And, thirdly, he should use that time to follow events and ascertain if they could improve prospects for commencing the negotiations—particularly if a new government emerged under Paredes.

Then came word that in late December Herrera's government indeed had collapsed. The central issue driving the anti-Herrera forces had been the president's willingness to negotiate with the United States, which was interpreted widely and angrily as a willingness to sell portions of northern Mexico. Now the general who had fomented much of that outrage was in charge, and he wasn't likely to entertain negotiations with Slidell and his despised associate, William Parrott. Herrera had represented Washington's final opportunity to negotiate a settlement, but even he had succumbed to the anti-U.S. hostility within his constituency.

Worse, the Mexican polity was in progressive deterioration, as Slidell explained in his cable to Buchanan. Yet another constitution was in the works, possibly to include provisions for a monarch to be imported from Spain, which inevitably would set off yet another round of civic strife. During that process—an estimated thirteen months—Paredes would exercise uncontrolled power—"unless . . . ," said Slidell, "some discontented generals succeed in making a counter-revolution." This could only be avoided if Paredes could pay the army, but he had no money with which to do so. Already the government's civilian employees had not been paid for months, and the expense of the army exceeded the country's entire revenue. In these circumstances the prospect for serious negotiations between the United States and Mexico seemed remote.

Thus it wasn't surprising that War Secretary William Marcy sent new orders to General Zachary Taylor: "Sir: I am directed by the President to instruct you to advance and occupy, with the troops under your command, positions on or near the east bank of the Rio del Norte." Taylor's men, nearly six months at Corpus Christi, were becoming restless, and the stolid commander welcomed the opportunity for a major maneuver to the west. He began preparations for the move.

ON JANUARY 22 the powerful foreign policy issues occupying Polk's mind receded temporarily when a political crisis erupted closer to home. The Senate rejected Polk's nomination of George Woodward to the Supreme Court. The entire Whig caucus had voted against, along with six Democrats—Cameron, Benton, Ambrose Sevier and Chester Ashley of Arkansas, and David Yulee and James Westcott of Florida. Polk knew Cameron, Sevier, and Westcott were intimate friends of Buchanan, presumably susceptible to entreaties from the secretary to support the president. Clearly, Buchanan had not supported the administration in its hour of need.

Worse, Polk heard that Buchanan had expressed hopes of getting the job even before the Woodward vote. "The information given me . . . ," wrote Polk to his diary, "left the painful impression that Mr. Buchanan had been willing to see . . . Mr. Woodward rejected by the Senate in order to obtain the office himself." Later that evening the president received visits from Vice President Dallas, Senator Daniel Dickinson of New York, and Allen of Ohio. They were indignant. The six errant Democrats had ignored all arguments in favor of the highly qualified Woodward, they reported, and voted simply for political effect. Cameron was the apparent ringleader, they said, and immediately after the vote rumors began floating across the Senate floor that Buchanan would be the next nominee. Sure enough, Polk shortly received a letter from Benton recommending Buchanan for the job.

In a long diary disquisition Polk complained of Buchanan's inordinate sensitivity to presumed slights regarding presidential appointments. "I cannot surrender the appointing power to any one else, and if, because I will not do so, Mr. B. chooses to retire from my Cabinet I shall not regret it." But he stopped short of taking action based on reports that Buchanan actively had opposed Woodward and had fostered the six-senator Democratic rebellion. One thing he made clear: Buchanan would not get the court vacancy.

A few days later Attorney General Mason stopped by the White House to relay a conversation he had with Buchanan, who clearly was trying to extricate himself from a bad situation. He protested that he had had nothing to do with Woodward's rejection and suggested that, had he been consulted on the matter, he could have ensured the man's confirmation. Polk considered this evidence of "conniving" because it proved the secretary could have reversed the outcome had he wanted to. Mason also revealed Buchanan had asked the attorney general to support him for the court vacancy.

All this constituted sufficient grounds for firing Buchanan—or perhaps putting him on the court simply to get rid of him. But, beyond fulminations to his diary and vows that further such behavior would elicit a serious response, Polk chose to put up with his meddlesome secretary—seemingly unmindful that such forbearance in the face of Buchanan's behavior undermined his executive authority throughout a watchful capital. The president told Mason that, if he discovered any cabinet member conspiring with a Democratic faction to join with Whigs in opposing his administration, that person "would find me a lion in his path, and . . . I would not submit to it." To his diary, he added, "Mr. Buchanan will find that I cannot be forced to act against my convictions, and . . . if he chooses to retire I will find no difficulty in administering the Government without his aid."

But such bravado to intimate associates and his diary wasn't accompanied by any overt actions that gave it credibility. And around Washington a perception was gathering that James Polk, for all of his firm conviction, stubbornness, and power, could be mauled and outmaneuvered with impunity. James Buchanan was Exhibit A.

14 · END OF A TREATY

Diplomacy and Politics at War with Each Other

ON FEBRUARY 7, 1845, a backbench Democratic congressman named John D. Cummins rose in the House to add
his voice to the territorial debate that had absorbed Congress for nearly two months. He was from the western state of Ohio,
and hence he surprised no one with his call for U.S. acquisition of the
entire Oregon expanse. But his vision and eloquence went beyond
expectation.

Cummins dismissed those, such as Virginia's Senator Archer, who
deprecated the value and richness of the disputed lands. They were,
said Cummins, nothing less than "the master key of the commerce
of the universe." Get that territory into U.S. jurisdiction, he argued,
and soon it would fill up with "an industrious, thriving, American
population" and "flourishing towns and embryo cities" facing west
upon the Pacific within four thousand miles of vast Asian markets.
Now contemplate, he added, ribbons of railroad track across America,
connecting New York, Boston, and Philadelphia to those burgeoning
West Coast cities and ports that would spring up once Oregon was in
American hands.

Now, Cummins continued, think about how the "inevitable eternal laws of trade" would render America the necessary passageway
for "the whole eastern commerce of Europe." Traversing the American continent on their way to Asia, European goods could get there
in little more than seven weeks, whereas the traditional sea routes
around Cape Horn or Good Hope generally required seven months.
"The commerce of the world would thus be revolutionized," he said.
"The East India Company would be broken down; Great Britain must

lose her commercial supremacy in the Pacific; and the portion of its commerce which forced its destination there must pay tribute to us."

Cummins's bold vision was easily dismissed as hopelessly fanciful in a world utterly dominated by Great Britain. And yet it crystallized a fundamental element of the era's politics—the widely shared conviction that America was a nation of destiny, that one day it would supplant Britain as the world's dominant power, that Oregon represented merely an interim step toward realization of that vision. Of course in the world of everyday politics, such rarefied concepts of destiny inevitably encountered messy realities of skepticism and counterconcerns about the price to be paid. That was the essence of the congressional debate on Oregon.

In the House on February 9, destiny carried the day. The chamber approved, by a vote of 163 to 54, a resolution calling on the president to notify Great Britain that the United States intended to abrogate the Convention of 1827 at the end of twelve months. The House added language inviting the president to pursue "negotiations for an amicable settlement" but rejected by a "heavy vote" a provision that would have recommended pursuit of a compromise. The matter then went to the Senate.

Ohio's Senator Allen, as Foreign Relations chairman, led off with a rousing defense of the abrogation notice and a fervent prediction that Britain "dare not go to war with this country single-handed on the subject of Oregon." So earnest was his call for unity on the issue that the galleries—filled "almost to suffocation," according to the *Union*—erupted in applause. Though rebuked by the Senate president, it reflected, said the *Union*, "the intensity of the public feeling on the great question of the time." The next day John M. Clayton of Delaware, a highly respected Whig, echoed Allen in a speech that lasted an hour and a half. On this great issue, he said, there was but one party, the national party.

These expressions of Senate unity would prove false, and the unfolding drama would ensnare President Polk in a troubling predicament as his diplomatic approach abroad conflicted with his political approach at home. His audacious decision to withdraw his 49th parallel offer and refuse absolutely to present another was paying off. Britain was coming around to a reasonable compromise. But the president's stoic stubbornness on the issue split his party into two warring camps. After all, the president at different times had advocated two opposing outlooks—compromise at the 49th parallel, embraced by those consumed with war fears; and the claim of Oregon's entirety up to 54-40, embraced by those who felt anything less would dishonor the nation.

Now each camp claimed to speak for the president and desperately desired the executive to say as much. Not from James Polk. Any effort to assuage these animosities and harmonize his party would unravel his delicate diplomatic gamesmanship. And so Polk could only fall back upon the language of his Annual Message and let the Senate descend into bitter political discord that split not just the chamber but his own party.

Across the Atlantic in London, political developments were playing nicely into Polk's diplomatic game. The ruling Tory government, led by Sir Robert Peel, collapsed over the incendiary issue of the Corn Laws—a shorthand term denoting the country's centuries of protectionist trade policies on farm goods. Pressures were mounting to repeal those high tariffs and move into a new era of free trade, much like the Jacksonian policies of America's Democratic Party. In quick succession, the protectionist Peel lost his cabinet consensus and resigned as prime minister. Lord John Russell, opposition leader and a strong free trader (but also a bellicose opponent of America's Oregon claims), sought to form a cabinet but failed. Queen Victoria rejected Peel's resignation and urged him to renew efforts to form a government. And so he put together a new reform cabinet dedicated to Corn Law repeal. He also retained Lord Aberdeen as foreign minister.

All this benefited Polk in three ways. The anti-American Lord Russell was denied the prime minister's job. The new Peel administration suddenly found itself looking to the Polk government as a model on trade policy and potential commercial ally. And the harrowing political threats weathered by the Peel government, coupled with the risky repeal effort ahead, generated a strong governmental desire to dispose of the Oregon question. Aberdeen, a man of conciliatory temperament, was well positioned to do that.

By early February, the mails brought to America editions of the London *Times* "marked by a *decorum and reserve* of expression, and a new moderation of spirit," as the *Union* happily put it. A few weeks later came news of parliamentary speeches by Peel and even Lord Russell that reflected, said the *Union,* "an amicable and courteous tone towards us." A subsequent London *Times* editorial hailed free trade across the Atlantic as "the surest safeguard of peace." Puncturing the dire warnings of America's congressional doves, the editorial welcomed the abrogation notice as "no less desirable to us than it is to them."

But the peace process needed a reciprocal signal from Polk, and it wasn't forthcoming. Accompanying the placatory expressions from London were dispatches from U.S. ambassador McLane urging Polk to seek a compromise at the 49th parallel, which he said Britain would readily accept. McLane revealed the frustrations of London officials who had been waiting in vain for a softening in Polk's hard-line position. Peel and his government began to suspect Polk had fired up the western expansionists to such a pitch that compromise would be impossible. As Aberdeen put it in a letter to Pakenham, "I imagine the President and his Government are more afraid of the Senate than they are of us." Reflecting this frustration, Peel's government moved ostentatiously to bolster its military readiness.

On February 3, McLane dispatched a stark report to Buchanan warning of a growing war fever in London born of discontent over Polk's silence. This spurred two days of urgent cabinet discussions in Washington, beginning on February 24.

Buchanan, perceiving that Polk now feared war, seized the opportunity. He recommended instructing McLane to inform Aberdeen that nothing said or done before had closed the door to any forthcoming British proposal; and further that if Britain proposed a 49th parallel compromise accompanied by British navigation rights to the Columbia for seven to ten years, Polk would seek prior counsel from the Senate in executive session. Since the Senate was considered highly likely to endorse such an outcome, this was tantamount to acceptance. After considerable cabinet discussion, Buchanan offered to draft a letter designed to pull together the sentiments of his cabinet colleagues. A special meeting was scheduled to discuss the draft at eight o'clock the following night.

But that evening the president received a visit from William Haywood, a close friend since the two had been students together at the University of North Carolina. Haywood, now a North Carolina senator and loyal Polk ally, warned that a scheme was afoot by Calhoun, McDuffie, and others to seize the Oregon issue from the president by fostering a resolution pushing for compromise. Calhoun and his group, said Haywood, would settle the Oregon question on just about any terms demanded by the British. Haywood himself vehemently opposed such a move but also harbored concerns that William Allen and other Northwest senators, in demanding all of Oregon, would precipitate a war.

An hour later Allen arrived for a two-hour visit marked by his insistence that Polk never compromise America's full right to all of Oregon. Contending that the cunning South Carolinians, Calhoun and McDuffie, were pushing compromise merely to "break . . . down" the president and "destroy [his] popularity," Allen predicted a compromise at the 49th parallel would cost Democrats many congressional seats in nine or ten states in the West and Southwest.

The next morning at ten-thirty, in the midst of a snowstorm, Calhoun arrived at the White House with Senator Walter Colquitt, a former Methodist preacher from Georgia. Calhoun delivered to Polk a letter from McDuffie, unable to attend because of ill health. Polk read McDuffie's letter as the others looked on. It pleaded for a U.S. conciliatory gesture, and Calhoun echoed the sentiment by threatening to press a Senate resolution, to be passed in executive session, advising the president to reopen negotiations on the basis of the 49th parallel. He said McDuffie would sponsor the resolution.

"I must frankly say," replied Polk, "that I cannot in the present state of the question advise such a course."

No executive session could guarantee the secrecy of such an action, he argued, and the consequence would be disastrous to his entire diplomatic effort. The president revealed his intention to submit such a proposal, if it came from Britain, to the Senate for its prior advice. And he engaged Calhoun in a bit of debate on the importance of reserving to America full Columbia River navigation rights after a prescribed period. Calhoun clearly would yield on that point to forge a quick settlement.

Polk later expressed to his diary suspicions that Calhoun, as usual, had an unstated motive—in this instance, to extricate himself from his previously stated hard-line opposition to the abrogation notice, which had become a ridiculous position in light of the congenial signals emanating from London. That night the cabinet met until eleven to discuss Buchanan's letter to McLane, which was approved substantially as the secretary of state had initially proposed it. This letter constituted Polk's first olive branch since withdrawing his compromise proposal the previous July.

But the political battle at home continued to threaten his delicate diplomatic dance. On March 5 a Senate exchange erupted between the compromise-minded Senator Haywood and two western hawks—Senators Allen and Hannegan—that threw the party into turmoil. It began when Haywood expressed faith that the president remained willing to compromise at the 49th parallel. His actions, said Haywood, "require of us not to doubt that his purpose was pacific—that he had not placed himself in the perilous position of plunging his country into war." No, added the senator, the president's initial compromise offer "had been actuated by a strong sense of public duty," and nothing in his message "countenanced the idea that the negotiation had terminated."

Hannegan rose to pose a question to his colleague: "I ask him if he has the authority of the President, directly or indirectly, for saying to the Senate that it is his wish to terminate the Oregon question by compromising with Great Britain on the 49th degree of north latitude?"

"It would be unwise and impolitic," replied Haywood, "for the President to authorize any Senator to make such a declaration as that implied in the question of the Senator from Indiana."

Allen interjected that he would "construe the answer of the Senator from North Carolina into a negative."

"Then I desire to say that my friend from Ohio only proves . . . that he is a very bad hand at construction."

"Well, then," said Allen, "I will adopt the other construction, and consider his answer as an affirmative; and I put the question, and demand an answer to it as a public right."

"I deny the right of any Senator to put questions to me in this way," replied Haywood. "I have not assumed to speak by authority of the President."

Allen: "Then the Senator takes back his speech."

Haywood: "Not at all; but I am glad to see that my speech *takes*."

Allen: "With the British."

From there the discourse deteriorated.

"What is this, need I ask," demanded Hannegan, "but charging upon the president conduct the most vile and infamous?" He then predicted history's judgment on Polk would be extremely harsh if the president actually wanted to settle the matter at the 49th parallel, as Haywood had implied. "So long as one human eye remains to linger on the page of history, the story of his abasement will be read, sending him and his name together to an infamy so profound, a damnation so deep, that the hand of resurrection will never be able to drag him forth. He who is the traitor to his country can never have forgiveness of God. . . . I ask the Senator whether he came here charged with missives from the President, or whether he assumed the dogmatic style on his own responsibility, and—"

At this point North Carolina's Senator Willie Mangum interjected: "I call the Senator to order. I protest against these remarks."

But the damage had been done. Within twenty-four hours Polk was besieged by agitated visitors who lamented the party split. First came Cass, who vowed to force Hannegan to "put the matter right" and do Polk justice at the next senatorial session. McDuffie stopped by the next day with similar expressions, as did Tennessee's Senator Turney and Mississippi's Jesse Speight, who warned that the Northwest "ultras" were getting up a caucus to pressure Polk on the issue. All said they were aghast at the turn of events. To all of these expressions Polk replied blandly—and disingenuously—that he held no views beyond his Annual Message. More sincerely, he said no one was authorized to speak for him.

On March 7, Hannegan called on the president and worked himself into a state of high dudgeon. "Do you go for the whole of Oregon up to 54°40'," he demanded, "or will you compromise and settle the question at 49 degrees?"

Polk replied that what he had done thus far on Oregon was before the world and had been approved by the country and, as he thought, by Hannegan himself.

"Yes, that is so," said the senator.

"Wait then until I act," said Polk, "and then approve or condemn what I may do." He expressed frustrations that Senate Democrats would attack him for what they thought he *might* do.

Hannegan seemed mollified, but then Allen showed up and denounced Haywood's speech as a direct attack on himself. He too wanted to know if the North Carolinian spoke for Polk. The president gave the same answer in the same measured tone. But Polk reminded Allen that the senator once had recommended the president submit to the Senate any British proposal at the 49th parallel. He revealed that other Northwest ultras, including Cass, had offered the same counsel. And so had Haywood. Thus, he suggested, the matter ultimately would rest with the Senate, not with him.

But so intense was Allen's feeling that he came back the next afternoon to read remarks he intended to deliver in the Senate—a firm announcement that he was authorized to say the president continued to assert the U.S. title to Oregon up to 54-40. Polk adamantly stood by his position that no one was authorized to speak for him.

It fell to the *Union*, Polk's newspaper, to try to quell the intraparty strife. Democratic senators, said the paper, "may exhibit, now and then, some evanescent flashes of momentary feeling," but ultimately they will rise "superior to all such excitements, will preserve the equanimity of their temper, and along with it their union, their power, their invincibility." In light of the rhetoric rising on the Senate floor, this seemed like wishful thinking.

As for Polk, he seemed unmindful that he himself had injected much of this venom into the body politic with his own ambiguity of leadership. He blamed the presidential aspirations of various Democrats, including Allen, Cass, and Calhoun—and Haywood's alliance with presidential aspirant Silas Wright. They all wanted to exploit the administration for their own purposes, he believed, and likely would "so divide and weaken the Democratic party . . . as to . . . render my administration unsuccessful and useless." He would not be swayed by such maneuverings, he vowed with characteristic self-righteousness. "I will do my duty to the country & if my measures fail the responsibility shall rest where it belongs."

As DISTURBING AS these developments were, they didn't keep the president's attention away from that other foreign policy crisis—Mexico. A thick fog of intrigue had descended upon the White House on February 13 with the arrival of a mysterious figure named Colonel Alejandro T. Atocha. Born in Spain, with an extensive background as Mexican banker, he claimed to be a naturalized U.S. citizen. More important, he was a close associate of that flamboyant figure, Antonio López de Santa Anna. In fact, his association with the discredited general had gotten him expelled from Mexico the previous December when Santa Anna himself had been exiled upon pain of death. Atocha had visited Polk the previous June in an effort to get his reparation claim added to the dozens of outstanding claims that remained a major contention point between the United States and Mexico.

But now he pressed a different agenda. Lately he had been visiting Santa Anna in Havana, Atocha said, adding that the general had supported the recent Paredes revolution and might soon get back into power in Mexico. If so, the general would seriously pursue a treaty with the United States that would grant a substantial portion of Mexican land in exchange for cash. He mentioned lands east of the Rio Grande and north of the Colorado River down through San Francisco Bay. All this could be ceded to the United States, he suggested, for as little as $30 million—sufficient, he said, to pay down on much of Mexico's public debt, support the army, and establish the government on a sound footing.

But Atocha told Polk that Santa Anna wondered why Polk had removed his naval forces from Veracruz and kept Taylor's army so far from the Rio Grande? If he wanted to treat with Mexico, said Atocha, Polk must place his forces in a more threatening position. No Mexican government could survive after making concessions to the despised United States unless he did so under some military duress. Polk took care to say nothing of substance in reply to Atocha's information, but he invited the man back for a subsequent visit a few days later.

When Atocha returned on February 16, Polk suggested that if Mexican officials wanted to put forth a proposition, it would be considered when made. Atocha said Polk had missed his point. No Mexican government would dare make such a proposition, he said, because it would instantly invite another revolution. There had to be an appearance of being forced. That's why he now wanted Polk to get his navy back to Veracruz and his army to the Rio Grande. Order Slidell away from Jalapa and onto a naval ship off Veracruz, he counseled, and then have him demand payment of all outstanding reparation claims. Everyone knew Mexico had no money with which to make such a payment. And hence the people—and the archbishop, who was owed half a million dollars from the government—would see the necessity of a settlement.

Atocha said Santa Anna expected to be back in Mexico in April or May and likely would assume power in collaboration with Paredes and his top general, Juan Nepomuceno Almonte, both of whom favored this settlement concept. But they would need money to stabilize the country—perhaps half a million dollars up front to sustain themselves for a few months until the balance could be paid. Atocha gave Polk Santa Anna's last words to him: "When you see the President, tell him to take strong measures, and such a treaty can be made & I will sustain it."

Polk didn't know what to make of Atocha. But he was intrigued. This might be the break he was looking for—an opportunity to get the land he wanted without bloodshed. The next day he spoke to his cabinet in a manner suggesting he was pondering the words of the mysterious Spaniard. He felt the United States must take strong measures toward Mexico in order to reach a settlement. He suggested Slidell should be instructed to demand an early decision on whether the country would receive him—and, if so, whether it would make speedy reparation payments. If Mexico refused one or both, Slidell should leave the country immediately and take a position aboard a naval vessel off Veracruz to await further instructions. If Mexico then refused a final demand, Polk would send a message to Congress seeking authorization to "take redress into our own hands by aggressive measures."

Everyone agreed with the approach—except Buchanan, "manifestly in a bad mood," as Polk noted to his diary, as indeed he had been in such a mood since it had become clear he would not get the open Supreme Court seat. Polk continued to vow to his diary that he would not tolerate rebellious behavior from Buchanan but continued to do so. Polk delayed the dispatch to Slidell in part because Buchanan seemed hostile to it, in part because he desired more information from Mexico before making his next move.

More information came on March 9 with a dispatch from Slidell saying he remained at Jalapa pending word on whether the Paredes government would receive him. Polk and Buchanan managed to agree on an appropriate instruction for Slidell. He was not to leave Mexico before making a formal demand that he be received by the new government, which represented a revolutionary departure from the old one. Upon Slidell's empty-handed return, said Buchanan, Polk would recommend "energetic measures" against Mexico, "and these might fail to obtain the support of Congress, if it could be asserted that the existing government had not refused to receive our minister."

Slidell, anticipating the instruction, had issued the demand on

March 1 in bold diplomatic language. He had been prepared to request his passport following Herrera's rebuff, Slidell told the new foreign minister, Joaquín María Castillo y Lanzas. But in light of subsequent events the president was "unwilling to take a course which would inevitably result in war, without making another effort to avert so great a calamity." So now it was up to Mexico "whether it shall give place to friendly negotiation, or lead to an open rupture."

Fifteen days later he got his answer. The Mexican republic, declared Castillo, had been "despoiled, outraged, contemned" by the United States. "The sentiment of her own dignity will not allow her to consent to such ignominy." Slidell promptly demanded his passport and made plans to proceed to New Orleans via Veracruz. The long diplomatic dance was over.

MEANWHILE, CONGRESS REMAINED fixed on Oregon. As it became clear the Senate would pass a notice resolution, the question narrowed down to the form of the language. Allen's Committee on Foreign Relations recommended a simple resolution without embellishment—referred to colloquially as a "naked notice." The House version had invited the president to pursue further negotiations but didn't request or demand it. But Georgia's Colquitt had proposed language declaring the Senate "earnestly desired that the long-standing controversy . . . be speedily settled by negotiation and compromise." This was totally unacceptable to Polk, who feared such language would embolden Britain to abandon its recent flexibility and hold out for concessions.

This was the state of affairs on March 11 when Thomas Benton stopped by the White House for a chat. Polk reported later that "Col. B was in a pleasant temper and spoke in a kind spirit." The two men shared their mutual irritation at Allen, Calhoun, and other Democratic troublemakers.

"I regret the division and excitement," the president complained, "which seems to prevail among the Democratic Senators on the subject of the form of the notice."

Benton agreed and predicted the Colquitt amendment likely would pass the Senate, with a few dissident Democrats joining the united Whigs, unless an alternative approach could be found. The Missourian embraced Polk's plan to submit a reasonable British proposal to the Senate before responding. But if the British demanded permanent navigation rights on the Columbia, said the president, he would reject it outright. Benton concurred in that as well.

But new problems emerged with the president's premier cabinet member and premier malcontent, James Buchanan. Suddenly his convictions on Oregon had gone through a remarkable transformation. After months of fervently urging compromise and issuing dire warnings of war, Buchanan now suddenly turned bellicose and manifested "a disposition to be warlike" in recommending language for a report to Congress on the country's military readiness. Polk had no difficulty in surmising the cause of this abrupt sea change. Buchanan had been noting in casual conversation that Lewis Cass seemed to be gaining political stature with his extreme views on Oregon, and it now seemed clear the secretary wanted to "supersede Gen'l Cass before the country," as Polk put it to his diary. He added a lament: "I cannot rely upon his honest and disinterested advice."

The Senate's Oregon debate raged throughout March and into April. Reverdy Johnson, a Maryland Whig, said if war emerged from America's rejection of a compromise at the 49th parallel "there will be from one end of the civilized world to the other, unmixed and absolute reprobation of the American character." Calhoun offered an elaborate rationale for why he had opposed notice some months before but could vote for it now since prospects for compromise looked brighter than ever. But he insisted upon Colquitt's amendment calling for "negotiation and compromise" and spun out a scenario of global woe should the United States and Britain stumble into war.

Daniel Webster of Massachusetts said a consensus had emerged in America—and probably Britain—for a logical compromise line. "I am of opinion," declared the famous Whig, "that this matter must be settled upon the 49th parallel." Louisiana's Whig senator Alexander Barrow said the president seemed to be sitting on a fence, "that he

might fall on either side as might be desirable" based on the preponderance of political sentiment that emerged. He said Polk had mis-
managed the entire matter from the beginning.

Cass vehemently stuck with his call for all of Oregon. "I am among
those," he said, "who mean to march, if we can, to the Russian boundary." He painstakingly picked apart Benton's rationale for confining
U.S. claims to the Columbia River Valley. McDuffie, speaking with
vigor despite deepening ill health, endorsed the Colquitt compromise
language.

And so it went until April 16, the day of the vote, some sixty-five
contentious days after Allen of Ohio had opened the debate with a call
for unity. Emotions remained highly charged when the chamber heard
from the last Whig to speak, John Crittenden of Kentucky, longtime
friend of Henry Clay. The problem with the naked notice as requested
by the president, said Crittenden, was "that it would not facilitate
negotiation, and might possibly be looked upon as an unfriendly proceeding." But if the notice should be "given in terms of amity and
respect, and without offence, the matter would become one of necessity, and be taken up by the people to avoid the dangers of war."

Besides, he argued, the people of the United States were "the great
first-born of the continent," and the continent was falling into their
hands by virtue of demographics, superior technology, the industrious
impulses handed down from their forefathers. "Why then pluck green
fruit," he asked, "that to-morrow will fall ripe into our hands?"

As the chamber moved toward a vote, Reverdy Johnson offered two
amendments that essentially rewrote the House resolution based on
language put forth earlier by Crittenden. The most important change
was the insertion of a long preamble urging "that the attention of the
governments of both countries may be the more earnestly and immediately directed to renewed efforts for the amicable settlement of all
their differences and disputes in respect to said territory." Johnson's
language was accepted, and the debate shifted to the new language.

Allen attacked it as inappropriate because it presumed to advise
the president on how he should exercise his treaty-making power,
which the Senate had no jurisdiction to do. Besides, in authorizing

the president "at his discretion" to give notice, argued Allen, the Senate was seeking to dodge the issue and place the entire onus upon Polk. The president had charged Congress to act, said Allen, and then the "law-making power returns the subject to him, and with erratic, halting, cramped, manacled action, with timid unwillingness to meet responsibility." Could anyone think, asked Allen, moving his arms in emphasis in his own characteristic manner, that with passage of such language Great Britain, "whose trident already keeps in awe the waters of the ocean, will stoop and go on her knees to us?"

That was too much for the usually courtly Crittenden. "On what meat," he demanded, "did this our Caesar feed, that he came here to lecture the Senate in the style he did. Who gave him his commission to do so?" He and his colleagues, declared Crittenden, were not accustomed to putting up with such unfounded charges, "however vehemently made and enforced by all sorts of gesticulation."

"I speak here," declared Allen in response, "under the commission of a State as respectable, in every particular, as any other State in this Union." He took singular umbrage at Crittenden's reference to his arm gestures. "His jeers, his grimaces, have no effect upon me," he said. "He speaks of my manner. Well, . . . it is his manner to make faces—it is mine to make gestures. He thought that I alarmed the audience by my vehement gesticulation. Well, they must have quite forgotten their terror in amusement created by his grimaces."

The exchange continued for several minutes until mercifully the yeas and nays were called for. The vote was 40 to 14, reflecting strong sentiment in the Senate for presidential efforts to settle the simmering dispute at the 49th parallel. Now this language would have to be reconciled with the more accommodating House version. Polk immediately concluded it would be best for the House to accept the Senate language. He didn't particularly like it, "but still it authorized the notice to be given & that was the main object," he concluded. He feared a House rejection could cause interminable delays, and so he dispatched Buchanan, Marcy, and Cave Johnson to the Hill to lobby House Democrats on the preferred approach.

The efforts proved unavailing. On April 18 the House amended the

Senate version by saying the president was "authorized and requested" to serve notice of abrogation, thus accepting a measure of congressional responsibility in the matter. Two days later the Senate rejected that language and sent the issue to a conference committee. It crafted a final version almost identical to the Senate measure, and on April 23 both Houses approved it—142 to 46 in the House; 42 to 10 in the Senate. The *Union* gushed, "With one accord we have met a great crisis nobly." But Polk groused about the unwanted preamble and the time it took Congress to finally act on the matter. He added to his diary, "After all, however, Congress . . . have sustained the first great measure of my administration, though not in a form that is altogether satisfactory or one that was preferred."

But the Oregon crisis seemed controllable for the first time in years. The Mexico crisis, on the other hand, was gaining fire. On April 11, word reached Washington that Slidell had been turned away by the Paredes government. He was headed back to Washington. Polk and his cabinet decided to keep the matter private, aside from consulting a few trusted legislators, until the envoy's arrival. In the meantime, Polk was girding for an escalation in hostilities. As he told Calhoun on April 18, U.S. relations with Mexico had "reached a point where we could not stand still but must assert our rights firmly." He could perceive, he said, "no alternative but strong measures towards Mexico."

15 · WAR

"Every Consideration of Duty and Patriotism"

T O JAMES POLK'S many critics, he didn't seem to view himself as they often saw him. Through his own eyes he was a
man of rectitude, seriousness, and sincerity, often beleaguered
by the deceits and hypocrisies of those he had to deal with in order
to press his grand and pure national aims. To others he seemed frequently to display his own deceits and hypocrisies. As Gideon Welles,
a civilian naval official of the time, put it, "he possessed a trait of sly
cunning which he thought shrewdness, but which was really disin-
genuousness and duplicity." Welles gave him one quality: that "few
men could better keep their own counsels."

These characteristics were evident at the cabinet meeting of Saturday, March 28, when Polk once again brought up the subject of Mexico by suggesting John Slidell soon would be received by the Paredes
government. In fact, there was no reason to believe any such thing.
Slidell's mission already had been rejected by Herrera, and Slidell's latest communication had offered little hope that Paredes would be any
more hospitable. Indeed, within just two weeks Washington would
learn that Slidell had been rebuffed by Paredes.

But Polk had a purpose in his phony optimism. He told the cabinet
that Slidell's biggest obstacle in getting a deal was his lack of authority
to make a prompt cash payment at signing. Paredes's military regime,
he noted, depended upon the army for its longevity. Unless Paredes
could acquire money fast to feed, clothe, and pay his troops, he could
find himself the object of another military rebellion. But if Slidell
could pay down a half-million dollars or perhaps a million, then Paredes could maintain himself in power until the treaty could be ratified

and subsequent payments made. That, mused Polk, "might induce him to make a Treaty." The president sought cabinet views on whether he should seek congressional approval for such a payment.

Polk had done his homework. "I called their attention," he wrote to his diary, "to an act appropriating two millions, which had been passed in 1806 in Mr. Jefferson's administration"—money, he noted, to facilitate Jefferson's desired purchase of Florida. After considerable discussion, during which Buchanan, as usual, expressed misgivings, it was agreed the president should consult with some key senators on the matter.

That evening, Polk sought Benton's counsel in the president's White House study. "Col. B. entered very fully into all my views," noted Polk to his diary. He urged the president to consult also with Senators Allen, Cass, and Haywood. Allen and Cass seconded Benton's endorsement, but Cass suggested the president should discuss it also with Calhoun. Allen agreed. If Calhoun opposed it, said Allen, the matter would die, so they might as well find out beforehand. Polk promptly called in Calhoun.

The South Carolinian pronounced himself sympathetic to Polk's aim of getting a settlement with Mexico to include U.S. acquisition of large tracts of southwestern territory. But he expressed fears the matter, when made public, would complicate the delicate effort to settle the Oregon dispute. He asked for a few days to ponder the issue and consult his trusted ally, McDuffie. Four days later he returned to say it would be "inexpedient at present to move in the matter in Congress." That killed the idea—for the moment.

It was true Polk considered his up-front-cash initiative to be crucial to his plans and ambitions regarding Mexico. But this had nothing to do with Slidell's doomed mission. More likely he was thinking of the words of Santa Anna as conveyed by Alejandro Atocha: He must impress Mexican officials with the threat of military action before a settlement could be reached. He must expect to treat with Santa Anna himself once the irrepressible general managed to get back into power. And he must be prepared to supply the forthcoming regime of Paredes and Santa Anna with up-front cash to help stabilize the country.

Before he could ratchet up his belligerence toward Mexico, he needed justification, something that would stir Americans with heightened patriotism and hostility toward the southern neighbor. If Slidell were to return empty-handed after suffering insult from Mexican authorities, that could serve the purpose. Indeed, back in November Polk had written Slidell that, should his mission fail, "we must take redress for the wrongs and injuries we have suffered into our own hands, and I will call on Congress to provide the proper remedies." Thus, while Polk was willing to *risk* war to fulfill his designs on Oregon, it appeared he might actually *need* war to get what he wanted from Mexico.

In any event, decisions made in both capitals were setting the two countries on a course toward war. One of those decisions was Polk's order, conveyed by Marcy on January 13, that General Taylor march his army of 3,550 officers and men to the Rio Grande. By March 8 Taylor had set his advance guard upon the winding, 120-mile trek, and by March 28 he had his army planted on the Del Norte, directly across the river from the dusty little Mexican town of Matamoros. The troops dubbed their little outpost Fort Texas and ran up the Stars and Stripes as a band played "The Star-Spangled Banner." Then they positioned their artillery to fire directly upon the town.

Across the river, some hundred yards away, was the Mexican army of General Francisco Mejia, three thousand strong and well fortified. Mejia had local civil authorities send Taylor a message warning war would ensue if he didn't withdraw his troops. The U.S. general, mindful his orders emphasized he was not to treat Mexican forces as enemies, sought to send a message to Mejia by hand of General William Worth. Mejia sent word he would speak only with Taylor, but he sent his artillery commander, Rómulo Díaz de la Vega, to meet with Worth on the west bank of the river.

It was a tense exchange. Both men—and both nations—accepted that this was disputed territory, but Polk felt justified in securing the sparsely populated lands, claimed by Texas from the beginning, until the matter could be resolved through negotiations. Mexican authorities, on the other hand, considered this an act of war. When Worth asked to see the American consul at Matamoros, he was refused.

"Has Mexico declared war against the United States?" asked Worth.
"No."
"Are the two countries still at peace?"
"Yes."

But it was a precarious peace, residing in the hands of these two armies and their commanders, far from their respective governments. On April 11, a famously sadistic and self-important Mexican general named Pedro de Ampudia arrived with an additional three thousand troops. He promptly initiated plans to attack Taylor's force. First he sent a message: "I require you . . . to break up your camp and return to the east bank of the Nueces River while our Governments are regulating the pending question in relation to Texas." If he refused, added Ampudia, "arms, and arms alone, must decide the question." Taylor responded: "I regret the alternative which you offer; but, at the same time, wish it understood that I shall by no means avoid such alternative."

Taylor, viewing Ampudia's ultimatum as an act of war, responded by blockading the mouth of the Rio Grande. This cut off all supplies to the six thousand Mexican troops around Matamoros—and forced the Mexican generals to break the delicate status quo. As Taylor expressed it, "It will . . . *compel* the Mexicans either to withdraw their army from Matamoros, where it cannot be subsisted, or to assume the offensive on this side of the river." Already two popular U.S. officers had been killed on the disputed side. First, Colonel Truman Cross disappeared during a routine horseback ride. Then, some days later, a search party under Lieutenant David Porter, on a mission to find Cross, came under attack. Porter was killed. Shortly thereafter, Cross's body was found.

Tensions ran high on both sides of the river when yet another Mexican general arrived with orders to take command of his country's forces at Matamoros and drive Taylor's army from the Rio Grande Valley. This was the highly regarded Mariano Arista, forty-three, with sandy hair and freckled face. To test Taylor's resolve, Arista on April 25 sent some 1,600 cavalrymen across the river a few miles north of the U.S. general's army. The next day Taylor sent an interdiction force of sixty-three dragoons under Captain Seth Thornton. The superior Mexican force ambushed the U.S. patrol, killed eleven soldiers, wounded six, and captured the rest, including Thornton. Instantly, the tense Rio Grande face-off had escalated to war, with Taylor's seriously outnumbered troops in a precarious position.

But it was merely an unofficial war in a far-off frontier while word of the spilled blood made its way to the respective capitals. In the meantime James Polk was pondering how to get his country into the war he long since had concluded was necessary to his territorial aims. On Friday morning, May 8, he spent an hour with Slidell, freshly returned from his failed Mexican mission. The envoy said the United States had only one course of action now—"to take the redress of the wrongs and injuries" suffered at the instigation of Mexico "and to act with promptness and energy." Polk agreed and said he would be sending a tough communication to Congress soon.

The next day, at the regular cabinet session, there was consensus that any Mexican act of hostility against Taylor's forces should prompt an immediate war message to Congress. Polk reminded his cabinet that the country already had "ample cause of war." He propounded it his duty to send a message to Congress recommending "definitive measures." The country, he said, was "excited and impatient on the subject," and failure to act would constitute a dereliction of duty.

He then went around the room seeking the opinions of his men. All supported the message except Bancroft, who said he preferred they wait for an actual act of hostility. Buchanan, in a rare display of cooperation, agreed the country had sufficient cause for war. The cabinet resolved to devote its Tuesday meeting to final editing on a message to Congress, much of which already had been drafted at Polk's direction. The meeting broke up around two o'clock.

Four hours later the army's adjutant general, Roger Jones, delivered to the White House the latest dispatches from Taylor, just arrived with the southern mail. Thus did Polk learn the fate of Thornton's mission and the outbreak of hostilities on the Rio Grande. Before he could finish reading the dispatches, Marcy rushed in with the same news. Polk said he was calling an emergency cabinet meeting for seven-thirty that night.

Small of stature and drab of temperament, James Polk was often underestimated by Whig opponents and sometimes by his own Democratic allies, despite his early political accomplishments in Congress. He struck many as a smaller-than-life figure with larger-than-life ambitions. But he harbored an absolute conviction that he was a man of destiny, and his unremitting tenacity ultimately produced a successful presidency.

James Polk, as a young congressman, loyally served the political interests of his great mentor and father figure, Andrew Jackson. Jackson in turn fostered Polk's rise to Ways and Means chairman, to House speaker, and later to Tennessee governor.

This cabin in North Carolina, designed as a replica of Polk's birthplace, stands on the location of his birth. At that time Polk's father was in a period of economic transition before moving to Tennessee, where he amassed considerable wealth as land speculator and planter.

4

5

Polk, who idolized Jackson and never deviated from his political creed, hung Sully's famous Jackson portrait (*top*) in his White House office. "The contrast between your appearance now and then is very great," he wrote to his mentor. By then Jackson was descending toward death, as captured by this photograph (*bottom*) taken at his beloved Hermitage. "I thank my god that the Republic is safe," Jackson wrote upon hearing of Polk's presidential election, "& that he had permitted me to live to see it." He died barely three months into Polk's presidency.

6

7

8

Among Polk's presidential predecessors, probably his most bitter rival was John Quincy Adams (*top left*), defeated for reelection by Jackson in 1828. Later, as an elder statesman in the House, Adams greeted Polk's presidential victory with near despair. New York's Martin Van Buren (*top right*), like Polk a Jackson protégé, succeeded his mentor but lost the presidency four years later during the Panic of 1837. He hungered for a White House return in 1844, but his opposition to Texas annexation prompted Jackson to abandon him in favor of Polk. Virginia's John Tyler (*left*), who succeeded to the White House upon the death of President William Henry Harrison, set in motion the events leading to Texas annexation. His primary motivation was a hope that the issue could help him retain the White House in his own right.

Speech bubble (Polk): *We've got up so far that the water grows shallow. I think I could get out & wade now.*

Label: *Polk.*

Speech bubble (Van Buren): *I never sailed so far up this river before. We must be near the head of navigation.*

Speech bubble (Benton): *By the eternal! Polk don't give up the ship.*

Labels: *Van Buren. Benton. Dallas Jackson*

Boat/steamer: **STEAMER BALLOT BOX**

POLK & Cº GOING UP SALT RIVER.

The opposition Whigs anticipated a Polk defeat in 1844, as reflected in this cartoon showing prominent Democratic politicians going up "salt river" and running aground. Polk seems resigned to defeat, but Jackson characteristically implores him to keep fighting. In the end, Polk and his running mate, George Dallas of Pennsylvania, won the election narrowly against Henry Clay.

Sarah Polk was her husband's only true confidante. "None but Sarah," the president once wrote, "knew so intimately my private affairs." Her enveloping warmth was viewed by many as an antidote to her husband's stiff demeanor.

The pressures of the presidency took a severe toll on Polk's health and appearance, as reflected in the contrast between the photograph with Sarah above and this earlier likeness. Elected president at age forty-nine, he soon looked older than his years and suffered from multiple persistent ailments.

This 1848 photo of Polk's cabinet was the first photograph taken in the White House. Seated, left to right: Navy Secretary John Y. Mason, War Secretary William L. Marcy, President Polk, and Treasury Secretary Robert J. Walker; standing, Postmaster General Cave Johnson and Attorney General Isaac Toucey. (Missing: Secretary of State James Buchanan.)

Secretary of State Buchanan displayed an erratic temperament and proclivity to stir things up for sport. Buchanan's advice to Polk seemed always filtered through his overweening presidential ambition. The president chafed at the secretary's transparent maneuverings but couldn't bring himself to fire the man.

Among Polk's opponents, none loomed larger than Henry Clay of Kentucky (*top left*), one of the greatest legislators of the nineteenth century and founder of the Whig party. But his brand of politics was not as popular as the Jackson-Polk outlook, and the Kentuckian fell to both men in two of his three White House bids. South Carolina's Senator John C. Calhoun (*top right*) was brilliant and erratic, mesmerizing and polarizing. Polk never knew when the South Carolinian would offer support for his policies (tepid at best) or attack them with a vengeance. Missouri's Senator Thomas Hart Benton (*left*), a big man with powerful whims and a prodigious intellect, offered Polk abundant counsel and support during his early presidency but then turned against the president with a withering brutality.

As a freshman congressman in 1846, David Wilmot of Pennsylvania transformed American politics with his famous proviso, designed to bar slavery from lands acquired through a peace treaty with Mexico. The proviso turned the war debate into a slavery debate and set in motion the forces that would lead to the Civil War.

A rich and erudite empire builder from Michigan, Lewis Cass served his country as Ohio legislator, Indian fighter, army general, Michigan's territorial governor, secretary of war, and minister to France. As a senator during Polk's presidency, he was a powerful presidential ally. Polk secretly favored Cass as his successor.

Polk and his fellow expansionists crushed the Whigs on the Texas annexation issue, as demonstrated in this cartoon showing the inevitable outcome of statehood leaving Whig opponents scrambling to avoid catastrophe. Polk welcomes the Texas "ship," while the two Texans aboard evince varying degrees of enthusiasm.

Old Hickory's namesake and nephew, Andrew Jackson Donelson, was raised by Andrew and Rachel Jackson and later served as his uncle's military aide de camp and White House secretary. He played a key role in Texas annexation as U.S. minister to the Republic of Texas.

Two of Polk's generals hated each other with an intensity that seriously disrupted the U.S. military command in Mexico. The bombastic and prickly Winfield Scott (*top*) was Polk's antithesis in temperament and outlook, but he was the only available man to lead the president's war effort in the field. His battlefield brilliance led Britain's Duke of Wellington to call him "the greatest living soldier." Gideon Pillow (*bottom*), a close Polk confidant, leveraged his relationship with the president to undermine Scott. This enraged Scott and led to a Pillow court martial, but Scott himself ultimately faced a court martial as well.

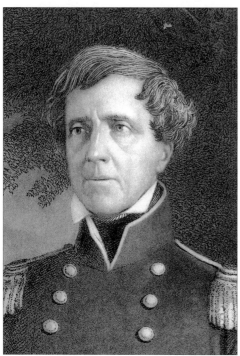

America's "war in the West" featured three men of destiny seeking glory for their country and themselves. Stephen Kearny (*top left*) by temperament probably the army's finest high-ranking officer, conquered New Mexico without firing a shot, then headed west to help with the California campaign then being led by the western explorer John C. Frémont (*top right*) and naval Commodore Robert Stockton (*left*). Frémont, Thomas Hart Benton's son-in-law, refused to submit to Kearny's superior rank and found himself facing a court martial. Stockton, known for his audacity and dash, previously had sought to foster a war between Texas and Mexico so America could swoop down and grab Mexican territory.

Known as "Old Fuss and Feathers" for his love of elaborate military regalia and ritual, General Winfield Scott is shown here reviewing his troops in Mexico during the war. Scott landed an army at Veracruz and marched to Mexico City, winning every battle he fought along the way.

Antonio López de Santa Anna managed to insert himself into nearly every military and political development of his country over twenty-five years. From his Cuban exile, he snookered Polk into believing he would negotiate a peace settlement if allowed back into Mexico. Polk let him through the U.S. blockade, but Santa Anna promptly turned belligerent.

GENERAL D. ANTONIO LÓPEZ DE SANTA-ANNA

Scott's officers, contemplating the invasion of Mexico City, urged the general to attack from the south and avoid the fortified castle of Chapultepec to the west of the city. Scott rejected their advice and sent his troops directly against the castle, which proved more vulnerable than anticipated. Scott took the castle and the city.

Nicholas Trist was probably the only American diplomat ever to negotiate a peace treaty with a foreign nation after being stripped of his diplomatic portfolio. The headstrong Trist justified his unauthorized actions with a view that Polk's wrongheaded policies had to be circumvented. Though livid, Polk sent the treaty to the Senate for ratification.

30

General Zachary Taylor defeated Santa Anna decisively at Buena Vista, in the Mexican heartland, but Polk faulted Taylor for violating orders to keep his army dug in at Monterrey, away from military action that served no strategic purpose. The American people, however, were thrilled with the victory.

Taylor's military victories brought him immense national popularity and led the Whigs to embrace him as their presidential candidate. Polk considered the stolid and unimaginative Taylor to be "exceedingly ignorant of public affairs, and . . . of very ordinary capacity." Nevertheless, Taylor succeeded Polk as president.

Upon taking office in 1845 (with a promise to serve a single term), President Polk vowed privately to achieve four major political accomplishments: acquire California from Mexico; acquire Oregon territory from Britain; reduce tariff rates; and create an "independent treasury" to ensure currency stability. He achieved all four, then retired to his home state of Tennessee, where he died less than four months after leaving office.

The cabinet members gathered in Polk's study with solemn faces. They agreed unanimously, and without debate, that Polk must send a message to Congress on Monday reporting on the new developments—"recommending vigorous & prompt measure[s] to enable the Executive to prosecute the War," as Polk put it to his diary. Clerks were called in to help with the drafting and editing. Instructions were issued to collect the administration's official correspondence with Slidell and Taylor. Members of Congress—"greatly excited at the news," as Polk described them to his diary—arrived to discuss the dramatic development. The cabinet adjourned at ten o'clock, and Polk immediately began work on his message, with Bancroft and Buchanan remaining to help.

The president rose early the next morning to resume the effort and stayed with it through most of the day, breaking only to attend church with Sarah. Once the draft was in final form he turned his attention to discussions with key members of Congress. At five o'clock he conferred with Representative Hugh Haralson of Georgia, chairman of the House Military Affairs Committee, and Illinois congressman Edward Baker. Later he called for William Allen, Texas senator Sam Houston, Congressman Joseph Ingersoll, House Ways and Means Committee chairman James McKay of North Carolina, and Congressman Barclay Martin of Tennessee. All either read the message or had it read to them. All approved. Haralson said his committee had met in emergency session that morning and unanimously supported legislation appropriating $10 million to prosecute the looming war and authorizing the president to raise fifty thousand troops.

The next morning Polk called for Cass and Benton. The message was read to Cass, who "highly approved it." Benton was another matter. After reading the document to himself in a quiet anteroom, he returned to express serious misgivings. He could support men and money to defend U.S. territory, he said, but not to wage aggressive war against Mexico. He added he had opposed from the beginning Polk's order to send his army to the Rio Grande but had never said so publicly out of respect to the president. He suggested Texas territory didn't extend beyond the Nueces River.

This was an ominous development. After wooing Benton and soliciting his support for more than a year, Polk now found the maverick senator opposing him on the most important issue of his presidency. Worse, he could see prospects for precisely the congressional alliance he had been working most intently to prevent—between Benton and Calhoun, those two powerful and irascible titans of the Senate.

The message, sent to Capitol Hill at noon, was brilliantly crafted to leverage the death of American troops for maximum political effect. Recounting the events surrounding the Slidell mission, Polk said the envoy was rejected "upon the most frivolous pretexts." Slidell had been invested with full diplomatic powers, the president explained, because the reparations issue had become "inseparably blended" with the territorial dispute. "I could not for a moment entertain the idea that the claims of our much-injured and long-suffering citizens . . . should be postponed or separated from the settlement of the boundary question."

Polk recounted all the reasons for contending that Texas included the disputed lands west of the Nueces—Texas had declared it so from the beginning; it had been part of the annexation process; it currently had representation in the U.S. Congress; Congress had declared it part of Texas, and the U.S. government had sent a revenue officer there. "It became, therefore, of urgent necessity to provide for the defense of that portion of our country." Hence his decision to send Taylor's army to the Rio Grande. But, said Polk, the army had been "under positive instructions to abstain from all aggressive acts . . . and to regard the relations between that Republic and the United States as peaceful unless she should declare war or commit acts of hostility indicative of a state of war."

The Mexican forces at Matamoros, said Polk, "assumed a belligerent attitude" from the beginning, resulting in the April 26 attack on Thornton's unit on the east side of the Rio Grande. The president concluded:

The cup of forbearance had been exhausted even before the recent information from the frontier of the Del Norte. But now, after reiterated menaces, Mexico has passed the boundary of the United States, has invaded our territory and shed American blood upon the American soil. She has proclaimed that hostilities have commenced, and that the two nations are now at war.

As war exists, and, notwithstanding all our efforts to avoid it, exists by the act of Mexico herself, we are called upon by every consideration of duty and patriotism to vindicate with decision the honor, the rights, and the interests of our country.

Polk asked Congress to recognize the existence of war and give him the authority and resources necessary to wage it with such vigor as to bring "the existing collision with Mexico to a speedy and successful termination."

THE DEMOCRATIC-CONTROLLED HOUSE took up the matter Monday afternoon under procedures designed to sweep any dissidents along with the majority. The leadership allotted just two hours of debate, much of it devoted to reading Polk's message and accompanying documents. Then the House took up the bill from Haralson's committee authorizing the president to call up fifty thousand volunteers and expend $10 million to prosecute the war.

Jacob Brinkerhoff of Ohio, a member of Military Affairs, offered an amendment attaching a preamble that declared "by the act of the republic of Mexico, a state of war exists between the United States and that republic." He said the initial committee bill was deficient in that it failed to acknowledge the existence of war and confined the U.S. response to defensive actions. He could not support merely a defensive war: "It will be expensive; it will be vexatious; it will be disastrous; it will be long continued; it will have no end; it will enable the enemy to choose his point of attack." No, said Brinkerhoff, the country needed to fight the war "in such manner that our enemy shall be at once crushed—such a war as should fully, instantly, at once bring them to our feet, and compel an honorable peace."

As majority Democrats tinkered with the language of the amend-

ment, antiwar Whigs and Calhounites could see the debate had been
transformed by Brinkerhoff's amendment. Now, if they voted for the
resources needed to support Taylor in his imperiled frontier position,
they also would be voting for Polk's version of events leading up to
that necessity. Many recoiled at that prospect since they didn't buy
the Polk rendition.

"Have the powers of Mexico declared war?" asked Elias Holmes,
a Whig from New York. "If they have there is war, and you need
not respond but at the cannon's mouth. But the point is this: We
know nothing more than that the two armies have come into collision
within the disputed territory, and I deny that war is absolutely, necessarily, the result of it." He said his colleagues needed both action and
reflection—action in sending troops to support Taylor and reflection
on how all this came to pass. Garrett Davis, who represented Henry
Clay's old district in Kentucky, was more blunt. "The river Nueces is
the true western boundary of Texas," he declared. "It is our own President who began this war."

But, as Polk had anticipated, the nation's blood was up, and an
opposition vote struck most members as highly dangerous to their
careers. Besides, a nay vote meant leaving Taylor exposed on the Texas
frontier. After brushing aside efforts to delete or dilute the preamble,
the House embraced the resolution 173 to 14. Even Garrett Davis
joined the majority.

The Senate's heritage as Congress's more deliberative body raised
hopes in opposition forces that the upper chamber might halt or slow
the rush to war. And the man to do it, if it could be done, was John
C. Calhoun, whose famous polemical force mixed powerfully with his
consistent aversion to war. He did not shrink from the challenge. The
very language of the resolution, he argued, raised serious constitutional questions because it declared a state of war based on the president's say-so.

"There may be invasion without war," he declared, "and the President is authorized to repel invasion without war. But it is *our* sacred
duty to make war, and it is for *us* to determine whether war shall be
declared or not. If we have declared war, a state of war exists, and not

till then." He urged his colleagues to give the matter "that high, full, and dispassionate consideration which is worthy of the character of the body and the high constitutional functions which it is called on to exercise."

Delaware's John Clayton, like Holmes in the House, raised a distinction between Congress's responsibility to assess events leading to hostilities and its need to support Taylor's troops. "I will not undertake to decide, in the first instance, whether it was right or not," he said. "But I go for the soldiers, and the millions at once to support the honor of the country and the army."

Then Thomas Hart Benton rose in the well of the chamber to bring to the matter his considerable bulk, acknowledged stature, and capacity for reasoned discourse. Yes, he said, there were two distinct questions before the body, and each required a different form of action. The first was the president's right and responsibility to repel invasion, which was a military matter and "proper for the action of the Military Committee," of which he happened to be chairman. But the rest concerned the country's foreign policy and hence should go to Allen's Foreign Relations Committee.

It was a master stroke—separating the two questions Polk had wanted to keep as one and doing so with the least prospect for raising political hackles. Allen, whose role would be enhanced, instantly pronounced Benton's idea "very proper," and Cass rose to praise Delaware's Clayton for his balanced view. "He goes for the country first, and then intends to ask who brought the country into this position," said Cass. "That is a very fair course." Calhoun leaped to concurrence. "Now I hope," he said, "that there will not be the slightest difference of opinion, but the utmost unanimity and promptitude of action in repelling invasion."

But war issue emotions were too raw for complete civility. And, while senators generally praised the issue split, some couldn't forbear from expressing themselves on the question of responsibility. Ambrose Sevier of Arkansas said he welcomed the eventual reckoning on that question. "The Executive," he declared, "has done precisely what the national interests required, and what the constitution and laws justified." Clayton vehemently disagreed. "If the acts of the Executive do not amount to acts of war," he argued, "they are acts which necessarily tend to provoke war, and to bring on war." Therefore, he added, "I condemn the conduct of the Executive."

That prompted Allen to plead for restraint from Polk's critics. It was "extremely unjust towards the President," he argued, to denounce him at this early stage "by charging errors on the government, and accusing it of being the aggressor, before there is time to examine the state of the case." It was, he added, "a very bad beginning" that threatened to undermine the entire war effort. They all agreed on the necessity of sending help to Taylor, he said, so they should concentrate their thoughts and arguments on that for the present.

There was little point in further debate, as the measure had been split in its assignment to two committees, and the Senate turned to routine business in anticipation of two separate debates over the next several days. For Polk this was a looming disaster, rendered all the more ominous by the prospect of a Benton-Calhoun opposition alliance. That evening Benton arrived for a candid discussion with Polk, Buchanan, and Marcy, and despite their earnest entreaties he seemed implacable on the issue. Afterward, wrote Polk to his diary, "Mr. Buchanan, Mr. Marcy, and myself were perfectly satisfied that he would oppose the Bill . . . and that if the Whigs on party grounds acted with him the Bill might be defeated." It could only be saved, he concluded, by "the fear of the people by the few Democratic Senators who wish it defeated."

Polk moved to action as the evening waned. He got some of the Senate's Van Burenites, including New York's John Dix, to warn Benton that a vote against the resolution would harm him politically, perhaps irreparably. No dice. Then Dix, "in distress," sought help from Francis Blair out at his Silver Spring mansion. The retired newspaperman rushed to Washington early the next morning to reason with the stubborn Missourian. He expressed surprise that Benton would make common cause with his despised rival Calhoun and emphasized the political reality that opposition to the war would render him "a ruined man."

"I see *you are right*," declared Benton finally, and then joined forces with Allen to have their respective committees report out the House bill. The opposition was stunned at this reversal of fortune, with the measure now on the floor for a brief debate and quick action. Political angers flowed copiously on the Senate floor that afternoon.

Mangum of North Carolina set the tone with an impassioned speech declaring himself "unwilling to pass the bill in its present form, because the fact is not to be disguised that it is to all intents and purposes equivalent to a solemn declaration of war. I am not prepared for that. But I am fully prepared this day—this very moment—if the political question be separated from the bill—to vote for the raising of supplies."

Calhoun pleaded with his colleagues to split off the preamble for a later debate so the chamber could quickly and unanimously vote for the supplies. "Mr. President," said he, "it is as impossible for me to vote for that preamble in the present state of my information as it would be for me to strike a dagger to my own heart." Declaring he would withhold his vote from the measure altogether, he added:

> I know not whether there is a friend to stand by me. . . . But here I stand, and stand immovably. . . . If I could not stand here on a question of truth and veracity, I should be little worthy of the small degree of respect which I am desirous to retain. I cannot vote for this bill without further information, because I will not agree to make war upon Mexico by making war upon the constitution. . . . As the facts now stand, there is no hostility—no conflict but that between the two armies on the Rio del Norte; and yet you affirm . . . that mere local conflict, not authorized by either government, is a state of war! that every American is an enemy of every Mexican! . . . The doctrine is monstrous.

Cass countered that the mere effort to repel an invasion was folly because it placed the U.S. military in a defensive posture that was ultimately untenable militarily. "A Mexican army is upon our soil," he said, adding:

Are we to confine our efforts to repelling them? Are we to drive them to the border, and then stop our pursuit, and allow them to find a refuge in their own territory? And what then? To collect again to cross our frontier at some other point, and again to renew the same scenes, to be followed by a similar immunity? What sort of a condition of things would this be, sir? The advantage would be altogether on the side of the Mexicans, while the loss would be altogether ours. . . . Now, sir, no vote of mine shall place my country in this situation.

Cass dismissed Calhoun's suggestion that the Mexican government had not sanctioned the spilling of American blood at the Rio Grande. After all, he noted, Mexican officials had been threatening war in word and deed since the first stirrings of the latest annexation effort. They called annexation a casus belli. They withdrew their minister and broke off diplomatic relations. They refused to receive our minister or negotiate points of disagreement. They collected an army upon the U.S. frontier. Their military threatened war if Taylor didn't retreat from what the United States considered sovereign land. That military then commenced the war by killing Americans on the disputed land. "Now, sir, I appeal to every senator on the other side of the chamber, if he does not believe that all this has been done by order of the Mexican government."

Slowly it became clear to opposition senators that they had little maneuver room. Democrat James Westcott of Florida said he had been prepared to vote against the measure on Monday, but "calm and cool reflection" had changed his mind. This was no time for verbal criticism, he said, but rather for "prompt, decisive action." Even die-hard Whigs now expressed themselves in measured terms, knowing they were talking about a bill they eventually would have to vote for.

Crittenden of Kentucky, conceding he didn't have all the facts in the case, nonetheless criticized the president's decision to send his army to the Rio Grande—"for the hazarding of those consequences which every sensible man must have foreseen." It was impossible to imagine, he said, "that the angry armies of two angry and quarrelling nations should day after day face each other with cannons pointed at each other, and only a fordable river between them, and conflict not result." Sure, it was disputed territory, said Crittenden, but what right did that give the United States to occupy it before the matter had been resolved? He added, though, that he would not press that view at present in deference to the need to pass the bill so Taylor could get his reinforcements.

At six-thirty, after numerous peace amendments had been voted down, the final roll call commenced. Vice President Dallas, surveying the scene from his perch as Senate president, felt the Whigs "almost got on their knees to beg to be spared from voting on the preamble." But the Democrats had no intention of softening their tough stance. Only John Davis of Massachusetts and Delaware's Clayton hazarded nay votes, while two Whigs responded, "Aye, except for the preamble." As promised, Calhoun declined to answer the roll call; he was joined by two Whigs. The final tally was 40 to 2. And so James Polk now had his war.

The congressional action loomed as a testament to Polk's manifold political talents—his steady nerve, operational stealth, ability to assess political sentiment, readiness to take risks, willingness to crush the opposition. But, as Polk set about the monumental task of prosecuting his war, a legacy of bitterness was left behind that masked the lopsided votes in the two congressional chambers. As long as the conflict was successful and retained voter support, that bitterness remained a small matter in the political firmament. But, should the war effort turn sour or appear hopeless, that legacy would rise up to threaten the very foundation of Polk's presidency.

In the meantime, as the president had foreseen, the country rallied enthusiastically to the cause. In part this was a natural surge of patriotism brought on by reports of spilled American blood and longtime frustration with the struggling Mexican nation. But in part also it was attributable to that impulse of expansionism that had been driving American politics for the past two years. This was crystallized by a leading officer of a liberal organization called the American Union of Associationists, devoted to salving the social wounds brought on by industrialization. "The questions of war and slavery," declared Parke Godwin in opposing an antiwar resolution within his organization, "are only incidental ones, which can easily be put aside, but the question of extending *constitutional republican institutions* over this whole continent is one of the broadest, noblest and most important that was ever presented to any nation."

16 · VAGARIES OF WAR

"And May There Be No Recreant Soul to Fail or Falter Now"

O F ALL THE powerful officials in the U.S. government at the dawn of the Mexican War, probably no two men were more different or naturally antagonistic than the nation's commander-in-chief and his top army general, Winfield Scott. To Polk's slight physical stature, Scott presented a towering bulk of six feet five inches. To Polk's reserved and suspicious manner, Scott presented human magnetism and a kind of in-your-face bluster. In contrast to Polk's inclination to absorb slights and avoid confrontation, Scott demonstrated an impetuous haste to hostility whenever he felt insulted, which could be easily triggered. To Polk's Presbyterian resolve to keep his ego in check, Scott manifested a lavish vanity probably unequaled in governmental circles.

Beyond the catalytic chemistry of temperament was a history of mutual distrust, brought on in part by Scott's feuds with Andrew Jackson that nearly led, in one instance, to a duel. Besides, Scott was a Whig, and the president didn't trust Whigs—particularly those positioned to affect the success or glory of his administration.

For three decades Scott had basked in his status as one of the nation's most illustrious military men. Born in Virginia in 1786 into a declining landed family, he was orphaned at seventeen and forced to make his way without inherited advantage. He set his sights on a legal career, but growing hostilities with Britain lured him into the Regular U.S. Army. Intensely ambitious, he maneuvered relentlessly for promotion and rose quickly to lieutenant colonel at the start of the War of 1812.

There followed an extraordinary career marked by signal battlefield actions, uncommon bravery, social success—and a tendency to let his personal flaws undercut his professional standing. Even before the 1812 war his career was nearly upended by his verbal attacks on a superior officer named James Wilkinson. He called the man a traitor, a "liar and a scoundrel," and vowed to "blow up General Wilkinson" when the opportunity arose. He was court-martialed, convicted of "unofficer-like conduct," and sentenced to a year of suspension without pay.

Like Jackson, he manifested a tendency toward insubordination when superiors failed to earn his respect. This was attributable in part to his vanity, which seemed to surge whenever he donned his officer's uniform. Indeed, when he first obtained the raiment, he was so taken with it that he cleared out the furniture of his largest room, placed two mirrors at diagonal corners, and strutted back and forth for two hours of self-indulgent preening. If anyone had seen him, he quipped years later, the embarrassment would have forced him to kill the person.

He developed a reputation as an exacting commander who put his troops through arduous training while he marched about in his gaudy uniforms—hence his eventual nickname: "Old Fuss and Feathers." In his first battle in the War of 1812, he was captured by the British but later released. He broke his collarbone at the Battle of Fort George, took a bullet to the shoulder at Lundy's Lane, and emerged from the war a hero and brigadier general—at twenty-seven the youngest army general at the time. Later exploits in various Indian wars and political deftness in Washington contributed to his military rise, leading in 1841 to his appointment as the army's general-in-chief.

Intellectually ambitious, he read constantly, developed an impressive expertise in military history and tactics, mastered French, and kept up on the latest developments in the law. But his vanity and its attendant traits never remained in check for long. "The chief ruling passion of the general," wrote a junior officer who served under him, "was ambition and its uniform attendant, jealousy."

Now, with war declared, the fifty-nine-year-old warrior found himself positioned for even more glory, perhaps enough to carry him into the White House. All he had to do was ensure his personal traits didn't get in the way of his military brilliance.

AS NEWS OF the Mexican War spread across America, the nation rallied to the cause. "The general fact is well known," said the *Union*, "that the whole country is roused to the most earnest and vigorous action." In the Senate, Pennsylvania's Simon Cameron told of a mass meeting in Philadelphia that drew twenty thousand citizens "of all parties [who] had forgotten their political predilections, and come together to sustain the country in its emergency." Representative Seaborn Jones of Georgia speculated on the House floor that, had Polk refrained from protecting the Texas frontier, "one general burst of indignation would have risen against him. . . . He would have been called a poor craven wretch."

The *Union* ran a poem from a Washington writer labeled "E.M.H.":

WAR!

Ho! Ho!—fling out our starry flag unto the sunny sky!—
Let sound the bugle and the drum with stirring notes and
high!—
Grasp now the slumbering musket, and harness on the sword
And stand erect and ready, for our Country's voice is heard!

· · · · · · · · · · · · · · · ·

The Mexican hath pressed our soil—his hand hath shed the
blood
Of brave and gallant bosoms—and, fiend-like, he hath stood,
Gloating with all murderer's joy, as his poor victims lay
Unburied on the desert shore—the loathsome vulture's prey!

· · · · · · · · · · · · · · · ·

Then, ho!—shout out the battle-cry!—draw forth the glitter-
ing brand!
And from the soil of freemen expel the invading band!—
Our cause is just and righteous—meet with dauntler's brow—
And may there be no recreant soul to fail or falter now!

But the Polk opposition quickly crafted a counter-legend. The war, declared Representative Columbus Delano, a Whig from Ohio, was a "presidential war—a war commenced by the President in an unconstitutional manner and by illegal means." With that sentence Delano crystallized the Whig position. Slowly the argument expanded to include the allegation that Polk had perpetrated his war solely to cadge southwestern territory from the hapless Mexicans.

Ritchie's *Union* vectored in on the soft underbelly of the Whigs' argument—"That is, if Congress would, by its silence, admit our war was *aggressive and indefensible,* THEN the Whigs would cheerfully vote the men and money to fight it out!" For the moment, in the patriotic fervor that gripped the land, the Democratic outlook prevailed. But everyone knew that would continue only with success on the battlefield. And Polk knew military success required unity within his inner circle and among Hill Democrats. Within his inner circle, that unity appeared tenuous. The reason was two outsized personalities—Buchanan and Scott.

The Buchanan problem emerged immediately. On May 13, 1846, the secretary brought to the cabinet a draft dispatch for U.S. ministers at London, Paris, and other foreign courts, outlining what they should tell those host governments. They should say, said the dispatch, the United States had no intention of acquiring Mexican territory in the war. This was a remarkable bit of mischief, perpetrated in full knowledge of Polk's oft-stated goal of acquiring California, New Mexico, and perhaps other Mexican lands. Polk brushed aside the proposed language as "unnecessary and improper" and said his own statements to Congress offered sufficient guidance to U.S. envoys.

"Then you will have war with England as well as Mexico," retorted Buchanan, "and probably with France also, for neither of these powers will ever stand bye and [see] California annexed to the U.S."

Polk, agitated, said he would wage that war with England and France "or all the Powers of Christendom" and would "stand and fight until the last man among us fell in the conflict." Neither as a citizen nor president, he added, would he "permit or tolerate any intermeddling of any European Power on this continent."

Treasury Secretary Walker attacked Buchanan's arguments with considerable heat, and Bancroft, Mason, and Johnson all opposed the secretary. Buchanan refused to yield until Polk stepped to his desk, wrote out a substitute draft, and handed it to Buchanan. Then the secretary wordlessly picked up his papers and left the room.

As for Scott, Polk's wartime relations with the general began amicably enough. When the two met on May 13, along with Army Secretary Marcy, the president offered Scott the position of commander of U.S. troops in the field. The general avidly accepted.

The next evening the three met again and agreed the primary strategy would be to capture northern Mexico and hold it until a peace could be negotiated. They also agreed to call up for immediate service some twenty thousand volunteers, largely from southern and western states. Afterward, Polk couldn't prevent his dislike for the general from seeping into his thinking. "Gen'l Scott did not impress me favourably as a military man," he wrote to his diary, adding the general seemed "rather scientific and visionary in his views." He felt Scott's insistence on recruiting twenty thousand volunteers went a bit beyond necessity but kept silent for fear of getting blamed should things go awry with fewer troops than requested.

Then a series of developments unfolded that soured relations between the two men. At the May 19 cabinet meeting, Polk noted rumors that Scott planned to remain in Washington until September. This was unacceptable, the president told Marcy, adding that Scott "must proceed very soon to his post" or Polk would "supersede him in the command." He urged Marcy to take charge and ensure his orders were obeyed.

For his part, Scott also was hearing disturbing rumors—that the president was working with Benton on legislation authorizing two new major generals and four new brigadier generals. Since Scott was the army's only major general, he quickly "smelt the rat"—an apparent plan to push him aside. His anger was heightened by hints the president might elevate Benton, thirty years out of military uniform, to major general, thus massaging the egotistical senator's conceit that his capacity for military heroism, if given sufficient rein, would round out his career and perhaps elevate him to the White House.

Scott confronted Marcy with these rumblings on the evening of May 20. The secretary promptly countered by revealing the president's displeasure with his timetable for getting to the Rio Grande. Upon hearing this, the impetuous general began a slow boil that erupted the next day in a letter to Marcy that manifested more rage than sense. At great length he catalogued the arduous labors attending his effort to get to the front, then added a passage dripping with self-pity:

> In the midst of these multitudinous and indispensable occupations I have learned from you that much impatience is already felt, perhaps in high quarters, that I have not already put myself in route for the Rio Grande; and now, with fourteen hours a day of preliminary work remaining on my hands for many days, I find myself compelled to stop that necessary work to guard myself against, perhaps, utter condemnation in the quarters alluded to. . . .
>
> Not an advantageous step can be taken in a forward march without the confidence that all is well behind. . . . I am, therefore, not a little alarmed, nay, crippled in my energies, by the knowledge of the impatience in question. . . . My explicit meaning is, that I do not desire to place myself in the most perilous of all positions—*a fire upon my rear from Washington, and the fire in front from the Mexicans.*

Before this remarkable outburst could reach the president, Polk happened upon another Scott letter sent privately to Virginia's Senator Archer. It accused the president of rejecting Whigs for all army officer positions in the West and reserving those slots for Democrats. Polk was outraged. The letter, he wrote to his diary, "proved to me that Gen'l Scott was not only hostile, but recklessly vindictive in his feelings towards my administration." In fact, Polk had taken steps to ensure the wartime officers' corps contained both Whigs and Democrats and rejected all Democratic entreaties that he reserve those slots for his own party members. Later, Polk got wind of efforts by Scott and others to kill his legislation to expand the army's contingent of generals. Polk considered this "highly censurable"—evidence that Scott and his allies would "throw every obstacle in the way of my prosecuting the Mexican War successfully."

When Polk later read Scott's letter to Marcy, he instantly concluded the general lacked the requisite stability and sense for the field command. He read the letter aloud at the next cabinet meeting and asked what should be done. Walker echoed Polk's private views, whereupon the president replied that, if he could find any other qualified officer, he would supersede Scott.

He found his officer that night when exciting news arrived from the Rio Grande that Zachary Taylor had scored two brilliant victories. After hostilities had broken out with the Thornton ambush, Taylor found himself in a dilemma. He had his army at Fort Texas without supplies, and he had his supply depot at Point Isabel, some twenty-five miles away, without an army to protect it. He marched the bulk of his troops back to his supply depot, secured its defense, then proceeded to march back to Fort Texas. On May 8, at a point called Palo Alto, he encountered Mexico's General Arista with a force that outnumbered his own by three to one. Taylor's army held firm and battled the superior Mexican force to a standoff. The Americans' newly designed artillery devastated the enemy. Only four American troops died, while forty-two were wounded. Arista lost five hundred soldiers, most of them killed at long range.

The next day Arista fell back some six miles and repositioned his army for a follow-up battle at what was known as the Resaca de la Palma. Taylor, in pursuit, sent a cavalry force to capture Arista's main artillery battery while his U.S. infantry overran the retreat routes back to the Rio Grande. The Mexicans faltered, then retreated, then turned and fled in panic. In the rush to safety, many soldiers drowned in the Rio Grande. Within forty-eight hours Taylor had eliminated any danger of a Mexican invasion and demonstrated superior American tactics and resolve. He lost thirty-four killed and 113 wounded during the two battles while capturing seven pieces of artillery, large caches of ammunition, and a hundred prisoners, including General Díaz de la

Vega. It was estimated the Mexicans lost 1,200 killed and wounded, while some three hundred drowned in the panic flight across the Rio Grande. That night Taylor sent a message to Washington: "Our victory has been complete."

Washington was elated, and so was Polk. The exhilarating victories not only affirmed the president's war policy but also expanded his range of options in the matter of Winfield Scott. On May 25, Polk called a special cabinet meeting to consider Marcy's draft reply to the general's remarkable letter. Everyone agreed it was an appropriate response, and Polk instructed Marcy to deliver it that day.

It was a masterpiece of pained condescension. After quoting Scott's letter at length, Marcy said it falsely alleged "most unworthy motives in the Executive government—of bad faith toward yourself—of a reckless disregard for the interests of the country—of a design to carry on a war against you while you are sent forth to carry on a war against the public enemy." Meanwhile, said Marcy, the volunteers rushing to serve would be arriving at the battlefront by June, and their brief enlistments could be over by the time Scott managed to show up under his proposed timetable. "Every consideration of economy and duty," wrote Marcy, "forebade that the troops should, if thus collected, be permitted to remain inactive, by reason of the absence of the general officer, who . . . was to direct their movements."

On what basis, asked Marcy, did Scott conclude the president wished to open fire upon his rear? "Had not the President, in a frank and friendly spirit, just intrusted you with a command on which the glory and interest of the country depended, to say nothing of the success of his own administration?" Since Scott clearly felt the president intended to place him in "the most perilous of all positions" for the purpose of doing him in, and since the general had adopted that fear "entirely without cause or even the shadow of justification," the president would be negligent "if he were to persist in his determination of imposing upon you the command of the army." Thus, concluded Marcy, Scott would remain in Washington; he would not command the troops in the field.

Scott wasted no time in responding with an almost desperate effort to get himself reinstated. But his ego and self-regard impaired his ability to hit an appropriate tone. He began: "Sir: Your letter of this date, received at about 6, p.m., as I sat down to take a hasty plate of soup, demands a prompt reply." He noted that Marcy had taken four days to craft a reply that accused him of official and perhaps personal disrespect to his commander-in-chief. And, if the president shared this view, said Scott, "I am placed under very high obligations to his magnanimity—may I not add, *to his kindness?*—in not placing me instantly in arrest, and before a general court-martial." Since no such arrest had taken place, he averred, he had to conclude Marcy's indictment was not shared by the president.

Then, dissecting the language of his letter, he expressed bewilderment that Marcy could possibly think he had directed his criticisms at the president, of all people. He had not said this impatience was manifest "in the highest quarters," after all, but rather "in high quarters"—by which he obviously meant not the president but Marcy himself and some members of Congress who were said to be grousing about Scott's timetable for action. "My letter was written, in part, to guard both the President and myself against such a result, which would have been fatal, not only to me, but perhaps . . . to the service of the country."

Having found himself in a hole, Scott dug furiously. When Marcy sent over a blistering reply in which he defended himself from the allegations that previously had seemed directed at the president but now were aimed at him, Scott responded with a combination of defensiveness and sycophancy. Seeking with great orotundity to explain his previous expressions and ingratiate himself with his superior, he urged reconsideration of the president's decision to keep him in Washington. Marcy sent back a terse reply saying Polk wasn't inclined to reverse his previous judgment. Polk already had sent to Congress a message nominating General Taylor for promotion to the brevet rank of major general. Taylor would be the president's man at the battlefront.

The Marcy–Scott letter exchange, which would be released to Congress and made public within a few weeks, would prove devastating to the ambitious general, whose presidential aspirations probably came a cropper over those words of easy ridicule—"a hasty plate of soup."

But Polk had more on his mind than relations with his cantankerous general-in-chief. As early as May 13 the president instructed Navy Secretary Bancroft to issue a brief order to Commodore Conner, whose Home Squadron had blockaded all Mexican ports in the Gulf. It read: "Commodore: If Santa Anna endeavors to enter the Mexican ports, you will allow him to pass freely." Clearly, Polk's visit with Santa Anna's friend Atocha was on his mind. Also on the 13th, Polk met with Benton to discuss plans for an invasion of California. Benton favored the idea, and the president began a series of cabinet discussions on the matter.

On May 26 the cabinet unanimously embraced a proposal to send an expedition immediately against Upper California if sufficient mounted regiments could be assembled and marched from Independence, Missouri, before winter set in. A few days later Polk made his move. He would place some thousand mounted volunteers, then mustered at Independence, under the command of Colonel Stephen Kearny, a dignified and resourceful officer whose exploits in the Far West had become legendary. Kearny would take Santa Fe and then, if deemed feasible, proceed toward California, perhaps with another contingent of dragoons that would be made available. Meanwhile, Polk would ponder the question whether he should send reinforcements by sea.

The president's war strategy was coming into focus. Taylor would capture enough territory in northern Mexico to force a settlement; in the meantime, the United States would conquer the Mexican lands Polk wished to obtain in that settlement, notably New Mexico and California, encompassing all of present-day California, Nevada, Arizona, and Utah; half of New Mexico; and segments of Kansas, Oklahoma, Colorado, and Wyoming (the other half of present-day New Mexico already had been acquired with Texas annexation). By capturing New Mexico and California, the reasoning went, he would enhance his bargaining clout at treaty time.

Polk, knowing such plans would raise hackles with the congressional opposition, carefully kept them secret. But the congressional opposition went after him anyway. On June 2 the House took up the bill to increase the number of generals, and Kentucky's Garrett Davis went on the attack. This action, declared the Whig politician, was "totally unnecessary" because the war would soon be over. Thus he could see but two motives behind it—first, to do in Scott and exclude him from command; and, secondly, to do in Taylor, who had proved his military competence and "ought to remain, no matter under what name he might be called."

This was pure partisan politics born of the Whigs' most pressing political imperative. They desperately needed a leader who could rally their forces and carry them into the White House. Henry Clay, though much loved, clearly wasn't that leader. Now the war was about to generate some military heroes, most likely Whigs, as most army generals were Whigs—notably Scott and Taylor. Whig politicians were painfully aware their party's only presidential victory had been at the behest of a military hero—William Henry Harrison in 1840. So this looked promising—unless Polk managed to replace Scott and Taylor with Democratic generals. They couldn't allow that. Though the measure passed the Senate, the House sliced the bill to authorize only one additional major general and two brigadiers. Thus, unless Polk was willing to take the political heat that would ensue if he fired Scott or Taylor, they would remain his top military command for the war.

WITH ALL THE activity surrounding Mexico, it might have been easy to forget Oregon. But the British didn't forget. On June 3, Polk received a dispatch from Ambassador McLane at London saying Pakenham shortly would present to Buchanan a British proposal for settling the nettlesome diplomatic issue. McLane's description of the proposal was sketchy, but Polk immediately concluded he probably couldn't accept it. He pondered his options. If he declined to send it to the Senate for prior advice and declined to offer a counterproposal, "the probable result will be war." If he submitted it to the Senate and the chamber recommended acceptance, which was likely, he then would have to accept that judgment, however reluctantly. Polk called a special cabinet meeting for the next day.

The cabinet first pondered the probable terms. It seemed the British would accept a boundary line at the 49th parallel from the Rocky Mountains to the Strait of Juan de Fuca, then through the strait so Vancouver Island would remain entirely British. The strait itself would be considered open sea to both nations, and British subjects holding farms and lands between the Columbia River and the 49th parallel would be granted title to their property. Free navigation rights to the Columbia would be granted not to British subjects generally but only to the Hudson's Bay Company and those trading with it.

The sticking point was the Columbia navigation rights. But Buchanan noted the Hudson's Bay Company charter in the territory ran only to 1859, and hence those rights could be construed as expiring in that year. That put a new construction on the matter, and the cabinet coalesced around the view that the proposal should be submitted to the Senate.

Two days later the cabinet returned to the subject, this time with Pakenham's actual language, which matched McLane's previous report. One by one, Polk's men expressed satisfaction with the terms and urged it be submitted. Then Buchanan posited a different view. He said the 54-40 men were the true friends of the administration, and he didn't think Polk should back out of his previous claim to that boundary.

Buchanan's cabinet colleagues were stunned. Here was the cabinet's premier Oregon dove, the man who had been wringing his hands for months over the prospect of war over Oregon and pleading for concessions, now urging a course almost certain to generate war—at a time when the nation already was fighting a war. Polk "felt excited at the remark" but sought to hide his indignation. Walker made no such effort. He began a verbal attack on Buchanan that Polk felt obliged to cut off lest the meeting erupt into open hostility. Before that happened, however, Walker made clear he would oppose any submission to the Senate that wasn't supported unanimously by the cabinet. Polk assured Walker any action on his part would have full cabinet support.

The president then outlined the message he would attach to the British proposal, should he decide to send it up. It would reiterate his views as expressed in his Annual Message but then express deference to subsequent congressional debates and the precedents of former presidents. Further, he would say he would embrace a Senate recommendation of acceptance if it received the constitutional majority (two thirds) necessary for treaty ratification. If it didn't he would reject the British proposal.

When Buchanan expressed lukewarm support for such an approach, Polk asked him to draft the message. The secretary declined. The president, in accepting the task himself, harbored no illusions about his secretary of state. The Pennsylvanian clearly was nurturing his presidential ambitions, seeking to undermine Cass's powerful standing among westerners bent on getting all of Oregon. "My impression," wrote Polk to his diary, "is that Mr. Buchanan intends now to shun all responsibility for the submission . . . but still he may wish it to be done without his agency, so that if the 54-40 men shall complain, he may be able to say that my message submitting it did not receive his sanction."

On May 8, Polk had two conversations with Buchanan that accentuated the secretary's strange behavior. Buchanan, saying he wished to have "no agency" in drafting the presidential message on Oregon, complained about Walker's attack. And he revealingly sought to exclude certain dispatches penned by himself from documents to be sent to the Senate with the presidential message. Clearly, he sought to shield himself from public knowledge of his previous position. Then Buchanan went too far.

"Well," he said, "when you have done your message I will then prepare such an one as I think ought to be sent in." Polk became angry but characteristically sought to control it.

"For what purpose will you prepare a message?" he asked. "You have twice refused, though it is a subject relating to your Department, to give me any aide in preparing my message; do you wish, after I have done, to draw up a paper of your own in order to make an issue with me?"

Buchanan feigned injury. It struck him, he said, "to the heart," and he asked if Polk actually thought him capable of such a thing.

Polk reiterated his complaint that Buchanan had been uncooperative, leaving it to Polk to do work that rightfully belonged to the secretary's portfolio. He inquired again why Buchanan would now seek to submit an alternative draft. Then Polk, who now had the secretary firmly in his crosshairs, buckled. "I . . . told him that I thought I had cause to complain that he had not aided me when requested," the president told his diary, "but that if I had misunderstood him, I retracted the remark." A presidential retreat. This led to "mutual explanations that seemed to be satisfactory," and Polk disclaimed any unkind feelings toward his secretary of state, "personally or politically." Buchanan likewise expressed "his friendship for me and for Mrs. Polk."

The episode revealed a fundamental Polk trait. Though capable of outmaneuvering his opponents with brutal disregard for their political sensibilities and of sanctifying his actions through rationalization, he often lacked the fortitude necessary for face-to-face confrontation. Judging from his diary, Polk apparently felt he had brought Buchanan to heel, but it was the secretary who had manipulated the president.

That became clear during a five-hour cabinet session on June 9 devoted mostly to the Oregon message. All agreed on Polk's language except Buchanan, whose recalcitrance generated frustration and irritation among his colleagues. Finally Polk crafted compromise language that passed muster with everyone, and the cabinet signed off on the submission plan. Polk called in a number of prominent senators for consultation in preparation for the move. Most endorsed the plan but Allen of Illinois not surprisingly urged the president to reject the British proposal outright. Cass, conceding the president was bound to submit the proposal, vowed nevertheless to vote against it. The British proposal went to the Senate on June 10, and two days later Polk got word the Senate, in executive session, had recommended, by a vote of 38 to 12, that he accept the British treaty language. (Later official accounts would put the vote at 37 to 12.) Polk promptly sent it up, and three days later the Senate ratified it, 41 to 14. The long boundary conflict with Great Britain was over.

It took days for news of the Senate action to seep into the public consciousness, but when it did the *Union* promptly placed credit squarely upon the president. Though the Whig press sought to attribute the outcome to the Senate, in truth—said the paper—the Senate's meddling probably prevented further concessions from the British. But the final terms, "such as they are," argued the *Union*, "would never have been conceded to us, had it not been for the firm and energetic, though not offensive, stand taken by the President."

The *Union* had it about right in this instance. For decades the British had utterly refused to give up navigation rights to the Columbia and full control over the lush harbors of Puget Sound. When Polk went public with his firm statement of U.S. demands, the immediate result was outrage—in Britain and as well as among concession-minded Americans either fearful of war or disdainful of the expansionist impulses driving the issue in America. To many, Polk's approach seemed foolhardy, risky, and unjust. But it turned out he knew what he was doing. With his willingness to go right to the brink of war, he kept everyone guessing as to his true intentions—not least, perhaps, himself. His nerve and defiance yielded up a choice and strategically priceless stretch of land—"about three degrees of seacoast on the Pacific, with the eventual exclusive navigation of the chief river on the western slope of our continent," as the *Union* put it. This acquisition, along with Texas, moved the country a far distance toward that heady vision that had animated American politics so forcefully over the past two years—conquest of the full midsection of North America from sea to sea.

17 · PRESIDENTIAL
TEMPERAMENT

"I Prefer to Supervise the Whole Operations of the Government"

ALTHOUGH OREGON AND Mexico consumed most of the president's time and energy throughout his first eighteen months in office, he never lost sight of his domestic ambitions—tariff reduction and the independent treasury. Others might shrink from pressing so many major initiatives simultaneously, particularly in wartime. But not Polk.

Thus in late April the president invited Alabama senator Dixon Lewis to the White House for a touching demonstration of intellectual attainment by about thirty blind students, who read, solved math problems, and sang—all with a new communication method of "raised letters." Afterward Polk took Lewis to his office for a political chat aimed at getting the senator moving on the president's domestic agenda.

A devoted ally of John C. Calhoun, Lewis was chairman of the Senate Finance Committee, which meant he had his hand on the Senate's spigot of revenue legislation. He was positioned to assist Polk's aims or thwart them. Lately he had seemed inclined to thwart them—possibly, Polk surmised, because of Calhoun's ongoing hostility to his administration. Responding to a Senate floor query from Daniel Webster, Lewis had said his committee would take up the independent treasury matter only after it had disposed of what Polk considered lesser bills. The president feared Lewis's priorities could sink the independent treasury and also his tariff reductions as time ran out on the legislative session.

In his office, the president told Lewis he felt great anxiety about the fate of the tariff and monetary bills because he had identified them repeatedly as presidential priorities. If they went down, said Polk, his political power and the glory of his administration would be seriously damaged. Apparently Polk was persuasive. "My suggestions seemed to strike him forcibly," he informed his diary. Lewis promised to ensure action on the presidential priorities.

This episode reflected Polk's presidential temperament. He was his own chief lobbyist. He also was his own chief political strategist, chief speechwriter, chief policy analyst, chief scheduler. He insisted upon being involved in the minutiae of the departments represented in his cabinet. He delegated little and pulled a vast expanse of administrative and decision particulars into his own ambit, particularly on matters of the military. Even when Polk consciously intended to assign decision-making to his cabinet—in the matter of minor patronage jobs, for example—he couldn't resist his meddlesome ways. In part this stemmed from his congenital affinity for the martyrdom of duty, in part from his lack of trust that others could handle any tasks as competently as he could. As he would write to his diary:

> The public have no idea of the constant accumulation of business requiring the President's attention. No President who performs his duty faithfully and conscientiously can have any leisure. If he entrusts the details and smaller matters to subordinates constant errors will occur. I prefer to supervise the whole operations of the Government myself . . . and this makes my duties very great.

Indeed, so great were those duties that he did in fact enjoy almost no leisure time. Seldom did he leave the White House, except for a brief morning walk and a longer evening stroll. Occasionally Marcy or Mason would lure him out for an afternoon horseback ride, but most often their entreaties, issued in part out of concern for the president's fragile health, were rebuffed. On April 1, 1846, he ventured forth to spend an evening hour of quiet conversation with Cave Johnson—

and noted in his diary that it was only his fifth such evening excursion during thirteen months in office. The Polks did attend church nearly every Sunday—usually the Presbyterian congregation favored by Sarah but occasionally the Foundry Methodist Church at 14th and G streets, the president's preference.

As for travels outside Washington, they almost never occurred. By August 1846, Polk had ventured beyond the capital only three times during his presidency—for a day trip to Mount Vernon, another to Francis Blair's Silver Spring mansion in Maryland, and finally for several days at Fortress Monroe near Norfolk, where the president took ill with a severe fever that marred the outing.

At the White House, when he did leave his desk for some diversion organized by Sarah, he often felt distracted—or slightly contemptuous. He was lured downstairs at eight o'clock one evening for a juggler act that stirred wonder and delight among some fifty guests. Polk felt the display contributed little to the guests' "edification or profit" and considered his own time in attendance "unprofitably spent."

The Polk White House served as focal point of social Washington, and Sarah glistened in her role as the city's premier hostess. "Reception night" occurred twice a week at the mansion, and the couple frequently had important political players in for well-orchestrated dinner parties. Sarah allowed no spirituous liquors, but wine was available in abundance. No dancing, though; Sarah considered such amusements an assault on the dwelling's requisite decorum.

Polk usually attended White House receptions, at least briefly, before returning to his desk for an hour or two of work or retreating for a chat with an important legislator. If he spent any appreciable time at social events, he would rise earlier than normal the next morning to compensate for the lost toil. During receptions or dinners, of course, he worked the room in behalf of his legislative aims. At one reception in April, when the Oregon "notice" legislation was before Congress, the president earnestly urged five congressmen to embrace the Senate version in order to facilitate a speedy resolution of the matter.

Sarah's warm personality was evidenced at White House receptions, which were open to anyone "without ceremony and without invitation." On one occasion she spotted an old man in humble garb who tottered into the room with a cane. Sarah singled him out for special attention, discovered he was 108 years old, and conversed with him at length about his adventures during the Revolutionary War and before. As one participant later noted, "when other guests claimed her ear she followed the old man with her eye and directed that the venerable visitor should be treated with special respect."

Through Polk's presidency, the captivating Sarah continued to serve as a social antidote to her husband's famous reserve. She was described variously as "extremely affable," "perfectly self-possessed," "endowed with regal stateliness," and "a most auspicious domestic influence." More significantly, she was her husband's only intimate adviser and his unofficial secretary and helpmate. "None but Sarah," the president once wrote, "knew so intimately my private affairs."

One thing Sarah could not accomplish was to lure the president away from his conviction that republican principles required a willingness to open the White House to streams of visitors, most of them job seekers. Yet he came to detest this ritual that left him contemptuous of the citizenry. His diary is filled with expressions of irritation that increased in frequency and intensity as time went on. "It is one of the most painful of my duties," he wrote in February, to receive supplicants "who are so patriotic as to desire to serve their country by getting into fat offices." He had become, he said, "greatly disgusted" with the whole business. He possessed a self-righteous tendency to assess others through a prism of jaundiced superiority.

This was most pronounced in his feelings toward fellow politicians, whose motives he attributed largely to base ambition. Seldom did he accept opponents' actions as products of honest conviction. As he wrote during the fight over the Oregon "notice": "In the midst of these factions of the Democratic party I am left without any certain or reliable support in Congress. . . . Each leader looks to his own advancement more than he does to the success of my measures." Of course, self-interest drives much of Washington's political maneuverings, but Polk's narrow tendency to view his opponents in only one way left him susceptible to a bitterness that often guided his political thinking.

AND IT WAS true, of course, that Congress constantly tried to thwart his aims and policies. On May 25 word reached Polk that the Senate had rejected his nomination of Henry Horn, an old House colleague, to Pennsylvania's top patronage job, collector for the Port of Philadelphia. The deed had been orchestrated by Senator Simon Cameron, a great friend of Buchanan in the Senate. Cameron had waited for a number of Senate Democrats to be away at the funeral of a colleague's son, then called up the nomination for certain defeat in what Polk called "a thin Senate." Cameron, Calhoun, and James Westcott of Florida joined a solid Whig phalanx in voting down the nomination.

Polk dismissed Cameron as a "managing, tricky man in whom no reliance is to be placed . . . little better than a Whig." As for Calhoun, Polk felt "his ambition is destroying him," while Westcott was simply a Whig in Democratic garb. After canvassing the absent senators and concluding Horn could be confirmed in a full Senate, the president sent his name up for a second vote. But the tricky Cameron, bent on controlling patronage in his state, corralled sufficient Democrats to reject him again. "The selfishness of some members of Congress who make their public duties bend to their personal interests, proves at least that they are no better or purer than the mass of other men," declared the president to his diary. He sent up a second nominee even more distasteful to Cameron (and to Buchanan) than Horn. When the president refused to yield to Buchanan's entreaty that he choose someone else or at least consult the Pennsylvania delegation, Cameron retreated before the stubborn president, and Polk's nominee went through.

But the episode marked a turning point in Polk's congressional standing. Calhoun's southerners, seeing how easily the president could be rebuffed on nominations, adopted a tack of joining with the solid Whig opposition on such votes, and soon it became clear the president's position in Congress was eroding. Vice President Dallas perceived "a wretched condition in both Houses of Congress," with the situation "likely to get worse and worse." It was becoming clear why Polk needed to press Congress to move as quickly as possible on his favored initiatives.

ONE OF THOSE, the independent treasury measure, was reported by the House Ways and Means Committee in March 1846. It authorized the president to deposit government monies in treasury vaults until they were disbursed in the course of governmental business. Later it was amended to stipulate that only specie was to be received by the government. Hence, the measure, as amended, ensured that government funds could not be deposited in private banks, that the government must confine itself to hard money policies, and that the government could not print money as needed. The debate was framed by the measure and a floor amendment designed to gut it—federal custodianship of federal monies vs. custodianship by private banking interests; and hard money vs. soft money. The Jacksonians had always believed federal custodianship and hard money offered the greatest security for the country's financial system.

On April 2, with solid Democratic support and a considerable Whig tally, the measure cleared the House by a substantial margin. Reaching the Senate the next day, it was referred to Dixon Lewis's Finance Committee, where it languished until April 22. That's when the ever-alert Polk invited Lewis to the White House for the deaf students' performance and subsequent chat in the president's office. After the president managed to break down the chairman's resistance, the measure cleared the Finance Committee and obtained Senate passage on August 1. On August 5 the House accepted all Senate amendments, and Polk had his independent treasury. Another of Polk's major policy goals was secured.

The tariff initiative would prove more nettlesome. On April 14, the House Ways and Means Committee had reported a bill based on language provided by Polk and Treasury Secretary Walker. Its primary feature was that it substituted the specified dollar tariffs of the 1842 bill (imposed irrespective of import commodity prices) with ad valorem taxes, meaning percentage rates that would fluctuate with price. This was viewed by Democrats as fairer in that it ensured that commodities within certain groupings would be taxed at the same rate.

It was not truly a free trade measure. The ad valorem rates on a few commodities would reach as high as 100 percent, and rates on some products—wine and some apparel items, for example—actually would increase. But the vast majority of items would carry tariffs of just 30 percent, a substantial drop from the 1842 policy. And it would eradicate the idea that import taxes should be imposed strictly for purposes of protecting particular industries. Such protection, argued Seaborn Jones of Georgia, floor manager for the bill, distorted economic activity through governmental selection of favored and nonfavored industries—"bringing forth exotics which the soil and climate would not naturally produce."

Whigs attacked the bill by arguing it would damage the economy and slash federal revenue to dangerous levels in wartime. But on July 3, the Democratic-controlled House passed it easily, 114 to 95. "Will the protectionists longer resist this irresistible phalanx?" asked the *Union*. "Will they learn wisdom, and permit the present bill to pass through the Senate?"

That was the question on Polk's mind. By July 11 he feared many northeastern Democrats would line up against the bill—in part, he surmised, because of lingering animosities over his patronage decisions. "There is more selfishness among members of Congress which is made to bear upon great public measures, than the people have any knowledge of," he wrote. Some days later Polk heard that even his old college friend, William Haywood, planned to oppose the bill.

On July 23, when Polk called Haywood to the White House to discuss the issue, the North Carolinian appeared highly agitated about the bill.

"I would rather die than vote for it," he declared.

Haywood's central concern wasn't the bill itself but the abrupt manner in which it would be put into effect. If its effective date were delayed, he said, he could vote for it.

"The principal objection to such an amendment," replied Polk, "would be that it might put in jeopardy the fate of the Bill."

Later that day the two had another conversation, and Polk ratcheted up the rhetoric. The bill was his highest domestic priority, said the president, and it had received unanimous support among southern Democrats. Haywood's opposition would harm the administration, harm the nation, and—added Polk as a friend—destroy Haywood. Polk brought up rumors that Haywood was thinking of resigning his seat over the issue. "I begged him not to do so," Polk informed his diary. He told Haywood a resignation was tantamount to a negative vote, as his tally was needed to generate a Senate tie that could then be trumped by Vice President Dallas.

Haywood went away appearing intractable. So Polk turned his attention to Tennessee's Senator Spencer Jarnagin, a Whig, who was in a ticklish position. He opposed the bill on principle but had been instructed by the Tennessee legislature to vote for it.

On Saturday, July 25, three developments occurred in staccato sequence: Jarnagin, in the cabinet's presence, assured Polk he would vote for the measure; Haywood resigned his Senate seat out of a conviction that he could not accept his state legislature's instruction on the issue; and rumors began flying around official Washington that Jarnagin would resign also. Without Jarnagin's vote, the measure appeared dead.

"THE REVENUE BILL IN DANGER!" ran the headline in the *Union* that afternoon. It added: *"North Carolina betrayed!—Resignation of Senator Haywood!"*

The president felt genuine sadness over Haywood's decision. His career success had been a source of pride for Polk, who judged Haywood's tariff issue actions to be ill-considered and a likely result of his being "nervous, and in an excited state." But Polk harbored no ill feelings toward his friend, whose behavior he considered to be "from good motives."

On Monday, after a "stormy and violent debate," the Senate

embraced, by one vote, a procedural action that placed the tariff bill in further jeopardy. Jarnagin, voting with the majority, enraged Polk by abandoning his earlier promise to support the measure. The Tennessean, complained Polk, "holds the fate of the bill in his hands, and there is no reliance to be place upon him."

But the next day the measure cleared the Senate by a single vote, which turned out to be Jarnagin's. The maverick senator had voted his conscience, or ducked out, on all procedural tallies but had accepted his legislative instruction on final reading. The House promptly accepted the Senate's lone minor amendment, and with Polk's signature some days later the measure became law. "The long agony is now over," crowed the *Union*.

THAT POLK SUCCEEDED in getting congressional approval for his two domestic priorities was a testament to his political resolve and acumen. These were the two issues of lingering potency left over from the days of the great Jackson-Clay rivalry, and Polk now had put them to rest as matters of disruptive political contention. On domestic policy, the country was moving into a new era.

This was particularly true of federal money management. Alexander Hamilton's concept of placing that management in the hands of corporate executives beholden to shareholders was now dead. Jackson's expediency of transferring those funds to state "pet banks" also was dead. The people's money now would be in the hands of the people's government. Polk's system would last for seventy years, until creation of the Federal Reserve System in 1913, with its matrix of central banks throughout the country regulated by an independent board in Washington. Meanwhile, discovery of huge California gold reserves and a large influx of British investment capital prevented Polk's hard money approach from constricting U.S. economic activity unduly. The result was that the issue lost much of its sting, and Polk's approach became firmly embedded in American financial policy.

The tariff victory was less definitive, as various trade policy wars would emerge in American politics over the decades. But the economic forces unleashed during Polk's time would blunt the call for protectionist policies in coming years. A railroad boom generated huge demand for Pennsylvania iron and steel, and textile manufacturers soon discovered high tariffs only spawned troublesome domestic competitors. More significantly, the world was moving in the Jacksonian direction, as reflected in Britain's repeal of its Corn Laws. As Ritchie's *Union* pointed out, Britain's closed ports had been put forth "again and again, and in every form of ingenuity and emphasis" as justification for America's own high tariffs. But now Britain embraced free trade, and that argument was gone. Indeed, the booming British-American commerce was fueling much of the prosperity that undercut the protectionist rationale. As historian Michael F. Holt would later observe, "All in all, the Whig demand for higher tariffs had become moot."

All in all, indeed! The politics of the Jackson-Clay rivalry was receding rapidly, overwhelmed by the politics of expansionism, which had dominated American discourse since the spring of 1844. But the politics of expansionism was spawning in turn a new era, the politics of slavery. And nothing seemed more potent in bringing this new era into ascendancy than Polk's final presidential aim—acquisition of California and New Mexico, which had necessitated his Mexican War. Now that war would dominate his presidency just as its residues would dominate American politics for decades to come.

18 · WILMOT'S PROVISO

Transformation of the War Debate

I N EARLY JULY 1846 a young American arrived in Havana, Cuba, and sought out the city's U.S. consul, R. B. Campbell. In a satchel he carried a letter from Secretary of State Buchanan and a copy of Navy Secretary Bancroft's May 13 instruction to Commodore Conner ensuring free passage into Mexico for General Santa Anna. In his brain the young man carried unwritten instructions from the president of the United States on what he should say if he managed to get an audience with that wounded but willful Mexican exile.

The messenger was Alexander Slidell Mackenzie, a naval officer and nephew of Polk's rejected envoy to Mexico City, John Slidell. With Campbell's help Mackenzie secured his interview with Santa Anna—and made his first mistake. Contrary to Polk's unwritten instructions, the young courier had crafted a written memorandum, which he proceeded to read to the Mexican general. It stated the United States remained bent on prosecuting what it considered a just and necessary war. And Polk would wage that war with brutal aggression. But he preferred a quick negotiated settlement and considered Santa Anna both able and willing to effect such a settlement. Hence, "the President of the United States would see with pleasure his restoration to power in Mexico."

Mackenzie then stated the president's terms. The Rio Grande must be accepted as the boundary of Texas, and Mexico must grant to the United States a sufficient expanse of California to include San Francisco Bay. The president would pay handsomely for any acquired Mexican lands, and he wasn't inclined to demand any indemnity for the costs of the war.

Santa Anna seemed receptive to Polk's proposal. He quibbled a bit initially about the Rio Grande boundary but eventually relented on that issue and all others. He even extended his considered judgment on which American military actions—including occupation of Tampico—might most effectively bring leverage over his nation. Believing this martial advice to be highly valuable, Mackenzie made his second mistake. Violating his instructions to return directly to Washington, he rushed to the Rio Grande to deliver Santa Anna's views to Zachary Taylor, who dismissed the information as unimportant.

The president didn't wait for Mackenzie's report before pursuing a second diplomatic channel. On July 27, Buchanan, at Polk's instruction, sent a letter to Mexico's foreign minister offering to send an envoy to Mexico or receive one in Washington "to terminate . . . the present unhappy war." Around the same time, in discussions with Benton, Polk resurrected his old plan for a congressional appropriation allowing him to lubricate any settlement with an up-front payment of some $2 million. "I had but little doubt," he explained later, "that by paying that sum in hand at the signature of a Treaty we might procure California . . . and that in the present impoverished condition of Mexico the knowledge that such a sum would be paid in hand might induce Mexico to Treat, when she might not otherwise do so."

Benton approved. Now Polk could vigorously pursue his strategy, which was to seek a negotiated peace while waging aggressive war—with the "$2 million bill," as it became known, paving the way toward the negotiated peace. But that legislation posed two troubling challenges. The first was procedural—how to ease the bill through Congress without unleashing a political firestorm. The second involved political perception—presidential acknowledgment, implicit in the bill, that the war issue now involved the president's resolve to acquire Mexican territory. This had been suspected, of course, and hurled at the president in the form of accusation by congressional Whigs and the *National Intelligencer*. But Polk had always finessed the matter. Now the finesse would be over.

Polk addressed the first challenge in discussing his plan with Senator Cass, one of the president's most stalwart supporters. He thought it best, said Polk, to send his request privately to the Senate for consideration in executive session. If the senators approved without undue opposition, the Senate then could take up the measure in open session. The secret would be out, but by then he would have achieved mastery over the issue. Cass endorsed the approach.

Polk addressed the second challenge in discussions with Senator McDuffie, who recently had replaced William Allen as chairman of Foreign Relations. The president drew a fine distinction between conquest of Mexican lands, which he had no wish to pursue in any manner whatsoever, and acquisition of such lands through a just peace process. Given this peace would ensue only after the United States managed to bring Mexico to heel militarily, it wasn't clear just what kind of logic girded this distinction. But McDuffie seemed to buy it.

On August 1, after getting his cabinet's consensus on the issue, Polk instructed Buchanan to draft his message to the Senate. Two days later came word from Mackenzie that Santa Anna had accepted the president's terms for settling the two countries' differences and intended soon to reclaim his lost mantle of Mexican leadership. Thus, if Polk's peace overture to the Paredes regime was rejected, which appeared likely, there was insurance in the form of Santa Anna's resolve to supplant that regime—made possible by his safe passage through Polk's Mexican blockade. James Polk, the political chess master, was arraying his pieces for maximum effect on the chessboard of statecraft.

THROUGHOUT THIS TIME of complex maneuvering on the war, Polk grappled also with the congressional fate of his beleaguered tariff legislation. And he struggled simultaneously with a number of other high-intensity issues—notably two vetoes and his ongoing relations with James Buchanan.

On June 10, Polk surprised his secretary of state by extending to him the Supreme Court seat that had remained vacant since George Woodward's Senate rejection. The president didn't explain to anyone, including his diary, why he would make such an offer to a man who, just weeks earlier, had been suspected of complicity in Wood-ward's defeat. But Polk seemed to have an underlying need to ingrati-ate himself with his annoying foreign secretary, and the June 10 offer certainly served that purpose. "After a long conversation," the presi-dent reported to his diary, Buchanan "retired, manifestly changed in his feelings and in a very pleasant humor."

On June 28, Cave Johnson arrived at the White House with a mes-sage from Buchanan: He would accept the court nomination. That led to a Polk-Buchanan conversation on July 1 in which the presi-dent said he would send up the nomination shortly before the close of the current congressional session. Buchanan, seemingly taken aback, requested an immediate nomination. Polk said that wasn't possi-ble, given the lingering policy matters in Congress as its late-session crunch loomed. Buchanan seemed to accept the rationale.

But Buchanan never fully accepted any outcome that went against his wishes, and the next day he returned to the White House to express urgency in the matter. Rumors were rife about his impending nomi-nation, he said, and he feared a groundswell of opposition. When Polk dismissed that possibility, Buchanan suggested Britain might inter-vene somehow in the Mexican War, thus precluding his departure from the cabinet. Highly unlikely, replied the president. Buchanan accepted Polk's judgment, "but with great reluctance."

On July 12, Polk, concerned about Buchanan's lingering reluc-tance, told the secretary he needed a definitive commitment as he was about to write to U.S. ambassador Louis McLane in London with an offer to become Buchanan's successor. Buchanan waffled once more, reiterating his desire for an immediate nomination. Polk responded with a lengthy and pungent political analysis of what would occur if he sought to replace Buchanan at State too soon. Every member would put forth his pet nominee, said the president, and the result would be a donnybrook of competing interests. As soon as members learned their favorites were rejected, the resulting angers would jeop-ardize the president's entire agenda.

"My position," the president told Buchanan, "would be one of per-fect torment & vexation until the close of the Session."

Buchanan once again relented, but suggested Polk refrain from sending his letter to McLane, as he might change his mind. Polk speculated later that Buchanan probably feared Senate opposition stemming from his correspondence with McLane on Oregon. Before his abrupt and inexplicable conversion into a 54-40 man, he had been openly dovish on the issue and perhaps now feared the Cass followers would hold that against him. Also, his alignment with a free trade administration could stir opposition among northeastern protectionists, most notably his own fellow Pennsylvanians.

Two weeks later Buchanan, through Cave Johnson, stunned Polk with the news he would remain in the cabinet. Later that day Buchanan personally delivered his decision, which Polk accepted in good grace. For good or ill, he would have Buchanan in his cabinet for the remainder of his presidency.

Polk next turned his attention to other personnel matters. He offered the London ambassadorship to Bancroft, who readily accepted. He asked Mason to return to the Navy Department, which he had headed in the Tyler years. Always the good soldier, Mason accepted the president's wishes. Then Polk set about, without much urgency, to select a successor at Justice.

More urgent was his response to domestic legislation under the rubric of the "river and harbor bill," an appropriations measure that had become a kind of catch-all for pet pork barrel items desired by legislators. Henry Clay himself could not have asked for a measure more in keeping with his American System of internal improvements. By the time it reached Polk, the appropriations in the bill had ballooned to a million and a half dollars. Polk drafted a veto message in consultation only with Mason, whom he knew would approve the decision; anticipating opposition from other cabinet members, he kept them out of the loop until August 1, when the message was completed.

Sent up on August 3, the message was a pure distillation of the Jacksonian philosophy of strict construction and limited government. "The whole frame of the Federal Constitution," wrote Polk, "proves that the Government which it creates was intended to be one of lim-

ited and specified powers." But the river and harbor bill implied a
constitutional construction so broad that it "tends imperceptibly to a
consolidation of power in a Government intended by the framers to be
thus limited in its authority." In addition to being unconstitutional
and inexpedient, said the president, the measure represented "a dis-
reputable scramble for the public money."

Ritchie's *Union* naturally applauded the action. "It is one of the
strongest vetoes which ever emanated from the executive department
on this subject," said the paper. The *Intelligencer*, seeing national crisis
in the Whigs' ongoing political defeat, saw the veto as evidence "that
our government is fast degenerating into a mere quadrennial elective
despotism!" On August 4 the House took up the veto and failed, by a
vote of 96 to 91, to override it.

Around the same time, Polk vetoed the so-called French spoliation
bill designed to provide $5 million in land scrip to Americans who
claimed they had been damaged by French plundering prior to 1800.
Polk couldn't see why the U.S. government should assume responsibility for the actions of a foreign nation so many years before. Benton
was so delighted with the president's decision that he offered to help
draft the veto message. The veto was easily sustained.

As the congressional session neared a dramatic denouement,
however, political attention became riveted on the $2 million bill,
which everyone knew would kick up intense controversy. On August
4, Polk sent to the Senate his confidential message outlining the state
of affairs with Mexico and requesting an executive-session, sense-of-
the-Senate vote on the $2 million appropriation. Noting two prece-
dents for this approach dating back to the Jefferson administration,
the message emphasized Polk's intention to use the appropriation to
help secure an honorable peace.

Two days later, in secret session, the Senate took up two resolutions
brought forth by McDuffie's Foreign Relations Committee. The first
declared the Senate's "strong desire that the existing war with Mexico
should be terminated by a treaty of peace" and urged the president

"to adopt all proper measures for the attainment of that object." The second declared:

> 2d. *Resolved, further,* That the Senate deem it advisable that Congress should appropriate a sum of money to enable the President to conclude a treaty of peace, limits, and boundaries with the republic of Mexico, and to be used by him in the event that such treaty should call for the expenditure of the money so appropriated, or any part thereof.

The first resolution prevailed with only two dissenting senators—David Atchison of Missouri and Thomas Rusk of Texas, both Democrats. The second passed 33 to 19, with no discernible party-line breakdown. Eight Whigs voted aye, while three Democrats opposed it. It was a signal victory for the political chess master in the White House.

Then things began to go awry. Several Democratic senators, including Benton, urged Polk to send a similar confidential message to the House and get a corollary executive session action from that chamber before the Senate went public. Polk recoiled at the thought. No confidential message to the House could possibly be kept secret for long, he protested, adding such a move would be "a perfect farce."

The most effective approach, argued the president, would be for the Senate to pass the measure without debate in open session and send it to the House, where it could be acted upon "without attracting much public attention." But word soon arrived that several Whig senators, including some who had voted for the bill in executive session, now were saying they would oppose it unless the president took responsibility for recommending it. Of course Polk had done so in his confidential message to the Senate, but he dutifully ordered Buchanan to draft an open message to the appropriate Senate and House committees asking for the appropriation.

On his way to deliver the missives, Buchanan ran into Benton, who strenuously questioned the president's judgment in rejecting his counsel and refusing to send a secret message to the House. Stung by the rebuke, Buchanan returned to the White House at around 9 P.M. with the undelivered letters. A frustrated Polk said he absolutely would not send up such a secret letter and dispatched Buchanan once again to deliver the open letters.

The next day, Saturday, August 8, Polk heard from his Senate sources that the Whigs were uniting in opposition to the $2 million bill on the pretext that the president hadn't adequately accepted responsibility for it. Once again the weary president summoned Buchanan to help draft yet another message to both houses of Congress—to be delivered, he insisted, in open session. The aim was to place the onus on Congress if the measure went down.

In the new message Polk identified the most difficult issue in any peace negotiation as "the adjustment of a boundary between the two republics, which shall prove satisfactory and convenient to both, and such as neither will hereafter be inclined to disturb." In settling such a boundary, he added, the United States "ought to pay a fair equivalent for any concessions which may be made by Mexico." Once again he outlined the Jeffersonian precedents and suggested the money would be needed to assist Mexico as the slow ratification process unfolded.

The House received the language of Polk's message as a beehive receives the poke of a stick. Whig Joseph Ingersoll of Pennsylvania sought to have the matter referred to the Ways and Means Committee, where it could be delayed or perhaps buried. But Virginia's Democratic representative George Dromgoole foiled that ploy by moving a procedure that ensured immediate floor consideration. The House then took up the measure, presented in the form of a bill by North Carolina's James McKay, chairman of Ways and Means. It provided the $2 million "for the purpose of defraying any extraordinary expenses which may be incurred in the intercourse between the United States and foreign nations . . . to be applied under the direction of the President of the United States, who shall cause an account of the expenditure thereof to be laid before Congress as soon as may be."

After considerable procedural maneuverings on the bill, the House agreed to take it up at five o'clock, following a two-hour recess. It was during this respite that a legislative resolve emerged in the conscious-

ness of a Pennsylvania freshman named David Wilmot. It was never
clear if Wilmot, a staunch Democrat, fully understood the explosive
nature of his resolve or just how decisively it would alter the course
of American politics. But he clearly knew it would stir up a raucous
floor debate, and he welcomed the verbal fracas with a kind of grim
obstinacy.

Wilmot, then thirty-two, was a curious sort. Reared in relative
affluence in rural Pennsylvania, he excelled at his studies, embraced a
legal career, gravitated to politics, and impressed audiences with his
rich and melodious voice tied to a defiant display of conviction. But
he was slovenly, careless in dress and manner, and sometimes profes-
sionally listless. These traits occasionally dulled the force of his intellect. He was a big man, blunt-spoken and impetuous, with a chaw of
tobacco ever-present in his mouth. And, when he set himself upon a
course, he did so with fearless grit, as when he defied his Pennsylvania
colleagues to cast the delegation's only vote for Polk's tariff bill. Now
he was about to set himself upon a momentous course in opposition
to his president.

During the recess, Wilmot lingered with members of a political coterie of antislavery Democrats informally led by that resolute
New York Barnburner, Preston King. Devotees of Van Buren and
Silas Wright, these men were developing an intense antipathy toward
Polk, and it occurred to them, as they discussed the coming evening
session, that the $2 million bill presented an exquisite opportunity
to strike a blow at the president. The idea was to amend the bill to
exclude slavery from any territory acquired through the Mexican War.
It wasn't clear who within the King coterie actually came up with the
idea; most likely it was fashioned jointly. But Wilmot resolved himself to be the man to force the issue on the House floor.

It was in many ways a peculiar maneuver for the Pennsylvanian.
Never before had he demonstrated such defiance against his party or
his president. Neither was he an opponent of the war. Moreover, he
was not by any measure an abolitionist; as a states' rights Democrat,
he had consistently and forcefully opposed federal meddling with the
South's controversial institution of servitude. His dislike of slavery

and opposition to its expansion into new territories were not tied to any sense of moral outrage, such as that displayed with flamboyant emotion by Joshua Giddings or John Quincy Adams. His motivation was not anguish over black bondage but rather a reverence for the free toil of his own kind. "I would preserve," he once pronounced, "for free white labor a fair country, a rich inheritance where the sons of toil of my own race and own color, can live without the disgrace which association with negro slavery brings upon free labor."

Whatever his true motivation, young Wilmot entered the five o'clock House session poised to pounce at the opportune moment. The debate began with Hugh White, a fiery New York Whig, who took the occasion to denounce the war as "unnecessary, uncalled for, and wholly unjustifiable; offensive in its inception, and I fear of conquest and subjugation in its ending." He could not vote for the $2 million bill, he said, unless it was amended to "forever preclude the possibility of extending the limits of slavery." He added: "I call upon the other side of the House to propose such an amendment . . . as an evidence of their desire to restrain that institution within its constitutional limits."

Robert Winthrop of Massachusetts, a Daniel Webster protégé, argued the bill gave too much sway to a president bent on territorial acquisition. "Give him no countenance," said Winthrop, "in his design to take advantage of the present war to force Mexico into the surrender, or even the sale, of any of her provinces." If anybody wanted a better harbor on the Pacific, he added, "let him wait till it can be acquired with less of national dishonor."

But Whig Joseph Ingersoll of Pennsylvania defended the president and hailed what he called "the rainbow of peace." All branches of government, he said, must "unite with the President in making peace as they had united in making war." A Tennessee Whig named Henry Grider added that, though he opposed the war, he favored the appropriation as a vehicle for ending it.

Then Wilmot rose to declare the war both "necessary and proper." Nor did he consider it a war of conquest. If it were, he said, he would oppose it "in every form and shape." At the same time he considered it "earnestly desirous" that the country should acquire some Mexican lands on the Pacific, including San Francisco harbor, but only by "fair and honorable means, by purchase or negotiation—not by conquest."

But, he added solemnly, he would oppose "now and forever" the extension into those acquired lands of "this 'peculiar institution' that belongs to the south." He had voted for annexation of Texas as a slave state, he averred, only because slavery had already been established there. "But if free territory comes in, God forbid that I should be the means of planting this institution upon it." Then he presented his amendment:

> *Provided.* That, as an express and fundamental condition to the acquisition of any territory from the republic of Mexico by the United States, by virtue of any treaty which may be negotiated between them, and to the use by the Executive of the moneys herein appropriated, neither slavery nor involuntary servitude shall ever exist in any part of said territory, except for crime, whereof the party shall first be duly convicted.

Immediately the war debate took on a new cast, intertwined now with the slavery question, the most emotional and ominous of all controversies facing the nation. It didn't matter that none of the lands under discussion for possible acquisition contained slavery or even seemed hospitable to it. It didn't matter that no one was advocating the introduction of slavery into those lands or that any effort to do so would almost surely fail. It was as if a giant hand had reached down from above, grabbed the war discussion, and crumpled it up into an entirely new debate.

Over in the Senate, Benton watched with disbelief the emergence of this Wilmot Proviso, as it became known. The amendment, he wrote later in his memoir, "was nugatory and could answer no purpose but that of bringing on a slavery agitation. . . . Never were two parties so completely at loggerheads about nothing." Polk not surprisingly was outraged. It was "a mischievous and foolish amendment," he wrote, adding: "What connection slavery had with making peace with Mexico it is difficult to conceive."

On the House floor that afternoon, this intermingling of the war and slavery issues seeped into the chamber's collective consciousness only slowly. Some members seized upon it immediately while others kept their focus on the merits and flaws of the $2 million bill. No doubt the amendment's import was obscured by the intensity of attention directed at so many competing interests as Congress struggled to wrap up the session.

A New York Whig named Washington Hunt said he could perhaps support the bill and the acquisition of California in a war settlement, but not without the Wilmot Proviso. By contrast, Alexander Sims of South Carolina, a Democrat, decried the proviso as an unnecessary agitation and said he could never vote for Polk's request with Wilmot's amendment attached. Kentucky's bombastic Garrett Davis ignored the proviso in his assault on Polk's war. The president, said Davis, wants congressional complicity in his aim of extracting Mexican territory by force. "In one hand," pronounced the Kentuckian, "he already brandishes over weak, distracted, and prostrate Mexico the bloody sword; in the other, he asks Congress to place two millions of dollars that he may present to [Mexico] . . . the tempting lure, with the alternative of desolating her with war's havoc."

Quincy Adams announced he would vote for the appropriation with the same fervor with which he initially had opposed the war. In both instances his vote reflected his distaste for the conflict. "Sir," said the former president, "we have whipped [Mexico] already more than the most cruel task-master ever whipped a slave, without cause and without necessity. . . . And one of the reasons why I shall heartily vote for . . . this bill is that . . . instead of whipping Mexico, the President shows a desire to make peace with that republic." As for the Wilmot Proviso, he proclaimed it unnecessary, as there was no slavery in any Mexican territory. But he supported the proviso nonetheless as a statement of principle.

As the time for voting approached, McKay offered a substitute amendment designed to add clarity to Congress's intent on the $2 million appropriation. Wilmot then moved his amendment to McKay's substitute. James Dobbin of North Carolina promptly issued a point of order: The Wilmot amendment was out of order, he declared, because the subject of slavery had nothing to do with the $2 million bill. The chairman overruled Dobbin's point of order, whereupon the North Carolinian appealed the decision. The floor upheld the ruling, 92 to 37.

William Wick of Indiana put forth an effort to amend Wilmot's language so it applied only to territory north of 36°30' north latitude, the Missouri Compromise line. It failed. Then came the vote on the Wilmot Proviso. By now it was twenty minutes past eight, and word of the proviso had spread through the city. The gallery was filled with interested spectators. On the floor, reported the *New York Herald,* "Nearly every member was on his feet," and "newspaper fans and ice water were in great demand." James Buchanan arrived at the House lobby, soon followed by Cave Johnson and George Bancroft. Polk got regular updates over in the vice president's office on the Senate side, where he had repaired earlier in the day to sign legislation as it rolled out during the late flurry of congressional activity.

Then came the proviso vote. It passed, 83 to 64. Finally, after disposition of further legislative maneuverings, the House voted on McKay's modified bill, as amended by Wilmot. It passed, 87 to 64. Almost absentmindedly, the House had transformed the war debate into a slavery debate.

On Monday morning the Twenty-ninth Congress's first session resumed its legislative activity under a previous agreement to adjourn *sine die* precisely at noon. An hour before the appointed adjournment hour the Senate took up the $2 million bill under the floor management of Alabama's Dixon Lewis, Finance Committee chairman. Upon moving consideration of the bill, Lewis demanded the yeas and nays and refused to yield for any other purpose. Then, just before the third and final reading of the bill, the chairman moved to strike the Wilmot language.

John Davis of Massachusetts, an earnest Whig and supporter of Wilmot's proviso, rose to inquire as to Lewis's reasoning for striking out the antislavery proviso. There was, snapped Lewis, "no time now for giving reasons or making explanations."

Well, said Davis, this seemed like "legislating under a high degree of steam pressure." He proceeded to discuss the details of the bill at length, and it soon became clear he was "talking against time," as senators put it when a member sought to dispatch legislation by talking it to death.

Lewis sought to reclaim the floor, noting anxiously that only twenty minutes remained in the session. If the senator from Massachusetts wished to make a floor speech, said Lewis, perhaps he would not object to a resolution delaying the time of adjournment.

"I do object," said Davis, adding he didn't plan to talk beyond the adjournment hour. After a few minutes Lewis again sought to gain the floor.

"Does the senator from Massachusetts yield the floor?" asked the presiding officer.

"For a question of order," replied Davis. "Otherwise not."

"I merely wished to state the fact," said Lewis with a tone of pained resignation, "that the House has adjourned."

The game was up. Without the House in session, the Senate debate fizzled. Polk's hope of getting his $2 million appropriation in the 1846 session was now dead, leaving him without the leverage he most desired in his efforts to negotiate a peace with Mexico. Davis later insisted his ploy had been to talk just long enough to preclude a conference with the House, thus requiring the Senate to take the bill with Wilmot's proviso intact. But he hadn't calculated that the House clock ran about eight minutes ahead of the Senate clock, and hence his effort was foiled.

Antislavery politicians throughout the nation expressed outrage at this political fumbling. "Ten political lives of ten John Davises, spent in the best direction," wrote Ohio politician Salmon P. Chase, "could not compensate for this half-hour's mischief." Pro-war Democrats were equally angry. "Had the appropriation been passed," wrote Polk to his diary, "I am confident I should have made an honorable peace by which we should have acquired California, & such other territory as we desired, before the end of October." Should the war now linger, he added, "the responsibility will fall more heavily upon the head of Senator Davis than upon any other man, and he will deserve the execrations of the country."

THOUGH STUNG BY the defeat, the president had reason to celebrate the congressional session just ended. Seldom in American history up to that time had any president dominated a congressional session as Polk had dominated this one or filled any eighteen-month period with so many political accomplishments. Taking power at a critical moment in the Texas annexation matter, he thwarted European efforts and Lone Star intrigues to derail the outcome. Thus he played a decisive role in bringing Texas into the American union. He successfully choreographed a complex and dangerous diplomatic and political dance that brought the most desirable expanses of Oregon into the Union. He pushed through Congress his two most cherished domestic goals—tariff reduction and the independent treasury. And he engineered a war that seemed a necessary step in his aim of acquiring large tracts of Mexican land—territory that, pieced together with Oregon and Texas, would position America to dominate its continent and, eventually, two oceans.

This record was played back to Polk during his late August visit to Fortress Monroe at Hampton, Virginia, during which he held a dinner party that included Virginia's highly acclaimed Littleton Waller Tazewell, former congressman, senator, and governor. Tazewell had befriended Polk during the Tennessean's early congressional years, and the president viewed the Virginian as one of the greatest Americans he had ever met—"a man of great purity and uprightness of character," as he put it to his diary. The governor extolled Polk's accomplishments and said he had "disposed of and settled more important public subject of great interest" in the first eighteen months of his administration "than any of [his] predecessors had ever done in eight years."

Polk's pride in receiving such praise was manifest in his diary entry of that day. "I was surprised but of course gratified to hear these opinions from such a man as Gov. Tazewell," he wrote, "and expressed my gratification to him."

19 · THE WAR IN THE WEST

Patriotism, Duty, Adventure, and Glory

ON AUGUST 18, 1846, a week after James Polk's congressional defeat on the $2 million bill, a powerful development occurred some sixteen hundred miles to the west. On that day Stephen Watts Kearny, freshly promoted to brigadier general, brevet rank, rode into Santa Fe, capital of the Mexican department of New Mexico, with three divisions of mounted dragoons. Passing wary and sullen-faced inhabitants aligned motionless against their adobe dwellings, he made his way to the town plaza, dismounted before the Palace of the Governors, and raised his hand as a command of silence.

"I, Stephen W. Kearny, General of the Army of the United States, have taken possession of the province of New Mexico," he intoned. "In the name of the government of the United States I hereby instruct the inhabitants to deliver their arms and surrender absolutely. . . . I am your governor—look to me for protection."

Thus did the United States conquer a large expanse of Mexican territory containing eighty thousand inhabitants without firing a shot or shedding a drop of blood. Now Mexico had lost not just Texas and the portion of Texas it considered eastern New Mexico. It had forfeited the remainder of that remote and forbidding department as well. For Mexico, it was beginning to look like a costly war.

And more costly still with events occurring some seven hundred miles further west in California. On August 17, just a day before Kearny's march into Santa Fe, that irrepressible naval adventurer and Texas intriguer, Robert Stockton, issued a similar proclamation at the small town of Los Angeles. He declared the whole of California to be

United States territory, with himself now serving as both commander-in-chief and governor. The commodore then sat down and penned a report to President Polk, replete with abundant praise of his own signal role in the triumph. So intent was Stockton on indulging his characteristic self-absorption that he overlooked a budding resistance movement that would prove troublesome in the weeks ahead.

But a new era had begun in the intertwined story of Mexico and the United States. That Polk actually could conquer these lands with just a few thousand men was a testament to the haplessness of Mexico and the audacity of those itinerant soldiers and their leaders. They came west for a host of reasons—patriotism, duty, adventure, glory. The men of destiny among them—notably, Kearny, Stockton, and that military explorer and Thomas Benton son-in-law, John C. Frémont—were focused particularly on glory. And thus it was perhaps inevitable, as the Mexican War story unfolded, that these ego-driven combatants would find themselves in heated controversy with one another, and one would return to Washington under arrest and facing court-martial.

The War in the West had germinated in the Polk mind early in his presidency. On October 11, 1845, nearly seven months before American blood was spilled on the Rio Grande, word reached the White House that Britain's Hudson's Bay Company had offered Mexico abundant money and arms to reassert national dominance over the errant department of California, edging toward an independence movement as streams of U.S. immigrants entered the territory. This struck Polk as ominous. Already he had heard that Britain was bolstering its Pacific fleet against the possibility of war with the United States over Oregon. And rumors had circulated that a Father Eugene McNamara had devised plans to settle ten thousand Irish Catholics in California. Thus it seemed Britain was preparing to take control of that western territory.

Two weeks later, Polk and Senator Benton agreed Britain must not be allowed to snatch California under any circumstances. Benton also took pains, in the same conversation, to mention the third western expedition, then in progress, of his son-in-law, Frémont. The famous

explorer, said Benton, would be veering into California before returning to St. Louis.

This suggested a hint of intrigue. At the time, Frémont was a U.S.
Army officer, accompanied by a contingent of some sixty armed civilians. Officially, he was operating under the auspices of the Corps of
Topographical Engineers, which meant his mission was that of a mapmaker, assigned to explore the eastern slope of the southern Rocky
Mountains. But here was his father-in-law, one of the country's leading
politicians, telling the president that the young man and his armed
followers intended to enter upon the sovereign soil of a neighboring
nation—a nation with which the United States had a precarious relationship. In his diary that night, the president seemed untroubled by
the prospect.

Six days later Polk summoned Marine Lieutenant Archibald Gillespie and sent him on his secret mission—to deliver confidential
messages to Thomas Larkin, U.S. consul in Monterey, California;
Commodore John D. Sloat, commander of the U.S. Pacific Squadron; and Frémont, wherever he might be found. Gillespie, a lithe,
tough, cocky man of thirty-three, set off on a remarkable journey
as presidential courier—by ship to Veracruz; then overland to Mexico City and on to the West Coast city of Mazatlán; from there to
Hawaii aboard an American whaling ship; and finally to Monterey
aboard a U.S. man-of-war. During his Mexican land trek, the bilingual Gillespie took on a disguise and gleaned valuable intelligence
on the country's seething anger toward the United States. War, he
concluded, was inevitable.

Gillespie carried much of his secret messages in his head, and history has never revealed just what Polk wanted from the three Americans—or from Gillespie. But one written instruction, from Buchanan
to Larkin, hints at the president's thinking. The United States, vowed
Buchanan, would "make no effort and use no influence to induce California to become one of the free and independent States of this Union."
At the same time, said Buchanan, "should California assert and maintain her independence, we shall render her all the kind offices in our
power as a Sister Republic." And, he went on, should the people of

California wish to join the U.S. republic, "they would be received as brethren, whenever this can be done without affording Mexico just cause of complaint."

But, added Buchanan, should Britain or France attempt to absorb California, the United States would "vigorously interpose" to prevent that. And of course should war break out between the United States and Mexico, California would be ripe for conquest according to the laws of war.

It was typical Polk, delicately maneuvering between the imperative of diplomatic propriety and the aim of national expansion. By hand of the same courier, the president also designated Larkin a secret U.S. agent. In addition to his consular duties, he would be charged with gathering and reporting intelligence on developments within California. Larkin, well connected throughout the region, already had been working quietly to nudge events toward a peaceful transfer of the territory to U.S. jurisdiction. No doubt Polk wished these activities to continue.

For insurance, the same messages were dispatched to Stockton, then in Norfolk, Virginia, outfitting the frigate *Congress* for duty in the Pacific. He was to transmit them to the same three men. Gillespie arrived at Monterey Bay on April 17, 1846, nearly six months after getting his assignment, and conveyed his secret instructions to Larkin. Then he set out overland in search of Frémont. Stockton arrived three months later, by which time news of the war had reached the region.

WHATEVER POLK'S WESTERN aims before the war, those aims became clear to Washington insiders afterward. As soon as Congress declared a state of war and authorized volunteers, Polk decided those mustered into service in Missouri would be sent west along the famous commercial route known as the Santa Fe Trail, that seemingly endless umbilical that for some twenty-five years had linked the American civilization of St. Louis with the trading opportunities of Santa Fe. He called on Missouri governor John Edwards to recruit some thousand mounted volunteers to bolster Kearny's small contingent of regulars.

He negotiated with leaders of Mormon groups fleeing persecution in Illinois for another five hundred or so troops. And he ordered Kearny to find another thousand or so from among Americans living in New Mexico and working on the commercial caravans whose way west had been thwarted by the war.

Kearny was the right man for this expedition. By temperament he was probably the army's finest high-ranking officer, well known for thorough planning, sound judgment, and fairness toward his troops. He had a knack for maintaining absolute discipline without sinking to preoccupations over petty matters that breed disaffection among soldiers. An easterner by birth and a connoisseur of fine wines and a well-spread table, he nevertheless was completely comfortable in the roughs of remote mountains, prairies, and deserts. Just the previous year he had led a vigorous round-trip expedition between Fort Leavenworth and the South Pass of the Rocky Mountains—twenty-two hundred miles in ninety-nine days without a casualty.

Now he collected his troops at Leavenworth, on the edge of American civilization, where he drilled them into a knot of disciplined soldiery to prepare them for the two-month journey through nine hundred miles of unforgiving wilderness. Before setting out, Kearny issued an assignment to James W. Magoffin, a longtime trader whose business acumen and force of personality had rendered him a well-known fixture along the trail. Fluent in Spanish and popular in Santa Fe, Magoffin had been summoned to Washington by Senator Benton in early June to discuss American objectives with Benton, Marcy, and Polk. His assignment was to travel to Santa Fe ahead of Kearny's army and persuade New Mexico's governor Manuel Armijo, an old friend, to abandon any plans to fight. History doesn't record whether he was to do this merely with words or perhaps with suggestions of more material inducements.

On June 16, Kearny and his troops set out upon the Santa Fe Trail. Waiting for them was Governor Armijo. Cunning, brutal, vainglorious, and obese ("a mountain of fat," as one traveler described him), Armijo was given to spouting flowery pronouncements that never seemed to say anything. He was utterly corrupt, brazen in his official thievery. He had emerged as a rich potentate by becoming customs collector for the Santa Fe Trail and then levying huge tariffs against American traders and pocketing large proportions of the proceeds. Now as governor he had the job of stifling this invasion of Anglo-Saxons. He never seemed particularly committed to the challenge. Indeed, following his session with Magoffin, he liquidated his business assets and appropriated considerable riches from the region's churches.

Kearny's Army of the West, as he called it, set out in stages during June with 1,458 men, to be followed shortly by another thousand. They dragged along twelve six-pound guns and four twelve-pound howitzers. Also in the train were 1,556 supply wagons, 459 horses, 3,658 draft mules, and nearly 15,000 cattle and oxen. The men would march through 537 miles of heat, dust, and privation before reaching a semblance of civilization at Bent's Fort, on the north bank of the Arkansas River. From there the Army of the West turned south toward Santa Fe. On August 14, Kearny entered the dusty town of Las Vegas, recently beset by a brutal Navajo attack. Standing atop an adobe building facing the town square he spoke to the townsfolk through the interpretation of the mayor.

"I have come amongst you by the order of my government to take possession of your country," he said, adding that he and his army came "as protectors, not as conquerors. Henceforth, I absolve you of all allegiance to the Mexican government." Then, noting the recent Indian attack, he derided the Mexican government's inability to protect its citizens. "My government," he said, "will *correct* all this. It will protect you in your persons and property." The townsfolk didn't know what to make of this bold warrior who marched into their midst with such bravado. But they seemed subdued by his confidence and his promise to honor their religious sensibilities and pay for all provisions taken by his army.

Along the trail, Kearny had heard from Armijo, who dispatched a number of fast couriers to deliver letters that were as ambiguous as his famous pronunciamentos. "You have notified me that you intend to take possession of the country I govern," said one letter. "The people of the country have risen en masse in my defense. If you take the country, it will be because you are strongest in battle. I suggest you to stop . . . and we will meet and negotiate on the plains."

Armijo seemed caught between his patriotic duty and a growing desire to flee with his riches. Many of his subordinates pressed him to rise to the occasion, and plans were laid to intercept the weary and bedraggled Kearny force some twelve miles outside Santa Fe at a juncture called Apache Canyon, where huge masses of rock and mountain pinched the trail into a narrow passageway.

This is where Armijo and his lieutenants amassed some four thousand armed Mexicans and Indians, stationing them for maximum military effect on the west side of the narrow canyon and high above the pass whence they could rain armaments down upon the invading Americans. But as the invaders approached, Armijo lost his nerve. He suddenly dismissed his troops and fled south into Chihuahua. He wrote a final missive to Kearny filled with his characteristic false bravado. "I do not *deliver* to Your Excellency the province of New Mexico," he clarified. "I only make a temporary military retreat, until I shall receive further orders from my government." But he was gone— and gone for good.

It was left to the mayor of a neighboring town to deliver the news and letter to Kearny. He galloped into the general's camp the evening of August 17, dismounted in a cloud of dust, and exclaimed with a shout of laughter, "Armijo and his troops have gone to hell! The canyon is all clear!"

And so by the following evening the conquest of New Mexico was complete. Kearny promptly set about consolidating his position with a combination of tact, efficiency, and gentle toughness. He established a civil government, named Charles Bent of Taos as territorial governor, and issued a code of laws. He didn't actually have authority to establish a civil government in such lands, and his action later generated some controversy back in Washington. But in New Mexico it generated stability, allowing Kearny to embark upon his next expedition, the trek into California. On September 25, with a contingent of three hundred mounted dragoons, Kearny set out for the Pacific, where events had reached a state of turbulence since word of the Mexican War had arrived.

CALIFORNIA'S TURBULENCE BEGAN on December 9, 1845, when Frémont and a few of his men rode into Sutter's Fort, at the confluence of the Sacramento and American rivers. Why he entered into Mexican territory has never been fully understood. His orders clearly confined his explorations to the Arkansas and Red rivers. But Frémont viewed these instructions as too restrictive for a man of his destiny. He wanted to find a convenient wagon route to California, which would have bolstered the migration of U.S. citizens into the region and hastened California's entry into the American union. Not coincidentally, such a route, if found, likely would have been called the Frémont Trail, thus cementing his name forever to the fate of California.

But Frémont also had something else in mind. Should his country slip into war with Mexico, he would be the only U.S. Army officer anywhere near the U.S. settlers needing protection from Mexican authorities. And war also would render the conquest of California diplomatically acceptable. And so, projecting himself as a mere mapmaker, he set about collecting intelligence and making contacts among the province's American expatriates.

Still, he sought initially to observe certain diplomatic niceties. He left the bulk of his force outside California during his early sojourn there. He also sought permission from Comandante General José María Castro, California's military governor, to garrison his force in the San Joaquin Valley for the winter, before proceeding north to Oregon in the spring. Permission was granted, whereupon Frémont promptly ignored the terms of the agreement. He wandered with his heavily armed force about California's coastal regions and hovered around Monterey, the provincial military capital.

This was too much for Castro. At stake, he believed, was the fate of a region that everyone knew would someday become a global pivot point. It encompassed some five thousand square miles of exquisite real estate, with a coastline that stretched some eight hundred miles along the Pacific. Its harbors at San Diego and San Francisco, located as gateways to the Orient, were among the world's finest. It boasted some of the most fertile soil to be found anywhere. Grass grew luxuriantly in the northern reaches, and conditions throughout vast areas were ideal for the cultivation of wheat, corn, grapes, and cattle.

It had been settled by Spanish clerics who built some twenty-one Catholic missions along the coast from San Diego to San Francisco and beyond. Eventually they presided over vast estates with thousands of acres under cultivation and immense herds of cattle, sheep, and horses. In the tradition of their faith, they brought thousands of Indians under their protection and tutelage and received in return abundant labor for the maintenance of their missions. And they cleared the way for the later influx of landowners and cattle barons who became the elite of the province.

But this centuries-old system of settlement was upended when Mexican authorities sought to break the power of the Church, and soon the missions atrophied and declined. In a mere twelve years, from 1834 to 1846, the Indian population of the twenty-one missions declined to 4,450 from 30,650. Cattle within the missions' herds dropped to 28,220 from 424,000. The number of horses, donkeys, and mules declined to 3,800 from 62,500. Most of the Indians returned to their tribes, and California found itself beset by the familiar Mexican problem of population stagnation.

In 1842 California had only about five thousand white inhabitants—about four thousand of Spanish origin, some four hundred U.S. immigrants, and the rest of European origin. About thirteen hundred lived around San Diego, another thousand at Monterey and some eight hundred each at Santa Barbara and San Francisco. The rest were scattered throughout the province. The only significant population dynamism was coming from U.S. immigrants, and this posed a serious risk to Mexican authorities. They knew, as did Polk and many other American expansionists, that if current trends continued California would go the way of Texas.

It was Comandante Castro's job to prevent that. On his side he had Mexican law, which prohibited this inflow and authorized local officials to expel unauthorized foreigners. On March 5, 1846, Castro ordered Frémont's immediate departure. He sent a letter also to Monterey's consul Thomas Larkin urging him to "inform said Capt. Fremont that since he entered this department with an armed force, whether through malice or error, he must now either blindly obey the authorities, or . . . experience the misfortunes which he has sought by his crimes."

Frémont responded with such outrage that it diminished his judgment, not to mention his survival instinct. He led his men to the top of a small mountain northeast of Monterey called Gavilan Peak, where he constructed a fort and prepared for a melodramatic last stand. He converted a nearby sapling into a flagpole and hoisted an American flag upon Mexican soil in a brazen act of defiance that almost seemed like a suicide wish. When Larkin sent a fast courier up to him with a letter urging a retreat, he responded with defiance. "We have in no wise done wrong to the people or the authorities of the country," he wrote, "and if we are hemmed in and assaulted here, we will die, every man of us, under the flag of our country."

But from his perch above the coastal valley Frémont could see Castro mustering a force that would indeed spell certain death for his entire force, and he began to reconsider a martyrdom that would mark him forever as a fool rather than a hero. He broke camp and slowly made his way north into Oregon, stopping upon the southern shores of Klamath Lake. There he waited.

He didn't wait long. Into his camp one evening strode Archibald Gillespie, carrying the secret instructions from Washington as well as a passel of letters from Frémont's wife and his famous father-in-law. Gillespie also told of episodes during his trek through Mexico that had convinced him war was inevitable. Within a day Frémont would decide to return to California—where, he was convinced, his fate was intertwined with that of his expanding country. After a spree of Indian killing in revenge for the slaughter of three members of his party by a Klamath Lake tribe, the American pathfinder set his path southward toward the West's great geographic prize.

When Frémont got there things were beginning to break. On

April 17, Castro had ordered all noncitizens out of California and vowed to stop U.S. immigration once and for all. He also reportedly had induced the area's Indian tribes to attack American settlers. This enflamed passions among the American expatriates, and in June one motley contingent initiated a rebellion in Sonoma aimed at ripping California from Mexican control and creating a new nation called the Bear Flag Republic. Frémont did all he could to encourage the revolt while studiously avoiding any overt action that could be construed as belligerent. But, when Castro quite understandably sent a military force toward Sonoma to quell the uprising, the pathfinder became an open combatant, self-charged with protecting Americans from aroused Mexican authority.

Frémont recruited some 160 expatriates from the Sacramento Valley, commingled them with his sixty men, and created what he called the California Battalion. By this time news of the Rio Grande skirmish had reached Commodore Sloat, who, concluding Frémont had word of actual war or perhaps had received new orders authorizing his military initiatives, commenced some aggressive actions of his own. On July 7 he seized Monterey without bloodshed. Two days later his top lieutenant, Commander John Montgomery, seized San Francisco bloodlessly. In both instances the Americans announced the existence of war and declared California to be U.S. territory. They promised fair treatment of all locals, and then hoisted American flags over the respective customs houses.

A week later Stockton arrived at Monterey, and four days thereafter Frémont managed to get there as well. It was then that Commodore Sloat, commander of the U.S. Pacific Squadron, learned that Frémont had initiated his military actions without knowledge that the U.S.-Mexican war had begun and without authorization from Washington. Sloat was aghast to learn Frémont's actions provided no cover for his own. So rattled was the commodore that he placed Stockton in charge of his squadron and set sail for home.

Now the two highest-ranking U.S. officials in California were Stockton and Frémont, who not surprisingly developed a high degree of camaraderie. Both were super-patriots hungry for fame and glory in the name of the United States. Both valued action over contemplation and demonstrated little patience for those who disagreed with them. Both harbored contempt for groups or peoples arrayed against their country. And both displayed a penchant for boldness that often undercut their judgment. Neither would serve as a check on the other.

Stockton incorporated Frémont's Bear Flag rebels into a military unit he dubbed the California Battalion of United States Troops, which he hoped could recruit some two thousand men. He promoted Frémont to major and put him in charge, with Gillespie, now a captain, as his second in command. Together, the three Americans raised volunteer units in major towns around northern California, and Stockton then issued a proclamation that was so bellicose and disrespectful of Mexican sensibilities that it precluded a peaceful conquest.

Stockton devised a military plan that called for Frémont to land at San Diego with a contingent of troops while he would emerge at San Pedro with another band and move inland. The idea was to catch Castro in a pincers movement and end the war on U.S. terms. Before a shot was fired, it had the desired effect. Castro contacted Larkin, the Monterey consul, with an offer of truce and a promise to parley with Stockton about ending hostilities. This was a breakthrough, but Stockton promptly booted the opportunity by making demands that Castro couldn't accept. Seeing the futility of his position, Castro dissolved his force and departed the field. This seeming victory was actually an unfortunate development, for now Stockton had no one to negotiate with—and hence no one who could enforce an end to hostilities.

Mistaking this lull in the fighting for victory, Stockton issued his August 17 proclamation and penned his self-congratulatory—and premature—letter to Polk. Within a month an insurrection erupted in Los Angeles, hotbed of anti-American sentiment, and soon the war was on again. Gillespie, garrisoned at the town with forty-eight troops, lost ten when they were ambushed and captured. He found himself besieged at his headquarters but managed to reposition himself and his troops upon higher ground—only to discover the higher ground lacked water. Forced to surrender, he was unceremoniously kicked out of town.

With Frémont now well positioned near Monterey, Stockton moved his force to San Diego, whence he planned a march on Los Angeles. Before he could set out, however, he learned that Stephen Kearny, making his way from the west, was not far off. He sent Gillespie to meet the brigadier general with thirty-nine troops and a plan for assaulting the main Mexican force outside the city. The resulting battle turned into a near disaster, and Kearny found himself pinned down without access to food, water, or medicine. Stockton had to send another contingent to rescue the general and his men. Kearny's losses numbered some thirty men, killed and wounded.

Notwithstanding these fumblings, ultimately the Mexican forces were no match for the Americans when Stockton moved a consolidated force toward Los Angeles. At every potentially decisive confrontation, the Americans prevailed and soon found themselves triumphantly in possession of Los Angeles once again. Frémont, meanwhile, moving down from Monterey, mopped up any lingering pockets of resistance to the north. Soon the conquest that Stockton had pronounced on August 17 actually was reality.

But another war then commenced—a bureaucratic war involving Kearny, Stockton, and Frémont. Kearny, putting forth his superior rank and his specific orders from Washington, informed Stockton that he expected the naval officer to stand down so he could assume the territorial governorship. Stockton refused and defiantly named Frémont governor of the territory. When Kearny demanded that Frémont yield to his superior rank, the pathfinder likewise refused. To Stockton and Frémont, it was natural that they should retain command as California was in U.S. hands only through their own actions. In their view, Kearny's orders to take California were now null and void because California already had been taken.

Kearny didn't see it that way. And, while he lacked capacity to enforce his commands, he had no intention of accepting what he considered abject insubordination. He would bide his time but never relinquish the high ground. On January 17, 1847, he wrote to Frémont that, "as I am prepared to carry out the President's instructions to me, which you oppose, I must, for the purpose of preventing a collision between us . . . remain silent for the present, leaving with you the responsibility of doing that for which you have no authority, and preventing me from complying with the President's orders."

The matter was settled when Commodore W. Branford Shubrick arrived and established himself as the highest-ranking naval officer on the Pacific Coast. He and Kearny promptly reached an accommodation that placed Kearny in command of all military and civilian matters in California. Now the general set about the difficult task of bringing Frémont to heel. This included ordering him to return to Missouri with Kearny's party, leaving California on May 31, 1847. They reached Fort Leavenworth on August 22, at which point Kearny promptly placed Frémont under arrest and sent him to Washington to face military charges of insubordination.

For James Polk this was an unfortunate turn of events. It would set off within the volcanic Thomas Benton, Frémont's father-in-law, fiery eruptions of outrage and high dudgeon, and it would prove impossible for the president to get out of the way of the falling debris.

But Polk was elated with the broader events in New Mexico and California. The earnest president had vowed repeatedly that he would never seek to acquire Mexican lands through conquest, and he still believed that. These lands would be purchased as part of a peace settlement freely entered into by the two parties—entered freely, everyone understood, as soon as the United States applied sufficient military pressure on Mexico. But of course America's western conquests would enhance Polk's bargaining leverage once those negotiations got underway. And, in any event, he had no intention of ever relinquishing any of those conquered lands.

20 · THE NEW FACE
OF WAR

"We Are Yet to Have a Long and Wearisome Struggle"

As August in Washington descended into its final sultry days, James Polk pondered his situation. Intimations of political and military adversity gnawed at him, and it became difficult to maintain any sense of optimism about the war. His defeat on the $2 million bill was a serious blow that could dash his hopes for an early negotiated peace with Mexico. He knew a protracted war could sap his political standing at home and breed military persistence in his excitable adversaries to the south. Hence, failure could breed more failure, which could generate in turn even more.

It occurred to Polk that he would have to look at the war differently—as a possibly persistent struggle requiring greater military boldness than he had anticipated or wanted. Mexico, so far silent in response to his peace overture of July 27, seemed disinclined to seek a negotiated settlement. So the president retreated to the exquisite solitude of his White House writing table and personally devised a new military plan. On Saturday, August 29, he presented it to his cabinet.

The idea, he said, was to initiate an amphibious landing at Veracruz, Mexico's leading Gulf port. This could be effected only after the return of the yearly "healthy season," when coastal folks weren't under constant assault from the dreaded yellow fever, colloquially known in those parts as *vómito*. The troops would have to take special care to avoid the hazards of the Fortress of San Juan de Ulloa, a seemingly impregnable sentinel protecting the city. But if a landing party could join up with Commodore Conner's blockading squadron, perhaps they could lay siege to the fortress and force its capitulation. The fortress then could be blown up, permitting an army to move on to Mexico City via the same route taken by the great conqueror Cortés toward his bloody triumph more than three centuries before.

These thoughts, Polk later reported to his diary, "met with a favourable consideration." The cabinet also agreed the U.S. military should probably seize Tampico, some three hundred miles north on the coast, as Santa Anna helpfully had suggested to Alexander Mackenzie in Cuba two months before.

Polk did glimpse a few fragments of hope that all this might prove unnecessary. On September 1 the president got word, generously delivered through the British embassy, of the U.S. Navy's bloodless California victories at Monterey and San Francisco, as well as Frémont's success in forcing Comandante Castro's troops into retreat. This led Polk to calculate that a California conquest, particularly if joined by a similar New Mexico victory, might induce the Mexicans to negotiate an end to the war.

And a reporter for the *New York Tribune,* writing from Havana, dispatched an intriguing piece, reprinted in the *Union* on September 7. It said that Mexican army elements were agitating for Santa Anna's return to power. President Paredes himself had promised to "liberate all persons confined for political offences." This, said the reporter, "indirectly offers the olive branch to Santa Anna himself," clearing the way for an alliance between the two men. Thinking back to the exiled general's own olive branch to the United States, Polk saw the promise of a possible negotiated settlement. The president was heartened to learn from Commodore Conner that Santa Anna had freely passed the U.S. blockade and entered Veracruz amid much fanfare and civic tumult.

But despite these glimmerings Polk continued to fret about the state of the war effort. He confronted the army's quartermaster general, Thomas Jesup, about the man's apparent inability to get New York troops shipped to California in a timely manner. He inserted himself into the matter of whether General Taylor should transport supplies in wagons or on mules. He generally chafed at what he considered "entirely too much delay and too much want of energy & promptness in execution on the part of many of the subordinate officers."

And he became increasingly uneasy about Taylor, who seemed to lack the "grasp of mind" for a major command. Though brave and willing to take orders, the general displayed little planning initiative and seemed "unwilling to express any opinion or to take any responsibility on himself." Yet Polk was stuck with Taylor. The army had no one else who seemed fit for the job.

On the evening of September 19, Navy Secretary John Mason and War Secretary William Marcy called on the president to deliver more bad news—Mexico's reply to Polk's peace overture. The matter had been postponed until the new Mexican Congress convened on December 6. This amounted to an out-and-out rejection. Polk's war plans would have to change.

First he would cease his generous policy of paying liberally for provisions obtained in Mexico's conquered lands; now the necessary stores would be seized as booty of war. With Marcy and Mason he drafted orders for an assault on the Mexican coast by land and sea. Marcy was ordered to determine which troops could be spared for the new campaign, while Mason drafted orders for Commodore Conner to take Tampico.

As these official actions unfolded the country too was beginning to sense the war's new face. The *New Orleans Picayune*, probably the country's most sagacious analyst of Mexican affairs, reported that Mexico seemed bent on scoring a major military victory before entering into negotiations. Only after such a victory, the reasoning went, could Mexico expect a reasonable peace. This reality was beginning to sink into American thinking also, said the *Picayune*, adding that "the public mind is settling down in the conviction that we are yet to have a long and wearisome struggle."

Hopes were also dimming that Santa Anna harbored any thought of bucking the defiance of his countrymen. The *Union* quoted the general as vowing to drive Zachary Taylor all the way back to the Sabine

River and reclaim the entirety of Texas. Arriving in Mexico City on September 15, Santa Anna had declared:

> Mexicans! There was once a day, and my heart dilates with the remembrance . . . you saluted me with the title of Soldier of the People. Allow me to take it again, never more to be given up, and to devote myself, until death, to the defence of the liberty and independence of the Republic!

Clearly, the wily general and his unctuous agent, Alejandro Atocha, had snookered the president of the United States. Now that he was back in Mexico, Santa Anna wanted power and national acclaim, available only through glorious victory against the despised Americans.

On October 1, the *Union* sought to prepare its readers for the new policy. If Mexico wouldn't entertain any peace discussions until December, said the paper, "the intervening months will witness the rapid and victorious progress of our arms into the heart of the country, and . . . our arms will bristle upon its strong holds, while our squadrons beleaguer and threaten its coast, and . . . all this will be done in the spirit and purpose of effectual and invasive war."

The next day Polk received two important letters. One, from Taylor, reported he was approaching Monterrey, on the Mexican plateau, where he anticipated a major battle. The other, from Kearny, announced he had conquered New Mexico and would soon depart for California. "Gen'l Kearny," wrote Polk, "has thus far performed his duty well."

BEFORE POLK'S RECEIPT of Taylor's letter, events would unfold in northern Mexico confirming the general's valor and tactical competence. But his strategic judgment would be called into question. Following Taylor's victory at Resaca de la Palma in May, the general settled in at Fort Texas, across from Matamoros. Mexico's General Arista quickly abandoned the dusty Rio Grande town and led his bedraggled troops to Monterrey. Shortly thereafter Taylor crossed the

Rio Grande and planted his army upon undisputed Mexican soil—
the first time a U.S. army had invaded foreign territory since Andrew
Jackson's incursion into Spanish Florida in 1818.

Mexico's northern army, now under that heartless warrior, General
Pedro de Ampudia, settled in at Monterrey, a fortress of a town nes-
tled between the Santa Catarina River to the south and a collection
of hills that constituted the beginnings of the majestic Sierra Madre
range. Soon he had collected more than seven thousand troops, well
protected behind hastily but sturdily constructed fortifications around
the town and upon the surrounding hills. His aim was to employ his
armored position as a bastion against the U.S. advance.

Taylor's orders from Marcy were vague. "Prosecute the war with
vigor, in the manner you deem most effective," the secretary had written in late May. In June he instructed Taylor to "dispose the enemy
to desire an end to the war . . . in the shortest space of time practicable." Taylor, lacking political acumen but possessing a generally surly
temperament, responded to such blurry instruction by curtailing his
communication with Washington. This infuriated both Marcy and
Polk. But Taylor was no status quo general.

In July he moved his troops to a staging area at Camargo, a dilapi-
dated town of three thousand inhabitants on the San Juan River. In
late August and early September he began moving his army toward
Monterrey. As he approached, he instantly recognized Ampudia's tactical folly. The Mexican general had fortified his troops in all the natural locations, but his fortifications were so far removed from each
other that none could assist another effectively if it came under attack.
And he had placed no troops in reserve to reinforce beleaguered units
as needed.

Taylor sent Brigadier General William Worth's division in a
wide sweep to the west and south to cut off Ampudia's supply route
from Saltillo, then ordered an assault upon the Mexican fortification atop Federación Hill, southwest of the town. Both maneuvers
proved successful. After capturing the Saltillo road, the Americans
routed the Mexican defenders atop the hill and quickly employed an
abandoned nine-pound cannon to rain devastation upon defenders

of nearby Fort Soldado. Worth had established his position to the west of Monterrey.

Meanwhile, Taylor led a separate attack on its eastern fortifications, particularly well-entrenched positions called El Tenería and El Diablo. On the first day the U.S. troops managed to take El Tenería. But the cost was high—some 394 casualties—and Taylor's performance was unimpressive. Through vagueness and indecision, he allowed a diversionary feint to turn into an actual unplanned assault, which had accounted for the heavy losses.

On September 22, the battle's second day, Taylor rested his eastern forces while Worth's men west of town expanded their perimeter by capturing the important Bishop's Palace atop the eastern portion of Independencia Hill. Ampudia, blustery in conversation but passive in battle, withdrew his men from all outlying fortifications and consolidated his force inside Monterrey. That set the stage for the battle's third and final day.

Taylor's men moved into the city slowly and cautiously, avoiding dangerous streets and moving briskly from building to building. They blew holes in the walls separating adjacent structures, killing Mexican troops on ground floors, then stormed upstairs to remove the enemy from upper floors and rooftops. Worth took a similar tack in moving in from the west. He dragged with him a ten-inch mortar that pounded the Central Plaza.

Before daybreak the next day, Ampudia sent a courier with an offer to abandon the city if Taylor would accept his terms—most notably, permission for his men to leave with their weapons, including artillery. He reported, falsely, that the United States and Mexico had entered into peace negotiations, which negated any need for the Americans to take his men as prisoners. Taylor initially rejected this demand outright, then wavered, then met twice with Ampudia, then generally accepted his terms. Ampudia's seven-thousand-man army, with six artillery pieces, would be free to depart—and fight again later. Taylor also accepted an eight-week armistice between the two armies.

Polk got word of the battle late on the evening of October 11. Immediately he concluded Taylor had squandered his victory. At a hastily convened cabinet session the next day, the president's men expressed similar sentiments. The group perceived only two reasons to justify Taylor's concessions—first, if he believed he held no prospect of capturing Ampudia's army; and, second, if he had serious reason to believe the war was nearing a negotiated conclusion. But Taylor offered his Washington superiors no information suggesting he lacked an opportunity for a Monterrey victory. And, if Taylor actually believed peace was at hand, then he had allowed himself to be misled by his crafty adversary. Either way, it seemed difficult to justify the general's actions.

The enraged cabinet unanimously agreed that, had Taylor managed to capture the Mexican army, he could have deprived Ampudia's troops of their arms and discharged them upon their parole of honor not to fight against the United States for the rest of the war. Such a blow to Mexico might have ended the war outright.

In truth, Taylor's army had suffered grievously during the three-day battle. Exhausted by arduous maneuvers in and around Monterrey, haggard from lack of food and sleep, exposed to harsh heat by day and cold rains by night, the U.S. troops were at a low ebb of morale and organizational crispness when Taylor cut his deal with Ampudia. Thus, there was at least an element of justification for his decision. But the stakes were high enough and the door-to-door city assault was succeeding well enough that the better judgment probably would have been to hold firm and fight on.

Either way, Polk didn't want a messy public dispute over the matter. It was agreed Taylor should be ordered to terminate the armistice and prosecute the war with vigor. But the terms of the order should be free of condemnatory language. Polk turned his attention toward his resolve to open up a new military front on the Gulf Coast.

On October 17 the president met with diplomat F. M. Dimond, who had served many years as U.S. consul at Veracruz. Polk pumped Dimond for details on the geography of the area and insights on how an amphibious landing might be accomplished. Dimond said a landing party should take the island of Sacrificios, about four miles south of San Juan de Ulloa and well out of reach of that stout fortress's powerful guns. From that position, said Dimond, the Americans could lay siege to the castle and establish a staging area for moving troops onto the mainland and behind Veracruz. Meanwhile, the navy would cut off the city and castle from the sea. Delighted with the briefing, Polk pressed army officials to determine precisely which troops should be diverted to the Veracruz expedition.

That left open the question of Taylor's strategic aims—whether he should march further into the Mexican interior or hold his position at Monterrey to allow for greater troop deployments at Veracruz. On October 20, cabinet members agreed he should stand pat. Ampudia, after all, still had some seven thousand troops ready for war, thanks to Taylor's armistice agreement, and Santa Anna had vowed to combine Ampudia's army with a larger contingent from Mexico City. Thus Taylor's army soon would be outnumbered four or five to one. Besides, there was no clear objective discernible in a Taylor advance that could outweigh the risk. He couldn't ultimately get to Mexico City over the rough terrain before him, and even a victory south of Monterrey wasn't likely to force a Mexican truce. A special courier was dispatched the next day to deliver these views to Taylor.

Although the cabinet discussion didn't reflect political considerations, they were never far from Polk's mind. With a protracted war sapping his political standing, he did not want to invest money and blood on campaigns that could not hasten an end to hostilities. Complicating his calculation was a disturbing article in a Spanish-language newspaper at New Orleans called *La Patria*. It was reprinted in the *New Orleans Delta* and later in the *Union*.

Its substance was a letter sent to the *Patria*'s Havana correspondent from "a man of high standing in Mexico, and of considerable intellectual ability." The letter suggested some intriguing developments had attended the Mexican return of Santa Anna, who "has been assiduously occupied in directing manoeuvres extremely strange and mysterious to those who are not well informed of the meshes in which this affair is entangled." It seems, said the letter writer, that the general had obtained from the U.S. government a "safe-conduct, in order that Com. Conner should not prevent him from landing at Vera Cruz," and this safe conduct had been given "under *conditions and arrangements* of a character extraordinarily *Machiavellian*."

The letter reported that Santa Anna had promised to profess interest in a vigorous Mexican war effort but, in fact, "by pre-arrangement with the government of the United States," would conduct hostilities in a manner designed to ensure U.S. success. In this way the Mexican people and their leaders would conclude no victory was possible, and they would accept a settlement highly favorable to both the United States and Santa Anna. The latter, according to rumor, would rule as dictator for eight or ten years under a U.S. protectorate, after which the United States would annex portions of Mexican territory at Santa Anna's behest.

Though incorrect in its most outlandish particulars, the letter contained just enough truth to generate interest and also to be highly injurious to Polk's political standing. The *Union* labeled the speculations "absurd" and predicted they would "amuse some of our readers by their extravagant improbability." But the paper acknowledged the report's political potency and predicted it would "probably not fail to reappear in the columns of some of the whig journals."

Democrats also felt a growing threat in waves of abolitionist sentiment emerging among northeastern Whigs. "Every mail which we receive from the north, brings us new and stronger proof of the breadth and strength of the whig movement towards abolition," warned the *Union* on October 10. A few days later the paper argued this agitation threatened the Union itself, then asked, "Yet who can deny that the whig party, as a national party, is throughout large sections of our country steadfastly laboring to bring the whole topic of slavery into the next presidential canvass?" The paper didn't need to remind its readers that this agitation constituted a serious threat to Democratic unity. With slavery interjected into partisan politics, prospects mounted that fissures would emerge among northeastern Democrats as some would find irresistible the political pressures generated by Whig antislavery agitations.

Polk's political standing suffered a more immediate blow with the fall election results. The Whigs of the Thirtieth Congress, set to convene a year hence in December 1847, would have 115 House seats to the Democrats' 108. Clay's party had picked up thirty-one seats in the elections, while Jackson's had lost twenty-eight. It was a swing of fifty-nine seats—a signal defeat for the Democrats, leavened only slightly by the party's four-seat gain in the Senate. It was only the second time in the Whigs' history that they had captured the House, the lone previous success having been fostered by Harrison's 1840 presidential victory. Then it was economic turmoil that had generated the Democratic rebuff. Now it seemed to be the war.

Whatever it was, the Whigs picked up fourteen additional House seats in New York, five in Pennsylvania, three in Ohio, and one each in New Jersey and Georgia. The Whigs also gained governorships in Ohio, North Carolina, and Massachusetts—and in New York, where voters, with unsentimental finality, upended the career of that dignified and eloquent Democratic mainstay, Silas Wright.

Polk felt particularly stung by Wright's fate. Despite the lingering awkwardness between Polk and his New York friend over the unfortunate events surrounding Polk's cabinet decisions, the president harbored deep affection for the man. He attributed Wright's defeat to New York's obstinately rebellious Hunker faction that despised Van Buren's Barnburners with internecine passion. "This faction shall hereafter receive no favours at my hands if I know it," the president vowed to his diary.

The electoral results also caused further difficulties with James Buchanan, who attributed the Democrats' Pennsylvania losses to Polk's tariff bill. In conversation with the president on November 5, the *Union*'s Ritchie reported rumors Buchanan was preparing an anti-tariff article for a Pennsylvania newspaper. Later that day Buchanan himself stopped by to express concerns about the tariff policy. Polk brushed aside his concerns, saying he would oppose changes in the law until it had a chance to prove itself.

Two days later the cabinet met to ponder the president's war policy and the troop levels needed to prosecute it. Marcy had advocated a forty-thousand-man army—fifteen thousand regular troops and 25,000 volunteers. With cabinet approval Polk reduced this to

35,000—fifteen thousand in the Regular Army, ten thousand more that could be either enlisted or regular, and an additional ten thousand to be kept in reserve if needed. But the cabinet snagged on the question whether the military strategy should be merely to hold captured territory or to prosecute the war into the heart of Mexico.

The same day Polk received a visit from Benton, freshly returned to Washington for the Twenty-ninth Congress's "lame duck" second session, set to begin on December 7. The Missourian was in a sprightly mood, though somewhat agitated by reports that Mexican General José María Castro was about to publish an account of his California dealings with Frémont. Benton feared Castro's account would malign Frémont and, by extension, America. This, he said, would undermine the country's standing in foreign capitals "unless it was met & contradicted in an authentic manner," as Polk put it to his diary. Benton proposed a letter from himself to Polk, to be published in the *Union,* that would counter Castro's account and set the record straight. Polk embraced the idea.

Benton also advised Polk against any passive war policy aimed at merely holding captured territory. That could extend the war for years, warned the Missourian, and destroy the Democrats.

"Ours is a go ahead people," he said, "and our only policy to obtain peace and save ourselves is to press the war boldly."

He advocated not only the seizure of Veracruz but also "a rapid, crushing movement" against Mexico City. Benton added that the invading army should be accompanied by a commission of prominent Americans, of both parties, authorized to negotiate peace terms with Mexican officials. This, said the erudite Missourian, had often been done in European wars.

"I am willing to accompany the army as one of these commissioners of peace," said Benton. Polk readily assured the senator that, should he consider the plan expedient, he would be happy to make Benton a commissioner.

But Polk had bigger plans for Benton, as he suggested when the two men talked again on November 10. Polk suggested he could take Veracruz with a relatively small contingent, but any push to Mexico City would require congressional approval for a much larger force.

This was in part because Polk didn't expect Taylor to cooperate in transferring significant numbers of troops at Monterrey. In fact, he didn't expect much cooperation from Taylor at all unless he commanded the Veracruz expedition. Polk didn't consider Taylor up to that challenge. Benton agreed.

"Who," asked the president, "would be the proper officer to command so important an expedition?"

Benton fell silent, apparently pondering the question. Polk asked about Winfield Scott.

"I have no confidence in him," said Benton.

Polk mentioned the names of several other officers, none of whom elicited any enthusiasm from Benton.

The senator digressed upon the question in a broader framework. What Polk needed, he said, was a lieutenant general who would serve as the army's overall general-in-chief, overseeing and coordinating all military operations. This must be a military man, of course, and someone of unquestioned bravery. But the job also required a man of broad talents and energy not always found in military men. Then the Missourian allowed as how he himself might fit the bill if such an office were created by Congress.

"I would be willing to accept the command," he said.

Polk expressed confidence in Benton and said he would be pleased to see him leading the army if Congress would create such a position. Benton, noting Whig efforts to exploit the war for political ends, offered unstinting support in Polk's hour of need.

"I will give you any support in this war in my power," he said.

Polk expressed gratitude and added he had never harbored any but the most cordial sentiments toward the Missourian. After further discussion on the war, Benton left.

POLK'S NEW THINKING on the war was taking shape. He must force a Mexican surrender as quickly as possible, and that would require the Veracruz landing and subsequent conquest of Mexico City. That in turn would require additional troops and greater competence and loyalty in his military leadership. He also would have to find ways to fund the expedition. And all this would require congressional approval at a time when his political standing was sinking. Democrats would still command both houses of Congress in the coming lame-duck session, but the Whigs' recent electoral victories certainly would embolden the congressional opposition and weaken the resolve of many Democrats. Clearly, the president faced a fearsome political and military challenge.

Just getting full cooperation within his cabinet, Polk felt, would take some effort. Buchanan, displaying his characteristic maverick impulses, was signaling opposition to any march on Mexico City. And there were further complications from Taylor, who responded to Marcy's most recent requests for military information and recommendations in a most desultory and unhelpful fashion.

The various decision elements occupied the November 14 cabinet session, which focused entirely on the war. The question, said Polk, was whether he should call up additional volunteers and march into the Mexican heartland. Marcy promptly said yes. Buchanan strenuously countered that an assault on Mexico City would cost too much money, present a high risk of failure, and wouldn't end the war even if successful. He would go along with Marcy's call for more troops, but only reluctantly. Ultimately it was agreed the president should call up nine additional regiments from the states to serve out the war. Polk decided to proceed with the Veracruz attack but defer the Mexico City expedition for a later date.

Turning their attention to Taylor, the cabinet members agreed he was unfit to command either the Veracruz expedition or any march to Mexico City. But no consensus emerged on who might qualify for the assignment. A few days later the cabinet reluctantly concluded the only viable candidate was the cantankerous and prickly Winfield Scott. Before acting on the matter, Polk consulted Benton, who agreed Scott was the only option. The two men also agreed that, should Polk get Congress to accept creation of a lieutenant general to command the entire war effort, the president would offer the job to Benton and Benton would accept.

Polk scheduled a session with Scott at the White House on November 19. The president disliked the man as much as ever, didn't trust him, and only reluctantly accepted the necessity of his promotion. But he sought to put the best face possible upon the situation. Polk outlined the logic for an assault on Veracruz. Scott concurred. Polk added that the man in command of the expedition must have confidence in the administration and, conversely, the administration must have confidence in the man in command. Scott again agreed. Polk then said that, notwithstanding the previous unpleasantness, he did possess confidence in Scott's ability and was inclined to give him the command.

Scott erupted in paroxysms of gratitude and joy. "He was . . . so much affected that he almost shed tears," the president later reported. With great conviction and at fulsome length, Scott expressed complete trust and faith in Polk and his government, added his willingness to accept completely Polk's recommendations on subordinates, and vowed to prove his gratitude upon the field of battle. "He left," reported the president, "apparently the most delighted man I have seen for a long time."

There remained the increasingly uncooperative Zachary Taylor, who had not responded well to Marcy's most recent letter. The secretary had suggested that, since his army now was idle at Monterrey, he could spare the troops needed for Veracruz. But the question had been left to Taylor's discretion. Replying "in very bad taste and in worse temper," as Polk saw it, Taylor protested against such interference, which he said thwarted his ability to operate as chief-in-command of the army in Mexico. "I have no prejudice against him," wrote Polk, "but think he has acted with great weakness and folly." It seems, he added, the general had become "giddy with the idea of the presidency."

He wasn't alone. Many prominent Whigs demonstrated a similar giddiness at the same idea and flooded the nation's political consciousness with scornful attacks on the president. Daniel Webster, speaking to a rapt Whig audience in Boston, declared Polk's war policy to be "illegal in its character" and "a great misjudgment on the part of the President . . . a clear violation of his duty . . . an impeachable offence." The latter suggestion generated explosive applause. Senator John Clayton of Delaware attacked Polk's tariff policy, calling for the immediate and unconditional restoration of the 1842 tariff. "Until that end is obtained," he declared, "we hearken to no compromises, we listen to no half-way measures."

Polk, looking ahead to the second congressional session of his presidency, fully anticipated this drumbeat of attack to intensify as the Whig opposition sought to undermine his fortitude and destroy his party's chances of retaining the White House at the next election. But the indomitable occupant of the White House would not falter or retreat. True to his past and his nature, he would seek to ignore the slings and arrows of outrageous opposition and forge ahead to what he knew would be military and political victory.

21 · THE POLITICS OF RANCOR

Constitutional Usurpation vs. Moral Treason

THROUGH THE LATTER days of November and into December, as members of Congress drifted into Washington and settled in for the second session of the Twenty-ninth Congress, everyone knew this would be a season of political enmity. The war was driving a wedge through official Washington, and even by the political standards of the day, which encompassed a certain acceptance of rhetorical malevolence, the atmosphere was highly charged.

James Polk liked to think he was above all that. He would let others succumb to the lure of political excess, even when they aimed their truculence directly at him. He would suffer in silence and then unburden himself to his diary with manifest pride that he was one politician in Washington who wasn't tempted by the politics of rancor.

But the attacks of his enemies were eating at him, and he found it increasingly difficult to resist responding in kind. In weaving together his second Annual Message, he penned the following passage:

> The war has been represented as unjust and unnecessary, and as one of aggression on our part upon a weak and injured enemy. Such erroneous views, though entertained by but few, have been widely and extensively circulated not only at home, but have been spread throughout Mexico and the whole world. A more effectual means could not have been devised to encourage the enemy and protract the war than to advocate and adhere to their cause, and thus give them "aid and comfort."

By placing quotation marks around "aid and comfort" he labeled his critics traitors, for those words formed the constitutional definition of treason. The reaction from Whigs was swift and angry.

The offending passage, declared the *Intelligencer*, "defaces" Polk's arguments and required "no delay of reprehension." The paper attacked the president for taking what he apparently considered the "necessary precaution" of warning the nation that any doubt about his war rationale "was not permitted" and would be silenced by allegations of the highest crime against the nation. The *Union* responded the next day by drawing a distinction between overt acts of treason and the kinds of advocacy that encouraged an enemy and thus protracted a war. The former, said the paper, was punishable "by the law in pursuance of the constitution." But the latter, which "exists only in the embryo of an intent substantially treasonable . . . is punished, not by the law's avenging power, but by the open and burning shame of 'MORAL TREASON!'"

"Moral Treason" was an epithet hurled three decades earlier by War of 1812 supporters—including the *Intelligencer*—at war opponents. Then, as now, it pushed against the limits of acceptable debate. But probably no more so than the allegations flung at Polk—that he had trampled the Constitution and deceived the electorate to manufacture an illegal war for nefarious purposes unsupported by public sentiment.

Aside from Polk's uncharacteristic "aid and comfort" thrust, he sought generally to fashion his Annual Message as a measured political defense focused on what he considered the facts in the case. Recounting in intricate detail the events leading up to the war, he argued the United States had sufficient grounds for hostilities, even before the Rio Grande bloodshed, based on Mexican abuses against U.S. citizens. He traced the history of Texas independence and disputed the notion that annexation represented any kind of insult to Mexico. "From the day that the battle of San Jacinto was fought until the present hour," he argued, "Mexico has never possessed the power to reconquer Texas."

Defending Texas's claim to the Rio Grande as its western boundary, Polk recounted the full history of the issue, including actions by both the Texas legislature and the U.S. Congress that stamped the disputed territory as part of Texas and, hence, now part of the United States. A U.S. refusal to defend that territory, said Polk, "would have been a violation of good faith toward the people of Texas."

No, said the president, it wasn't the United States that had precipitated the war but Mexican officials who declared America's Texas annexation a casus belli and ordered their armies across the Rio Grande to conquer not just the territory between that river and the Nueces but the full Texas expanse all the way to the Sabine.

The president recounted in detail his various peace initiatives, with particular emphasis on the bellicose response of Paredes, whom Polk branded a usurper, a monarchist, and a "sworn enemy of the United States." Hence, said Polk, it was only "expedient" for him to allow Santa Anna back into Mexico. It was hoped, said Polk, that the former exile would take a more conciliatory approach to the war. He had to acknowledge, though, that only time would tell whether that hope was realistic.

The president extolled the efficiency and valor of U.S. forces, which had taken military possession of wide expanses of northern and western Mexico. "Well may the American people be proud of the energy and gallantry of our regular and volunteer officers and soldiers," he wrote, adding the best way to end the war was to let those troops prosecute it as vigorously as possible.

As for the conquered territories, Polk said he anticipated little resistance from inhabitants there to the "temporary governments which have thus, from the necessity of the case and according to the laws of war, been established." He added it might prove necessary to ensure the security of these conquests "by making adequate appropriation for the purpose of erecting fortifications and defraying the expense necessarily incident to the maintenance of our possession of authority over them."

Turning to what he needed from Congress, Polk renewed his call for the $2 million bill—the appropriation aimed at securing a settlement with Mexican leaders in need of official funds, pending Senate ratification of a peace treaty. He requested congressional approval for a government loan of from $19 million to $23 million—enough to prosecute the war, if necessary, through the middle of 1848. And he called on Congress to give "early and favorable consideration" to the troop recommendations encompassed in Secretary Marcy's corollary report—a total force of 36,000 troops, including nearly seventeen thousand regulars, some 9,400 volunteers, and a "contingent force" of ten thousand volunteers, "to be . . . called into the service if needed."

As Polk expected, his message ignited a fierce congressional war debate. In the House, Kentucky's fiery Garrett Davis introduced a resolution requesting release of all orders to military and naval officers related to the creation of civil governments in conquered lands. Had Kearny and Stockton, he demanded, received presidential authorization to create such governments in New Mexico and California? If so, he wished to understand "by what imperial or regal authority his majesty undertook to act in the premises." It had, he said, the ring of usurpation.

Stephen Douglas of Illinois, a rising House member and staunch Polk defender, took elaborate pains to explain that the Kearny and Stockton proclamations had been misunderstood. These men did not annex this territory into the United States, he insisted, but merely stated the fact of conquest, which had brought the territories under U.S. control. Once that had taken place, according to the laws of war, it was necessary for the commanders on the ground to create civil governments to ensure peace and protect the citizenry. "It was therefore," he said, "the act of conquest which annexed the territory, and it did not require the proclamation of General Kearny or Commodore Stockton."

Polk faced a bit of a problem here. Both Kearny and Stockton had indeed exceeded their authority by proclaiming the people of New Mexico and California to be U.S. citizens. Only Congress could do that. Their proper charge as military officers in conquered lands was merely to ensure adequate civil governance, not to effect an official annexation. But Polk had never authorized those misguided proclamations, and the two military men had merely misunderstood the limits of their authority. In truth it was a minor matter, but it represented too rich a target for the Whigs to pass up.

Accompanying the political cynicism, however, was a new reality—the country's complete unfamiliarity with the kinds of questions now descending upon it. The conquest of other nations' territories on such a scale was an alien experience for America, and it wasn't surprising that no consensus could easily emerge as to how to proceed while preserving the sacred precepts of the Constitution.

Was there merit, for example, in the argument that the conquest of foreign lands was in itself unconstitutional because the Constitution makes no provision for such actions? Or that the creation of civil governments on such foreign lands was a perversion of the American mission? Noting that Stephen Douglas had spoken of "the right of conquest," Representative Cornelius Darragh suggested these were "new terms to be used under the constitution of the United States." The Pennsylvania Whig said it was "democratic doctrine that a war of conquest could not be waged, and that territory could not be acquired by conquest."

Or was it perhaps more reasonable to argue that such actions were entirely within all nations' understanding of the international laws of war? Indeed, was it defensible to contend, as Tennessee's Frederick Stanton did, that the creation of such governments was "not only in the power of our military commanders . . . but that it was their duty to do so—a duty founded upon the laws of war, as well as on the general laws of humanity"?

Upon such questions did the debate take flight, and it lasted for weeks as both houses grappled with the complex implications of conquest. But nothing injected emotion into the proceedings quite like the president's "aid and comfort" allegation. "A grosser attack upon the principles of free discussion in [this] House of Congress . . . [has] never been made," declared Massachusetts representative Robert Winthrop. He added, "As if no man, after the war commenced, should call in question the consummate wisdom or purity of motive on the part of the Executive in the initiatory steps of that war!"

But Tennessee's Frederick Stanton defended his president with vigor:

Those who regard this war as unjust have the right to say so. Those who regard it as an Executive war may so characterize it when and where and as often as they please. Those who behold our brave volunteers marching to the mouth of the cannon and falling on the bloody field of battle, and yet believe that they are engaged in an unjust cause, have a right, if they choose, to dampen the spirits of our armies, and animate the hearts of the foe, by saying so. . . . But if we say that by such language they are affording "aid and comfort" to the enemy, we claim but the same right to characterize their conduct as it deserves to be characterized.

If Polk's defense was amply stated in his carefully crafted Annual Message, the Whigs' attack centered on three deadly accusations: that when Polk ordered Taylor to the banks of the Rio Grande, he committed an act of war without authority of law; that Polk was waging a war of conquest unauthorized by law and hence a usurpation of power; and that, under the pretense of securing military possession of enemy territory, Polk in effect had annexed these lands illegally and in a way that constituted further usurpation of presidential authority. As Joshua Giddings put it, the president's message "was exactly such a defense as the President would make were he upon trial on impeachment. The same distortion of facts—the same misrepresentation of the truth—the same sophistry."

Polk sought to ignore this raging debate as he set about clearing the way for his policies and plans. Foremost in his mind was the need to place the war into the hands of a military officer with whom he could work effectively. He needed a lieutenant general to command the entire army, but that required congressional approval, and the early signs weren't good.

On December 12 the president sent Marcy to broach the subject with Lewis Cass, one of the president's most ardent Senate defenders. Marcy reported back that Cass "would not withhold his assent if the Government desired it," but he didn't recommend such a course and didn't think Congress would go along.

Polk discussed the plan with a number of loyal House members, including Douglas and Stanton. They fully appreciated the president's predicament with Winfield Scott and Zachary Taylor but didn't think Congress would ever consent to supersede them. Later, on his regular afternoon walk, the president ran into Cass, who said rumors were spreading through town that Polk planned to appoint Benton to the position of lieutenant general if Congress created the title. That didn't help the cause, warned Cass. The Missourian's many rivals and detractors were bent on ensuring he never would get a sure pathway to the presidency.

Polk did manage to get support from Senator Ambrose Sevier of Arkansas, the new chairman of Foreign Relations. John Niles of Connecticut also seemed agreeable. But on December 19, Polk sat down for a long chat with Calhoun, and the South Carolinian expressed adamant opposition to the lieutenant general idea. "I found that his mind was settled upon the subject," the president reported later, "and that it was useless to press it." But Calhoun, seemingly in high spirits, proved accommodating on other matters. He would support the $2 million bill enthusiastically, so long as it didn't come with the Wilmot Proviso prohibiting slavery in territories acquired from the war. He would support U.S. acquisition of Mexican territory, including New Mexico and California. Finally, expressing flexibility on the price for those lands, Calhoun said he would "not stand on a few millions of dollars."

As Polk maneuvered, Congress continued to struggle with the implications of the war. In the Senate, Democrat James Westcott of Florida, trying to be helpful, offered a resolution calling for legislation to bring the governance of the conquered territories under congressional jurisdiction. Those lands shouldn't be left in the hands of military officers even for a few months, he said. Benton, insisting Westcott had the whole thing wrong, pleaded with him to withdraw his amendment. It would not be proper, argued Benton, for Congress to extend U.S. law over these lands. Congress simply needed to appropriate sufficient funds to the military commanders there to administer those territories according to the laws of war.

"Spare me," cried Benton, "from the exhibition of the Senate of the

United States . . . deliberating about the establishment of civil governments in territories acquired by our armies . . . which never in our country can be considered as presenting a soil or field upon which our laws and constitution can operate." Benton carried the day, and Westcott's resolution was placed aside.

But House Whigs continued to pummel the president with accusations of official malfeasance. Tennessee's fervent Meredith Gentry led the way. "Let those whose servility of soul qualified them for the menial task truckle to the Executive," he declared. He and his friends, pursuing "a nobler destiny," felt "no disposition to truckle to the petty usurper, who came into power against the wishes of the great men of his own party, and whose personal character was unworthy [of] the favor of the meanest minion that shouted in his train."

As for America's claim to the disputed territory east of the Rio Grande, Gentry declared, "No man in his senses could be deceived by the sophistry of the President on that point; he sought to make the people believe a lie."

That was too much for many Polk defenders. Particularly aggressive in rebuttal was Tennessee's Barclay Martin, who castigated Gentry for favoring the war with his vote and then attacking the president charged with prosecuting the war he had voted for. Gentry and his allies, said Martin, were saying, "We voted for this war, but it is an unjust war . . . it is an unholy war!" Weren't such words, he asked, guaranteed to "paralyze the heart-strings of the gallant volunteer? Would it not cause him to sheath his sword, and pause in sorrow in the midst of his glorious career?"

Georgia's Seaborn Jones protested that Gentry had "used the most opprobrious terms the vocabulary could furnish for the purpose of expressing his disgust—his hatred—his violence of feeling against the President." This language, he added, was "not proper in this House, and most certainly unfit to be applied to the President of the United States."

Gentry protested. "I never have entertained, and do not now entertain, the slightest feeling of personal ill-will towards the President."

Jones said he was pleased to hear it, but certainly it was to be expected that "the coarseness and vulgarity of the gentleman's remarks should have suggested the idea that some personal pique existed."

GENTRY: I beg to say that when I seek instruction in elegance of language, I will not apply to the gentleman from Georgia.

JONES: I dare say not. . . . Yet I still hope that "the sober second thought" of the gentleman will convince him that his remarks on that occasion were entirely too vulgar.

GENTRY: Not at all.

JONES: They were quite too coarse to come from a member of this House, if not too coarse to be applied to the President of the United States. Does the gentleman approve of the lie direct from one gentleman to another?

GENTRY (with much agitation): Mr. Chairman, I must and will correct this. [Cries of "order."]

JONES: I cannot be corrected in that. It must be in the recollection of all that he applied these epithets to the government of the United States.

The exchange degenerated into a go-round on whether Gentry had called Polk a liar.

JONES: Did [the gentleman] not say the President made false assertions with regard to the causes of the war?

GENTRY: Certainly.

JONES: Pray, then, is it not that charging the President with a lie?

GENTRY: I abide by what I said. . . . I drew a distinction between the character of the man and the character of the President.

JONES: I do not understand that system of ethics which draws a distinction between a straightforward, honorable, veracious, and pure-minded man in private life, and a deceitful scoundrel as a public officer.

It was a noteworthy exchange, capturing the passions and angers that rippled through both houses of Congress and fueled a debate that seemed endless. As the session progressed, Whigs intensified their barrage against Polk's policies and character while Democrats increasingly wondered rhetorically why the Whigs, and their Federalist forerunners, always seemed to fault their own government in every war. Even the hint of possible hostilities, argued New York's Samuel Gordon, would find "the same party . . . in the same attitude of hostility to their own government."

The emotions of these debates spilled over into other aspects of Washington life. At one late December White House reception, the Polks noticed that few Whigs attended. "This," wrote Polk to his diary, "is probably to be attributed to the excitement growing out of the party debate . . . on the subject of the Mexican War and my course in conducting it." That day Tennessee's Barclay Martin had attacked Meredith Gentry as "an advocate of Mexico and of Mexican aggression! Yes, and I cannot but feel amazed at the manner in which my colleague attempts to excuse himself."

The December 19 cabinet session took up a delicate matter—the Garrett Davis resolution, passed by the House on December 15, calling on the president to submit all correspondence related to the civil governments established in New Mexico and California. Buchanan recommended ignoring the resolution, but Polk's sense of constitutional duty wouldn't permit such defiance of legislative prerogative. Still, there was a problem—Kearny's declaration that New Mexico had become sovereign territory of the United States. The general had even taken steps to send a delegate from the territory to the U.S. Congress.

It was agreed the president must disapprove these actions publicly while refraining from censuring Kearny. The president's message accompanying the documents constituted a measured and accurate legal brief on how a nation should conduct itself following territorial conquests in wartime. Any "excess of power," said Polk, had been the "offspring of a patriotic desire to give to the inhabitants the privileges and immunities so cherished by the people of our own country." He added these actions had generated "no practical injury" and would be "early corrected." Though many Whigs remained belligerent on the point, the released documents demonstrated no conscious effort on the part of the government to gain territory through a subversion of constitutional precepts. As the *Union* put it, "No instructions have been given to exercise any other authority than are, under the laws of war, applicable to territory conquered by the force of arms."

On December 21, Benton called on Polk at the White House to discuss the lieutenant general issue. Polk shared his political judgment, based on numerous conversations with sympathetic lawmakers, that he simply couldn't get the plan past Congress. Perhaps, said Polk, he should just let it go. Benton recoiled at the thought. He urged Polk to "make the proposition at all events, and if Congress rejected it the responsibility would be theirs." The country would then see, said the senator, that Congress had refused to grant the president the means he needed to prosecute the war. Benton became so vehement on the matter that Polk could see the Missourian and his friends would be "greatly dissatisfied" with a decision to abandon it.

The next day's cabinet discussed the challenge faced by Polk in getting his $2 million bill through Congress if the Wilmot Proviso reemerged. In that event, it was agreed, there wasn't much point in pressing for the appropriation. On December 23, Polk conversed at length with David Wilmot about the difficulties the Pennsylvanian had interposed in the president's path with his famous antislavery measure. He needed the $2 million bill, said the president, to bring about a speedy end to the war. And congressional sentiment overwhelmingly favored the appropriation. But, he added, if Wilmot's proviso were attached, southern opposition would kill it. That likely would prolong the war.

Wilmot said he favored the $2 million bill and would vote for it even without his proviso, which he felt no need to reintroduce. But, if someone else moved the antislavery amendment, he would feel duty-bound to vote for it. Polk replied that he had no wish to extend slavery, and anyway there was hardly any chance it would ever appear in either New Mexico or California. But, should he be forced by the proviso to attach antislavery language to any peace treaty with Mexico, it would never get sufficient votes for Senate ratification. Wilmot seemed sympathetic but somewhat stuck in the position he had created for himself.

The next day James and Sarah Polk entertained nearly forty members of Congress and their wives at a formal Christmas Eve White House dinner. Afterward, Calhoun lingered at the president's request for a private chat, and Polk promptly renewed his call for the lieutenant general position. Calhoun dismissively brushed it aside. He wanted to talk about the president's war strategy. He felt a march on Mexico City posed "insuperable difficulties" and could end in failure—at the least, a prolongation of the war. He recommended instead a "cordon" approach designed to hold and protect all captured Mexican territory as a kind of indemnity pending Mexico's willingness to negotiate a settlement. Calhoun's suggestion, though unpalatable to Polk, indicated some members at least were prepared to stop arguing about the causes of the war and start seeking effective ways of ending it.

On Christmas Day the president spent much of his time drafting his message to Congress calling for the lieutenant general position. There was almost no chance it would pass, and in fact Polk likely would have abandoned the matter entirely except for the need to mollify Benton. But such was his devotion to duty that he thought little of devoting his holiday to an arduous task that was essentially nugatory.

A week later the new year dawned in the form of an unseasonally bright and balmy day. The *Union* greeted 1847 by looking back on 1846 with astonishment at all the grand events that had unfolded at the behest of James Polk. Texas officially had entered the United States on February 19. On June 15 the country acquired what the *Union* called "a vast region on the Pacific slope of our continent, soon to be civilized by our people and our institutions." Prosperity got a boost, added the paper, through the president's leadership on tariff rates and England's dramatic move toward free trade—developments that had "opened a new source of wealth and prosperity both to the Old World and to the New."

And then there was the war—characterized by the *Union* as a conflict "waged in the highest interests of independence, justice, and the faith of treaties, on which the peace of the world depends." And to the extent it flowed from Texas annexation, said the *Union*, it should be seen as "a continuation of the great struggle of the Anglo-Saxon race on this continent for self-government."

The *Union*'s encomium to American expansionism represented the majority sentiment in the country. But that body of sentiment was under assault by a minority outlook growing in magnitude and intensity as the war dragged on. And in official Washington the two vastly different outlooks appeared more and more evenly divided in influence and power. The Whigs smelled political opportunity in James Polk's increasingly overextended political position, and they weren't about to let up now in their relentless effort to obliterate the long Democratic hegemony that had begun with Andrew Jackson's presidential victory nearly two decades before. It was clear on that lovely false spring day that 1847 loomed, even more than 1846, as a year of relentless and pitiless political combat.

22 · DILATORY CONGRESS

The Challenge of Presidential Leadership

O N THE SATURDAY morning of January 2, 1847, James
Polk's cabinet met at eleven for a three-hour war-planning
session. The central question was whether the president
should order a march on Mexico City following the anticipated seizure of Veracruz. Polk favored the move, but his advisers were nervous.

Secretary of State Buchanan spoke first and strongly opposed the
idea. Even if the army could bring off such a maneuver, he said, it
would merely "excite a feeling against us of races & religions" and
hence forestall the war's end. He favored the Calhoun approach—hold
and defend New Mexico and California, then wait for Mexico to recognize the immutable fact of conquest. Buchanan added the United
States should seek no more territory than was already under military
dominion. But he said other northern provinces should be encouraged
to revolt against Mexico City and form their own governments—in
which case, "we should furnish them aid & assistance."

William Marcy agreed. He expressed skepticism that any Mexico City expedition could succeed—a result, it appeared, of his lack
of confidence in Winfield Scott and Zachary Taylor. Robert Walker,
the cabinet hawk who frequently clashed with Buchanan, this time
endorsed his views. Even Cave Johnson ventured his concern about the
enterprise. The cabinet's newest member, Attorney General Nathan
Clifford, raised a lone voice in support of Polk's position. The former
Maine congressman added, however, that he would go along with any
final decision. The president decided once again to defer his decision
on Mexico City until after the Veracruz assault.

Turning their attention to the lieutenant general initiative, Polk's advisers predicted Congress wouldn't pass it. Polk agreed but said he would ask for it anyway as part of his forthcoming request for an increase in the army's regular forces. The healthy season in Mexico would end at midyear, he noted, and the enlistments of many volunteers at the front would soon expire. If Congress didn't act quickly on his request for ten new regiments of regular troops, the war could drag on indefinitely.

When the cabinet next took up the matter of war financing, Walker predicted difficulty in getting loans if Congress didn't accept some means of raising revenue. Polk had recommended a temporary duty on coffee and tea, but Congress thus far seemed hostile to the idea.

That night the president carried on extensive political conversations with several members of Congress, then retired around eleven o'clock "much fatigued & exhausted." Polk felt fatigued and exhausted more and more often these days as the burdens of his office grew inexorably and settled upon him with increasing weight. Though barely into his fifties, he began to look old—his pale blue eyes sinking into their sockets, his cheeks contracting inward, his jaw increasingly taut. The presidency was taking its toll upon James Polk.

As he retired that night, Polk fully understood the day's cabinet session had reflected a fundamental political reality descending upon Washington: He was losing control of the game. In contrast to his dominance of the previous congressional session, the president now faced an almost insolent legislature. He reaped little benefit from the Democrats' sizable majorities in both houses because his party was so divided on so many issues that it couldn't be controlled or swayed.

On January 4, Polk learned to his chagrin that New York's Preston King had introduced the mischievous Wilmot Proviso in the House, and Hannibal Hamlin of Maine was expressing opposition to Polk's call for the ten regiments. These Democrats, like others, apparently felt no particular loyalty to the president. As Polk saw it, many Hill Democrats freely abandoned party principle in favor of petty patronage angers, preoccupations with slavery, or passions centered on the coming contest for the Democratic presidential nomination. Meanwhile, as Polk complained to his diary, the Whigs "are united, and delighted at the unnecessary and foolish division in the Democratic party."

Polk found himself in a political predicament. Though he held out little hope for the lieutenant general bill, the rest of his legislative agenda was critical to his war aims. The call for more regular troops, now dubbed the Ten Regiment Bill, was necessary for taking the war into the Mexican interior. Along with the added troops, he needed authority to reorganize the army and add at least three new major generals to the officer corps. To bolster his dual strategy of waging aggressive war while offering a path to peace, he needed his $2 million appropriation, which now had ballooned to $3 million. A loan authorization and a corollary revenue initiative were required so he could pay for the war.

It wasn't clear whether he would get any of it. An early test came on January 9 when New York Democrat George Rathbun sought to gut the Ten Regiment Bill with a floor amendment that would have confined any troop increases to volunteers, for which Polk already had ample authority. It failed by a single vote, leading Polk to pour into his diary musings of anguish and anger. He castigated opposition Democrats as "without exception disaffected and unsound men." And it wasn't just the New Yorkers now but also former Democratic stalwarts from Illinois. He harbored no doubt these Illinois mavericks "vented their spite towards me" because of a Land Office appointment they had opposed. It was, wrote Polk, "sickening to the heart of a patriot."

In truth the deterioration in Polk's political standing could be attributed in part to a character trait that was now becoming more apparent: his lack of natural leadership ability. Unlike his great mentor, Andrew Jackson, he inspired neither loyalty nor fear. Nor could he manipulate men to his will with Henry Clay's smooth efficiency. He possessed no guileful capacity to offer carrots of political incentive and administer sticks of political punishment, and thus the city's power brokers were concluding with increasing confidence that they could ignore his wishes—or attack him frontally—without paying any price. Polk's relationship with Buchanan crystallized the point. Official Washington knew the secretary of state had treated his boss time and again with disrespect and yet always managed to get away with it. The president was beginning to look like an easy mark.

But James Polk did possess one trait his adversaries always underestimated—his iron-willed political perseverance. To his diary he expressed disillusionment with the petty figures of officialdom. Yet he still took pride in his own rectitude, harboring faith that his famous persistence would propel him on to ultimate political success.

ON JANUARY 11 that mysterious agent of Santa Anna, Colonel Alejandro Atocha, reappeared on the scene. He called on Buchanan with what he purported to be important letters from Santa Anna and also from General Juan Almonte, Santa Anna's great rival, who had become, in the way of Mexican politics, his current political ally. Atocha said he would show the letters soon to Senator Benton. Three days later Polk received a note from Benton saying the correspondence from Santa Anna and Almonte indeed appeared "very important." The letters were written in Spanish, dated the previous November, and addressed to Atocha. Taking them to the White House, the bilingual Benton read them aloud to Polk, translating as he went along.

Benton's translation left little doubt that Atocha was there at the behest of Santa Anna, who was now renewing his call for a peace settlement. The only question was whether this was a sincere gesture or a ploy designed to maneuver Mexico into an advantageous position. Given the recent history, suspicions were in order. But Polk, perhaps owing to his fervent desire for peace, chose to credit the letters as well as Atocha's face-to-face representations to Benton.

The terms were simple. The Mexicans would accept the Rio Grande boundary, with some space east of the river serving as a kind of buffer zone. They would cede California for a consideration of some $15 million to $20 million. They suggested a negotiating session in Havana, with the United States in the meantime withdrawing its blockade at Veracruz. Polk asked about New Mexico. Benton replied that Atocha didn't seem to know Santa Anna's position on that. But Benton expressed confidence in Atocha's veracity and suggested his overture should be pursued. Polk was inclined to agree.

Reviewing the matter later, the cabinet also credited the overture. But there could be no buffer zone; some of New Mexico would have to be relinquished; and there would be no suspension of the blockade. Later, after Atocha expressed misgivings about Polk's blockade position, the president accepted a compromise allowing U.S. negotiators to recommend a blockade suspension based on Mexico's conduct in the talks. Buchanan was instructed to draft a letter to Mexico's foreign minister outlining these conditions and proposing appointment of commissioners to meet in Havana. Atocha was dispatched aboard a fast U.S. ship to deliver the message.

In the meantime, the president continued to struggle with the political forces arrayed against him. As he complained to Benton, Taylor was becoming increasingly uncommunicative and petulant. Scott, it seemed, "either through his inordinate vanity or some other cause," had revealed his Veracruz strategy to a New Orleans newspaper, which had published it. And Congress continued to dither through endless debates without taking action on his requests.

"With a large nominal majority in both Houses, I am practically in a minority," rued Polk to his diary.

And now the president's situation took on an ominous cast. Reports were reaching Washington from New Orleans newspapers, the country's window on Mexico, indicating that Santa Anna was moving a huge army toward Taylor's force at and near Monterrey. Taylor had divided his troops, much to Polk's displeasure, and now Santa Anna apparently saw an opportunity to fall upon one or another of these scattered forces—"and by superiority of numbers cutting it to pieces," as the *New Orleans Mercury* put it. If true, the reports indicated the war's outcome could depend upon the military acumen of one man— Zachary Taylor.

In Washington the House finally moved on Polk's agenda, passing the Ten Regiment Bill on January 11 by a wide margin. In the Senate, however, it promptly became embroiled in wrangling over proposals to tender land grants to war veterans. Congress's languid pace of action continued to agitate Polk. On January 19 he told the cabinet he was more anxious than ever for a negotiated peace because congressional lassitude raised questions about whether he could prosecute the war effectively. Unless this situation changed, he added, "my administration and with it the Democratic party must be overwhelmed."

The *Union*'s Ritchie gave public vent to the problem on January 18:

And how has Congress hitherto met [its] most grave and momentous responsibility? . . . Half of the session has already passed. The treasury is unsupplied. The measures to sustain the credit of the country are not yet adopted or perfected. The organization of the army is not completed. . . . And in such a state of things, if we may judge from the action of the few past days, the popular branch of the American Congress . . . turns to convulse the public mind, and to distract the public councils by . . . irrelevant and premature topics of agitation, which must be profitless, which may be baneful, and which, at all events, swallow up the precious hour which patriotism needs for the highest and noblest purposes.

An example of what Ritchie was talking about occurred on the House floor three days later when the chamber took up the bill to authorize war loans of up to $23 million. The House passed the bill overwhelmingly but not before Tennessee's John Crozier offered an amendment for the sole purpose of opening up the measure for a long and spirited disquisition on the war's lack of legitimacy. The haughty young Whig traced the decisions leading to the war with the purpose of demonstrating the president had no right to send Taylor's army to the Rio Grande. He excoriated Polk for his "aid and comfort" language—"remarkably bold and rash," he suggested wryly, in a man "usually spoken of as a remarkably cautious man—even to timidity." He traced the controversies between the president and Winfield Scott, defending Scott at every turn. He sought to deflect all criticism of Taylor from administration allies, including Mississippi's Jacob Thompson, with whom he engaged in an extensive and vehement debate on the matter. And then, when the roll was called, he joined 165 colleagues in voting for the measure against only 22 nay votes.

On January 25 word reached Washington that the *New York Express,* a highly partisan Whig newspaper, had published a letter from Zachary Taylor to an anonymous friend (soon identified as General Edmund Gaines) that not only heaped criticism on his commander-in-chief but revealed military secrets, including his own troop deployments. The letter revealed Taylor's lingering animosities toward his Washington superiors for questioning his armistice with General Ampudia and for letting Mexican troops leave Monterrey. In fact, Taylor's complaints against the government reached back to the aftermath of his victories at Palo Alto and Resaca de la Palma, when the prickly general had felt slighted by what he considered the president's tardiness in getting off to him a congratulatory letter.

"Was I a prominent or ambitious aspirant for civil distinction or honors," the general had written to his son-in-law, "I might very readily suppose there was an intention somewhere among the high functionaries to break me down." In fact, the general was emerging rapidly as an ambitious aspirant for the country's highest civil distinction, and that was beginning to color his outlook. But his natural tendency toward dark musings and suspicions was contributing also to his questionable behavior. Polk's cabinet agreed that Marcy must send the general a condemnatory letter, but there was no talk of firing him. The letter was a "decided rebuke," in the words of Polk, who felt Taylor and Gaines could justifiably face courts-martial for what they had done. The cabinet also agreed the president should accept congressional calls for releasing publicly the correspondence with Taylor; this, said the members, was the only way to stem the attacks from Whig politicians and newspapers.

The attacks were relentless. George Ashmun of Massachusetts rose in the House to defend Taylor against what he depicted as a Polk character assassination. The president couldn't stand having a Whig general at such a lofty military station, said Ashmun, and hence sought to disgrace Taylor and get rid of him "in the most summary mode." That's what the whole lieutenant general matter was all about, he said—to supersede a good and honorable general with someone more under the president's thumb. And what about that evidence that Polk secretly had allowed Santa Anna back into Mexico? He had no intention of charging Polk with giving "aid and comfort" to the enemy with such an action, said Ashmun slyly, but that certainly had been the effect.

"Mr. Polk," said the Massachusetts Whig, "had, in effect, given a lieutenant general to Mexico, and after that achievement for the benefit of the enemy, perhaps he thought that it would be nothing more than was fit and becoming to appoint a lieutenant general over the forces of the United States."

Polk supporters defended the president, none more effectively than that rising star from Illinois, Stephen Douglas, who cleverly pointed out the contradiction in Ashmun's readiness to praise Taylor for his sterling success in what Ashmun condemned as an unjust and unholy cause. Essentially he was saying, argued Douglas, "that [Taylor] had succeeded with extraordinary ability in the work of plunder, robbery, and murder." This elicited cries of "good!" and "go it, Douglas!" from the House floor. But the Ashmun tirade reflected the growing appetite among Whigs for flaying the president.

On January 27, Polk received a welcome victory when the Senate passed the loan bill and sent it to the White House for a presidential signature. Three days later the Senate passed the Ten Regiment Bill and sent it back to the House for its consideration of Senate amendments. The vote was 39 to 3, reflecting a pattern emerging in Congress. It now seemed the president might get what he wanted, but Congress would set the timetable and would slice up the president with plenty of rapier rhetoric in the process. Before clearing the bill the Senate spent days haggling over amendments designed to gut the measure.

On February 5, when the Senate took up the $3 million bill, as it was now called, Georgia's venerable John Berrien rose to redirect the debate. Berrien—once a devout Democrat and attorney general in the Jackson administration, now a resolute Whig—offered an amendment declaring the war could not be prosecuted "with any view to the dismemberment of [Mexico], or to the acquisition, by conquest, of any portion of her territory." It called for immediate negotiations to end the war on whatever terms the United States could get.

Democrats were outraged that the Senate must now pause to debate this language of capitulation when the president's war needs were so pressing. The *Union* described the amendment as "calculated to disgrace our arms—to humble our nation—and to invite further aggressions from [Mexico], and from all other powers." Though Berrien's amendment had no chance of passage, it soaked up valuable congressional time and added to Polk's anxiety. "I am much embarrassed by the want of support in Congress to the measures which I have recommended," Polk wrote to his diary, as the Ten Regiment Bill languished in Congress even though versions of it had cleared both houses. And, while the loan bill had become law, Congress seemed in no hurry to enact the revenue measures needed to buttress the country's creditworthiness. Polk began to ponder the idea of sending a stern message to Congress aimed at putting members on the defensive with the American people.

Then on the evening of February 8, Senator Cass arrived with terrible news. The Senate had just rejected the conference report on the Ten Regiment Bill, effectively killing it. The unified Senate Whigs had joined with the Calhoun faction to thwart the president's most important war measure. The president was outraged and expressed himself "in terms of great indignation" to the many senators who called that evening to express their anger. The *Union* called the action "nothing less than a great national calamity."

The next day Polk fulminated against his opponents' lack of patriotism to anyone who ventured near the White House. He pored over his stern message to Congress, making it even sterner. But that evening, on his daily walk, he encountered Vice President Dallas, who told him the Ten Regiment Bill had been resurrected and assigned to a new conference panel. The next day the measure cleared both houses, and the day after that Polk signed it into law. It took two months of congressional wrangling, but he now had the needed authority to augment his army.

He still needed the $3 million bill and revenue measures, how-ever, and Congress appeared no more willing to move quickly. On February 13 the president sent to Congress his plea for action in lan-guage designed to generate pressure on lawmakers from their constit-uents back home. He expressed gratitude for the Ten Regiment Bill but noted he still needed authority to organize those regiments and appoint generals to lead them. He also needed authority to replenish volunteer units as needs arose. And he urged action allowing him to raise money through specified import duties, preferably on coffee and tea, and to reduce the price of public lands to induce greater sales and hence greater revenue.

"The worst state of things which could exit in a war with such a power as Mexico, would be a course of indecision and inactivity on our part," wrote the president. The public good and their shared responsi-bilities to the American people, he concluded, "imperiously demand that I should present them for your enlightened consideration, and invoke favorable action upon them before the close of your present session."

Even before the president's message reached the Hill, the war debate moved into a new phase. The discourse now focused more and more on the best strategy for ending the troublesome conflict. The man who initiated this new phase was John C. Calhoun, whose long and brilliant career reflected not just his famous eloquence but also a mastery over political dialectic as a means of directing and shaping the course of discussion.

The South Carolinian rose on the Senate floor on February 9 to expound upon his thesis that the United States should fall back to its conquered territory, defend it thoroughly, cease offensive operations against Mexico, and wait for the enemy to sue for peace. Calhoun declared his "defensive position" would ensure a "successful termina-tion . . . with the least sacrifice of men and money." Why, he asked, invade Veracruz simply to "compel the Mexicans to acknowledge as ours what we already hold?"

He fully accepted the argument that Mexico owed the United States a territorial indemnity for U.S. claims against that country and also

for the war's costs. He agreed with Democratic hawks who wanted all
of New Mexico and California, including the long peninsula of Lower
California (later called Baja California). He accepted the Rio Grande
as the legitimate Texas boundary.

And he described with equal respect Polk's rationale for pursuing
the war and his critics' reasons for opposing it. He declined to get into
that thicket of debate, he said, in the interest of advocating a means
of effecting a just conclusion at the least cost. What was important
now, he argued, was to draw a line of indemnity, defend it, and pursue a policy of "masterly inactivity." Stop the battles, the killing, the
deaths from yellow fever, the growing racial and religious tensions
between the two countries—and, he suggested, the slavery agitations
that would ensue from any further U.S. conquest of southern Mexican lands.

Calhoun's speech stirred up a flurry of political emotions. "Why,
we are at war!" declared Ritchie's *Union*. "And what is inactivity in
war . . . but delay and feebleness, and, in the long run, cruelty?"

Lewis Cass threw his considerable senatorial stature into the fray
with a tightly reasoned critique of Calhoun's expressions and an eloquent defense of the motives, angers, visions, and sentiments of honor
leading to the war. "A strong desire pervades this country," said Cass,
"that a region extending west of our present possessions to the Pacific
ocean should be acquired." It would provide wide expanses for settlement and cultivation, he added, connect the country to "the great
western ocean," extend America's dominion of the Pacific coastline
some thirteen or fourteen degrees of latitude, provide "the magnificent
bay of St. Francisco, one of the noblest anchorages in the world," and
give America a "commanding position" over the trade of the northern
Pacific. The Cass vision was, in short, the vision of Manifest Destiny.

The senator placed blame for the war squarely on the dysfunctional
Mexican nation. "Her government is ephemeral. Its members are born
in the morning, and die in the evening. Administrations succeed one
another, like the scenes of a theatre." That was the reality that had
led to hostilities, he argued, adding: "We are at war with Mexico,
brought on by her injustice."

Particularly pointed was Cass's critique of Calhoun's military judgment. The country faced three possible "plans of operation" in the war, he said. The first, suggested by Senator Berrien and others, was abandonment of the war and a return to prewar borders. "I cast it from me with contempt," declared Cass.

The second was Calhoun's proposal of "masterly inactivity." It couldn't work militarily, said Cass, because such an extended boundary was indefensible so long as the enemy could amass his troops at points along the border of greatest U.S. vulnerability. Then, after overwhelming U.S. forces at their weakest points, he could scurry back across the proclaimed border to regroup for another like mission against other points of weakness. "You cannot pursue him into his country, for the moment you do that, you confess the folly of your plan. . . . If you cross your boundary you must cross it to hold on, and then you have a new boundary, or in other words, a system of unlimited operations."

Thus, the only sensible approach was the Polk approach—"vigorous prosecution of the war, agreeably to the public expectation, and the experience of the world." Only such an approach can bring the war to a certain end. "I consider offensive wars," said Cass, "as necessary means for the attainment of certain just objects"—in this case, a redress of wrongs through territorial indemnity.

When Calhoun saw his proposal wasn't generating serious attention in Congress, he abandoned the rhetorical evenhandedness of his February 9 speech and joined the Polk attackers in attributing the war to the president's actions. "The immediate cause of the war," he declared on the Senate floor, "was the marching of our forces . . . to the banks of the Del Norte." He had opposed the war for many reasons, he said, but particularly for "high considerations *connected with the manner in which it was brought on.*"

This was too much for Thomas Benton, whose hatred of the South Carolinian was flowing as copiously as ever. He was delighted to have such a rich opportunity to go on the attack, and he seized it with a vengeance. Pulling together his famous eloquence, erudition, wit, and pugnacity into an hour-long floor speech, Benton argued it was simply silly to suggest the Rio Grande march had caused the war. It hadn't caused the war any more than the British march on Concord and Lexington had caused the American Revolution or Caesar's crossing of the Rubicon had caused the Roman civil war. "The causes of this Mexican war were long anterior to this march," declared Benton. Then he added with dramatic flair, "The senator from South Carolina is the author of those causes, and therefore the author of the war."

It all began, explained Benton, with the Adams-Onís Treaty of 1819, which ceded Texas to Spain in exchange for Florida. For years southerners had blamed John Quincy Adams, then secretary of state under President Monroe, for giving up that valuable land. He was motivated, according to the legend, by his hostility to the South and West and his desire "to clip the wings of the slaveholding States." But that wasn't true, said Benton. It was Calhoun, then secretary of war, who had promoted the idea in the Monroe cabinet. Adams had said as much, and Calhoun had never contradicted him. He added:

> [He], therefore, stands admitted the co-author of that mischief to the south and west which the cession of Texas involved, and to escape from which it became necessary, in the opinion of the senator from South Carolina, to get back Texas at the expense of war with Mexico. This conduct of the senator in giving away Texas when we had her, and then making war to get her back, is an enigma which he has never yet condescended to explain, and which, until explained, leaves him in a state of self-contradiction, which, whether it impairs his own confidence in himself or not, must have the effect of destroying the confidence of others in him, and wholly disqualifies him for the office of champion of the slave-holding States.

Benton pointed out that Calhoun had advocated annexation of Texas almost from the moment Washington received word of San Jacinto. Thus, said Benton, he advocated "plunging us into instant war with Mexico. I say, instant war; for Mexico and Texas were then in open war; and to incorporate Texas, was to incorporate the war at the same time." And he harbored those same views right into his tenure as Tyler's secretary of state, when he pursued Texas annexation with a zeal and aggressiveness almost guaranteed to generate tensions with Mexico, which adamantly had equated annexation with an act of war.

Indeed, said Benton, Calhoun had assured Texas during annexation discussions that Tyler would "use all the means placed in his power by the constitution to protect Texas from all foreign invasion." This, he averred, was an explicit promise "to lend the army and navy to the President of Texas, to fight the Mexicans while they were at peace with us. That was the point—at peace with us."

So there it was, said Benton—Calhoun's history as America's leading catalyst of war with Mexico. He added:

> The state of war existed legally: all the circumstances of war, except the single circumstance of bloodshed, existed at the accession of Mr. Polk; the two countries, Mexico and the United States, stood in a relation to each other impossible to be continued. The march upon the Rio Grande brought on the conflict—made the collision of arms—but not the war. The war was prepared, organized, established by the Secretary of State, before he left the department. It was his legacy to the democracy, and to the Polk administration—his last gift to them, in the moment of taking a long farewell. And now he sets up for a man of peace, and throws all the blame of war upon Mr. Polk, to whom he bequeathed it.

Of all the attacks unleashed by all the legislative combatants throughout the war debate, probably none hit its target with such force as this clever philippic lodged against Calhoun by his longtime adversary and tormentor. The South Carolinian put forth a rebuttal, but his point-by-point response seemed forced and his words sounded defensive. Certainly he would not be silenced and probably had not felt seriously chastened. But he seemed at least momentarily taken aback by this assault of such rare potency. Still, by Senate standards if not his own, he gave a good account, and, while the *Union* pointedly refrained from calling the exchange "a war of giants," the paper did consider it "a very interesting contest between two of the strongest members of the Senate . . . [and] conducted with much general ability on both sides."

But Polk wanted action more than words. On the day after the Calhoun rebuttal, the president learned that House Democrats had scheduled a caucus to seek some harmony among themselves—"and thus," as he put it, "secure the action of Congress upon the important war Measures which I have repeatedly recommended." He wasn't optimistic. The party, he wrote, continued to be "torn by factions & so divided that I am not sustained in either House of Congress."

But slowly, as Congress moved toward its planned March 3 adjournment, the various elements of the Polk agenda began falling into place. In the last days of February and into March the two Houses grappled with the remaining business, various conference committees, and pressures of the clock. Finally, in the terminal twenty-four hours of the session, the House passed the $3 million bill, stripped of the Wilmot Proviso. It had been attached by the House initially but cast aside by the Senate. Now Wilmot, violating his promise to Polk, moved his famous proviso once again in the final hours. It failed by five votes, whereupon the House approved the $3 million measure 115 to 81.

Another last-minute triumph for Polk was legislation authorizing him to organize the new regiments and appoint three new major generals and two brigadiers to command them. But there would be no lieutenant general—and hence no opportunity to place Benton in command of the army. And Congress rejected Polk's call for revenue measures—targeted import duties and a reduction in the price of public lands—designed to bolster the nation's creditworthiness as it sought war loans. "The democratic majority in Congress," lamented the *Union,* "has fallen far short of its usual patriotism and foresight in permitting these measures to fail." But early fiscal signs indicated Polk's policy of reduced tariffs was generating more trade and hence more revenue than the 1842 tariff law, so perhaps those measures wouldn't prove necessary.

The president traveled to the Capitol the evening of March 3 to be on hand for signing bills and advising his allies during the last-minute legislative crunch. At about one o'clock in the morning, he was informed that Congress had adjourned *sine die*. He invited members to the vice president's offices for refreshments, and many wandered in, including those from both parties. "Good feeling prevailed" reported Polk to his diary, adding he returned to the White House a bit after two. It had been a harrowing and frustrating congressional session, but in the end the president got what he needed to prosecute his war. Now he faced the need to turn his attention aggressively to his job as commander-in-chief.

23 · VERACRUZ AND BEYOND

Grappling with Mexico's Military Defiance

WHEN NEWS TRAVELS slowly and arrives in fragments, it breeds suspense. It took Mexican War news generally a month or more to reach Washington, and often it arrived in bits of information covering military developments unfolding over time. In March of 1847 reports began filtering into the capital that Zachary Taylor's army had suffered a devastating defeat at the hands of Santa Anna. Suspense throughout the city reached levels of fevered concern.

Nowhere was that concern more intense than in the White House, where James Polk fully understood such a defeat would likely devastate his administration. Already his political standing was eroding rapidly, and it could collapse entirely with a battlefield humiliation in this persistent and increasingly unpopular war.

In a series of articles beginning on March 5, the *Union* cited New Orleans newspaper reports that Taylor had encamped with six thousand men at Saltillo, about sixty miles southwest of Monterrey. Further, there were indications of "a more active campaign on the part of Santa Anna," who threatened "an attack upon Saltillo, Matamoros, &c." It seemed the relentless Mexican general was on the move with some twenty thousand troops, and rumors were persistent that he had forced a battle upon Taylor.

In the midst of all this, word reached Washington via the itinerant Alejandro Atocha that Santa Anna would negotiate an end to the war only if Polk ended the Veracruz blockade and removed all U.S. forces from Mexican soil. That was untenable; there would be no negotiations pending further Mexican defeats. But at a subsequent cabinet meeting Buchanan renewed his opposition to any march on Mexico City. Polk reacted with a rare display of agitation.

"I differ with you in opinion," he declared. "I would not only march to the City of Mexico, but would pursue Santa Anna's army wherever it was, and capture or destroy it." All he needed, he added, calming down a bit, was a general willing and able to fight aggressively.

On March 21, Polk reported to his diary that he had received "more detailed rumours" of Taylor's "critical situation" and noted also his own "painful apprehensions." It had been understood that Taylor would keep his army at Monterrey, the site of his previous decisive victory against General Ampudia and a well-fortified, easily defended outpost. Now it seemed Taylor had ventured forward into less defensible territory, and Polk wasn't happy about it. He found himself in "painful suspense" as fragments of information filtered in, all noting Taylor's force was heavily outnumbered and outgunned.

"I have great fears for the safety of Gen'l Taylor's army, and for the whole line of our military operations in his rear & on the Rio Grande," Polk wrote to his diary. He initiated a flurry of activity designed to get fresh troops to Mexico as quickly as possible.

On March 28, Polk received "exciting rumours," as he later described them, that Taylor's force had fared better than initially understood, although it apparently remained vulnerable. "If Gen'l Taylor is in any danger, as I greatly fear he is," wrote Polk, "it is in consequence of his having, in violation of his orders, advanced beyond Monter[r]ey." He added: "The truth is that from the beginning of the War he has been constantly blundering into difficulties, but has fought out of them, but at the cost of many lives."

That summed up Taylor's performance in the most recent battle. It began when he chose to ignore Polk's policy of consolidating Taylor's position at Monterrey while Scott moved on Veracruz. Scott himself, now in command of the entire Mexican theater, had issued a direct order to Taylor that read in part: "I must ask you to abandon Saltillo, and to make no detachments . . . much beyond Monterrey."

Brushing aside that command, Taylor abandoned his previous military judgment that a march further into the Mexican interior served little military purpose. Now he concluded a march to Saltillo was "much the safest course," as he wrote to Kentucky's Senator Crittenden, a friend and supporter. Thus he abandoned the relative safety of Monterrey and moved his troops south, where Santa Anna was maneuvering his huge army into position to pounce on the invading force.

By February 21, Santa Anna had placed his army within six miles of Taylor's battalions, and Taylor knew he had been forced into battle against a greatly superior force. He quickly fell back, repositioning his army at the Angostura Pass, a restricted valley in front of the Hacienda de Buena Vista. It was ideal terrain for defense, and Taylor's men dug in for a protracted stand. With his typical tactical brilliance, Taylor positioned his forces for maximum protection.

Santa Anna, by contrast, had exhausted his troops by rushing them to Angostura Pass in a deadening heat, and he was slow to get into position for battle. But he did take possession of the commanding heights to the east of Taylor's army, and this fueled his confidence that victory would soon be his. On February 22 he sent a message to the American commander under a flag of truce. "You are surrounded by twenty thousand men, and cannot in any human probability avoid suffering a rout and being cut to pieces with your troops," declared the vain Mexican. But, as Taylor deserved "consideration and particular esteem," he would allow the American to surrender.

"I beg leave to say," Taylor responded, "that I decline acceding to your request." The battle commenced at three o'clock that afternoon and raged for a day and a half in a series of maneuvers, feints, thrusts, and bloody clashes. On the second day Taylor's men managed to repel a frontal assault on their main force, but Santa Anna routed the Americans' left flank. Taylor's force now seemed hopelessly vulnerable. As the commander returned to the fray with fresh troops from Saltillo, a dejected General John Wool poured out his pessimism.

"General, we are whipped," he exclaimed.

"That," replied Taylor, "is for me to determine."

The commander promptly ordered an assault upon the Mexican

forces menacing his left flank. It proved successful, but a contingent of Mexican lancers, passing a full half mile beyond Taylor's force, threatened to outflank it. Taylor dispatched a force of mounted troops to intercept the enemy lancers while he turned his devastating artillery upon them. Again, Taylor's decisive actions carried the moment. But Santa Anna wasn't finished. He sent a large force to take a ridge to Taylor's extreme left. Again, he nearly succeeded. Again, Taylor repulsed the maneuver. Taylor then ordered an attack on Santa Anna's retreating forces, but the Mexican general got reinforcements in place to blunt the effort and initiate a counterattack. Taylor's vulnerable forward units were saved only by his able artillery but not before a number of brave soldiers perished in the battle's last skirmish.

That night Santa Anna, realizing his effort to destroy the invading American army had failed, vacated the field. Taylor once more had demonstrated his nimble tactical brilliance, chalking up another victory that would stir appreciation and adulation among his countrymen back home. But Polk was right in concluding this was a victory without strategic significance in what was probably an unnecessary battle. And the cost was substantial—some 665 officers and men killed, wounded, or missing out of the 4,594 sent into the fight. And Santa Anna's army would be available to fight in future battles.

One of the officers killed at Buena Vista was young Lieutenant Colonel Henry Clay, Jr., West Point–educated son of the acclaimed politician whose opposition to James Polk's war was famous for its intensity. He died a hero, fending off a contingent of attacking Mexicans so his men could scurry to safety behind him. As he lay wounded on the ground, he had been surrounded by enemy soldiers and bayoneted to death. The senior Clay got the word as he was dining one spring evening at his Ashland estate. The father broke down, wept uncontrollably, buried his head in his hands, and cried out against the cruelties of the universe. "Alas," he wrote later, "there are some wounds so deep and so excruciatingly painful, that He only can heal them, by whose inscrutable dispensations they have been inflicted. And the death of my beloved son is one of them."

The elder Clay was now nearing seventy. His six daughters already had reached the grave, while two other sons had suffered mental breakdowns. And of course Prince Hal's political career never had quite reached the pinnacle of his dreams. And so young Henry had been one of the father's lingering joys of life—a lanky, industrious, earnest young man who resembled his father in looks, demeanor, and capacity to rise above other men and serve his country with extraordinary ability. Now he was gone, killed in an unnecessary war, in Clay's view, brought on by the protégé of his greatest rival and nemesis, Andrew Jackson. It was an excruciating development in a life whose grand accomplishments seemed always mixed with disappointment and pain.

The *Union* noted young Clay's death as it would that of any other officer, neither mentioning the father nor extending so much as a bow of respect to the man who had sacrificed so much in furtherance of the war he opposed. And the president wasn't sufficiently moved by the event to mention it to his diary.

WHILE TAYLOR'S BUENA Vista triumph was much heralded in the land as another reflection of America's growing military strength, Polk chafed at the fact that it did nothing to hasten the war's end. It did, however, contribute to the Whigs' hopes for an 1848 presidential victory. The opposition party now was looking more and more fervently to Taylor as its standard-bearer in the coming election, and everyone knew this beloved military hero, whatever his capacity for political leadership, would be formidable. It rankled Polk that this man whom he respected so little could actually pose such a threat to his party.

Also on the president's mind was the question of his relationship with Benton. A delicate development had arisen since Polk had decided to offer the Missourian one of the new major generalships created by Congress. Benton had accepted, and Congress had ratified the choice. But the glory-hungry Benton concluded the honor wasn't worth much unless he could be placed at the head of all U.S. forces in Mexico and given diplomatic powers to negotiate the eventual peace treaty. Polk was inclined to give it to him, but a study of military protocol revealed he could supersede the other major generals in Mexico only by recalling them. This wasn't politically tenable, so Benton was allowed to resign his newly acquired commission.

Both men took pains to ensure that these developments would not bruise their mutually advantageous friendship. And Polk still turned avidly to Benton for political and military counsel. He embraced the Missourian's creative suggestion that he withdraw the Veracruz blockade and instead impose a duty on goods shipped through the port city. This could supply the war funding that Congress had declined to provide. After receiving assurances from the attorney general and others that the approach was legal, Polk issued an order directing such levies be imposed at all Mexican ports that fell into U.S. military hands.

While the war dominated Polk's concerns, another development was increasingly agitating his consciousness—the growing intensity of the slavery issue. For months he had watched with foreboding as New York and other northern states had succumbed more and more to the politics of abolition. Northeastern Whigs were particularly energized on the issue and in some areas quite united in their opposition to slavery. But pockets of abolitionist sentiment were emerging among northeastern Democrats as well. Now a southern backlash was developing under the charismatic leadership of John C. Calhoun.

On March 10 the citizens of Charleston called a meeting to protest what they considered the aggressive anti-southern actions of the North. They got up a committee, appointed officers, drafted bylaws, and passed resolutions. One stated:

> That, in the opinion of this committee, the developments of the last year . . . indicate a condition of things, in regard to the domestic institutions, peculiar to the South, requiring the most grave and earnest consideration of the whole people of the slave-holding States. Your committee think they perceive, in the events of the session of Congress which has just closed and of the latter part of the preceding session, in the tone and temper of the northern press during the interval, and in the action of the legislatures

of most of the non-slaveholding States, conclusive evidence of a fixed determination . . . that slavery shall not hereafter exist in any of the Territories of the United States, and that no State shall be admitted into the Union, whose constitution tolerates its existence.

The committee cited particularly the Wilmot Proviso votes in the House and resolutions passed by nine northern state legislatures denouncing slavery and protesting against its extension. The committee then endorsed a recently passed Virginia resolution that stated such actions in the North rendered it "the duty of every slaveholding State, and all the citizens thereof, as they value their dearest privileges, their sovereignty, their independence, their rights of property, to take firm, united, and concerted action in this emergency."

After the vote Calhoun rose to speak. The South labored under a numerical disadvantage, he said, as northern states soon would outnumber slaveholding ones. He added the South had truth and the Constitution on its side. But those advantages wouldn't count for much if the North united behind an antislavery banner, and that was all the more likely if the South accepted the entreaties of many politicians to keep the slavery issue under wraps. Southern Democrats, he said, must agitate the issue to prevent southern politicians from uniting with northerners at the next Baltimore nominating convention and bringing forth "a man unsound on this question, so vital to the south." He added: "If this course is pursued, our ruin is inevitable." Following Calhoun's remarks the assembled delegates "manifested their concurrence . . . by the most enthusiastic cheering," according to a Charleston newspaper.

There was no cheering at the offices of the *Union,* which called Calhoun "a political Ishmael . . . an injudicious leader, and an unsafe statesman." Polk considered Calhoun's agitations "not only unpatriotic and mischievous, but wicked." He told Navy Secretary Mason that Calhoun, desperate to initiate a presidential run, had issued his tirade as his "only means of sustaining himself in his present fallen condition."

But the president was equally irritated with the North's slavery agitators. Benton told Polk a few days earlier that New York's Democratic congressional delegation, nearly united in its support of Silas Wright for president, planned to exploit Calhoun's mischief in efforts to stir up abolitionist sentiment in the Northeast in behalf of Wright's candidacy. "The truth is," Polk wrote to his diary, "there is no patriotism in either faction. . . . Both desire to mount slavery as a hobby and . . . secure the election of their favourite upon it."

ON APRIL 5 word reached Washington that Winfield Scott's forces, with help from Commodore Conner's naval squadron, had landed near Veracruz on March 9, within sight of both the city and the Fortress of San Juan de Ulloa. "The whole army reached the shore in fine style," Scott wrote to Marcy in a letter published in the *Union*, "and without direct opposition (on the beach), accident, or loss, driving the enemy from the ground to be occupied." The general, in a flawless operation, had landed an army of twelve thousand men onto Mexican soil some three miles south of the city.

Five days later Polk received a telegraphic message from the *Baltimore Sun* reporting the paper had received word via ship from Pensacola that Veracruz and its castle fortress had both surrendered to the combined U.S. land and naval forces. "This was joyous news," wrote the president.

After his landing, Scott built a well-concealed and fortified battery for big guns, and soon he had implanted twenty-two such weapons of various size and impact, including cannon lugged ashore from Conner's ships. Before unleashing the merciless barrage, Scott issued an ultimatum to Mexican General Juan Morales to surrender city and castle. The general, unaware of what was in store, defiantly refused.

The shelling went on for nearly three days, with devastating effect. On the afternoon of March 25 representatives of England, France, and Prussia pleaded with Scott to halt the barrage temporarily so foreigners and civilians could leave. Scott refused, but Morales soon initiated steps for a truce. Two days later an agreement was signed, and the United States had a new route to Mexico City and a new source of revenue.

"We have taken the Gibraltar of the western continent," crowed the *Union*. "We have added new laurels to our wreath. The gratitude and admiration of a free people are due to Maj. Gen. Scott. We congratulate our country again upon the prowess of their army and navy."

The victory brought to the fore another pressing matter—selection of an envoy to travel with Scott and negotiate a settlement with Mexico as soon as its leaders had finally accepted the reality of defeat. This question occupied the cabinet meeting of March 10. The problem, said Polk, was that the party was so hopelessly riven by faction and contention that any selection would set off rivalries and agitation. That could jeopardize the ratification. The cabinet agreed. Polk said he favored sending Buchanan, but Mexico's refusal to name commissioners rendered that untenable, as there was no assurance he would be received within any reasonable time frame.

Then Buchanan suggested Nicholas Trist, his chief clerk and a man of considerable experience and talent. The idea, said the secretary, would be to have Trist on hand for any negotiations that emerged from the looming battles, but if Mexico formally named commissioners to treat with the United States he could report that fact back to Washington, and Buchanan could then rush to the scene. Everyone agreed it was a good solution.

Nicholas Philip Trist was a man on the make who wasn't always able to make of his career precisely what he wished. Born 1800 into a prominent Virginia family, he gravitated to the law and successfully courted Thomas Jefferson's granddaughter, Virginia Jefferson Randolph. Through that marriage he became a devoted friend and avid protégé of the former president, to whom he ministered tirelessly throughout Jefferson's final months of enfeebled life. During a brief stint at West Point he befriended Andrew Jackson Donelson and through that friendship became an administration fixture during the presidency of Andrew Jackson. Eventually succeeding Donelson as Jackson's private secretary, Trist established a relationship with Old Hickory much like his Jefferson friendship. He served as helpmate, factotum, confidant, tireless supporter, and avid cheerleader. Through both of these mentorships he became extremely well connected throughout Washington's top governmental and social circles.

Appointed consul at Havana, Cuba, in 1833, he spent eight years in the post, gaining fluency in Spanish and prominence in Caribbean diplomatic and trade circles. But his fortunes began to slide in 1839 when he was the subject of a congressional investigation into allegations of inefficiency, failure to support American interests, and abetting the slave trade. Though exonerated, he suffered an erosion of reputation, and when the new Whig administration took power in 1841 he was relieved of his post. But his previous years of nurturing Washington connections had brought him into friendship with James Buchanan—who, upon becoming Polk's secretary of state, made Trist the State Department's number two official.

Trist was tall and lean, with curly brown hair receding from his forehead, thin expressive lips, and small, dartlike eyes. Towering physically over most men, he gave off an appearance of looking down on them as inevitably inferior. And acquaintances couldn't help noticing certain stark idiosyncrasies, such as his inordinate fear of illness, his conviction that Virginians were superior to other Americans, and a pugnacity of manner when challenged. Most intriguing was his habit of crafting interminably long official and personal letters that betrayed a lack of ability to distinguish the important from the trivial. This seemed most pronounced whenever he ventured into controversy with others, and a natural defensiveness gained sway over his judgment.

As soon as the April 10 cabinet session ended, Polk and Buchanan called Trist over from the State Department for a conversation on his new assignment. In typical fashion Polk emphasized the need for absolute secrecy, an imperative the president stressed further by calling to his office William Derrick, the single State Department clerk who would be allowed to work on the Trist mission. He told Derrick the same thing he had said to Trist: He must treat his assignment with absolute secrecy, lest the entire enterprise die aborning.

On April 13 the cabinet took up the question of the negotiating stance Trist would take with him to Mexico. It was decided the boundary must be the Rio Grande up to the point where it meets the southeastern corner of New Mexico, then west to the Pacific. Thus all of New Mexico and both Upper and Lower California would become U.S. territory. Mexico would cede to the United States a right of passage and transit across the Isthmus of Tehuantepec, the most narrow point in Mexico between the Gulf and the Pacific. The United States would assume all U.S. citizen claims against Mexico and pay, in addition, a sum of $15 million, in annual installments of $3 million.

Polk said he hoped to get all this for less than $15 million but would pay as much as $30 million. After all, he noted, the annual cost of the war far exceeded that figure, and all that land, in terms of market value, was worth multiples of $30 million. The cabinet agreed that Trist should be empowered to offer the $30 million if necessary, but he would be confined to $25 million if he could not get access to the Tehuantepec isthmus. And, if Lower California also proved unavailable, then the top figure would be $20 million.

In the following days final instructions were issued for Trist, and letters were dispatched to Scott and Commodore Matthew Perry, Conner's successor as squadron commander, informing them of Trist's imminent arrival. If Trist managed to negotiate a favorable treaty that received Mexican ratification, the two military leaders were told, they should suspend hostilities until instructed further.

THE TRIST MISSION did not begin auspiciously. On April 21, Polk learned that two letters in the *New York Herald* revealed minute details of the mission. "I have not been more vexed or excited since I have been president than at this occurrence," declared Polk, who became nearly obsessed with identifying the culprit who leaked the information. He harbored no doubt that opposition politicians and journalists, with knowledge of the mission, would attempt to undermine him by sending couriers to Mexico to discourage that country from negotiating.

The president berated Buchanan in uncharacteristically strong language on the theory that the culprit was Derrick, the State Department clerk. Buchanan denied it. Polk then speculated it might be Trist himself or perhaps a member of the cabinet. He interrogated Derrick, consulted the *Union*'s Ritchie in hopes he might know something, and probed other cabinet members. All to no avail. Then the mischievous Buchanan said he knew the identity of the cabinet officer who had violated governmental secrecy—but he declined to reveal his name. Polk would have to swallow his frustration and move on.

Adding to the frustration was a growing groundswell of Whig support for Taylor's presidential nomination. As the *Mobile Register* put it, "The nomination of General Taylor as the party candidate of the *whigs,* is making quite a stir within that party, of which the external symptoms, though subdued by prudential considerations, are sufficiently manifest." The *Union* twitted opposition politicians for wanting to bring this man directly from the battlefield to the White House without so much as a hint of what he actually stood for. They didn't know, said the paper, whether he favored or opposed the 1846 tariff, or Polk's independent treasury, or the aim of extracting territorial concessions from Mexico. They didn't even know how he felt about the Wilmot Proviso. "And yet," said the *Union,* "in this utter darkness and ignorance as to all his political principles, the Federal leaders would force General Taylor into the presidential canvass as their party candidate solely and avowedly on the ground that he has fought with success and glory in a war which they abhor!"

That war was never far from Polk's mind. The president was spending more and more time with Marcy and getting into ever more intricate details of the war effort. On April 28 he met with Marcy and the army's adjutant general to assign regiments to the theaters of war: Scott would get twenty thousand troops, Taylor twelve thousand, and the Santa Fe occupation 2,500. About the same time, word filtered back to Washington of the embarrassing contretemps between Kearny and Frémont, now returning to Washington from their California adventures. This was horrible news. Polk quickly surmised

Kearny was in the right, but any acknowledgment of that on his part risked his important wartime alliance with Benton.

On May 7, Polk received a telegraphic message that Scott had scored a stunning victory over Santa Anna on the so-called National Road from Veracruz to Mexico City. The Mexican general had positioned some fifteen thousand troops at a strong pass called Cerro Gordo, or "wide ridge." There, fortified by the Plan del Rio to his right and numerous steep hills on his left, Santa Anna expected to mow down Scott's advancing army as it sought to proceed through his entrenched position. But the wily American crafted an assault plan that proved too much for the defending Mexicans. Through a series of thrusts over little more than three hours of battle, Scott dislodged the enemy troops from their strongholds and sent them scurrying in panicked retreat. Santa Anna himself barely managed to escape, trudging through the chaparral on a mule. He left behind $6,000, presumably his army payroll, and three thousand captured Mexican troops, including four generals.

The Cerro Gordo victory, secured at a cost of sixty-three U.S. soldiers killed, cleared the way for Scott's army to march all the way to Mexico City. For Mexico and its vainglorious president-general, this was not simply a defeat but a humiliation. Surely, thought many Americans, the Mexican Republic—oft-defeated, without a single military victory to hail after a year-long war—would now treat for peace. "In this emergency," asked the *Union*, "what remains for Mexico?" The reply: "Nothing but peace." And yet the proud Mexicans gave no sign of any inclination to sue for peace or enter into any kind of negotiations.

The Cerro Gordo victory generated another cause of tension between the president and his top general that would in time deflect the course of history. In this instance the man in the middle was Gideon Pillow, Polk's old Tennessee friend and the figure most responsible for his nomination at Baltimore in May 1844. Pillow harbored visions of military glory, followed perhaps by political glory, and Polk had nurtured these visions when he gave Pillow one of the new major generalships. It turned out at Cerro Gordo that the man lacked the steadiness of mind and battlefield savvy necessary for military success. He complained bitterly of orders from Scott, finally accepting the mission with a complaint that he fully expected to leave his bones on the field of battle. Later he quarreled with underlings, demonstrated indecisiveness, chose an inferior route into battle, and finally left the conflict following a minor wound.

Scott's initial report to Marcy gave no hint of this. "Brigadier General Pillow and his brigade twice assaulted with great daring the enemy's lines of batteries on our left," wrote Scott, "and though without success, they contributed much to distract and dismay their immediate opponents." It seemed clear Scott was seeking to avoid frictions with the president, known as one of Pillow's closest friends and confidants. But Scott never fully trusted Pillow after that, and relations between the two generals deteriorated badly.

On the morning of May 28 the president embarked on a rare nine-day excursion outside Washington—to Chapel Hill, North Carolina, to attend the commencement of his alma mater. He discovered during his journey that, while he had generated strong feelings of antipathy in Washington, he still enjoyed a reservoir of support out in the country. He had with him an entourage that included Sarah and her niece, a Miss Rucker; Navy Secretary Mason, Polk's chum from college days; and Mason's son, daughter, and son-in-law. At the Richmond rail depot the president was greeted by an enthusiastic crowd "without distinction of political party," as Polk proudly noted to his diary. Later at the state capitol he attracted a throng of many thousands and an artillery salute.

The entourage continued its rail journey through the night, arriving at the North Carolina town of Gaston at 4 A.M. on May 29. Later that morning the group was greeted by a delegation from Chapel Hill's University of North Carolina. Heading the delegation was a local potentate named John D. Hawkins, who regaled the president with flights of enthusiasm.

"Thirty years ago, Mr. President!" exclaimed Hawkins, noting the years since Polk had attended the university. "What changes have come over the face of the world in thirty years! In all that elevates man—in the improvements of advancing civilization, the last thirty years present greater results than three hundred years preceding. Little then did we dream of the achievements that steam and electricity were to bring about. Little then did either of us think, sir, that in thirty years you should be traveling through the heart of the country by steam to visit your native State."

Proceeding to Raleigh and then to Chapel Hill, the president and his entourage encountered glowing crowds everywhere, military displays, cannon salutes, a fireworks display, and plenty of welcoming rhetoric. When the group reached Chapel Hill it was "overflowing with people," as one newspaper put it, "and they continue to pour in from all quarters—a number of persons having arrived all the way from Tennessee."

Following the commencement ceremony, the presidential party returned directly to Washington, where a delighted Polk characterized his traveling experience to his diary as "exceedingly agreeable . . . all that I could have wished it to be." He noted that of all the politicians along his route, only one had declined to pay his respects. The lone holdout was North Carolina's Senator George Badger, a Whig appointed the previous year to fill the vacancy left by William Haywood's resignation. "It was a matter of perfect indifference to me," wrote Polk with typical disdain, "whether he did so or not."

24 · SCOTT AND TRIST

A Clash of Policy and Temperament

O N MAY 31, during Polk's North Carolina trip, a packet of correspondence arrived at the desk of War Secretary William Marcy that would cause any ordinary man to toss up his hands at the reckless folly of Winfield Scott and Nicholas Trist. It seemed the two men, consumed with hubris and overcome with poor judgment, had entered into a venomous spat that threatened to undermine the president's military-diplomatic strategy. Marcy took steps to defuse the situation, but the Scott-Trist affair would run its own course in a tale of personalities as bizarre as any to beset the James Polk presidency.

The tale begins on May 6 with Trist's arrival at Veracruz. He carried with him Marcy's letter to Scott outlining the Trist mission. He also carried a sealed letter from Buchanan to Mexico's foreign minister informing him that Trist would be with Scott and available whenever Mexico wished to negotiate based on terms outlined in the letter. Although that diplomatic communication was sealed, Trist possessed a copy for Scott's perusal.

Marcy's letter to Scott said if Trist succeeded in arranging a suspension of hostilities, Scott must respond accordingly. "Should he make known to you, in writing, that the contingency has occurred in consequence of which the President is willing that further military operations should cease," wrote Marcy, "you will regard such notice as a directive from the President to suspend them until further orders from the department, unless continued or recommended by the enemy." Marcy also directed Scott to transmit Buchanan's diplomatic dispatch to the country's central government by delivering it under truce to the commander of Mexican forces, who would then forward it on.

Upon arriving in Veracruz, Trist ignored the normal courtesy of proceeding immediately to Scott, presenting himself with a full measure of respect, and delivering personally the packet of correspondence. Instead, Trist dispatched a courier to Scott with the Marcy letter and sealed Buchanan dispatch (without the unsealed copy), along with a terse cover note announcing his arrival and indicating he was himself instructing the general in the matter of the diplomatic dispatch. That was all it took for Scott to explode into a fit of wrath remarkable even for this famously vainglorious man.

"I see," Scott wrote immediately to Trist, "that the Secretary of War proposes to degrade me, by requiring that I, the commander of this army, shall defer to you, the chief clerk of the Department of State, the question of continuing or discontinuing hostilities." This was untenable, he said, adding "the question of an armistice or no armistice is most peculiarly a military question, appertaining, of necessity, if not of universal right, in the absence of direct instructions, to the commander of the invading forces." So if Mexico actually decided to entertain Trist's overtures, said Scott, the diplomat should turn the matter over to him. "The safety of this army demands no less."

As for the communication to Mexico City—"(sealed!)," as the insulted Scott exclaimed in his letter—the general said, "I very much doubt whether I can so far commit the honor of my government as to take any direct agency in forwarding the sealed dispatch." He would hold it for Trist to reclaim and handle as he saw fit, said Scott, adding: "Should you . . . visit the moveable headquarters of this army, I shall receive you with the respect due to a functionary of my government, but whether you would find me here . . . depends on events changeable at every moment."

Scott sent Marcy a copy of his letter along with a cover note declaring he was "too much occupied with the business of the campaign" to deliver Buchanan's diplomatic dispatch.

When a stunned Marcy read this outburst he attributed it to Scott's injured feelings at not getting the diplomatic portfolio. But the imbroglio also seemed partly traceable to Trist's indelicate approach to a potentially awkward situation. Marcy's response to Scott offered clarification mixed with admonition. He expressed "sincere regret that a letter of such an extraordinary character was sent . . . and I cannot doubt it will be no less regretted by yourself on more reflection and better information."

Trist should have delivered the letters in person and clarified all matters surrounding his mission, Marcy conceded. But he added this lapse did not absolve Scott from the directive that he transmit the diplomatic dispatch. This, said Marcy, was "a positive instruction to yourself to send that dispatch forward; and it is expected you will have acted upon it without waiting for the arrival of Mr. Trist." Marcy pointed out that, under the president's policy, Trist could effect an armistice only after a negotiated treaty had been ratified by the Mexican government. He added:

> It will not be questioned that a commissioner of peace may be properly vested with the power of agreeing to a suspension of hostilities in a definitive treaty, negotiated and already ratified by one party, while waiting the ratification of the other. As the negotiator is the first to know the fact that a treaty has been concluded and so ratified, it is, beyond dispute, proper that he should be directed to communicate the knowledge of that fact to the commanding general; and it cannot, in my view of the case, be derogatory to that officer to be placed under instructions to act with reference to that fact, when duly notified of it by the commissioner.

Marcy's impeccable logic failed to mollify the riled general, in part because the self-important and condescending Trist already had weighed in with his own response. "In a word, sir," he wrote to Scott, "the course determined upon by our government . . . is what any man of plain unsophisticated common sense would take for granted that it must be; and it is not what your exuberant fancy and over-cultivated imagination would make." In letters to his wife, Trist called Scott "decidedly the greatest imbecile . . . that I ever had any thing to do with." Noting he expected his correspondence to become public, he added, "If I have not *demolished* him, then I give up."

When Scott got Trist's reply, his fulminations overflowed—and were directed equally at Trist and Polk. On May 20 the general wrote to Marcy with injured tones protesting what he considered a decision to place his command under this civilian clerk. Of course these actions didn't surprise him, said Scott, because the president already had revealed his desire to supersede him with Thomas Benton if Congress would consent. "I entreat to be spared," he wrote, "the personal dishonor of being again required to obey the orders of the chief clerk of the State Department." The general added Trist had arrived at his camp some six days earlier but had not deigned to approach him—an implicit confession that he had offered no official welcome.

When this letter reached Washington on June 12, an enraged Polk told his cabinet the "insubordinate" Scott should be dismissed. The cabinet agreed, but Polk characteristically shied away from such a bold step until after Scott replied to Marcy's latest stern rebuke. Much upset, Polk wrote that "the golden moment to make a peace . . . may be lost because of Gen'l Scott's arrogance & inordinate vanity." But there wasn't much to do now but wait in hopes the two willful men would come together and fulfill their obligations.

As he waited, Polk decided to build upon his successful North Carolina trip by scheduling a northern journey. During two weeks of travel he visited Baltimore, Wilmington, Philadelphia, New York, Hartford, Boston, and Augusta, Maine, among other Eastern Seaboard locations. "No President could have performed so long a journey, and seen so much of his country in so short a time," noted the *Union*, "because of the present immense facilities afforded to travelling by steamboats and railroad cars." Polk's return trip, from Portland, Maine, to Washington, took only two and a half days. He was back in Washington on July 8.

Throughout his northern stops, the president encountered robust crowds, rousing cheers, military salutes, and displays of enthusiasm.

Delighted to be away from Washington's persistent office seekers and poisonous political ethers, he basked in the obvious respect of his countrymen. "My reception was everywhere respectful & cordial," he wrote to his diary upon returning. "Not an unpleasant incident occurred to mar its pleasure."

Looking relaxed and trim, Polk seemed actually buoyant as he greeted his fellow Americans with expressions of wonder at the brilliant experiment in government forged by the Founders some seventy years before. Speaking at Philadelphia's Independence Hall on June 24, he said:

> This is the hall in which sat that venerable body of men—here sat John Hancock—here sat Thomas Jefferson—here sat your own Franklin and Rush—that venerable, that illustrious body of men, (God bless their memories!) who made the astounding declaration to the world—that a nation of freemen lived!
>
> Seventy years have gone since that glorious event—the birth of our nation—and when seventy more years shall have passed away—when other Presidents shall have enjoyed the honor which I now enjoy, of being thus warmly welcomed by the citizens and municipal government of this city, I would ask—what human sagacity can foresee the prosperity and greatness of my beloved country? May our constitution ever be held sacred, our Union unbroken and inviolate!

Back in Washington, Polk discovered the war circumstances hadn't improved much. The feud between Scott and Trist had intensified as the two men resided at Scott's military encampment at Puebla, along the National Road to Mexico City. Scott, refusing to transmit Buchanan's diplomatic dispatch to Mexico's foreign minister, had returned the sealed envelope to Trist—who, in Polk's view, had no authority to do anything with it and hence "committed a great error in receiving it."

Scott's insolence reached a high pitch in a letter received by Marcy during Polk's northern journey. He wryly referred to Trist as "a flank battery planted against me," and added: "Considering the many cruel disappointments and mortifications I have been made to feel . . . or the total want of support and sympathy, on the part of the War Department, which I have so long experienced, I beg to be recalled from this army."

Polk was prepared to oblige the general while also placing him before a court-martial—and tossing out Trist for good measure. But private conversations with his cabinet yielded a consensus that, while both men deserved to be fired, such an action would be highly disruptive at a delicate and critical time in the war. Citing the cabinet consensus, Polk said he would defer action pending further developments from Mexico. He ordered Marcy and Buchanan to issue further letters of reprimand to both men, demanding that they put aside petty sentiments and get on with the important tasks of serving the nation's interests.

UNBEKNOWNST TO MARCY and Buchanan as they wrote those stern letters, or to Polk when he edited them, was the improbable fact that the Scott-Trist rift had entirely healed. The two men had, from the fires of their contention, forged an emotional bond so strong and meaningful that it would blossom into a lifelong friendship—nurtured initially by the realization that they had in common a powerful sentiment: They both hated James K. Polk.

The second chapter in the Polk-Trist relationship began amid diplomatic developments of potentially far-reaching significance. In early June, Trist began pondering ways to get Buchanan's dispatch to Mexico City. He had no official authority to do anything with it, of course, except deliver it to Scott. But the resourceful envoy hit upon the idea of seeking help from the British legation, headed by Minister Charles Bankhead, whom Trist had met during Bankhead's diplomatic tour in Washington some years earlier. Bankhead was pleased to help.

On June 10 the minister sent his chargé, Edward Thornton, to visit Trist and Scott. Thornton received the sealed packet from Trist and delivered it to Bankhead in Mexico City. The minister in turn delivered it to Mexican foreign minister Domingo Ibarra, who turned the matter over to the Mexican Congress. Shortly thereafter Thornton returned to Puebla with the news that Santa Anna had called a special congressional session to consider the matter.

Prospects now brightened that some serious negotiation might actually commence, and that necessitated a Trist communication to Scott advising him of the new developments. He sent that communication on June 25 along with a copy of his commission for Scott's inspection. Scott sent a cordial if correct official reply. As Trist later noted to Buchanan, this "constituted the commencement of our official intercourse with reference to the duties with which I am charged." A week later Scott heard Trist was confined to bed with what appeared to be a severe illness. Succumbing to the kindness of heart that was as prominent a trait as his explosive temper, the general promptly sent over a jar of guava marmalade, by chance a Trist favorite from his Havana years. The gesture utterly destroyed any lingering Trist animosity toward his old adversary. It demonstrated, wrote Trist to Buchanan, "so much good feeling that it afforded me the sincerest pleasure to meet it as I did, in a way which should at once preclude all constraint & embarrassment between us."

Indeed, the two men were soon meeting regularly for long, rambling conversations about past adventures, mutual friends, the war situation, and their meddlesome bosses in Washington. All past insults and enmities were forgotten as the two discovered in each other soul mates of brotherly affinity. Both wrote to their Washington patrons requesting removal from official files of their previous letters about each other. Those Washington patrons must have smiled at the requests; not only did the letters remain in the files but soon they would become public.

Hardly had the new Scott-Trist friendship germinated before it was directed toward an initiative that would threaten grave embarrassment to Polk's administration. The two men, along with a few others, entered into a conspiracy to commit diplomatic bribery—to pay a Mexican official and his minions $1 million to bring about peace. Not surprisingly, the Mexican official was Generalissimo Santa

Anna, who never missed an opportunity to gratify his personal appetites as he went about his arduous role of serving, with great ostentation, the Mexican Republic.

The conspiracy seems to have begun with Edward Thornton, the British envoy. A flurry of letter-writing that ensued upon Thornton's return to Puebla indicates Thornton had brought with him a suggestion that Santa Anna might settle matters in exchange for an under-the-table payment. Scott and Trist were still feuding, and the suggestion got no serious attention.

But they were fast friends by July 15, when they engaged in a lengthy private conference on the subject. The next day, in a typically prolix letter to Scott, Trist embraced Santa Anna's suggestion. "We are both convinced," he wrote, " . . . that the only way in which the indefinite protraction of this war can possibly be prevented . . . is by the secret expenditure of money at the city of Mexico." He named a "necessary and sufficient" figure of $10,000 in advance and $1 million at ratification. Trist embraced an earlier Scott suggestion that the money could come out of the general's war funds. Of course, he added, the U.S. government had authorized no such action, but he felt "a duty to disregard" this absence of authority in the interest of the government's primary imperative—ending the war. If Scott would join him in pledging such payments, said Trist, together they could "entirely supersede the necessity for the occupation of the capital."

Scott already had demonstrated enthusiasm for the scheme, but upon getting Trist's letter he solicited the views of his generals—particularly prominent Democrats Gideon Pillow, John Quitman, and James Shields. According to one participant, Pillow initially expressed misgivings but slowly relented after Scott postulated that such payments were customary in dealing with dysfunctional nations such as Mexico. While Quitman appreciated the motives involved, he said he couldn't get comfortable with the idea. Shields went along reluctantly so long as Scott was shielded from direct participation. Other officers seemed to go along without enthusiasm.

The next day Scott replied to Trist's letter: "I fully concur with you, with several of the general officers of this army & with many foreigners of high standing, here & at the capital, who have volunteered their opinions" that further Mexican occupation wasn't likely to bring peace—*"without the administration, or pledge in advance, of douceurs to some of the principal authorities in this miserably governed country."* They had learned, he added, "thro' the most unquestionable channels," that such payments were "invited & expected as an indispensable condition precedent to any negotiation." Scott revealed he already had sent the up-front payment of $10,000.

But soon the bribery plan fizzled. Santa Anna sent word to Puebla, through Thornton, that the Mexican Congress had declined to repeal an earlier law denying Santa Anna the power to negotiate an end to the war. His hands were tied, he reported, and hence Scott would have to move his army to the edge of Mexico City before any negotiation could take place. Scott informed Santa Anna that his army soon would be there, and the result would be either a peace negotiation with Trist or another major Mexican humiliation in full view of the capital.

BACK IN WASHINGTON, Polk knew nothing of the Scott-Trist rapprochement, the communications with Santa Anna, or the bribery scheme. Waiting for news from Mexico, he focused primarily on two things: latest developments in the 1848 presidential contest; and a brewing financial scandal involving the army's quartermaster general and Treasury Secretary Robert Walker.

The state of presidential politics was captured nicely by the *Cincinnati Morning Signal* in late June. The presidential canvass, said the paper, was in "utter confusion." No Whig enjoyed anything approaching party dominance. Antiwar factions of the Northeast and Ohio's Western Reserve favored Senator Thomas Corwin of Ohio, while southerners hoped for a Scott victory of sufficient magnitude to catapult him forward.

Then there was that giant of the past, Henry Clay, now seventy years old. A Whig publication called the *North American* bitterly lamented Clay's fate at the last election, which had occurred, said the paper, "amid evil times,—times of confusion, passion, and folly . . . under which thousands of men voted against their own wishes and interests." But now, said the paper, as Clay moved once again amidst his countrymen, "touched by affliction, they accompany him whithersoever he bends his steps, deepened by the reverence which a free people can only accord to the most worthy and most honored of public men."

Hovering over this speculation was Zachary Taylor, whose military victories had fired the public spirit and whose persona stirred confidence and respect. The country knew him as sober, solid, steady, and dependable—traits that compared favorably to the public image of Scott as egotistical, erratic, and explosive. Even Scott's longtime nickname, Old Fuss and Feathers, drooped next to Taylor's hearty moniker of Old Rough and Ready.

Of course the American people didn't know their hero's petty and petulant side, or his languid temperament, or his lack of imagination and intellectual curiosity. He was their hero, and that was good enough—and good enough also for the Whig establishment, which saw in Taylor a rare chance for presidential victory. By summer the Whig conventions of Maryland and Georgia had thrown their support behind Taylor, and Whig newspapers were touting him everywhere.

Responding to a May query from the *Cincinnati Morning Signal*, Taylor acknowledged that "my services are ever at the will and call of the country, and . . . I am not prepared to say that I shall refuse if the country calls me to the presidential office." But he added a curious proviso: *"In no case can I permit myself to be the candidate of any party, or yield myself to party schemes."*

This was a remarkable statement, suggesting this soldier felt he could reach the presidency through some kind of immaculate ascension. Many Whigs recoiled at such apparent naïveté. "If Gen. Taylor adhere to this resolution," declared the *Richmond Times and Compiler*, "we are constrained to express an opinion that the whig party cannot be expected to surrender their organization and their principles for the purpose of elevating him to the presidency." The *American and Gazette* of Philadelphia was more blunt: "The power of one man, if it be such as to set aside all the cherished principles of honest and patriotic parties, is nothing more nor less than despotism."

In early August, seeking to recover from his political blunder, Taylor wrote to a Philadelphia supporter saying he considered himself a Whig. In the last election, he said, he had favored Clay, whose "views and those of the whigs, for the most part are more nearly assimilated, as regards political matters, to those of Mr. Jefferson than their opponents—in whose political creed I was reared, and whose opinions, in matters of state, I have never lost sight of."

The *Union*, howling at this seeming political confusion about the parties' political etymology, suggested either the general was attempting to deceive voters or had been deceived himself by Whig propaganda. Some Taylor supporters urged him to cease his conspicuous correspondence. "If Taylor keeps writing letters," said one New Yorker, "Clay will be nominated."

As for the Democrats, the *Cincinnati Morning Signal* suggested the heartiest candidates, assuming Polk's sincerity in forswearing a second term, were Cass, Calhoun, and New York's Silas Wright, whose recent gubernatorial defeat hadn't dampened his northeastern support. Meanwhile, said the paper, the party could find itself turning to Van Buren, "the statesman of the party, who will probably never again join the political *melee*, but might prove more available . . . than many men whose names are frequently heard in the present connexion." Clearly, the Democrats remained fractured, far from any kind of coalescence behind any single man or political philosophy.

The Whigs, on the other hand, seemed increasingly united on one fundamental political principle—the United States should acquire no Mexican territory from the war. As a Whig newspaper in Auburn, New York, put it, the Whigs should "surrender up" the Wilmot Proviso debate "and adopt in its stead *no more territory*, free or slave. This is striking at the root of the matter; and we have little doubt that the great mass of even southern whigs will be found co-operating with the whigs of the north, heart in hand, in favor of such a policy."

This was politically brilliant, escaping the double-edged sword of Wilmot and leaving that dangerous and divisive issue to the Democrats. The *Intelligencer* said it best when it expressed regret that so many northern Whig newspapers heralded the Wilmot Proviso as the election's central question. "Do they not see," asked the paper, "that if this issue be made by the north, it must of necessity be made by the south? Are they not already authoritatively advised that it is *the issue* now most desired by our opponents of the south?" Let the followers of Calhoun and Van Buren rend the Democrats apart over Wilmot, said the paper, while the Whigs remained safely above that fray, concentrating on an issue—no new territory—upon which all Whigs from all regions could agree.

Ritchie's *Union* attacked this cynical political avoidance, but not without recognition of its potency. "And to what end have the whig leaders put their party in this position?" it asked, then answered: "It is avowedly in order to unite their party in an effort to clutch the spoils of office."

ON AUGUST 17, Polk received a visit from Benton, who seemed obsessed with the military fate of his son-in-law, that California adventurer, Lieutenant Colonel Frémont. He had written a letter to the army's adjutant general requesting a court-martial as the only way to exonerate the man. Polk replied he hoped the case could be resolved without the necessity of a court-martial.

"I am glad to hear from you, Sir, as President of the U. States," roared Benton, "that there has been nothing in Col. Fremont's conduct which requires a Court Martial in his case."

Polk quickly emphasized he could not extend any opinion on the matter, given the fact that the case might eventually rise to the level of presidential review. But he did hope the unfortunate episode could be handled administratively. Benton understood, but said he intended to initiate a full Senate inquiry into "the whole California business." The senator, wrote Polk later, "was evidently much excited, but suppressed his feelings and talked in a calm tone." How long the Missourian would stay calm remained an open question.

The president didn't react calmly the next day when Buchanan suggested he should delay further troop call-ups because the U.S. treasury seemed to be running out of money. Polk was astonished.

Nothing ever seemed to be fully under control in his administration, and now he faced a financial crisis that could prove highly embarrassing. He set off on a flurry of fact-finding, none of which seemed to get to the bottom of this mystifying turn of events. Marcy, suffering from an illness, was heading to New York to recuperate. Polk put Mason in charge of the War Department and instructed him to investigate the matter. The president spoke with a top treasury official and functionaries of the army's office of the quartermaster general. Nobody seemed to have an explanation for the missing money.

On August 20 the president discovered the problem resided primarily in the army's quartermaster and commissary departments. An "astonishingly large amount" of funds, it appeared, had been withdrawn from those two accounts in the past two months. Polk summoned from New York the army's quartermaster general, the incompetent military bureaucrat Thomas Jesup, whose office held custodianship over much of the depleted funds. "When Gen'l Jesup arrives," Polk wrote hopefully to his diary, "he will be able to explain how the matter stands. The accounts are badly kept in his office, or his clerks would be able to give more satisfactory explanations of their actual condition."

Jesup appeared on August 21 to explain that some $4 million in war funds had been extended to disbursing officers in New York and New Orleans. Much of that money remained unexpended, said Jesup, so there was no need for concern. He said Polk could resume calling up the six thousand troops anticipated in the Ten Regiment Bill approved by Congress earlier in the year. But the president remained vexed—and curious as to why Jesup's underlings didn't have sufficient records on hand to provide that explanation during Jesup's absence.

His curiosity increased three days later when Jesup revealed he now understood another $2 million also had been sent out to disbursing officers. Polk expressed further astonishment that Jesup didn't have a sufficient grasp of the finances under his jurisdiction to say, at any moment, precisely where all the money was. "I told him," Polk wrote later, "that his books should be kept in such manner that any one familiar with accounts should be able on inspection to see at once the amounts drawn from the Treasury, in whose hands the funds were, and the amounts remaining undrawn."

The next day Jesup returned to the White House with a bombshell revelation. It seems the last $2 million mentioned by Jesup had been deposited at the banking house of Corcoran & Riggs, which had invested the funds in stock securities pending any need for disbursement to army officials at New Orleans. This had been done, said Jesup, at the insistence of the treasury's chief clerk, McLintock Young, who had appeared at Jesup's office the previous June with a Mr. Corcoran from the banking house and requested the funds transfer. Jesup said some $400,000 had since been disbursed to New Orleans for war purposes, and another $500,000 was set to be sent down soon. That would leave $1.1 million in the hands of the private bankers, who reportedly were investing it for their own personal gain.

Polk sent for Buchanan and expressed his "utter astonishment" at the revelation. He had not been so troubled since his presidency began, said Polk, adding the episode almost made him sick. When Polk confronted Walker about the matter later that day, the treasury secretary evinced a casualness of outlook on it. Speaking in vague generalities, he said he couldn't recall the precise transaction but defended the practice of depositing government funds in private banks pending governmental need for them. Polk disagreed, ordered an immediate investigation, and directed Walker to rescind any federal war funds being held in private banks. "The matter troubles me very greatly," he wrote to his diary.

The next day Walker reported the investigation was underway and would yield results soon. Polk replied he didn't understand why his questions couldn't be answered immediately. But a day later Walker still didn't have answers. "I told him," reported Polk later, "that it was strange to me that the information I wanted could not be furnished in an hour from the Books of his Department." All he wanted to know, said Polk, was how much money had been drawn from the treasury upon requisition of the quartermaster general, when it had been drawn, in whose hands it was being held, and under what contract or arrangement it was being held. When Walker emphasized no funds had been transferred except under requisition from the War Department, Polk dismissed the point as unresponsive to his queries.

By the next day's cabinet meeting, Walker could add only that some $600,000 remained in the hands of the bankers and would be distributed to the army by September 15. Polk said that, even if the mode of transfer had been legal and proper, "the time given had been too long and the amt. too large, for the safety of the funds." Buchanan said he saw nothing illegal in the practices adopted, and the matter soon faded from the president's consciousness as it became clear he had sufficient funds to wage his war. Was some kind of chicanery going on? That question was never answered, but it is noteworthy that, throughout this unfolding drama, Polk never recalled to his diary Andrew Jackson's dire warning at the beginning of his presidency that Walker wasn't a man to be trusted with the nation's cash.

AMONG THE MATTERS that diverted the president's attention was a telegraphic report that New York's Silas Wright had died of a heart attack on August 28—"struck down without warning," said the *Union,* "in the splendid maturity of his great faculties, and in the midst of bright and almost boundless prospects of future usefulness and renown." He was a giant of his time, a leader of moderate views and measured temperament who had emerged as the standard-bearer of the Democratic Party's Van Buren faction. Born the same year as Polk, he was just fifty-two at his death. "He was a great and good man," recalled the president. "I was intimate with him when he was in Congress. He was my personal and [political] friend, and I deeply regret his death."

As summer faded into fall, Polk knew he was politically vulnerable to powerful opposition attacks if the war lingered into the new congressional session scheduled to begin in early December. He would need an articulated war strategy designed to blunt those attacks and also to bring the war to a speedy close. But the cabinet discussions on the subject served to illustrate the paucity of available options.

At a September 4 cabinet session, Polk outlined his current think-

ing. If Mexico wouldn't negotiate for peace, he said, he favored com-
bining the Scott and Taylor forces for a major assault on Mexico City
and all other vital regions of the country. Also, since the cost of the
war had ballooned because of Mexican obstinacy, he now would insist
on smaller payments and greater tracts of territory than previously
authorized in Trist's instructions.

Three days later, at the next cabinet meeting, it became clear the
president's formulations had introduced a new debate into the government's war deliberations. The question was: How much territory
should the United States acquire? Walker and Attorney General Clifford advocated taking the entire state of Tamaulipas, which included
the port of Tampico. Buchanan, Mason, and Johnson recoiled at such
territorial ambitions. Clifford argued that, if Mexico refused to negotiate even after a U.S. conquest of Mexico City, the president should
announce to the world that he was withdrawing his envoy and would
overrun and subdue the entire country of Mexico. Walker quickly
endorsed that view. Polk agreed partially, saying he wouldn't likely
recall Trist in such an eventuality. Finally it was agreed to postpone
any definitive decision until after further news arrived from the battlefront.

A week later word arrived that Scott on August 20 had scored
two major victories against Santa Anna just outside Mexico City. The
American commander had moved his army from Puebla along the
fabled National Road, which would have brought it to the eastern
entrance to Mexico City. Some eight miles from that entrance, at El
Peñón, Santa Anna established his forward defensive position, some
seven thousand men and thirty cannon for maximum devastation upon
the approaching Americans. But the flexible and resourceful Scott had
veered off the National Road, moved his troops through rugged territory around the wide expanse of Lake Chalco, then up through a
narrow passage between Lakes Chalco and Xochimilco, approaching
Mexico City from the south.

Santa Anna, seeing Scott's bold maneuver, redeployed his troops
south of the city, moving some twenty thousand soldiers into a defensive perimeter by August 19. Scott, with half as many troops, probed

for weaknesses in Santa Anna's perimeter, but soon a major force under Colonel Bennett Riley found itself in a precarious position near a town identified as Contreras. A bold overnight maneuver by Colonel Persifor Smith positioned a brigade to protect Riley's unit and then join with it for a daybreak assault on Mexican General Gabriel Valencia's northern army. The assault succeeded, aided by Santa Anna's lethargic battlefield decision-making. The Americans, with 4,500 men pitted against seven thousand Mexicans (and twelve thousand more positioned within sight), routed Valencia's army, killing seven hundred and capturing more than eight hundred, including four generals.

Seeing the victory at Contreras, Scott pounced with his combined forces, unleashing three attacks on Santa Anna's remaining positions near a town called Churubusco. All succeeded, and Santa Anna was forced to retreat with his army into what was now the besieged capital of Mexico. In a single day, the Mexican general had lost four thousand soldiers killed or wounded and another three thousand captured (including eight generals, two of them former presidents). Scott lost 139 men killed and some eight hundred wounded. Santa Anna, with his numerical superiority in a defensive battle, had been positioned to devastate the invading army and shatter the American president's standing back home. Instead, he had presided over the single greatest day of national humiliation in the history of the Mexican Republic.

25 · MEXICO CITY

The Pivot of Personality

THE FATE OF James Polk's war policy, and his standing in history, now resided in the hands of a few powerful men— Winfield Scott and his top generals, Nicholas Trist, Santa Anna, a handful of key Mexican officials, and the president himself. With Scott's army positioned just beyond the protective causeways of Mexico City, prospects for a lasting peace became palpable for the first time since Texas annexation some two years before. But the opportunity for peace was fragile and could crumble if the big players at the vortex of events proved incapable of rising to the occasion.

Unfortunately, these men were all flawed, and their flaws now contributed to confusion and turmoil. Polk's final push for peace would be as messy and circuitous as the rest of his troubled presidency. And his own suspicious nature and self-righteous tendencies would contribute to his difficulties.

On August 20, Santa Anna arrived in the heart of Mexico City a broken and desperate man. But he quickly seized the political initiative and forged a consensus among his nation's leaders. They would seek a truce with the enemy. Some Mexican officials, seeing the hopelessness of their cause, urged immediate surrender. But Santa Anna brushed aside those sentiments. He needed time to reorder his army for a last-ditch defense, and a truce would give him that time.

The next day, as Scott positioned his troops to assault the capital, a delegation arrived from within the city with a sealed packet for Trist. It contained a letter to James Buchanan from J. R. Pacheco, the latest in the unfolding string of Mexican foreign ministers. He was ready to receive Trist, said Pacheco, and to weigh the terms contained in

Buchanan's famous communication delivered through Trist the previous June. The minister also proposed a truce during which a permanent peace could be negotiated.

Trist and Scott discussed the matter and embraced a brief truce. Scott knew he could conquer Mexico City in short order, but the resulting damage to civilian security and sensibilities could "scatter the elements of peace," as Scott later put it, "excite a spirit of national desperation, and thus indefinitely postpone the hope of accommodation." To forestall such stubborn resistance and demonstrate his own conciliatory outlook, Scott sent to Santa Anna an offer of armistice. "Too much blood has already been shed in this unnatural war," wrote the general, adding he was "willing to sign, on reasonable terms, a short armistice." Then he dispatched a letter to Marcy saying his army had "very cheerfully sacrificed . . . the *éclat* that would have followed an entrance—sword in hand—into a great capital."

On August 22 representatives of the two sides met to craft an elaborate cease-fire that forbade either army from resuming military activity, including building fortifications within ninety miles of the capital. Normal traffic into and out of Mexico City would be allowed, and the Americans would be permitted to obtain supplies from within the city. Prisoners would be exchanged, the wounded tended to, and the civil rights of Mexicans within American-held lands would be respected. The agreement could be abrogated by either side through a forty-eight-hour notice.

Almost from the beginning the agreement unraveled.

True to his nature, Santa Anna immediately violated the terms by fortifying his military positions. Then Americans were blocked from seeking supplies in the capital, first by Mexican mobs and then by Santa Anna's own army. On September 7 a frustrated Scott summarily terminated the truce. In the meantime, Trist had opened up negotiations with his Mexican counterparts, and some important developments had occurred.

Trist's negotiating leeway was constricted, of course, by his instructions from Polk: The Rio Grande boundary must remain inviolate; New Mexico and Upper California would go to the United

States; Lower California would go also if possible, along with transit rights across the Isthmus of Tehuantepec; the United States would assume all U.S. citizen claims and pay Mexico between $15 million and $30 million, depending on how much territory was conveyed.

But the Mexican negotiators, led by ex-President Herrera, brought some constraints of their own. Santa Anna felt considerable political pressure from his country's so-called Puros, the traditionalist faction that saw treason in any negotiation with the despised Americans. Santa Anna faced enough danger just sending a delegation to treat with Trist; he wasn't going to enflame his political foes further by letting his negotiators accept inordinate concessions.

Thus, the two parties became deadlocked. The Mexican negotiators, refusing to accept the status of a vanquished party, demanded the Nueces border as well as indemnities from the United States for injuries suffered by Mexican citizens during the war. They offered a portion of California north of San Diego for a pecuniary consideration but refused to yield any of New Mexico or Lower California and declined to cede any transit rights across Tehuantepec. Trist receded on Lower California and Tehuantepec, as his instructions allowed, but held firm on Upper California, New Mexico, and the boundary question. Then he blinked. Previously, while at Puebla, the American had mused aloud about the possibility of the territory between the Nueces and Rio Grande becoming a neutral zone providing both countries a protective buffer. The Mexicans slyly tossed Trist's ill-considered words back at him with the suggestion this might be a fitting compromise.

Trist was in a bind. Sent there to negotiate as America's military victories softened up Mexican resistance, he found those victories only seemed to stiffen the resistance. Now it seemed his old idea of a neutral zone might be his only avenue for bringing about peace and foreclosing the necessity of a bloody assault on Mexico City. He offered to submit the idea to his government, along with a recommendation that Scott extend the truce by forty-five days so Washington would have time to respond. On September 4 he sent the proposal to Buchanan for cabinet review.

Trist's proposal hit Washington like a brick hurled through a stained glass window. It now became clear that Polk and Trist saw the diplomatic challenge differently. Polk was waging his war so he could negotiate the accumulation of vast lands he coveted for his country. Trist was negotiating the territorial question so he could terminate Polk's war. The two men were on a path of collision.

Polk was already disturbed when, on September 15, he got word of Scott's victories at Contreras and Churubusco and his subsequent acceptance of an armistice. Though pleased with the victories, Polk felt Scott should have issued an immediate ultimatum to Santa Anna— accept Trist's authorized terms or suffer a devastating assault on the capital. He suspected correctly that Santa Anna was merely buying time to fortify his position. And he fretted that ten days had apparently elapsed since Scott's victories without any discernible progress on a peace agreement. "I shall wait very anxiously for further information from the army," he wrote to his diary.

As he waited, Polk increasingly felt that Trist's mission was heading toward failure. This was reinforced by rumors, apparently emanating from the Mexican side, that Trist had shown flexibility on the Rio Grande boundary and had proposed a forty-five-day truce extension. Polk wasn't inclined to credit these rumors, nor was Ritchie's *Union*. "The propositions said to be made by Mr. Trist must be grossly misrepresented," the paper declared. "He could scarcely have asked 45 days for any purpose—much less to consider of a proposition to limit our boundary to the Nueces. . . . All this, of course, is out of the question."

But Polk was troubled. Confined to his bed with a severe fever, the president pondered whether he should summon Trist back to Washington on the ground that his usefulness had expired. By the time he returned to work on October 4, he had made his decision. He instructed Buchanan to draft a letter informing Trist that he was being recalled. Buchanan's letter instructed the envoy to return to Washington with any treaty that may have been negotiated; if none had been, he was to return anyway "by the first safe opportunity." Polk also directed Marcy to craft a letter instructing Scott to support his army by levying contributions from the conquered Mexicans.

Scott was in a good position to levy such contributions because in mid-September he had conquered Mexico City and planted the flag of American hegemony atop the defeated country's National Palace. The city had posed some peculiar military challenges for Scott. It could be entered only along the causeways, or elevated roadbeds, that cut through the marshes and waterways surrounding the city. Hence any attacking unit, spread out along the causeways, would be vulnerable to Mexican defensive units positioned at the inner end of the causeways like Horatius at his bridge. On the other hand, those bunched-up defensive units could be vulnerable to Scott's superior artillery.

Before initiating his attack, Scott on September 8 sent General William Worth to capture a complex of stone buildings, called Molino del Rey, that once had housed a cannon foundry and, according to reports, was now being used to forge big guns from the city's many church bells. If the reports were true, the complex posed a serious artillery threat. Worth, with some 3,500 men, set off toward what he and Scott assumed would be a relatively minor skirmish to secure the area. But Santa Anna had anticipated the move and rushed to the molino a large contingent of troops, including five brigades with artillery support and some four thousand cavalry. Once again, the Americans were seriously outnumbered.

A brutal two-hour battle followed. It was marked by superior U.S. combat mobility and characteristically sluggish Mexican decision-making. Worth took the foundry, but at a cost of 116 men killed, 665 wounded, and eighteen missing. Santa Anna lost some two thousand soldiers killed or wounded and another 685 taken prisoner. But the rumors of a cannon factory had been false. Thus, the mission served no useful tactical purpose. Scott still had to determine which causeways to choose as his routes into the fortified Mexican capital.

Most of his officers favored the three southern causeways, in part because they allowed U.S. troops to skirt the fortified castle of Chapultepec to the west. Scott was inclined to hit directly at Chapultepec via two western causeways. Though he invited plenty of discussion and listened respectfully as some of his officers argued vehemently for the southern routes, Scott held firm. Planning immediately commenced for a western assault.

It began at dawn on September 12 with a relentless bombardment of the Chapultepec fortification and a feint aimed at lulling Santa Anna into a conviction that the attack would come from the south. The Mexican general wasn't fooled. But, lacking reliable intelligence on Scott's troop movements, he spread his troops at various points throughout the city to meet an attack from any likely direction. Still, his forces vastly outnumbered the Americans, and he enjoyed the added advantage of defending fortified territory against troops forced to place themselves into vulnerability just to initiate an assault.

When the American assault actually commenced, Santa Anna once again demonstrated he was no match for the resourceful and deft Scott, whose insistence on the western approach proved brilliant. The castle turned out to be more vulnerable than Scott's men had supposed— first, to the artillery bombardment, which destroyed much of the roof and blasted holes in its walls; and then to the ground assault and subsequent scaling parties that clambered up the walls after Santa Anna's infantry defenders had been routed. It required just two hours for the Americans to take the castle and begin the hand-to-hand cleanup operation that would result in the slaughter of the remaining Mexican defenders.

Santa Anna lost some 1,800 men that morning, four times the U.S. casualties. Generals Quitman and Worth ordered their troops to rush into the city and take possession of all the remaining causeways. By day's end they had captured the key strategic points at the city's northwest and southwest corners, and Mexican resistance was fading away. The elusive Santa Anna slipped out of the city overnight with the remnants of his army. The next afternoon Old Fuss and Feathers, atop a spirited bay charger and displaying his favorite military regalia, including his famous plumage, rode triumphantly down the streets of Mexico City, past his cheering troops, to the plaza in front of the ministerial palace. He then named General Quitman governor of the city.

For the imperious Scott it was the crowning victory in a military

campaign marked by a rare degree of martial brilliance from beginning to end. Upon reading of the American's exploits, Britain's Duke
of Wellington, probably the world's most renowned military man,
called Scott "the greatest living soldier" and said his campaign "was
unsurpassed in military annals." The Mexico City effort illustrated
the point. Cut off from his supply bases and with fewer than eleven
thousand troops, Scott had faced an army of some thirty thousand,
well dug in to protect their most sacred city. In the face of those odds,
he had killed or wounded some seven thousand enemy troops, had
taken an additional 3,730 prisoners, and captured seventy-five cannon. It was a remarkable military achievement that thrilled his fellow
countrymen.

But not James K. Polk. Beleaguered by his increasingly aggressive political enemies, the president didn't feel any spirit of generosity toward the general who had performed his assigned mission with
such aplomb. And Scott, true to form, continued to nettle his superiors in Washington, who received news reports about the Mexico City
battle on October 20, along with rumors Santa Anna had relinquished
the presidency to Peña y Peña, but got nary a word of official description from the commanding general for weeks thereafter. Polk became
convinced that Scott was not truly the mastermind of the Americans'
signal triumphs on the road to Mexico City.

This wasn't merely a product of prejudice. He was told as much by
his old friend and benefactor, Gideon Pillow, whose dream of military glory hadn't been realized on the battlefield. Though clearly brilliant as lawyer, planter, and political operative, the man lacked the
steadiness of mind and leadership traits of the successful general officer. Worse, his compulsive ambition and manipulative impulses, so
beneficial in settings such as the Baltimore convention back in 1844,
proved disruptive in the military setting. One young officer with
manifest potential as combat warrior, Lieutenant William Tecumseh
Sherman, described the general as "a mass of vanity, conceit, ignorance, ambition and want of truth."

Pillow, apparently coveting Scott's command, set out to undermine
the commander through a letter-writing campaign to the president.

And Polk was only too happy to receive these letters and credit Pillow's criticisms. Pillow, after all, was part of Polk's Tennessee inner circle, a close friend of both Cave Johnson and Aaron Brown. Indeed, Brown had married Pillow's sister in 1845 after the death of his first wife. It was perhaps inevitable that the normally skeptical Polk, who seldom extended himself in behalf of even his most loyal followers, would make an exception in the case of Pillow. "I have great confidence in Pillow," the president wrote in August 1847, "but he is young in the service & the country do[es] not know his merits as well as I do."

With his power base in Washington unmatched among his fellow officers, Pillow developed delusions of grandeur. "I can only say," he wrote to his wife, Mary, after the Churubusco battle outside Mexico City, "my part was far more brilliant and *conspicuous* than I myself, in my most sanguine moments ever hoped for." After the Chapultepec assault, during which Pillow suffered a wound to the ankle, he described himself to Mary as "a gentleman who has now the name in the army of the '*Hero of Chapultepec*.'" He added: "I know I am not mistaken when I say it will give my name a place in history which will live while our Republic stands."

Unfortunately, Pillow didn't confine these flights of vainglory to his private correspondence. In submitting his reports of the Churubusco and Chapultepec battles to Scott, he inflated his own role with elaborate grandiloquence while diminishing his colleagues. Though irritated, Scott merely instructed Pillow to modify the language and correct obvious errors about the roles of the various players. He didn't want a public spat with the presidential favorite.

But then he read an article that had appeared in the September 10 *New Orleans Delta,* signed by someone who called himself "Leonidas." The writer hailed Pillow's Contreras performance as the instrument of victory. The anonymous correspondent wrote:

> [Pillow's] plan of battle and the disposition of his forces, were
> most judicious and successful. He evinced in this, as he has done
> on other occasions, that masterly military genius and profound

knowledge of the science of war, which has astonished so much the mere martinets of the profession. . . . During this great battle, which lasted two days, General Pillow was in command of all the forces engaged, except General Worth's division, and this was not engaged. . . . (General Scott gave but one order and that was to reinforce General [George] Cadwalader's brigade.)

Not surprisingly, Scott erupted in outrage. Further aftershocks emerged when he read similar pieces printed subsequently in the *New Orleans Picayune* and the *Pittsburgh Star.* The general dashed off General Order No. 349, which reminded his officers of an 1825 regulation forbidding them from discussing military matters in print. He expressed disbelief that the officers lauded in those articles had no agency in getting them published. Then, in characteristically venomous prose, he added, "False credit may, no doubt, be obtained at home, by such despicable self-puffings and malignant exclusion of others; but at the expense of the just esteem and consideration of all honorable officers, who love their country, their profession, and the truth of history."

Scott had no doubt Pillow had written the *Delta* piece, and he was right. The ego-driven general had submitted the account to a correspondent named James L. Freaner, who brushed it aside as a suspect document from a glory-hungry officer. But Pillow's adjutant, Archibald W. Burns, then edited the document a bit and submitted it anonymously to the newspaper. Scott had no intention of tolerating such actions, even from the president's friend.

Pillow then found himself in a highly vulnerable position when one of the Mexican howitzers captured at Chapultepec turned up missing, then was discovered in Pillow's personal baggage wagon. It appeared the Tennessean had stashed it away as a battlefield trophy. Confronted, Pillow professed ignorance of the matter and sought to deflect blame to two of his lieutenants. Then he demanded a court inquiry to clear his name. It was a mistake. Though the court assigned most of the blame to Pillow's subordinates, it faulted the general for moving too slowly to return the contraband. Pillow's reputation within the command, already diminished because of his exorbitant ego, now was frayed further.

He fought back, appealing the court decision to Marcy and seeking Polk's intervention. That was it for Scott. On November 22, he ordered Pillow to face a court-martial for violating the chain of command. For good measure he also arrested General Worth for submitting self-laudatory battlefield descriptions to the *Pittsburgh Post* and the *New Orleans Picayune*. Worth's artillery chief, Lieutenant Colonel James Duncan, also was charged. Pillow wrote to Polk complaining of the commander's "assassin-like tactics."

But the mails were slow, and Polk knew nothing of this disintegration of military decorum and order in Scott's command as he struggled with a lack of information from Mexico, his need to craft a new military strategy to counter the enemy's intransigent ways, his deteriorating relationship with Thomas Benton, and a series of threatening political developments. At the October 12 cabinet meeting, the president outlined his new thinking on the war.

He said the conflict now must be prosecuted with renewed vigor. He would not withdraw the army under any circumstance or retreat to a defensive line as recommended by Calhoun and others. He would hold all ports, towns, cities, and provinces then under U.S. dominion, and he would expand the army's zone of dominance as far as possible. He would support U.S. forces by levying contributions from the enemy. He favored establishing more stable and permanent governments over the conquered lands, and he contemplated recommending to Congress that New Mexico and California be claimed by the United States as indemnity. He would propose creating permanent territorial governments over both. Already Polk had vowed to the cabinet that he would offer no new peace proposals but would instead wait stoically until Mexico sued for peace in the face of America's ongoing military onslaught. The cabinet concurred in all of Polk's thinking.

A week or so later the president received a visit from Benton, who made it clear he intended to do all in his power to protect his son-in-law's good name against Kearny's allegations. The current charges against John Frémont, he said, didn't encompass sufficient scope to lay bare all the events in California that would exonerate the beleaguered colonel. Hence, he said, Frémont planned to ask Marcy to expand the charges so the full story could be aired. If Marcy declined, he warned, he would force courts-martial against four other officers, including Kearny. "Mr. Benton became excited & exhibited much deep feeling on the subject," wrote Polk later, adding he himself took pains to avoid any expressions that could trigger the senator's famous temper. The president said simply he would act justly in the matter, and Benton expressed confidence in the president's fair-mindedness.

The next day, October 23, the cabinet took up the state of the Trist negotiations as understood in Washington based on the latest official dispatches. The president was livid that Trist had violated his instructions by entertaining a neutral zone between the Rio Grande and Nueces rivers and only a partial transfer of Upper California to the United States. The envoy's flexibility on the Texas territory particularly rankled the president. Didn't Trist understand, he wondered, that to accept that proposal would be to negate the entire rationale for the war and destroy the president's credibility on the matter of whether Mexico had spilled American blood on American soil? It was almost as if Trist was seeking to serve the president's Whig tormentors.

Polk's anger was mixed with anxiety lest Trist negotiate terms he couldn't accept. He also feared Mexico now would insist upon the terms entertained by Trist, which could diminish chances for peace. "I am much embarrassed by Mr. Trist's course," wrote the president. "I thought he had more sagacity and more common sense than to make the propositions he has made." He instructed Buchanan to write another letter to the envoy reiterating in strong language his recall and the imperative that he cease all negotiations at once.

Equally ominous for Polk was a political development brewing in the Northeast—the emergence of Wilmot Proviso Democrats who threatened to drive a wedge through the Democratic Party. These activists were gaining force particularly in New York, where they bolted from the party convention at Syracuse, in protest of its choice of the nominees for the coming elections, and threatened to stage a mass meeting of dissident Democrats at Herkimer in late October. The actual Herkimer meeting turned out to be, as the *Union* put it, "ludicrously small, when compared with . . . the objects which it sought to accomplish." One observer numbered the participants as "about 700 persons, including the ladies."

But the *Union*'s extensive coverage of these events evinced a recognition of their potential to disrupt Democratic unity. "The Wilmot-Proviso party," declared the paper, "have done great injustice to the administration in attributing the war to a desire on the part of its friends to extend the bounds of slavery." Indeed, the *Union* echoed the sentiment of the Democratic establishment in suggesting this development posed a grave threat to the Union itself. "There is no rock on which there is the slightest danger of shipwreck but the question of slavery," said the paper. "There is no other which can excite such agitations and passions as are calculated to override that deep devotion to the Union, which mingles itself with the very life-blood of our countrymen."

The 1848 political season was just beginning, and already it was reaching a white-hot intensity—kindled in part by that dynamic dynast of American politics, Henry Clay, whose magnified presence shone over the nation like a late afternoon sun over the sea. He was seventy-one now, with a slower gait but a greater air of dignity. The fires of ambition that had fueled his nearly forty-year political career still smoldered with undiminished heat. And, while he knew his party hankered for that stolid hero of the war, Zachary Taylor, he still harbored hopes of turning the tables with a speech.

His speech venue would be his hometown of Lexington, where he would declare a manifesto for his party and his time. The day was November 13, 1847; the occasion was a mass meeting of the party faithful. His aim was to galvanize the antiwar sentiment throughout the nation and forge it with the growing contingent of antislavery Whigs, now often dubbed Conscience Whigs. He began by excoriating the war and its author in terms as brutal as ever he had hurled at his opponents. "It was created," he declared, "by the act of Mr. Polk" in sending Taylor's army to the Rio Grande. And it was ratified by

Congress, whose members "voted, *whigs and all,* for what they knew to be false." Thus, he averred, it was a war "with a palpable falsehood stamped on its face"—a lie, he added, that he would have sniffed out and opposed. "Almost idolizing truth, as I do," he said, "I never, never, could have voted for that bill."

But Congress *had* voted for it, said Clay, and now it continued without any justifiable object or discernible end. Congress must speak up and seize the initiative from the executive in order to define the limits of American ambition in the war. He disclaimed any U.S. right to acquire Mexican territory and said the country should limit its aims to settling the Texas boundary question. "This is no war of defence, but one unnecessary and of offensive aggression," he said. "It is Mexico that is defending her fire-sides, her castles, and her altars—not we."

Clay warned against what seemed like a growing desire on the part of some Americans to annex the whole of Mexico. "Supposing the conquest to be once made, what is to be done with it?" he asked. "Does any considerate man believe it possible that two such immense countries . . . with populations so incongruous, so different in race, in language, in religion, and in laws, could be blended together in one harmonious mass, and happily governed by one common authority?" It wouldn't work, he said. "Murmurs, discontent, insurrections, rebellion, would inevitably ensue," with a likely result that "our present glorious Union itself would be dissevered or dissolved." He cited "the warning voice of all history," including the ongoing struggles within divided nations such as Spain during the Moorish ascendancy, modern-day Canada with its English and French identities, and Britain with its ongoing troubles with its Irish.

As for slavery, Clay took an absolute stand against its extension in any lands acquired by the United States. "I have ever regarded slavery as a great evil," he declared. "I should rejoice if not a single slave breathed the air or was within the limits of our country." Thus, Clay sought—as the *Union* instantly recognized—"to propitiate the abolitionists of the north and some of the Proviso men of New York."

Indeed, the entire speech was designed as a philosophical framework for his party in the coming elections. At its end he cleverly bundled his sentiments into a collection of "resolutions" that served as a call to action for opposition Americans sick of the war and wary of its lingering ramifications. He exhorted them to pressure Congress to take control of the war policy as envisioned in the Constitution, narrow the government's aims in the conflict, forswear any intent to annex Mexico to the United States, and "disclaim and disavow any wish or desire" to expand slavery.

It was a brilliant speech, distilling opposition sentiment into a potent capsule of political exhortation and displaying all the force and lilt that Americans had come to associate with the man. Reprinted in newspapers across the country, the speech quickly generated comment and debate, and soon everyone knew it would serve as the framework for the Whig Party platform of 1848. But, while it brought to the fore Clay's compelling dialectic, it didn't bring him to the fore. The party he had founded, grateful and respectful as ever, continued to press its flirtation with Zachary Taylor.

THOUGH STUNG BY these political developments, Polk professed little interest in them. Adamant in his decision to confine his presidential tenure to a single term, he also refused to involve himself in his party's succession. His focus now was the war. He had embraced the one-term promise initially because of his longtime opposition to entrenched power and also in hopes of quieting for a time the presidential ambitions of his Democratic rivals. But now he was motivated primarily by a yearning to be free of his public duties. At his fifty-second birthday on November 2, he noted to his diary that he had passed through two-thirds of his presidency and added, "I . . . most heartily wish that the remaining third was over, for I am sincerely desirous to have the enjoyment of retirement in private life."

This feeling deepened in late November when Benton broke officially with the administration. He sent Polk a private letter revealing that he would relinquish his chairmanship of the Senate Military Affairs Committee because he considered Marcy's handling of the Frémont matter to be censorious. Having seen it coming, Polk resigned himself to the unfortunate development. He showed Benton's "singular communication" to Marcy and vowed to "stand by him, if any improper attack was made on him."

As the war effort moved into its next phase of greater U.S. aggressiveness, Polk's cabinet grappled with the territorial consequences of the new policy. Buchanan, who previously had insisted U.S. territorial aims should be confined to New Mexico and the Californias, now seemed inclined to incorporate the entire Mexican nation into the United States. On November 20, as the cabinet grappled with the language of the president's forthcoming Annual Message, Polk's advisers paused over what would happen if Mexico simply refused to negotiate an end to the war. Buchanan offered language saying such circumstances meant "we must fulfil that destiny which Providence may have in store for both countries"—a veiled suggestion the country could swallow up the whole of Mexico. Polk, viewing this language as too vague and potentially too encompassing, offered language limiting any future territorial claims to indemnities stemming from Mexico's level of intransigence. Polk noted the cabinet seemed to favor Buchanan's version over his own.

Two days later Polk submitted compromise language that was embraced by all cabinet members save Buchanan, who didn't press the point. But the episode reflected a new reality in the war debate: The territorial question was taking on more and more urgency. Everyone knew this would enflame the Washington debate set to begin afresh in early December when the new Congress convened—with the House of Representatives under Whig control.

MEANWHILE, EVENTS IN Mexico began taking on an intriguing new cast. Trist, still doing business in Mexico City, saw two encouraging developments. One was Santa Anna's fall from power and the temporary elevation of the former foreign minister, Manuel Peña y Peña. Peña lacked force and charisma, but his reputation for honesty and long national service gave him serious stature with his countrymen—and with Scott and Trist. Further, Peña was a product of the Moderado party, far more realistic about the state of events than the bellicose Puros and hence more willing to seek a negotiated peace. After a hurriedly called election on November 11, Peña relinquished the presidency to General P. M. Anaya, a Moderado stalwart who promptly made Peña foreign minister.

The second development was the defeat in the Mexican Congress of legislation to bar government officials from relinquishing any Mexican territory in peace talks with the Americans. The 46 to 29 vote represented a major Moderado triumph over the Puros.

Trist, unaware of his recall, saw these developments as impetus for a new round of peace talks. Knowing the Texas boundary question remained the primary sticking point, Trist sent to Mexican Minister of Relations Luis de la Rosa a cogently argued rationale for Texan and American convictions on the matter. The Rio Grande boundary, he stated, had been established through force of arms long before the United States initiated annexation efforts, and it represented the line of greatest security not just for the United States but also for Mexico. The letter—uncharacteristically brief for Trist, which contributed to its effectiveness—was delivered by the British legation, along with an impassioned British call for renewed talks. De la Rosa asked for time to consider the matter, which Trist interpreted as a favorable sign.

But on November 16 Trist received the two recall dispatches from Buchanan. These letters, particularly that of later date, were notable for their clipped and cool tone, and Trist quickly realized he had fallen from his government's good grace. It was mutual. He didn't feel good about his government either.

He particularly disliked the instruction to inform his Mexican counterparts that no further American proposals would be forthcoming. Prospects for peace, in Trist's view, had never been brighter. Trist had discussed Polk's terms with Mexican negotiators, and the response had been surprisingly receptive. Indeed, when Trist informed Peña of his recall and Washington's termination of peace talks, the foreign minister wept.

What's more, the next Mexican Congress, likely to be dominated by the Moderados, would convene on January 8, 1848, and it could be America's last hope to deal with a Mexican Congress inclined toward peace. Trist believed Polk was bungling an exquisite opportunity for peace on his own terms.

But he prepared to depart as soon as Scott could organize an escort across Mexico to Veracruz. Unfortunately, or fortunately, no escort party was available until at least December 4. As he lingered in Mexico City, further evidence emerged that the opportunity for peace was now entirely propitious.

On November 24 he received a letter from Peña saying Anaya had appointed a delegation to treat with him on peace terms. Peña, knowing Trist held no diplomatic portfolio, clearly was suggesting he should negotiate for his country anyway. Others offered similar counsel. Edward Thornton, Trist's friend from the British legation, expressed a strong conviction that the peace forces in Mexico had gained the upper hand and fervently wanted a settlement. General Scott urged Trist to proceed on the ground that no treaty within the bounds of the president's instructions could possibly be rejected by either Polk or Congress.

Hungry for glory, Trist found himself beguiled by the idea. Such breathtaking defiance, if it should produce the desired result, would catapult his name to the forefront of the American consciousness. And yet the risks were immense. On November 28 he wrote to his wife, Virginia, saying he had decided to leave public life forever. "Say so to Mr. Buchanan, with my kindest regards," wrote the envoy, adding the secretary would soon understand "the impossibility of . . . my having anything to do with Mr. Polk." She might also convey, wrote Trist, his utter disgust and disdain for the manipulative general whom Trist considered responsible for most of what had gone wrong in Mexico— Gideon Pillow. "Say to him from me that a baser villain and dirtier scoundrel does not exist out of the penitentiary or in than Genl Pillow," wrote Trist.

But the situation born of willful men and sluggish communications continued to gnaw at Trist's sensibilities. He knew Polk had turned more bellicose in the war and more grasping in his resolve to acquire Mexican territory. He knew also that these new policies, devised in ignorance of the opportunity at hand, would quickly snuff out that very opportunity. And, once it was gone, events very likely could spin out of control to the severe detriment of both countries. As it became clear to Trist that Polk had no intention of replacing him, the fired envoy became almost desperate to salvage the situation.

On December 4 he received a visit from his friend James Freaner, the young correspondent for the *New Orleans Delta*. The two men enjoyed each other and frequently shared drinks and intimate conversation. On this occasion Trist revealed his temptation to defy his recall and renew the negotiation. Freaner practically leaped from his chair.

"Mr. Trist, make the Treaty," he intoned. "Make the Treaty, Sir! It is now in your power to do your country a greater service than any living man can render her. . . . You are bound to do it. Instructions or no instructions, you are bound to do it. Your country, Sir, is entitled to this service from you. Do it, Sir!"

This burst of enthusiasm demolished Trist's indecision on the spot. "I *will* make the Treaty," he replied with equal fervor. He asked Freaner to stay on through the negotiations and carry the final document back to Polk.

THREE DAYS LATER in Washington, the new Thirtieth Congress convened. James Polk was about to enter a new and dangerous phase of his presidency. Politically, his standing was in serious erosion, and the new Congress loomed as a body of heightened hostility bent on seizing control of the war policy.

What's more, though he didn't fully know it yet, the president was losing control of his administration and his war effort. His secretary of state, consumed with his own political ambitions, dispensed counsel that was erratic at best. Polk never knew where Buchanan would come down on any issue or what conspiratorial impulses would drive his opinions. Even Treasury Secretary Walker now was showing inclinations to defy the president on matters of high policy. In crafting his

Treasury report to Congress, he sought to sneak into the document language advocating the annexation of all Mexico in defiance of Polk's clear opposition to that troubling concept.

In Mexico, Scott's war machine was sputtering in the wake of its victories. His command was a mess of petty jealousies, personality clashes, and competing ambitions. Word hadn't yet reached Washington of the turmoil within the general's command stemming from the discouraging fact that three of his top officers faced courts-martial. Nor did the president yet know that Scott and Trist had involved themselves in a scheme to bribe Mexican officials to get a peace settlement. Word of this unfortunate plan would reach Polk courtesy of Pillow, who would use his knowledge of it to undermine Scott while finessing his own role in the affair.

And here was Nicholas Trist, a private citizen without portfolio and a man who enjoyed no confidence of the president, entering into negotiations with a foreign country on the matter of greatest import and delicacy within the president's ambit.

All this was soon to hit the administration, creating a swirl of troubles for the president and an arsenal of political weapons for his enemies. Compounding the situation was what Polk thought, erroneously, to be Mexico's ongoing intransigence in the face of its humiliating defeats. As far as he could see, his only option was to double down on his war policy, capturing ever more Mexican territory and bringing military dominance over greater numbers of Mexican citizens. The outcome of such a policy was difficult to predict, but it was sure to generate powerful opposition.

Confronting all this, the man in the White House proceeded doggedly with his agenda, worked tirelessly into the night, brushed aside all diversions, and directed hardly a thought to his own health or happiness. He wasn't enjoying the job now at all, but he did derive a measure of satisfaction in devoting his waking hours to what had always captured his inner self—the martyrdom of duty.

26 · THE SPECTER OF CONQUEST

"Have We Conquered Peace? Have We Obtained a Treaty?"

ON DECEMBER 6, 1847, with the start of the Thirty-first Congress, James Polk's presidency entered a new phase. The opposition Whigs now controlled the House of Representatives. If Polk felt the previous, Democratic-controlled Congress had beset his White House with more frustrations than he deserved, now his situation would only get worse. This became clear as soon as he sent up his third Annual Message. While studiously avoiding incendiary language such as his "aid and comfort" thrust of the previous year, Polk knew his message would nonetheless kick up a political ruckus. Largely ignoring his critics, he laid out a dispassionate rationale for his wartime decisions and actions. This time the president seemed to be writing for posterity more than for the day's political arena, and that only enraged his adversaries all the more.

Polk began by playing the spotted Mexican card. He said it was well known that only through a cession of territory could Mexico extend an indemnity—"in satisfaction of the just and long deferred claims of our citizens." The entire U.S. rationale for the war, he added, hinged on this reality: "The doctrine of no territory is the doctrine of no indemnity, and, if sanctioned, would be a public acknowledgment that our country was wrong, and that the war declared by Congress with extraordinary unanimity, was unjust, and should be abandoned; an admission unfounded in fact, and degrading to the national character."

The president noted that, in international law, a state of war abrogates all previous agreements between warring nations. Hence any peace treaty without indemnities would nullify U.S. citizens' claims against Mexico. "Our duty to these citizens," he declared, "must forever prevent such a peace, and no treaty which does not provide ample means of discharging these demands can receive my sanction."

But Mexico had refused to negotiate, said Polk, even after receiving his generous terms via Nicholas Trist. So he would send no further peace overtures and would "press forward our military operations" with added aggressiveness, taking as much territory as possible through force of arms. "In the meantime . . . we should adopt measures to indemnify ourselves, by appropriating permanently a portion of her territory"—specifically, California and New Mexico.

Polk rejected both the Whig notion of withdrawing entirely from Mexico and Calhoun's suggestion of withdrawing to a designated line from which to hold and defend conquered territory. He argued, "To withdraw our army altogether from the conquests they have made by deeds of unparalleled bravery, and at the expense of so much blood and treasure, in a just war on our part, and one which, by the act of the enemy, we could not honorably have avoided, would be to degrade the nation in its own estimation and in that of the world." And withdrawing to a designated line would simply embolden the Mexicans to fight on and hence protract the war indefinitely. He embraced Cass's argument that a purely defensive war would render the defenders inherently vulnerable to guerrilla attacks at the points of greatest U.S. weakness.

Polk emphasized his resolve to preserve the Mexican Republic, although in smaller form. "It has never been contemplated by me, as an object of the war," he said, "to make a permanent conquest of the republic of Mexico, or to annihilate her separate existence as an independent nation." He had waged the war with the olive branch of peace always in one hand, he said, and Mexico could have averted its fate of conquest by simply accepting that olive branch. Perhaps, he mused, Mexicans had developed a "false inference from the supposed division of opinion in the United States." But all that would now change as "the adoption and prosecution of the energetic policy proposed must soon undeceive them."

Polk argued Mexico lacked the population and power to hold California and New Mexico in any event, and if the United States abandoned those territories they likely would fall under the sway of voracious European powers, particularly Great Britain. "This," he said, alluding to the Monroe Doctrine, "for our own safety, and in pursuance of our established policy, we should be compelled to resist."

Turning to economic issues, Polk reported that, during the last year of Tyler's high tariffs, federal trade receipts had been just under $23 million. During the first year of his low tariff program, receipts had swelled to nearly $32 million. Clearly, the high tariffs had constricted trade and curbed tariff revenue, while his policy had reduced trade barriers, spurred commerce, and plenished federal coffers. Hence, he added, "all the great interests of the country have been advanced and promoted."

But the cost of the war still far exceeded the government's revenue under current law, and so Polk renewed his call for import duties on tea and coffee, which had been suspended under his Tariff of 1846. He would oppose such duties in peacetime, he said, but the necessities of war now took precedence.

Finally, Polk admonished his countrymen on the urgency of preserving the confederated union, "to which we are so much indebted for our growth in population and wealth, and for all that constitutes us a great and happy nation." He urged Americans to "scrupulously . . . avoid all agitating topics which may tend to distract and divide us into contending parties, separated by geographical lines, whereby it may be weakened or endangered." He was talking, of course, about slavery, that ominous issue that had been generating increasing civic emotion since David Wilmot had forced it into the war discussions. To Polk's undisturbed slaveholder's mind, the nation would be just fine so long as this issue could be kept out of the hands of abolitionist firebrands.

WHIG REACTION TO Polk's message was swift and furious. The *National Intelligencer* compared Polk unfavorably to "the very savage of the court-yard . . . that most brutal of mankind, the bully of the bailiwick, who chewed up an ear or nose, or scooped out with thumb a prostrate adversary's eye." But such a bully, said the paper, "was humane, was generous" in comparison with Polk, for the bully fought others his own size—"nor, when his rival champion lay gasping and helpless under him, game to the last, and ready to die sooner than utter the craven word 'enough,' would *he* have ever thought of *proceeding to mutilate the vanquished, by way of forcing him to confess himself conquered*, and then, moreover, *have helped himself to whatever he could find in the maimed man's pockets.*"

Everyone knew this sentiment would find echo in the looming congressional war debates, and the *Union* quickly responded in tones that would also reverberate in Congress. Ritchie's paper declared:

> This American people—proud and patriotic as they are—will crush and grind to powder . . . the political life of any party leader who shall ask them *to confess, by their votes,* that this just Mexican war—*their* war, which they have *volunteered* to fight, which they have fought so gloriously, and which they are resolved to fight out till its great ends of peace and justice are obtained—*is only the demoniac work of savage bullies, and gougers, and pickpockets* whom they have set in high places in the executive cabinet, and in the halls of Congress, to govern them, and under whose lead they have elected to go forth to Buena Vista, and Churubusco, and the National Palace of Mexico!

Soon the message faded in political force as other events interceded—including arrival of Pillow's report to Polk revealing the Scott-Trist plan to pay Santa Anna $1 million to get a treaty. Relaying this information to his cabinet on December 11, Polk condemned such actions "in the strongest terms," and Buchanan said that, if the allegations proved accurate, Scott should be fired. Since Generals Shields and Quitman were scheduled to arrive in town soon, it was decided to withhold action pending an opportunity to talk with them.

A few days later John Calhoun rose in the Senate to submit two resolutions for future consideration. They read:

Resolved, That to conquer Mexico, and to hold it either as a province or to incorporate it in the Union, would be inconsistent with
the avowed object for which the war has been prosecuted; a departure from the settled policy of the government; in conflict with
its character and genius; and in the end subversive of our free and
popular institutions.

Resolved, That no line of policy in the further prosecution of the
war should be adopted which may lead to consequences so disastrous.

On December 20, when Calhoun requested a date for floor consideration of his resolutions, Ohio's William Allen inquired whether
Calhoun opposed any acquisition of Mexican territory. Not at all, said
the South Carolinian. He knew the United States was likely to acquire
Mexican land, perhaps a substantial amount of it.

"I believe," he explained, "the pressing question at this moment is,
whether we shall conquer Mexico, and hold her as a subjected province, or incorporate her into our Union. That . . . would involve the
nationality of Mexico, and it was to that point that my resolutions
referred."

Cass of Michigan expressed a hope that Congress's pressing war
business wouldn't be superseded by a debate that seemed of little
practical importance. After all, he said, "there is no man in this nation
in favor of the extinction of the nationality of Mexico."

Calhoun disagreed, citing a dinner in Ohio in which a commis-
sioned combat veteran from the Mexican War had described army
sentiment there as favoring a full Mexican conquest before U.S. forces
would ever return from that country. This view, said Calhoun, "was
applauded by the assembly, and endorsed by the official paper of that
State."

But, continued Calhoun, he was talking more about the unfore-
seen consequences of powerful governmental actions, particularly in
war. Polk's avowed war strategy, after all, was to "conquer a peace."
But, he added, "The whole progress towards the accomplishment of
this avowed object . . . has been marked by an earnest desire eagerly

to prosecute the war until we find ourselves where no man expected." It was to avert a continuation of this pattern, said Calhoun, that he introduced his resolutions—"while the public mind is yet sound, and while the Senate . . . is prepared almost unanimously to vote against such an end of the war."

Thus began a powerful new strain of the war debate, centering on the question of what would be the final outcome—and what *should* be the outcome—of Polk's new strategy of seizing greater and greater portions of Mexican territory. Calhoun was correct in perceiving a nascent movement toward the view that America should simply annex Mexico or perhaps dominate it in conquest as ancient Rome did its provinces. After all, the president's own treasury secretary, Robert Walker, favored incorporating all of Mexico into the United States. And Calhoun understood further that, once Mexico had become largely conquered, this movement would gain force. His aim was to head it off while such an incorporation still seemed unthinkable to most Americans.

Polk harbored no such fears. He had no intention of moving in that direction, as he made clear in his Annual Message. And he was, after all, the president. But the unfolding history of his presidency suggested he didn't always have the keenest awareness of where events were taking him. He had not wanted or expected a protracted war, but he got one. He hadn't anticipated a need to conquer Mexican territory he didn't want, but he had done so and now faced the necessity of expanding that strategy. He certainly hadn't anticipated the breakdown in Scott's command, but reports filtering into Washington suggested he faced a serious crisis on that front.

This was reflected foremost in the reports of a Scott-Trist bribe offer to Santa Anna. "Neither Gen'l Scott, Mr. Trist, or any one else had the slightest authority to make such a proposition" wrote Polk to his diary. "This subject has given me great pain, but it must be investigated, and the censure fall where it is due, whatever may be the consequences to the officers concerned." And yet he didn't seem inclined to let any censure fall upon his friend Pillow. Though he suspected Pillow may have "assented with reluctance in the first instance," he felt certain his friend later had protested against the scheme.

A week later Polk met with General Shields, who sought to win the president's favor by speaking glowingly of Pillow's "bravery & gallantry." When Polk asked about Scott's conference on the possible bribe payment, Shields sought to finesse the matter, emphasizing that the discussion had not centered on a bribe but rather on whether it would be proper to pay, in advance of Mexico's treaty ratification, a portion of the money earmarked for a territorial transfer. Polk did not seek clarification on this vague distinction, nor did he question Shields closely on who was at the meeting and what was said by whom.

Then on December 30, Marcy arrived with Scott's bombshell report of his court-martial charges against Generals Pillow and Worth, and Lieutenant Colonel James Duncan—and Worth's countercharges against Scott. The president immediately placed the blame on Scott's "vanity and tyrannical temper." He speculated that Trist had manipulated the general's "malignant passions" to foster a loathing toward Pillow and others "who are supposed to be friendly to me." Scott was angry, suggested Polk, at the published letters because "Gen'l S. is not made the exclusive hero of the War." It struck the president as inconceivable that these letters could justify such an assault on the army's "harmony and efficiency" in enemy territory.

The next day, in a conversation with Senators Cass and Jefferson Davis of Mississippi, Polk began discussing the terms and timing of Scott's recall. The three men agreed Scott had been irresponsible in crafting the incendiary language attending his general order on unauthorized public statements by officers. The senators agreed further "in strong and decided terms" that Scott should be fired. As to who should succeed the general, Davis favored Taylor while Cass supported William O. Butler, a Kentucky Democrat who had fought with Andrew Jackson in the War of 1812, had served four years as a congressman, and had distinguished himself as a Mexican War major general. That same conversation yielded an intriguing bit of news from Davis, who had just received a letter from General David Twiggs in Mexico saying prospects for a peace agreement with the Mexican government seemed brighter than ever.

Over the next few days Polk held numerous conversations with cabinet members and congressional allies on the multiple decisions he faced regarding Scott's command. Finally, in several cabinet sessions between January 3 and January 8, he packaged his thinking into a series of decisions covering most of the pressing questions before him. Scott would be recalled immediately and replaced by Butler. The courts-martial would be reduced in scope to courts of inquiry aimed at determining whether courts-martial were in fact necessary. The three men would be ordered released from arrest, and Worth's charges against Scott would be aired also through a court of inquiry. These proceedings would commence at the town of Perote, between Veracruz and Mexico City, then continue at Mexico City as needed.

That left a big question stemming from numerous reports that the Mexican government, now in the hands of the peace faction, was ready to negotiate seriously: Should Polk invest Butler with diplomatic powers to treat with these commissioners or send another civilian envoy to take over for Trist? Polk deferred his decision.

In the midst of all this, on January 4, Buchanan received unofficial reports from a British courier that Trist actually had resumed negotiations with the Mexican commissioners. This stunned Polk. Trist had acknowledged his recall and hence fully understood he had no authority to represent his government in any capacity with anyone. "He is acting, no doubt, upon Gen'l Scott's advice," wrote Polk, who by now could see none but dishonorable motives in anyone outside his immediate circle. "He seems to have entered into all Scott's hatred of the administration, and to be lending himself to all Scott's evil purposes."

Ten days later Buchanan received an incendiary communication from Trist that topped everything the egotistical envoy had ever done before. Having decided to negotiate without portfolio, Trist could have communicated this maverick decision in terms designed to reassure Washington that his actions were motivated by the purest of intentions toward his country, his government, and his bosses. Perhaps, in doing so, he could have brought Buchanan and Polk around to the view that he had actually acted nobly in attempting to seize this rare and perishable opportunity for peace.

Instead, Trist fired off a sixty-five-page letter to Buchanan encapsulating every one of his many character flaws—the obsession with self, the quickness to querulous defensiveness, the unnecessary resort to insult, the tendency toward interminable expression, the inability to distinguish the important from the trifling. Nicholas Trist was treating with a foreign power illegally while poking his president in the eye.

Trist castigated the president falsely for wishing to conquer all of Mexico. He assaulted Polk's man Pillow as an "intriguer" with an "incomprehensible baseness of character." Polk's "blind confidence" in Pillow, said Trist, had distorted the president's understanding of events so that "everything was seen upside down." He added Pillow habitually presented himself as "the *maker* of the President (by having procured his nomination at the Baltimore convention), and as the President's *other self*—a pretension which I have reason to believe but too well founded."

In "justice" to Polk, Trist said, he was inclined to attribute the man's shortcomings to his naive friendship with Pillow. But then he added that "infallibility of judgment . . . is not among the attributes of the President of the United States." Trist defended Scott's armistice decision against critics, including Polk and his newspaper, the *Union*—whose attacks, he said, were "balderdash," "stuff" and "nonsense" that wouldn't be swallowed by anyone outside Washington, "however low in understanding."

When this missive reached the White House on January 15, Polk instantly saw Trist's action as "arrogant, impudent; and very insulting to his Government, and even personally offensive to the President." He ordered Buchanan to fire off "a short, but stern and decided rebuke."

POLK'S PROBLEMS WITH Scott and Trist constituted only a small part of the political challenge bearing down on him as he crossed into the last full year of his presidency. Now Congress was partially dominated by Whigs and fully dominated by members more and more skittish over an increasingly unpopular war. As the *Union* complained, "The whig members of the House of Representatives are piling resolutions upon resolutions against the war." Even obscure freshmen were getting into the act. One was Abraham Lincoln, a lanky Illinois legislator in his late thirties, with a hero-worship regard for Henry Clay. He called on the president to answer eight questions designed to elicit an admission that the war's first blood had been spilled not on American soil but on disputed soil.

Later Lincoln rose on the House floor to direct his considerable rhetorical flair against the beleaguered president. He accused Polk of seeking "to avoid the scrutiny of his own conduct . . . by fixing the public eye upon military glory—that rainbow that rises in showers of blood—that serpent's eye that charms but to destroy." The president "talked like an insane man," the combative freshman said, adding, "His mind, taxed beyond its power, is running hither and thither, like an ant on a hot stove."

Polk was becoming an easy mark for such attacks. On January 3, House Whigs pushed through the chamber, on a vote of 85 to 81, an amendment declaring the war had been "unnecessarily and unconstitutionally begun by the President of the United States." The House then passed a resolution calling on Polk to disclose documents related to John Slidell's instructions as envoy to Mexico and to Santa Anna's safe passage into Mexico from Cuba. This posed a serious dilemma for Polk.

Defying Congress in such a highly charged time would generate abundant hostility, and yet the president and his cabinet believed diplomatic instructions such as those issued to Slidell could not be divulged without harming future negotiations with Mexico. The president, with cabinet concurrence, decided to decline that House request. He did agree to submit Bancroft's order instructing Commodore Conner to let Santa Anna through the Veracruz blockade. But a more sensitive issue was Alexander Slidell Mackenzie's written communication to Santa Anna, which he had read to the Mexican general during his secret Havana mission. The young naval officer had been instructed to refrain from putting anything on paper, but there in the naval archives was his unfortunate lapse in written form. Worse, he had sent to Washington a dispatch detailing his conversation with Santa Anna, including the general's fulsome assurances that he desired peace with the United States.

Polk quickly perceived that these communications, if made public, "would exhibit me in a ridiculous attitude"—demonstrating a naïveté about Santa Anna that would generate howls of derision. Buchanan argued that while the memos reflected no official wrongdoing they would signal to foreign officials that the United States couldn't be trusted to keep sensitive diplomatic discussions confidential. No government, he said, "would ever trust us again." The cabinet unanimously recommended that the president rebuff the House on Slidell's instructions and Mackenzie's communication.

Polk's reply to the House arrived on January 12, and the response was swift. "This House," declared John Quincy Adams in all his majesty, "ought now to assert, in the strongest manner, this right to call for information; and especially in such cases as those where questions of war and peace are depending." Ohio Whig Robert Schenk posed a powerful rhetorical question: "Should it go abroad that all the power we have here, as the people's representatives, is to record the edicts of a master?"

The debate occupied the House over several days, affording angry Whigs ample opportunity to attack the president with a crescendo of invective. Meanwhile, over in the Senate a more fundamental debate had emerged, fostered by John C. Calhoun's December 20 resolutions disavowing U.S. interest in incorporating Mexico. Over the decades the South Carolinian's congressional colleagues had struggled to identify the inevitable hidden agendas in his legislative maneuverings, the secret motivations in his complex ploys and thrusts. He was the master at casting the debate in ways that created new fault lines of political combat and new oppositional coalitions. It wasn't always clear, as he entered the fray with his Machiavellian flair, precisely what he was trying to accomplish.

But sometimes there was no hidden agenda. Sometimes Calhoun was propelled simply by pure political conviction. Such was the case with his fervent opposition to Polk's May 1846 war resolution and the president's legend on how the war had commenced. Such was the case now with his throbbing expressions of concern lest the country slip into a full conquest of Mexico. The South Carolinian rose on the Senate floor in early January to deliver an hour-long speech on the subject.

He had opposed the war, declared Calhoun, not simply because he considered it unnecessary and avoidable or because he thought Polk had no authority to seize disputed territory or because he rejected the allegations upon which Congress had sanctioned it. No, he said, his central concern was that "I believed it would lead to great and serious evils to the country, and greatly endanger its free institutions."

After the war commenced, said Calhoun, he "acquiesced in what I could not prevent" and directed his efforts to thwarting "the evil and danger with which, in my opinion, [the war] threatened the country and its institutions." That's why he had proposed the strategy of a defensive line, and that's why he rose now to defend it as necessary to preserve the essence of America.

If Polk wanted a territorial indemnity, as he insisted, said Calhoun, then he already had captured all the territory he needed for his indemnity. What's more, the Mexican territory in U.S. control was the most desirable because it was the least populated. "For I hold it, in reference to this war," he said, "a fundamental principle, that when we receive territorial indemnity, it shall be unoccupied territory."

Calhoun next laid out his interpretation of the war thus far. He had advocated a measured approach designed to minimize the conquest of territory. But Polk advocated a vigorous prosecution of the war—not for conquest, which he disavowed, but to force Mexico to sign a treaty incorporating a territorial indemnity. And Polk's policy had yielded a string of glorious military victories, without a single defeat. But, asked Calhoun, "what has been accomplished? What has been done? Has the avowed object of the war been attained? Have we conquered peace? Have we obtained a treaty? Have we obtained any indemnity? No, sir." Indeed, said Calhoun, "We have for all our vast expenditure of money—for all the loss of blood, and men—we have nothing, but the military glory which the campaign has furnished."

And, he went on, Polk had nothing further to recommend than more of the same—"to suppress all resistance in Mexico, to overpower and disperse her army, to overthrow her civil government, and to leave her without any further power of resistance." Once that is accomplished, declared Calhoun, Polk will have been defeated by his own success. "For if the war should be so prosecuted, where will be the nationality of Mexico? Where her separate existence? Where this free republic with whom you desire to treat? Gone!"

Calhoun dismissed those who believed America could build up, from the ashes of Mexico's defeat, a free and independent republic that would operate like the United States. He couldn't see, he confessed, how such a republic could grow up under the protection and authority of its conqueror. An aristocracy, yes; a "kingly government," perhaps; a despotism, certainly. But he added, "I had always supposed that republican government was the spontaneous work of the people—that it came from the people—from the hearts of the people—that it was supported by the hearts of the people, and that it required no support, no protection, from any quarter whatever." The Mexican people, he said, lacked the mystical spark for such a government.

Here's where Calhoun moved into ideological territory commonly occupied by Americans at the time but slowly abandoned over succeeding decades. He saw his country's identity wrapped up not just in the Northern European, Protestant culture that was its heritage and not just in the elaborate and profound democratic creed bequeathed by its Founders, but also in its racial and ethnic makeup—Caucasian and Anglo-Saxon. And he saw in a conquest of Mexico a fundamental threat to the racial and ethnic identity of the United States. "I know . . . , sir," said Calhoun, "that we have never dreamt of incorporating into our Union any but the Caucasian race—the free white race. To incorporate Mexico, would be the very first instance of the kind of incorporating an Indian race. . . . Ours, sir, is the government of the white man. . . . And yet it is professed and talked about to erect these Mexicans into a territorial government, and place them on an equality with the people of the United States. I protest utterly against such a project."

Beyond that, Calhoun concluded, it wasn't possible for America to be an empire and a republic at the same time because such imperial ambitions would lead inevitably to ever greater concentrations of power in the federal government. "Sir," intoned the South Carolinian, "he who knows the American constitution well—he who has duly studied its character—he who has looked at history, and knows what has been the effect of conquests of free States invariably, will require no proof at my hands to show that it would be entirely hostile to the institutions of the country to hold Mexico as a province." There was no historical precedent of such a conquest on such a scale, he added, "without disastrous consequences. . . . This Union would become imperial, and the States mere subordinate corporations."

When he sat down, Calhoun accepted a motion by Ambrose Sevier of Arkansas to lay his resolutions on the table, and the Senate moved on to legislation authorizing the ten regiments needed by Polk to continue his war. The *Union* quickly dismissed Calhoun's defensive line strategy as "neither peace nor war." The essential element of peace was security, said the paper, and the essential element of war was action. Calhoun's approach encompassed neither but was a kind of "half-breed, hybrid hostility, involving the danger and the cost of war, without its force or its glory."

But the South Carolinian had laid down an important rhetorical marker for the coming debate, which he foresaw, over the idea of a full Mexican conquest. Those, like Cass, who considered the issue moot for lack of any serious agreement for such an incorporation, would seek to ignore Calhoun's sentiments as irrelevant. Those who harbored latent hopes for taking the full expanse of Mexico would seek to ignore the South Carolinian as a way to skirt the force of his arguments. Ultimately, though, his words could not be ignored.

In the meantime the Senate grappled with the Ten Regiment Bill. Cass, the new chairman of the Military Affairs Committee, had hoped this could be handled routinely since the body was called upon merely to confirm an authorization approved by Congress in the previous session. But war opponents couldn't pass up the opportunity to fulminate against the president as the man who had manufactured this unfortunate conflict. Maryland's Reverdy Johnson declared his opposition to any accession of territory by conquest or force as unworthy of the country's national character. If the war had that object, he vowed, he would not vote a dollar.

But the question of just how the country would dispose of greater expanses of conquered territory bedeviled the debate at times, as Calhoun had foreseen. At one point Delaware's John Clayton suggested Winfield Scott himself had intimated that the president's desire for a fifty-thousand-man army had been put forward "in case the administration should design to subjugate—to reduce all Mexico."

"Oh! No," replied Cass.

"That is the amount of it, as I understand," said Clayton.

Cass carefully explained that the administration had no such plans but wished on the contrary "to keep the central government [of Mexico] in motion." Clayton acknowledged the correction, then commenced to hurl at the administration all the Whig arguments against the war and the regiment bill.

As Congress plodded through its war debates, the country was becoming increasingly aware that another presidential campaign was gaining force—and that events were propelling Zachary Taylor toward a Whig ascendancy. Taylor had asked for—and received—a six-month leave of absence the previous November, and by mid-December he arrived in New Orleans as a war hero of the first order. The *Baltimore Sun* reprinted a dispatch from the *New Orleans Mercury* recounting the soaring grandeur of Taylor's triumphant entry into that gateway city. Above the piece the *Sun*'s editors had affixed the following headline:

> *The grand procession. — Unprecedented enthusiasm. —*
> *Presentation of a sword. — Speech of Old Rough and Ready. —*
> *The embarkation. — His passage through the Triumphal Arch. —*
> *Welcome to the city. — The General's reply to the Mayor's address. —*

The Te Deum. — Description of the procession. —
The dinner at the St. Charles Hotel. — Visit to the theatres. —
Applause of the ladies. — A beautiful incident. —
The illumination, fireworks, &c.

Zachary Taylor was on the march, and this was no military campaign.

27 · TREATY

From Trist to Polk to the Senate

SHORTLY AFTER NOON on February 4, 1848, as James Polk was working at his writing table, his porter entered to say the president had a visitor in the parlor below stairs. It was Henry Clay. This was an intriguing surprise. Polk knew the famous Kentuckian had been visiting Washington for several weeks, but he hadn't anticipated a courtesy call from the man who had raged against just about every political initiative of the Jackson-Polk party for two decades. He rushed downstairs to receive his visitor with all the warmth at his command.

Clay appeared remarkably fit for a man of his seventy years. Certainly friends and acquaintances had long since begun to notice that he was taking on the appearance of an old man. But he was still trim, still ramrod straight in his posture, and he still moved with his famous easy grace, though more slowly than in his suave youth. And he exuded the same exuberance of spirit. Just a few months before, on his way to Washington, he had stopped off at Cape May, New Jersey, to, in his words, "enjoy a Sea bath" for the first time. He had dashed into the ocean surf, swimming atop the breakers, cavorting with the ladies, and "frolicking like a man half his age," as one biographer later put it. Though Clay had suffered his share of tragedy and disappointment, he still met life head-on.

Clay greeted the president with a warm smile and apparent high spirits. He wished to apologize, he said, for not calling sooner, but he had been much occupied with old friends. He wished to say he harbored "no feelings of an unkind character" toward the president.

"I entertain none such toward you," replied Polk. In fact, he added, "there is no citizen of the U.S. whom I would be more gratified to see in my parlor."

When Clay inquired about Mrs. Polk, the president promptly had Sarah summoned. Clay greeted her with his famous florid courtliness, then turned his attention back to the president. He said he would have called sooner but wasn't sure Polk would welcome such a visit. Then he had run into their friend in common, Supreme Court Justice John Catron, who had assured him Polk would receive him avidly.

"I determined to call very soon," said Clay.

"I am gratified that you have done so," the president replied.

The three conversed pleasantly for about a half hour before Clay rose to depart. Turning to Sarah, he said he would visit her drawing room soon. Then he broke into his famous sly smile.

"Madame," he said in his elaborate way, "I must say that in all my travels, in all companies and among all parties, I have heard but one opinion of you. All agree in commending in the highest terms your excellent administration of the domestic affairs of the White House."

Sarah smiled. Then Clay, nodding toward the president with a twinkle in his eye, continued.

"But as for that young gentleman there," he said, "I cannot say as much. There is some little difference of opinion in regard to the policy of his course."

The three broke into laughter.

"Indeed," replied Sarah with genuine warmth, "I am glad to hear that *my* administration is popular. And in return for your compliment, I will say that if the country should elect a Whig next fall, I know of no one whose elevation would please me more than that of Henry Clay."

That generated "a hearty laugh" and set the stage for a cordial leave-taking.

The touching episode reflected an underlying reality of American politics: However intensely the battles are fought and however copiously the animosities flow, all parties are expected to accept the political outcomes in good grace and refrain from the kinds of personal enmities that could undermine the delicate balance of democracy. Of course during the Jackson era, this conviction was often honored in the breach—but never abandoned entirely. And now, after all those years of animosity, these two men, representing the two rival political philosophies, paid a measure of obeisance to that principle. Not even Clay's loss of a beloved son—in a war commenced by Polk over the Kentuckian's opposition—would be allowed to thwart this symbolic nod to the principle of harmonious democratic contention.

Beyond that, these were the two surviving lions of the old politics, and of course senior lions like to mingle with other lions. But the old era of politics was fading now, and these gentlemen of the old era were fading with it. Looking back on all the battles and battle scars of their political rivalry, they shared a commonality of nostalgia that could never be appreciated by the younger lions of either party vying for dominance of the nation.

AT THE TIME of the Clay visit, Polk was still grappling with the problem of his renegade envoy, Nicholas Trist. On January 23 he called in Senators Cass and Sevier to inform them of Trist's "reprehensible conduct." The senators shared the president's outrage and recommended that he order General Butler to expel Trist from the country and inform Mexico that the man had no authority to negotiate. Polk expressed concern that Trist might in the meantime send to Washington a treaty consistent with his April instructions. Should he send such a treaty to the Senate for ratification, he asked, even if it had been negotiated illegally?

Sevier said yes, while Cass recommended deferring the question pending further developments. Given the blood and treasure expended since Trist's instructions were issued, said Polk, he was inclined to demand more now than he had proposed the previous spring. Both men agreed.

But Buchanan subsequently advised Polk that, if there was any prospect he would accept a Trist treaty, he shouldn't force Trist's expulsion. It could be politically awkward, said the secretary, to send such a treaty to the Senate after the president had placed himself on record as disavowing any outcome wrought by the recalled diplomat. That led to further cabinet discussions on whether a treaty based on the April ultimatum should in fact be sent to the Senate.

Marcy and Mason said yes, while Buchanan, as usual, equivocated. Polk was still so enraged at Trist's behavior (and Scott's) that he couldn't bear the thought of accepting any outcome generated by this two-man cabal. But he was in a box. By nurturing his anger he was positioning himself to act irresponsibly should a reasonable treaty reach Washington. Indiana's Senator Edward Hannegan, as angry as Polk at Trist's behavior, expressed it best in an early conversation with the president. He probably wouldn't negotiate a treaty now along the lines of the April ultimatum, said Hannegan, but it would be "very embarrassing" for Polk to reject such a treaty if it should materialize.

In the end the president decided to send the letter instructing Butler to expel Trist. He concluded such an expression didn't constrict his range of options unduly, and in any event he didn't anticipate getting an acceptable treaty.

Congress, meanwhile, continued to pepper Polk with resolutions calling for war documents. The aim was to generate controversy that could be turned against the Polk administration. Both the Senate and House called for the War Department correspondence with General Taylor that related to the decision to send his army to the Rio Grande. Polk promptly complied, which set off further debate over whether that decision had caused the war and whether Polk had acted unconstitutionally in making it.

But some Polk loyalists fought back. When Democratic officials in New York City organized a Tammany Hall rally to support the president, thousands of citizens jammed into the pavilion and raucously approved ten resolutions endorsing the president's war policies. The *New York Globe* reported that "one feeling prevailed; and that was an enthusiastic determination to sustain the administration in the prosecution of the war until an honorable peace is obtained." The president's congressional defenders also sought to rally public sentiment. Sevier of Arkansas took the Senate floor for a long and detailed disquisition on the war's essential justice, with particular attention to the sanctity of the Texas boundary. "I am one of those who have ever contended, and do now contend," he said, "that the territory lying between the Nueces and the Rio Grande . . . rightfully and properly belongs to Texas, by the title of conquest and possession." Stephen A. Douglas of Illinois attacked more forcefully, labeling the president's critics hypocrites. They poured invective upon the executive, he said, for prosecuting a war they themselves had supported repeatedly with their votes. He added,

> Do gentlemen suppose that they can throw the responsibility of their own acts upon the President of the United States? Do they imagine that they can make the people believe that the Executive is alone responsible for all the consequences that may flow from the faithful execution of the laws which they enact, and, under the constitution, compel him to execute? If it be a war of iniquity and injustice, you are the transgressors! If it be a war of robbery, you are the robbers! If it be a war against and in violation of the constitution, yours is the treason!

At the end of January, Polk received a visit from Senators Hopkins Turney of Tennessee and Arthur Bagby of Alabama. Their mission, said the two Democrats, was to persuade Polk to consider the idea of seeking a second presidential term. The party might find it necessary to nominate Polk at the Baltimore convention in the spring, they said, and, if so, it would be his duty to run again. Other prominent Democrats had made similar entreaties. Polk gave each the same response: He would not run under any circumstances. "I sincerely hope," he wrote to his diary, "that the Democratic party may yet be able to unite & harmonize on some other candidate."

On February 2, Polk got word of the verdict in the court-martial of John C. Frémont. Since November the military trial had been unfolding, with Thomas Benton serving as his son-in-law's legal counselor. The famous explorer had been charged with three offenses, each buttressed with multiple "specifications," or distinct instances of wrongdoing. One charge was "mutiny" against his military superior, General Stephen Kearny. This carried eleven specifications. Next was "disobedience of the lawful command of his superior officer," with seven specifications. An accusation of "conduct to the prejudice of good order and military discipline" carried five specifications. All stemmed from his relations with Kearny from January to May 1847, the period between Kearny's arrival in California and his order that Frémont accompany him back to the United States for court-martial.

Under Benton's guidance, Frémont based his defense on two bulwarks—that the matter fundamentally centered on a legitimate dispute of command between the two men; and that Kearny was a vindictive witness willing to testify falsely in order to destroy his rival. Frémont also brought in that flamboyant dandy, Commodore Robert Stockton, to testify in his behalf. It all failed. The court found Frémont guilty on all charges and all specifications. His sentence: dismissal from military service.

But six of the twelve jurors recommended that Polk demonstrate clemency to the convicted officer because of his past service to the nation. And the presiding officers issued "Remarks of the Court" suggesting that, because of the ambiguities surrounding those distant events and Frémont's previous military contributions, the court "respectfully commend Lieutenant Colonel Fremont to the lenient consideration of the President of the United States."

This was a bizarre twist that gave the proceedings an unsavory appearance—as though the court didn't stand behind its own verdict. To many, it seemed the outcome had been the result of military politics more than judicial rectitude. And of course this was just the opportunity Thomas Benton needed to rail against the injustice of it all. It fell to the president to sort out the mess and render a suitable outcome. After extensive cabinet discussions, Polk dismissed the mutiny charge. Everyone agreed, however, that Frémont was guilty of the other two counts. Still, given the complexities of the case and Frémont's previous service, Polk decided to remit the sentence and restore him to duty. Frémont declined the remittance because it carried with it an implicit acceptance of guilt. But Polk felt satisfied with his resolution of this "painful and responsible duty" and concluded he had performed it "with the best lights before me."

Thereafter Benton promptly set himself in defiant opposition to the Polk presidency at every turn. Gone now were the friendly private sessions in which the president sought the Missourian's advice on major decisions of state. For Benton this wasn't merely a breach in their political relationship; he wouldn't even acknowledge the president's existence when the two men encountered each other in church on Sundays.

But Polk was pleased with his new friendship with Henry Clay. On February 16 the Polks held a White House dinner for the Kentuckian. The forty guests—including senators, representatives, Justice Catron, and New York journalist John O'Sullivan—were carefully chosen to represent Whigs and Democrats in equal number. The party was "exceedingly pleasant," wrote Polk later, "& I was much gratified to have it in my power to pay this mark of respect to Mr. Clay."

The president had no intention of paying such respect to Nicholas Trist. The envoy had not been idle in his self-assigned role as U.S. negotiator in Mexico. Throughout January he met regularly with commissioners appointed by Mexico's Moderado-dominated government. The meetings took place in Guadalupe Hidalgo, a few miles north of Mexico City, where Trist sought to wend his way through a thicket of conflicting claims and interests while maintaining a strict adherence to the Polk ultimatum of the previous spring. The early sessions produced an air of hopelessness as the Mexican commissioners insisted on a a host of demands fundamentally at odds with the Polk formula. Knowing only success could protect him from the wrath of his government, Trist worked methodically with his counterparts, bringing to the challenge all the forbearance, civility, and creativity he could muster.

Though prepared to forgo Lower California to get Upper California, Trist was intent on including the precious San Diego harbor within the U.S. sector. He employed Winfield Scott's trusted engineering officer, Robert E. Lee, to show the harbor was part of Upper California, then adjusted the boundary line slightly northward in order to get a Mexican compromise that assured U.S. possession of that maritime jewel.

The level of U.S. payments to Mexico proved more difficult. Trist had been authorized to offer $30 million if he could get all that Polk wanted, but any compromise on territory must result in a lesser sum. Trist offered $15 million on the ground that the final figure must acknowledge Mexico's unnecessary prolongation of the war and its resulting cost to the United States. The Mexican commissioners, though miffed, sent the matter to their government for guidance.

On the issue of U.S. citizen claims against Mexico, Trist proposed U.S. payment of all such claims up to a total of $3 million, provided the claims had been filed prior to May 13, 1847. When the Mexicans objected that this wouldn't absolve their government of claims above that ceiling, Trist raised the ceiling to $3.25 million. The Mexicans, satisfied this would cover the extent of the claims, accepted the compromise.

Other matters proved easier to deal with. Mexicans living in the ceded territories could stay or leave at their own volition, and those leaving would not be taxed for any property they took with them. Those staying would become U.S. citizens after a year unless they stipulated a desire to remain Mexican citizens. Church property would remain in Church hands in perpetuity. The United States would assume responsibility for Indian tribes in the ceded lands, including the burden of protecting Mexico from cross-border raids.

By January's end the mutual efforts had been tied up into a neat package ready for consideration by the temporary Mexican government at Querétaro. Trist made sure his Mexican counterparts understood the entire effort could be obliterated by Scott's replacement, who likely would be empowered, and perhaps ordered, to remove Trist from the country. Trist used that knowledge to emphasize that the Mexicans must ratify the treaty promptly if they wanted to end the war. The approach worked. The Mexican government, once again in the hands of Peña y Peña, accepted all terms of the draft treaty, including the modest $15 million compensation package and the transfer to the United States of the vast lands of Upper California and New Mexico.

On February 2, the appropriate Mexican officials signed the "Treaty of Peace, Friendship, Limits and Settlement" between the United States and Mexico, later known popularly as the Treaty of Guadalupe Hidalgo. As he was about to affix his name to the document, the Mexican official Don Bernardo Couto said to Trist, "This must be a proud moment for you; no less proud for you than humiliating for us." Replied Trist, "We are making *peace*. Let that be our only thought."

In fact, Trist viewed the war as a shameful display of naked American power, and he had sought assiduously to render an outcome that would limit Mexico's humiliation as much as possible while still getting approval in Washington. He remained convinced throughout his life that, had he not taken such a balanced tack, he never could have obtained Mexico's assent to the document, and both nations would have lost their last hope for cessation of the bloody war under reasonable terms.

BACK IN WASHINGTON, Polk and his team concentrated on the usual congressional battles over the president's war measures while also waiting for news from the renegade envoy Trist. On February 17, the House passed one of the president's most important priorities—legislation authorizing him to borrow up to $16 million on U.S. credit for prosecuting his war. It was a welcome victory.

The next day around two o'clock Buchanan arrived at Polk's office with a telegraphic dispatch dated that day from Charleston. Written in cipher, the message had been garbled in transmission, and the two men managed to decipher it only with considerable difficulty. Slowly they concluded it was from Trist, though his name was not on it. It appeared he was telling them he was in Charleston with a peace treaty signed and ratified by the Mexican government.

Not quite. The treaty was on its way to Washington by hand of James Freaner. The newspaperman arrived the evening of February 19 with the document. Buchanan delivered it to the president at nine o'clock, and the two men pored over it. Before retiring that night,

Polk acknowledged to his diary that the treaty's terms "are within his instructions which he took out in April last, upon the important question of boundary and limits." He added, "Mr. Trist has acted very badly . . . but notwithstanding this, if on further examination the Treaty is one that can be accepted, it should not be rejected on account of his bad conduct." Polk's sense of realism was gaining sway over his sense of outrage.

The next day, February 20, the president devoted most of his attentions to the six-thousand-word treaty, reading it carefully, weighing its details, and discussing it with members of his cabinet. He "deemed prompt action upon it so indispensable," said Polk to his diary, that he ordered a special cabinet session for seven that evening. At the meeting the treaty was read aloud and the question put before the presidential advisers—"*viz,* whether the Treaty should be rejected by me or sent to the Senate for ratification."

John Mason, William Marcy, Cave Johnson, and Nathan Clifford urged sending it to the Senate. Opposition, not surprisingly, came from Walker, still bent on bringing all of Mexico into the United States. More surprising was Buchanan, if the secretary still possessed a capacity to surprise his colleagues. Nothing less than a boundary line at the Sierra Madre mountains, said the secretary with considerable vehemence, would satisfy him.

This was a bit more than Polk could bear. He reminded Buchanan of his "total change of opinion on the subject." On the very day war was declared, recalled the president, Buchanan had insisted the country proclaim to the world that it sought no territory at all from the war. The president recounted this episode in considerable detail in an effort to embarrass his erratic secretary of state. Polk added that Buchanan had consistently opposed the acquisition of any Mexican territory right up to the previous April and then had fully concurred in Trist's instructions when they were crafted. He repeated these facts, said the president, "because it [is] proper that we should understand our relative positions on the subject, formerly and now."

Buchanan's cabinet colleagues responded with silence, but the secretary seldom opted for silence in any controversy. He replied airily that Polk was absolutely correct, and he might have added further that Buchanan also had opposed the military expedition to Mexico City and that he had been overruled on that as well. But since then, he added with some intensity, the country had "spent much money and lost much blood," and therefore he now wasn't satisfied with this treaty.

Polk wasn't fooled by Buchanan's machinations. Though the conversation "was unpleasant to me," he put in his diary, " . . . I thought I ought to rebuke him, and let him understand that I understood the motive that governed him"—namely, Buchanan's presidential ambition. He wished Polk to send up the treaty against his advice because he would then be well positioned irrespective of the outcome. "If it was received well by the country," speculated the president, "being a member of my administration, he would not be injured by it in his Presidential aspirations, for these govern all his opinions & acts lately; but if, on the other hand, it should not be received well, he could say, 'I advised against it.'"

The next day Polk convened another special cabinet session and informed his advisers that he had decided to send the treaty to the Senate. If he were crafting a treaty now, he said, he would demand more territory. But Mexico, having accepted the U.S. terms of the previous April, would never accept such a demand. The result would be resumed hostilities. And consider, he added, the domestic political consequences. If he rejected the treaty, House Whigs would promptly shut off all authorization for soldiers and money for the war. Thus, the army of occupation in Mexico would be "constantly wasting and diminishing in numbers." He might even be compelled to withdraw U.S. troops simply for their own protection, with the result that both New Mexico and California could be lost.

In short, concluded Polk, if he were now to reject his own terms, he didn't see how it would be "possible for my administration to be sustained."

That night Polk got word that John Quincy Adams, eighty years old and infirm but still full of fight, had collapsed at his desk on the House floor as he rose to address the speaker. The former president had been carried, barely conscious, to a nearby sofa, then to the speaker's private chambers. There he languished in what appeared to be a state of semiconsciousness from which he didn't seem likely to recover.

Congressional activity stopped while Adams slipped toward death. On February 22, Polk sent word that, because of the Adams situation, he would not be attending a ball to which he had been invited; shortly afterward he learned the ball had been postponed in deference to Mr. Adams. Few called at the White House that evening, but one who did was Henry Clay, who expressed a desire to pay his respects before heading to Philadelphia the next morning.

That next day Polk's private secretary, James Walker, was on hand when the Senate convened. He delivered the treaty, and the chamber went into executive session to consider it. That night, at twenty minutes past seven, Adams died. During a moment of consciousness the day before, he had asked to see the founder and leader of his beloved Whig Party, Henry Clay, and the Kentuckian had rushed over. Just before dying, the old warrior murmured, "This is the last of earth—I am composed."

Official Washington came to a standstill. Even the *Union*, representing a heritage of vehement opposition to everything Adams had stood for, bordered its columns in black and evinced a deep respect for the man's immense contributions to his country. Ritchie referred to Adams's death as a "mournful and deeply impressive event" and added he had died "amid the universal sympathy of this community."

Polk issued an order placing all executive offices at Washington in mourning and suspending all governmental business for two days. Black crepe was draped over the front door of the White House. Congress suspended business following several eulogies expressed in both chambers. The former president lay in state in the Capitol Rotunda on Friday, February 25, then was removed to the House chamber for a memorial service on Saturday that brought together members of Congress, the cabinet and top government officials, the justices of the Supreme Court, an array of diplomats "in their striking and superb costumes of state," distinguished officers of the army and navy, and the former president's extended family. The galleries were filled with bereaved citizens, reported the *Union,* adding, "The hall was dressed in mourning."

THE OUTPOURING OF sentiment for Adams soon gave way to a national obsession over the senatorial fate of the Trist treaty. Nearly everyone viewed the document as representing the country's last hope for peace under conditions palatable to most Americans. The treaty constituted a hinge of history. Continuation of the war would further divide the nation, deplete its treasury, and heighten the agony over the ongoing loss of American blood. It would raise further questions about the war's morality as more and more Mexican citizens came under U.S. sway. And it would add life to the ominous issue regarding the conquest of all of Mexico. Treaty ratification, on the other hand, would end the killing, the outflow of public monies, and the increasingly hate-filled domestic debate. It would bring into the Union highly valuable lands that could be easily absorbed and incorporated. It would seem to be an easy call for senators.

Most of the press seemed to agree. In a rare display of convergence, the *Union* and *National Intelligencer* strongly supported the treaty. Ratification, said the *Intelligencer*, would "avoid a greater national evil" inherent in the war's continuation. The editors acknowledged they could not reject the treaty and still oppose the conflict. Even Horace Greeley's *New York Tribune*, a beacon of Whig bellicosity, urged ratification. "Admit all its faults," said the *Tribune*, "and say if an aimless and endless foreign war is not far worse than any honorable treaty of peace could be."

Unfortunately, the political calculus in the Senate wasn't that simple. The usual war debates flared up. Some Whigs were outraged at the idea of grabbing any Mexican territory at all, while certain Democrats weren't satisfied with the magnitude of the acquisition envisioned in the treaty. Others suggested any treaty negotiated by Trist must be rejected as tainted. Then there was Thomas Hart Benton, who set himself against it without offering much of a reason why. Of course everyone knew why—his anger over the Frémont episode. All this raised concerns about the treaty's Senate prospects. It would take a two-thirds majority in the chamber to ratify the document, which meant a mere nineteen senators could kill it.

And so an anxious nation waited as the Senate grappled with the matter in secret. No one was more anxious than James Polk, whose presidency and legacy hinged on the outcome. On February 28, two days after the Adams funeral, the president heard from Ambrose Sevier that the Foreign Relations Committee had convened a meeting and recommended rejection. The committee wanted the president to appoint a commission of eminent Americans to proceed to Mexico and negotiate an agreement along the very lines of the Trist treaty. In other words, most members didn't oppose the terms per se, just the negotiator's role in crafting them. But some committee members, including Webster, Benton, Mangum, and Hannegan, expressed outright opposition. Only Sevier favored ratification.

Polk was stunned. It made no sense, he thought, for senators to reject a treaty they agreed with on merely procedural grounds. Further, it was something of a spectacle to see Daniel Webster, who favored no territorial acquisition, teaming up with Edward Hannegan, who wanted all of Mexico. The committee eventually sent the treaty to the floor without a recommendation.

Then new complications arose from a familiar source, James Buchanan. It began when a disturbed Lewis Cass stopped by the White House to express concerns about rumors that the president was dissatisfied with his stewardship of the Military Affairs Committee. These rumors mystified Polk. Where had they come from? It seemed they were fomented by a *New York Herald* correspondent named John Nugent, who wrote under the pseudonym of "Galviensis," among other pen names. But where did Nugent get such a report, wondered Polk, when in fact Cass was his private favorite for the Democratic nomination? Only the president's resolve to avoid all intrusion into the political process had kept him from expressing openly his high opinion of Cass.

Soon this "Galviensis" was directing his *Herald* attacks at the president, suggesting among other things that he secretly hankered for

a second term. Cass and former New Hampshire senator Levi Woodbury, another prominent candidate for the Democratic nomination,
came under constant attack from "Galviensis," while Buchanan
received garlands of praise. What was going on? Polk wondered.
He soon got his answer: John Nugent was a close friend of James
Buchanan and was frequently seen hanging around the State Department offices.

Polk held his tongue on the matter until Buchanan, on February
23, confronted the president with rumors that he was soon to be fired
because of Nugent's writings. He had talked with Nugent, Buchanan
acknowledged, but only in efforts to secure the journalist's support for
the war. He added that if the president so desired he would terminate
all conversation with the man.

Polk replied "in a stern manner" that Buchanan would have to
judge his own behavior but "it presented a very singular appearance
that a member of my Cabinet should be holding familiar intercourse
with an unprincipled newspaper letter-writer who was in the daily
habit of calumniating and abusing me." To his diary that night Polk
blustered, "If I obtain any reliable proof that Mr. Buchanan has given
countenance to Galvienses he shall not remain in the Cabinet." Characteristically, the president added, "He denies that he has done so, and
I am bound to believe him."

A couple of days later Polk heard from Cave Johnson that Buchanan
and Walker had been working behind the scenes against the treaty.
Further, said Johnson, Walker apparently had been corresponding
with Zachary Taylor and expressing his support for the general's presidential candidacy. Polk in his diary lamented this "spectacle" of a cabinet member supporting an administration opponent for president. Of
course, he added, he would have to fire the man if the Johnson suggestions proved accurate, but he would require "strong proof . . . before
I can believe it to be true."

Polk's presidency had reached perhaps its most critical juncture,
with his political fate and historical standing in the balance, and yet
his inner circle seemed rampant with political disloyalty and intrigue.
"The truth is," he wrote, "that the scheming and intriguing about

the Presidential election, and especially by Mr. Buchanan, is seriously embarrassing my administration."

Such intrigues were all the more disturbing because it seemed increasingly likely the treaty was headed toward defeat. On February 28 the Senate approved two resolutions calling for all correspondence between the administration and Trist. Polk considered the correspondence, particularly Trist's abusive missives following his recall, to be "impertinent, irrelevant, and highly exceptionable." But he sent the material on to the Senate to avoid any actions that could jeopardize the treaty.

The next afternoon Polk got further word the treaty was in trouble on the Senate floor. Polk figured a dozen Democrats might vote against, largely because they wanted more territory. (Benton had taken to justifying his opposition on the ground that the true Texas boundary was the Nueces River.) If Democratic opposition approached or reached that number, which seemed likely, Polk calculated, it would take only seven or eight opposition Whigs to kill the treaty. "The result is extremely doubtful," he wrote to his diary.

The next day, March 1, doubtfulness turned to near hopelessness. Polk spent much of the day talking with supportive senators, accumulating information and crafting arguments for the executive session debates. He spoke with Cass, Sevier, Solomon Downs of Louisiana, and Arthur Bagby of Alabama. All supported the treaty; all expected it to go down. That night Cass called again to say he considered the treaty's fate to be "extremely doubtful." Later Maine's Senator Wyman Moor stopped by to share his pessimism.

March 2 brought a snowstorm that lasted all day. Perhaps the snow turned the atmospherics in the Senate chamber somewhat brighter. After days of rhetorical fulminations from both Whigs and Democrats, a natural drift toward ratification seemed to emerge. Whig opponents had attacked the treaty as illegitimate because of Trist's recall. They branded it an instrument of slavery expansion. And they raged against its mindless territorial expansionism. But all their amendments were tabled or killed. On the Democratic side, Sam Houston put forth a measure to incorporate Lower California and most of northern Mexico to 22 degrees latitude, which would have included Tampico and San Luis Potosí. Jefferson Davis of Mississippi offered a more modest territorial proposal that still went considerably beyond the treaty's provisions. Davis's measure received only ten votes, while Houston's never reached a tally. After these maneuvers ran their course, it now became clear to most senators that ratification seemed likely, and they began falling into line.

After surveying the situation during the day of snow, Polk concluded the treaty "may be ratified, but by a very close vote." By the next day it appeared Benton might collect a dozen Democratic votes against the treaty, but more likely the number would be ten or fewer. Webster's nay votes seemed confined to six or eight. Polk calculated that many Whig senators would like to see the treaty defeated but only if the onus of defeat could be placed on the Democrats. Thus, if Democratic opposition reached a sufficient mass to attribute the defeat to the majority party, the Whigs would pile on. But, if not, Whig senators would hold back. It now seemed that the Democratic opponents wouldn't be numerous enough to draw a significant bloc of Whigs into opposition.

Still, over the next several days the treaty's prospects rose and fell like the tide. On March 6 its fate seemed sufficiently bright that Polk began seeking an envoy to take the document to Mexico and get that government's agreement to a number of minor modifications inserted by the Senate. But then came word that the Whigs were at it again, seeking to kill the pact through a new tactic—attaching amendments "of such a character," as Polk described it, "to jeopard its ratification by Mexico." Sevier told Polk the Whig ploy was to destroy the treaty while avoiding responsibility for the deed.

It didn't happen. At around ten o'clock on March 10, Secretary of the Senate Ashbury Dickins arrived at the White House with the news: After nine hours of intense debate, the Senate had ratified the treaty by a vote of 38 to 14, with four senators not voting. Upon getting the word in the White House parlor, Polk rushed to his office, summoned Marcy, and set in motion plans to have a fast courier dispatched to Mexico City with messages for Butler and Mexico that the treaty had been ratified with small modifications. The president would shortly send the document to Mexico by hand of a commissioner with full plenipotentiary powers.

That very night the *Union* rushed to the streets with an extra edition to spread the word. It noted that both Democrats and Whigs contributed to both sides of the vote tally. In fact, there was neither a clear partisan pattern in the vote nor a clear geographic pattern. Among the eighteen senators who voted no or abstained, ten were Whigs while eight were Democrats. Among those no votes and abstentions were seven northerners, five southerners, and six westerners.

"We congratulate the country upon the result—as furnishing some hope and some augury of the restoration of peace," wrote the *Union*. The paper added another hope, that the Mexican government would "not be so blind to the true interests of both countries, as to refuse its final ratification." It concluded, "We shall rejoice if the blessings of peace shall now succeed to the clash of arms."

28 · PEACE

California, New Mexico, and the Union

JAMES POLK didn't linger over his Senate victory, nor did he pause to insert into his diary expressions of enthusiasm or even satisfaction. Indulging his characteristic pessimism, he fretted that peace, now so close at hand, would prove unavailing due to the Senate's added amendments and prospects that Mexican officials would thus refuse to ratify the document. In fact, these modifications were too minor to cause any real difficulty, but Polk was a worrier, even when there wasn't much to worry about. He also was a man incapable of stepping back to savor a sweet victory. With matter-of-fact precision and his all-consuming sense of duty, he moved to keep events progressing in the right direction.

His first task now was to commission an envoy with plenipotentiary powers to take the treaty to Mexico. On March 11, the day after the Senate's ratification, he proposed to his cabinet the name of Senator Ambrose Sevier, the forty-seven-year-old chairman of Foreign Relations. Born in Tennessee, Sevier had migrated as a young man to Little Rock, Arkansas, where he emerged as a leading lawyer and politician. Even before Arkansas statehood, he represented his territory as a congressional delegate and staunch Andrew Jackson loyalist. With statehood in 1836, he obtained a Senate seat and became an effective and influential Democratic stalwart, strongly backing Indian removal, low tariffs, Texas annexation, acquisition of Oregon, and the Mexican War. Polk credited him with a major role in getting the war treaty ratified, and he particularly appreciated Sevier's opposition to the annexation of all Mexico.

Walker and Buchanan expressed some misgivings about Sevier,

but it became clear the president had settled on his choice. Indeed, Polk already had invited Sevier to the White House for a three o'clock conversation that afternoon. When the president offered Sevier the mission, the senator reacted first with apparent surprise, then with a respectful decline. He had no desire to leave the Senate, he said, and he feared acceptance would leave an appearance that his steadfast support for the treaty had been intermingled with an ambition to get this plum diplomatic role. Polk urged acceptance and promised to allay any suspicions about his motive in supporting the treaty. Sevier relented enough to think it over.

The next day he accepted with the request that the president, in sending up his name to the Senate, make good on his promise to emphasize the assignment had never been discussed before ratification. Polk promptly set about to explain the circumstances to key senators. He also asked Robert M. Walsh, a Pennsylvania lawyer who was fluent in Spanish, to serve as secretary to the Sevier mission. Walsh, a former U.S. diplomat to Brazil, accepted.

Events then moved in rapid succession on numerous fronts. On March 14, Polk sent to the Senate the names of Sevier and Walsh. Within the hour they were confirmed unanimously. The next day Polk learned of a move afoot in the Senate to disclose publicly the treaty debates, along with the treaty itself and the presidential message that had accompanied it. This would have been a disaster, in Polk's view, because it would reveal to the Mexican authorities precisely how contentious the issue had been. Polk was able to squelch the move.

On March 16 the president, acting on testimony before the army court of inquiry in Mexico, ordered the court to investigate the allegations that Scott and Trist had offered Santa Anna bribe money to induce him into a peace treaty. The next day Polk got word that Sevier's departure had been delayed because he had taken ill. The president decided another commissioner must proceed immediately with the treaty. "It was a case of emergency and no time was to be lost," he wrote later. He asked Attorney General Nathan Clifford—"a very discreet, sensible man," in Polk's view—to undertake the mission and the next day sent his name to the Senate for confirmation. Clifford left Washington at three o'clock the morning of March 19. It was assumed that Sevier would follow in a few days after his recovery, and the two men would then work together.

While the country was moving toward a cessation of hostilities and Congress was settling into a policy of supporting the peace process, the Whig opposition refused to curtail its verbal assault upon the president and his war. Daniel Webster marshaled his rhetorical force and logical rigor to dispute the president's constitutional right to levy import fees on goods and merchandise entering Mexico. Later he rose to denounce the war, the treaty, and the prospect of any territorial acquisition. He declared his opposition to the creation of new, sparsely populated states in the West with multiple senators representing few citizens but interjecting exotic new arguments into the national debate.

If expansionists embraced a vision of a great world power straddling a continent and dominating the commerce of two oceans, Webster wanted nothing to do with it, nor with the acquisition of Mexican territory as a war indemnity. "I resist it to-day, and always," he declared, adding, "I say, sir, that according to my conscientious convictions, we are now fixing upon the constitution of the United States and upon our form of government a monstrosity—a disfiguration—an enormity."

Joseph Root of Ohio brought to the House floor the fiery contempt of western Whigs in attacking the president's war. He called the treaty "nothing but a piece of land jobbing" and reinserted the Wilmot Proviso into the debate in language approaching a call to arms. "The strife between slavery and anti-slavery . . . cannot be avoided," he declared. "Depend on it, northern obstinacy will be a match for your southern chivalry. You will be in the field first, and we will not be first to leave it."

Polk sought to dismiss these assaults as the price to be suffered in furtherance of the national vision. But he couldn't dismiss the *New York Herald*'s March 23 publication of his message accompanying the treaty to the Senate. Polk was shocked. He had managed to suppress the Senate's desire to make public such documents, but now they were being divulged piecemeal, without regard to their potential damage to the nation. The Senate immediately initiated an investigation into the matter.

The next day brought more public revelations. The *Herald* published the full text of the treaty and confidential correspondence related to Washington's diplomatic efforts with Mexico. Later in the day Polk heard that the Senate's investigative committee had interrogated John Nugent, the *Herald*'s "Galviensis," and the letter writer had acknowledged furnishing the documents to the paper. He denied getting them from any senator. Asked if they had come from the president's cabinet or other executive offices, Nugent had declined to answer. North Carolina's Senator Mangum reported it was "pretty well understood" among senators that the documents had been slipped to Nugent from the State Department.

Later Senator Hannegan called on Polk and said Senator Westcott in executive session had stated his belief that the leak had come from Buchanan himself. Hannegan said he agreed. It was known among senators, said Hannegan, that Nugent "was in habits of intimacy with Mr. Buchanan." Many senators, he revealed, had been turned away in efforts to visit Buchanan in his office because the secretary was so often "closetted" with Nugent. This corresponded with what Polk had been hearing around town—that Nugent was seen constantly huddled with Buchanan at the State Department and also at Buchanan's home.

Of course, if Polk could prove Buchanan actually had instigated the attacks on him, wrote the president, he would dismiss the man from his cabinet immediately. But the evidence, while strong, was not conclusive, so once again he essentially shrugged it off, even knowing Buchanan's behavior stemmed from his powerful presidential ambitions.

Yet Polk held in his files Buchanan's letter of February 1845 stating he wouldn't seek the presidency while serving the administration unless Polk expressly consented. The secretary actually sent a request that Polk send him a copy of this letter as he apparently had misplaced his own copy. "Mr. Buchanan has been publicly a candidate for the Democratic nomination for the Presidency for some months past," wrote Polk, "& this is the first time that he seems to have remembered the promise contained in his letter." Polk poured into his diary expressions of woe and frustration at Buchanan's behavior. "He has been selfish," he wrote, "& all his acts and opinions seem to have been controlled with a view to his own advancement, so much so that I can have no confidence or reliance in any advice he may give upon public questions."

But, added the president, grasping for yet another excuse for passivity, he couldn't fire the man while the war raged on and while he faced "a talented and powerful opposition in Congress."

Of course, this tortuous rationale, typical of Polk's efforts to avoid reality in such matters, revealed a fundamental presidential weakness. He lacked the fortitude for the face-to-face encounter that must attend a dismissal. He certainly wasn't afraid of taking controversial or unpopular stands, as he had demonstrated repeatedly during his presidency. But when it came to direct confrontation, any excuse for inaction would be seized upon. This difficulty became manifest when he finally confronted Buchanan about the matter—an action, he acknowledged to his diary, that he "had felt a delicacy and reluctance" to pursue. Buchanan responded with an elaborate and defiant denial, followed by a direct question as to whether Polk believed he had furnished the documents to Nugent.

"I do not," replied the president. With that answer he lost another round to his manipulative secretary of state—and ensured he would have Buchanan around to continue his menacing ways into the indefinite future.

The matter finally receded from the Washington consciousness when Nugent signed a statement absolving Buchanan of any involvement in the matter. "I am myself gratified that Mr Buchanan is thus relieved from so injurious an imputation," wrote the president. "He will now, I hope, learn a profitable lesson." The Senate expressed its frustration by taking Nugent into custody for contempt of Congress for refusing to answer the questions put to him. But the matter eventually blew over.

AS POLK GRAPPLED with such unsavory matters in Washington, the army court of inquiry proceeded through its long and contentious hearings in Mexico, first at Perote and Puebla, then in Mexico City. After Scott's recall and Polk's action in downgrading the magnitude of the court proceedings, the general seemed inclined to let the matter drop. But Pillow, bent on inflicting a blow upon his erstwhile commanding officer, insisted on his day in court as a means of exonerating himself. Scott did, however, withdraw the charges against James Duncan, while Worth dropped his against Scott. That still left Pillow, Worth, and Scott in the dock, and the proceedings unfolded as a kind of spectacle in which the participants sought to protect themselves by destroying their former comrades.

Nicholas Trist lingered in Mexico long enough to testify in behalf of Scott (and, in the process, attack Pillow), then set out on his home journey on April 8. He had parried General Butler's gentle admonitions that he leave the country by defiantly insisting the president's departure order carried no weight, as he had been fired and thus was a private citizen not subject to presidential directives. He had added he would have left willingly but now couldn't do so because it would appear his departure represented "acquiescence in usurped authority." He left with a residue of bitterness toward Polk, who petulantly had directed that Trist not be paid for time served beyond the point at which he had received his recall notice. The maverick envoy was left to make his way home on his own meager resources. On May 4 he arrived in New Orleans a wayworn and nearly forgotten man.

In Mexico, however, Trist retained a measure of esteem. The peace party issued a formal statement extolling "the noble character and high endowments" of the man—toward whom, said the statement, "there remains in Mexico none but grateful and honoring recollections."

Scott meanwhile suffered through the ordeal of the court's inquiries, then on April 22 departed Mexico City by mule train amid the cheers of adoring U.S. soldiers thronged along his path. He left Veracruz on May 1 and reached his home in Elizabethtown, New Jersey, on May 20. He didn't have much time for renewal. The court of inquiry was scheduled to resume its deliberations in Frederick, Maryland, on June 5.

Even before Scott's Mexico City departure, Sevier and Clifford reached the capital—Clifford on the 11th with the Senate-ratified treaty and Sevier on the 15th. Their arrival set off a new round of bitter political warfare as the war faction in Mexico dredged up all the old warnings about national shame, humiliation, and oblivion at the hands of the despised *americanos*. But the peace faction remained steadfast in support of a settlement, and the only question was whether the peace forces would manage to retain their governmental dominance in the face of the enraged opposition.

BACK IN AMERICA the campaign year was generating plenty of civic interest. In April, Henry Clay once again put himself forward as a candidate for the Whig presidential nomination. The seventy-one-year-old politician had developed, confessed Clay to his countrymen, "a strong disinclination" to seek the presidency this time and had left Lexington the previous December "under a determination to announce to the public, in some suitable form, my desire not to be thought of as a candidate." But then he had consulted his friends, said Clay, and they expressed "the strongest appeals and the most earnest entreaties, both verbally and written, to dissuade me from executing my intended purpose." Such a decision, they told him (as Clay recalled it), could be "fatal to the success, and perhaps lead to the dissolution of the party." And so he had decided to run in the interest of party and country.

Clay's earnest self-absorption stirred the *Union* to have a little fun at his expense. Quoting the Kentuckian's expressions of agony over his decision with a bit of mockery, the paper said it would not "be so discourteous to the 'whig Embodiment' as to charge him with imposture." But it asked, "Is there an impartial man in the country who will . . . believe in the anxiety of Mr. Clay to decline the object of all his aspirations for nearly thirty years?" Just so. For this particular politician, there had been and would be no cure for the presidential bug.

Zachary Taylor wasted no time in saying Clay's candidacy would not alter his own decision to seek the presidency. Nor would he withdraw his name from the canvass, *"whoever may be the nominee of the national convention, either of the whig or democratic party."* In the cryptic vagueness of language that had become his trademark, he seemed to be saying he would run for president as a Whig if awarded that party's nomination but would press on under his own banner should the party turn to someone else. More ominously, he seemed to be saying, as the *Union* put it, that he would force his candidacy upon the Whigs or seek to force the election into the House of Representatives. With the Whigs' Philadelphia convention only weeks away, this caused considerable consternation among some party members.

But congressional Whigs, their eyes on the general election, saw an opportunity in a long letter of bitter complaint unleashed upon Secretary Marcy by General Scott, a hero to his nation if not his president. In language only slightly less self-serving than that of his famous "hasty plate of soup" letter, Scott poured out his anger at how his government had treated him—from Polk's effort to place a lieutenant general over him to the final indignities surrounding his recall, the official charges against him, and Polk's meddling in the court-martial cases. Scott wrote:

It was that budget of papers that caused the blow of power, so long suspended, to fall on a devoted head. The three arrested officers, and he who had endeavored to enforce a necessary discipline against them, are all to be placed together before the same court; —the innocent and the guilty, the accuser and the accused, the judge and his prisoners, are dealt with alike. Most impartial justice! . . . While the parties are on trial—if the appealer [Pillow] is to be tried at all, which seems doubtful—two are restored to their corps . . . and I am deprived of my command! There can be but one step more in the same direction: —throw the rules and articles of war into the fire, and leave all ranks in the army free to engage in denunciations and a general scramble for precedence, authority, and executive favors.

As a private expression of resentment, Scott's letter posed a valid point about the chaos created by presidential interventions in his command. But the letter wasn't intended as a private expression. No sooner had Marcy received the missive than its contents became known throughout Congress, and elements also found their way into Baltimore and Richmond newspapers. House Whigs quickly pushed through a resolution calling on the executive to make the document available to legislators, which meant it would be printed and distributed publicly. Polk complied but assigned Marcy to craft a hurried reply so it could be sent up along with the Scott letter.

The Whigs had not counted on a Marcy reply and didn't want it to blunt their planned attack on Polk. Alabama's Henry Hilliard moved to add some audacious language to the resolution directing the printing of the documents: "Excepting, however, from printing, a letter found among said documents, signed by the Secretary of War, and purporting to have been written to Major General Scott four days after the passage of the resolution calling for the correspondence." The ploy failed, and Marcy's detailed and stern rebuke to Scott was printed along with the general's written attack. But the episode reflected a fundamental political reality: For all the heat and tumult of the debates thus far in the Polk presidency, they were only going to get more brutal and desperate as the election season drew nigh.

In early May the *Union* published a buoyant letter, dated April 13, from a correspondent in Mexico City writing under the pen name of "Mustang." The Mexican Congress had not yet reached a quorum for purposes of considering the treaty, reported "Mustang," but prospects were good this would happen within the week. As for the treaty's fate, he added, his informants in the governing city of Querétaro had informed him "that but six deputies and two senators are opposed to its ratification."

Polk was gratified at such news, and he had further cause for good cheer the same day when he traveled to the Senate chamber to attend a memorial service for Senator Chester Ashley of Arkansas. As the senators left the chamber, Thomas Benton stopped at the door, turned around toward the president, bowed in a conspicuous display of respect, and saluted. Polk saluted back—and reported the incident to his diary that night as a welcome gesture from a man who had shunned him since the Frémont trial.

On May 13, Polk paused to note to his diary that precisely two years before, Congress had passed its war resolution. "They have been two years of unceasing labour and anxiety with me." The labors and anxieties yielded a resolve that his name would not be put before the Democrats' looming Baltimore convention. Friends and allies were coming by with growing frequency now to implore the president to seek a second term. To all he said the same thing: He would not run and would not change his mind. But to forestall prospects that the convention might bring forth his name to break a nomination deadlock, he crafted a letter to be read to the convention. The aim, as he explained to numerous friends and advisers, was "to relieve the Convention of any embarrassment which the presentation of my name might produce."

THE CONVENTION OPENED at five minutes to noon on May 22 in the Universalist Church on Baltimore's North Calvert Street. Immediately it became clear that the assembled Democrats must deal with two controversies before getting to the presidential balloting. One was that old bugaboo, the two-thirds rule. By now this nominating principle had guided the Democrats' last three conventions, and delegates embraced the supermajority concept with relative serenity. No contention emerged to match the emotional confrontation of four years before.

The other controversy wasn't so easily disposed of. New York Democrats brought to the convention their lingering strife between the Hunkers and Barnburners, the two warring factions of New York Democratic politics. Initially, the split between them had been over relatively benign issues related to banking and currency policies, but now the issue was slavery, beginning with the Wilmot Proviso and extending to the Barnburners' increasingly intense abolitionism. Each faction had sent its own delegation, insisting its contingent was the proper and duly constituted one. When the credentials committee awarded New York's floor seats to the Hunkers, a raucous four-hour floor debate ensued that inevitably called forth the slavery issue. Alabama's William Lowndes Yancey, responding to a question that suggested an abolitionist underpinning, unleashed a philippic of southern sensibility that deprecated the Barnburners as "factious Whigs in disguise and abolitionists" and hailed slavery as "one of the fundamental pillars of the constitution . . . so recognized alike by New York and South Carolina." He then introduced a resolution awarding New York's floor seats to the Syracuse Hunkers.

It appeared pandemonium might reign, but during the later evening session Yancey withdrew his resolution, and the convention accepted, by a two-vote margin, a compromise resolution allowing both delegations to be seated and to cast the state's votes in concert. When the proceedings continued the next day both factions rejected the compromise, thus forfeiting New York's floor vote during the ensuing balloting for the presidential nomination. That balloting commenced only after the convention listened to a reading of Polk's remarkable message declaring he would not under any circumstances accept a second nomination. "If," wrote the president, "on reviewing the history of my administration, and the remarkable events, foreign and domestic, which have attended it, it shall be the judgment of my countrymen that I have adhered to [my] principles, and faithfully performed my duty, the measure of my ambition is full, and I am amply compensated for all the labors, cares, and anxieties which are inseparable from the high station which I have been called to fill."

With Polk out, the presidential balloting focused on three serious candidates—Cass, Buchanan, and Woodbury. The first ballot yielded 125 votes for Cass, 55 for Buchanan, and 53 for Woodbury. Cass looked like the prohibitive favorite unless the other two could cut into his vote substantially on the second ballot. It didn't happen. Cass got 133 second-ballot votes, then increased his total to 156 on the third ballot. By the fourth he was over the top with 179 votes against the needed two-thirds total of 170. "The announcement of this result by the CHAIR," reported the *Union,* "was followed by . . . the members of the various delegations almost universally springing to their feet, and uniting in one spirit-stirring shout of approbation."

Though the *Union* sought to gloss over the fact, this burst of enthusiasm was misleading. Strong currents of anti-Cass sentiment ran through the politics of both the South and the Northeast. Robert Barnwell Rhett told Polk on the eve of the convention that he could never support Cass if he got the nomination, and South Carolina "could not and would not support him." Alabama's Yancey actually had walked out of the convention after it rejected his platform amendment declaring the party's commitment to ensuring all new U.S. territory would be open to slaveholders and their property. The pyrogenic southerner had pressed the amendment because of concerns that Cass wasn't sufficiently imbued with southern thinking on the Wilmot Proviso. Though Cass opposed Wilmot, he had flirted with the "popular sovereignty" precept that inhabitants of the territories should decide for themselves whether slavery would be allowed within their jurisdictions. Anti-Cass sentiment was not leavened by the selection of Major General William O. Butler, Winfield Scott's successor as commander of U.S. forces in Mexico, as the Democrats' vice presidential candidate.

In the Northeast, meanwhile, New York's antislavery Barnburners were leading the way to rebellion against the presidential candidate. The *New York Evening Post*, upon hearing of a forthcoming New York visit by Thomas Benton, inquired whether he was planning "to propose over the grave of Silas Wright a disgraceful co-operation with his assassins!" And the *New York Globe* suggested Benton and other New York visitors were bent on establishing a slaveholder dominion over all acquired U.S. territory. Soon the Barnburners would be planning a serious assault upon the Cass candidacy.

The Whig convention in Philadelphia began on June 7 amid a growing perception that Henry Clay, not Zachary Taylor, would get the party nod. The Kentuckian's hometown newspaper, the *Lexington Observer and Reporter,* declared, "The indications everywhere point to Mr. Clay as the whig candidate for the Presidency." Horace Greeley's *New York Tribune* castigated other newspapers that perceived a movement toward Taylor, and the *Union* pronounced it "quite clear that the chances of General Taylor's nomination by the whig convention are daily diminishing." Meanwhile, New England Whigs were seeking to unleash a boomlet for their regional favorite son, Daniel Webster—whose candidacy, declared the *Boston Atlas,* if coupled with a vice presidential selection of, say, Kentucky's John Crittenden, "would sweep through the free States like fire on a dry prairie."

These prognosticators all proved wrong. On the first ballot on June 8, Taylor received 114 votes to Clay's 97. The general rose steadily through the next three ballots, finally capturing the nomination on the fourth ballot with 171 votes. By then Clay's support had collapsed to a mere 32 votes. The convention nominated for vice president New York's former congressman Millard Fillmore—"an out-and-out partisan," said the *Union,* "a man of considerable talent—a high-tariff, abolition, Wilmot-Proviso, United-States-bank Whig."

The choice of the colorless and politically indistinct Taylor, as even many Whigs acknowledged, was in part a cynical one, designed to fuzz up differences between the Democratic agenda and Whig precepts. Horace Greeley called the Philadelphia convention "a slaughterhouse of Whig principles." Clay was disgusted as well as disappointed. "I fear," he said, "that the Whig party is dissolved and that no longer are there Whig principles to excite zeal and stimulate exertion." The *Union* professed jubilation at the choice of Taylor. "He cannot be elected," declared the paper.

THE NEWS FILTERING into Washington from Mexico, meanwhile, was decidedly mixed. Rumors and counter-rumors ricocheted off the pages of nearly all the major newspapers, and it was impossible to know what was actually happening in Mexico. Finally on June 7 the president received a definitive dispatch from Sevier and Clifford. The Chamber of Deputies had ratified the treaty, and there seemed little doubt the Senate would do likewise. "There is now, I hope, a good prospect for a speedy peace," wrote Polk to his diary. But he wrote it on June 8, a day after he got the news. The reason, as he explained to his diary, was that he had forgotten to mention this stunning news when he penned his diary entry the previous evening.

On June 9, the *Union* ran a late dispatch headlined: "IMPORTANT FROM MEXICO! Peace! Peace! Peace!!!" The Deputies' ratification vote had been 51 to 35, said the paper, and the Senate was expected to follow suit immediately. Just twenty-four hours later the paper was able to report the Senate vote under a headline larger than any seen in the paper: "PEACE!!!" the *Union* exulted:

> We have at length the exquisite pleasure of announcing to our countrymen the ratification of the treaty, and the establishment of peace between Mexico and the United States. We are satisfied that we proclaim no intelligence that would diffuse greater joy throughout our country—not peace only, but an honorable and an advantageous peace—as the result of one of the most brilliant wars that ever adorned the annals of any nation.

About a half-dozen members of Congress called at the White House that day to congratulate Polk on his successful war. Notwithstanding the celebratory mood among his guests, the president received them in his usual modulated fashion. Afterward, he summoned Marcy for discussions on the immediate actions needed to demobilize the army in Mexico and return the U.S. military as quickly as possible to a peacetime status. Then, turning to other matters in characteristic fashion, he directed to his diary not the slightest expression of pleasure or relief.

WITH WAR'S END came the culmination of Polk's presidential ambition. Texas, Oregon, the tariff bill, and the independent treasury had all fallen into his hands with relative ease and without much of a political or personal toll. And now he added the successful outcome of the Mexican conflict, ending in the acquisition of some 600,000 square miles of continental expanse and the dominance of a vast Pacific coastline with some of the best harbors in the world. Few presidents would prove capable of enhancing their country's geopolitical standing on such a scale.

But, unlike Polk's previous triumphs, this one carried a high personal and political price. Even as he received news of Mexican ratification, Polk was not well. He felt "indisposed" with chills and a fever that had bedeviled him for days. He received his cabinet in his bedchamber at one point, did not attend church the next Sunday, and had his doctor prescribe medications on at least two occasions. The fever would recede but then recur in greater magnitude a week later. This was not an unusual occurrence for the driven and overworked president, who was frail by nature and who pursued a schedule that surely added to his frailty. But never had his schedule been as frenzied or consuming as during the war. Beyond that was the psychological toll stemming from the torments and sorrows of a conflict that claimed 13,780 American lives and cost some hundred million in U.S. dollars. It resulted in a sacrifice of nearly 25,000 Mexicans.

The two-year ordeal accentuated the president's quiet force as national leader and political visionary. He had embraced an American aspiration that many articulated but few could fashion into a concrete plan with serious prospects of fulfillment. And, through grit, persistence, and flexibility of action, he had turned that aspiration into a reality that transformed a nation. But the ordeal also magnified the man's weaknesses—his suspicious sanctimony, his inability to establish a culture of teamwork, his tendency toward transparently sly maneuvers, his lack of personality traits used by true political leaders to bend others to their will.

Did these limitations contribute to the war's apparent intractability and its droning two-year time span? Could another leader with the same vision have rendered a successful outcome more quickly and more smoothly by generating less bitterness among top lieutenants and less rancor from political opponents? It's impossible to know. What we do know is that over its long tenure the war unleashed powerful crosscurrents that transformed not only the country's geographic outline but also its political sensibilities and fault lines.

It all left James Polk a diminished man. He was diminished politically as he faced his remaining eight months in office without an agenda and with an energized and bellicose opposition. He was diminished personally as small irritations took on ever greater magnitude in his consciousness until they began to sap his fortitude and strength. On June 14, when he might have been communing a bit with his diary about his great geopolitical triumph, he was instead complaining bitterly about citizens approaching the White House in search of federal jobs. He wrote:

> The number and importunities of office seekers was quite as great as they have been any day for months passed. I . . . am much disgusted with the unceasing pressure for them which occurs daily. A great portion of those who thus annoy [me] have no claims upon the public & are wholly unworthy. All of them had much better engage in some honest employment for a livelihood than to seek to live on the public.

Thus lacking a sense of proportion and thus preoccupied with unimportant vexations, the president brought upon himself more pressures and anxieties than his health could endure.

29 · FINAL MONTHS

"Solemnly Impressed with the . . . Emptiness of Worldly Honors"

J AMES POLK ROSE on the Fourth of July with anticipation. Though weak from a lingering fever, he would on this Independence Day attend a ceremony honoring the country's premier historical figure, George Washington. Between the White House and the Potomac, on a patch of land designated as a locale of national commemoration, the cornerstone was to be laid for the gigantic spear of a monument to the first president. At ten o'clock the cabinet assembled at the White House for the carriage trip to City Hall, where a procession was formed for the ceremonial ride to the construction site. There the president witnessed the political ritual and listened to an address by House Speaker Robert Winthrop, the stormy Whig and Polk rival, who managed to keep partisanship out of his remarks.

Later that afternoon, back at the White House, Polk received a courier bearing the official treaty from Mexico, ratified and signed. The president instructed Buchanan to prepare an official proclamation announcing the definitive conclusion of the war. He set to work himself on a message to be sent with the treaty to Congress. At eleven o'clock he signed the proclamation, then continued working on the message long into the night. He retired "exceedingly fatigued."

This was a pivotal day for America. With the war now officially over, that brief but explosive era of 1840s expansionism had come to an end. It was Polk's era. With his stubborn persistence and capacity to absorb political punishment, he had shaped and directed the swirling forces of Manifest Destiny into a powerful conclusion—Texas, Oregon, and now California and New Mexico. The continental United States had taken its shape—and taken on a new world image.

"The results of the war with Mexico," said Polk in his message to Congress, "have given to the United States a national character abroad which our country never before enjoyed."

Now the new territories needed territorial governments, which could only be established by Congress. Unfortunately, Congress would prove incapable of fulfilling this responsibility with dispatch and smoothness. The reason: slavery. Polk set about dealing with key legislators in hopes of crafting a territorial accommodation shaped around Henry Clay's old Missouri Compromise legislation of 1820 and 1821. This famous compromise had designated a line of demarcation—north latitude 36 degrees, 30 minutes—between northern territory without slaves and a southern region where slavery would be permitted if the citizens there chose to embrace it. For a generation this brilliant agreement had muted the slavery issue as the country carved new states out of Louisiana Purchase lands, absorbed Texas, and grappled with economic controversies such as the Bank of the United States and tariff rates. But now, in the wake of the Mexican War and its territorial acquisitions, the Missouri Compromise seemed to be losing its force.

Polk set himself against this erosion and pressed his pro-compromise arguments upon key members of Congress. On July 12 the Senate, embracing a resolution by Delaware's John Clayton, created a special committee to handle the territorial matter. The eight-member panel, designed to be evenly divided to foster a compromise spirit, would consist of four Whigs and four Democrats; and four southerners and four northerners. The next day the Senate awarded the panel's chairmanship to Clayton, a broad-faced lawyer whose strong Whig convictions were mixed with an instinct for legislative cooperation.

On Sunday evening, July 16, Calhoun, a member of the Clayton panel, called at the White House to discuss the closed-door proceedings. The men took tea with the Polk family in the parlor before retreating to the president's office to talk business.

The question, said Polk, "ought to be settled upon the Missouri or Texas compromise line."

That didn't seem possible, replied Calhoun. The Missouri Compromise language couldn't get a committee majority, and the panel seemed likely to adopt a novel idea posed by New York's Daniel Dickinson—essentially ignore slavery in hopes the issue would be settled later by the courts. On July 18 the committee embraced this concept and sent its territorial bill to the floor, where John Clayton described the innovative compromise in detail.

First, he said, the panel members agreed Oregon would never be a slaveholding region, and so they would essentially defer to the wishes of the territory's people, who already had prohibited bondage through temporary laws adopted pending creation of a territorial legislature. This Oregon policy could be adopted, said Clayton, "without any sacrifice of principle" on the part of southerners. Then California and New Mexico territories would be organized by allowing the appointment of a governor, senator, and judges who would act together in a legislative capacity—"but without the power to legislate on the subject of slavery." Thus, explained Clayton, the right to introduce or prohibit slavery would be determined by the judges, whose rulings in response to litigation on the matter could be appealed to the U.S. Supreme Court.

The idea was that the high court would settle this troublesome issue once and for all while Congress could avoid the nasty conflict in establishing territorial governments. The problem with a legislative solution, warned Clayton, was that any congressional action would simply stir up prompt and persistent agitations for repeal. "But this bill," he said, "resolves the whole question between the north and the south into a constitutional and a judicial question." At the White House, Polk expressed satisfaction with this approach. "There is now some prospect," he wrote, "that the question may be settled at the present session of Congress, and I sincerely hope it may be."

But Polk harbored no illusion about the ominous new era the country had entered. This was particularly clear in New York, where the increasingly agitated Barnburners were stepping up their bursts of political pyrotechnics. Their rallying cry was the Wilmot Proviso. Their vision was an entirely new alignment of American politics.

The vision was articulated with bold defiance by the *New York*

Globe. The Barnburners, said the paper, could never support Cass for president, largely because he embraced the "popular sovereignty" notion that territorial inhabitants should be allowed to decide for themselves whether to introduce slavery into their lands. "His defeat," declared the *Globe,* "must be made certain." That would bring to the White House an empty suit of a man without any discernible principles or convictions. A four-year Taylor administration, said the paper, "would create an opportunity for the real democracy of the Union to unite in 1852, and the result then would show a complete democratic triumph"—a triumph, in the *Globe's* view, of northern antislavery sentiment.

Later this New York Barnburner movement, now also encompassing Democrats from Ohio, Wisconsin, Connecticut, and Massachusetts, assembled at Utica, New York, for a convention of fiery dissension aimed at creating a new antislavery party of disgruntled Democrats and like-minded Whigs. Samuel Young of Saratoga, elected president of the assemblage, declared his pride at being called a Barnburner and noted that lightning itself was known to burn down some barns from time to time. Later Benjamin Butler read a letter from Martin Van Buren, written in response to the convention's inquiry as to whether the Lindenwald sage would consent to having his name placed in nomination for president. The answer was yes.

But Van Buren had a problem—his previous image as a Jackson protégé untroubled by slavery. Indeed, he had actively opposed outlawing slavery in the District of Columbia, had declared himself "altogether with the South against abolitionism," and had been described as "a northern man with southern principles." So with elaborate reasoning Van Buren explained how his current abolitionist sentiments actually were consistent with his previous views. Never had he doubted the power of Congress to outlaw slavery anywhere outside the original thirteen states, he said; he simply hadn't thought such actions were propitious in the political circumstances of the past. But now the time had arrived to employ Congress's inherent powers to halt the spread of slavery, and he demanded that Congress exercise those powers.

"We are called upon to do this," declared Van Buren, "at a period when the minds of nearly all mankind have been penetrated by a conviction of the evils of slavery, and are united in efforts for its suppression—at a moment, too, when the spirit of freedom and reform is everywhere far more prevalent than it has ever been."

So delighted were the delegates to have Van Buren carrying their standard that they easily glossed over his past. It was probably the most remarkable political conversion of the era—a Jacksonian politician known as a smooth and calculating slyboots now becoming the leader of a dissident minority bent on destroying the old political order on behalf of a moral conviction. Polk was aghast at his old friend's apostasy. "This is a most dangerous attempt to organize Geographical parties upon the slave question," he wrote. "Mr. Van Buren's course is selfish, unpatriotic, and wholly inexcusable." The *Union* declared that any politician who goes for sectional parties "is virtually worse than a whig."

The Barnburners and their allies, taking up a new catchphrase of "free soil," scheduled another convention for August 7 in Buffalo, which they hoped would surpass the Utica gathering in size and political energy.

In Congress these developments contributed to a sense that the old order was indeed fading. Maryland's Reverdy Johnson warned on the Senate floor that, if the matter wasn't settled by the Clayton compromise, it would be settled "by blood, or by disunion." But some southern senators remained bent on preventing any exclusion of slavery from the new territories. Calhoun took the floor for two hours to demand that the South be allowed to enjoy full advantages from the territorial acquisitions. Southern blood had contributed to those acquisitions, he argued, and southerners should have the right to enter those lands with their property. Georgia's Senator John Berrien, a Whig who once had served as Jackson's attorney general, argued Congress had no constitutional right to exclude slavery from any lands, including Oregon, beyond the original thirteen states. The Oregon precedent, declared Berrien, would never get his vote.

Opposition came also from northerners of both parties bent on establishing Congress's right to prohibit slavery in all territories, particularly in California and New Mexico, where Mexico already had outlawed slavery. Regarding the Clayton compromise, the fiery *New York Evening Post* wrote, "Congress may pass it, but it will not quiet the agitation. The free soil party will not be satisfied with anything short of an express confirmation . . . in favor of personal freedom."

On July 26 the Senate took up the Clayton bill under a previous commitment to bring the matter to a vote. Throughout the night senators voted down numerous amendments and repeated motions to adjourn. Only one amendment was approved—a Reverdy Johnson measure to grant territorial residents a right to appeal judicial rulings regarding slavery directly to the U.S. Supreme Court. Finally a few minutes before eight on the morning of July 27, the Senate passed the Clayton bill, 33 to 22.

The next day the *Union* noted with satisfaction that the favorable vote had come from members of both parties and both regions. But when the compromise bill arrived at the House the same day, Georgia's Alexander H. Stephens, a highly partisan Whig, moved to lay it on the table and called for the yeas and nays. This was a privileged motion, which meant the House would be voting essentially to kill the bill without any debate on its merits. The House became so feverish over the matter that Speaker Winthrop nearly lost control of the floor. After repeated cries of "Order," he finally warned that nobody would be recognized until members took their seats and restored themselves to decorum. Finally the yeas and nays were demanded, and the tabling motion passed 112 to 97. The Senate compromise was dead. The House promptly took up a measure to establish a territorial government only in Oregon.

Even more ominous than the vote was its sectional breakdown. All northern Whigs supported Stephens, while all southern Democrats voted against, joined by all but eight Whigs. Those southern Whigs represented the margin of Stephens's victory. Had they rallied with their southern brethren, the Stephens motion would have died.

Whig political calculations came into play also. Had Congress approved the Clayton bill, with its implied denial that Congress had any right to exclude slavery from the territories, northeastern abolitionists would have rallied to Van Buren's Free Soil Party and degraded Zachary Taylor's political standing. The *Union* quoted one prominent Massachusetts Whig as declaring passage of the compromise bill would have ensured that "General Taylor would not get a vote in 'a free state.'"

At the White House, a crestfallen Polk harbored no doubt that presidential politics contributed to the outcome. "The result of leaving the slavery question an open one, to be agitated by ambitious political aspirants & gamblers and their friends," he wrote, "[will be] to produce an organization of parties upon geographical lines, which must prove dangerous to the harmony if not the existence of the Union itself."

Polk knew now that a territorial bill was unlikely to pass in the current congressional session, set to end on August 14. But Congress seemed ready to send him a bill establishing a territorial government in Oregon, along with a restriction on slavery there. Should he sign it? Polk posed that question at the August 8 cabinet meeting. His own answer, he said, was yes because Oregon was situated above the Missouri Compromise line of 36°30'. But, said the president, for territory below that line he would not accept a slavery restriction. Absent a new congressional compromise, he would adhere to the Missouri formula. The cabinet generally agreed.

Then he asked if he should explain his position at the time of signing. This was trickier. Buchanan quickly noted that, if Polk denied Congress's right to restrict slavery in the southern territories, antislavery Democrats in the North would flock to the Van Buren banner, and Cass likely would lose the November election. Walker suggested a more indirect approach, perhaps an editorial in the *Union* outlining the president's reasoning. Everyone agreed that Polk should not put his own stamp on any explanatory statement until after the election. The president asked Buchanan and Walker to collaborate on a paper that could be used either as a statement or an editorial. But that night he told his diary he was inclined to issue it as a statement.

Hopes brightened the next night when the Senate, trying once more to craft a territorial compromise, voted 33 to 22 to attach the Missouri Compromise extension to its territorial bill. But on August 11 the House once again killed the Senate's initiative, this time with an 82 to 121 vote that reflected the country's powerful push toward sectionalism. Every southern member of both parties voted for the compromise language, while all but four northern members voted against. The *Union* called the vote "a melancholy sign of the times."

The president was feeling melancholy too—exhausted much of the time and frustrated with the turn of events. He began work on a veto message to be used if Congress passed a threatened public works bill but soon postponed the effort because of his persistent exhaustion. "I find myself greatly fatigued & worn down by my labours," he wrote to his diary.

Around the same time Polk learned the Free Soil agitators, meeting at Buffalo, had nominated Charles F. Adams as their vice presidential candidate on the Van Buren ticket. Adams, son of John Quincy Adams, was an avowed abolitionist. "Mr. Van Buren," wrote Polk, "is the most fallen man I have ever known."

At breakfast on August 13, Polk learned the Senate had been in session all night grappling with the Oregon bill. Finally around ten o'clock, the chamber passed it, along with a slavery restriction, and adjourned until nine the next morning. Convinced the Oregon legislation would pass, Polk set his attention to completing his Oregon message. Occupying the president until after midnight, this labor included plenty of discussion with various confidants along the way.

Essentially, Polk wanted the vexing slavery issue to go away so America could resume its pursuit of national greatness on the world stage. The Missouri Compromise had served to mute this issue for a generation. Therefore, he would defend and support the compromise in his Oregon statement. Thus, when Buchanan vehemently urged him to abandon any notion of issuing that statement, he promptly rejected the advice. Buchanan, used to handling the president, then urged him to avoid any veto threat against later territorial legislation that prohibited slavery south of the Missouri Compromise line. But Polk said no. When the *Union*'s Thomas Ritchie, who arrived around ten o'clock that night, submitted tougher veto-threat language than Polk had crafted, the president also rejected Ritchie's approach as too incendiary. Polk's aim was to placate the South without enflaming the North.

When Calhoun arrived at the White House to urge Polk to veto the Oregon bill, the president displayed a rare degree of vehemence.

"I have made up my mind to sign it, though I will do so reluctantly," said Polk. He added he intended to explain his action in a message to the House.

Calhoun insisted the bill was unconstitutional.

Polk rejected that argument. Congress, he noted, had restricted slavery on numerous occasions in the past. This question, he said, affected "the very existence of the Union," and politicians should yield individual opinions in deference to actions by their predecessors.

Polk said he had been willing to accept either the Missouri Compromise language or the Clayton approach (which, he noted pointedly, Calhoun had voted for). Both had failed. So how could he now veto the Oregon bill, "inasmuch as all the territory of Oregon lay North of the Missouri compromise line"? Previous efforts to establish an Oregon territorial government in 1844 and 1846 had passed the House with slavery restrictions, he noted, and had garnered numerous southern votes. And nearly every territorial bill before the present Congress had contained the slavery restriction for Oregon and yet had collected southern votes.

"These Bills contained provisions of compromise also," replied Calhoun.

"That fact did not change a constitutional principle," retorted Polk.

Oregon desperately needed a government, he said, and its location north of 36°30' precluded any reasonable objection on the part of the South. Besides, if he were to veto the bill "in the present excited state of Congress & of the public mind, I should do more to inflame that excitement & to array the country into geographical parties and to rend the Union, than any act which [has] ever been done by any President or any man in the country."

The next morning, the final day of the congressional session, Polk went to the Capitol to sign bills before the designated noon adjournment. As he signed legislation in the ornate vice president's room, Calhoun entered and sought out John Mason for an animated private conversation over in a corner. Mason then approached Polk to say the South Carolinian wished to speak with him.

Clutching a piece of legislation that needed signing, Polk stepped hastily to Calhoun. The senator argued against any presidential message on the Oregon bill. The president brusquely rejected the suggestion, returned to his table, and signed both the Oregon bill and his message.

Precisely at noon, both houses adjourned, and Polk returned to the White House to receive members of Congress who wished to express farewell sentiments before returning to their districts.

Later the president sat back to savor a moment of rest. He was "heartily rejoiced" that the long congressional session was over, but he felt spent and weak. It occurred to him that he hadn't been more than two or three miles away from the White House in some thirteen months. The next day he told the cabinet he planned a ten-day vacation at a resort in Bedford Springs, Pennsylvania.

Polk was disappointed that Sarah couldn't join him because of previous social commitments; she had invited a collection of family members for an extended White House stay. But the president would be joined by his brother and other family members, as well as William Day, a "free man of colour," who had served as Polk's faithful servant throughout his presidency. Along the way, at a halfway house where the party procured fresh horses for the luxurious presidential coach, Polk engaged a number of farmers who had congregated in hopes of shaking his hand. A voluble man named Cisney proudly told Polk the region was as solidly Democratic as any area of the country. At one nearby polling place, he said, Polk and Dallas had received 192 votes out of 208 cast. Cisney and his friends struck Polk as "honest farmers."

Cisney asked Polk to stop by to see his eighty-eight-year-old brother a mile or so up the road, but the presidential party arrived at the brother's farmhouse to discover the lifelong Democrat was away visiting a nearby "squire." When the man's distraught wife said he would be "almost beside himself" to learn he had missed a chance to shake Polk's hand, the president promised to stop by on his return trip.

Polk's stay at Bedford Springs was just what he needed. The walkways and grounds of the resort were tidy and well shaded, and the establishment exuded an appearance of comfort and luxury. He walked into the nearby mountains, drank the spring water, and visited with local citizens, who asked for nothing and hence endeared themselves to him particularly in comparison with the despised office seekers back in Washington. On the return trip he took pains to stop at the farmhouse of the old Mr. Cisney, whom he found to be a "remarkable person." He arrived back in Washington on August 29.

With Congress out of session and the election campaign absorbing national attention, the crush of official business subsided. Still, Polk didn't know how to relax. On September 23 he noted to his diary that most of his cabinet had been away from Washington since the end of the congressional session. But, he added with a touch of pride, he had become so familiar with the duties and workings of the government—"not only upon general principles, but in most of its minute details"—that he had little difficulty in governing even without the cabinet.

A few weeks later, on November 2, he penned a birthday entry into his diary. "Upon each recurrence of my birthday," he wrote, "I am solemnly impressed with the vanity & emptiness of worldly honors and worldly enjoyments." He noted he had lived about three fourths of the time allotted most men. "I have filled the highest station on earth," he wrote, "but I will soon go the way of all the earth. I pray God to prepare me to meet the great event."

For most Americans, the looming event of greatest interest was the election on November 7. And now, with the transformation wrought by Samuel Morse's magnetic wires, the results from far-flung corners of the country could be flashed to New York or Baltimore or Washington in record time. Within a day of the polls closing, Polk got word that the likely winner was Zachary Taylor. The news hit Polk like a blow to the temple. He viewed Taylor as a limited man of no opinions and little judgment whose presidency would be dominated by Federalist power grabbers bent on reversing the entire Polk agenda.

But the *National Intelligencer* crowed that Taylor's victory "will revive the heroic age of the republic." History, said the *Intelligencer*, produced two classes of military men—those brilliant on the battlefield but unfit for much else; and those few who, "in their military conduct display, like Washington, *eminent civic endowments*." Zachary Taylor, said the paper, belonged to the latter class. This was ridiculous, and *Intelligencer* editor Joseph Gales probably knew it. But it was natural that the Whig victory would generate flights of rhetorical rapture on the part of those who had been so long in the political wilderness.

When the final votes were counted, Taylor received 47.3 percent of the popular vote to Cass's 42.5 percent and Van Buren's 10.1 percent. Detailed analyses of the vote totals indicated Van Buren's candidacy probably didn't affect the outcome. But the results constituted a warning sign for Democrats. More than 80 percent of the Free Soil vote in New York, New Jersey, and Pennsylvania came from former Democrats disaffected by their party's nominee and his opposition to the Wilmot Proviso. The Free Soil insurrection probably didn't destroy the Democratic Party's Cass wing, as Free Soil strategists had planned, or create a hapless Whig administration that would be vulnerable to Free Soil attacks in 1852. But both of those things had happened anyway, and that was enough to keep the Free Soil agitators going.

On December 5, when Congress reconvened, James Polk was ready with his final Annual Message, which was sent to both legislative houses on the first day of the session. The message explained and defended all the principles and policies that had animated Polk's party since the earliest days of Jackson. The party's tariff policies, said the president, had brought prosperity and ample funds into federal coffers, while the independent treasury had stabilized the currency. But he particularly extolled his expansionist successes. "It would be difficult," he wrote, "to calculate the value of these immense additions to our territorial possessions." And America now was positioned to dominate the Pacific. The powers of Europe, far removed from that ocean, he said, "can never successfully compete with the United States in the rich and extensive commerce which is opened to us."

He presented an impassioned argument for settling the territorial question through some version of the Missouri Compromise or Clayton's judicial approach. But he firmly denied the right of Congress to interfere with any slavery policies that might emerge south of 36°30'. And he urged Congress to dispose of the issue quickly because the people of California and New Mexico were crying out for governmental protection.

In fact, Polk harbored private fears that those rich territories could be lost if Congress didn't move quickly to establish governments there. Particularly in California, which was experiencing a massive influx of immigrants drawn by newly discovered gold fields, the lack of U.S. legal protections could stir the people to organize an independent government, perhaps beseeching Oregon to join them. That in turn could induce congressional Whigs to agitate for relinquishing the whole thing, thus protecting Taylor from the ravages of Wilmot Proviso agitations. At the December 12 cabinet meeting, Polk outlined these fears and his hopes for a compromise plan that empowered territorial inhabitants to deal with slavery as they desired.

The congressional session unfolded, alas, much like the previous session, with plenty of agitation and no discernible consensus on how to handle the intractable slavery issue. And the Barnburners intensified their antislavery exhortations throughout the North and West. In mid-December, John Van Buren, the former president's quarrelsome son, attended a public White House reception, thus surprising Polk and irritating Sarah. So aghast was she at the young man's famous arrogance that she repeatedly had stricken his name from White House dinner invitation lists. At one point she had actually burned an invitation addressed to him, an uncharacteristic act of pique that had stirred her husband's amusement. Now young Van Buren was crisscrossing the country, attacking Polk in bellicose language and extolling the Free Soil advocacy of his father. Yet there he was in the president's house, enjoying his refreshments. "I, of course," wrote Polk to his diary, "treated him courteously in my own parlour."

The slavery agitations in Congress were looking increasingly ominous. The House in rapid succession passed a resolution instructing the Committee on Territories to report a bill excluding slavery from New Mexico and California; then passed a resolution instructing the Committee on the District of Columbia to report a bill abolishing the slave trade in the District; then cast 79 votes for a Joshua Giddings resolution calling for a poll of all District residents, including slaves, on the question of whether slavery should be abolished there.

Stung by these agitations, angry southerners in late December laid plans for a meeting aimed at producing a kind of southern manifesto on the slavery issue. Polk, despising both northern and southern agitators with equal vexation, began to feel a bit lonely in his effort to save the Union from this brewing civil strife. He considered such agitations wicked and reprehensible—the work of demagogues and political strivers who put their own ambitions ahead of the Union.

At dusk on December 22 he received a visit from a Tennessee congressman named James Thomas, who represented Polk's old House district. The young man wanted advice on how he should handle the southern meeting. He had declined to sign the statement calling for the meeting, he said, but was inclined to attend in order to assess the tenor of events. Polk gave Thomas the same counsel he later would give others—go ahead and attend such meetings for informational purposes but refrain from signing anything or participating in any way. The *Union* later reported that sixty-eight members of Congress attended the meeting, which called for a series of resolutions to be drafted for discussion at a subsequent gathering on January 15.

All this crystallized the political reality facing Polk. As the president explained it to Stephen Douglas, no territorial bill could pass the House without the Wilmot Proviso. But, if he should get a bill applying the proviso to territory below 36°30', he would have to veto it. That of course would set off a firestorm of agitation throughout the country. On the other hand, said Polk, legislation granting immediate statehood to California might pass without the proviso. Thus, he urged Douglas, chairman of the Committee on Territories, to craft such legislation for California while taking a territorial approach to New Mexico. If the Wilmot agitation delayed action on New Mexico, Polk reasoned, that would be less troublesome because New Mexico, being an interior region, would be less likely to break off from the United States in frustration.

On Christmas Day, Polk enjoyed one of the most peaceful days of his term. Outside it was damp and gloomy, but inside the White House fires burned warmly, and only two visitors called. When Sarah and visiting family members went off to church, the president sat down to produce a message to the House in response to calls for official documents related to wartime import levies in Mexico. He enjoyed the work and particularly the fact that he was under no time pressure to complete it.

But the slavery turmoil was never far from his mind. On January 14, Polk heard that Calhoun had spearheaded an address of the southern states, to be put before the delegates at the next day's scheduled meeting. It warned of dire consequences for the South if the North should gain the power to monopolize the territories and, with that power, the force to "emancipate our slaves under color of an amendment to the Constitution." The South would be destroyed, warned Calhoun, but not without a bitter and bloody war between the sections because the South would resist "without looking to consequences."

It was not an address designed to unite the eighty southerners who gathered in the Senate chamber for the January 15 meeting, and most Whigs and some Democrats refused to sign a document dripping so baldly with warnings of disunion. This was precisely what Polk did not want to see. Now, he feared, the division among southerners would encourage northern abolitionists to step up what Polk considered their assault on southern rights.

The next day Calhoun appeared at the White House, obsessed with the imperative that southerners resist "the aggressions of the North upon their rights." The two longtime adversaries reprised the arguments they had hurled at each other for years. When Polk outlined his delicate strategy for bringing California into the Union as a state, Calhoun would have none of it. But, if California could be admitted as a state, said Polk, "the whole difficulty would be settled, and . . . the Free-soil agitators or abolitionists of the North would be prostrate and powerless . . . the country would be quieted, and the Union preserved." Calhoun dismissed all this "in excited terms" and insisted that slavery must be allowed into territories below 36°30'.

The discussion reflected the growing despair surrounding the issue. Polk urged his southern friends to unite behind his plan for California statehood as a means of settling the slavery question and neutralizing northern abolitionists. Repeatedly he emphasized his devotion to the Union and his opposition to any movement that could disturb its harmony. He urged members to pursue solutions in Congress and not in caucuses such as the southern meeting. But it was clear that many members preferred agitation to compromise. And all congressional actions aimed at settling the issue seemed to be sputtering, while Whig calls for abandoning the territories altogether were gaining currency. Dining with Rhode Island's Whig senator John Clarke on January 18, Polk expressed concerns about losing California.

"Let her go," replied the senator.

On February 24, Zachary Taylor arrived in town and took up residence at Willard's Hotel a couple blocks east of the White House. He sent word that he would call on Polk on February 26. At the appointed hour he arrived, along with an entourage that included Senator Clayton, designated as his secretary of state, and Mississippi senator Jefferson Davis, his son-in-law. Mrs. Polk joined the group in the White House parlor, along with other family members and Supreme Court Justice John Catron. The half-hour meeting was marked by "courtesy and cordiality," as Polk expressed it. The president, like others encountering the general for the first time, found him an unprepossessing man—as one visitor to Willard's later reported, "the plain, respectable, painstaking ordinary citizen." Polk invited the president-elect to a White House dinner on March 1, and the general avidly accepted.

The dinner was a grand affair for about forty guests, including

Lewis Cass, Vice President—elect Millard Fillmore, Senators James Pearce of Maryland and John Bell of Tennessee, the *Union*'s Thomas Ritchie, and all members of the cabinet along with the wives of Walker, Marcy, and the new attorney general, Isaac Toucey. Polk seated Taylor between Mrs. Polk and his erstwhile rival, Senator Cass. The food was French and the conversation casual. "Not the slightest allusion was made to any political subject," Polk reported later. The party broke up around eleven o'clock.

On March 3, Polk accepted the resignations of his cabinet members, then devoted himself, as he later expressed it, to "all the business on my table down to the minutest detail and at the close of the day left a clean table for my successor." At dusk he departed the White House for the last time, took up temporary lodgings at the Irving Hotel, then proceeded to the Capitol for the traditional end-of-session bill signing. He was prepared to veto any "internal improvement" bills of the kind beloved by Henry Clay, but no such legislation reached final passage. He had with him also a veto message to accompany any necessary rejection of the Wilmot Proviso if Congress applied it to lands south of the Missouri Compromise line.

No such veto message was necessary, however, as Congress proved unable to pass a territorial bill with or without the proviso. The outcome remained in doubt late into the night, and Polk became particularly agitated by a last-ditch effort by proviso forces to attach an amendment to the territorial bill that would have retained in force all Mexican laws applying to New Mexico and California at the time of U.S. acquisition. Since Mexico had outlawed slavery, that prohibition would have carried forward for both territories. After extensive discussions with his cabinet, Polk resolved to veto that measure should it get into any final legislation.

It didn't, although it generated tremendous angst and anger among southerners and fiery debate into the night. Polk, weary and feeling a bit put upon, left the Capitol at nearly four o'clock the morning of March 4. At six a congressional delegation arrived with two bills for his signature—an appropriations measure and a default bill extending U.S. revenue laws over California and New Mexico. There would be no territorial governments established for those newly acquired lands. The matter was out of Polk's hands forever.

Later the president and Mrs. Polk attended their last services at the First Presbyterian Church, where congregants gathered around them afterward in a gesture of affectionate friendship and farewell. James and Sarah spent a mellow evening at the Irving, receiving friends and preparing for the next day's inaugural ceremony. "I feel exceedingly relieved that I am now free from all public cares," Polk wrote that night before retiring.

March 5 dawned blustery and chilly, but the skies were blue, and there would be no rains this year to dampen the inaugural proceedings. Taylor's open carriage, escorted by a hundred mounted marshals, arrived at the Irving Hotel around eleven-thirty that morning, and Polk joined the carriage party, including the president-elect, the Washington mayor, and outgoing Speaker Robert Winthrop. Polk was seated, according to protocol, to Taylor's right. He was shocked to hear Taylor express the view, during the ride up Pennsylvania Avenue, that California and New Mexico were so distant from the rest of the United States that it would perhaps be better if they were to become independent states. "Gen'l Taylor is, I have no doubt," Polk wrote later, "a well meaning old man. He is, however, uneducated, exceedingly ignorant of public affairs, and, I should judge, of very ordinary capacity."

After the procession reached the Capitol, Polk and Taylor entered the Senate chamber to solemn ceremonial silence. "They said nothing," reported the *Union*, "except a few private remarks to the gentlemen around them, after they had taken their seats." Then they and their entourage were escorted to the Capitol's east portico, looming before some ten thousand spectators and enthusiasts.

Taylor's speech was characterized by one observer as "remarkable only for its brevity, simplicity, good idiomatic English, and the absence of great promises in high sounding phrases." The *Union* said it consisted of "common-place, non-commital generalities" and gave off a whiff of being "ultra whig." In truth, its greatest mark of distinction was its lack of any mention whatever of the slavery crisis then enveloping the nation.

James and Sarah Polk wasted no time in fleeing the cares and controversies of Washington. Around midnight they boarded the steamboat that would take them to New Orleans, thence up the Mississippi River toward Nashville, where the ex-president planned to take up residence in the spacious home once owned by his early mentor, Felix Grundy. The boat left at three on the morning of March 6, and the Polks departed Washington with the expectation that they would never see it again.

During the trip Polk's health, never robust and particularly wan in recent months, began to deteriorate further. He suffered from chronic diarrhea and fatigue throughout much of the journey. Once in Nashville, as he set about the task of renovating and refurbishing the Grundy mansion, he seemed to improve a bit. But then his home labors caused a relapse. With fatalist stoicism he accepted his looming death, was baptized by a Methodist minister, and completely embraced Christianity for the first time in his life. On June 15, 1849, at age fifty-three, he died peacefully in his bed.

EPILOGUE: LEGACY

The Price of Presidential Accomplishment

WHEN NEWS REACHED Washington of James Polk's unexpected and early death, President Taylor ordered a suspension of all public business in the capital. But Taylor's order took on a measured and essentially ungenerous tone. The new president employed neutral language, without praise, in calling upon the nation "to mourn the loss of one, the recollection of whose long services in its councils will be forever preserved in the tablets of history."

Thus did the controversies that dogged James Polk during his lifetime follow him into death. Democratic newspapers naturally expressed unabashed veneration. The *Baltimore Clipper* called upon Americans to "unite in according to him sincere honesty of purpose, elevated patriotism, and lofty aspirations for the promotion and welfare of his country. As a man and a Christian, he was without blemish, and as a statesman, honest and pure." And the *Baltimore Sun,* proudly neutral in its politics, predicted Polk's period of leadership "will be recorded as one of the most brilliant in the annals of the nation—an epoch fraught with influences so great and important that they will be felt upon this continent and throughout the world till the last syllable of recorded time."

But that bastion of Whig passion, the *New York Evening Post*, noted it had viewed many of Polk's actions "in terms of reprobation, which we still think were fully deserved." The paper described the dead president as "very laborious" and added he had "little sensibility" and displayed "a low tone of character."

Those words stirred Ritchie's *Union* to note that, while even many ardent Whig newspapers were "bearing magnanimous testimony" to

Polk's private virtue and character, the *Post* proved itself "unable even under such circumstances, to control its savage temper." It added, "Surely, the viper should be shaken from the skirts of democracy."

When it comes to Polk's standing in history, the viper has never been far from the story. Many historians, like many of the man's contemporaries, have found him an easy mark, a natural target for criticism and repudiation. No doubt that has contributed to a certain paradox of Polk's reputation: Probably no other president presents such a chasm between actual accomplishment and popular recognition. Eugene Irving McCormac, whose two-volume Polk biography was published in 1922, pondered this paradox in noting that the country's eleventh president had remained largely "'forgotten' notwithstanding the fact that his tariff policy led to prosperity; that his 'constitutional treasury' proved to be successful; that his 'Polk Doctrine' [expounding U.S. resistance to European meddling in the affairs of the Western Hemisphere] has been approved and extended; and that his expansion policy added over five hundred thousand square miles of territory and gave the United States free access to the Pacific." McCormac adds that these successful policies were conceived largely by the president himself and brought to fruition through his own persistence and political deftness.

McCormac speculates that Polk's lack of personal magnetism and inability to pull large numbers of fond acolytes to his side contributed to his relative obscurity in later generations. Unlike other successful presidents, he had no appreciable personal following to breathe life into his story and promote his standing in history.

But McCormac also quotes an earlier historian, James Schouler, as suggesting Polk's reputation was undermined by the powerful crosscurrents of political emotion unleashed upon the nation by the slavery issue. As America slipped into the crucible of that irrepressible conflict, in large part through Polk's own expansionist zeal, his detractors found it easy and inviting to suggest his expansionism was in truth a conspiracy to extend slavery. This allegation, without foundation, has made its way into our time through lingering interpretations by various historians.

Leaving aside this false imputation, it seems reasonable to conclude the swirling forces of enmity that enveloped the nation over slavery simply swamped any reasoned consideration of Polk's presidential accomplishments. And then, in the wake of the bloody Civil War and its aftermath, there was little historical impetus to go back and rummage through events so overwhelmingly superseded by the subsequent conflagration.

No doubt all of this contributed to the paradox of Polk's popular standing—largely forgotten among Americans of later generations and yet highly rated by subsequent presidential historians. In his "Editor's Note" to John Seigenthaler's brief biography of Polk, the late Arthur M. Schlesinger, Jr., one of his generation's most noted historians, places Polk in a category of "forceful and persuasive presidents" that included Thomas Jefferson, Andrew Jackson, Theodore Roosevelt, and Ronald Reagan. These were men, said Schlesinger, who, even in the absence of first-order crisis, were "able to impose their own priorities on the country."

In 1948, when Schlesinger's father, Arthur M. Schlesinger, Sr., first polled noted scholars of American history on how they would rate the presidents, Polk ranked tenth—within the near-great category. The senior Schlesinger's subsequent 1962 poll of historians brought the Tennessean up to eighth place. An aggregate ranking of some twelve academic polls conducted since 1948 would place Polk at eleventh among all presidents, with a high of eighth and a low of fourteenth.

And yet, among American intellectuals Polk still generates abundant controversy down to our time in much the same way he did during his own presidency. Whereas the contemporary critics of John Adams, Thomas Jefferson, Abraham Lincoln, and the two Roosevelts exercise almost no lingering influence on those presidents' historical reputations, Polk's historical standing seems trapped in the arguments and controversies that swirled around him during his momentous White House years.

Thus, he is seen by many today as an imperialist manipulator who bent the truth and the nation's will to his questionable objectives. The Whig attacks on the man back in the 1840s continue to stalk his reputation some 160 years after his death—that he usurped illegitimate power to manufacture an unnecessary war; that he lied to the American people about the actual events that generated hostilities with Mexican troops; that he stole territory from a weaker nation lacking the resources to fight back; that he cast his nation into the role of international aggressor.

This view is widespread today. Former Democratic vice president Al Gore stated flatly in 2008, before a huge national television audience, that Polk's war had been "condemned by history." Historian John H. Schroeder, in a book about the war's critics, says the conflict emerged from "dubious beginnings and questionable motives." When a documentary producer named Sylvia Komatsu sought to produce a public-television film on the "U.S.-Mexican War" in 1998, the subject generated so much controversy that normally generous corporations declined to back the project for fear of getting caught in an ideological crossfire. One adviser to the effort, Ron Tyler, director of the Texas State Historical Association, extolled the documentary for presenting the notion "that this is the War of Yankee aggression and to call it anything else is wrong."

Such critics also delight in quoting Polk's contemporary critics, particularly Lincoln and Ulysses S. Grant, a lieutenant in the war, who called it "the most unjust war ever waged by a stronger against a weaker nation. . . . an instance of a republic following the bad example of European monarchies."

This lingering sentiment is not surprising in a nation with a powerful strain of foreign policy liberalism—a philosophy that deprecates wars fought for national interest and glorifies those fought for humanitarian ideals. When the United States fought the Mexican War, it decisively chose national interest over humanitarianism, and that breeds still a sense of discomfort among some Americans.

The humanitarian critique of Polk's war is not without traces of truth. Every American war, including those of Woodrow Wilson and Franklin Roosevelt as well as those of Lyndon Johnson and George W. Bush, has generated its own special hypocrisy and presidential deceit. And James Polk certainly contributed his share to that historical record.

But the critics of Polk's war consistently ignore the role of Mexico in those momentous events. British historian Paul Johnson probably had it right when he wrote that, while America was hypocritical in its war policies, Mexico was "foolish" in its approach to its powerful neighbor. Polk wanted war because he wanted California, says Johnson, but he didn't want to start it. He adds, "The Mexicans played straight into his hands by allowing their pride to overcome their prudence."

Texas, after all, had won its independence honorably from a dictatorship far more brutal and threatening than the British rule tossed aside by the American colonists in their own Revolution some eighty years earlier. In winning their independence, the Texans arguably also won the right to define their own boundaries, as the Americans had done. For nine years the Republic of Texas had claimed the Rio Grande as its western border, and Mexico had made no effort throughout that time to take back that disputed land from a defiant nation far weaker than the United States.

Surely the United States possessed a right, according to international law, to treat with this new nation, widely recognized by countries throughout the world, based on that nation's own terms and its own self-definition. But Mexico said no, withdrew its ambassador, cut off relations with the United States, and declared Texas annexation an act of war. That clearly was tempting fate by any reckoning. Then Mexico fired the first shots, inflicted the first casualties, and dared the United States to accept this bloodletting as a natural and acceptable outcome of the dispute.

Then there was Mexico's truculence in the matter of reparations for U.S. citizens—and also Europeans—whose lives were menaced and fortunes destroyed by criminal actions on the part of Mexicans. Many historians have taken pains to brush aside the significance of this ongoing dispute between the two nations, but that effort seems misplaced. No self-respecting nation can allow such abuse of its citizens to continue indefinitely. Long before America took action, France had actually attacked Mexico to get redress, while Britain later accomplished the same outcome by threatening military reprisals.

Beyond that, the moralistic impulse, when applied to the Mexican War, misses a fundamental reality of history: It doesn't turn on moral pivots but on differentials of power, will, organization, and population. History moves forward with a crushing force and does not stop for niceties of moral suasion or concepts of political virtue. Mexico was a dysfunctional, unstable, weak nation whose population wasn't sufficient to control all the lands within its domain. The United States by contrast was a vibrant, expanding, exuberant experiment in democracy whose burgeoning population thrilled to the notion that it was engaging in something big and historically momentous. The resulting energy—demographic, military, philosophical—generated a political compulsion toward expansion into largely unpopulated lands that seemed to beckon with irresistible enticement.

Then, once the concept of Texas annexation entered the national consciousness with Tyler's 1844 initiative, this generalized exuberance and national self-confidence quickly transformed itself into a powerful vision. It was the vision of a new kind of nation the likes of which the world had never before known—a nation that straddled an entire continent, positioned to dominate the commerce of two oceans. With ribbons of rail beds, miles of telegraph lines, a population explosion, and the force of democratic rule, this actually seemed feasible for the first time. And America, then as now a country of vast designs, collectively embraced this heady vision of national destiny.

In that sense Polk was simply a product of his time and an instrument of the prevailing political sentiment. There were contemporary nay-sayers, of course—including two of the country's most influential and articulate politicians, Henry Clay and Martin Van Buren. But their opposition, though passionately and eloquently expressed, did not sway the electorate. Instead, the electorate cast both men aside.

And so it was left to Polk, with all of his limitations of temperament and leadership, to bring the vision to a reality, and he did so with a fire of purpose that transcended anything that had been articulated with any seriousness up to that time. By embracing the notion of acquiring not only Texas and Oregon but also California and New Mexico, Polk brought to his presidency imperatives of boldness, persistence, force of will, and guile that went beyond anything anyone had before seen in him. Yet he brought those traits to the fore in such a way as to accomplish all of his ambitious presidential aspirations. Therein lies whatever greatness he may claim to a place in history.

In any event, his legacy comes down to us in a number of forms, but particularly in the map outline of the continental United States, which is very close to what Polk bequeathed to his nation. The only difference is a 30,000-square-mile segment in southern Arizona and New Mexico acquired from Mexico in 1853 for $10 million—the so-called Gadsden Purchase—to allow for a southern railroad route across the United States. To look at that map, and to take in the western and southwestern expanse included in it, is to see the magnitude of Polk's presidential accomplishments.

It did not come easily or cheaply. It depleted the country's treasury and absorbed substantial blood of its young men. It unleashed civic forces that hadn't been foreseen and couldn't be controlled. It sapped his own political standing and his health. It exposed his personal lapses and his least impressive traits. It engulfed him in controversy that would diminish his place in his country's historical consciousness. But in the end he succeeded and fulfilled the vision and dream of his constituency. In a democratic system that is the ultimate measure of political success.

NOTES

ABBREVIATIONS AND SHORT CITES

AJ	Andrew Jackson
JKP	James K. Polk
JKP, *Diary* I, II, III, IV	*The Diary of James K. Polk During His Presidency, 1845–1849,* Vols. I–IV
McCormac, *Polk* I	Eugene Irving McCormac, *James K. Polk: A Political Biography to the Prelude of War, 1795–1845*
McCormac, *Polk* II	Eugene Irving McCormac, *James K. Polk: A Political Biography to the End of a Career, 1845–1849*
Remini, *Jackson* I	Robert V. Remini, *Andrew Jackson and the Course of American Empire, 1767–1821*
Remini, *Jackson* II	Robert V. Remini, *Andrew Jackson and the Course of American Freedom, 1822–1832*
Remini, *Jackson* III	Robert V. Remini, *Andrew Jackson and the Course of American Democracy, 1833–1845*
Sellers, *Jacksonian*	Charles Sellers, *James K. Polk, Jacksonian, 1795–1843*
Sellers, *Continentalist*	Charles Sellers, *James K. Polk, Continentalist, 1843–1846*

INTRODUCTION: RITUAL OF DEMOCRACY

PAGE

1 *roar of cannon:* "Inauguration of the American President," *Illustrated London News,* April 19, 1845, vol. 6, pp. 243–44, Library of Congress Web site.

1 *Coleman's:* "Inaugural Procession," *National Intelligencer,* March 5, 1845.

2 *"This nomination":* *National Intelligencer,* quoted in "The Presidential Ticket of the Democracy Completed," *Washington Globe,* May 30, 1844.

2 *"he would be":* Quoted in Charles Sellers, *James K. Polk, Continentalist, 1843–1846* (Princeton: Princeton University Press, 1966; reprinted: Nor-

walk, Conn.: Easton Press, 1987), pp. 191–92 in Easton version. Herein-after Sellers, *Continentalist.*

3 *suite:* Ibid., p. 192.

3 *charcoal sky:* "The Inauguration," *National Intelligencer,* March 5, 1845.

3 *"office seekers":* Ibid.

3 *pallets upon their floors:* Ibid.

3 *mile-and-a-half ride:* "Order of the Procession," *Daily Globe,* March 4, 1845.

3 *"a long line":* Quoted in *Illustrated London News.*

4 *chief marshal and his aides:* "Inaugural Procession," *National Intelligencer.*

4 *"young hickory":* "Inauguration of the American President," *Illustrated London News.*

4 *procession:* "Order of the Procession," *Daily Globe.*

4 *Adams declines:* John Quincy Adams, *Memoirs of John Quincy Adams: His Diary from 1795 to 1848,* Vol. XII (Philadelphia: J. B. Lippincott & Co., 1877), p. 178.

4 *"I mused":* Quoted in Paul C. Nagel, *John Quincy Adams: A Public Life, a Private Life* (Cambridge: Harvard University Press, 1997), p. 402.

4 *Military plumes:* Ibid.

4 *Senate called to order:* "The Inauguration, &c.," *Daily Globe,* March 4, 1845.

4 *galleries filled:* "The Inauguration," *National Intelligencer.*

5 *"elegant man":* Quoted in John Reed Bumgarner, *Sarah Childress Polk: A Biography of the Remarkable First Lady* (Jefferson, N.C.: McFarland, 1997), p. 56.

5 *"I am resolved":* Quoted in Sellers, *Continentalist,* p. 194.

5 *"The citizen":* Quoted in "The Inauguration, &c.," *Daily Globe.*

6 *"the most raving":* Quoted in Oliver Perry Chitwood, *John Tyler: Champion of the Old South* (Newtown, Conn.: American Political Biography Press, 2003; originally published: American Historical Association, 1939), p. 364.

8 *"this long-conceived":* Quoted in Sellers, *Continentalist,* 110.

8 *"Before answering":* Quoted in ibid., p. 126.

8 *"cheers of welcome":* "Inauguration of the American President," *Illustrated London News.*

8 *"looking well":* Ibid.

8 *Spanish appearance:* Bumgarner, *Sarah Childress Polk,* p. 23.

8 *"dresses with taste":* Quoted in Sellers, *Continentalist,* p. 193.

9 *gown of satin:* Bumgarner, *Sarah Childress Polk,* p. 57.

9 *"rather too showy":* Quoted in Sellers, *Continentalist,* p. 193.

9 *"to a large assemblage of umbrellas":* Adams, *Memoirs of John Quincy Adams,* Vol. XII, p. 179.

9 *protected from the rain:* "Inauguration of the American President," *Illustrated London News.*

9 *"to assume no powers":* James K. Polk, Inaugural Address, Avalon Project, Yale University Web site, www.yale.edu/lawweb/avalon.

10 *crafted by Amos Kendall:* Aaron V. Brown, letter to JKP, December 23, 1844, *Correspondence of James K. Polk,* Vol. VIII, *September–December 1844,* Wayne Cutler, Robert G. Hall II, and Jayne C. Defiore (eds.) (Knoxville: University of Tennessee Press, 1993), p. 456 (Kendall identified in notes, p. 459). Hereinafter *Correspondence* VIII.

10 *"I thank my god":* Quoted in Robert V. Remini, *Andrew Jackson and the Course of American Democracy, 1833–1845* (New York: Harper & Row, 1984), p. 508. Hereinafter Remini, *Jackson* III.

10 *"in a voice so firm":* "Order of the Procession," *Daily Globe.*

10 *more polite than enthusiastic:* "Inauguration of the American President," *Illustrated London News.*

10 *"I feel so truly rejoiced":* Roger B. Taney, letter to JKP, November 20, 1844, *Correspondence,* Vol. VIII, p. 338.

11 *"a richly gilt Bible":* "Inauguration of the American President," *Illustrated London News.*

11 *presented to Sarah Polk:* Bumgarner, *Sarah Childress Polk,* p. 58.

11 *"preserve, protect":* Michael Nelson (ed.), *Guide to the Presidency* (Washington, D.C.: Congressional Quarterly, 1989), p. 33.

11 *twenty-eight-gun salute:* "Order of the Procession," *Daily Globe.*

11 *at Tyler's right:* "Inauguration of the American President," *Illustrated London News.*

11 *"draggle-tail":* Adams, *Memoirs of John Quincy Adams,* Vol. XII, p. 179.

11 *greeted visitors:* Bumgarner, *Sarah Childress Polk,* p. 58.

11 *two inaugural balls:* Ibid.

11 *"deeply fringed":* Quoted in ibid.

11 *"but supped with the true-blue":* Adams, *Memoirs of John Quincy Adams,* Vol. XII, p. 179.

CHAPTER 1: YOUNG HICKORY

PAGE

13 *Beginning in summer 1717:* David Hackett Fischer, *Albion's Seed: Four British Folkways in America* (New York: Oxford University Press, 1989), pp. 605–782. The description of the borderland migrants comes from this work.

14 *"Extreme inequalities":* Ibid., p. 754.

14 *one to 2 percent:* Ibid., p. 613.

14 *Jackson as gentleman:* Ibid., p. 642.

14 *Undwin's descendants:* William R. Polk, *Polk's Folly: An American Family History* (New York: Doubleday, 2000), pp. 9–10.

14 *first of ten children:* Eugene Irving McCormac, *James K. Polk: A Political Biography to the Prelude of War, 1795–1845* (Newtown, Conn.: American Political Biography Press, 1995; originally published: University of California Press, 1922), p. 2. Hereinafter McCormac, *Polk* I.

14 *born November 2, 1795:* Ibid.

15 *Pollock:* William R. Polk, *Polk's Folly,* p. 10.

15 *five-hundred-mile journey:* John Seigenthaler, *James K. Polk* (New York: Times Books, 2003), p. 18.

15 *path of betterment:* Ibid., p. 17.

15 *a thousand acres:* William R. Polk, *Polk's Folly,* p. 157.

15 *ninety-two grandchildren:* Ibid.

15 *weak and sickly:* McCormac, *Polk* I, pp. 2–3.

16 *urinary stones:* Seigenthaler, *James K. Polk,* pp. 19–20.

16 *"diligent in his studies":* Quoted in McCormac, *Polk* I, p. 3.

16 *"literary merit":* Quoted in ibid.

16 *first honors:* McCormac, *Polk* I, p. 4.

17 *studied law under Felix Grundy:* Seigenthaler, *James K. Polk,* p. 23.

17 *"She's beautiful":* Quoted in Bumgarner, *Sarah Childress Polk,* p. 24.

17 *"Why, of course I do":* Quoted in ibid.

17 *"The one who will never":* Quoted in ibid., p. 25.

18 *congressional seat:* McCormac, *Polk* I, p. 6.

18 *game of intrigue:* Robert V. Remini, *Henry Clay: Statesman for the Union* (New York: W. W. Norton, 1991), p. 58.

18 *deadly serious business:* Ibid.

19 *Clay loved the legislative game:* Ibid., pp. 58, 64.

19 *Jackson hated the ceaseless debates:* H. W. Brands, *Andrew Jackson: His Life and Times* (New York: Doubleday, 2005), p. 96.

19 *Jackson born 1767:* Marquis James, *The Life of Andrew Jackson* (Garden City, N.Y.: Garden City Publishing, 1940), p. 10.

19 *moved in with the Crawfords:* Ibid.

19 *early childhood:* Brands, *Andrew Jackson,* pp. 17–18.

20 *almost no formal schooling:* Ibid., p. 18.

20 *Tarleton's Raiders:* Ibid., pp. 22–24.

20 *courier and scout:* Ibid., p. 24.

20 *cousin killed:* Ibid., p. 25.

20 *sword incident:* James, *The Life of Andrew Jackson,* pp. 25–26.

20 *lost his brothers and mother:* Ibid., pp. 28–29.

20 *apprenticed in the law:* Brands, *Andrew Jackson,* p. 36.

20 *wild young man:* Ibid., p. 37.

20 *gaze of his eyes:* Ibid., p. 40.

20 *"a kind of majesty":* Quoted in ibid., p. 41.

20 *first congressman:* Brands, *Andrew Jackson,* p. 79.

20 *senator:* Ibid., p. 82.

21 *importance of militia:* Ibid., p. 61.

21 *Old Hickory nickname:* Robert V. Remini, *Andrew Jackson and the Course of American Empire, 1767–1821* (New York: Harper & Row, 1977), pp. 171–79. Hereinafter Remini, *Jackson* I.

21 *Jackson thwarts a mutiny:* Ibid., pp. 200–201.

21 *2,037 British casualties:* Ibid., p. 285.

21 *thirteen killed:* Ibid.

22 *Clay born 1777:* Bernard Mayo, *Henry Clay: Spokesman of the New West* (Boston: Houghton Mifflin, 1937), p. 1.

22 *comfortable Virginia family:* Remini, *Henry Clay,* p. 3.

22 *early life:* Ibid.

22 *"I always relied":* Quoted in ibid., p. 6.

22 *secretary to George Wythe:* Remini, *Henry Clay,* p. 9.

23 *indulgence with women:* Ibid., pp. 47, 51, 239, 251, 650.

23 *"Yes, and you seem resolved":* Quoted in ibid., p. 11.

23 *early career: Biographical Directory of the American Congress, 1774–1996* (Washington, D.C.: Congressional Quarterly, 1997), p. 825.

23 *Clay heading off to bed:* Remini, *Henry Clay,* p. 109.

23 *"savior of his country":* Quoted in ibid., p. 192.

24 *"Even the outer entries":* Quoted in ibid., p. 162.

24 *"Beware":* Quoted in Merrill D. Peterson, *The Great Triumvirate: Webster, Clay, and Calhoun* (New York: Oxford University Press, 1987), p. 56.

24 *"His opposition":* Adams, *Memoirs of John Quincy Adams,* Vol. IV, p. 243.

24 *February 17, 1825:* Remini, *Henry Clay,* p. 268.

24 *Clay had even rebuffed:* Ibid., pp. 259–60, 271.

25 *four of six presidents:* Brands, *Andrew Jackson,* p. 394.

25 *Jackson at Gadsby's:* Robert V. Remini, *Andrew Jackson and the Course of American Freedom, 1822–1832* (New York: Harper & Row, 1981), p. 84. Hereinafter Remini, *Jackson* II.

25 *Old General received the news:* Ibid., p. 98.

25 *"So you see":* Quoted in ibid.

25 *"When we behold":* Quoted in ibid.

25 *"shudder for the liberty"*: Quoted in ibid.

25 *1824 popular vote*: Brands, *Andrew Jackson,* p. 382.

25 *1824 electoral vote*: Nelson (ed.), *Guide to the Presidency,* p. 1406.

25 *"I cannot believe"*: Quoted in Remini, *Henry Clay,* p. 253.

26 *"cheating," "corruption," and "bribery"*: Quoted in ibid., p. 269.

26 *"Your speech"*: AJ to JKP, May 3, 1826, *Correspondence of James K. Polk,* Vol. I, Herbert Weaver and Paul H. Bergeron (eds.) (Nashville: Vanderbilt University Press, 1968), p. 41. Hereinafter *Correspondence* I.

26 *"I feel greatly obliged"*: AJ to JKP, December 4 [24?], 1826, ibid. Jackson dated the letter December 4, but events described show that he misdated it.

26 *JKP's reelection*: Seigenthaler, *James K. Polk,* p. 169.

26 *"It was a great triumph"*: JKP to Alfred Flournoy, December 6, 1827, *Correspondence* I, p. 100.

27 *Sarah's dismay*: Bumgarner, *Sarah Childress Polk,* pp. 27–28.

27 *Sarah as helpmate*: Walter R. Borneman, *Polk: The Man Who Transformed the Presidency and America* (New York: Random House, 2008), p. 26.

27 *Sarah in the House gallery*: Bumgarner, *Sarah Childress Polk,* p. 31.

27 *Sarah's stamina during travels*: JKP, letter to John Coffee, November 27, 1832, *Correspondence* I, p. 537.

27 *murder, adultery, etc.*: Seigenthaler, *James K. Polk,* p. 40.

27 *One particularly vicious handbill*: Ibid., p. 41; JKP to AJ, March 3, 1828, April 13, 1828, *Correspondence* I, pp. 169, 175.

27 *"Treat every thing"*: JKP to AJ, September 8, 1828, ibid., p. 196.

27 *"My friend Col Polk's"*: Ibid., p. 198n.

28 *"I receive my Dr. Sir"*: AJ to JKP, September 16, 1828, ibid., p. 200.

28 *transformation in presidential politics*: Michael F. Holt, *The Rise and Fall of the American Whig Party: Jacksonian Politics and the Onset of the Civil War* (New York: Oxford University Press, 1999), p. 8.

28 *a new political alignment*: Ibid., p. 7.

29 *Jackson and Adams vote totals*: Nelson (ed.), *Guide to the Presidency,* p. 1439.

29 *Democrats sweep Congress*: Mary Cohn (ed.), *Congressional Quarterly's Guide to Congress,* 4th edition (Washington, D.C.: Congressional Quarterly, 1991), p. 95-A.

29 *"await my allotted time"*: Quoted in Nagel, *John Quincy Adams,* p. 305.

29 *"I yet think"*: Quoted in Remini, *Henry Clay,* p. 335.

29 *"I would humbly prostrate"*: Quoted in ibid., p. 334.

29 *"We must but passively await"*: Quoted in Holt, *The Rise and Fall of the American Whig Party,* p. 10.

29 *"Everything valuable"*: Quoted in Claude G. Bowers, *The Party Battles of the Jackson Period* (Boston: Houghton Mifflin, 1922), p. 171.

30 *Isaac Hill episode:* Ibid., p. 87.

30 *Van Buren episode:* Ibid., pp. 177–81.

30 *"You have broken a Minister":* Quoted in ibid., p. 181.

30 *"His preference for the useful":* "The Democratic Nominees: James K. Polk," *Daily Globe*, June 1, 1844, reprinted from *Democratic Review*, May 1838.

CHAPTER 2: TENNESSEE AND WASHINGTON

PAGE

31 *May 27, 1830, veto:* Remini, *Jackson* II, p. 254.

31 *"prudent system of expenditure":* Quoted in ibid. All Jackson quotes on the Maysville Road episode come from this source.

32 *"the brilliant, resourceful, bitter":* Bowers, *The Party Battles of the Jackson Period*, p. 172.

32 *"and at times":* "The Democratic Nominees: James K. Polk," *Washington Globe*, June 1, 1844, reprinted from *Democratic Review*, May 1838.

32 *boardinghouse arrangements:* Anson Nelson and Fanny Nelson, *Sarah Childress Polk: Wife of the Eleventh President of the United States* (Newtown, Conn.: American Political Biography Press, 1994, originally published: Anson D. F. Randolph & Co., 1892), pp. 30–31.

32 *early housemates:* Ibid., p. 31.

33 *"Sarah, I wish you would not say that":* Quoted in ibid., p. 49.

33 *"That was the strongest rebuke":* Quoted in ibid.

33 *"Oh, why did you not go with me to-day":* Quoted in ibid. All quotes from this exchange are taken from this source.

33 *tying up the Maysville Road bill:* Seigenthaler, *James K. Polk*, p. 46.

33 *JKP helped draft message:* Remini, *Jackson* II, p. 253.

34 *"pronounced . . . that the people":* Quoted in Brands, *Andrew Jackson*, p. 403.

34 *public lands issue:* Bowers, *The Party Battles of the Jackson Period*, pp. 195–200.

35 *Second Bank of the United States corruption:* Remini, *Jackson* II, pp. 27–28.

36 *"hydra-headed monster":* Quoted in Remini, *Henry Clay*, p. 397.

36 *simple political calculus:* Holt, *The Rise and Fall of the American Whig Party*, p. 16.

36 *Biddle personality:* Bowers, *The Party Battles of the Jackson Period*, pp. 212–13.

36 *"Emperor Nicholas":* Ibid.

36 *On January 6, 1832:* Remini, *Jackson* II, p. 343.

36 *"Should Jackson veto it":* Quoted in Remini, *Henry Clay,* p. 398.

36 *"attack incessantly":* Thomas Hart Benton, *Thirty Years' View; or a History of the Working of the American Government from 1820 to 1850,* Vol. I (New York: D. Appleton & Co., 1854), p. 235.

36 *Benton commands congressional effort:* Remini, *Jackson* II, p. 362.

37 *Clayton's role:* Ibid.

37 *"the strongest speech of his congressional career":* Bowers, *The Party Battles of the Jackson Period,* p. 215.

37 *"rotten in the state of Denmark":* Quoted in McCormac, *Polk* I, p. 28.

37 *three reports:* Bowers, *The Party Battles of the Jackson Period,* p. 216.

37 *"I congratulate":* Quoted in Remini, *Jackson* II, p. 365.

37 *"chiefly the richest class":* AJ, *Veto Message Regarding the Bank of the United States, July 10, 1832,* The Avalon Project at Yale Law School, www.yale.edu. All quotes are taken from the veto address retrieved from this Web site.

38 *"Clay had unwittingly":* Bowers, *The Party Battles of the Jackson Period,* p. 227.

38 *"The bank":* Quoted in Brands, *Andrew Jackson,* p. 500.

39 *"a perversion":* Quoted in Remini, *Henry Clay,* p. 399.

39 *thirty thousand copies distributed:* Bowers, *The Party Battles of the Jackson Period,* p. 221.

39 *"It has all the fury":* Quoted in ibid.

39 *1832 election results:* Nelson (ed.), *Guide to the Presidency,* p. 1439.

39 *JKP to Ways and Means:* Remini, *Jackson* III, p. 118. Remini implies the Jackson men elevated JKP to Ways and Means chairman at the end of 1832 when in fact he was merely given a spot on the committee, as reflected in the *Biographical Directory of the American Congress,* pp. 1673, 143. Nevertheless, the citation reflects the influence of Jackson in congressional personnel decisions and his interest in positioning JKP for maximum value to his cause.

39 *"The Bank feels no vocation":* Quoted in Bowers, *The Party Battles of the Jackson Period,* p. 315.

39 *"the hydra of corruption":* AJ to JKP, December 16, 1832, *Correspondence* I, p. 575.

40 *document from Taney:* Roger B. Taney to JKP, January 3, 1833, *Correspondence of James K. Polk,* Vol. II, Herbert Weaver and Paul H. Bergeron (eds.) (Nashville: Vanderbilt University Press, 1972), p. 6. Hereinafter *Correspondence* II.

40 *"It is of the utmost importance":* Reuben M. Whitney to JKP, January 27, 1833, ibid., p. 54.

40 *"I communicate to you":* Reuben M. Whitney to JKP, February 11, 1833, ibid., p. 69.

40 *Verplanck report:* McCormac, *Polk* I, p. 31.

40 *JKP on the three percents:* Ibid., pp. 32–33.

41 *"When the President of the Bank":* Quoted in ibid., p. 33.

41 *"unauthorized and improper":* Quoted in ibid., p. 34.

41 *"are well apprised":* Andrew Jackson Donelson to JKP, May 30, 1833, *Correspondence* II, p. 80.

41 *"an angry and most violent contest":* JKP to Cave Johnson, June 20, 1833, ibid., p. 85.

41 *70 percent of the vote:* Seigenthaler, *James K. Polk*, p. 51.

41 *"small peep":* AJ to JKP, August 31, 1833, *Correspondence* II, p. 106.

42 *JKP becomes Ways and Means chairman:* Biographical Directory of the American Congress, pp. 1673, 143.

42 *Jackson stacks Ways and Means:* Remini, *Jackson* III, p. 119.

42 *two powerful documents:* McCormac, *Polk* I, p. 37.

42 *deft legislative maneuvering:* Ibid., pp. 37–38.

42 *"previous question":* AJ to JKP, December 18, 1833, *Correspondence* II, p. 182.

42 *debate rages for two months:* McCormac, *Polk* I, p. 39.

42 *"The committee cannot condemn":* Quoted in ibid., p. 43.

42 *broader Ways and Means report:* McCormac, *Polk* I, pp. 43–45.

42 *JKP bill clears House:* Ibid., p. 46.

42 *"perfectly irresistible":* "Mr. Polk's Bank Report," *Daily Globe,* March 6, 1833.

42 *"Polk for the hard service":* Quoted in McCormac, *Polk* I, p. 40.

43 *JKP loses speakership race:* Seigenthaler, *James K. Polk,* p. 170.

43 *Polk wins speakership:* Ibid., p. 56.

43 *"a test of the administration strength":* Benton, *Thirty Years' View,* Vol. I, p. 569.

43 *"The principal reason for this":* Exchange quoted in Bumgarner, *Sarah Childress Polk,* p. 41.

43 *Van Buren described:* Bowers, *The Party Battles of the Jackson Period,* pp. 55–57.

44 *"the Magician":* Remini, *Jackson* II, p. 41.

44 *Hugh Lawson White described:* Bowers, *The Party Battles of the Jackson Period,* pp. 427–28.

44 *Van Buren's victory margin:* Holt, *The Rise and Fall of the American Whig Party,* p. 45.

44 *"Jackson played the tyrant":* Quoted in Remini, *Jackson* II, p. 496.

44 *"I shall escape":* Quoted in ibid.

44 *White captures Tennessee:* Remini, *Jackson* II, p. 496.

45 *"a cycle of recession":* Holt, *The Rise and Fall of the American Whig Party,* p. 61.

45 *Specie Circular:* Seigenthaler, *James K. Polk,* pp. 58–59.

45 *"dead shot":* Quoted in ibid., p. 63.

45 *"a cancer on the body politic":* Quoted in ibid., p. 62.

46 *decision to run for governor:* McCormac, *Polk* I, p. 123.

46 *"the highest and most valued":* Quoted in ibid., p. 137.

46 *JKP's victory margin:* Seigenthaler, *James K. Polk,* p. 65.

46 *"genteel horse fanciers":* Charles Sellers, *James K. Polk, Jacksonian, 1795–1843* (Princeton: Princeton University Press, 1957; reprinted: Norwalk, Conn.: Easton Press, 1987), p. 378 in Easton version. Hereinafter Sellers, *Jacksonian.* The description of Polk's inauguration day, including Jackson's pronouncement of being *"mighty happy,"* comes from this source, pp. 378–80.

47 *"ridicule, sarcasm":* Quoted in Seigenthaler, *James K. Polk,* p. 67.

47 *"as the little fellow":* Quoted in McCormac, *Polk* I, p. 186.

47 *JKP loses by 3,243 votes:* Seigenthaler, *James K. Polk,* p. 67.

48 *JKP loses by 3,833 votes:* Ibid., p. 68.

CHAPTER 3: THE 1844 ELECTION

PAGE

49 *August 14, 1843:* Sellers, *Continentalist,* p. 3.

49 *sitting in retreat:* Ibid.

50 *"Mr. Polk, you and your friends":* Quoted in Nelson and Nelson, *Sarah Childress Polk,* p. 40.

50 *"What about the steamcar?":* Quoted in Bumgarner, *Sarah Childress Polk,* p. 47.

50 *new political developments:* Sellers, *Continentalist,* p. 16.

51 *yellow-brown eyes:* Bowers, *The Party Battles of the Jackson Period,* p. 92. (Bowers notes that in Jefferson Davis's *Memoirs,* Davis, who knew Calhoun well, describes his eyes as "yellow-brown.")

51 *"the great 'I am'":* Quoted in Sellers, *Continentalist,* p. 23.

51 *"He liked very much":* Quoted in ibid.

51 *"Vote for a Northern":* Quoted in Joel H. Silbey, *Martin Van Buren and the Emergence of American Popular Politics* (Lanham, Md.: Rowman & Littlefield, 2002), p. 104.

52 *Old Dick's background:* Sellers, *Continentalist,* p. 21.

52 *"the damndest political whore":* Quoted in ibid.

52 *Cass background:* "Biographical information," Lewis Cass Papers, William L. Clements Library, University of Michigan, www.clements.umich.edu.

52 *Cass physical description:* Sellers, *Continentalist,* plate VII.

52 *Cass avoided political identity:* Ibid., p. 22.

52 *"A hypocritical friend":* Quoted in ibid., p. 9.

53 *"capital error":* JKP, letter to Silas Wright, February 9, 1844, *Correspondence of James K. Polk,* Vol. VII, Wayne Cutler and James P. Cooper, Jr. (eds.) (Nashville: Vanderbilt University Press, 1989), p. 59. Hereinafter *Correspondence* VII.

53 *Nicholson ploy:* Sellers, *Continentalist,* pp. 9–10.

53 *Cave Johnson as young man:* "Cave Johnson, 1793–1866," *Tennessee Encyclopedia of History and Culture,* http://tennesseeencyclopedia.net.

53 *"the nuisance of the House":* Quoted in ibid.

53 *"when tangible rewards":* Sellers, *Continentalist,* p. 5.

54 *Laughlin persona:* Ibid.

54 *convention strategy:* J. G. M. Ramsey, letter to JKP, October 12, 1843, *Correspondence of James K. Polk,* Vol. VI, Wayne Cutler and Carese M. Parker (eds.) (Nashville: Vanderbilt University Press, 1983), p. 342. Hereinafter *Correspondence* VI.

55 *"If V. Buren, or his folks":* Quoted in Sellers, *Continentalist,* p. 12.

55 *Nicholson effort:* JKP, letter to Martin Van Buren, November 30, 1843, *Correspondence* VI, p. 364.

55 *convention endorsements:* McCormac, *Polk* I, p. 210.

55 *Polk controls delegates:* JKP, letter to Martin Van Buren, November 30, 1843, *Correspondence* VI, p. 364.

55 *"a few discontented members":* Ibid.

55 *"No explanations":* Martin Van Buren, letter to JKP, December 27, 1843, ibid., p. 395.

56 *contact with Silas Wright:* Cave Johnson, letter to JKP, December 9, 1843, ibid., p. 372.

56 *Johnson reports good news:* Ibid.

56 *"as if by accident":* Ibid.

56 *"bad aspect":* Ibid.

56 *This remarkable show of strength:* Ibid.

56 *Johnson reiterates his secondary interest:* Cave Johnson, letter to JKP, December 15, 1843, *Correspondence* VI, p. 377; JKP, letter to Andrew Jackson Donelson, December 20, 1843, ibid., p. 382.

56 *Calhoun withdraws:* John C. Calhoun, "Address of Mr. Calhoun to His Political Friends and Supporters," December 21, 1843, printed in the *Daily Globe,* February 2, 1844.

56 *"all the fragments of our party"*: Cave Johnson, letter to JKP, December 11, 1843, *Correspondence* VI, p. 376.

57 *"I think both the B's"*: Cave Johnson, letter to JKP, December 15, 1843, ibid., p. 378.

57 *"He regretted"*: Cave Johnson, letter to JKP, December 30, 1843, ibid., p. 400.

57 "Ohio *I regard to be the* pivot": JKP, letter to AJ, December 25, 1843, ibid., p. 393.

57 *"modestly couched"*: Samuel Laughlin, letter to JKP, January 1, 1844, *Correspondence* VII, p. 3.

57 *Ohio convention results:* Ibid., p. 20n.

57 *"It will not be the first time"*: JKP, letter to Samuel Laughlin, January 9, 1844, ibid., p. 20.

58 *"and can help the cause"*: "Amicus," "Communication. To the Editor of the Globe," *Daily Globe,* January 8, 1844.

58 *"How* could *Col. King"*: "A Tennessee Democrat," "Communication. To the Editor of the Globe," *Washington Globe,* January 15, 1844.

58 *"There is already"*: Cave Johnson, letter to JKP, January 13, 1844, *Correspondence* VII, p. 26.

59 *Polk's delicate position:* Ibid.

59 *"in good temper"*: Aaron Brown, letter to JKP, February 2, 1844, ibid., p. 51.

59 *"I deem this"*: JKP, letter to Cave Johnson, January 21, 1844, ibid., p. 42.

59 *Mississippi for Van Buren–Polk:* James M. Howry, letter to JKP, January 17, 1844, ibid., p. 32.

59 *statement proved worthless:* Sellers, *Continentalist,* p. 35.

59 *"has given us much trouble"*: JKP, letter to Silas Wright, February 9, 1844, ibid., p. 59.

59 *"regret"*: Ibid., p. 60.

59 *"I of course could have"*: Ibid.

60 *"frankness and confidence"*: Silas Wright, letter to JKP, February 27, 1844, ibid., p. 73.

60 *"A serious & earnest movement"*: Cave Johnson, letter to JKP, March 6, 1844, ibid., p. 79.

60 *"My own opinion"*: JKP, letter to Samuel Laughlin, March 7, 1844, ibid., p. 81.

60 *"Colo Polk is now encountering"*: Aaron Brown, letter to Sarah Polk, quoted in Sellers, *Continentalist,* p. 40.

61 *"There is a good deal"*: Ibid.

61 *"If Van was withdrawn"*: Cave Johnson, letter to JKP, March 7, 1844, *Correspondence* VII, p. 79.

62   *"any consolation":* Quoted in Holt, *The Rise and Fall of the American Whig Party,* p. 60.

62   *"There is everywhere":* Quoted in Remini, *Henry Clay,* p. 523.

62   *"Off in East Tennessee":* Incident recounted in ibid., p. 565.

63   *"Hurra for Jackson":* Incident recounted in ibid., p. 620.

63   *"the occupation of Oregon":* Quoted in ibid., p. 628.

63   *took to apologizing:* Remini, *Henry Clay,* p. 634.

CHAPTER 4: TEXAS

PAGE

65   *"The advantages of the* Princeton*":* Robert F. Stockton, "The Princeton," letter to *Daily Globe,* February 14, 1844.

65   *"more important results":* Ibid.

65   *"A nobler and a hardier man":* Quoted in Donald B. Webster, Jr., "The beauty and chivalry of the United States assembled . . . ," *American Heritage Magazine,* AmericanHeritage.com.

65   *February 28 cruise:* Benton, *Thirty Years' View,* Vol. II, p. 567.

66   *"great number of ladies":* Ibid.

66   *four hundred guests:* Ann Blackman, "Fatal Cruise of the Princeton," *Navy History,* www.military.com.

66   *cloudless sky:* Ibid.

66   *"sumptuous collation":* Benton, *Thirty Years' View,* Vol. II, p. 567.

66   *Benton repositions himself:* Ibid., p. 568.

66   *Explosion:* Ibid.

67   *Tyler's annexation plan:* Sellers, *Continentalist,* p. 52.

68   *either secession or annexation: Madisonian* position characterized in Elbert B. Smith, *Magnificent Missourian: The Life of Thomas Hart Benton* (Philadelphia: J. B. Lippincott, 1958), p. 192.

68   *"If the Union is to break":* Quoted in ibid.

68   *"the ripened pear":* Benton, "Texas and the United States: Letter from Senator Benton," *Washington Globe,* April 29, 1844.

68   *"on the part of some":* Benton, *Thirty Years' View,* Vol. II, pp. 582–83.

68   *cleanse the party of Calhoun:* Benton aim identified by Smith, *Magnificent Missourian,* p. 189.

69   *Crittenden's warning:* Remini, *Henry Clay,* p. 635.

70   *precise boundaries unknown:* "Territory to Statehood," a Web history of the Cabildo, Louisiana State Museum, http://lsm.crt.state.la.us/cabildo.

70   *"neutral strip":* Ibid.

70   *Adams treaty:* Samuel Flagg Bemis, *John Quincy Adams and the Foundations of American Foreign Policy* (New York: Alfred A. Knopf, 1949), p. 323.

70 *"a gratuitous and unaccountable sacrifice":* Benton, "Texas and the United States."

70 *a societal elite:* T. R. Fehrenbach, *Lone Star: A History of Texas and the Texans* (New York: Collier, 1968), p. 45.

71 *forty thousand inhabitants:* Joel H. Silbey, *Storm over Texas: The Annexation Controversy and the Road to Civil War* (New York: Oxford University Press, 2005), p. 7.

72 *Charles Elliot's plan:* Smith, *Magnificent Missourian,* p. 190.

72 *"open and honest efforts":* Quoted in Benton, *Thirty Years' View,* Vol. II, p. 607.

72 *Duff Green's private warning:* Smith, *Magnificent Missourian,* p. 191.

72 *"as an indemnity":* Quoted in Benton, *Thirty Years' View,* Vol. II, p. 606.

72 *Tyler's Texas hint:* Benton, *Thirty Years' View,* Vol. II, p. 599.

73 *"took fire at his words":* Ibid., p. 582.

73 *"the prosperity & permanent happiness":* Quoted in Remini, *Jackson* III, p. 493.

73 *Calhoun letter:* Described in Sellers, *Continentalist,* p. 59.

73 *"Texas bombshell":* Quoted in ibid.

74 *"I regard slavery":* Quoted in Remini, *Daniel Webster: The Man and His Time* (New York: W. W. Norton, 1997), p. 591.

74 *"With such a barrier":* AJ, untitled letter, reprinted in *Daily Globe,* March 20, 1844.

74 *Polk views solicited:* Salmon P. Chase, letter to JKP, March 30, 1844, *Correspondence* VII, p. 99.

75 *"I have no hesitation":* JKP, letter to Salmon P. Chase, April 23, 1844, ibid., p. 105.

75 *"a new element":* Henry Clay, "Mr. Clay's Letter," *National Intelligencer,* April 27, 1844.

76 *"so many of whom":* Martin Van Buren, "To the Editor of the Globe," *Daily Globe,* April 27, 1844.

77 *Democratic spirits had sunk:* Cave Johnson, letter to JKP, April 28, 1844, *Correspondence* VII, p. 110.

77 *"If Van Buren is to be thrown":* Cave Johnson, letter to JKP, April 30, 1844, ibid., p. 113.

78 *"Vans opponents":* Cave Johnson, letter to JKP, May 3, 1844, ibid., p. 116.

78 *"Texas is all now":* Quoted in Sellers, *Continentalist,* p. 66.

78 *"roars like a madman":* Quoted in ibid.

78 *Jackson wondered aloud:* Smith, *Magnificent Missourian,* p. 201.

78 *"a dead political Duck":* Quoted in James, *The Life of Andrew Jackson,* p. 768.

78 *"I knew Clay"*: Quoted in ibid. This Hermitage scene is taken entirely from this source.

79 *"I have shed tears"*: Quoted in Remini, *Jackson* III, p. 498.

79 *"impossible"*: Quoted in ibid.

79 *"I am particularly anxious"*: Andrew Jackson Donelson, letter to JKP, May 10, 1844, *Correspondence* VII, p. 131.

79 *"no difference on this subject"*: AJ, letter to the *Nashville Union*, reprinted in *Washington Globe*, May 27, 1844.

79 *"ruined"*: JKP, letter to Cave Johnson, May 14, 1844, *Correspondence* VII, p. 136. The Hermitage discussion is taken from this letter and also from JKP to Cave Johnson, May 15, 1844, *Correspondence* VII, p. 139.

80 *"This I do not expect"*: JKP to Cave Johnson, May 14, 1844, *Correspondence* VII, p. 137.

80 *"because you was known"*: Cave Johnson, letter to JKP, May 8, 1844, ibid., p. 125.

CHAPTER 5: BALTIMORE

81 *"You will find Pillow"*: JKP, letter to Cave Johnson, May 4, 1844, *Correspondence* VII, p. 119.

81 *"Whatever is desired"*: JKP, letter to Cave Johnson, May 15, 1844, ibid., p. 140.

81 *Pillow defends William Polk*: Sellers, *Continentalist*, p. 331; Borneman, *Polk*, p. 97.

82 *Pillow background and character*: Tennessee Encyclopedia of History and Culture, http://tennesseeencyclopedia.net.

82 *Pillow physical appearance*: Photo in ibid.

82 *"ridiculous"*: JKP, letter to Cave Johnson, May 15, 1844, *Correspondence* VII, p. 140.

82 *Pillow's Washington arrival*: Gideon Pillow, letter to JKP, May 22, 1844, ibid., p. 145.

83 *"If they continue"*: Ibid.

83 *"My great effort"*: Ibid.

83 *Jones and Johnson rebellion*: Gideon Pillow, letter to JKP, May 24, 1844, ibid., p. 151.

83 *"They . . . said that if Polks friends"*: Ibid.

83 *"I do not think V."*: Ibid., p. 152.

83 *"I would not still"*: Ibid.

84 *"I am satisfied"*: Gideon Pillow, letter to JKP, May 25, 1844, ibid., p. 155.

84 *"We of the south":* Ibid.

84 *convention opens:* "Democratic National Convention, Baltimore; May 27, 1844," *Daily Globe,* June 4, 1844.

84 "Resolved": Ibid.

84 *Walker described:* Sellers, *Continentalist,* p. 52; "History of the Treasury; Secretaries of the Treasury," http://www.ustreas.gov.

85 *"wheezy voice":* "History of the Treasury."

85 *"We were successful":* Robert J. Walker, convention speech, "Democratic National Convention, Baltimore; May 27, 1844," *Daily Globe.*

86 *"the well established usages":* Romulus Mitchell Saunders, convention speech, ibid.

86 *"Mr. Jefferson said":* Benjamin F. Butler, convention speech, ibid.

87 *"From what we can learn":* Cave Johnson, letter to JKP, May 27, 1844, *Correspondence* VII, p. 157.

88 *"so soon as we ascertain":* John W. Tibbatts, convention speech, "Democratic National Convention; Second Day," *Daily Globe,* June 5, 1844.

88 *"great applause":* "Democratic National Convention; Second Day," *Daily Globe.*

88 *roll call on two-thirds rule:* Ibid.

88 *nomination roll call votes:* Ibid.

89 *"the* damned rotten corrupt venal": Quoted in Sellers, *Continentalist,* p. 91.

89 *Miller motion:* "Democratic National Convention; Second Day," *Daily Globe.*

90 *"There is, I think":* Gideon Pillow, letter to JKP, May 28, 1844, *Correspondence* VII, p. 158.

90 *Bancroft's national fame:* "Biography of George Bancroft," http://www.2020site.org/literature.

91 *Bancroft seeks out Pillow:* George Bancroft, letter to JKP, July 6, 1844, *Correspondence* VII, p. 317.

91 *"it flashed on my mind":* Ibid. The rendition of Bancroft's convention activities is taken from this letter unless otherwise noted.

92 *eighth ballot unfolds:* "Democratic National Convention; Wednesday, May 29, 1844," *Daily Globe,* June 6, 1844.

93 *"the bosom friend":* Reah Frazer, convention speech, ibid.

93 *"brotherly affection":* Samuel Medary, convention speech, ibid.

93 *"The enthusiasm":* "Democratic National Convention; Wednesday, May 29, 1844," *Daily Globe.*

93 *"with a bleeding heart":* William Roane, convention speech, ibid.

93 *"Thunders of applause":* "Democratic National Convention; Wednesday, May 29, 1844," *Daily Globe.*

94 *"ties equal to those":* Butler, convention speech, ibid.

94 *"a continued and heartfelt burst":* Williamson Smith, letter to JKP, May 29, 1844, *Correspondence* VII, p. 165.

95 *"that our title":* Quoted in Sellers, *Continentalist,* p. 99.

Chapter 6: Polk vs. Clay

PAGE

96 *rumor reached Polk:* JKP, letter to Cave Johnson, June 8, 1844, *Correspondence* VII, p. 218.

96 *"I need scarcely say":* JKP, letter to Robert J. Walker, June 8, 1844, ibid., p. 221.

96 *"If the nomination":* JKP, letter to John K. Kane, June 8, 1844, ibid., p. 220.

96 *"I am under many personal":* JKP, letter to Cave Johnson, June 8, 1844, ibid., p. 218.

96 *"Are our Democratic friends":* Quoted in Remini, *Henry Clay,* p. 647.

96 *"It is a literal disbanding":* Quoted in Sellers, *Continentalist,* p. 101.

96 *"a farce":* Quoted in Holt, *The Rise and Fall of the American Whig Party,* p. 173.

96 *"I hardly believe":* Quoted in Sellers, *Continentalist,* p. 101.

96 *"Who is James K. Polk?":* Quoted in Holt, *The Rise and Fall of the American Whig Party,* p. 173.

97 *astute Whigs knew:* Sellers, *Continentalist,* p. 101.

97 *"one question":* Robert J. Walker, letter to JKP, May 30, 1844, *Correspondence* VII, p. 168.

98 *"He stood up all the time":* Andrew J. Donelson, letter to JKP, May 31, 1844, ibid., p. 169.

98 *"wanderers of 1840":* Robert J. Walker, letter to JKP, June 18, 1844, ibid., p. 263.

98 *"harmonize, as far as possible":* Ibid.

99 *"I am in favour":* JKP, letter to John K. Kane, June 19, 1844, ibid., p. 267.

99 *"Your discreet & well advised":* James Buchanan, letter to JKP, September 23, 1844, ibid., p. 109.

99 *"I have at all times":* Quoted in Sellers, *Continentalist,* p. 121.

100 *"Having declared the general principles":* JKP, letter to John W. Goode et al., September 25, 1844, *Correspondence* VIII, p. 123.

100 *"satisfactory nomination":* JKP, letter to AJ, August 3, 1844, *Correspondence* VII, p. 431.

100 *"The Whigs are aghast":* Albert Gallup, letter to JKP, September 5, 1844, *Correspondence* VIII, p. 24.

100 *Tyler's 150,000 supporters:* Robert J. Walker, letter to JKP, July 10, 1844, *Correspondence* VII, p. 337.

100 *Jackson writes to Mason:* Andrew J. Donelson, letter to JKP, July 1, 1844, ibid., p. 303 (explained in note p. 304).

101 *"a most disagreeable duty":* Robert J. Walker, letter to JKP, July 10, 1844, ibid., p. 337.

102 *"Mr Blair's columns":* George M. Dallas, letter to JKP, July 10, 1844, ibid., p. 332.

102 *"I know of none":* JKP, letter to Andrew J. Donelson, July 22, 1844, ibid., p. 379.

102 *"I wish the tone":* JKP, letter to AJ, July 22, 1844, ibid., p. 381.

102 *"I believe":* JKP, letter to Andrew J. Donelson, July 23, 1844, ibid., p. 384.

102 *"There is certainly no necessity":* JKP, letter to AJ, July 23, 1844, ibid., p. 388.

103 *"great want of common sense":* AJ, letter to JKP, July 26, 1844, ibid., p. 401.

103 "received as brethren": Quoted in Sellers, *Continentalist,* p. 136.

103 *"as to the proper course":* Quoted in Chitwood, *John Tyler,* p. 382.

103 *"I pray you":* Quoted in ibid.

103 *Tyler's* Madisonian *letter:* Chitwood, *John Tyler*, p. 382.

103 *"I need not say":* Aaron Brown, letter to JKP, May 30, 1844, *Correspondence* VII, p. 166.

104 *"I shall enter upon":* JKP, letter to Henry Hubbard et al., June 12, 1844, ibid., p. 241.

104 *"Upon every principle":* Silas Wright, Jr., letter to JKP, June 2, 1844, ibid., p. 184.

104 *"Texas excitement":* JKP, letter to Silas Wright, Jr., June 12, 1844, ibid., p. 245.

104 *"cheerfully and proudly":* Quoted in Sellers, *Continentalist,* p. 115.

105 *Van Buren's endorsement:* Sellers, *Continentalist,* p. 115.

105 *"a sort of rally":* Cave Johnson, letter to JKP, June 10, 1844, *Correspondence* VII, p. 228.

105 *"the war will go on":* Cave Johnson, letter to JKP, June 13, 1844, ibid., p. 248.

105 *southern convention gains:* Cave Johnson, letter to JKP, June 21, 1844, ibid., p. 270.

105 *Wright's warning:* Ibid.

106 *"Can not you see him":* Ibid.

106 *"I assure you":* AJ, letter to JKP, June 29, 1844, ibid., p. 299.

106 *Rhett's previous name: Biographical Directory of the American Congress,* p. 1724.

106 *"vain, self conceited":* Quoted in Sellers, *Continentalist,* p. 45.

107 *Pickens's visit:* Sellers, *Continentalist,* pp. 126–28.

107 "Everything is completely satisfactory": Quoted in ibid.

107 *"throw off the burthen":* Quoted in ibid.

108 *500,000 copies:* Sellers, *Continentalist,* pp. 128–29.

108 *"From all quarters":* AJ, letter to JKP, September 2, 1844, *Correspondence* VIII, p. 3.

109 *"Polk and Texas":* Quoted in Remini, *Henry Clay,* p. 659.

109 *"Personally":* Quoted in ibid.

109 *"national dishonor":* Quoted in ibid., p. 660.

109 *"an ugly letter":* Quoted in ibid.

109 *"I feel pretty tolerably angry":* Quoted in Peterson, *The Great Triumvirate,* p. 364.

110 *electoral results:* John L. Moore, Jon P. Preimesberger, and David R. Tarr (eds.), *Congressional Quarterly's Guide to U.S. Elections,* 4th edition, Vol. I (Washington: Congressional Quarterly, 2001), pp. 649, 732.

CHAPTER 7: THE VICTOR

PAGE

112 *a fast horseman:* Sellers, *Continentalist,* p. 157.

112 *"Reid of Louisville":* Robert Armstrong, letter to JKP, November 15, 1844, *Correspondence* VIII, p. 320.

112 *"I can say":* Quoted in Remini, *Jackson* III, p. 508.

113 *"and again and again":* "What Is to Be Anticipated from the Next Administration," *Daily Globe,* November 20, 1844.

113 *"the blow came":* National Intelligencer, quoted in ibid.

113 *"the general wreck":* Quoted in Remini, *Henry Clay,* p. 664.

113 *Senate ratification vote:* Silbey, *Storm over Texas,* p. 50.

114 *"We should . . . carefully distinguish":* Cave Johnson, letter to JKP, May 5, 1844, *Correspondence* VII, p. 122.

114 *Hermitage conference:* Sellers, *Continentalist,* pp. 165–67.

114 *"a hotter bed":* Quoted in ibid., p. 162.

114 *"if a 'rotten egg'":* Quoted in ibid.

115 *"I desire that you will accept":* JKP, letter to Silas Wright, Jr., December 7, 1844, *Correspondence* VIII, p. 410.

115 *"but tempered with moderation":* Aaron Brown, letter to JKP, December 9, 1844, ibid., p. 416.

115 *"no earthly probability":* Ibid.

115 *"I am not at liberty":* Silas Wright, Jr., letter to JKP, December 20, 1844, ibid., p. 446.

116 *"confidently anticipated"*: JKP, letter to Martin Van Buren, January 4, 1845, *Correspondence of James K. Polk,* Vol. IX, January–June 1845, Wayne Cutler and Robert G. Hall (eds.), (Knoxville: University of Tennessee Press, 1996), p. 19. Hereinafter *Correspondence* IX.

117 *"he will retire"*: Aaron Brown, letter to JKP, January 5, 1845, ibid., p. 24.

117 *"solemn pledge"*: Ibid., p. 22.

118 *"a marvel"*: Quoted in Sellers, *Continentalist,* p. 166.

118 *"reputation in this State"*: Martin Van Buren, letter to JKP, January 18, 1845, *Correspondence* IX, p. 54.

119 *Polk's initial cabinet*: Sellers, *Continentalist,* p. 184.

119 *"fearlessly carry out"*: Quoted in ibid.

119 *Polk's trip to Washington*: Sellers, *Continentalist,* pp. 189–91.

120 *"A controlling majority"*: John Tyler, Message to Congress, December 2, 1844, reprinted in *Daily Globe,* December 3, 1844.

121 *Milton Brown resolution*: Described in Silbey, *Storm over Texas,* p. 86; also, Holt, *The Rise and Fall of the American Whig Party,* p. 220.

121 *House vote on Brown resolution*: Holt, *The Rise and Fall of the American Whig Party,* p. 220.

121 *"We congratulate the democracy"*: "Vote Reannexing Texas as a State," *Daily Globe,* January 25, 1845.

121 *"weak and groundless pretexts"*: Benton speech, reprinted in Benton, *Thirty Years' View,* Vol. II, p. 605.

122 *"I shall not engage"*: Ibid., p. 620.

122 *"antagonistical"*: Aaron Brown, letter to JKP, December 23, 1844, *Correspondence* VIII, p. 458.

122 *Missouri General Assembly instructions*: Smith, *Magnificent Missourian,* p. 203.

122 *Benton's new approach*: Ibid.

122 *"just as fully"*: Quoted in ibid.

122 *support for Benton's approach evaporates*: Sellers, *Continentalist,* p. 189.

123 *Walker compromise*: Ibid., p. 205.

123 *"He is for Texas"*: Quoted in ibid.

123 *Butler works Dix*: Sellers, *Continentalist,* p. 206.

123 *Polk's new approach*: Ibid.

123 *Polk's refinement on Walker idea*: Ibid.

123 *"have the audacity"*: Quoted in ibid., p. 207.

124 *Senate vote*: Silbey, *Storm over Texas,* p. 87.

124 *"could not . . . accept"*: James Buchanan, letter to JKP, February 18, 1845, *Correspondence* IX, p. 115.

124 *Cave Johnson accepts*: Cave Johnson, letter to JKP, February 26, 1845, ibid., p. 139.

124 *Walker letter not sent:* JKP, letter to Robert Walker, February 19, 1845, unsent draft, Polk Papers, Library of Congress.

125 *cabinet shift:* Sellers, *Continentalist,* p. 196. Sellers's rendition of this chain of events, painstakingly pieced together from multiple fragments of evidence, is the most thorough to date.

125 *"great difficulties interposed":* JKP, letter to Martin Van Buren, February 22, 1845, *Correspondence* XI, p. 127.

125 *"distinguished individual":* Ibid.

125 *"Would you give":* Ibid.

125 *"I most sincerely hope":* JKP, letter to Benjamin F. Butler, February 25, 1845, ibid., p. 135.

125 *"domestic and prudential":* Benjamin F. Butler, letter to JKP, February 27, 1845, ibid., p. 140.

126 *Van Buren to Albany:* Sellers, *Continentalist,* p. 199.

126 *"has caused me considerable":* Martin Van Buren, letter to JKP, February 27, 1845, *Correspondence* IX, p. 143.

126 *"I hope this appointment":* JKP, letter to Martin Van Buren, March 1, 1845, ibid., p. 156.

126 *"as nervously as if":* Quoted in Sellers, *Continentalist,* p. 201.

127 *"utterly paralyze the party":* Quoted in ibid., p. 202.

127 *"endeavor to rectify":* Quoted in ibid.

127 *final cabinet:* Seigenthaler, *James K. Polk,* pp. 105–8.

127 *"It is an evil":* Quoted in Sellers, *Continentalist,* p. 203.

127 *Tyler's actions on resolution:* Benton, *Thirty Years' View,* Vol. II, p. 636.

127 *"It was not a barren fraud":* Ibid., p. 638.

128 *"Thus was Texas":* Ibid.

128 *Manifest Destiny:* Holt, *The Rise and Fall of the American Whig Party,* p. 232.

129 *"like a fire bell":* Thomas Jefferson, letter to John Holmes, April 22, 1820, Library of Congress, www.loc.gov/exhibits/jefferson.

129 *Democratic dominance thin:* Sellers, *Continentalist,* p. 170.

130 *"I will if I can":* JKP, letter to Cave Johnson, December 21, 1845, *Correspondence* VIII, p. 456.

Chapter 8: Taking Charge

PAGE

131 *Polk slapped his thigh:* George Bancroft, untitled typescript, beginning draft of a JKP biography, Bancroft Collection, New York Public Library.

131 *four goals:* Ibid.

132 *population seventeen million:* Daniel Walker Howe, *What Hath God Wrought: The Transformation of America, 1815–1848* (New York: Oxford University Press, 2007), p. 538.

132 *3.9 percent growth rate:* Ibid.

132 *"We are now reaching":* "Our Country," *Wilmington* (Delaware) *Gazette,* reprinted in *Daily Union,* May 1, 1845.

133 *450 locomotives:* Howe, *What Hath God Wrought,* p. 563.

133 *3,200 miles of track:* Ibid.

133 *more than seven thousand track miles:* Ibid., p. 564.

133 *Clay's travel time:* Ibid.

133 *"the improvement":* Benton, *Thirty Years' View,* Vol. II, p. 578.

133 *from Baltimore to Washington:* Howe, *What Hath God Wrought,* p. 4.

133 *Morse at inauguration:* "Inauguration of the American President," *Illustrated London News,* April 19, 1845, vol. 6, pp. 243–44, Library of Congress Web site.

133 *"America is the country":* Quoted in Howe, *What Hath God Wrought,* David M. Kennedy, "Editor's Introduction," p. xiii.

134 *Thomas Sully's portrait:* JKP, letter to AJ, May 22, 1845, *Correspondence* IX, p. 402.

134 *"The contrast":* Ibid.

135 *"corrupt speculators":* AJ, letter to JKP, June 6, 1845, ibid., p. 432.

135 *Buchanan's effeminacy:* Jean H. Baker, *James Buchanan* (New York: Times Books, 2004), pp. 25–26.

135 *"an inept busybody":* Quoted in ibid., p. 31.

135 *"Aunt Nancy":* Quoted in ibid., p. 25.

135 *"Aunt Fancy":* Quoted in ibid.

135 *"Buchanan & his wife":* Quoted in ibid.

136 *Polk's March 7 instruction:* JKP, letter to Andrew Jackson Donelson, March 7, 1845, *Correspondence* IX, p. 180.

136 *"most speedily":* Buchanan, letter to Andrew Jackson Donelson, State Department document, March 10, 1845, reprinted in *Daily Union,* December 19, 1845.

137 *"with a great deal of feeling":* Andrew Jackson Donelson, letter to JKP, March 18, 1845, *Correspondence* IX, p. 205.

137 *"very indignant":* Archibald Yell, letter to JKP, March 23, 1845, ibid., p. 227.

137 *"occupying a doubtful position":* Archibald Yell, letter to JKP, March 26, 1845, ibid., p. 236.

137 *"if H. doubts":* Ibid.

137 *"the thousand difficulties":* Ibid.

138 *"every possible inducement":* "Texas," *New York Herald,* quoting an anonymous source in the *Richmond Enquirer,* reprinted in *Daily Globe,* April 1, 1845.

138 *Blair background:* "Blair, Francis Preston, 1791–1876," *Columbia Encyclopedia,* http://columbia.thefreedictionary.com/Blair,+Francis+Preston.

138 *"The corrupted intriguers":* Francis Blair, letter to Martin Van Buren, reprinted in *The Francis Preston Blair Family in Politics*, Vol. I, William Ernest Smith (New York: Macmillan, 1933), p. 170.

139 *"certain prominent men":* JKP, letter to AJ, March 17, 1845, *Correspondence* IX, p. 197.

140 *letter apparently destroyed:* Sellers, *Continentalist,* p. 280.

140 *"I am sick":* AJ, letter to Francis Blair, quoted in ibid.

140 *Polk-Blair meeting:* JKP, letter to AJ, March 26, 1845, *Correspondence* IX, p. 233.

140 *"All I said":* Ibid.

140 *Blair editorial:* "The Passage of the Texas Act," *Daily Globe,* March 24, 1845.

141 *"This is placing me":* JKP, letter to AJ, March 26, 1845, *Correspondence* IX, p. 233.

141 *"How loathsome it is":* AJ, letter to Francis Blair, quoted in Sellers, *Continentalist,* p. 281.

141 *"If he will do this":* JKP, letter to AJ, March 26, 1845, *Correspondence* IX, p. 233.

141 *Heiss to Richmond:* Sellers, *Continentalist,* p. 277.

141 *financial arrangements:* Ibid., pp. 278–79; Smith, *The Francis Preston Blair Family in Politics*, Vol. I, p. 180.

142 *One Polk biographer:* Sellers, *Continentalist,* p. 279.

142 *"But my dear friend":* AJ, letter to JKP, April 11, 1845, *Correspondence* IX, p. 278.

142 *"to make enemies":* Untitled editorial, *Daily Globe,* April 14, 1845.

142 *"Pledged to no candidate":* "Prospectus, For publishing at Washington a newspaper, to be called 'THE UNION,'" *Daily Union,* May 1, 1845.

143 *"It must soon take me off":* Quoted in Sellers, *Continentalist,* p. 281.

143 *"both white & black": Andrew Jackson,* Jr., letter to Alfred O. P. Nicholson, reprinted in ibid., p. 281.

143 *"Oh! do not cry":* Ibid.

143 *"with perfect serenity":* Sam Houston, letter to JKP, June 8, 1845, reprinted in *Daily Union,* June 16, 1845.

143 *"His life is a volume":* Obituary, "Death of Gen. Jackson," *Daily Union,* June 16, 1845.

143 *"the death of a great man":* Headline, *Daily Union,* June 16, 1845.

143 *"There was an almost total":* "Honors to the Memory of Gen. Jackson," *National Intelligencer,* June 28, 1845. The description of the day's events comes from this item.

143 *"on the most exalted ground":* Ibid.

143 *"Andrew Jackson is no more!":* JKP, presidential statement, "By the President of the United States," June 16, 1845, reprinted in *Daily Union,* June 16, 1845.

144 *"the greatest man":* JKP, letter to A. O. P. Nicholson, June 28, 1845, *Correspondence* IX, p. 470.

144 *"There is no doubt":* Daniel Webster, remarks before the New York Historical Society, June 17, 1845, reprinted in *Daily Globe,* "Mr. Webster on Gen. Jackson," June 24, 1845.

144 *He has occupied:* "The Death of Gen. Jackson," *National Intelligencer,* June 17, 1845.

CHAPTER 9: ANNEXATION COMPLETE

PAGE

145 *April 2 orders:* Glenn W. Price, *Origins of the War with Mexico: The Polk-Stockton Intrigue* (Austin: University of Texas Press, 1967), p. 76.

145 *May 12 arrival:* "Latest from Texas," *Daily Union,* June 2, 1845.

146 *entered college at thirteen: Encyclopedia of World Biography,* http://www.bookrags.com/biography/robert-field-stockton/.

146 *"He appears":* "Report of the Naval Court of Inquiry into the Conduct of Capt. Stockton, &c.," reprinted in *Daily Globe,* March 14, 1844.

146 *"God and nature":* Robert Stockton speech, September 24, 1844, quoted in Price, *Origins of the War with Mexico,* p. 66.

147 *Wickliffe's disdain for lower classes:* Wikipedia, http://en.wikipedia.org/wiki/Charles_A._Wickliffe.

147 *"the Duke":* Ibid.

147 *Wickliffe's political service: Biographical Directory of the American Congress,* p. 2053.

147 *Sherman background:* Handbook of Texas Online, http://www.tsha.utexas.edu/handbook/online/articles/SS/fsh27.html.

147 *Houston rival:* Herbert Gambrell, *Anson Jones: The Last President of Texas* (Garden City, N.Y.: Doubleday, 1948), p. 270.

147 *Jones's early life:* Ibid., pp. 3–12.

147 *"I had struggled":* Anson Jones, *Memoranda and Official Correspondence Relating to the Republic of Texas, Its History and Annexation,* quoted in ibid., p. 1.

147 *Jones's successes:* Texas State Library and Archives Commission, http://www
.tsl.state.tx.us/exhibits/presidents/jones/grow.html.

148 *Colonneh:* The Handbook of Texas Online, http://www.tsha.utexas.edu/
handbook/online/articles/HH/fho73.html.

148 *Houston a lawyer, major general, etc.: Biographical Directory of the American
Congress,* p. 1241.

148 *marriage falls apart:* Marshall de Bruhl, *Sword of San Jacinto: A Life of Sam
Houston* (New York: Random House, 1993), pp. 100–102.

148 *thrashing of congressman:* Ibid., pp. 129–34.

148 *"So long as you continue":* Mark R. Cheathem, *Old Hickory's Nephew: The
Political and Private Struggles of Andrew Jackson Donelson* (Baton Rouge:
Louisiana State University Press, 2007), p. 20.

148 *second in his class:* Tennessee Encyclopedia of History and Culture, http://
tennesseeencyclopedia.net/imagegallery.php?EntryID=D042.

149 *Smith-Elliot meeting:* Gambrell, *Anson Jones,* pp. 385–86.

149 *March 6 message:* Ibid., p. 386.

149 *Saligny informed:* Ibid.

149 *Donelson's March 24 departure:* Ibid., p. 392.

149 *Donelson's March 27 arrival:* "From Texas," *National Intelligencer,* April 16,
1845.

149 *Electra's Galveston arrival:* Gambrell, *Anson Jones,* p. 388.

150 *"but the agent of the people":* Quoted in ibid., p. 391.

150 *"breach of faith":* Quoted in ibid.

150 *Smith uncommunicative:* Ibid., p. 393.

150 *"some settled scheme of delay":* Quoted in ibid.

150 *"If annexation":* Andrew Jackson Donelson, official correspondence to Ebenezer Allen, March 31, 1845, reprinted in *National Intelligencer,* July 16, 1845.

150 *Donelson's April 2 letter:* Donald Braider, *Solitary Star: A Biography of Sam
Houston* (New York: Putnam's, 1974), p. 240.

150 *Houston demurs:* Ibid.

151 *"I am in favor":* Sam Houston to Andrew Jackson Donelson, April 9, 1845,
Texas State Library, http://www.tsl.state.tx.us/exhibits/annexation/part-
5sam_houston_apr9_1845_1.html.

151 *"Tell Uncle":* Andrew Jackson Donelson, letter to Elizabeth Donelson,
April 16, 1845, quoted in Braider, *Solitary Star,* p. 241.

151 *"go on shore":* George Bancroft, confidential letter to Robert Stockton,
April 22, 1845, quoted in Price, *Origins of the War with Mexico,* p. 48.

152 *Wickliffe's arrival:* Price, *Origins of the War with Mexico,* p. 108.

152 *"He has my confidence":* JKP, letter to Andrew Jackson Donelson, March 28,
1845, *Correspondence* IX, p. 241.

152 *Yell reports Wickliffe arrival:* Archibald Yell, letter to JKP, May 5, 1945, ibid., p. 347.

152 *"is now safe":* Ibid.

152 *"I have been greatly vexed":* Andrew Jackson Donelson, letter to JKP, May 11, 1845, ibid., p. 366.

152 *"authorizes the declaration":* Andrew Jackson Donelson, letter to JKP, May 14, 1845, ibid., p. 372.

152 *"wonderfully preserved":* "Sketch of Gen. Sam Houston," *Daily Union,* June 5, 1845.

152 *"coquetted a little":* Untitled article, *New Orleans Commercial Bulletin,* indeterminate date, reprinted in *National Intelligencer,* June 7, 1845.

152 *"He said":* Ibid.

153 *"I will do the best I can":* Robert Stockton, letter to George Bancroft, May 21, 1845, quoted in Price, *Origins of the War with Mexico,* p. 110.

153 *"far superior":* "Complimentary Ball to Commodore Stockton and Officers of the United States Squadron," *Galveston News,* May 24, 1845, reprinted in *Daily Union,* June 9, 1845. All further quotes and details from the ball come from this dispatch.

153 *"consented to call out the troops":* Robert Stockton, letter to George Bancroft, May 22, 1845, quoted in Price, *Origins of the War with Mexico,* p. 119.

154 *"Orders will be given":* George Bancroft, letter to Robert Stockton, June 2, 1845, quoted in ibid.

154 *My Dear Sir:* Robert Stockton, letter to George Bancroft, May 27, 1845, reprinted in ibid., p. 122.

154 *Stockton leaves May 28:* "A Strong Movement," *National Intelligencer,* June 5, 1845, includes extract of undated article from *New Orleans Republican,* May 27, 1845.

154 *Wickliffe's seasickness:* Charles Wickliffe, letter to JKP, June 3, 1845, *Correspondence* IX, p. 422.

154 *Sherman-Wright visit to Jones:* Anson Jones, *Memoranda and Official Correspondence,* quoted at length in Price, *Origins of the War with Mexico,* pp. 111–12. This episode is taken largely from this source.

155 *"The important event":* "A Strong Movement," *National Intelligencer.*

156 *"This was not correct":* Andrew Jackson Donelson, letter to James Buchanan, June 2, 1845, quoted in Price, *Origins of the War with Mexico,* pp. 125–26.

156 *"to hear through Genl Sherman":* Charles Wickliffe, letter to JKP, June 3, 1845, *Correspondence* IX, p 423.

157 *Wickliffe's second letter:* Charles Wickliffe, letter to JKP, June 4, 1845, ibid., pp. 425–26.

157 *"I do hereby declare"*: Anson Jones, proclamation, reprinted in *National Intelligencer,* June 26, 1845.

157 *Jones's apparent aim:* Gambrell, *Anson Jones,* p. 403.

157 *Jones's second proclamation:* "By the President of the Republic of Texas, A Proclamation," reprinted in *National Intelligencer,* June 2, 1845.

157 *"Public sentiment is rushing":* "The Signs in Texas—The Question Settled," *Daily Union,* June 2, 1845.

157 *triple alliance:* Article, *Galveston News,* quoted in *National Intelligencer,* June 16, 1845.

157 *"dictatorial":* Statement issued by citizens' meeting in Bastrop, Texas, reported in ibid.

158 *"pilloried as a villain":* Texas State Library and Archives Commission, http://www.tsl.state.tx.us/exhibits/annexation/part5/page4.html.

158 *"demagogues, emissaries":* Quoted in Gambrell, *Anson Jones,* p. 402.

158 *unanimous votes:* Dr. John Wright, statement delivered upon arrival of *Princeton* at Annapolis, reprinted in *Daily Union,* July 3, 1845.

158 *"The Senate are so much afraid":* Quoted in Gambrell, *Anson Jones,* p. 404.

158 *request for troops:* Dr. John Wright, statement delivered upon arrival of *Princeton* at Annapolis, *Daily Union.*

158 *"Our duties":* Thomas J. Rusk, speech at state convention, quoted in Gambrell, *Anson Jones,* p. 406.

158 *single dissenting vote:* Gambrell, *Anson Jones,* p. 406.

158 *"The act":* "Interesting Intelligence from Texas—Ratification by the People in Convention," *Daily Union,* July 28, 1845.

159 *"stood forth":* Sam Houston, letter to Andrew Jackson Donelson, December 9, 1845, quoted in Price, *Origins of the War with Mexico,* p. 151.

CHAPTER 10: THE UNITED STATES AND OREGON

PAGE

161 *We are beginning:* "To the Democratic Press," *Daily Globe,* April 29, 1845.

162 *"We run the hazards":* "The Oregon Question," *National Intelligencer,* April 29, 1845.

163 *360,000 square miles:* "The Oregon Question," *National Intelligencer,* June 12, 1845.

164 *seven thousand American whites:* Joseph Ingersoll, House floor speech, January 3, 1846, *Daily Union,* January 3, 1846.

164 *"contains a population":* Letter, "Oregon City, July 8, 1844," printed in *Ithaca Journal,* reprinted in *Daily Globe,* March 18, 1845.

164 *"A regular convention":* Letter, "Falatine Plains, Oregon, Nov. 4, 1844," printed in *Platte* (Missouri) *Argus,* reprinted in *Daily Union,* August 22, 1845.

165 *Juan de Fuca exploration:* "The Oregon Question," *National Intelligencer,* June 12, 1845, reprinted from *London Examiner,* April 25, 1845.

165 *Juan Pérez exploration:* Ibid.

165 *Bruno Heceta exploration:* "The Sovereignty of Oregon—The British View of the Question," *Daily Union,* December 23, 1845.

165 *Drake exploration:* Adam Thom, *The Claims to the Oregon Territory Considered* (London: Smith, Elder & Co., 1844), p. 6.

165 *Cook exploration:* "The Oregon Question," *Daily Union,* June 7, 1848, reprinted from *Democratic Review,* June 1845.

166 *Robert Gray exploration:* Ibid., pp. 8–10.

166 *Gray meets Vancouver:* Ibid., pp. 10–11.

166 *Vancouver sails 150 miles:* "The Oregon Question," *National Intelligencer,* June 12, 1845.

166 *John Meares episode:* "The Sovereignty of Oregon," *Daily Union,* December 23, 1845; "The Oregon Question," *Daily Union,* June 7, 1845, reprinted from *Democratic Review,* June 1845.

167 *Lewis and Clark navigate three hundred miles:* World Atlas, http://encarta .msn.com/map_701510612/Columbia.html.

167 *Simon Fraser exploration:* Wikipedia, http://en.wikipedia.org/wiki/Fraser_ River.

167 *"rights, claims, and pretensions":* James Buchanan, letter to Richard Pakenham, July 12, 1845, reprinted in *Daily Union,* December 9, 1845.

167 *Russian treaties:* " 'Greenhow's History of Oregon and California.'—New Edition," *Daily Union,* May 20, 1845.

168 *Treaty of 1818:* Bemis, *John Quincy Adams and the Foundations of American Foreign Policy,* p. 292.

168 *"free and open":* Ibid.

168 *"It will certainly":* Quoted in ibid.

168 *extension of 1818 provisions:* Bemis, *John Quincy Adams and the Foundations of American Foreign Policy,* p. 532.

169 *"If Spain could not make good":* Quoted in John C. Calhoun, letter to Richard Pakenham, September 20, 1844, reprinted in *Daily Union,* December 9, 1845.

170 *"nothing in the Nootka":* Ibid.

170 *Everett's formula:* Sellers, *Continentalist,* pp. 239–40.

170 *"Our title":* James K. Polk, Inaugural Address, March 4, 1845, the Avalon Project at Yale Law School, http://www.yale.edu/lawweb/avalon/presiden/ inaug/polk.htm.

171 *thirty-six-hour delay:* "Later from England," *National Intelligencer,* April 25, 1845 (originally a dispatch from London in the *New York Commercial Advertiser*).

171 *"the most temperate":* "Debates on Oregon, House of Lords," April 4, 1845, reprinted in ibid.

171 *"blustering announcement":* Ibid.

171 *"in the most explicit manner":* *Times* (London), April 4, 1845, reprinted in ibid.

171 *frigates in the vicinity:* Sellers, *Continentalist,* p. 235.

171 *"insolent tone":* "War with England," *Daily Union,* April 25, 1845.

171 *"England cannot be serious":* "England and the United States," *Daily Union,* April 28, 1845.

172 *"an indiscreet":* "The Oregon Question," *National Intelligencer,* May 5, 1845.

172 *"palpable knavery":* "From the Tribune," under headline, "The Oregon Question—Prospects," *Daily Union,* May 9, 1845.

172 *sentiment in the old Northwest:* Sellers, *Continentalist,* p. 237.

172 *"This is the rattling":* AJ, letter to JKP, May 2, 1845, *Correspondence* IX, p. 332.

172 *"The arrogant tone":* JKP, letter to AJ, April 27, 1845, ibid., p. 321.

173 *Pakenham's fears:* Sellers, *Continentalist,* p. 248.

173 *"embarrassed, if not committed":* James Buchanan, letter to Richard Pakenham, July 12, 1845, reprinted in *Daily Union,* December 9, 1845.

173 *backchannel communications:* Sellers, *Continentalist,* pp. 247–48.

174 *historical analysis:* "The Debate in Parliament," *Daily Union,* May 2, 1845.

174 *"Mr. Polk will not fight":* Untitled excerpt, *Portland Advertiser,* reprinted in ibid.

174 *Less than two weeks:* Sellers, *Continentalist,* p. 250.

174 *"be prepared":* Quoted in ibid.

CHAPTER 11: THE UNITED STATES AND MEXICO

PAGE

176 *"as offensive to Mexico":* Luis G. Cuevas, letter to Wilson Shannon, March 28, 1845, reprinted in *National Intelligencer,* April 28, 1845.

176 *"could be arranged":* Wilson Shannon, letter to Luis G. Cuevas, March 31, 1845, ibid.

176 *"which has . . . usurped":* Luis G. Cuevas, letter to Wilson Shannon, April 2, 1845, ibid.

176 *"the probabilities of a war":* "Mexico," *New Orleans Jeffersonian Republican,* July 7, 1845, reprinted in *Daily Union,* July 15, 1845.

177 *"War between this country"*: Letter, June 24, 1845, printed in the *Baltimore American,* July 17, 1845, reprinted in the *National Intelligencer,* July 18, 1845.

177 *"probable"*: Report from "An American," "The Late News—Measures to Be Adopted," *Daily Union,* August 16, 1845.

177 *"one of those beautiful"*: Alexis de Tocqueville, quoted in Timothy J. Henderson, *A Glorious Defeat: Mexico and Its War with the United States* (New York: Hill & Wang, 2007), p. 5.

178 *"was destroyed like a sunflower"*: Oswald Spengler, *The Decline of the West,* abridged edition by Helmut Werner, prepared by Arthur Helps from the translation by Charles Francis Atkinson (New York: Modern Library, 1952), pp. 239–40.

178 *"spiritual conquest"*: Enrique Krauze (translated by Hank Heifetz), *Mexico— Biography of Power: A History of Modern Mexico, 1810–1996* (New York: HarperCollins, 1997), p. 33.

178 padrecitos: Ibid.

179 *New Laws:* Ibid., p. 37.

179 *approaching 40 percent:* Ibid., p. 52.

180 *"the Spanish sword"*: Justo Sierra, *Political History,* quoted in ibid., p. 73.

180 *"the country of inequality"*: Alexander von Humboldt, quoted in Henderson, *A Glorious Defeat,* p. 11.

180 *U.S. and Mexican income:* Henderson, *A Glorious Defeat,* p. 18.

180 *U.S. population, 1790–1840:* "Demographic History of the United States," Wikipedia, http://en.wikipedia.org/wiki/Demographic_history_of_the_ United_States.

180 *Mexican Population, 1790–1840:* Robert McCaa, "The Peopling of Mexico from Origins to Revolution," Table 4 (preliminary draft), Cambridge University Press, December 8, 1997, http://www.hist.umn.edu/~rmccaa/ mxpoprev/cambridge3.htm.

181 *hundreds dead:* Henderson, *A Glorious Defeat,* pp. 19–20.

181 hombres de bien: Ibid., p. 21.

181 *"well made"*: "A Sketch of Santa Anna—His Fortunes Within a Few Years," *Daily Globe,* April 22, 1845.

182 *"to all appearance an outlaw"*: "Antonio López de Santa Anna," *Daily Union,* June 20, 1845.

183 *solemn burial ceremony:* "A Sketch of Santa Anna—His Fortunes Within a Few Years," *Daily Globe.*

183 *"a most cynical attack"*: Herbert Ingram Priestley, *The Mexican Nation: A History* (New York: Macmillan, 1923), p. 295.

183 *"constitutional despotism":* Ibid.

184 *"forced to yield":* "Antonio López de Santa Anna," *Daily Union.*

184 *catalogue of Mexican abuses:* "The War—Its Causes and Its Prosecution," *Daily Union,* January 6, 1847.

185 *ninety-five episodes:* Ibid.

185 *"wanton . . . outrages":* AJ, Message to Congress, February 6, 1837, in Rep. No. 752, House of Representatives, 29th Congress, 1st Session.

185 *"We should act":* Ibid.

185 *"with justice":* Report of Senate Committee of Foreign Relations, February 19, 1837, quoted in "Mexico—No. 7," *Daily Union,* May 16, 1845.

185 *"ample cause exists":* Report of House Committee on Foreign Relations, February 24, 1837, quoted in ibid.

185 *Mexican viewpoint:* Sellers, *Continentalist,* pp. 233–34.

186 *"has rendered herself":* Abel Upshur, letter to Waddy Thompson, July 25, 1843, quoted in "Mexico—No. 9," *Daily Union,* May 19, 1845.

186 *$2 million:* Sellers, *Continentalist,* p. 234.

187 *Thompson's suggestion:* Ibid.

187 *Polk's justification:* McCormac, *Polk* II, p. 374. (McCormac cites this as Donelson's justification, but Polk embraced the arguments.)

188 *Taylor description:* K. Jack Bauer, *Zachary Taylor: Soldier, Planter, Statesman of the Old Southwest* (Baton Rouge: Louisiana State University Press, 1958), pp. xxi–xxiii; John S. D. Eisenhower, *So Far from God: The U. S. War with Mexico, 1846–1848* (New York: Random House, 1989), pp. 29–30.

188 *"placed and kept":* William Marcy, letter to Zachary Taylor, May 28, 1845, quoted in Eisenhower, *So Far from God,* p. 30.

188 *two thousand soldiers:* Eisenhower, *So Far from God,* p. 30.

188 *"unless an actual state of war":* William Marcy, letter to Zachary Taylor, July 8, 1845, quoted in McCormac, *Polk* II, p. 375.

189 *"That you may precisely":* George Bancroft, letter to David Conner, July 11, 1845, quoted in ibid.

189 *"it being the determination":* Ibid.

189 *"but for the appearance":* JKP, letter to Alfred O. P. Nicholson, July 28, 1845, Polk Papers.

189 *"we should sacrifice":* "Our Troops in Texas," *Daily Union,* August 7, 1845.

189 *"But it is apparent":* Editorial, *National Intelligencer,* quoted in "Boundaries of Texas—Duties of the United States," *Daily Union,* August 8, 1845.

Chapter 12: Britain and Mexico

190   *"Let the British minister"*: JKP, *The Diary of James K. Polk During His Presidency, 1845–1849* Vol. I, edited and annotated by Milo Milton Quaife (Chicago: A. C. McClurg & Co., 1910; reprinted: Chicago Historical Society), August 26, 1845, p. 3. Hereinafter JKP, *Diary* I.

190   *"If we do have war"*: Ibid., p. 4.

191   *"We should do our duty"*: Ibid., p. 5.

191   *"God won't have"*: Quoted in ibid.

191   *"hesitancy and indecision"*: JKP, ibid.

192   *"able and admirable"*: Ibid., August 27, 1845, p. 7.

192   *a number of propositions*: Ibid., August 29, 1845, p. 9.

192   *"Well, the deed is done"*: Quoted in ibid., August 30, 1845, p. 11.

192   *"I'm glad"*: JKP, ibid., p. 12.

193   *"deter and prevent"*: Ibid., September 1, 1845, p. 13.

193   *$690,000 claim*: Joseph Wheelan, *Invading Mexico: America's Continental Dream and The Mexican War, 1846–1848* (New York: Carroll & Graf, 2007), p. 67.

193   *Parrott's reputation*: Sellers, *Continentalist*, p. 230.

193   *Buchanan's distrust*: Wheelan, *Invading Mexico*, p. 68.

193   *"might with comparative ease"*: Quoted in Sellers, *Continentalist*, p. 263.

193   *"The prejudices existing"*: Quoted in Wheelan, *Invading Mexico*, p. 69.

194   *"one great object"*: JKP, *Diary* I, September 16, 1845, p. 34.

194   *territory sought*: Depicted on map, Krauze, *Mexico*, p. 146.

194   *"For such a boundary"*: JKP, *Diary* I, September 16, 1845, p. 34.

194   *"breathing a war spirit"*: Ibid., September 17, 1845, p. 35.

195   *"disposed to stand"*: James Buchanan, letter to John Black, September 17, 1845, reprinted in *Daily Union*, May 18, 1846.

195   *"it would be far better"*: Quoted in Sellers, *Continentalist*, p. 263.

195   *"but not in negotiation"*: Quoted in ibid.

195   *state of Mexican government*: "Later from Mexico," *Daily Union*, September 29, 1845.

196   *Buchanan and the court*: JKP, *Diary* I, September 29, 1845, p. 45.

196   *shrewd bit of politicking*: Ibid., October 12, 1845, p. 55.

197   *"in terms not very courteous"*: Ibid., October 21, 1845, p. 63.

197   *"inevitably lead to war"*: Quoted in JKP, ibid.

197   *"improper"*: JKP, ibid., p. 64.

197   *Pakenham's state of mind*: James Buchanan, report to JKP, ibid., October 23, 1845, p. 66.

198 *"very cheerfully"*: JKP, *Diary* I, October 24, 1845, p. 69.

198 *"strongly inclined"*: Ibid., p. 70.

199 *"Col. B"*: Ibid., p. 72.

199 *U.S. immigration to California*: Hampton Sides, *Blood and Thunder: An Epic of the American West* (New York: Doubleday, 2006), p. 69.

200 *should sleep on it*: JKP, *Diary* I, October 28, 1845, p. 77.

200 *"with some earnestness"*: Ibid., p. 78.

201 *"The result of the whole"*: Ibid., p. 82.

201 *"confidential conversation"*: Ibid., October 30, 1845, p. 83.

201 *"would receive an envoy"*: John Black, letter to Manuel de la Peña y Peña, October 13, 1845, reprinted in "The Mexican Document," *Daily Union,* May 18, 1846.

201 *"disposed to receive"*: Manuel de la Peña y Peña, letter to John Black, October 15, 1845, reprinted in ibid.

201 *"envoy extraordinary"*: JKP, *Diary* I, November 19, 1845, p. 93.

201 *Parrott assignment*: Ibid.

202 *meeting with Allen*: Ibid., November 17, 1845, p. 96.

202 *Allen forty-one*: *Biographical Directory of the American Congress*, p. 571.

202 *"entirely satisfied"*: JKP, *Diary* I, November 19, 1845, p. 97.

202 *"well satisfied"*: Ibid., p. 99.

203 *"channels of information"*: Ibid., November 29, 1845, p. 107.

203 *"warlike tone"*: Ibid.

203 *"The truth is"*: Ibid.

203 *Robert McLane visit*: Ibid., November 27, 1845, p. 103.

CHAPTER 13: THE TWENTY-NINTH CONGRESS

PAGE

205 *"the sword"*: JKP, First Annual Message, December 2, 1845, reprinted, American Presidency Project, http://www.presidency.ucsb.edu/index.php.

207 *"Never, in the period"*: "The President's Message," *Daily Union,* December 2, 1845.

207 *"You have struck"*: Quoted in JKP, *Diary* I, December 2, 1845, p. 110.

207 *"We Pennsylvanians"*: Quoted in ibid.

207 *"moderation"*: Editorial, *National Intelligencer,* quoted indirectly in "The Message—The Tone of the Press," *Washington Union,* December 6, 1845.

207 *"appearance of a charitable donation"*: "The Message—The Tone of the Press," *Washington Union,* December 6, 1845.

207 *"But . . . suppose"*: Quoted in JKP, *Diary* I, December 9, 1845, p. 119.

208 *"Should that Government"*: JKP, *Diary* I, December 13, 1845, p. 122.

208 *"had better prepare"*: Quoted in ibid.

208 *"A crisis is fast approaching"*: Lewis Cass, Senate floor speech, December 15, 1845, *Daily Union,* December 15, 1845.

209 *"Could any man calculate"*: William Archer, Senate floor speech, December 15, 1845, ibid.

209 *Cass resolution passes:* "Congressional," *Daily Union,* December 16, 1845.

209 *Slidell arrives December 6:* John Slidell, letter to James Buchanan, December 17, 1845, reprinted in *Washington Union,* May 18, 1846.

209 *"manifested great surprise"*: Ibid.

210 *December 20 rejection:* Manuel de la Peña y Peña, letter to John Slidell, December 20, 1845, reprinted in ibid.

210 *"Mr. Slidell cannot be admitted"*: Ibid.

210 *"abstain from the full expression"*: John Slidell, letter to Manuel de la Peña y Peña, December 24, 1845, reprinted in ibid.

211 *"a fine humor"*: JKP, *Diary* I, December 22, 1845, p. 131.

211 *"will be very soon"*: Ibid., p. 132.

212 *Polk would consult senators:* Ibid., December 23, 1845, p. 135.

212 *appropriate course:* Ibid., December 24, 1845, p. 139.

212 *"almost mad"*: Quoted in JKP, ibid., p. 140.

212 *White House Christmas:* JKP, *Diary* I, December 25, 1845, p. 143.

212 *eagle feather:* JKP, letter to Robert Armstrong, December 29, 1845, *Correspondence of James K. Polk,* Vol. X, *July–December 1845,* Wayne Cutler and James L. Rogers II (eds.) (Knoxville: University of Tennessee Press, 2004), pp. 443–44n. Hereinafter *Correspondence* X.

213 *Buchanan agitated:* JKP, *Diary* I, December 25, 1845, pp. 143–46.

213 *"a sound, original"*: Ibid., December 24, 1845, p. 138.

213 *"act on my own convictions"*: Ibid., December 25, 1845, p. 146.

213 *Polk went around the room:* Ibid., December 27, 1845, p. 147.

213 *"part and parcel"*: Edward Hannegan, Senate resolution, introduced December 30, 1845, reprinted in *Daily Union,* December 30, 1845.

214 *"not abandon the honor"*: John C. Calhoun, Senate resolution, introduced December 30, 1845, reprinted in ibid.

214 *"war would be one"*: John C. Calhoun, Senate floor speech, December 30, 1845, ibid.

214 *"If it is rashness"*: Edward Hannegan, Senate floor speech, ibid.

214 *"Get children"*: Charles Ingersoll, quoting Benjamin Franklin, House floor speech, January 3, 1845, *Daily Union,* January 3, 1846.

214 *"tokens of assent"*: Editorial aside, *Daily Union,* ibid.

214 *"that it should demonstrate"*: Preston King, House floor speech, ibid.

215 *"in its own nature"*: Robert Winthrop, House floor speech, ibid.

215 *"I am led"*: Joshua Giddings, House floor speech, January 5, 1846, *Daily Union*, January 5, 1846.

216 *"In one breath"*: James McDowell, House floor speech, ibid.

216 *"their natural rights"*: Quoted in Online Encyclopedia (originally appearing in Vol. 12, 1911 Encyclopaedia Britannica), http://encyclopedia.jrank.org/ GEO_GNU/GIDDINGS_JOSHUA_REED_1795_1864_.html.

217 *"plain, unequivocal war"*: Robert Barnwell Rhett, House floor speech, January 5, 1846, ibid.

217 *"I am for the whole"*: Leonard Sims, House floor speech, ibid.

217 *"The only way"*: JKP, *Diary* I, January 4, 1846, p. 155.

217 *Calhoun visit*: Ibid., January 10, 1846, pp. 158–63.

218 *"Notice to terminate"*: "The 'Notice' to Great Britain," *Daily Union*, January 12, 1846.

218 *"as to throw the whole odium"*: Buchanan, letter to John Slidell, January 20, 1846, reprinted in *Daily Union*, May 19, 1846.

219 *"unless . . . some discontented"*: John Slidell, letter to James Buchanan, February 6, 1846, reprinted in ibid.

219 *"Sir: I am directed"*: William Marcy, letter to Zachary Taylor, January 13, 1846, quoted in Eisenhower, *So Far from God*, p. 49.

220 *Senate rejects Woodward*: JKP, *Diary* I, January 22, 1846, pp. 183–86.

220 *six Democrats*: Ibid.

220 *"The information given me"*: Ibid.

220 *"I cannot surrender"*: Ibid., January 24, 1846, p. 190.

221 *"conniving"*: Ibid., January 26, 1846, p. 195.

221 *"would find me a lion"*: Ibid., p. 196.

221 *"Mr. Buchanan will find"*: Ibid., January 28, 1846, p. 201.

CHAPTER 14: END OF A TREATY

PAGE

222 *"the master key"*: John D. Cummins, House floor speech, February 7, 1846, *Daily Union*, February 7, 1846.

223 *vote of 163 to 54*: McCormac, *Polk* II, p. 592.

223 *"negotiations for an amicable settlement"*: Quoted in ibid.

223 *"heavy vote"*: "Abrogation Notice," *Daily Union*, February 9, 1846.

223 *"dare not go to war"*: William Allen, Senate floor speech, quoted in "Congressional," *Daily Union*, February 11, 1846.

223 *"almost to suffocation"*: Ibid.

223 *"the intensity"*: Ibid.

223 *but one party:* "Congressional," *Daily Union,* February 12, 1846.

224 *Corn Law repeal:* R. B. Mowat, *A New History of Great Britain* (London: Oxford University Press, 1926), pp. 744–46.

225 *"marked by a* decorum": "The 'Times,' on the Oregon Question," *Daily Union,* February 2, 1846.

225 *"an amicable and courteous":* "Arrival of the Cambria," *Daily Union,* February 20, 1846.

225 *"the surest safeguard":* "From the London Times," *Daily Union,* March 6, 1846.

225 *"I imagine the President":* Lord Aberdeen to Richard Pakenham, quoted in Sellers, *Continentalist,* p. 376.

225 *McLane's February 3 warning:* Ibid., p. 381.

225 *Buchanan's recommendation:* JKP, *Diary* I, February 24, 1846, pp. 244–46.

226 *Haywood's warning:* Ibid., pp. 246–48.

226 *"break . . . down":* Allen, Quoted in ibid., p. 248.

226 *Calhoun's proposal:* Ibid., February 25, 1846, pp. 249–52.

227 *McLane letter approved:* Ibid., p. 253.

227 *"require of us":* William Haywood, Senate floor speech, *Congressional Globe,* March 5, 1846. The entire exchange among Haywood, Hannegan, and Allen is taken from this account.

228 *"I call the Senator":* Willie Mangum, Senate floor declaration, ibid.

228 *"put the matter right":* Quoted in JKP, *Diary* I, March 5, 1846, p. 268.

228 *senatorial visits:* JKP, *Diary* I, March 6–March 7, 1846, pp. 268–78.

229 *"ultras":* Quoted in ibid., p. 270.

229 *"Do you go":* Quoted in ibid., p. 273.

229 *"Yes, that is so":* Quoted in ibid.

229 *"Wait then":* JKP, *Diary* I, March 6–March 7, 1846, p. 273.

229 *Allen's second effort:* Ibid., March 8, 1846, pp. 278–79.

229 *"may exhibit, now and then":* "The Wise and Celebrated Maxim," *Daily Union,* March 6, 1846.

230 *"so divide and weaken":* JKP, *Diary* I, March 8, 1846, p. 280.

230 *Atocha's visit:* Ibid., February 13, 1846, pp. 222–25.

231 *Atocha's return:* Ibid., February 16, 1846, pp. 227–30.

232 *new Slidell instructions:* Ibid., pp. 233–35.

232 *"take redress":* Ibid.

232 *"manifestly in a bad mood":* Ibid., p. 234.

232 *"energetic measures":* James Buchanan, letter to John Slidell, March 12, 1846, reprinted in *Daily Union,* May 20, 1846.

233 *"unwilling to take a course":* John Slidell, letter to Don J. Castillo y Lanzas, March 1, 1846, reprinted in ibid.

233 *"despoiled, outraged"*: Don J. Castillo y Lanzas, letter to John Slidell, March 12, 1846, reprinted in ibid.

233 *"naked notice"*: Foreign Relations Committee language, described in "The Terms of the 'Notice' in the Senate," *Daily Union,* March 17, 1846.

233 *"earnestly desired"*: Colquitt amendment to notice resolution, reprinted in ibid.

233 *"Col. B"*: JKP, *Diary* I, March 11, 1846, p. 287.

233 *"I regret the division"*: Ibid., p. 285.

234 *"a disposition to be warlike"*: Ibid., March 22, 1846, pp. 296–98.

234 *"supersede Gen'l Cass"*: Ibid., p. 297.

234 *"I cannot rely"*: Ibid.

234 *"there will be"*: Reverdy Johnson, Senate floor speech, "Special Order—Oregon—'The Notice,'" *Daily Union,* March 11, 1846.

234 *Calhoun's rationale:* John C. Calhoun, Senate floor speech, March 16, 1846, "Speech of Mr. Calhoun," *Daily Union,* March 19, 1846.

234 *"I am of opinion"*: Daniel Webster, Senate floor speech, *Daily Union,* March 30, 1846.

234 *"that he might fall"*: Alexander Barrow, Senate floor speech, *Daily Union,* ibid.

235 *"I am among those"*: Lewis Cass, Senate floor speech, *Daily Union,* April 2, 1846.

235 *McDuffie endorses Colquitt:* "Congressional," *Daily Union,* April 4, 1846.

235 *sixty-five days:* William Allen, Senate floor speech, *Daily Union,* April 16, 1846.

235 *"that it would not facilitate"*: John Crittenden, Senate floor speech, ibid.

235 *"that the attention"*: Johnson amendment, reprinted in ibid.

236 *"law-making power"*: William Allen, Senate floor speech, ibid.

236 *"On what meat"*: John Crittenden, Senate floor speech, ibid.

236 *Crittenden-Allen exchange:* Ibid.

236 *40 to 14:* Ibid.

236 *"but still it authorized"*: JKP, *Diary* I, April 17, 1846, p. 334.

237 *"authorized and requested"*: "Congressional," *Daily Union,* April 23, 1846.

237 *142 to 46:* Ibid.

237 *42 to 10:* Ibid.

237 *"With one accord"*: "The Deed of the Day," *Daily Union,* April 23, 1846.

237 *"After all, however"*: JKP, *Diary* I, April 23, 1846, p. 348.

237 *"reached a point"*: Ibid., April 18, 1846, p. 337.

CHAPTER 15: WAR

PAGE

238 *"he possessed a trait"*: Quoted in Richard R. Stenburg, "President Polk and California: Additional Documents," *Pacific Historical Review* 10, no. 2 (June 1941): 219.

239 *"might induce him"*: JKP, *Diary* I, March 28, 1846, p. 306.

239 *"I called their attention"*: Ibid.

239 *"Col. B entered"*: Ibid.

239 *Allen conversation*: Ibid., March 29, 1846, p. 309.

239 *Cass suggestion*: Ibid., March 30, 1846, pp. 310–11.

239 *Calhoun conversation*: Ibid., pp. 311–14.

239 *"inexpedient at present"*: Quoted in ibid., April 3, 1846, p. 317.

240 *"we must take redress"*: JKP, letter to John Slidell, November 10, 1845, quoted in Stenburg, "President Polk and California," p. 218.

240 *3,550 officers and men*: Eisenhower, *So Far from God*, p. 52.

240 *March 8*: Ibid., p. 51.

240 *120-mile trek*: Wheelan, *Invading Mexico*, p. 64.

240 *March 28*: Eisenhower, *So Far from God*, p. 51.

240 *"The Star-Spangled Banner"*: Wheelan, *Invading Mexico*, p. 84.

240 *three thousand strong*: Eisenhower, *So Far from God*, p. 61.

241 *"Has Mexico declared war"*: "Minutes of an interview between Brig. General W. J. Worth, United States army, and Gen. Romulo Vega of the Mexican army, held on the right bank of the Rio Grande, 28th March, 1846," *Daily Union*, May 11, 1846.

241 *additional three thousand troops*: Eisenhower, *So Far from God*, p. 63.

241 *"I require you"*: Quoted in Wheelan, *Invading Mexico*, p. 89.

241 *"I regret the alternative"*: Quoted in ibid., p. 90.

241 *"It will . . . compel"*: Quoted in ibid.

241 *Thornton's mission*: Wheelan, *Invading Mexico*, p. 92.

242 *"to take the redress"*: Quoted in JKP, *Diary* I, May 8, 1846, p. 382.

242 *"ample cause of war"*: JKP, ibid., May 9, 1846, p. 384.

243 *"recommending vigorous"*: Ibid.

243 *breaking for church*: Ibid., May 10, 1846, p. 387.

243 *conferred with members*: Ibid.

243 *"highly approved it"*: Ibid., May 11, 1846, p. 390.

243 *Benton's opposition*: Ibid.

244 *"upon the most frivolous pretexts"*: JKP, "Message of President Polk," May 11, 1846, The Avalon Project at Yale Law School, http://www.yale.edu/law-

web/avalon/president/messages/polk01.htm. All quotes from the message are taken from this source.

245 *two hours of debate:* Sellers, *Continentalist,* p. 416.

245 *fifty thousand volunteers:* War measure from the House Military Affairs Committee, taken up on the House floor May 11, 1846, "House of Representatives: Relations with Mexico," *Daily Union,* May 11, 1846.

245 *"by the act":* Jacob Brinkerhoff, amendment offered on House floor, ibid.

245 *"It will be expensive":* Jacob Brinkerhoff, House floor speech, ibid. All quotes from this debate are taken from this source unless otherwise noted.

246 *"The river Nueces":* Garrett Davis, House floor speech, May 11, 1846, reprinted in Sellers, *Continentalist,* p. 417.

246 *173 to 14:* "House of Representatives: Relations with Mexico," *Daily Union.*

246 *"There may be invasion":* John C. Calhoun, Senate floor speech, "In Senate," *Daily Union,* May 11, 1846. All quotes from this debate are taken from this source.

248 *"Mr. Buchanan, Mr. Marcy":* JKP, *Diary* I, May 11, 1846, p. 392.

248 *"the fear of the people":* Ibid., p. 393.

248 *"in distress":* Quoted in Sellers, *Continentalist,* p. 418.

248 *"a ruined man":* Quoted in ibid.

249 *"I see you are right":* Quoted in ibid.

249 *"unwilling to pass":* Willie Mangum, Senate floor speech, "In Senate," *Daily Union,* May 12, 1846. All quotes from this debate are taken from this source.

251 *At six-thirty:* Sellers, *Continentalist,* p. 419.

251 *"almost got on their knees":* Quoted in ibid.

251 *"Aye, except for":* Quoted in ibid.

251 *40 to 2:* "In Senate," *Daily Union.*

252 *"The questions of war":* Quoted in Sellers, *Continentalist,* p. 420.

CHAPTER 16: VAGARIES OF WAR

PAGE

253 *six feet five inches:* John S. D. Eisenhower, *Agent of Destiny: The Life and Times of General Winfield Scott* (New York: Free Press, 1997), p. 2.

253 *almost a duel:* Ibid., p. 114.

253 *Scott born 1786:* Ibid., p. 1.

254 *"liar and a scoundrel":* Quoted in ibid., p. 18.

254 *"unofficer-like conduct":* Quoted in ibid., p. 19.

254   *strutted back and forth:* Eisenhower, *Agent of Destiny,* p. 11.

254   *"The chief ruling passion":* Quoted in ibid., p. 143.

255   *"The general fact":* "Military Movements," *Daily Union,* June 10, 1846.

255   *"of all parties":* Simon Cameron, Senate floor speech, "In Senate: *The Mexican War,*" *Daily Union,* May 15, 1846.

255   *"one general burst":* Seaborn Jones, House floor speech, "House of Representatives," *Daily Union,* May 14, 1846.

255   *Ho! Ho!:* "E.M.H.," "War," *Daily Union,* May 21, 1846.

256   *"presidential war":* Columbus Delano, House floor speech, "House of Representatives: Personal," *Daily Union,* May 16, 1846.

256   *"That is, if Congress would":* "Whig Views of the War," *Daily Union,* June 27, 1846.

256   *"unnecessary and improper":* JKP, *Diary* I, May 13, 1846, p. 397.

256   *"Then you will have war":* Quoted in ibid., p. 398.

256   *"or all the Powers":* JKP, ibid.

257   *twenty thousand volunteers:* Ibid., May 14, 1846, p. 400.

257   *"Gen'l Scott":* Ibid., p. 401.

257   *"must proceed very soon":* Ibid., May 19, 1846, p. 408.

257   *"smelt the rat":* Quoted in Eisenhower, *Agent of Destiny,* p. 224.

258   *In the midst of these:* Winfield Scott, letter to William Marcy, May 21, 1846, reprinted in *Daily Union,* June 8, 1846.

258   *"proved to me":* JKP, *Diary* I, May 21, 1846, p. 414.

259   *"highly censurable":* Ibid., May 22, 1846, p. 418.

259   *Polk's plan to supersede Scott:* Ibid., May 23, 1846, p. 425.

259   *Taylor's victories, May 8–9:* Eisenhower, *"So Far from God,"* pp. 71–85.

260   *"Our victory":* Quoted in ibid., p. 84.

260   *Marcy's draft reply:* JKP, *Diary* I, May 25, 1846, p. 424.

260   *"most unworthy motives":* William Marcy, letter to Winfield Scott, May 25, 1846, reprinted in *Daily Union,* June 8, 1846.

261   *"Sir: Your letter of this date":* Winfield Scott, letter to William Marcy, May 25, 1846, reprinted in ibid.

261   *Further Scott–Marcy correspondence:* Reprinted in ibid.

262   *"Commodore: If Santa Anna":* George Bancroft, letter to David Conner, reprinted in Eisenhower, *So Far from God,* p. 91.

262   *Polk meets with Benton:* Eisenhower, *So Far from God,* p. 91.

262   *expedition to California:* JKP, *Diary* I, May 26, 1846, p. 429.

262   *president's war strategy:* JKP, ibid., May 30, 1846, pp. 437–38.

263   *"totally unnecessary":* Garrett Davis, House floor speech, June 2, 1846, "House of Representatives: Mexican War," *Daily Union,* June 3, 1846.

263   *dispatch from McLane:* JKP, *Diary* I, June 3, 1846, pp. 444–45.

263 *"the probable result"*: Ibid.

264 *terms of British proposal*: JKP, ibid., June 4, 1846, p. 447.

264 *"felt excited"*: JKP, ibid., June 6, 1846, pp. 453–54.

265 *"My impression"*: JKP, ibid., June 7, 1846, p. 456.

265 *"no agency"*: Quoted in JKP, ibid., June 8, 1846, pp. 457–60. This entire exchange is taken from this *Diary* entry.

266 *five-hour cabinet session*: JKP, ibid., June 9, 1846, pp. 461–62.

266 *vote of 37 to 12*: Sellers, *Continentalist*, p. 412.

267 *vote of 41 to 14*: Ibid.

267 *"such as they are"*: "The Treaty," *Daily Union*, June 20, 1846.

267 *"about three degrees of seacoast"*: Ibid.

CHAPTER 17: PRESIDENTIAL TEMPERAMENT

PAGE

268 *"raised letters"*: JKP, *Diary* I, April 30, 1846, pp. 366–68. The entire episode is taken from this source.

269 *The public have no idea*: JKP, *The Diary of James K. Polk During His Presidency, 1845–1849*, Vol. IV, Milo Milton Quaife, editor and annotator (Chicago: A. C. McClurg, 1910; reprinted: Chicago Historical Society), December 29, 1848, p. 261. Hereinafter JKP, *Diary* IV.

270 *fifth excursion*: JKP, *Diary* I, April 1, 1846, p. 316.

270 *church attendance*: Ibid., November 2, 1845, p. 86.

270 *"edification or profit"*: Ibid., February 6, 1846, p. 213.

270 *no spirituous liquors or dancing*: Bumgarner, *Sarah Childress Polk*, p. 73.

270 *April reception lobbying*: JKP, *Diary* I, April 17, 1846, p. 335.

271 *"without ceremony"*: Quoted in Sellers, *Continentalist*, p. 307.

271 *"when other guests"*: Quoted in Bumgarner, *Sarah Childress Polk*, p. 72.

271 *"extremely affable"*: All quotes from ibid., pp. 68, 70.

271 *"None but Sarah"*: JKP, quoted in ibid., p. 68.

271 *"It is one of the most"*: JKP, *Diary* I, February 27, 1846, p. 255.

271 *"In the midst of these factions"*: Ibid., March 4, 1846, p. 265.

272 *"a thin Senate"*: Ibid., May 25, 1846, p. 426.

272 *"managing, tricky man"*: Ibid.

272 *"his ambition"*: Ibid., p. 427.

273 *"a wretched condition"*: Quoted in Sellers, *Continentalist*, p. 356.

274 *as high as 100 percent*: "Tariff of 1842 and 1846 Compared," *Daily Union*, July 28, 1846.

274 *some rates increased*: Ibid.

274 *most at 30 percent*: Ibid.

274 *"bringing forth exotics"*: Quoted in McCormac, *Polk* II, p. 673.

274 *114 to 95:* "The Revenue Tariff Passed," *Daily Union*, July 3, 1846.

274 *"Will the protectionists"*: Ibid.

274 *"There is more selfishness"*: JKP, *The Diary of James K. Polk During His Presidency, 1845–1849,* Vol. II, Milo Milton Quaife, editor and annotator (Chicago: A. C. McClurg & Co., 1910; reprinted: Chicago Historical Society), July 11, 1846, p. 20. Hereinafter JKP, *Diary* II.

274 *"I would rather die"*: Quoted in ibid., July 23, 1846, p. 43.

275 *"The principal objection"*: JKP, ibid.

275 *"I begged him"*: Ibid.

275 *July 25 events:* Ibid., July 25, 1846, pp. 47–49.

275 *"THE REVENUE BILL"*: *Daily Union*, July 25, 1846.

275 *"nervous"*: JKP, *Diary* II, July 25, 1846, p. 48.

275 *"from good motives"*: Ibid.

275 *"stormy and violent debate"*: Ibid., July 27, 1846, p. 51.

276 *"holds the fate"*: Ibid.

276 *Senate vote margin:* "The Revenue System Reformed," *Daily Union*, July 29, 1846.

276 *"The long agony"*: Ibid.

277 *"again and again"*: "The Tariff," *Daily Union*, June 20, 1846.

277 *"All in all"*: Holt, *The Rise and Fall of the American Whig Party,* p. 687.

CHAPTER 18: WILMOT'S PROVISO

PAGE

278 *Alexander Mackenzie's mission:* McCormac, *Polk* II, p. 439.

278 *"the President of the United States"*: Ibid.

279 *"to terminate"*: James Buchanan, letter to the Mexican Minister of Foreign Affairs, July 27, 1846, reprinted in "Affairs of Mexico," *Daily Union*, August 13, 1846.

279 *"I had but little doubt"*: JKP, *Diary* II, July 26, 1846, p. 50.

280 *JKP's discussion with Cass:* Ibid., July 31, 1846, p. 57.

280 *JKP's fine distinction:* Ibid., July 30, 1846, p. 56.

280 *JKP instructs Buchanan:* Ibid., August 1, 1846, p. 60.

280 *word from Mackenzie:* McCormac, *Polk* II, p. 440.

281 *"After a long conversation"*: JKP, *Diary* I, June 10, 1846, pp. 464–65.

281 *Cave Johnson arrives:* Ibid., June 28, 1846, p. 492.

281 *Polk-Buchanan conversation:* Ibid., July 1, 1846, pp. 1–2.

281 *"but with great reluctance"*: Ibid., July 2, 1846, pp. 4–5.

281 *"My position"*: Ibid., July 12, 1846, pp. 21–24.

282 *Buchanan informs Polk:* Ibid., August 1, 1846, p. 58.

282 *"The whole frame":* JKP, veto message, quoted in McCormac, *Polk* II, p. 679.

283 *"It is one of the strongest vetoes":* "The Veto," *Daily Union,* August 3, 1846.

283 *"that our government":* National Intelligencer editorial, quoted in "The Groans of the Whig Organ," *Daily Union,* August 3, 1846.

283 *Benton delighted:* JKP, *Diary* II, August 6, 1846, pp. 68–69.

283 *August 4 message:* "Affairs of Mexico," *Daily Union,* August 13, 1846.

283 *"strong desire":* Quoted in ibid.

284 2d. Resolved, further: Ibid.

284 *only two dissenters:* "The Two Million Appropriation," *Daily Union,* August 12, 1846.

284 *vote of 33 to 19:* Ibid.

284 *Eight Whigs voted aye:* Ibid.

284 *"a perfect farce":* JKP, *Diary* II, August 7, 1846, p. 70.

284 *"without attracting much":* Ibid., p. 71.

285 *"the adjustment of a boundary":* JKP, Message to Congress, August 8, 1846, reprinted in "Relations with Mexico," *Daily Union,* August 8, 1846.

285 *maneuverings on the bill:* Ibid.

285 *"for the purpose":* $2 million bill, reprinted in ibid.

286 *Wilmot described:* "Traveler's Diary," *New York Globe,* 1843, reprinted in Charles Buxton Going, *David Wilmot, Free-Soiler: A Biography of the Great Advocate of the Wilmot Proviso* (New York: D. Appleton & Co., 1924), pp. 35–36.

286 *During the recess:* Sean Wilentz, *The Rise of American Democracy: Jefferson to Lincoln* (New York: W. W. Norton, 2005), pp. 594–96.

287 *"I would preserve":* Frederick J. Blue, *No Taint of Compromise: Crusaders in Antislavery Politics* (Baton Rouge: Louisiana State University Press, 2005), p. 193.

287 *"unnecessary, uncalled for":* Hugh White, House floor speech, August 8, 1846, reprinted in "Message—Foreign Intercourse," *Daily Union,* August 10, 1846. All quotes from this Saturday debate, as well as vote totals, are taken from this source.

288 *"was nugatory":* Benton, *Thirty Years' View,* Vol. II, p. 695.

288 *"a mischievous and foolish":* JKP, *Diary* II, August 10, 1846, p. 75.

290 *"no time now":* Dixon Lewis, Senate floor debate, quoted in Going, *David Wilmot, Free-Soiler,* p. 102. All quotes and descriptions of this Senate floor drama are taken from the same source.

291 *"Ten political lives":* Salmon P. Chase, letter to Charles Sumner, December 2, 1847, quoted in ibid., p. 103.

291 *"Had the appropriation"*: JKP, *Diary* II, August 10, 1846, p. 77.

292 *"a man of great purity"*: Ibid., August 22, 1846, p. 94.

CHAPTER 19: THE WAR IN THE WEST

PAGE

293 *"I, Stephen W. Kearny"*: Quoted in Sides, *Blood and Thunder*, p. 106.

293 *eighty thousand inhabitants*: "Capture of Santa Fe," *Daily Union*, October 2, 1846, includes reprint from "Capture of Santa Fe by Gen. Kearney," *St. Louis Republican*, September 24, 1846.

293 *Stockton's declaration*: Ibid., p. 100.

294 *JKP's California fears*: Neal Harlow, *California Conquered: The Annexation of a Mexican Province, 1846–1850* (Berkeley: University of California Press, 1982), p. 56.

295 *Frémont veering into California*: JKP, *Diary* I, October 24, 1845, pp. 71–72.

295 *Gillespie summoned*: Ibid., October 30, 1845, pp. 83–84.

295 *Gillespie's journey*: Ferol Egan, *Frémont: Explorer for a Restless Nation* (Garden City, N.Y.: Doubleday, 1977), pp. 328–29.

295 *"make no effort"*: Quoted in McCormac, *Polk* II, p. 387.

296 *Gillespie's Monterey arrival*: K. Jack Bauer, *The Mexican War, 1846–1848* (Lincoln: University of Nebraska Press, 1974), p. 166.

296 *Stockton's arrival*: Ibid., p. 172.

296 *JKP's western plans*: McCormac, *Polk* II, p. 422.

297 *twenty-two hundred miles*: Sides, *Blood and Thunder*, p. 26.

297 *"a mountain of fat"*: Quoted in ibid., p. 82.

298 *1,458 men*: Bauer, *The Mexican War*, p. 130. Other statistics related to the march come from this source.

298 *"I have come"*: Quoted in Sides, *Blood and Thunder*, p. 73.

298 *"You have notified me"*: Quoted in ibid., p. 83.

299 *four thousand men*: "Capture of Santa Fe," *Daily Union*, October 2, 1846.

299 *"I do not deliver"*: Quoted in Sides, *Blood and Thunder*, p. 102.

299 *"Armijo and his troops"*: Quoted in ibid., p. 103.

299 *three hundred mounted dragoons*: Phyllis Roberts, "Stephen Watts Kearny," Buffalo County Historical Society, http://bchs.kearney.net/BTales_197901.htm.

300 *December 9, 1845*: Bauer, *The Mexican War*, p. 164.

300 *five thousand square miles*: "The Californias," *Daily Union*, September 9, 1846, reprinted from the *N.Y. True Sun*.

301 *twenty-one missions:* "Sketch of California," *Daily Union,* October 9, 1846, reprinted from *Fisher's National Magazine.*

301 *Indian population decline:* Ibid. All numbers reflecting the decline of the missions are taken from this source.

301 *five thousand white inhabitants:* "The Californias," *Daily Union.* All population figures cited here are from this source.

302 *"inform said Capt. Fremont":* Manuel Castro, letter to Thomas O. Larkin, March 8, 1846, reprinted in *Daily Union,* November 9, 1846.

302 *"We have in no wise":* John C. Frémont, letter to Thomas O. Larkin, March 10, 1846, reprinted in ibid.

303 *Castro's April 17 order:* Egan, *Frémont,* p. 335.

303 *160 expatriates:* Bauer, *The Mexican War,* p. 169.

304 *Gillespie's forty-eight troops:* Ibid., p. 183.

305 *Gillespie's thirty-nine troops:* Ibid., p. 187.

305 *"as I am prepared":* Stephen W. Kearny, letter to John C. Frémont, reprinted in "General Stephen Kearny," Son of the South Web site, http://www .sonofthesouth.net/mexican-war/general-stephen-kearny.htm.

CHAPTER 20: THE NEW FACE OF WAR

PAGE

307 *Polk's Veracruz plan:* JKP, *Diary* II, August 29, 1846, p. 103.

308 *"met with a favourable consideration":* Ibid.

308 *word of California victories:* Ibid., September 1, 1846, pp. 107–8.

308 *"liberate all persons":* "From Mexico," *New York Tribune,* August 8, 1846, reprinted in *Daily Union,* September 7, 1846.

308 *confronting Jesup:* JKP, *Diary* II, September 5, 1846, p. 117.

309 *wagons or mules:* Ibid.

309 *"entirely too much delay":* Ibid.

309 *"grasp of mind":* Ibid.

309 *Mexico's rejection:* Ibid., September 19, 1846, p. 144.

309 *new war policies:* Ibid., p. 145.

309 *Mexican war strategy:* "The Route to Mexico," *Daily Union,* October 7, 1846, reprinted from the *New Orleans Picayune,* date not given.

309 *"the public mind":* Ibid.

310 *Santa Anna's boast:* "Negotiations with Mexico," *Daily Union,* September 26, 1846.

310 *Mexicans!:* Quoted in Eisenhower, *So Far from God,* p. 116.

310 *"the intervening months":* "Vigor in the War," *Daily Union,* October 1, 1846.

310 *two important letters:* JKP, *Diary* II, October 2, 1846, p. 169.

310 *"Gen'l Kearney":* Ibid., p. 170.

311 *"Prosecute the war":* Quoted in Bauer, *The Mexican War,* p. 85.

311 *"dispose the enemy":* Quoted in ibid., p. 86.

311 *Monterrey campaign:* Battle reconstruction taken from Bauer, *The Mexican War,* pp. 81–102; and Eisenhower, *So Far from God,* pp. 98–151.

312 *JKP's armistice reaction:* JKP, *Diary* II, October 11, 1846, pp. 181–82.

313 *cabinet reaction:* Ibid., October 12, 1846, pp. 183–85.

313 *meeting with Dimond:* Ibid., October 17, 1846, pp. 195–97.

314 *Taylor's strategic aims:* Ibid., October 20, 1846, pp. 198–200.

314 *"a man of high standing":* "Santa Anna's Mysterious Doings," *Daily Union,* October 10, 1846, reprinted from the *New Orleans Delta,* October 2, 1846. The initial report was printed in *La Patria,* Spanish-language publication at New Orleans, September 22, 1846.

315 *"absurd":* Ibid., *Daily Union.*

315 *"Every mail":* "The Whig Abolition Movement," *Daily Union,* October 10, 1846.

315 *"Yet who can deny":* "Rapid Progress of the Whig Abolition Movement," *Daily Union,* October 15, 1846.

316 *115 House seats:* Cohn (ed.), *Congressional Quarterly's Guide to Congress,* Appendix 94-A.

316 *fifty-nine-seat swing:* Ibid.

316 *fourteen seats in New York:* State statistics from Holt, *The Rise and Fall of the American Whig Party,* p. 238.

316 *"This faction":* JKP, *Diary* II, November 5, 1846, p. 218.

316 *troubles with Buchanan:* Ibid., pp. 217–18.

316 *troop level decision:* Ibid., November 7, 1846, pp. 219–21.

317 *"unless it was met":* Quoted in JKP, ibid., 219–23.

318 *"Who,":* JKP, ibid., November 10, 1846, pp. 226–28.

319 *decision elements:* Ibid., November 14, 1846, pp. 234–37.

320 *"He was . . . so much affected":* Ibid., November 19, 1846, pp. 244–45.

320 *"in very bad taste":* Ibid., November 21, 1845, pp. 248–49.

320 *"illegal in its character":* Quoted in "The Issues Between the Two Parties," *Daily Union,* November 10, 1846.

321 *"Until that end":* Quoted in "The Cry of 'Restoration,'" *Daily Union,* November 11, 1846.

CHAPTER 21: THE POLITICS OF RANCOR

PAGE

322 *The war has been:* JKP, Annual Message, December 8, 1846, reprinted in "Senate," *Daily Union,* January 8, 1846.

323 *"defaces":* National Intelligencer, December 9, 1846, editorial quoted and reprinted in part in "The Freedom of the Press Against the Country," *Daily Union,* December 10, 1846.

323 *"by the law":* Ibid.

323 *"From the day":* JKP, Annual Message. All quotes from the message are from this source.

325 *"by what imperial":* Garrett Davis, House floor speech, December 9, 1846, quoted in McCormac, *Polk* II, p. 459.

325 *"It was therefore":* Stephen Douglas, House floor speech, December 9, 1846, "House of Representatives," *Daily Union,* December 9, 1846.

326 *"new terms to be used":* Cornelius Darragh, House floor speech, ibid.

326 *"not only in the power":* Frederick Stanton, House floor speech, ibid.

326 *"A grosser attack":* Robert Winthrop, House floor speech, ibid.

327 *Those who regard this war:* Frederick Stanton, House floor speech, ibid.

327 *"was exactly such a defense":* Joshua Giddings, House floor speech, December 15, 1846, "House of Representatives," *Daily Union,* December 15, 1846.

327 *"would not withhold":* JKP, *Diary* II, December 12, 1846, p. 273.

328 *Douglas and Stanton views:* JKP, ibid., December 14, 1846, pp. 275–76.

328 *Cass view of Benton appointment:* Ibid.

328 *Sevier support:* Ibid., December 15, 1846, p. 277.

328 *Niles support:* Ibid., December 18, 1846, p. 281.

328 *"I found that his mind":* Ibid., December 19, 1846, pp. 282–84.

328 *Westcott effort:* James Westcott, Senate floor amendment, December 16, 1846, reprinted in *Daily Union,* December 16, 1846.

328 *"Spare me":* Thomas Hart Benton, Senate floor speech, ibid.

329 *"Let those whose servility":* Meredith Gentry, House floor speech, December 16, 1846, *Daily Union,* December 16, 1846.

329 *"We voted for this war":* Barclay Martin, House floor speech, December 22, 1846, "The War with Mexico," *Daily Union,* December 22, 1846.

329 *"used the most opprobrious":* Seaborn Jones, House floor speech, December 21, 1846, "The War with Mexico," *Daily Union,* December 21, 1846. The Jones-Gentry exchange is taken from this source.

331 *"the same party":* Samuel Gordon, House floor speech, December 24, 1846, "The War with Mexico," *Daily Union,* December 24, 1846.

331 *"This is probably":* JKP, *Diary* II, December 22, 1846, p. 288.

331 *"an advocate of Mexico"*: Barclay Martin, House floor speech.

331 *"excess of power"*: JKP, "Message of the President of the United States," delivered to Congress, December 22, 1846, reprinted in *Daily Union*, December 22, 1846.

332 *"No instructions"*: "Interesting Message and Accompanying Documents," *Daily Union*, December 22, 1846.

332 *"make the proposition"*: Quoted in JKP, *Diary* II, December 21, 1846, p. 286.

332 *"greatly dissatisfied"*: JKP, ibid.

332 *conversation with Wilmot*: Ibid., December 23, 1846, pp. 288–90.

333 *"insuperable difficulties"*: Quoted in JKP, ibid., December 24, 1846, pp. 292–93.

333 *"a vast region"*: "The New Year," *Daily Union*, January 1, 1847.

CHAPTER 22: DILATORY CONGRESS

PAGE

335 *"excite a feeling against us"*: Quoted in JKP, *Diary* II, January 2, 1847, pp. 300–303. All quotes and descriptions from this cabinet meeting are from this source.

336 *"much fatigued"*: Ibid.

336 *King and Hamlin*: JKP, ibid., January 4, 1847, pp. 304–05.

337 *"are united"*: Ibid., p. 306.

337 *failed by a single vote*: House vote, January 9, 1847, *Congressional Globe*, January 14, 1847.

337 *"without exception disaffected"*: Ibid., January 9, 1847, p. 318.

337 *"vented their spite"*: Ibid., p. 319.

337 *"sickening to the heart"*: Ibid.

338 *Atocha reappears*: Ibid., January 12, 1847, p. 323.

338 *"very important"*: Quoted in ibid., January 14, 1847, p. 325.

338 *Santa Anna's terms*: Ibid.

339 *cabinet view of Atocha*: JKP, ibid., January 16, 1847, pp. 331–32.

339 *"either through his inordinate"*: Ibid., January 14, 1847, pp. 327–28.

339 *"With a large nominal majority"*: Ibid., p. 328.

339 *"and by superiority"*: "From the Army," *New Orleans Mercury*, reprinted in "Army and Navy Intelligence," *Daily Union*, January 11, 1847.

339 *House passes Ten Regiment Bill*: House vote, January 11, 1847, "Increase of the Army," *Congressional Globe*, January 15, 1847.

340 *"my administration"*: JKP, *Diary* II, January 19, 1847, p. 341.

340 *And how has Congress*: "The Action of Congress," *Daily Union*, January 18, 1847.

340 *"remarkably bold and rash"*: John Crozier, House floor speech, January 21, 1847, *Congressional Globe*, January 23, 1847.

341 *Taylor's letter*: Zachary Taylor, letter to Edmund P. Gaines, reprinted in "General Taylor's Letter," *Daily Union*, January 26, 1847.

341 *"Was I a prominent"*: Zachary Taylor, letter to R. C. Wood, quoted in McCormac, *Polk* II, p. 431.

341 *"decided rebuke"*: JKP, *Diary* II, January 27, 1847, p. 359.

341 *"in the most summary mode"*: George Ashmun, House floor speech, January 30, 1847, *Daily Union*, February 1, 1847.

342 *"that {Taylor} had succeeded"*: Stephen Douglas, House floor speech, ibid.

342 *loan bill clears Congress:* "Congressional," *Daily Union*, January 27, 1847.

342 *Senate vote 39 to 3:* "Senate," *Daily Union*, February 1, 1847.

342 *"with any view"*: John Berrien amendment, introduced February 4, 1847, reprinted in "Senate," *Daily Union*, February 5, 1847.

343 *"calculated to disgrace"*: "The Proposed Amendment," *Daily Union*, February 4, 1847.

343 *"I am much embarrassed"*: JKP, *Diary* II, February 5, 1847, p. 368.

343 *"in terms of great indignation"*: Ibid., February 8, 1847, p. 372.

343 *"nothing less"*: "The Army Bill in the Senate," *Daily Union*, February 8, 1847.

343 *Ten Regiment Bill passes:* JKP, *Diary* II, February 10, 1847, p. 375.

344 *"The worst state of things"*: JKP, "Message from the President," February 13, 1847, *Congressional Globe*, February 17, 1847.

344 *"defensive position"*: John C. Calhoun, Senate floor speech, February 9, 1847, *Congressional Globe*, February 11, 1847.

345 *"Why, we are at war!"*: "Mr. Calhoun's View of the Conduct of the War," *Daily Union*, February 10, 1847.

345 *"A strong desire"*: Lewis Cass, Senate floor speech, February 10, 1847, *Daily Union*, February 11, 1847. All quotes from the Cass speech come from this source.

346 *"The immediate cause"*: John C. Calhoun, Senate floor speech, *Daily Union*, February 22, 1847.

347 *"The causes of this Mexican war"*: Thomas Hart Benton, Senate floor speech, February 24, 1847, "The Three Million Bill," *Daily Union*, February 24, 1847. All quotes from this speech are from this source.

349 *"a war of giants"*: "Scene in the Senate," *Daily Union*, February 24, 1847.

349 *"and thus"*: JKP, *Diary* II, February 25, 1847, p. 392.

349 *"torn by factions"*: Ibid.

349 *Wilmot fails by five votes:* "Three Million Bill," *Daily Union*, March 4, 1847.

349 *vote of 115 to 81:* Ibid.

349 *"The democratic majority":* "Close of the Last Session of the 29th Congress," *Daily Union,* March 4, 1847.

350 *"Good feeling prevailed":* JKP, *Diary* II, March 3, 1847, p. 406.

CHAPTER 23: VERACRUZ AND BEYOND

PAGE

351 *six thousand men:* "From the Army," *Daily Union,* March 5, 1847.

351 *"a more active campaign":* Ibid.

352 *"I differ with you":* JKP, *Diary* II, March 20, 1847, pp. 431–32.

352 *"more detailed rumours":* Ibid., March 21, 1847, p. 433.

352 *"painful suspense":* Ibid., March 22, 1847, p. 434.

352 *"I have great fears":* Ibid., p. 435.

352 *"exciting rumours":* Ibid., March 28, 1847, p. 444.

352 *"If Gen'l Taylor":* Ibid.

352 *"I must ask you":* Winfield Scott to Zachary Taylor, January 26, 1847, quoted in Eisenhower, *So Far from God,* p. 174.

353 *"much the safest course":* Zachary Taylor, letter to John Crittenden, January 20, 1846, quoted in ibid.

353 *"You are surrounded":* Gen. López de Santa Anna, letter to Zachary Taylor, February 22, 1847, reprinted in "From General Taylor's Camp," *Daily Union,* April 1, 1847.

353 *"I beg leave":* Zachary Taylor, letter to Gen. López de Santa Anna, February 22, 1847, reprinted in ibid.

353 *"General, we are whipped":* Quoted in Eisenhower, *So Far from God,* p. 188.

353 *"That is for me":* Quoted in ibid.

354 *665 officers and men:* Bauer, *Zachary Taylor,* p. 205.

354 *4,594 sent:* Bauer, *The Mexican War,* p. 217.

354 *"Alas, there are some wounds":* Quoted in Remini, *Henry Clay,* p. 685.

356 *levies on Mexican ports:* JKP, *Diary* II, April 5, 1847, p. 456.

356 *That, in the opinion:* Public meeting statement, "Meeting of the Citizens of Charleston," *Charleston Mercury,* March 10, 1847, reprinted in *Daily Union,* March 15, 1847.

357 *"the duty of every slaveholding State":* "Virginia Resolutions," reprinted in *Daily Union,* ibid.

357 *"a man unsound":* John C. Calhoun, "Remarks of Mr. Calhoun," *Charleston Evening News,* reprinted in *Daily Union,* ibid.

357 *"manifested their concurrence":* "Meeting of the Citizens of Charleston," reprinted in *Daily Union.*

357 *"a political Ishmael"*: "Mr. Calhoun's Movement Against a National Convention," *Daily Union*, March 27, 1847.

357 *"not only unpatriotic"*: JKP, *Diary* II, April 6, 1847, pp. 457–58.

357 *"only means"*: Ibid.

358 *"The truth is"*: Ibid.

358 *"The whole army"*: Winfield Scott, letter to William Marcy, March 12, 1847, reprinted in "From Our Army at Veracruz," *Daily Union*, April 5, 1847.

358 *"This was joyous news"*: JKP, *Diary* II, April 10, 1847, p. 465.

359 *"We have taken the Gibraltar"*: "Glorious Achievement," *Daily Union*, April 10, 1847.

360 *Trist selection*: JKP, *Diary* II, April 10, 1847, pp. 466–67.

360 *imperative of secrecy*: Ibid., p. 468.

361 *negotiating instructions*: Ibid., April 13, 1847, pp. 471–75.

361 *"I have not been more vexed"*: Ibid., April 21, 1847, pp. 482–83.

362 *Buchanan is mum*: Ibid., April 22, 1847, p. 486.

362 *"The nomination of General Taylor"*: "General Taylor," the *Mobile Register*, reprinted in *Daily Union*, April 22, 1847.

362 *"And yet in this utter darkness"*: "The Federal Leaders and Gen. Taylor," *Daily Union*, April 28, 1847.

362 *Scott's twenty thousand troops*: JKP, *Diary* II, April 28, 1847, p. 491.

363 *three thousand troops captured*: Eisenhower, *So Far from God*, p. 283.

363 *sixty-three U.S. soldiers killed*: Bauer, *The Mexican War*, p. 268.

363 *"In this emergency"*: "Mexico," *Daily Union*, May 11, 1847.

364 *"Brigadier General Pillow"*: Quoted in Eisenhower, *So Far from God*, p. 280.

364 *"without distinction"*: JKP, *The Diary of James K. Polk During His Presidency, 1845–1849*, Vol. III, edited and annotated by Milo Milton Quaife (Chicago: A. C. McClurg & Co., 1910); reprinted: Chicago Historical Society, May 28, 1847, p. 37. Hereinafter, JKP, *Diary* III.

364 *"Thirty years ago"*: Quoted in *Richmond Enquirer*, reprinted in *Daily Union*, June 7, 1847.

365 *"overflowing with people"*: *Richmond Enquirer*, reprinted in *Daily Union*, June 7, 1847.

365 *"exceedingly agreeable"*: JKP, *Diary* III, June 5, 1847, p. 50.

365 *"It was a matter"*: Ibid.

CHAPTER 24: SCOTT AND TRIST

PAGE

366   *"Should he make known"*: William Marcy, letter to Winfield Scott, April 14, 1847, reprinted in "Correspondence Between the War Department and General Scott," *Daily Union,* April 9, 1848.

367   *"I see"*: Winfield Scott, letter to Nicholas Trist, May 7, 1847, reprinted in ibid.

367   *"too much occupied"*: Winfield Scott, letter to William Marcy, May 7, 1847, reprinted in ibid.

368   *"sincere regret that a letter"*: William Marcy, letter to Winfield Scott, May 31, 1847, reprinted in ibid.

368   *"In a word, sir"*: Nicholas Trist, letter to Winfield Scott, May 9, 1847, reprinted in "Correspondence—Continued: *Mr. Trist to Major General Scott,*" *Daily Union,* March 26, 1848.

368   *"decidedly the greatest imbecile"*: Quoted in McCormac, *Polk* II, p. 498n.

369   *"I entreat to be spared"*: Winfield Scott, letter to William Marcy, May 20, 1837, reprinted in "Correspondence Between the War Department and General Scott," *Daily Union,* April 9, 1847.

369   *"insubordinate"*: JKP, *Diary* III, June 12, 1847, p. 58.

369   *"the golden moment"*: Ibid., June 15, 1847, p. 62.

369   *"No President"*: "The President of the United States," *Daily Union,* July 7, 1847.

369   *two and a half days:* Ibid.

370   *"My reception"*: JKP, *Diary* III, July 7, 1847, p. 73.

370   *This is the hall:* JKP, untitled, *Pennsylvanian,* June 25, 1847, reprinted in "The Visit of the President," *Daily Union,* June 26, 1847.

370   *"committed a great error"*: JKP, *Diary* III, July 9, 1847, p. 76.

370   *"a flank battery"*: Winfield Scott, letter to William Marcy, June 4, 1847, reprinted in "Correspondence Between the War Department and General Scott," *Daily Union,* April 9, 1848.

371   *Thornton visit on June 10:* McCormac, *Polk* II, p. 506.

372   *"constituted the commencement"*: Nicholas Trist, letter to James Buchanan, July 23, 1847, quoted in ibid., p. 507.

372   *"so much good feeling"*: Nicholas Trist, letter to James Buchanan, July 7, 1847, quoted in ibid., p. 509.

373   *"We are both convinced"*: Nicholas Trist, letter to Winfield Scott, July 16, 1847, quoted in ibid., p. 510.

373   *Scott's meetings with generals:* Ibid., p. 511; Eisenhower, *So Far from God,* p. 306.

373 *"I fully concur"*: Winfield Scott, letter to Nicholas Trist, quoted in McCormac, *Polk* II, p. 511.

374 *"utter confusion"*: "General Taylor and the Presidency," *Cincinnati Morning Signal*, April 13, 1847, reprinted in "General Taylor's Letter—The Presidency," *Daily Union*, July 1, 1847.

374 *"amid evil times"*: "Henry Clay," *North American*, August 17, 1847, reprinted in *Daily Union*, August 20, 1847.

375 *"my services are ever"*: Zachary Taylor, letter to *Cincinnati Morning Signal*, May 18, 1847, reprinted in "General Taylor's Letter—The Presidency," *Daily Union*, July 1, 1847.

375 *"If Gen. Taylor adhere"*: Untitled editorial, *Richmond Times and Compiler*, reprinted in "General Taylor's Letter," *Daily Union*, July 6, 1847.

375 *"The power of one man"*: Untitled editorial, *American and Gazette,* quoted in "General Taylor and His Too Hasty Friends," *Daily Union*, July 8, 1847.

376 *"views and those of the whigs"*: Zachary Taylor, letter to Joseph R. Ingersoll, August 3, 1847, reprinted in *Daily Union*, June 21, 1848.

376 *The* Union *howling:* "The Taylor Correspondence," *Daily Union*, June 21, 1848.

376 *"If Taylor keeps writing"*: Quoted in Bauer, *Zachary Taylor,* p. 227.

376 *"the statesman of the party"*: "General Taylor and the Presidency," *Cincinnati Morning Signal*, April 13, 1847, reprinted in "General Taylor's Letter—The Presidency," *Daily Union*, July 1, 1847.

376 *"surrender up"*: Untitled editorial, *Auburn* (New York) *Advertiser*, reprinted in *Daily Union*, September 7, 1847.

377 *"Do they not see"*: Untitled editorial, *National Intelligencer,* reprinted in *Daily Union*, September 7, 1847.

377 *"And to what end"*: "The Self-Styled 'Peace Party' and Their New Issue," *Daily Union*, September 13, 1847.

377 *"I am glad to hear"*: Quoted in JKP, *Diary* III, August 17, 1847, pp. 120–23.

377 *"was evidently much excited"*: JKP, *Diary* III, August 17, 1847, p. 123.

378 *"astonishingly large amount"*: JKP, ibid., August 20, 1847, p. 130. The story of the misappropriated funds is taken entirely from JKP, *Diary* III.

380 *"struck down without warning"*: "The Death of Silas Wright," *Daily Union*, August 30, 1847.

380 *"He was a great and good man"*: JKP, *Diary* III, August 29, 1847, p. 153.

380 *Polk's new war thinking:* Ibid., September 4, 1847, pp. 159–62.

381 *How much territory:* Ibid., September 7, 1847, pp. 163–65.

381 *seven thousand men:* Eisenhower, *So Far from God,* p. 313. All figures and descriptions of the August 20 battles come from this source, pp. 312–27, and from Bauer, *The Mexican War,* pp. 279–301.

CHAPTER 25: MEXICO CITY

PAGE

384 *"scatter the elements"*: Quoted in Eisenhower, *So Far from God*, p. 329.

384 *"Too much blood"*: Winfield Scott, letter to Santa Anna, quoted in ibid.

384 *"very cheerfully sacrificed"*: Winfield Scott, letter to William Marcy, quoted in ibid.

384 *August 22 truce terms*: Eisenhower, *Agent of Destiny*, p. 286.

384 *Truce breaks down*: Bauer, *The Mexican War*, pp. 307–8.

385 *Mexican demands*: JKP, Annual Message, December 7, 1847, reprinted in *Daily Union*, December 7, 1847.

385 *Trist's concession*: Wallace Ohrt, *Defiant Peacemaker: Nicholas Trist in the Mexican War* (College Station: Texas A&M University Press, 1997), p. 131.

385 *Trist's September 4 dispatch*: Nicholas Trist, letter to James Buchanan, with Enclosure No. 1, reprinted in *Daily Union*, February 3, 1848.

386 *"I shall wait"*: JKP, *Diary* III, September 15, 1847, pp. 171–72.

386 *"The propositions"*: "Accounts from Mexico," *Daily Union*, October 1, 1847.

386 *Polk's October 4 decision*: JKP, *Diary* III, October 4, 1847, p. 185.

386 *"by the first safe opportunity"*: James Buchanan, letter to Nicholas Trist, quoted in McCormac, *Polk* II, p. 519.

387 *Worth's 3,500 men*: Eisenhower, *So Far from God*, p. 334.

387 *Santa Anna's five brigades*: Ibid., p. 335.

387 *116 men killed, etc.*: Ibid., p. 336.

387 *Santa Anna loses two thousand soldiers*: Bauer, *The Mexican War*, p. 311.

388 *Scott's attack route*: Ibid., p. 312.

388 *Santa Anna loses 1,800 men*: Eisenhower, *So Far from God*, p. 342.

389 *"the greatest living soldier"*: Quoted in Bauer, *The Mexican War*, p. 322.

389 *seven thousand enemy troops*: Ibid.

389 *"a mass of vanity"*: Quoted in Ohrt, *Defiant Peacemaker*, p. 119.

389 *Pillow is Brown's brother-in-law*: The Tennessee Encyclopedia of History and Culture, Aaron V. Brown, 1795–1859, http://tennesseeencyclopedia.net.

390 *"I have great confidence"*: JKP, *Diary* III, August 7, 1847, pp. 112–13.

390 *"I can only say"*: Quoted in Borneman, *Polk*, p. 294.

390 *"a gentleman"*: Quoted in ibid., p. 295.

390 *"give my name a place"*: Quoted in ibid.

390 *{Pillow's} plan of battle*: "Leonidas," letter to the *New Orleans Delta*, September 10, 1847, quoted in Eisenhower, *So Far from God*, p. 353.

391 *"False credit"*: Winfield Scott, General Order No. 349, November 12, 1847, quoted in Eisenhower, *So Far from God*, p. 354.

392 *"assassin-like tactics"*: Gideon Pillow, letter to JKP, quoted in Borneman, *Polk,* p. 297.

392 *Polk's new war strategy*: JKP, *Diary* III, October 12, 1847, pp. 189–90.

393 *"Mr. Benton became excited"*: Ibid., October 22, 1847, pp. 197–98.

393 *"I am much embarrassed"*: Ibid., October 23, 1847, pp. 199–201.

394 *"ludicrously small"*: "The Herkimer Convention," *Daily Union,* October 30, 1847.

394 *"about 700 persons"*: Quoted in ibid.

394 *"The Wilmot-Proviso party"*: "The War," *Daily Union,* October 27, 1847.

394 *"There is no rock"*: "Compromise and Conciliation," *Daily Union,* September 24, 1847.

394 *"It was created"*: Henry Clay, speech of November 13, 1847, reprinted in *Daily Union,* November 24, 1847. All speech quotes are taken from this source.

395 *"to propitiate"*: "The New Whig Manifesto.-Mr. Clay's Resolutions and Speech," *Daily Union,* November 16, 1847.

396 *"I . . . most heartily wish"*: JKP, *Diary* III, November 2, 1847, p. 210.

397 *"singular communication"*: Ibid., November 22, 1847, p. 228.

397 *"stand by him"*: Ibid., November 23, 1847, p. 230.

397 *"we must fulfil"*: Ibid., November 20, 1847, p. 226.

397 *Polk submitted compromise*: Ibid., November 22, 1847, p. 228.

398 *46 to 29 vote*: Ohrt, *Defiant Peacemaker,* p. 133.

398 *Trist's Rio Grande rationale*: Ibid., p. 134.

398 *Peña wept*: Ibid.

399 *Peña's November 24 letter*: Eisenhower, *Agent of Destiny,* p. 305.

399 *"Say so to Mr. Buchanan"*: Nicholas Trist, letter to Virginia Trist, quoted in Ohrt, *Defiant Peacemaker,* p. 139.

400 *"Mr. Trist, make the Treaty"*: Ibid., p. 140.

400 *"I will make the Treaty"*: Ibid.

400 *Walker's ploy*: JKP, *Diary* III, December 7, 1847, pp. 241–42.

CHAPTER 26: THE SPECTER OF CONQUEST

PAGE

402 *"in satisfaction"*: JKP, Annual Message, "Message," *Daily Union,* December 7, 1847.

404 *"the very savage"*: National Intelligencer, quoted in "A New Whig Manifesto," *Daily Union,* December 13, 1847.

405 *This American people*: "A New Whig Manifesto," *Daily Union.*

405 *"in the strongest terms"*: JKP, *Diary* III, December 11, 1847, p. 245.

406   Resolved, *That to conquer:* John C. Calhoun, Senate resolutions, introduced December 15, 1847, reprinted in "The War with Mexico," *Daily Union,* December 15, 1847.

406   *"I believe":* John C. Calhoun, Senate floor debate, December 20, 1847, "Senate: The Conquest of Mexico," *Daily Union,* December 22, 1847.

406   *"there is no man":* Lewis Cass, ibid.

406   *"was applauded":* Calhoun, ibid.

407   *"Neither Gen'l Scott":* JKP, *Diary* III, December 20, 1847, p. 253.

407   *"assented with reluctance":* Ibid.

408   *"bravery & gallantry":* Quoted in ibid., December 28, 1847, p. 262.

408   *"vanity and tyrannical temper":* JKP, *Diary* III, December 30, 1847, p. 266.

408   *"in strong and decided terms":* Ibid., December 31, 1847, p. 269.

409   *"He is acting, no doubt":* Ibid., January 4, 1848, p. 283.

410   *"intriguer":* Nicholas Trist, letter to James Buchanan, December 6, 1847, quoted in McCormac, *Polk* II, pp. 525–27. All quotes from Trist's letter are taken from this source.

410   *"arrogant, impudent":* JKP, *Diary* III, January 15, 1848, p. 300.

410   *"a short, but stern":* Ibid., p. 301.

411   *"The whig members":* "More Resolutions," *Daily Union,* January 3, 1848.

411   *Lincoln's eight questions:* "The War with Mexico," *Daily Union,* December 22, 1847.

411   *"to avoid the scrutiny":* Abraham Lincoln, House floor speech, quoted in Frank van der Linden, *Lincoln: The Road to War* (Golden, Colo.: Fulcrum, 1998), p. 3.

411   *vote of 85 to 81:* "Thanks to General Taylor," *Daily Union,* January 3, 1847.

411   *"unnecessarily and unconstitutionally":* Ibid.

412   *"would exhibit me":* JKP, *Diary* III, January 8, 1848, p. 291.

412   *"would ever trust us":* Quoted in ibid., p. 292.

412   *"This House":* John Quincy Adams, House floor debate, January 12, 1848, "The Return of Santa Anna to Mexico," *Daily Union,* January 13, 1848.

412   *"Should it go abroad":* Robert Schenk, House floor debate, ibid.

413   *"I believed it would lead":* Calhoun, Senate floor speech, January 4, 1848, reprinted in "Speech of Mr. Calhoun," *Daily Union,* January 6, 1848. All quotes are taken from this source.

415   *"neither peace nor war":* "Mr. Calhoun's Policy—A Defensive Line," *Daily Union,* January 7, 1848.

416   *Reverdy Johnson's position:* "Mr. Reverdy Johnson," *Daily Union,* January 12, 1848.

416 *"in case the administration"*: John Clayton, Senate floor debate, January 11, 1848, "The Ten Regiment Bill," *Daily Union,* January 12, 1848. The full Clayton-Cass exchange is taken from this source.

416 The grand procession: *Baltimore Sun* headline, reprinted in "Reception of Gen. Taylor at New Orleans in a Blaze of Glory!" *Daily Union,* December 13, 1847.

CHAPTER 27: TREATY

PAGE

418 *"enjoy a Sea bath"*: Quoted in Remini, *Henry Clay,* p. 689.

418 *"frolicking"*: Remini, *Henry Clay,* p. 690.

418 *"no feelings of an unkind character"*: Quoted in JKP, *Diary* III, February 4, 1848, pp. 325–26. The entire episode is taken from this source, but some of the quotes are taken from Allan Nevins, *The Ordeal of the Union: Fruits of Manifest Destiny, 1847–1852* (New York: Scribners, 1947), p. 198. Nevins places the exchange at a White House dinner, and gives Clay a more elaborate mode of expression. I credit Polk's accuracy in placing the conversation in his parlor, given that Polk's rendition was crafted on the very day of the conversation. But Nevins's direct quotes appear more authentic than Polk's more clipped version.

420 *"reprehensible conduct"*: JKP, ibid., January 23, 1848, pp. 309–10.

420 *Buchanan's advice:* Ibid., January 24, 1848, p. 311.

421 *"very embarrassing"*: Quoted in ibid., January 25, 1848, p. 313.

421 *ten resolutions:* "The Great War Meeting at Tammany Hall. Tremendous Gathering of the People," *New York Herald,* January 30, 1848, reprinted in *Daily Union,* January 31, 1848.

421 *"one feeling prevailed"*: Untitled and undated commentary, *New York Globe,* quoted in "The Voice of the Empire City—Immense Rally to Sustain the War and the Cause of the Country," *Daily Union,* February 1, 1848.

422 *"I am one of those"*: Ambrose Sevier, Senate floor speech, February 4, 1848, *Daily Union,* February 23, 1848.

422 *Do gentlemen suppose:* Stephen Douglas, Senate floor speech, February 1, 1848, *Daily Union,* February 20, 1848.

422 *Turney and Bagby visit:* JKP, *Diary* III, January 29, 1848, pp. 319–20.

422 *"I sincerely hope"*: Ibid.

422 *details of Frémont court-martial:* Egan, *Frémont,* pp. 443–63.

423 *"respectfully commend"*: Quoted in ibid., p. 461.

424 *"painful and responsible duty"*: JKP, *Diary* III, February 16, 1848, p. 340.

424 *"exceedingly pleasant"*: Ibid.

425 *Trist offers $15 million:* Ohrt, *Defiant Peacemaker,* p. 144. Details of the negotiations are taken largely from this source.

426 *"This must be a proud":* Quoted in ibid., p. 145.

426 *"We are making peace":* Quoted in ibid.

426 *loan bill passes:* "The Loan Bill," *Daily Union,* February 17, 1848.

426 *telegraphic dispatch:* JKP, *Diary* III, February 18, 1848, pp. 343–44.

427 *"are within his instructions":* Ibid., February 19, 1848, p. 345.

427 *"Mr. Trist has acted":* Ibid.

427 *"deemed prompt action":* Ibid., February 20, 1848, p. 346.

427 *"viz, whether":* Ibid.

427 *"total change of opinion":* Ibid., February 21, 1848, pp. 347–51. The heated exchange between Polk and Buchanan is part of the February 21 entry, but Polk appends a note at the end saying the conversation actually took place on February 20.

428 *"was unpleasant to me":* Ibid.

428 *"constantly wasting":* Ibid.

429 *Clay calls:* Ibid., February 22, 1848, p. 352.

429 *"This is the last of earth":* Nagel, *John Quincy Adams,* p. 414. Adams's last words have been quoted variously, but Nagel considers this to be the most likely.

429 *"mournful and deeply impressive event":* "Death of Mr. Adams," *Daily Union,* February 23, 1848.

429 *"in their striking":* "Funeral Obsequies," *Daily Union,* February 26, 1848.

430 *"The hall was dressed":* Ibid.

430 *"avoid a greater national evil":* *National Intelligencer,* quoted in "The Treaty," *Daily Union,* February 28, 1848.

430 *"Admit all its faults":* *New York Tribune,* reprinted in "The Treaty," *Daily Union,* March 2, 1848.

432 *"in a stern manner":* JKP, *Diary* III, February 23, 1848, p. 354.

432 *"If I obtain":* Ibid.

432 *"spectacle":* Ibid., February 25, 1848, p. 361.

432 *"The truth is":* Ibid.

433 *"impertinent, irrelevant":* Ibid., February 28, 1848, p. 367.

433 *"The result":* Ibid., February 29, 1848, p. 368.

433 *"extremely doubtful":* Quoted in ibid., March 1, 1848, p. 369.

434 *Senate floor maneuvers:* David M. Pletcher, *The Diplomacy of Annexation: Texas, Oregon, and the Mexican War* (Columbia: University of Missouri Press, 1973), p. 562.

434 *"may be ratified":* JKP, *Diary* III, March 2, 1848, p. 369.

434 *"of such a character":* Ibid., March 9, 1848, p. 376.

434 *38 to 14:* Pletcher, *The Diplomacy of Annexation,* p. 563.

435 *party and geographic breakdown:* Ibid.

435 *"We congratulate the country":* "The Treaty Ratified by the Senate of the United States," *Daily Union,* March 10, 1848.

CHAPTER 28: PEACE

PAGE

436 *Polk fretted:* JKP, *Diary* III, March 10, 1848, p. 378.

436 *Walker and Buchanan misgivings:* Ibid., March 11, 1848, p. 378.

437 *Sevier meeting:* Ibid.

437 *Walsh appointment:* Ibid., March 13, 1848, p. 382.

437 *Sevier and Walsh confirmed:* Ibid., March 14, 1848, p. 383.

437 *a move afoot:* Ibid., March 16, 1848, p. 385.

437 *bribe investigation:* Ibid., March 16, 1848, p. 389.

437 *"It was a case of emergency":* Ibid.

437 *"a very discreet, sensible man":* Ibid., March 18, 1848, p. 391.

438 *"I resist it":* Daniel Webster, Senate floor speech, March 23, 1848, quoted at length and described in "Mr. Webster's Speech," *Daily Union,* March 28, 1848.

438 *"nothing but a piece of land jobbing":* Joseph Root, House floor speech, March 15, 1848, "House of Representatives," *Daily Union,* March 15, 1848.

439 *"pretty well understood":* Quoted in JKP, *Diary* III, March 24, 1848, p. 400.

439 *"was in habits of intimacy":* Quoted in ibid., p. 401.

439 *"closetted":* Ibid.

439 *"Mr. Buchanan has been publicly":* Ibid., p. 403.

440 *"He has been selfish":* Ibid., p. 404.

440 *"had felt a delicacy":* Ibid., March 25, 1848, p. 405.

440 *"I do not":* Ibid., p. 406. Actual diary language: "I told [him] I did not."

440 *"I am myself gratified":* Ibid., March 26, 1848, pp. 409–10.

441 *Trist departs April 8:* Eisenhower, *Agent of Destiny,* p. 316.

441 *"acquiescence in usurped authority":* Quoted in Ohrt, *Defiant Peacemaker,* p. 152.

441 *Polk cuts off Trist's pay:* Ibid., p. 155.

441 *May 4 New Orleans arrival:* Ibid., p. 152.

441 *"the noble character":* Quoted in ibid., p. 151.

441 *Scott's departure schedule:* Eisenhower, *Agent of Destiny,* pp. 318–19.

442 *"a strong disinclination":* Clay, statement entitled "To the Public," reprinted in *Daily Union,* April 13, 1848.

442 *"be so discourteous"*: "Mr. Clay's Letter," *Daily Union,* April 14, 1848.

443 "whoever may be the nominee": Zachary Taylor, public letter, quoted in "Gen. Taylor and His Letter of April 20," *Daily Union,* May 5, 1848.

443 *It was that budget:* Winfield Scott, letter to William Marcy, February 24, 1848, reprinted in "General Scott's Letter," *Daily Union,* April 30, 1848.

444 *"Excepting, however":* Henry Hilliard amendment, House floor, April 17, 1848, reprinted in "The Recent Correspondence Between General Scott and the War Department," *Daily Union,* April 29, 1848.

444 *"that but six deputies":* "Mustang," letter to *Daily Union* from Mexico City, April 13, 1848, printed May 2, 1848.

444 *Benton's display of respect:* JKP, *Diary* III, May 2, 1848, p. 442.

445 *"They have been two years":* Ibid., May 13, 1848, p. 448.

445 *"to relieve the Convention":* Ibid., p. 449.

445 *five minutes to noon:* "Democratic National Convention, First Day's Proceedings, May 22, 1848," *Daily Union,* May 22, 1848.

446 *"factious Whigs":* William Lowndes Yancey, convention speech, quoted in Wilentz, *The Rise of American Democracy,* p. 615.

446 *two-vote margin:* "Proceedings of the Democratic National Convention, Baltimore, May 24, 1848—Evening Session," *Daily Union,* May 27, 1848.

446 *"If on reviewing the history":* JKP, statement to Democratic National Convention, reprinted in "The Baltimore Convention—Nomination of President—the Present President of the United States," *Daily Union,* May 26, 1848.

446 *presidential balloting:* "Proceedings of the Democratic National Convention," *Daily Union,* May 27, 1848.

446 *"The announcement":* Ibid.

447 *"could not and would not":* Quoted in JKP, *Diary* III, May 22, 1848, p. 458.

447 *Yancey walks out:* Wilentz, *The Rise of American Democracy,* p. 616.

447 *"to propose over the grave":* Editorial, *New York Evening Post,* quoted in *Daily Union,* June 14, 1848.

447 *a slaveholder dominion:* Editorial, *New York Globe,* quoted in ibid.

447 *"The indications everywhere":* Editorial, *Lexington Observer and Reporter,* reprinted in *Daily Union,* May 26, 1848.

447 *Greeley castigates newspapers:* Editorial, *New York Tribune,* reprinted in ibid.

448 *"quite clear":* "The Prospects of Our Opponents," *Daily Union,* May 21, 1848.

448 *"would sweep through":* Editorial, *Boston Atlas,* reprinted in ibid.

448 *Whig convention balloting:* "The Whig Convention, Second Day's Proceedings," *Daily Union,* June 8, 1848.

448 *"an out-and-out partisan"*: "The Whig Nomination," *Daily Union*, June 11, 1848.

448 *"a slaughterhouse"*: Quoted in Wilentz, *The Rise of American Democracy*, p. 617.

448 *"I fear that the Whig party"*: Quoted in Holt, *The Rise and Fall of the American Whig Party*, p. 332.

448 *"He cannot be elected"*: "The Whig Ticket—Taylor and Fillmore," *Daily Union*, June 9, 1848.

448 *"There is now, I hope"*: JKP, *Diary* III, June 8, 1848, pp. 484–85.

449 *"IMPORTANT FROM MEXICO!"*: *Daily Union*, June 8, 1848.

449 *vote of 51 to 35:* Ibid.

449 *We have at length:* "PEACE!!!," *Daily Union*, June 9, 1848.

449 *600,000 square miles:* Ohrt, *Defiant Peacemaker*, p. 154.

450 *"indisposed"*: JKP, *Diary* III, various entries between June 8, 1848, and July 3, 1848.

450 *13,780 American lives:* Eisenhower, *So Far from God*, p. 369.

450 *hundred million in U.S. dollars:* Ibid.

450 *sacrifice of nearly 25,000 Mexicans:* The History Guy Web site, http://www.historyguy.com/mexican-american_war.html.

451 *The number and importunities:* JKP, *Diary* III, June 14, 1848, p. 491.

CHAPTER 29: FINAL MONTHS

PAGE

452 *cornerstone ceremony:* JKP, *Diary* IV, July 4, 1848, p. 1.

452 *"exceedingly fatigued"*: Ibid.

453 *"The results of the war"*: JKP, Message to Congress, July 6, 1848, reprinted in "The President's Message," *Daily Union*, July 7, 1848.

453 *"ought to be settled"*: JKP, *Diary* IV, July 16, 1848, p. 20.

454 *"without any sacrifice of principle"*: John Clayton, Senate floor speech, July 18, 1848, *Daily Union*, July 19, 1848.

454 *"There is now some prospect"*: JKP, *Diary* IV, July 19, 1848, p. 24.

455 *"His defeat must be made certain"*: *New York Globe*, quoted in *Daily Union*, June 15, 1848.

455 *Samuel Young's comment:* "The Utica Convention," *Daily Union*, June 25, 1848.

455 *"altogether with the South"*: Quoted in "Mr. Van Buren," *Daily Union*, June 28, 1848.

455 *"a northern man"*: "Mr. Van Buren," *Daily Union*, June 28, 1848.

456 *"We are called upon"*: Martin Van Buren, letter to Barnburner convention,

June 20, 1848, reprinted in "The Utica Convention," *Daily Union,* June 27, 1848.

456 *"This is a most dangerous attempt":* JKP, *Diary* III, June 24, 1848, p. 502.

456 *"is virtually worse":* "The Utica Convention," *Daily Union,* June 25, 1848.

456 *"by blood":* Reverdy Johnson, Senate floor speech, "Congressional," *Daily Union,* July 11, 1848.

456 *Calhoun and Berrien arguments:* "Congressional," *Daily Union,* June 28, 1848.

457 *"Congress may pass it":* Editorial, *New York Evening Post,* quoted in "The Compromise Bill," *Daily Union,* July 28, 1848.

457 *Clayton bill passes 33 to 22:* Ibid.

457 *party and regional votes:* Ibid.

457 *House vote of 112 to 97:* "House of Representatives," *Daily Union,* July 29, 1848.

457 *ominous sectional breakdown:* "Who Killed the Compromise?" *Daily Union,* July 29, 1848.

458 *"General Taylor would not get":* Quoted in ibid.

458 *"The result of leaving":* JKP, *Diary* IV, July 28, 1848, p. 33.

458 *August 8 cabinet meeting:* Ibid., August 8, 1848, pp. 60–63.

459 *33 to 22 Senate vote:* "Congressional," *Daily Union,* August 11, 1848.

459 *82 to 121 House vote:* "The Second Compromise Killed," *Daily Union,* August 12, 1848.

459 *"a melancholy sign":* Ibid.

459 *"I find myself":* JKP, *Diary* IV, August 10, 1848, p. 65.

459 *"Mr. Van Buren":* Ibid.

460 *"I have made up my mind":* Ibid., pp. 69–74. The account of JKP's activities on this day comes from this diary entry.

461 *Calhoun encounter at Capitol:* Ibid., August 14, 1848, p. 76.

461 *"heartily rejoiced":* Ibid., p. 78.

461 *"free man of colour":* Ibid., August 18, 1848, p. 86. The account of Polk's trip is taken from diary entries, August 18, 1848, to August 28, 1848.

462 *"not only upon general principles":* Ibid., September 23, 1848, pp. 130–31.

462 *"Upon each recurrence":* Ibid., November 2, 1848, p. 177.

463 *"will revive the heroic age":* *National Intelligencer,* quoted in "The Coming 'Heroic Age!," *Daily Union,* November 12, 1848.

463 *"in their military conduct":* Ibid.

463 *vote percentages:* Nelson (ed.), *Congressional Quarterly's Guide to the Presidency,* p. 1439.

463 *"It would be difficult":* JKP, Annual Message, December 5, 1848, reprinted in "Senate," *Daily Union,* December 6, 1848.

465 "I, of course, treated him courteously": JKP, *Diary* IV, December 19, 1848, p. 245.

465 *advice to Thomas*: Ibid., December 22, 1848, pp. 249–50.

465 *sixty-eight attendees*: "The Meeting of the Southern Members of Congress," *Daily Union*, December 24, 1848.

465 *Polk's talk with Douglas*: JKP, *Diary* IV, December 23, 1848, pp. 254–55.

466 *Christmas Day*: Ibid., December 25, 1848, pp. 256–57.

466 "*emancipate our slaves*": Quoted in Margaret L. Coit, *John C. Calhoun: American Portrait* (Boston: Houghton Mifflin, 1950), p. 475.

466 *eighty southerners*: Ibid., p. 476.

466 "*the aggressions of the North*": Quoted in JKP, *Diary* IV, January 16, 1849, pp. 285–88.

467 "*Let her go*": Quoted in JKP, ibid., January 18, 1849, p. 294.

467 "*courtesy and cordiality*": JKP, ibid., February 26, 1849, p. 353.

467 "*the plain, respectable*": Quoted in Bauer, *Zachary Taylor*, p. 253.

468 "*Not the slightest allusion*": JKP, *Diary* IV, March 1, 1849, p. 359.

468 "*all the business*": Ibid., March 3, 1849, p. 362.

469 "*I feel exceedingly relieved*": Ibid., March 4, 1849, p. 373.

469 *blustery and chilly*: Bauer, *Zachary Taylor*, p. 256.

469 *Taylor's territorial views*: JKP, *Diary* IV, March 5, 1849, pp. 375–76.

469 "*Gen'l Taylor is*": Quoted in ibid., p. 376.

469 "*They said nothing*": "The Scene in the Senate," *Daily Union*, March 6, 1849.

469 *ten thousand spectators*: Bauer, *Zachary Taylor*, p. 256.

469 "*remarkable only for its brevity*": Quoted in ibid., p. 257.

469 "*common-place*": "The Inaugural," *Daily Union*, March 6, 1849.

470 *Polks' departure*: JKP, *Diary* IV, March 5, 1849; March 6, 1849, pp. 376–77.

470 *baptism*: McCormac, *Polk* II, p. 721.

Epilogue: Legacy

PAGE

471 "*to mourn the loss*": Zachary Taylor, General Orders, No. 34, June 19, 1849, reprinted in *Daily Union*, June 20, 1849.

471 "*unite in according to him*": "Death of Ex-President Polk," *Baltimore Clipper*, June 19, 1849, reprinted in *Daily Union*, June 20, 1849.

471 "*will be recorded*": "Death of Ex-President Polk," *Baltimore Sun*, reprinted in *Daily Union*, June 20, 1849.

471 "*in terms of reprobation*": Editorial, *New York Evening Post*, reprinted in "A Stab at the Illustrious Dead," *Daily Union*, June 21, 1849.

471 *"bearing magnanimous testimony":* "A Stab at the Illustrious Dead," *Daily Union.*

472 *"'forgotten'":* McCormac, *Polk* II, p. 722.

472 *Schouler interpretation:* Discussed in ibid.

473 *"forceful and persuasive presidents":* Arthur M. Schlesinger, Jr., "Editor's Note," in Seigenthaler, *James K. Polk*, p. xv.

473 *Polk's academic poll rankings:* "Historical Rankings of United States Presidents," Wikipedia, http://en.wikipedia.org.

474 *"condemned by history":* Al Gore, speech at Democratic National Convention, 2008, quoted in Jake Tapper, "Gore Talks About What Might Not Have Been, Compares Obama to Lincoln," http://blogs.abcnews.com.

474 *"dubious beginnings":* John H. Schroeder, *Mr. Polk's War: America's Opposition and Dissent, 1846–1848* (Madison: University of Wisconsin Press, 1973), p. xiv.

474 *"that this is the War":* Ron Tyler, quoted in Diana Claitor, "Producers Must Tell Mexican War from Two Viewpoints, Far Apart," *Current,* August 24, 1998.

474 *"the most unjust war":* quoted in Eisenhower, *So Far from God,* p. xvii.

475 *"foolish":* Paul Johnson, *A History of the American People* (New York: Harper-Collins, 1998), p. 378.

BIBLIOGRAPHY

CORRESPONDENCE OF JAMES K. POLK

Correspondence of James K. Polk, Vol. I, 1817–1832, Herbert Weaver and Paul Bergeron, eds. Nashville: Vanderbilt University Press, 1969.

Correspondence of James K. Polk, Vol. II, 1833–1834, Herbert Weaver and Paul Bergeron, eds. Nashville: Vanderbilt University Press, 1972.

Correspondence of James K. Polk, Vol. VI, 1842–1843, Wayne Cutler and Carese M. Parker, eds. Nashville: Vanderbilt University Press, 1983.

Correspondence of James K. Polk, Vol. VII, January–August 1844, Wayne Cutler and James P. Cooper, Jr., eds. Nashville: Vanderbilt University Press, 1989.

Correspondence of James K. Polk, Vol. VIII, September–December 1844, Wayne Cutler, Robert G. Hall II, and Jayne C. Defiore, eds. Knoxville: University of Tennessee Press, 1993.

Correspondence of James K. Polk, Vol. IX, January–June 1845, Wayne Cutler and Robert G. Hall II, eds. Knoxville: University of Tennessee Press, 1996.

Correspondence of James K. Polk, Vol. X, July–December 1845. Knoxville: University of Tennessee Press, 2004.

OTHER BOOKS

Adams, John Quincy. *Memoirs of John Quincy Adams: His Diary from 1795 to 1848,* Vol. IV. Philadelphia: J. B. Lippincott & Co., 1877.

———. *Memoirs of John Quincy Adams: His Diary from 1795 to 1848,* Vol. XII. Philadelphia: J. B. Lippincott & Co., 1877.

Ames, William E. *A History of the National Intelligencer.* Chapel Hill: University of North Carolina Press, 1972.

Bailey, Thomas A. *A Diplomatic History of the American People.* New York: Appleton-Century-Crofts, 1958.

Baker, Jean H. *James Buchanan.* New York: Times Books, 2004.

Bartlett, Irving H. *Daniel Webster.* New York: W. W. Norton, 1978.

———. *John C. Calhoun: A Biography.* New York: W. W. Norton, 1993.

Bauer, K. Jack. *The Mexican War, 1846–1848*. Lincoln: University of Nebraska Press, 1974.

———. *Zachary Taylor: Soldier, Planter, Statesman of the Old Southwest*. Baton Rouge: Louisiana State University Press, 1985.

Bell, Jeffrey. *Populism and Elitism: Politics in the Age of Equality*. Washington, D.C.: Regnery Gateway, 1992.

Bemis, Samuel Flagg. *John Quincy Adams and the Foundations of American Foreign Policy*. New York: Alfred A. Knopf, 1949.

Benton, Thomas Hart. *Thirty Years' View; or a History of the Working of the American Government from 1820 to 1850,* Vol. I. New York: D. Appleton & Co., 1854.

———. *Thirty Years' View; or a History of the Working of the American Government from 1820 to 1850*, Vol. II. New York: D. Appleton & Co., 1856.

Bergeron, Paul H. *The Presidency of James K. Polk*. Lawrence: University Press of Kansas, 1987.

Bill, Alfred Hoyt. *Rehearsal for Conflict: The Story of Our War with Mexico, 1846–1848*. New York: Alfred A. Knopf, 1947.

Blue, Frederick J. *No Taint of Compromise: Crusaders in Antislavery Politics*. Baton Rouge: Louisiana State University Press, 2005.

Borneman, Walter R. *Polk: The Man Who Transformed the Presidency and America*. New York: Random House, 2008.

Bowers, Claude G. *The Party Battles of the Jackson Period*. Boston: Houghton Mifflin, 1922.

Braider, Donald. *Solitary Star: A Biography of Sam Houston*. New York: Putnam's, 1974.

Brands, H. W. *Andrew Jackson: His Life and Times*. New York: Doubleday, 2005.

Bumgarner, John Reed. *Sarah Childress Polk: A Biography of the Remarkable First Lady*. Jefferson, N.C.: McFarland, 1997.

Cheathem, Mark R. *Old Hickory's Nephew: The Political and Private Struggles of Andrew Jackson Donelson*. Baton Rouge: Louisiana State University Press, 2007.

Chitwood, Oliver Perry. *John Tyler: Champion of the Old South*. Newtown, Conn.: American Political Biography Press, 2003 (originally published by American Historical Association, 1939).

Cohn, Mary W. (ed.). *Congressional Quarterly's Guide to Congress*, 4th edition. Washington, D.C.: Congressional Quarterly, 1991.

Coit, Margaret L. *John C. Calhoun: American Portrait*. Boston: Houghton Mifflin, 1950.

Davis, William C. *Three Roads to the Alamo: The Lives and Fortunes of David Crockett, James Bowie, and William Barret Travis*. New York: HarperCollins, 1998.

De Bruhl, Marshall. *Sword of San Jacinto: A Life of Sam Houston*. New York: Random House, 1993.

DeConde, Alexander. *A History of American Foreign Policy*, Vol. II. New York: Scribner's, 1963.

De Voto, Bernard. *The Year of Decision, 1846*. Boston: Houghton Mifflin, 1942.

Egan, Ferol. *Frémont: Explorer for a Restless Nation*. Garden City, N.Y.: Doubleday, 1977.

Eisenhower, John S. D. *Agent of Destiny: The Life and Times of General Winfield Scott*. New York: Free Press, 1997.

——. *So Far from God: The U.S. War with Mexico, 1846–1848*. New York: Random House, 1989.

Fehrenbach, T. R. *Lone Star: A History of Texas and the Texans*. New York: Collier, 1968.

Ferrell, Robert H. *American Diplomacy: A History*. New York: W. W. Norton, 1975.

Fischer, David Hackett. *Albion's Seed: Four British Folkways in America*. New York: Oxford University Press, 1989.

Fuess, Claude M. *Daniel Webster*, Vol. I, *1782–1830*. New York: Da Capo, 1968 (originally published in 1930).

——. *Daniel Webster*, Vol. II, *1830–1852*. New York: Da Capo, 1968 (originally published in 1930).

Gambrell, Herbert. *Anson Jones: The Last President of Texas*. Garden City, N.Y.: Doubleday, 1948.

Garraty, John Arthur. *Silas Wright*. New York: Columbia University Press, 1949.

Going, Charles Buxton. *David Wilmot, Free-Soiler: A Biography of the Great Advocate of the Wilmot Proviso*. New York: D. Appleton & Co., 1924.

Handlin, Lilian. *George Bancroft: The Intellectual as Democrat*. New York: Harper & Row, 1984.

Harlow, Neal. *California Conquered: The Annexation of a Mexican Province, 1846–1850*. Berkeley: University of California Press, 1982.

Haynes, Sam W. *James K. Polk and the Expansionist Impulse*. New York: Longman, 2002.

Heidler, David S., and Jeanne T. Heidler. *Old Hickory's War: Andrew Jackson and the Quest for Empire*. Mechanicsburg, Penn.: Stackpole, 1996.

Henderson, Timothy J. *A Glorious Defeat: Mexico and Its War with the United States*. New York: Hill & Wang, 2007.

Holt, Michael F. *The Rise and Fall of the American Whig Party: Jacksonian Politics and the Onset of the Civil War*. New York: Oxford University Press, 1999.

Howe, Daniel Walker. *What Hath God Wrought: The Transformation of America, 1815–1848*. New York: Oxford University Press, 2007.

James, Marquis. *The Life of Andrew Jackson*. Garden City, N.Y.: Garden City Publishing, 1940.

Johannsen, Robert W. *Stephen A. Douglas*. New York: Oxford University Press, 1973.

———. *To the Halls of the Montezuma: The Mexican War in the American Imagination*. New York: Oxford University Press, 1985.

Johnson, Paul. *A History of the American People*. New York: HarperCollins, 1998.

Klein, Philip S. *President James Buchanan: A Biography*. Newtown, Conn.: American Political Biography Press, 1995 (originally published by Pennsylvania State University Press, 1962).

Krauze, Enrique (translated by Hank Heifetz). *Mexico—Biography of Power: A History of Modern Mexico, 1810–1996*. New York: HarperCollins, 1997.

Lincoln, Abraham. *Abraham Lincoln: Great Speeches*. New York: Dover, 1991.

Long, Jeff. *Duel of Eagles: The Mexican and U.S. Fight for the Alamo*. New York: Quill/Morrow, 1990.

Mayo, Bernard. *Henry Clay: Spokesman of the New West*. Boston: Houghton Mifflin, 1937.

McCormac, Eugene Irving. *James K. Polk: A Political Biography to the Prelude of War, 1795–1845*. Newtown, Conn.: American Political Biography Press, 1995 (originally published by the University of California Press, 1922).

———. *James K. Polk: A Political Biography to the End of a Career, 1845–1849*. Newtown, Conn.: American Political Biography Press, 1995 (originally published by the University of California Press, 1922).

McFaul, John M. *The Politics of Jacksonian Finance*. Ithaca, N.Y.: Cornell University Press, 1972.

Meacham, Jon. *American Lion: Andrew Jackson in the White House*. New York: Random House, 2008.

Merk, Frederick. *The Monroe Doctrine and American Expansionism, 1843–1849*. New York: Alfred A. Knopf, 1971.

Moore, John L., John P. Preimesberger, and David R. Tarr (eds.). *Congressional Quarterly's Guide to U.S. Elections,* 4th edition, Vol. I. Washington, D.C.: Congressional Quarterly, 2001.

Mowat, R. B. *A New History of Great Britain*. London: Oxford University Press, 1926.

Nagel, Paul C. *John Quincy Adams: A Public Life, a Private Life*. Cambridge: Harvard University Press, 1997.

Nelson, Anson, and Fanny Nelson. *Sarah Childress Polk: Wife of the Eleventh President of the United States*. Newtown, Conn.: American Political Biography Press, 1994 (originally published by Anson D. F. Randolph & Co., 1892).

Nelson, Michael (ed.). *Congressional Quarterly's Guide to the Presidency*. Washington, D.C.: Congressional Quarterly, 1989.

Nevins, Allan. *The Ordeal of the Union: Fruits of Manifest Destiny, 1847–1852*. New York: Scribner's, 1947.

Ohrt, Wallace. *Defiant Peacemaker: Nicholas Trist in the Mexican War*. College Station: Texas A&M University Press, 1997.

Peterson, Merrill D. *The Great Triumvirate: Webster, Clay, and Calhoun*. New York: Oxford University Press, 1987.

Pletcher, David M. *The Diplomacy of Annexation: Texas, Oregon, and the Mexican War*. Columbia: University of Missouri Press, 1973.

Polk, James K. (edited and annotated by Milo Milton Quaife). *The Diary of James K. Polk During His Presidency, 1845–1849*, Vol. I. Chicago: A. C. McClurg & Co., 1910 (reprinted by the Chicago Historical Society).

————. *The Diary of James K. Polk During His Presidency, 1845–1849*, Vol II. Chicago: A. C. McClurg & Co., 1910 (reprinted by the Chicago Historical Society).

————. *The Diary of James K. Polk During His Presidency, 1845–1849*, Vol. III. Chicago: A. C. McClurg & Co., 1910 (reprinted by the Chicago Historical Society).

————. *The Diary of James K. Polk During His Presidency, 1845–1849*, Vol. IV. Chicago: A. C. McClurg & Co., 1910 (reprinted by the Chicago Historical Society).

Polk, James K. (edited by Allan Nevins). *The Diary of a President, 1845–1849*. London and New York: Longmans, Green, 1952.

Polk, William R. *Polk's Folly: An American Family History*. New York: Doubleday, 2000.

Price, Glenn W. *Origins of the War with Mexico: The Polk-Stockton Intrigue*. Austin: University of Texas Press, 1967.

Priestley, Herbert Ingram. *The Mexican Nation: A History*. New York: Macmillan, 1923.

Procter, Ben, and Archie P. McDonald (eds.). *The Texas Heritage*. Arlington Heights, Ill.: Harlan Davidson, 1980.

Remini, Robert V. *Andrew Jackson and the Course of American Empire, 1767–1821*. New York: Harper & Row, 1977.

————. *Andrew Jackson and the Course of American Freedom, 1822–1832*. New York: Harper & Row, 1981.

————. *Andrew Jackson and the Course of American Democracy, 1833–1845*. New York: Harper & Row, 1984.

————. *Daniel Webster: The Man and His Time*. New York: W. W. Norton, 1997.

————. *Henry Clay: Statesman for the Union.* New York: W. W. Norton, 1991.

Riding, Alan. *Distant Neighbors: A Portrait of the Mexicans.* New York: Alfred A. Knopf, 1985.

Schlesinger, Arthur M., Jr. *The Age of Jackson.* Boston: Little, Brown, 1946.

Schroeder, John H. *Mr. Polk's War: American Opposition and Dissent, 1846–1848.* Madison: University of Wisconsin Press, 1973.

Seigenthaler, John. *James K. Polk.* New York: Times Books, 2003.

Sellers, Charles. *James K. Polk, Jacksonian, 1795–1843.* Norwalk, Conn.: Easton Press, 1987 (originally published by Princeton University Press, 1957).

————. *James K. Polk, Continentalist, 1843–1846.* Norwalk, Conn.: Easton Press, 1987 (originally published by Princeton University Press, 1966).

Shepherd, William R. *Shepherd's Historical Atlas*, 9th edition. New York: Barnes & Noble, 1964.

Sides, Hampton. *Blood and Thunder: An Epic of the American West.* New York: Doubleday, 2006.

Silbey, Joel H. *Martin Van Buren and the Emergence of American Popular Politics.* Lanham, Md.: Rowman & Littlefield, 2002.

————. *Storm over Texas: The Annexation Controversy and the Road to Civil War.* New York: Oxford University Press, 2005.

Simon, James F. *Lincoln and Chief Justice Taney: Slavery, Secession, and the President's War Powers.* New York: Simon & Schuster, 2006.

Singletary, Otis A. *The Mexican War.* Chicago: University of Chicago Press, 1960.

Smith, Elbert B. *Magnificent Missourian: The Life of Thomas Hart Benton.* Philadelphia: J. B. Lippincott, 1958.

Smith, William Ernest. *The Francis Preston Blair Family in Politics,* Vol. I (New York: Macmillan, 1933).

Sobel, Robert. *Conquest and Conscience: The 1840s.* New York: Thomas Y. Crowell, 1971.

Spengler, Oswald. *Decline of the West,* abridged edition by Helmut Werner, prepared by Arthur Helps from the translation by Charles Francis Atkinson. New York: Modern Library, 1952.

Thom, Adam. *The Claims to the Oregon Territory Considered.* London: Smith, Elder & Co., 1844.

Treese, Joel D. (ed.). *Biographical Directory of the American Congress, 1774–1996.* Alexandria, Va.: CQ Staff Directories, 1997.

van der Linden, Frank. *Lincoln: The Road to War.* Golden, Colo.: Fulcrum, 1998.

Wanniski, Jude. *The Way the World Works: How Economies Fail—and Succeed.* New York: Basic Books, 1978.

Watson, Harry L. *Andrew Jackson vs. Henry Clay: Democracy and Development in Antebellum America.* Boston: Bedford/St. Martin's, 1998.

Webb, James. *Born Fighting: How the Scots-Irish Shaped America.* New York: Broadway, 2004.

Wheelan, Joseph. *Invading Mexico: America's Continental Dream and the Mexican War, 1846–1848.* New York: Carroll & Graf, 2007.

Wilentz, Sean. *The Rise of American Democracy: Jefferson to Lincoln.* New York: W. W. Norton, 2005.

Williams, T. Harry. *The History of American Wars: From Colonial Times to World War I.* New York: Alfred A. Knopf, 1981.

NEWSPAPERS

Congressional Globe
Illustrated London News
National Intelligencer
Daily Globe
Daily Union

ARCHIVES

Bancroft Collection, New York Public Library
Andrew Jackson Papers, Library of Congress
James K. Polk Papers, Library of Congress

ARTICLES AND PAPERS

Bancroft, George. Untitled typescript, beginning draft of a JKP biography. Bancroft Collection, New York Public Library.

Blackman, Ann. "Fatal Cruise of the Princeton." *Navy History,* September 2005.

Claitor, Diana. "Producers Must Tell Mexican War from Two Viewpoints, Far Apart." *Current,* August 24, 1998.

Nugent, Walter. "The American Habit of Empire, and the Cases of Polk and Bush." *Western Historical Quarterly,* Spring 2007.

Stenburg, Richard R. "President Polk and California: Additional Documents." *Pacific Historical Review* 10, no. 2 (June 1941).

WEB SITES

www.americanheritage.com
http://bchs.kearny.net
http://blogs.abcnews.com

http://www.bookrags.com/biography/robert-field-stockton/
www.clements.umich.edu
http://columbia.thefreedictionary.com/blair
http://encarta.msn.com/map
http://encyclopedia.jrank.org
http://www.hist.umn.edu
http://www.historyguy.com
www.loc.gov/exhibits/jefferson
http://lsm.crt.state.la.us/babildo
www.military.com
http://www.sonofthesouth.net
http://tennesseeencyclopedia.net
http://www.tsha.utexas.edu
http://www.tsl.state.tx.us/
http://www.2020site.org/literature
http://www.ustreas.gov
http://wikipedia.org
www.yale.edu/lawweb/avalon

ACKNOWLEDGMENTS

This book began with a question: "What do you know about the Mexican War?" The questioner was Alice Mayhew, my editor at Simon & Schuster, well known for her passion for the narrative of American history. I replied that I knew a little about it, but I would learn a lot more if she wanted a book on the politics surrounding the war and the powerful wave of expansionist fervor that swept across America in that time. Thus did I embark on this project. And among those who helped nurture it with their support, counsel, and sound judgment, Alice Mayhew heads the list. I credit her with the initial idea and salute her unerring historical and literary acumen.

My friend Al Silverman, who fostered and supervised my first book project more than fifteen years ago, contributed an invaluable service on this one—a painstaking editing effort that honed the narrative, identified gaps in the story, and polished the language. Al's generosity of spirit has always been there whenever I undertook to produce a work of prose.

I express appreciation also to three friends who read segments of the manuscript and offered counsel on words and facts: the late Kenneth H. Bacon, whose observations on history, politics, and writing have influenced my thinking for some three decades; Gerald J. Baldasty, whose longtime passion for the newspapers and politics of Polk's era proved highly beneficial to my efforts; and Jerome Cramer, whose ministrations reflected his long career as writer, editor, and teacher. All offered suggestions that proved a great service to author and reader.

Philippa ("Flip") Brophy of Sterling Lord Literistic, Inc., served wonderfully as agent for this project, guiding me with particular insight through the early efforts to shape the story line. And two dedicated professionals at Simon & Schuster—Karen Thompson and Roger Labrie—helped usher the project to its conclusion. While the contributions of those noted here proved invaluable, they of course bear no responsibility for any faults embedded in the final product.

As always, many colleagues at Congressional Quarterly, Inc., offered assistance and support at critical junctures. Marilyn Gates-Davis produced the sterling map displaying the powerful waves of American expansionism in the 1840s. Nell Benton and her CQ research team reached back at crucial times for obscure tidbits of historical fact. And the omnicompetent and always ebullient Loesje Troglia, my executive assistant, supported the project throughout its duration with all manner of beneficence, most notably in securing the photographs and reproductions that grace the volume.

Andrew Corty, my boss for twelve years when *Congressional Quarterly* was owned by the Times Publishing Co. of St. Petersburg, Florida, extended plenty of encouragement and succor—particularly, it seemed, when I found myself most in need of such moral sustenance.

I convey appreciation also to the good folks at the Library of Congress's Documents and Periodical rooms, as well as those at the Martin Luther King Library's collection of Washington documents and newspapers.

An expression of gratitude goes to my family, beginning with children Rob, Johanna, and Stephanie, and to son-in-law John Derlega. Their unwavering support provided fuel to the effort. My father, Robert E. Merry, and brother, Jack Merry, extended their usual guidance and encouragement.

And, finally, a special note of appreciation and affection goes to Susan Pennington Merry, my closest friend and wife of forty years, whose support came encased in love and a sacrificial regard for the passions that drive my often consuming literary enterprises. All this was well reflected in the words I heard her say so often following one of our lovely conversational dinners; she would say with a tone of mock command: "I'll do the dishes; you go upstairs and get back to work!"

INDEX